The SCERTS® Model

*A Comprehensive
Educational Approach
for Children with
Autism Spectrum Disorders*

Volume II
Program Planning
& Intervention

The SCERTS® Model

A Comprehensive Educational Approach for Children with Autism Spectrum Disorders

Volume II
Program Planning & Intervention

by

Barry M. Prizant, Ph.D., Amy M. Wetherby, Ph.D., Emily Rubin, M.S.,
Amy C. Laurent, Ed.M., OTR/L, and Patrick J. Rydell, Ed.D.

Baltimore • London • Sydney

Paul H. Brookes Publishing Co.
Post Office Box 10624
Baltimore, Maryland 21285-0624

www.brookespublishing.com

Copyright © 2006 by Paul H. Brookes Publishing Co., Inc.
All rights reserved.

"Paul H. Brookes Publishing Co." is a registered trademark of
Paul H. Brookes Publishing Co., Inc.

SCERTS® is a registered trademark and the ⟨SCERTS⟩ logo is a trademark
of Barry M. Prizant, Amy M. Wetherby, Emily B. Rubin, Amy C. Laurent,
and Patrick Rydell.

Purchasers of *The SCERTS® Model: A Comprehensive Educational Approach for Children with Autism Spectrum Disorders (Volume II: Program Planning and Intervention)* are granted permission to photocopy the materials on pages 48 and 77–78 and in the Appendix of Volume II (pp. 365–372) for clinical or educational purposes. None of the forms may be reproduced to generate revenue for any program or individual. Photocopies may only be made from an original book. *Unauthorized use beyond this privilege is prosecutable under federal law.* You will see the copyright protection notice at the bottom of each photocopiable page.

The case studies in this book are fictionalized accounts based on the authors' clinical and research experience that do not represent the lives of specific individuals, and no implications should be inferred.

Typeset by Integrated Publishing Solutions, Grand Rapids, Michigan.
Manufactured in the United States of America by
Sheridan Books, Chelsea, Michigan.

Second printing, February 2007.

Third printing, November 2008.

Library of Congress Cataloging-in-Publication Data
The SCERTS model : a comprehensive educational approach for children with autism
 spectrum disorders / by Barry M. Prizant ... [et al.].
   v.   cm.
  Includes bibliographical references and index.
  Contents: v. 1. Assessment—v. 2. Program planning and intervention
  ISBN-13: 978-1-55766-689-5 (v. 1) — ISBN-13: 978-1-55766-809-7 (v. 2)
  ISBN-10: 1-55766-689-X (v. 1) — ISBN-10: 1-55766-809-4 (v. 2)
  1. Autistic children—Education.   2. Autism in children—Treatment.
  I. Prizant, Barry M.   II. Title.
 LC4717.S28 2006
 371.94—dc22   2005026703

British Library Cataloguing in Publication data are available from the British Library.

Contents
Volume II

Contents, Volume I vi
About the Authors vii
For the Reader ix
Acknowledgments x

    Chapter 1   Guide to SCERTS Model Educational Practices, Part I: Core Values and Guiding Principles, Practice Guidelines, Goal Setting, and Transactional Support 1

    Chapter 2   Guide to SCERTS Model Educational Practices, Part II: Transactional Support: Interpersonal Support and Learning Support and Learning and Playing with Peers 25

    Chapter 3   Transactional Support: Support to Families and Support Among Professionals 43

    Chapter 4   Linking Transactional Support Goals to Social Communication and Emotional Regulation Goals 83

    Chapter 5   Enhancing Social Communication, Emotional Regulation, and Transactional Support at the Social Partner Stage: From Assessment to Program Implementation 171

    Chapter 6   Enhancing Social Communication, Emotional Regulation, and Transactional Support at the Language Partner Stage: From Assessment to Program Implementation 227

    Chapter 7   Enhancing Social Communication, Emotional Regulation, and Transactional Support at the Conversational Partner Stage: From Assessment to Program Implementation 291

References 363

Appendix   SCERTS Assessment Process–Quality Indicators 365

Index, Volumes I and II 373

Contents
Volume I

Contents, Volume II
About the Authors
For the Reader
Acknowledgments

Chapter 1　Introduction
Chapter 2　Social Communication
Chapter 3　Emotional Regulation
Chapter 4　Transactional Support
Chapter 5　SCERTS Model Programmatic Priorities and Milestones
Chapter 6　Continuum of Current Intervention Approaches and the SCERTS Model
Chapter 7　The SCERTS Assessment Process: Overview and Implementation
Chapter 8　The SCERTS Assessment Process: Using the SAP-O Forms and Criteria

References

Appendix A　SCERTS Assessment Process Forms
Appendix B　Glossary

Index, Volumes I and II

About the Authors

Barry M. Prizant, Ph.D., CCC-SLP, Director, Childhood Communication Services, 2024 Broad Street, Cranston, Rhode Island, 02904; Adjunct Professor, Center for the Study of Human Development, Brown University, 133 Waterman Street, Box 1831, Providence, Rhode Island

Barry M. Prizant has more than 30 years of experience as a clinical scholar, researcher, and consultant to young children with autism spectrum disorders (ASD) and related communication and developmental disabilities and their families. Dr. Prizant has published more than 90 articles and chapters on ASD and pediatric communication disabilities, serves on the advisory board of six professional journals, and has presented more than 500 seminars and numerous keynote addresses at national and international conferences. Dr. Prizant also served on the Committee on Screening and Diagnosis of Autism Spectrum Disorders at the National Institutes of Health and co-authored the Practice Parameters published by the committee. He is co-editor (with Amy M. Wetherby) of the book *Autism Spectrum Disorders: A Developmental, Transactional Perspective* (Paul H. Brookes Publishing Co., 2000), a volume in the *Communication and Language Intervention Series*. Dr. Prizant is a Fellow of the American Speech-Language-Hearing Association and has received numerous awards as well as widespread recognition for his clinical and scholarly work.

Amy M. Wetherby, Ph.D., CCC-SLP, Laurel Schendel Professor, Department of Communication Disorders, and Executive Director, Center for Autism and Related Disabilities, Florida State University, Tallahassee, Florida 32306

Amy M. Wetherby has more than 20 years of clinical experience and is a Fellow of the American Speech-Language-Hearing Association. Dr. Wetherby has published extensively and presents regularly at national conventions on social and communicative profiles of children with autism spectrum disorders (ASD) and early identification of communication disorders in infants and toddlers. She served on the National Academy of Sciences Committee for Educational Interventions for Children with Autism. Dr. Wetherby is the Project Director of the FIRST WORDS Project (http://firstwords.fsu.edu), which is funded by a U.S. Department of Education Field-Initiated Research Grant on improving early identification of young children at risk for ASD, a Model Demonstration Grant on early intervention for very young children with ASD and their families, and a Doctoral Leadership Training Grant specializing in autism.

Emily Rubin, M.S., CCC-SLP, Lecturer, Yale University School of Medicine; Director, Communication Crossroads, Post Office Box 222171, Carmel, California 93922

Emily Rubin is Director of Communication Crossroads, a private practice in Carmel, California. She is a speech-language pathologist specializing in autism, Asperger syndrome, and related social learning disabilities. As an adjunct faculty member and lecturer at Yale University, she has served as a member of its Autism and Developmental

Disabilities Clinic. She has also served as an instructor for the Communication Sciences and Disorders Department of Emerson College in Boston, Massachusetts, where she has developed courses to prepare graduate-level students to address the needs of children with autism and their families. Her publications have focused on early identification of autism, contemporary intervention models, and programming guidelines for high-functioning autism and Asperger syndrome. She has participated as a member of the American Speech-Language-Hearing Association's Ad Hoc Committee on Autism Spectrum Disorders (ASD), a committee charged with developing guidelines related to the role of speech-language pathologists in the diagnosis, assessment, and treatment of ASD. She lectures internationally and provides consultation to educational programs serving children and adolescents with autism and related developmental disorders.

Amy C. Laurent, Ed.M., OTR/L, Occupational Therapist, Private Practice, North Kingstown, Rhode Island

Amy C. Laurent is a pediatric occupational therapist who holds a master's degree in special education. Currently in private practice, she is a New England affiliate of Communication Crossroads and Childhood Communication Services. Ms. Laurent specializes in the education of children with autism spectrum disorders (ASD) and related developmental disabilities. Through her practice, she provides comprehensive evaluations, direct therapeutic services, and consultations to educational programs for children with ASD. She also provides extensive educational and emotional support to families of children with ASD. Ms. Laurent has co-authored several journal articles and frequently lectures throughout the United States on topics related to therapeutic and educational intervention for children with ASD. Her areas of clinical interest include therapeutic intervention as it relates to the development of self-regulation and social-adaptive functioning across contexts (e.g., school, home, and community settings).

Patrick J. Rydell, Ed.D., CCC-SLP, Director, Rocky Mountain Autism Center, Post Office Box 620578, Littleton, Colorado 80162

Dr. Rydell has been in the field of autism and communication disorders for more than 24 years in public school, hospital, university, administration, and private practice settings. Dr. Rydell is the owner and director of Rocky Mountain Autism Center (RMAC), a private center dedicated solely to working with children with autism spectrum disorders and their families. RMAC is a model/demonstration site for the implementation of the SCERTS Model in Lakewood, Colorado. The center provides comprehensive center-, community-, and home-based assessments, programs, interventions, and training to individuals with autism, their families, and professionals.

Dr. Rydell earned his doctoral and master's degrees in the field of communication disorders and special education, with a primary program emphasis in autism and early childhood education. Dr. Rydell is a Fulbright Senior Specialist grant recipient (2005) and has previously co-authored five book chapters and numerous research articles on autism and unconventional verbal behaviors. In addition, he frequently speaks at international, national, and state levels on topics related to autism.

For the Reader

The SCERTS® Model: A Comprehensive Educational Approach for Children with Autism Spectrum Disorders is a two-volume manual. Volume I, *Assessment,* describes the three domains of the SCERTS Model—Social Communication, Emotional Regulation, and Transactional Support—with detailed information about developmental sequences and priorities for each domain. The SCERTS Model is also discussed in the context of the array of educational options for children with autism spectrum disorders (ASD). Volume I also describes in detail the SCERTS Assessment Process (SAP) and provides specific assessment criteria at three stages of communication development: Social Partner, Language Partner, and Conversational Partner. Appendix A contains a number of photocopiable forms for collecting information and monitoring progress for a child during the SAP.

Volume II, *Program Planning and Intervention,* addresses the how-to of implementing the SCERTS Model across home, school, and community settings. It describes how to prioritize goals and implement practices that fall under the Transactional Support domain, including how to link Transactional Support goals with Social Communication and Emotional Regulation goals. Volume II also presents in-depth vignettes about several children and their families at the three major developmental stages in the model. These vignettes include examples of completed forms used during the SAP. An appendix at the end of Volume II contains quality indicator rating scales that can be used to address program-level assessment and planning.

A glossary appears as Appendix B of Volume I. This glossary is placed in Volume I because most of the key terms defined in it are first presented in Volume I.

The index at the end of each volume is identical. It serves both books together, containing page references to both volumes.

Acknowledgments

The SCERTS Model and the manual *The SCERTS® Model: A Comprehensive Educational Approach for Children with Autism Spectrum Disorders* have resulted from support we have received over many years and from many different sources. The SCERTS Model collaborators would like to acknowledge those who have provided the "transactional support" that has made this manual possible.

First and foremost, we would like to thank the children and older individuals with autism spectrum disorders (ASD) and their families who have and who continue to teach us about their courage and humanity every day. We consider it a privilege that they have allowed us to be a part of their lives and their ongoing journeys. Their generous sharing of their spirit and wisdom provides the fuel that drives us in our life's work and helps us to strive to do our very best.

We would like to thank our families and friends, whose support and understanding helped to create the opportunities and space in our lives to do the painstaking and seemingly never-ending work during the years of developing the SCERTS Model and this manual. We hope their sacrifices are counterbalanced by the potential positive impact the SCERTS Model will have in the lives of individuals with ASD and their families.

We would like to thank our academic, clinical, and research mentors, who have instilled the values and beliefs that have guided our life's work and that are infused throughout the SCERTS Model. These values and beliefs are grounded in 1) an understanding that each child and family should be treated with respect and integrity, in recognition of the unique relationships we establish with them in our work, 2) that each individual, regardless of the challenges in his or her life, has interests and strengths that must be understood and enhanced, and 3) that an understanding of the complexities of human development is the most respectful guide to working effectively with children and families.

Finally we would like to acknowledge the staff of Paul H. Brookes Publishing Co., who have enthusiastically supported our efforts in developing and sharing the SCERTS Model. Their insistence on clarity and quality and their expertise at all levels of this project have contributed to a final product that we are proud to share.

With all of the support we have received, it is our sincere hope that this manual, in turn, will support the efforts of educators, therapists, family members, and other caregivers in promoting the most positive quality of life for individuals with ASD and related disabilities.

Chapter 1

Guide to SCERTS Model Educational Practices, Part I

Core Values and Guiding Principles, Practice Guidelines, Goal Setting, and Transactional Support

WHAT IS THE SCERTS MODEL?

As described in Chapter 1 of Volume I of this two-volume manual, the SCERTS Model is a comprehensive, multidisciplinary approach to enhancing communication and social-emotional abilities of individuals with autism spectrum disorders (ASD) and related disabilities. The acronym SCERTS refers to Social Communication, Emotional Regulation, and Transactional Support, which we believe should be the primary developmental dimensions targeted in a program designed to support the development of individuals with ASD and their families. In the SCERTS Model, it is recognized that most learning in childhood occurs in the social context of daily activities and experiences. Therefore, efforts to support a child's development within the model occur with caregivers and familiar partners in everyday routines in a variety of social situations, not primarily through work with a child in isolation. The SCERTS framework has been designed to target priority goals in social communication and emotional regulation through implementation of transactional supports (e.g., interpersonal support, learning supports) throughout a child's daily activities and across partners to facilitate competence within these identified goal areas. When a child's development in social communication and emotional regulation is supported with the strategic implementation of transactional supports, there is great potential for comprehensive, long-term positive effects on a child's development in educational environments and everyday activities.

We believe that an effective program for a child with ASD requires the expertise of a team of professionals working in a careful, coordinated manner in partnership with parents and other family members. Therefore, the SCERTS Model is best implemented as a multidisciplinary team approach that respects, draws from, and infuses expertise from a variety of disciplines, including general and special education, speech-language pathology, occupational therapy, child psychology and psychiatry, and social work.

ABOUT THIS MANUAL

Volume I of this manual describes the domains of the SCERTS Model, presents a detailed description of the SCERTS Assessment Process (SAP), and contains a number of helpful forms for collecting information and monitoring progress in the domains of Social Communication, Emotional Regulation, and Transactional Support for a child.

In this second volume, we address the how-to of implementing the SCERTS Model in a variety of settings. Chapters 1 and 2 describe how to prioritize goals and implement the first two components of the Transactional Support domain—*Interpersonal Support,* which includes teaching practices, interpersonal style, and issues related to inclusion and learning with and from peers, and *Learning Supports,* which include the design of functional and meaningful activities, use of visual supports, and curriculum modification. Chapter 3 discusses specific practices in implementing the two final components of Transactional Support—*support to families* and *support among professionals*. Chapter 4 demonstrates how the Social Communication, Emotional Regulation, and Transactional Support domains are linked in program planning. Finally, Chapters 5, 6, and 7 provide in-depth vignettes on a variety of children and their families, to illustrate implementation of the model and the identification of specific goals for children and their partners at the three major developmental stages in the model: Social Partner, Language Partner, and Conversational Partner. Some of these vignettes include filled-in SAP forms to illustrate how these forms are used in the assessment process.

Because 1) children with ASD and their families are very different from each other and 2) the SCERTS Model must be tailored to the individual needs of children and families, in this volume we make some generalizations that may hold for most but not necessarily all children with ASD. Furthermore, because the SCERTS Model is not a "one size fits all" model (i.e., it is not a prescriptive model that uses the same sequence of goals and activities for all children), we encourage professionals and caregivers to think creatively and individualize practices based on 1) each child's developmental profile, 2) family priorities, and 3) each child's motivations and functional needs, all of which are informed by the results of the SCERTS Assessment Process (SAP).

SCERTS MODEL CORE VALUES AND GUIDING PRINCIPLES

As mentioned in Chapter 1 of Volume I, one unique aspect of the SCERTS Model is that practices are guided by explicitly stated core values and guiding principles. They are as follows:

1. The development of spontaneous, functional communication abilities and emotional regulatory capacities, which support all aspects of development and independence, are of the highest priority in educational and treatment efforts.

2. Principles and research on child development frame assessment and educational efforts. Goals and activities are developmentally appropriate and functional, relative to a child's adaptive abilities and the necessary skills for maximizing enjoyment, success, and independence in daily experiences.

3. All domains of a child's development (e.g., communicative, social-emotional, cognitive, sensory, motor) are interrelated and interdependent. Assessment and educational efforts must address these relationships.

4. All behavior is viewed as purposeful. Functions of behavior may include communication, emotional regulation, and engagement in adaptive skills. For children who display unconventional and/or problem behaviors, there is an emphasis on determining the functions of the behaviors and supporting the children's development of more appropriate ways to accomplish those functions, within the context of enhancing emotional regulatory capacities.

5. A child's unique learning profile of strengths and weaknesses plays a critical role in determining appropriate accommodations (i.e., transactional supports) for facilitating competence in the domains of social communication and emotional regulation.

6. Natural routines across home, school, and community environments provide the educational and treatment contexts for learning and for the development of positive relationships. Progress is measured in reference to increasing competence and active participation in daily experiences and routines.

7. It is the primary responsibility of professionals to establish positive relationships with children and with family members. All children and family members are treated with dignity and respect.

8. Family members are considered experts about their child. Assessment and educational efforts are viewed as collaborative processes with family members, and principles of family-centered practice are advocated to build consensus with the family and enhance the collaborative process.

SEVEN ESSENTIAL SCERTS MODEL PRACTICE GUIDELINES FOR EDUCATING CHILDREN WITH ASD

We now highlight seven related operating guidelines that define practice in the SCERTS Model. We then expand the discussion throughout the remainder of this chapter and in subsequent chapters to address these practices in detail.

1. *In the Social Communication domain of the SCERTS Model, goals emphasize the functional use of language and communication in all natural settings, not simply the teaching of language and speech behaviors (e.g., vocabulary, grammar).* A first priority in education should be to help children with ASD develop competence in social communication for a variety of functions or purposes and not simply teach a set of verbal behaviors. Both verbal and nonverbal means of communication support the development of communicative competence. Developing language and communicative abilities should be an integral part of a child's ongoing educational and living experiences to have the greatest positive impact in a child's life.

2. *A child's emotional regulation and its effect on communication, social interaction, and learning are always considered, and arousal states are monitored constantly.* Problems in emotional regulation and modulation of arousal in children with ASD detrimentally influence attentional capacities and activity level and may, in turn, ultimately account for patterns of problem behavior and limitations in social interaction and social-emotional development. The development of mutual and self-regulatory capacities and the ability to recover from extreme dysregulation are high-priority goals. That is, children must develop the capacity to maintain an organized, well-regulated state independently (i.e., self-regulation); learn to request assistance or respond to others' efforts to support emotional regulation (i.e., mutual regulation); and recover successfully from states of heightened dysregulation (i.e., recovery from extreme dysregulation). Situations and factors known to be stressful or anxiety arousing for a child need to be modified in an effort to prevent dysregulation, and a child should be supported in developing specific emotional regulatory strategies to cope in those situations.

3. *Approaches to problem behavior are fully integrated with social-communicative programming and are determined by understanding the range of challenges to a child's emotional regulation.* The SCERTS Model views problem behavior within the larger developmental contexts of emotional regulation and social communication. Positive approaches to problem behaviors are now widely accepted as recommended practice for children with ASD, and the SCERTS Model is fully consistent with this philosophy. Many factors that underlie difficulties in emotional regulation and that may contribute to problem behavior are assessed systematically in the SAP. Empirically validated approaches to addressing problem behavior, such as teaching communicative replacements or functional equivalents for problem behaviors, are then implemented

as part of a broader emotional regulation plan. For example, children have as primary goals the acquisition of socially acceptable means to protest or reject, to support emotional regulation, and to preclude the acquisition and use of socially undesirable means to communicate. Furthermore, in the SCERTS Model, the dimension that examines behavior of partners (i.e., Interpersonal Support, which is part of the Transactional Support domain) and the effect of such behavior on emotional regulation is given careful consideration when attempting to understand and address problem behavior.

4. *Environments are arranged and activities are designed to foster motivation to encourage initiation of communication, a high-priority goal for children with ASD.* In the SCERTS Model, we emphasize a continuum of learning contexts, from planned activity routines to naturally occurring activities. Along this continuum, we prioritize teaching strategies that encourage children with ASD to initiate communication and language in everyday activities, to foster a sense of social control and communicative confidence. We refer to this dimension of Transactional Support programming as Learning Support. Thus, environments and activities are arranged to motivate communication and social engagement. For example, activities may include frequent opportunities for choice making, and other opportunities and needs to communicate are created in natural routines to encourage communicative initiation within shared reciprocal interactions and activities.

5. *Transactional supports are used to promote active and independent participation in activities.* Many children with ASD have difficulty participating in social activities, especially in less structured learning environments, where there is a lack of consistency and predictability. For children with ASD, consistency and predictability in life routines are essential, as they are a foundation for emotional regulation and such routines are the primary contexts for supporting children's development. Planned activity routines and more natural activities are effective learning contexts in which issues of motivation and generalization can be addressed. Transactional interpersonal and learning supports help children understand the purpose of activities, and such supports provide guidance, as needed, to help the children participate as successfully and independently as possible. The use of transactional supports for social communication and emotional regulation is effective in promoting motivation and active participation, developing flexibility, and building independence.

6. *Learning and playing with peers is an essential component of education and social learning.* Interacting with, and ultimately, developing positive relationships with peers may be particularly challenging for children with ASD and needs to be addressed in education. Therefore, a child with ASD is not the sole focus of educational goals. Goals are also targeted to support all partners, including peers, in engaging more effectively with a child with ASD, with the overriding goal of supporting positive relationships. Such goals address specific aspects of social communication as well as emotional regulation.

7. *The development of positive relationships among professionals and family members is the foundation for successful collaboration. A priority is placed on the development of mutually respectful relationships to enhance family members' sense of competence and trust. In turn, such relationships have a positive impact on fostering a child's development.* In most cases, family members are the most constant positive influences on a child's development,

and these influences are present across virtually all activities and settings. Family members include parents, brothers and sisters, and grandparents and other extended family members. Due to the nature of the social disabilities observed in ASD, family members often are significantly challenged in facilitating positive interactions and active learning opportunities for their child. Thus, family members are considered essential partners in all efforts designed to support their child's development. In the SCERTS Model, we attempt to foster as much positive change in the behavior of a child's social partners as we do for the child with ASD. Furthermore, we believe children with ASD are very capable of developing positive relationships with adults and children, despite their social challenges. The development of positive professional–family relationships is viewed as a critical factor in supporting optimal social, communication, and emotional development for a child and a productive, collaborative relationship with caregivers.

DETERMINING GOALS FOR CHILDREN

In implementing the SCERTS Model, progress for a child and his or her partners is based on targeting and measuring change in functional and developmentally appropriate goals. Thus, the identification of goals and objectives provides the foundation and focus for educational programming.

Social Communication, Emotional Regulation, and Transactional Support: The Foundation for Identifying and Prioritizing Goals in the SCERTS Model

The SCERTS Model prioritizes programmatic goals for children and families based on the most current research and understanding of ASD and of child development, with the priorities being on the developmental dimensions of social communication and emotional regulation and the implementation of a range of transactional supports. Therefore, we begin with the following questions when developing a comprehensive program or modifying an existing program for a child based on the SCERTS Model:

1. What are the social-communicative skills a child needs to be actively engaged and to participate and learn optimally in different activities and settings? What skills and strategies does a child already demonstrate to support such participation? To answer these questions, the requirements of specific activities or settings, as well as the child's social-communicative abilities (as documented in the SAP) must be taken into account. The answer to these questions then form the basis for establishing goals in Joint Attention and Symbol Use, the two major components of the Social Communication domain of the SCERTS Model.

2. What emotional regulatory abilities are needed to address the primary challenges to a child's emotional regulation in everyday activities or settings and to maximize a child's availability for social engagement and learning? In addition, what emotional regulatory strategies (mutual and self-regulatory) does a child already demonstrate to prevent or minimize dysregulation, allowing the child to actively participate and benefit from specific activities and settings? When a child experiences more extreme dysregulation, what strategies are most effective in supporting the child's ability to recover from that state? Once again, to answer these questions, the challenges inherent in specific activities or settings, as well as the child's emotional regulatory strategies and abilities (as documented in the SAP) must be taken into account. The answer to these questions then forms the basis for establishing goals in Mutual Regulation and Self-Regulation, the two major dimensions of the Emotional Regulation domain of the SCERTS Model, including recovery from extreme dysregulation.

3. Which transactional supports (interpersonal supports, including peer supports, and learning supports) does a child currently benefit from or may the child potentially benefit from to enhance social communication and emotional regulation and learning? What supports are already available to the child as documented in the SAP and the three rating forms that make up the SCERTS Assessment Process–Quality Indicators (SAP-Q)? (The SAP-Q forms appear in the Appendix in this volume.) Finally, what are the supports that may be provided to family members (support to families) and professionals (support among professionals) that will be most helpful in enhancing their success in engaging the child and supporting the child's development?

Thus, all of the major domains of the SCERTS Model (Social Communication, Emotional Regulation, and Transactional Support) must be addressed in an integrated and comprehensive manner across settings and partners when a team is planning new activities and modifying everyday activities to address specific goals. The program planning portions of the SCERTS Assessment Process–Summary Form (SAP Sum), which are the last 2 pages of the SAP Sum (see Figure 1.1), and the SAP Activity Planning Form (see Figure 1.2) are designed to assist in documenting how each of the domains of the model are addressed in the overall program and in specific activities for a child, respectively. (Full-size photocopiable master forms appear in Appendix A of Volume I, and sample completed forms are included in the in-depth "spotlights" on children in Chapters 5–7 of this volume.)

The process of determining appropriate developmental goals is of the utmost importance and forms the basis of a child's program. Goals are general statements of what a child will learn and of how partners will support a child and are the standards against which progress will be measured. These also are referred to as *benchmarks* in an individualized educational program (IEP). However, we must operationally define *learning* if we are to be clear about criteria for measuring true developmental progress.

What Is Learning?

In the SCERTS Model, we define learning in the following manner: *Learning* has occurred when a child is able to apply an acquired skill or set of skills across people, places, and circumstances in an appropriate manner. Inherent in this definition are a child's increasing conceptional and operational understanding of activities and the relevance of skills to life routines and events. The ultimate goal is for a child to understand how and when to use acquired skills as independently as possible and consistently apply them in a functional manner in meaningful activities.

How Are Goals Selected and Targeted for a Child?

Goals drive the design and selection of activities and may require modification of important activities that already occur in a child's life. Goals also determine the types of transactional supports that need to be developed and implemented. The SCERTS Model uses three major criteria in determining goals: 1) functionality, 2) family priorities, and 3) developmental appropriateness.

Goals Must Be Functional

For this criterion, the primary questions are, "What difference will this skill make in a child's life?" and "What is a child learning this skill for?" A related question is, "Why is this activity being used as the context for learning?" As discussed in Volume I, the SCERTS Model is not a model that teaches "readiness skills" with the hope that the child will know how to use the skills in other settings outside of the primary learning context or that the skills will be helpful for a child at some unspecified point in the future. For

Prioritize Weekly SCERTS Objectives

Child Social Communication and Emotional Regulation objectives	Partner Transactional Support objectives
1.	1.
2.	2.
3.	3.
4.	4.
5.	5.
6.	6.
7.	7.
8.	8.

Further Assessment—Key Results or Additional Recommendations

SAP Activity Planning

Identify key activities using the SAP Activity Planning Form for
❑ Morning schedule ❑ Afternoon schedule

SCERTS Family Support Plan

Educational Support		Emotional Support	
Activity	How often	Activity	How often

SCERTS Support Plan for Professionals and Service Providers

Educational Support		Emotional Support	
Activity	How often	Activity	How often

Figure 1.1. Program planning portions of the SAP Summary Form (SAP Sum). A full-size blank version of the SAP Sum for each communication stage appears in Appendix A of Volume I. Filled-in samples of this form appear in Chapters 5–7 of Volume II.

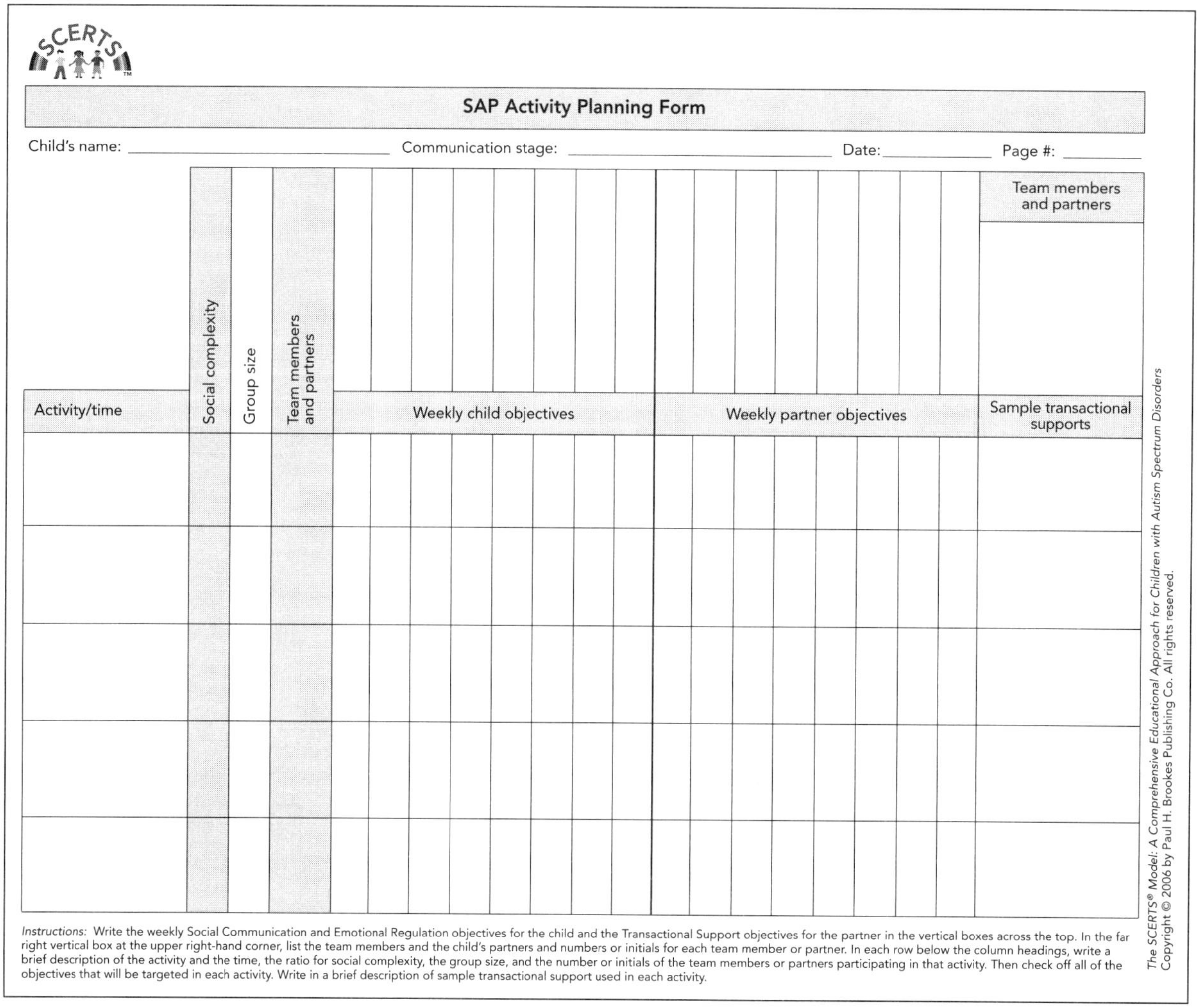
SCERTS™

SAP Activity Planning Form

Child's name: ______ Communication stage: ______ Date: ______ Page #: ______

Activity/time	Social complexity	Group size	Team members and partners	Weekly child objectives	Weekly partner objectives	Sample transactional supports

Team members and partners

Instructions: Write the weekly Social Communication and Emotional Regulation objectives for the child and the Transactional Support objectives for the partner in the vertical boxes across the top. In the far right vertical box at the upper right-hand corner, list the team members and the child's partners and numbers or initials for each team member or partner. In each row below the column headings, write a brief description of the activity and the time, the ratio for social complexity, the group size, and the number or initials of the team members or partners participating in that activity. Then check off all of the objectives that will be targeted in each activity. Write in a brief description of sample transactional support used in each activity.

Figure 1.2. SAP Activity Planning Form. A full-size blank version of the SAP Activity Planning Form for each communication stage appears in Appendix A of Volume I. Filled-in samples of this form appear in Chapters 5–7 of Volume II.

example, the teaching of matching skills, a common readiness skill taught in many programs (e.g., matching shapes, colors) would only be targeted in the SCERTS Model if it were to directly relate to supporting a child's active involvement in activities at school or in other settings, such as matching in meaningful activities at circle time or at home. An example of a more functional use of this ability would be matching picture symbols of functional objects, to help a child to become familiar with those symbols before adding them to his or her communication book to address a social-communicative goal, or matching pictures to play Lotto with friends, to address the interpersonal support goal of learning to play with peers.

Goals Must Address Family Priorities

Related to the issue of functionality is whether identified goals are consistent with the priorities and values of parents and other family members. In other words, how important are potential goals for a child in the life of the family and in the eyes of family members relative to their goals, hopes, and dreams for their child? In our experience, goals such as expressing emotions, maintaining a well-regulated emotional state, sharing experiences with parents about events or friends at school, and communicating and playing with other children and family members are examples of typical high-priority goals for parents.

However, it is important to note that in some cases, goals that are priorities for parents may appear to parents to be functional but may not be functional upon closer scrutiny. For example, some parents may be interested in goals that give the appearance of competence, such as those having to do purely with rote learning (e.g., counting up to high numbers in a rote manner; reciting the alphabet; reading flash cards; stating rotely learned facts, such as facts about history in response to a list of questions). However, in the teaching process, there may be little or no attention to helping the child understand the meaning or to comprehend the words or the facts. In such cases, there may be a need for discussion with parents as part of the educational aspect of family support. Some parents may not understand that such skills provide a superficial picture of competence, especially when progress is measured primarily in reference to a child performing the rotely learned skills in the same format in which they were taught. In reality, these skills may not contribute to the child's functional learning and integrated knowledge and therefore may have little positive impact in the life of the child. (It is important to note that some rotely learned skills can be functional for a child, such as a child learning one's home address, telephone number, and so forth.)

Goals Must Be Developmentally Appropriate

The last criterion of goal selection addresses the following question: "Are goals appropriate to a child's developmental capacities in social communication (e.g., language, play), emotional regulatory capacities, and social and cognitive understanding?" One of the most common problems we observe in some approaches that are not developmentally based is that the skills targeted in any of the areas just noted may significantly under- or overshoot a child's developmental capacities. In our experience, children with ASD often become very aware of activities or goals that are either too challenging or not challenging enough. In circumstances in which activities or goals are either significantly below or above a child's developmental capacities, the following problems may result:

1. The child may be either bored or, conversely, too challenged and stressed, leading to resistance to the activity (i.e., anticipatory avoidance) or attempts to escape the activity.

2. Lack of motivation may result in problems maintaining an optimal level of arousal for learning (e.g., a child with a low arousal bias may remain in that state).

3. The child may remain preoccupied and inwardly focused (e.g., on the inner world of videos, songs, and so forth), rather than shifting attention to social partners and engaging optimally with others to the extent that the child is able to do so.

4. If attempts are made to have the child respond to language or academic tasks well beyond his or her level of language comprehension or conceptual abilities, the child may resort to a rote memory strategy with retention but little understanding of the information being presented. Rote recitation of responses may give a spurious picture of developmental growth, when, in fact, little of value is being learned.

5. Ultimately, the child may develop negative emotional memories related to the activity or events, and future efforts to engage the child may trigger negative reactions, such as refusals or persistent attempts to leave or escape from an activity.

In the SCERTS Model, goals are developmentally based as they are derived from the SAP, a comprehensive assessment of a child's social-communicative and emotional regulatory abilities across a variety of settings and partners. The developmental basis for targeting goals is derived from research on child development as well as from developmental patterns documented in research on children with ASD (see Chapters 2, 3, and 4 in Volume I for a review). In the SCERTS Model, educational goals are organized according to the three primary developmental stages used in the SAP: Social Partner, Language Partner, and Conversational Partner (see Chapter 2 in Volume I for a detailed discussion of these stages).

It also is important to remember that the SCERTS Model focuses on supporting developmental change in underlying capacities, not simply teaching a laundry list of skills. Thus, overriding long-term goals are to support a child in moving from the Social Partner to the Language Partner to the Conversational Partner stage in joint attention and symbol use capacities, as well as to support a child in enhancing and expanding emotional regulatory capacities. Other important developmental capacities that are prioritized are a child's sense of competence and confidence as a communicator and social partner and the child's capacity to develop positive relationships, to be well regulated and organized, to experience joy in social engagement, and to develop a positive sense of self. We have referred to these in Volume I as Social-Emotional Growth Indicators and have operationalized them by targeting and measuring a child's 1) happiness, 2) sense of self, 3) sense of other, 4) active learning and organization, 5) flexibility and resilience, 6) cooperation and appropriateness of behavior, 7) independence, and 8) social membership and friendships.

In What Settings Are Goals Addressed?

Ideally, the answer to the question, "In which settings are goals addressed?" should be "everywhere." The SCERTS Model is designed to target goals across home, school, and community settings. In practice, goals are targeted and progress is measured in the settings a child experiences most frequently and where services are provided. This is determined, to some extent, by the child's age and whether the child is in a program with a predetermined schedule of activities (e.g., child care, preschool, school). For example, for very young children receiving services at home or in individualized therapy sessions (e.g., speech-language therapy, occupational therapy), professionals and parents have control over the design of the schedule and the activities selected. However, when children enter preschool programs and continue into the school years, social expectations require that children learn to participate successfully in an agenda designed for a group of children, and activities may be more difficult to individualize. In such cases, the goals of the preschool, kindergarten, or elementary school curriculum become an important part of a child's program, and these more complex social settings offer opportunities for more advanced goals in social communication, emotional regulation, and transactional supports. However, in the SCERTS Model, the goals of the school curriculum, and the specific activities selected to address those goals for a student with ASD still must meet the three criteria noted for goal selection (i.e., functionality, family priorities, developmental appropriateness). Goals identified in the SCERTS Model curriculum are designed to be flexible so that they may yield individualized objectives that are relevant to a school's curriculum, a family's priorities, and a child's functional needs.

Multiple Goals Are Targeted within Activities

Another clear distinction in contrasting how goals are targeted in the SCERTS Model compared with how goals are targeted in some other educational approaches for children is that any one activity may have multiple goals across the Social Communication, Emotional Regulation, and Transactional Support domains of the model and may target multiple skills. This is in contrast to approaches that isolate single skills and design training protocols focusing on those specific isolated skills. In the SCERTS Model, an activity would never be designed to focus solely on an isolated skill or single skill domain such as receptive language, expressive language, eye contact, matching, or motor imitation. To be sure, many of these skills may be necessary for successful participation in meaningful activities. However, in everyday activities, a child most often needs to apply coordinated skills to be successful; therefore, an activity may target as many as two to four primary goals, with measurement of progress for each of the goals. For example, a cooking activity might have as its primary goals social communication (e.g., making choices for requesting, commenting on observations), emotional regulation (e.g., maintaining active engagement over many turns in the activity, requesting assistance, requesting a break and returning to the activity when needed), and the use of transactional supports (e.g., using a picture sequence to follow the logical steps in the activity, taking turns with peers). It is the *coordination* of these skills, not application of each skill in isolation, that results in the highest level of competence and independence. In the SCERTS Model, we believe that understanding of and active, successful participation in activities and life routines is more than the sum of a sequence of skills taught in isolation and then "added" together. The meaningfulness of activities and events in the context of a child's life and how coordinated skills support the child's participation and understanding of such events is of the highest priority.

TRANSACTIONAL SUPPORT FOR LEARNING: LEARNING CONTEXTS

The design of activities and the identification and effective use of interpersonal and learning supports are critical factors when supporting a child's progress toward the achievement of high-priority goals.

General Guidelines for Designing Activities

Activities are designed to support success and independence in everyday routines by supporting learning across more varied natural activities and contexts. If a child is struggling in an activity, as evidenced by frequent problem behaviors such as attempts to escape or persistent inattention, it may be, in part, that more rehearsal and practice is needed for the child to develop familiarity with the activity and the skills necessary to succeed. In addition, infusing appropriate transactional supports such as visual supports and environmental modifications to enhance emotional regulation and participation may also be required.

The SCERTS Model incorporates activity-based learning as a primary method to support the development of children with ASD. Activities are developed based on the goals for and developmental capacities of a child and are provided systematically throughout the day. More structured activities, such as planned activity routines, may co-occur with learning opportunities in more natural routines and activities. Program content, goals, instructional strategies, and intensity of practice are based on results of the SAP, other individualized developmental assessments, the child's strengths and learning style, and child and family needs as expressed by caregivers. Activities for learning are selected based on their relevance to naturally occurring activities in everyday environments, incorporating a continuum of one-to-one, small-group, and large-group settings, with an emphasis on shared activities and interactions with other children. Skills are taught and maintained across people, places, and circumstances, with a focus on providing intrinsically motivating activities and natural contingencies by focusing on the learning strengths and interests of children.

Activities include planned activity routines and engineered, modified, and naturally occurring events that are used throughout the day for the purpose of supporting the development and practice of skills, as well as understanding of activities that are directly related to, and infused within the child's natural routines during other parts of the day. To ensure that activities are meaningful and purposeful, careful consideration is given to the learning contexts, or the types of situations in which children learn best. We refer to this approach in the SCERTS Model as the MA & PA approach, which is described next.

The MA & PA Approach for Selecting and Designing Learning Activities

The SCERTS Model places considerable effort into the design of individualized learning activities and modification of everyday activities to be both motivating and functional for a child. We refer to this as the MA & PA approach, which refers to the use of meaningful activities and purposeful activities. In developing the MA & PA approach, we have drawn from the work of Diane Bricker and colleagues on activity-based intervention (Bricker & Cripe, 1992; Bricker, 1998; Pretti-Frontczak & Bricker, 2004), and Lee McLean and colleagues (Snyder-McLean, Solomonson, McLean, & Sack, 1984) on joint action or joint activity routines. We also factor in knowledge of the benefits of consistency and predictability for children with ASD (Prizant, 1982), the need to consider both structure and flexibility in activities, and the importance of visually based and multimodal learning grounded in our understanding of the learning strengths and weaknesses of children with ASD (see Chapter 4 in Volume I for a detailed discussion). Careful planning of activities and the use of transactional supports are inherent parts of the MA & PA approach.

The MA & PA approach is clearly distinct from approaches that are primarily skill based, in which most "learning" occurs when skills are trained in a repetitive mass-trial format in isolation from meaningful activities. It is our belief, based on research as well as years of experience, that approaches that are primarily skill based and that do not use more natural activities from early on compound the problems that children with ASD have in making meaning of their experiences and therefore in applying what they have learned flexibly across settings and partners. However, we also recognize that it is rarely possible to use purely natural learning opportunities and simply follow the child's lead. Therefore, in designing and modifying activities, we find it helpful to think of naturalness along a continuum, which we will return to shortly.

Why the SCERTS Model Uses the MA & PA Approach

The SCERTS Model uses the MA & PA approach for the following reasons:

1. Children with ASD often have problems making sense of experience and reflecting on previous experiences to help in coping and adapting to new experiences. Therefore, they need support in meaningful activities that already occur or that can be scheduled to occur in everyday life.

2. Child development research has found that children organize their understanding of life experiences in reference to events and routines and learn meaningful skills most efficiently in these events and routines. However, if and when repetitive practice is needed, such as learning to request at snack time through use of a picture system or having the opportunity to practice motor skills in gym class, such practice can be arranged to occur within planned activity routines as well as naturally occurring activities. In this manner, the need for repetition and practice can be met without resorting to rote, nonfunctional practice routines outside of meaningful contexts.

3. Meaningful and purposeful activities are, by definition, integrated as part of a child's life routines and are thus more easily replicated across different settings. Activities focusing on isolated skill training are less easily integrated in a child's day across settings.

4. Most activities have a natural logical sequence, clear beginnings and endings, and offer greater opportunities for introducing flexibility than repetitive drill practice offers. Many activities also provide natural, concrete cues to indicate progress toward completion, such as steps in a cooking activity, a board game with friends, and so forth.

5. Activities are more likely to provide opportunities for active learning and engagement. It also is easier to include other children and brothers and sisters in more natural activities.

6. Activities are more likely to be motivating for all involved: children with and without disabilities and adult partners in the activity.

Levels on the Continuum of Naturalness in the MA & PA Approach

In the MA & PA approach, there are four levels on the continuum ranging from least to most natural:

1. Planned activity routines
2. Engineered activities and environments
3. Modified natural activities and environments
4. Naturally occurring events and environments

These levels of naturalness do not imply a strict hierarchical sequence in programming, in which programming must start with planned activity routines before moving to more natural activity structures. Many or all levels may occur simultaneously but may serve overlapping but slightly different purposes in a child's program. Figure 1.3 depicts this continuum, and Table 1.1 summarizes the levels in greater detail.

Planned Activity Routines

Planned activity routines target the instruction of specific skills through multiple learning opportunities for learning a specific skill or set of skills. The skills are only selected if they directly support other naturally occurring routines in other parts of the day. Planned activity routines may be incorporated throughout the day for those children who require a greater degree of individualized instruction and repetition to learn and apply specific skills effectively. These learning routines *are not* used to teach isolated skills that are part of a predetermined lock-step curriculum sequence, nor are the activities devoid of meaningfulness. However, the focus initially may be more on acquiring and practicing a skill with support rather than on independence within the

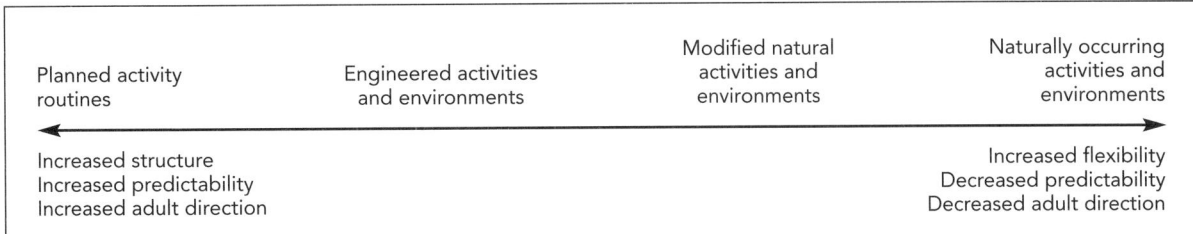

Figure 1.3. The continuum of naturalness in activities in the MA & PA approach of the SCERTS Model.

Table 1.1. Levels of naturalness in the MA & PA approach of the SCERTS Model

Level	Description	Purposes or goals
Planned activity routines	Planned activity routines target initial exposure to routines and activities and the instruction of specific skills through multiple learning opportunities for learning a specific skill or set of skills. The skills are only targeted if they directly support other naturally occurring routines in other parts of the day.	Help a child to learn and rehearse skills to be used within current or upcoming natural or modified routines. Provide multiple opportunities for learning and applying skills that are functional in a wide variety of settings. Help a child to practice a skill that has been identified as a relative weakness within a sequence of skills as part of an established natural routine. Teach a child how to work independently, progress through a sequence of related tasks, and complete preacademic and academic tasks with minimal adult assistance.
Engineered activities and environments	Engineered activities and environments are activities that may not occur naturally in the child's life but are designed and scheduled to provide consistent familiar and predictable formats for learning.	Provide consistent, predictable, and familiar routines from which the child can practice and maintain skills. Help a child to acquire familiarity with such activities and a sense and meaning of activities similar to those that are naturally occurring. Help a child to understand events and master skills within such events through multiple opportunities of predictable activities that can be repeated throughout the day and week.
Modified natural activities and environments	Natural routines, activities, and environments that are already a part of a child's life routines are modified to support optimal participation and engagement, through the addition of supports for social communication and emotional regulation.	Introduce significant changes in natural activities to support greater success when a child is significantly challenged in experiencing such success. The ultimate goal is to maintain the integrity of the activity or setting while supporting the child's active participation.
Naturally occurring events and environments	Naturally occurring events and environments are learning opportunities that occur within settings and activities that already are present in the life of a child and his or her family.	Provide learning opportunities that are most natural, with natural contingencies and motivations, without the need for significant additional supports. Other children may support the child naturally, but such support is neither planned by adults nor prompted.

Note: These levels of naturalness do not imply a hierarchical sequence in programming. All levels may occur simultaneously but may serve different purposes in a child's overall program.

event. Thus, there is a higher degree of support at this level, such as guided participation through prompting and modeling, use of visual supports, and so forth. Planned activity routines are particularly useful for the following:

1. *Learning and rehearsing skills to be used within current or upcoming natural or modified routines,* such as teaching and practicing imitative motor movements in a planned therapy session in preparation for applying these movements in an upcoming circle-time song such as "Head, Shoulders, Knees, and Toes."

2. *Providing multiple opportunities for learning and then applying skills that are functional in a wide variety of settings,* such as for a child at the Social Partner or emerging Language Partner stage, working on vocal imitation such as vocal production of "hi" and a high-five gesture for greeting practiced with friends in a classroom context, and then applying this skill when this student sees his or her friends in the hallway at school. For a child at the Conversational Partner stage, practice in a planned activity routine may involve learning to order food from a menu.

3. *Practicing a skill that has been identified as a relative weakness within a sequence of skills as part of an established natural routine.* Such a skill identified as a weakness requires additional and multiple practice opportunities outside of the natural activity for successful acquisition in order for a child to be independently successful within the more natural routine. For example, for a child at the Language Partner stage, practice in a planned activity routine may entail providing practice raising a hand in a small group to respond to the request, "Who wants a turn?" For a child at the Conversational Partner stage, practice in a planned activity routine may involve learning to explain a two- to three-step sequence in preparing food for a group cooking activity in the classroom. Planned activity routines are also useful in teaching children how to work independently, to progress through a sequence of related tasks, and to complete preacademic and academic tasks with minimal adult assistance.

Engineered Activities and Environments

At the next level in the MA & PA approach, environments and activities that may not occur naturally in a child's life may be developed to provide consistent, predictable, and familiar routines from which the child can practice and maintain skills and acquire a sense and meaning of events similar to naturally occurring events. Examples include social skill groups, Circle of Friends, and Friendship Groups. In engineered activities and environments, developmentally appropriate skills can be more consistently practiced by the child in the context of developing relationships because social expectations for participation, and goals of activities are relatively clear. Furthermore, such activities are designed so that when necessary, the child receives clear instructional feedback and consistent and contingent responses from an adult partner. Communicative initiations and confidence in applying acquired skills are more likely when the child understands the purpose of the activity or event and when both the child and his or her partner can predict outcomes across people, places, and circumstances. Understanding of events and the use of skills within such events are solidified through multiple occurrences of predictable activities that can be engineered and repeated throughout the day and week. Instructional materials used during these activities should be very similar to or the same as those within the naturally occurring environment. Through the engineering of predictable environments, the child's cognitive resources can be more efficiently and effectively applied toward learning and applying skills, with an understanding of the purpose of the child's participation.

Although engineering of activities and environments may initially require that professionals and parents introduce new experiences and events in a child's life, such activities and environments may become a natural part of a child's routine over time if scheduled with sufficient regularity and consistency that the child comes to anticipate and expect them to happen on a regular basis. For example, for a child at the Social Partner or Language Partner stage, a Circle of Friends program may be started in school or other structured learning environments for the child to develop friendships and learn the skills to participate in shared enjoyable activities such as sensory-motor routines or constructive play (e.g., building with blocks or Legos). At the Conversational Partner stage, a school-age child may have a Circle of Friends group focused on special-interest activities based on themes such as science (e.g., weather, outer space). The ultimate goal is to carry over such activities to settings outside of school with brothers and sisters or with playmates.

Modified Natural Activities and Environments

At this level in the MA & PA approach, natural routines, activities, and settings that are already a part of a child's life are modified to support optimal participation and engagement, by adding supports for social communication and emotional regulation. Significant changes may be introduced in such activities to support greater success when a child is significantly challenged in experiencing success. For example, a child at the Social Partner or Language Partner stage may be offered more opportunities for making choices, or visual supports and movement breaks may be added to the activity to support attention and emotional regulation. A child at the Conversational Partner stage may have the ability to select friends with whom to work or play and may negotiate with those friends about the activities they wish to engage in.

Naturally Occurring Events and Environments

At the most natural level in the SCERTS Model's MA & PA approach, learning opportunities are identified within naturally occurring environments and activities that are already a part of the life of a child and his or her family. No significant special supports are implemented nor are activity modifications made, as the child is capable of participating with natural cues and supports. This level typically involves a continuum of naturally occurring one-to-one, small-group, and large-group settings, with an emphasis on interactions with other children. Of course, a child's age would be an important factor at this level, as very young children have fewer natural opportunities to participate in large-group activities. Examples of naturally occurring events include full inclusion in a general education classroom for a child who is able to learn in that environment with no or minimal paraprofessional support, or playing with cousins during family visits on a regular basis. Other children may support the child naturally, but such support is not designed to occur nor is it prompted. In these more natural settings, interpersonal supports may come to play a greater role for the child with ASD, as the attunement and support of the social partners are critical factors for ensuring the child's success in more natural contexts.

As discussed previously, planned activity routines and engineered and modified activities may be incorporated throughout the day to support the development of skills that are directly related to and infused within a child's natural routines. Furthermore, the nature of supports and the specific goals addressed in planned activity routines and in engineered and modified activities may vary greatly according to the developmental abilities of the child relative to the Social Partner, Language Partner, and Conversational Partner stages.

Characteristics of Activities in the MA & PA Approach

Activity or event structure plays an important role for children with ASD, as an activity's characteristics may have an important impact on a child's success. As noted earlier, in the MA & PA approach, we incorporate characteristics of joint activity routines and activity-based intervention when designing activities. For example, we include the following specific characteristics of joint activity routines (Snyder-McLean et al., 1984) that are consistent with the social-communicative and emotional regulation focuses of the SCERTS Model:

1. An obvious unifying theme or purpose to support shared attention
2. A requirement for joint focus and interaction to support reciprocity
3. A limited number of clearly delineated roles
4. Exchangeable or reversible roles
5. A logical, nonarbitrary sequence
6. A structure for turn taking in predictable sequence
7. Planned repetition
8. A plan for controlled variation to enhance flexibility

Types of Activities

In the MA & PA approach, it is important to recognize that different activities may be engaged in for different purposes and that these activities have different types of structures, which may vary in difficulty for different children (see Table 1.2).

Goal-Directed Activities

Goal-directed activities have a clear sequence of steps with a clear, easily perceived end goal. For example, food preparation, such as making a sandwich, or constructive play, such as building towers or doing puzzles, typically must follow a logical sequence to conclusion. When the activity is concluded, there are clear, natural contextual cues such as eating the sandwich, knocking down the tower that was just built, or putting the final piece in a puzzle and then putting the puzzle away. These are goal-directed activities in that the primary function of engaging in such activities is to reach the end goal. However, such activities also may involve multiple goals such as social communication, independently following a sequence of steps, and problem solving, all in the service of completing the activity toward the predesignated goal.

Cooperative Turn-Taking Games

In contrast, cooperative turn-taking games do not necessarily have clear end goals in the same sense. The primary goal is in the success of social reciprocity, turn taking, and mutual enjoyment derived from such shared activities. For example, turn-taking games or routines, such as rolling balls back and forth, taking turns in playing musical instru-

Table 1.2. Types of activities with different structures

Goal-directed activities such as preparation or fabrication of a specific end product (e.g., food preparation, constructive play)

Cooperative turn-taking games or routines in which the goals are shared enjoyment and reciprocity (e.g., songs with spaces to fill, action routines, sports)

Theme-oriented activities organized around a plot or a theme, which may have multiple embedded components, with greater social-cognitive demands (e.g., daily living routines, preparation for bedtime, going to a restaurant)

ments, or singing songs, or sensory-motor games, such as taking turns going on a slide, playing on a seesaw, or tickling or chase games, have as their primary goal shared enjoyment. In a sense, for these activities, the goal is "in the journey," not in any one end result. The success of such activities is measured by qualities such as shared emotional experience, social reciprocity, and cooperation. Some activities may have elements of a reciprocal, cooperative game as well as a goal-directed activity, such as board games (e.g., Candy Land, Chutes and Ladders).

Theme-Oriented Activities

Theme-oriented activities are organized around and may have multiple embedded components, which may be related to functional skills in daily routines or even to imaginary events. For example, daily living routines such as preparation for bedtime, going to a restaurant, or taking a trip to the zoo involve sequences of smaller events that are organized in a logical manner. For example, for bedtime preparation, smaller events that are part of a larger whole may include brushing teeth, taking a shower, putting on pajamas, reading a book with Mom or Dad, and exchanging good-night kisses and hugs. Imaginary events may involve imaginative play sequences with toys or action figures or may involve role playing based on children's literature such as fairy tales or children's books. In general, there are more significant cognitive and social requirements for a child to participate in and understand activities organized around larger conceptual themes, which would be most appropriate for children at the more advanced Language Partner and Conversational Partner stages. There may be a greater need for use of transactional supports for children to participate successfully with the greatest degree of independence and understanding in theme-oriented activities.

Guidelines for Implementing Activities

The following guidelines for implementing activities are not designed to provide a cookbook approach that is to be applied inflexibly to all children with ASD. Rather, they provide a framework from which to develop a meaningful approach from both a developmental and functional perspective. The following sections provide guidelines for 1) implementing activities within natural settings and routines according to the MA & PA approach, 2) individualizing educational programming to meet the unique needs of each child with ASD, and 3) providing the transactional supports necessary to best support a child with ASD while implementing the program. Initial steps in implementing activities are as follows:

1. *Identify developmentally appropriate goals and outcomes.* Goals and objectives are determined from the SAP, which identifies 1) relative strengths and weaknesses in the domains of Social Communication, Emotional Regulation, and Transactional Support, 2) parent/family priorities, and 3) child functional needs. It is recommended that not more than two to three goals be targeted in each domain—Social Communication, Emotional Regulation, and Transactional Support.

2. *Identify at least three activities that are meaningful, purposeful, and motivational.* The purpose for a child's participation in each activity must be carefully considered. Activities selected should be functional, purposeful, and motivating so that the target skills can be best embedded and taught.

3. *Infuse goals across at least three activities across settings* so that the child learns to apply skills across people, settings, and activities.

4. *Identify/select optimal levels of social complexity in activities based on the child's learning needs and strengths.* For example, design an appropriate proportion of large-group, small-group, and one-to-one activities that best address target goals.

5. *Within Steps 2–4, identify the sequenced skills that are embedded into each activity* as part of the child's program and/or that are an inherent part of the steps of that activity that are relative weaknesses for the child. These skills would require a higher degree of adult instructional support.

6. *Identify appropriate transactional supports for social communication and emotional regulation.* Supports may include interpersonal supports, such as responsive strategies and level of language complexity used, and learning supports, such as changes in the ways the activity is organized, planned movement opportunities, the use of visuals, and so forth. Chapter 4 in this volume provides a detailed consideration on how to link transactional supports to Social Communication and Emotional Regulation goals.

7. *One-to-one or small-group planned activity routines may be provided as opportunities for increased practice or rehearsal of skills that require more instructional opportunities.* As noted earlier, planned activity routines can focus on teaching understanding of events and the necessary skills needed to actively participate in such events and will eventually be incorporated into the same learning environments in which the skills will be used most independently (modified natural routines and natural routines). As mentioned earlier, in using planned activity routines, it also is important to use the same or similar materials that are available in the natural learning environments. It is important for the child to practice and rehearse these skills within the context that he or she will eventually use them so that understanding of the natural cues of how and when to use the skills being taught is supported.

Specific Guidelines for Implementing Activities

The following specific guidelines are offered to support the introduction of activities, with the eventual introduction of variation and elaboration to support flexibility and learning.

1. Introduce the concept of the activity gradually. Start with simple activity routines based on 1) a child's motivations and interest, 2) functionality in the child's life, 3) the family's level of interest, and 4) whether the activity routine occurs or can be scheduled to occur as a regular activity in other settings.

2. Discuss, model, and/or demonstrate the purpose of the activity, or use a picture sequence and/or an example of a completed product to facilitate understanding of the goal. Initially, a greater degree of modeling and prompting will be necessary to establish routines. Fade prompts and support as routines become familiar, however, and ensure that visuals and other transactional supports are available for extra support for language comprehension or during states of dysregulation.

3. Provide consistency, predictability, and repetition until the child can participate actively with consistent success in the activity. Add variation as needed (see Step 5), but keep meaning or purpose constant.

4. Establish clear signals for initiation and termination of an activity. This may include rituals such as songs, movement, or greeting routines. Provide consistent simple language to mark dynamic aspects of the activity, such as action concepts.

5. Add flexibility and variation to activities, as well as needs and opportunities to communicate by doing the following:

    a. Sabotage the activity by interrupting or violating a routine once the activity is established and the child clearly demonstrates familiarity with the activity.

b. Omit necessary materials.

c. Add novelty by introducing new materials, by initiating familiar activities in new contexts, or by introducing new activities in familiar contexts.

d. Initiate an activity and "play possum," requiring that the child indicate how the activity needs to proceed. This strategy is especially effective with highly motivating and frequently recurring activities.

Other Considerations in Developing and Implementing Activities

There are a number of additional factors to consider to encourage and support active participation and learning and to address the most common challenges faced by children with ASD.

Create Communicative Opportunities

Children with ASD often are unable to initiate communication due to a number of challenges, which may include difficulties with 1) word retrieval, 2) processing of language and nonverbal cues, 3) emotional regulation, 4) understanding social-communicative conventions, and 5) motor planning difficulties. To compound these difficulties, children often are not provided the opportunities to initiate communication due to highly adult-directed verbal styles of interaction, such as a high frequency of questions and directives and excessive premature verbal or physical prompting. In daily activities, restrictive adult-directed patterns such as highly directive interaction styles can and should be modified to provide increased communicative opportunities so that children learn how and when to communicate within naturally occurring settings. In the SCERTS Model, this is addressed as Transactional Support goals under Interpersonal Support and Learning Support.

Design Activities to Be Intrinsically Motivating and Fun, Resulting in Positive Emotional Experiences

Natural incentives are one of the keys to learning within the SCERTS Model. The use of routines and activities that are meaningful, purposeful, and intrinsically motivating for the child with ASD are designed to maintain extended interactions with partners in activities. The goal is for a child to acquire a sense of confidence, competence, and enjoyment within activities, leading to positive emotional experience and positive emotional memories. Over time, as these cumulative positive emotional experiences become associated with people, activities, and settings, the child becomes intrinsically motivated to seek out and cooperate with others in the context of activities. Conversely, negative emotional memories, which may be instigated by disorganizing levels of stimulation, inappropriate levels of task difficulty, and/or an excessively directive and controlling partner style, may result in the child's refusing or avoiding people or activities when they are introduced at a later time.

Natural Interactions and Settings Are Most Desirable for Learning

As discussed earlier, the ultimate goal is for a child to be able to apply social communicative, emotional regulatory, and other functional skills in natural interactions across people, settings, and circumstances. Such learning involves the child's understanding and following of natural cues, conventions, and rules of interactions with adults and peers in a variety of contexts. Natural interactions and settings serve to promote more successful and emotionally satisfying interactions between the child and his or her partners across activities and settings.

Target Interrelated and Interdependent Skills within Activity Routines

Targeted skills should be taught as part of a naturally occurring sequence and combination of interrelated and interdependent skills embedded within activities. Naturally occurring sequences of skills are not a series of isolated skills but a seamless flow of interrelated skills that when applied in a sequential and organized manner lead toward active participation in an activity; efficient learning; goal-directed behavior; and, eventually, independence across settings. The child learns how and when to apply these skills based on natural cues inherent within routines. Thus, in essence, the child learns to become a problem solver, one who surveys the environment and acts accordingly based on an increasing understanding of activities.

Use Activity-Based Principles in School Settings

Classroom-based routines and activity-based learning can be complimentary. For example, children in the later elementary grades typically become involved in classroom math, reading, language arts, and so forth as opposed to doing developmental or center-based activities, which are more typical of early childhood settings and, in some cases, early primary grades. Math time in a typical classroom might involve an extended period of lecturing, demonstration, and teaching activities that might last for extended periods depending on the grade level and the teacher's style. A child with ASD who is included in a general education classroom for a math lesson may or may not be able to participate for an entire lesson, or possibly only certain aspects of this lesson may be relevant for that child. The concept of "partial participation" (Brown et al., 1979) may be applied in these situations. That is, the child only participates in the aspects of the math lesson that are meaningful, purposeful, motivating, and related to his or her IEP. Instead of remaining for the full duration of the activity, the child may instead participate in a planned activity routine that emphasizes and applies the math skills he or she is learning within a functional routine. This may occur within the classroom or in a separate learning area such as a resource room.

The routine might also incorporate interrelated and interdependent skills, as discussed previously. For instance, the child's math objective may include learning quantity from 1 to 10 in a one-to-one correspondence activity. An activity-based routine could be developed whereby the child practices quantity from 1 to 10 in the general education classroom's math time for the first half hour. The child then may participate in collecting checked-out books to be returned to the library, counting the number of books, writing the quantity number on paper, going to the library, placing the books in the returned books slot, and communicating to the librarian the number of books returned. In this example, the planned activity routine could relate to naturally occurring learning opportunities and systematic instruction across cognitive, academic, communication, adaptive, and motor skills while leading toward increasing independent life skills. All of the principles of planned activity routines described earlier could be applied within this activity.

Create a Balance in Activities Throughout the Day

The following dimensions are considered when planning a child's day to create a balance along different dimensions of activities:

1. Natural versus modified natural activities, engineered activities, and planned activity routines
2. Unfamiliar versus familiar routines
3. Adult-directed versus child-directed routines
4. Difficult versus easy or mastered routines
5. One-to-one versus small- and large-group routines
6. Preferred versus nonpreferred (but "must-do") activities
7. In-class versus out-of-class routines

8. Quieter versus noisier environments

9. Movement-based versus sedentary activities

This approach to creating a balance of activities during the day must take into consideration each child's developmental abilities in social communication and emotional regulation and his or her learning style. When such factors are considered, decisions regarding the child's level of participation for each activity at school or in other settings will be better informed. For example, a child should not be required to participate in learning a classroom activity or routine just because "that is what the other children are doing," without regard to the following questions: "Is the targeted classroom activity or routine, meaningful, purposeful, and/or motivating for that child?" and "Furthermore, are characteristics of the activity and the setting within the child's emotional regulatory capacities (with or without supports)?" If so, the child should be supported to participate at the level targeted by the team. If the child's learning style, learning capacity, and emotional regulatory abilities allow the child to participate only minimally or for only part of the activity routine, the program plan may call for a transition to another type of activity that better addresses the child's strengths and weaknesses for the remainder of that activity time period. The goal of counterbalancing activities along the dimensions just listed is to assist the child in continuing to participate in meaningful and purposeful learning activities with increasing active participation throughout the day, while reducing the potential for dysregulation caused by inflexibilities in program planning.

Other Issues Related to Learning Contexts

Classroom Structure

For school-age children, the activity-based approach used in the SCERTS Model places great importance on classroom structure. Children with ASD respond more positively in a classroom learning environment when there is a high degree of predictability and consistency, which minimizes the dysregulating effect of uncertainty. Problem behaviors resulting from emotional dysregulation are more likely to increase as the degree of uncertainty increases (Rydell & Prizant, 1995). Classroom predictability is increased through organizing the physical space with clear markers and boundaries and providing visually based environmental cues and supports for a child to follow in the flow of the classroom schedule. Consistent and systematic use of instructional strategies and transactional supports reduces the potential for confusion and excessive adult assistance or prompting and enhances the potential for independent success.

Role of Pull-Out Therapies

For the most part, an activity-based approach suggests that to the extent possible, skills should not be taught individually or in isolation from the settings in which they typically are needed and would be applied. Teaching individual skills outside of naturally occurring contexts may lead toward rigid learning patterns and generalization difficulties. Pull-out therapy or one-to-one therapy time to address communication, motor, and sensory difficulties is never the sole mode of providing services in the MA & PA approach of the SCERTS Model, and the extent to which it is needed is determined by a child's emotional regulatory abilities and how well a child can learn in more natural and complex activities. Ideally, therapeutic support specific to a discipline (e.g., occupational therapy, speech-language therapy, cognitive/developmental) is conducted mostly within planned activity routines and in engineered and modified activities, which are designed to directly support skill acquisition within the natural learning environment. Again, this approach emphasizes teaching of skills within the environment in which the skill will be applied, maintained, and naturally reinforced, to the extent that a child is able to be supported optimally, given the learning challenges inherent in more complex settings.

Criteria Defining the MA & PA Approach

In summary, the MA & PA approach of the SCERTS Model is defined by the following criteria:

1. Activities should make sense (i.e., be meaningful and purposeful) relative to a child's daily life activities and routines. That is, activities that occur across settings or that can readily be scheduled to occur outside of the school or teaching situation are designed and/or modified to support the learning of functional skills.

2. To the extent possible, activities should be selected on the basis of a child's motivations and strengths. If an activity is not inherently motivating (e.g., as may be the case with self-help skills), efforts should be made to infuse the activity with supports, topics, information, or qualities that support the child's learning and emotional regulation. For example, for a child who has problems attending during group circle but who likes Winnie-the-Pooh characters, such characters may be infused in circle time activities.

3. Activities should be designed and/or transactional supports should be used to provide a child with a clear sense of what the goal of the activity is, the logical sequence of the activity, the steps within the activity, and clear indicators of when the activity is completed. Whenever possible, visual supports should be used to support the child's understanding of the activity sequence, such as use of a within-activity schedule in a multistep science project.

4. Activities should provide a child with multiple and frequent opportunities for initiating communication, making choices, repairing breakdowns, and responding to the communication of partners.

5. Activities should have an understandable structure for social participation and turn-taking. Whenever possible, visual supports should be used to support a child's understanding of his or her role as a social partner.

6. Whenever possible, activities should involve the participation of children who provide good language and social models, to support the development of positive relationships.

Chapter 2

Guide to SCERTS Model Educational Practices, Part II

Transactional Support: Interpersonal Support and Learning Support and Learning and Playing with Peers

INSTRUCTIONAL STRATEGIES	Instructional strategies are viewed as a critical element of the Transactional Support domain of the SCERTS Model. We view instructional strategies broadly as all efforts to support a child's development, involving all partners who interact with the child on a regular basis, including professionals, parents and other caregivers, and other children. Instructional strategies are addressed in two components of Transactional Support: Interpersonal Support and Learning Support. More specifically, Interpersonal Support delineates the essential elements of the behavior of adult and child partners that support social communication, emotional regulation, and learning. Learning Support specifies how learning aids are used and how instructional strategies best support a child's engagement and learning.
ROLE OF THE ADULT PARTNER	The essence of the term *transactional* in the name *Transactional Support* is that there is an ongoing mutual influence between two or more partners in social exchange and that all partners bear some responsibility to make the exchange successful. We believe that to best support a child, an adult partner must be committed to engage in an ongoing process of self-reflection and, when necessary, behavioral change to best support the child's engagement and learning. This process is characterized by a partner's increasing *awareness, investment in change,* and *focused change* with respect to interpersonal style and use of learning supports.

1. *Awareness* involves a partner's general knowledge of the most effective interpersonal strategies and styles that best support a child's learning. It also includes self-awareness of one's own style and heightened sensitivity to a specific child's reactions to attempts at engaging the child. Without self-awareness of one's communicative and interactive style, there is little potential for a partner to adjust his or her behavior in a manner that supports the child's engagement, learning, and sense of competence.

2. *Investment in change* requires a partner's acceptance that his or her behavior plays a critical role in developing a positive relationship with a child and in supporting the child's motivation, engagement, and learning. An invested partner is willing to consciously assess the effect of his or her own behavior on the child's learning, especially when problems are apparent, and share responsibility for difficulties that arise in interactions. A partner who has little self-awareness and is not invested in change may blame the child for interactional and relationship difficulties, which

releases the partner from taking responsibility for difficulties a child may experience in social engagement and learning. Too often, children with ASD are blamed for interactional difficulties, even though educators and clinicians are well aware that difficulties experienced by children with ASD are often due to their extreme sensitivity to different levels of social complexity and more general stimulation in the environment, which may contribute to such difficulties.

3. *Focused change* involves a partner's concerted effort to make specific changes in his or her behavior, including interactive style and instructional strategies used, with ongoing systematic assessment of the positive or negative impact on a child as a result of the changes made. The process is one of ongoing hypothesis testing about the factors that create difficulties in interpersonal interactions and relationships, as well as the factors that are associated with the child's success in engagement and learning.

Another important role of the child's partner is to support the child's understanding of the activities and the expectations for participation and use of skills across activities and settings. The partner may initially serve as an important role model as skills are first being taught and may engineer a learning environment to control for novelty and uncertainty by using routines that highlight familiarity and predictability. It is most desirable for the support role of the adult partner to decrease over time as the child learns and participates with less direct support and applies newly acquired skills within familiar routines across people, settings, and circumstances. However, the support role of the adult partner and the child's learning and participation vary depending on the child's developmental capacities and progress. Overall, the emphasis is on supporting the child to be actively engaged and involved and not simply on "testing" the child or placing the child in the position of performing with the primary goal of eliciting the "correct" answers in inflexible routines.

TRANSACTIONAL SUPPORT: INTERPERSONAL SUPPORT

As noted in the SCERTS Assessment Process–Observation (SAP-O) forms and criteria in Chapter 8 in Volume I, the Interpersonal Support component of Transactional Support focuses on desirable characteristics of partner behavior and is divided into the following goals:

IS1 Partner is responsive to child

IS2 Partner fosters initiation

IS3 Partner respects child's independence

IS4 Partner sets stage for engagement

IS5 Partner provides developmental support

IS6 Partner adjusts language input

IS7 Partner models appropriate behaviors

Research has demonstrated that these aspects of partner interactive and instruction style are associated with effective practice that supports optimal engagement and learning for children with and without disabilities. We now provide examples of how these generic aspects of interpersonal support are operationalized into goals and objectives, with the understanding that instructional practices must be individualized for specific children based on results of the SAP and each child's profile of developmental abilities.

Partner Is Responsive to Child

Interpersonal support involves increased partner responsiveness to a child's attentional focus, communicative attempts, emotional expression, and signals of dysregulation. The specific nature of partner responsivity varies depending upon the developmental stage of the child. Nevertheless, it is broadly defined by the following characteristics in partner behavior. The partner

a. *Follows the child's focus of attention by looking at and/or talking about what the child is attending to:* If the partner uses language to comment on what the child is attending to, the language used would be simpler at the Social Partner and Language Partner stages than at the Conversational Partner stage.

b. *Attunes to the child's emotion and pace by mirroring the emotional tone of the child's behavior:* For example, the partner smiles and laughs in response to the child's positive emotion.

c. *Responds to the child's signals to foster a sense of competence by responding appropriately to the child's intended goal:* For example, if the child is requesting an object, the partner gives the child that object, and if the child is refusing an object, the partner removes that object.

d. *Recognizes and supports the child's behavioral and language strategies to regulate arousal by responding appropriately to the child's attempts at regulation:* For example, if a child at the Social Partner stage is trying to jump or move as an alerting and energizing behavioral strategy, the partner modifies the interaction to support or incorporate this strategy. If a child at the Conversational Partner stage uses language to regulate, by saying, for example, "Don't worry, it's okay" if feeling anxious, the partner may expand on the use of language to support regulation by commenting "Yes, everything is okay."

e. *Recognizes signs of dysregulation and offers support:* For example, when behavioral signs indicate that the child is not available for learning or engaging due to an arousal level that is too high, including distress or extreme excitement, appropriate assistance is provided contingent on the child's arousal state. For a child at the Social Partner stage, a partner might provide appropriate sensory input that is organizing, whereas for a child at the Language Partner or Conversational Partner stage, additional information such as when an activity will end might also be provided through language.

f. *Imitates the child's verbal and/or nonverbal behavior and gives the turn back to the child when appropriate to the context (Social Partner and Language Partner stages):* For example, when a child at the Social Partner stage acts on objects or vocalizes, the partner imitates or approximates these behaviors and pauses, waiting for a further response from the child. For a child at the Language Partner stage, this may involve imitating and expanding on the child's language production.

g. *Provides information or assistance to regulate state (Conversational Partner stage only):* For example, the partner observes the child becoming mildly frustrated or dysregulated and tells the child that after completing two more math examples, he or she can take a break. The partner asks the child if he or she needs assistance.

h. *Offers breaks from interaction or activity when the child's behavior suggests that a break is needed or when the child has been engaged in one activity for a long time:* The break is offered in a manner consistent with the child's developmental capacities and may include encouraging a child at the Social Partner or Language Partner stage to use a sign, picture, or simple oral language for "break" or encouraging a child at the Conversational Partner stage to use more complex language.

i. *Facilitates reengagement in interactions and activities following breaks when the child is demonstrating appropriate arousal level and emotional state to participate fully in ongoing activities:* For example, the child is helped to rejoin an activity after an episode of dysregulation leading to loss of attentionadn lack of participation in the activity. When the child's visual interest and more relaxed body posture indicates that the child is ready to reengage, the partner asks the child to take a turn in the activity.

Partner Fosters Initiation

Initiation is fostered in a number of ways and is noted by the following characteristics in partner behavior. The partner

a. *Offers choices nonverbally or verbally:* For example, choices may include what to eat, what to wear, what activity to participate in, and so forth. Choices are offered at a level appropriate to the child's developmental stage.

b. *Waits for and encourages initiations using nonverbal or vocal signals:* For example, when offered choices or when having needs to communicate, the child is allowed sufficient time to direct a nonverbal or verbal communicative signal to the partner, depending on the child's developmental abilities.

c. *Provides a balance of initiated and respondent turns, resulting in shared control and reciprocity:* A sense of shared control is fostered when the child is not relegated to a passive respondent role within the interaction and instead is supported in efforts to be actively involved.

d. *Allows the child to initiate and terminate activities when appropriate:* For example, the child may indicate that he or she is done with an activity nonverbally by walking away when finished or verbally by saying or signing "done." If the child is engaged in a must-do activity (e.g., dressing, washing) or if the activity is very close to successful completion, the partner verbally acknowledges the child's communicative bid to end the activity even if it is not possible for the activity to be terminated immediately.

Independence is respected in a number of ways and is noted by the following characteristics in partner behavior. The partner

Partner Respects Child's Independence

a. *Allows the child to take breaks to move about as needed when appropriate for the context:* For example, after the child has participated for some time, particularly in activities that require sitting, focusing attention, and processing language, the child is allowed to take a break.

b. *Provides time for the child to solve problems or complete activities at his or her own pace:* For example, the partner refrains from rushing the child or from providing premature prompting as long as the child is progressing in an activity and does not appear to need additional support.

c. *Interprets problem behavior as communicative and responds to problem behavior as communicative and/or regulatory:* For example, if the child pushes or hits to protest, the partner acknowledges the child's intent and models a more socially acceptable means for the child to protest (if appropriate), at a level consistent with the child's developmental abilities. Likewise, if the child is vocalizing loudly in an effort to block out disorganizing environmental sounds, the partner recognizes this and encourages the use of other regulatory strategies consistent with the child's developmental abilities.

d. *Honors protests, rejections, or refusals when appropriate:* For example, in situations in which the child clearly does not wish to accept offered items or engage in activities, the partner does not continue to demand that the child do so under appropriate circumstances, such as during nonessential activities, when other choices of foods or toys are available, and so forth.

Partner Sets Stage for Engagement

Setting the stage for engagement is another area in which strategies used by partners vary depending on a child's developmental stage. A partner sets the stage for engagement in the following ways. The partner

a. *Gets down on the child's level when communicating (Social Partner and Language Partner stages):* The partner positions him- or herself and gets down on the child's level to encourage face-to-face interaction or physical proximity when communicating to the child. However, for a child at the Conversational Partner stage, especially for a school-age child, this is not a strategy to be expected of a partner, and it is replaced with securing the child's attention and using appropriate proximity and nonverbal behavior to encourage interaction.

b. *Secures the child's attention nonverbally or verbally before communicating:* For example, for a child at the Social Partner stage, the partner touches the child to secure attention and may call the child by name before directing communicative signals to the child. For a child at the Language Partner or Conversational Partner stage, the partner calls the child's name.

c. *Uses appropriate proximity and nonverbal behavior to encourage interaction:* For example, for a child at the Social Partner stage, the partner comes close to the child and uses gestures, objects, and animated facial expression to engage the child rather than attempting to engage the child from a distance, such as calling to the child from across the room. For a child at a Language or Conversational Partner stage, there may be a greater expectation for the child to respond to verbal signals as well as nonverbal behavior.

d. *Uses appropriate words and intonation to support optimal arousal and engagement:* For example, the partner either uses exaggerated, more intense vocalizations or verbalizations for an alerting effect or quieter, less intense vocalizations or verbalizations for a calming effect, as appropriate.

e. *Shares emotions, internal states, and mental plans with the child (Conversational Partner stage only):* Partner informs the child of what the partner is feeling and is going to do, such as stating, "I am so happy that you have cleaned up so quickly. Now we can choose one more game to play before we go home."

Partner Provides Developmental Support	Developmental support must be appropriate to a child's developmental stage and is provided when the partner

a. *Encourages imitation following the child's attentional focus, waiting, taking turns, and modeling nonverbal and/or verbal behaviors for the child to imitate, appropriate to the child's developmental abilities (Social Partner and Language Partner stage):* The partner models clapping during a song for a child at the Social Partner stage or short phrases to fill in during a song for a child at the Language Partner stage, after the child has waited for his or her turn in a group activity.

b. *Encourages interaction with peers:* The partner encourages the child to interact with peers by drawing peers to the child, helping the child to respond to bids for interaction from peers, helping the child direct bids for interaction to peers, and mediating successful interactions with peers. The partner may use verbal and/or nonverbal means to encourage interaction.

c. *Attempts to repair breakdowns verbally or nonverbally by clarifying the meaning of the signal:* For example, the partner may repeat the verbal or nonverbal signal or may modify the signal by adding words or additional gestures depending on the child's conversational abilities.

d. *Provides guidance and feedback as needed for success in activities so that the child maintains optimal arousal and experiences success:* For example, the partner provides social praise or uses appropriate guided participation strategies, such as additional cues or prompts, without excessively prompting or directing the child.

e. *Expands on the child's play and nonverbal or verbal communication by adding to the child's behavior and following the child's attentional focus and topic of communication or play (Social Partner stage):* For example, when the child rolls a car to the partner, the partner puts a pretend figure in the car and rolls it back to the child. Or, when the child gives a jar of Cheerios or cookies to the partner to request that it be opened, the partner opens the jar and says "more Cheerios" or "open jar."

f. *Provides guidance on expressing emotions and understanding the cause of emotions (Language Partner and Conversational Partner stages):* For example, when the child appears angry that he or she cannot fit a puzzle piece into a puzzle, the partner models saying, "I'm mad. This piece does not fit."

g. *Provides guidance for interpreting others' feelings and opinions (Conversational Partner stage only):* For example, when the child curiously observes another child who is crying after she has fallen on the playground, the partner states, "Erica hurt her leg. Erica is upset. Let's ask her if she's okay."

Partner Adjusts Language Input	Adjustments must be appropriate to a child's developmental abilities and may involve the following changes in partner behavior. The partner

a. *Uses nonverbal cues to support understanding:* When talking to the child, the partner uses clear and appropriate nonverbal cues, such as gestures, facial expressions, and intonation, to support the child's understanding of the message. Words are not used in isolation as the only means to communicate at the Social Partner level, whereas language may be used without nonverbal cues at later Language Partner and Conversational stages.

b. *Adjusts complexity of language input to the child's developmental level:* For example, if the child does not yet understand words, the partner uses mostly single words or simple phrases when talking to the child, but if the child does understand more complex language, the partner uses levels of language appropriate to the child's degree of comprehension.

c. *Adjusts quality of language input appropriate to the child's arousal level, which may include adjustments in content, complexity, or paralinguistic features (e.g., stress, intonation), to support the child's arousal level:* For example, the partner uses a soothing vocal tone, less exaggerated intonation, and simplified language when the child is highly aroused or more exaggerated vocal tone and volume when child is underaroused.

Partner Models Appropriate Behaviors

The modeling of appropriate behaviors involves the partner modeling behaviors for social communication, emotional regulation, and learning. The partner

a. *Models appropriate nonverbal communication (e.g., gestures) and emotional expressions (e.g., smiling and laughing to indicate pleasure):* The partner models a pushing-away gesture when the child shows displeasure after tasting food or states "happy" or points to a picture for "happy" when the child shows excitement in an activity.

b. *Models a range of communicative functions verbally and nonverbally, including behavior regulation, social interaction, and joint attention:* The partner provides models for varied functions such as requesting or protesting, greeting and calling attention, and commenting at a level appropriate to the child's developmental abilities.

c. *Models appropriate play for the child's developmental level and provides a variety of experiences with sensorimotor, symbolic, and constructive play:* The partner models play at developmentally appropriate levels for the child during a variety of activities, such as pouring and dumping rice or water at a sensory table, feeding puppets in a kitchen or dining area, helping to construct towers in a block play area, or engaging in recreational activities.

d. *Models appropriate behavior when the child uses inappropriate behavior if the child is regulated enough to benefit from models:* For example, the partner models a pushing-away gesture and the word "no" if the child screams to reject a food item that is offered or models the use of a picture symbol, word, and/or sign for "all done" if the child is forcefully attempting to escape from an activity. Likewise, if the child is chewing on his or her clothing in an effort to self-regulate arousal, appropriate mouthing and biting activities are modeled and provided, such as providing chewy foods or a chewy. (A *chewy* is an object that is specifically designed to be chewed or mouthed safely to increase oral sensory input for regulation, such as tubes or plastic toys. Use of a chewy replaces less desirable activities that the child may engage in for oral sensory input, such as biting the wrist or chewing clothes or objects that are not safe or clean.)

It also is recognized that some inappropriate behaviors may fall into the category of problem behaviors if they are harmful to the child or others, disruptive, or socially stigmatizing for the child. In the SCERTS Model, prevention of problem behavior is targeted by supporting the development of socially acceptable means for social control, by supporting the development of mutual and self-regulatory strategies, and by using transactional supports to foster emotional regulation in challenging activities and settings.

e. *Models "child-perspective" language and considers the child's intentions and developmental level:* For example, if a child at the Social Partner stage screams to protest a snack being offered, the partner may physically support the child in pushing away the snack while modeling "no" or "no snack." If a child at the Language Partner stage physically positions him- or herself close to another child (i.e., uses proximity) to attempt to engage a friend in play, the partner may encourage the child to ask, "Want to play?" with the support of a picture strip if helpful. For a child at the Conversational Partner stage who is reproducing phrases (delayed echolalia) from a Disney video to comment on the characters he or she is drawing, the partner may model saying, "I'm drawing Captain Hook and Peter Pan!"

Summary of Transactional Support: Interpersonal Support

In summary, interpersonal support from partners plays a multifaceted role in fostering a child's development. Appropriate, supportive styles and interactional adjustments used by partners not only promote more successful activities but also establish a history of successful interpersonal experiences that lead to positive emotional memories of social engagement. These memories are the foundation for long-term relationships and trust, which are so essential for children to learn optimally and to take risks in a world that so often feels overwhelming and confusing. Table 2.1 presents the do's and don'ts of providing interpersonal support in the SCERTS Model.

TRANSACTIONAL SUPPORT: LEARNING SUPPORT

Learning supports are used to clarify expectations, support understanding of activities (e.g., the sequence of steps and end goal of an activity), support emotional regulation, and create natural and motivating opportunities for participation and communication. Learning supports involve aids such as visual supports and augmentative communication supports, as well as the strategies for implementation of these supports in instruction by partners.

As discussed in Chapter 4 in Volume I, children with ASD typically demonstrate relative strengths in processing visual information and typically respond better to nontransient rather than transient information. Visual supports are ways of presenting information using visual aids such as individual or sequences of objects, photographs, logos, or picture symbols, to enhance a child's active participation and understanding. Organizational supports are ways of organizing materials, physical space, or marking time concepts to enhance the child's organization.

Visual supports are important instructional tools because visual stimuli are nontransient and therefore remain consistent and predictable. Visual supports assist in developing a higher degree of awareness of activity expectations while reducing the need for oral language processing as the primary means to understand activities. The primary advantage of visually supported instructional methods is to increase structure and meaning so that a child is able to 1) more actively participate in all activities because the supports provide a road map for both the child and the partners; 2) be less dependent on adult prompts and direction; 3) be better regulated emotionally (i.e., prevent dysregulation related to confusion and anxiety that may result from a high degree of novelty and uncertainty); 4) make transitions between activities more effectively; and 5) understand expectations, predict outcomes, and benefit from consistency.

Table 2.1. Do's and don'ts of interpersonal support in the SCERTS Model

Do not...	Do...
Focus on compliance, respondent training, and passive learning	Encourage initiation, spontaneity, and active learning
Teach communicative skills exclusively in adult–child one-to-one teaching	Support the development of a child's communicative abilities with different partners in varied social contexts
Ask too many questions or give too many directions	Comment and expand upon a child's initiated communication and focus of attention
Persist in making a child "say the whole sentence" or focus on correct grammar	Respond to and expand on functional communication to support a child's self-confidence as a communicator
Remove visual supports as a child begins to speak or becomes familiar with a routine	Continue to use visual supports to enhance a child's communicative attempts, to build language, to support attention, and to serve as a safety net during times of dysregulation
Teach developmentally inappropriate communicative skills or skills that are not clearly functional, such as rote repetition of pictures, reading flash cards, and so forth	Support the development of communicative skills that are developmentally appropriate and that will have an immediate impact on a child's life in everyday activities
Focus primarily on labeling and requesting	Support a child's ability to communicate for a wide range of purposes
Teach fragmented skills in a repetitive, drill-like format outside of the context of meaningful and logical activities	Support a child's communicative growth in meaningful and purposeful activities that can be understood and make sense for the child
Make social-communicative activities stressful for a child (e.g., by withholding food or preferred activities until a child speaks)	Create motivating activities with many needs and opportunities to communicate, with modeling and support provided as needed
Ignore, punish, or extinguish echolalic speech or other unconventional communication	Respond to echolalia or unconventional communication specific to the functions that it serves for a child and model/teach more conventional means
Ignore a child's emotion regulation and emotional state or dismiss a child's behavior as noncompliant if he or she is dysregulated	Always monitor a child's emotion regulation and make the necessary accommodations or modifications to support emotion regulation, attention, and learning

Thus, the use of visual schedules with picture symbols, photographs, and transition cards (e.g., a *now–next* picture sequence) may prove to be highly effective in assisting with transitions, daily activities, and school expectations. Visual strategies are typically useful in assisting with 1) processing and understanding others' communicative attempts, 2) providing educational and instructional support, 3) giving information and directives, 4) establishing rules and behavioral expectations, and 5) providing emotional regulation support, all of which lead to greater independence, problem solving, and reduced need for adult assistance or prompting (Hodgdon, 1995, 1999). Work systems, using a series of work baskets or folders, are useful supports in structuring a visually organized method of teaching independent work skills and task completion (Schopler, Mesibov, & Hearsey, 1995).

Picture symbols or photographs that are either pointed to or used in exchange (Frost & Bondy, 1994) are transactional supports for facilitating communication for nonspeaking and even for speaking children. In the SCERTS Model, picture systems are introduced as a *primary* expressive means of communication and are initially used for children at the Social Partner stage, who are nonspeaking or minimally verbal. Such systems are particularly useful in encouraging communicative initiations (both verbal and nonverbal) and choice making. For speaking or nonspeaking children who are at the

Language Partner and Conversational Partner stages, picture supports may aid in word retrieval, may facilitate understanding of more advanced language structures, or may facilitate production of more complex utterances and even conversational discourse.

As noted in the SAP-O forms and criteria in Chapter 8 in Volume I, the Learning Supports component of Transactional Support, focusing on desirable characteristics of instructional strategies, is divided into the following goals:

LS1 Partner structures activity for active participation

LS2 Partner uses augmentative communication support to foster development

LS3 Partner uses visual and organizational support

LS4 Partner modifies goals, activities, and learning environment

Specific desirable instructional strategies that are assessed in the SAP and that may be targeted as Transactional Support objectives for each of these Learning Support goals are listed next. Once again, learning supports selected must be appropriate to a child's developmental abilities.

Partner Structures Activity for Active Participation

The partner structures an activity for active participation in the following ways. The partner

a. *Defines clear beginning and ending to activity:* For example, at the Social Partner and early Language Partner stages, the partner may use natural or planned rituals, such as beginning a swinging activity with "Ready, set, go," and ending with saying and signing "Stop," or marking the transition away from an activity with the words and sign for "all done." At the Conversational Partner stage, there may be a discussion of the steps in the activity before the activity as well as verbal supports provided throughout, such as saying, "We're almost finished, and then we'll have lunch."

b. *Creates turn-taking opportunities and leaves spaces for the child to fill in:* At the Social Partner stage or early Language Partner stage, the child's turn may be nonverbal or vocal or may involve very simple language. For example, when initiating an activity, the partner models "Ready, set . . . " and allows the child to vocalize "go"; the partner rocks with the child to music and pauses for the child to indicate verbally or nonverbally to continue; or the partner leaves spaces for the child to fill in during book routines that provide frequent repetition and carrier phrases (e.g., as found in the *Brown Bear, Brown Bear* books). At the Conversational Partner stage, there may be greater expectations for more elaborate verbal responses from the child when filling turns.

c. *Provides predictable sequence to activity by the nature of the activity itself, through repetition so that the steps become familiar or through the use of other supports to make it predictable to the child:* For example, the partner practices a constructive play activity with a fixed sequence of steps to completion, such as nesting cups or combining ingredients to create a product. For a child at the Social Partner and early Language Partner stages, the partner refers to a picture sequence to indicate progress in an activity and steps to completion, but a child at advanced Language Partner or Conversational Partner stages, the partner may rely more on written language.

d. *Offers repeated learning opportunities by consistently and predictably repeating aspects of activities across contexts throughout the child's day:* For example, the partner provides choice-making opportunities at snack, circle time, and lunch, or similar activities are repeated over time, such as pretend play with a feeding set one day and a grooming set another day, to provide predictable learning opportunities for the child.

e. *Offers varied learning opportunities by varying an aspect of the activity, which provides novelty for the child to learn from, within the context of repetition and expectation:* For example, once the child is familiar with a play activity (e.g., blowing bubbles), the partner may vary this routine by pausing just before blowing to provide an opportunity for the child to request continuation. Similarly, once the child is familiar with a snack routine, the partner may vary the activity by providing a cup while withholding the juice or milk to encourage an opportunity for the child to make a request. The nature of the expected responses varies depending on the child's developmental abilities.

Partner Uses Augmentative Communication Support to Foster Development

The partner uses augmentative communication support such as visual and organizational support to enhance socialization, communication, and emotional regulation.

a. *Uses augmentative communication support to enhance the child's communication and expressive language (i.e., nonspeech communication system, e.g., gestures, signs, objects, pictures, photographs, picture symbols):* For instance, the partner refers to sequences of picture symbols accompanying snack time on an activity board (e.g., "Steven drinks juice") to expand the child's use of single words into creative multiple-word utterances.

b. *Uses augmentative communication support to enhance the child's understanding of language and behavior:* For example, during greeting routines, the partner may show a picture of a familiar family member (e.g., Mom, Dad, a sibling) just before that person's arrival home to provide the child with a greater understanding of this social event.

c. *Uses augmentative communication support to enhance the child's expression and understanding of emotion:* The partner makes available and encourages the child to use an augmentative communication support to enhance the ability to express emotions and understand the emotions of others.

d. *Uses augmentative communication support to enhance the child's emotional regulation by enhancing the child's ability to regulate arousal level by providing a medium for mutual regulation,* such as requesting an organizing activity, a break from an activity, or assistance during an activity, through nonspeech means.

Partner Uses Visual and Organizational Support

The partner

a. *Uses support to define steps within a task:* For example, the partner refers to a "within-activity" picture sequence or a written list to define steps, depending on the child's developmental abilities.

b. *Uses support to define steps and time for completion of activities:* For example, a visual timer may provide visual depiction of the time remaining, or a count-down strip with pull-off Velcro numbers may indicate the steps remaining in an activity.

c. *Uses visual support to enhance smooth transitions between activities to support an optimal level of arousal:* For example, the partner uses a now–next visual sequence or refers to a picture schedule to indicate what is coming next. Likewise, a partner may use a visual timer to emphasize that a transition is about to occur.

d. *Uses support to organize segments of time across the day:* For example, the partner refers to a picture or object schedule to review upcoming activities as well as completed activities over a longer time than single transitions.

e. *Uses visual support to enhance attention in group activities:* The partner uses visual support to enhance the child's attention to the activity and to peers in group activities. For example, the partner uses photographs or picture symbols to cue the child to direct attention to the activity, by using copies of visual support used by the activity leader in circle time, or by exchanging pictures with peers as part of the activity.

f. *Uses visual support to foster active involvement in group activities:* The partner uses visual support to foster the child's initiation and active participation in group activities. For example, the partner uses visual support to offer choices within activities, including choices of songs, materials, play partners, and so forth.

Partner Modifies Goals, Activities, and Learning Environment

The partner

a. *Adjusts social complexity to support organization and interaction:* For example, the partner may provide a smaller group setting or one-to-one support as needed. The partner appropriately judges when to provide more or less social complexity.

b. *Adjusts task difficulty as needed to foster the child's success and help the child maintain an optimal level of arousal:* For example, the partner reduces the number of steps or simplifies steps in an activity.

c. *Modifies sensory properties of learning environment as needed to help the child maintain an optimal level of arousal:* For example, the partner adjusts lighting, and controls for noise level and visual distraction.

d. *Arranges learning environment to enhance attention and motivation:* For example, the partner may use chairs organized in a semicircle or small rugs to mark where children sit for small-group activities.

e. *Arranges learning environment to promote child initiation:* The partner modifies the arrangement of the learning environment as needed to help the child initiate interactions. For example, the partner organizes materials out of reach or sight to promote initiation of requests throughout daily routines rather than provide all materials in specified activities.

f. *Designs and modifies activities to be developmentally appropriate:* For example, activities are designed with appropriate expectations for communication, attention, and active participation for the child, relative to the child's developmental abilities.

g. *Infuses motivating materials and topics in activities:* For example, materials and topics are chosen based on the child's preferences and learning strengths (e.g., sensory-motor toys, gross motor play). The partner recognizes that the child's intrinsic motivation to communicate is fostered in these contexts in contrast to activities that are imposed on the child.

h. *Provides activities to promote initiation and extended interaction:* The partner designs activities such as music time to encourage and require the child to initiate requests for songs, to choose instruments, to take turns and to fill turns over multiple sequences during the activity.

i. *Alternates between movement and sedentary activities as needed:* The partner alternates between activities in which the child has the opportunity to engage in organizing movement activities with those in which the child is expected to be sedentary or still. The frequency and types of movement activities are selected with respect to the child's arousal bias.

j. *"Ups the ante" or increases expectations appropriately based on the child's developmental abilities to support active participation, communication, and/or problem solving when the child is being successful and is in a more optimal state of arousal:* This may occur through "sabotage," or holding out for more sophisticated communication or problem solving, with modeling or prompting as needed.

Summary of Transactional Support: Learning Support

In summary, learning supports provided by partners play an essential role in promoting understanding of activities and independence within activities. Children with ASD benefit from enhanced predictability and consistency and from information presented in a variety of modalities, especially the visual modality. The use of learning supports ensures that activities will be more successful. As with interpersonal support, this helps to establish a history of successful activities in daily life routines that leads to positive emotional memories of those activities. These memories are the foundation for building motivation to seek out and participate in those activities over time, which become the contexts for learning functional skills and for supporting participation in the "flow of life."

SUCCESSFUL INCLUSION AND LEARNING AND PLAYING WITH PEERS

As noted in the Learning Support goals and objectives just described, the SCERTS Model recognizes that learning and playing with peers (LAPP) is an integral component of programming for children with ASD and should become a part of a child's program from the outset, whenever feasible. To meet this goal, many of the Interpersonal Support and Learning Support objectives directly relate to peer interaction or can be targeted in LAPP activities. Examples include *Encourages interaction with peers, Provides guidance and feedback as needed for success in activities, Provides guidance for interpreting other's feelings and opinions, Uses visual support to foster active involvement in group activities, Provides activities to promote initiations and extended interaction,* and so forth.

For children receiving preschool and school services, LAPP typically occurs in the larger context of inclusive school programming. Given that this is such a crucial issue and priority goal for so many children with ASD, we now devote special attention to issues related to successful programming with peers in the SCERTS Model. Before discussing specific strategies to foster a child's success in LAPP activities, we must first address the issue of successful inclusive practices for children with ASD.

Essential Programmatic Elements for Successful Inclusion

Successful inclusion of students with ASD is a complex and ongoing process. In our experience, the following elements must be in place to support children with ASD, their families, and all others involved.

1. *Teamwork:* As noted, the SCERTS Model is best implemented as a team model. Open communication and trust among all team members (i.e., parents, professionals, paraprofessionals) is necessary to ensure coordination across all aspects of a student's program. Regular and systematic channels of communication, through regularly scheduled meetings and in writing, should be implemented. This

should occur between home and school and among educational staff, therapeutic specialists, and administrators. This may occur as part of or in addition to the SAP.

2. *Planning:* The full team, including parents, should begin to meet on a regular basis well before the beginning of the child's school program to plan inclusive elements of the child's program, anticipate any challenges that may arise, and develop provisional strategies for addressing those challenges (e.g., transactional supports for learning such as visual supports, curriculum modification). Transition plans to help the child adapt to a new inclusive setting as he or she progresses in school often are helpful (e.g., meeting the new teacher and visiting the school before the school starts). Contingency plans for unexpected difficulties should also be put into place (e.g., for a child more at risk for dysregulation, a step back from full to partial inclusion with more time in a special learning environment or resource room or if the child is not doing well in the complex classroom environment, even after transactional supports are in place). Once again, this may occur as part of or in addition to the SAP.

3. *Attitude:* The team must adopt an attitude that inclusion is a dynamic process, not simply an end goal. Regularly scheduled meetings during the school year underscore the need for programmatic monitoring, with adjustments made when necessary, based on progress documented in the ongoing SAP or on other information that is gathered. In addition, inclusion involves both academic/preacademic issues (e.g., cooperative learning) and social and social-emotional components (e.g., development of play skills, friendships). These components are not mutually exclusive, and all should be addressed by the team.

4. *Expectations:* Professionals, paraprofessionals, and parents need to have appropriate goals and expectations to judge the degree of success for a child in an inclusive program. The nature of the child's disability may result in slower than expected or uneven progress, as inclusive settings directly challenge the developmental weaknesses of many children with ASD (e.g., potential for noisier and busier settings, increase in uncertainty and unpredictability, increase in social and communicative demands). Although it is important to have high expectations, setting the bar too high may result in frustration for all. Expectations of social progress (including development of friendships) and of learning conventions of appropriate classroom behavior must be calibrated to allow for celebration of even small gains.

5. *Flexibility:* Inclusion does not work well in inflexible systems. Due to the challenges experienced by children with ASD, and their changing needs, flexibility is needed in the rules and schedules established for the children, how services are provided by staff, and how transactional supports are implemented. The following are just a few examples of flexible and supportive programming that may help a child succeed: breaks to support emotional regulation, early arrival for a settling-in time, team teaching, opportunities to choose playmates or learning partners, and so forth.

6. *Transactional supports* must be built in and provided at multiple levels.

    - *General education staff* must feel supported by members of the team with expertise in ASD (including parents) so that there are not significant additional burdens placed on them over and above those of educating all the children in the class.

- *Peers without ASD* must feel supported if they feel confused by the behavior of children with ASD. Such confusion may arise from feelings of being rejected ("He doesn't want to play with me") or from unconventional behavior (e.g., motor stereotypies, unconventional or difficult to read verbal or nonverbal communication).

- *Instructional assistants, aides, and paraprofessionals* are crucial and must feel supported by specialists on the team (e.g., occupational therapists, speech-language pathologists) to implement therapeutic strategies throughout the day, supported by general educators in helping a child academically, and supported by parents who often rely on assistants for daily communication.

- *Parents* must be supported by all staff and administrators in fulfilling their hopes and dreams for a more normalized educational experience for their child, fostering the development of positive relationships with peers, and carrying over efforts outside of the school setting (e.g., Circle of Friends programs).

- *The child with ASD* must feel supported by the team's use of strategies that have proved helpful (e.g., interpersonal supports, learning supports) and by the team's understanding of the challenges and difficulties from the child's perspective (e.g., sensory environment, abstract social rules, complex language).

With these elements in place, there is a much greater likelihood that inclusive programming will be successful. However, there also must be a systematic plan in place to develop the competencies specific to an individual child.

Implementing Activities Involving Learning and Playing with Peers

LAPP activities serve to promote peer-related competencies, including the ability to initiate and maintain successful social-communicative interactions across partners, settings, and activities, ultimately contributing to the development of positive relationships and friendships. A systematic approach to LAPP activities is important for a child with ASD, as we have come to understand 1) the wealth of learning opportunities LAPP provides and 2) the potential for the development of long-term relationships and friendships within a child's social community, which creates continuity and a feeling of community membership over time for the child and his or her family. However, parents, educators, and professionals also must be cognizant of 1) the learning style differences of children with ASD as compared with same-age peers without disabilities (discussed in Chapter 4 in Volume I), as well as 2) the social-communicative and emotional regulatory challenges inherent in more complex social interactions with peers. In addition, we have become more aware that social communication and play with peers is not easily learned naturally or in an incidental manner for many children with ASD. However, with appropriate transactional supports, opportunities for successful interaction and development of relationships between a child with ASD and his or her peers increase significantly.

The SCERTS Model approach to LAPP activities offers a child with ASD a systematic and semistructured means to learn and apply social-communicative and play skills in predictable and supportive activities, as well as in natural activities. Of primary importance is helping the child learn the meaning of social events to enhance active participation and how and when to use social-communicative skills in those events. This requires an increased understanding of social cues and conventions as well as the rules of the social, communication, and play activities that guide activities with peers. LAPP activities should be designed in such a manner as to increase the child's familiarity and expectations of social-communicative events and thus increase the likelihood of the child being well regulated and motivated to participate. Familiarity and predictability supports emotional regulation and therefore greater availability and resources for active participation. Conversely, if the activity and/or setting is unfamiliar and a high degree of novelty is contributing to emotional dysregulation, social-communicative breakdowns are more likely to occur and the likelihood of the child to experience success in initiating and maintaining interactions is reduced.

Our approach to LAPP activities is based on a number of guiding principles for increasing peer-related competencies and relationships. These principles offer a practical basis for special considerations in approaching LAPP activities in a variety of natural settings, such as school, home, child care, clinics, and other community environments. It will be evident that many of the principles discussed in Chapter 1 in this volume for developing a range of activities, from planned activity routines to natural activities, also are relevant for LAPP.

1. *Planned activity routines:* Social-communicative initiations and motivation to remain involved in social exchange are more likely when all children are familiar with both the steps within the activity and their roles in participating. Social-communicative abilities are enhanced through multiple opportunities to communicate throughout predictable routines. In specific reference to LAPP activities, a child may need to be prepared for such activities in less complex social situations such as planned activity routines that are introduced with an adult and child initially and then expanded to include other children. For example, a child might practice for integrated playtime by learning the rules of a specific activity or game ahead of time (e.g., "Ring Around the Rosy" for a child at the Social Partner stage, Barnyard Bingo for a child at the Language Partner stage, and Red Light, Green Light for a child at the Conversational Partner stage). This will reduce the possibility that the child will be challenged with the activity *and* the interaction with peers. Through planned activity routines, the child's social-cognitive and emotional regulatory resources may then be more efficiently and effectively applied toward learning and communicating with peers, rather than being used to engage in attempts to stay well regulated in these more challenging circumstances. Peers may also provide mutual regulatory supports as well as appropriate responses, further supporting emotional regulation.

2. *Natural interactions and settings:* On the other end of the continuum of activity structure, the ultimate goal for LAPP is for a child to be motivated to engage in social-communicative interactions in a range of activities across peer partners and settings, leading to the development of positive relationships. Naturally occurring interactions and settings provide many opportunities for LAPP activities that offer the potential for contingent interactions, reciprocal exchanges, and shared positive emotional experiences between the child and his or her peers, not just between the child and adults.

3. *Control for novelty:* Activities with peers, by definition, add increased stimulation, novelty, and unpredictability, and therefore the potential for dysregulation increases as compared with adult–child or isolated play. Even with well-designed activities, emotional dysregulation may occur when LAPP activities are offered in a manner of "too much too quickly," for example, with too many children or through activities that are too complex or overly stimulating. LAPP has the potential for increasing novelty, and therefore stress and emotional dysregulation, if

a child is being presented with unfamiliar social, communication, and play schemes in less structured settings. Systematic control for the presentation of novelty becomes an important consideration for LAPP, especially in the initial stages of program development.

4. *Shared control and reciprocity:* Ideally, LAPP activities, as with all activities, should have some degree of balance and shared control, not with one partner dominating or controlling the other partner, but rather with partners engaging in a process of initiating and maintaining social-communicative exchange as well as contingently responding to social overtures of one another. To support shared control, children with ASD must be supported in becoming familiar with the social, communication, and play schemes to be used with peers. Such previewing will increase understanding of the structure of activities, of how and when to initiate, with the goal of increasing motivation to remain engaged in activities with peers.

    Furthermore, the nature of shared control varies according a child's developmental abilities. For example, at the Social Partner stage, activities can be modified to support each child's awareness of the rotation of turns. For example, during a puzzle activity, the pieces can be placed in a bowl and passed between the child and one or more peers. Likewise, at the Language Partner stage, a visual support can be implemented to remind a child whose turn it is (e.g., a dial paired with a spinner to point to each child's picture). Last, at the Conversational Partner stage, a visual support can be used to indicate turn taking in conversation (e.g., a "talking ball" could be passed around to indicate the current speaker).

5. *Unconventional behavior and social play behaviors:* Unconventional communicative patterns (e.g., echolalia, incessant questioning) or unconventional play patterns (e.g., repetitive manipulation of toys) should not preclude children from being involved in LAPP activities. Rather, adult partners may help peers to recognize and understand the purpose and intent of these unconventional behaviors and design strategies to systematically increase means of social-communicative interactions (verbal and nonverbal) while replacing less conventional with more conventional means of interaction.

6. *Intrinsic motivation:* As noted, natural incentives are key to the SCERTS Model, and this is especially crucial for more challenging LAPP activities. Activity routines that are meaningful, purposeful, and intrinsically motivating are targeted as the most conducive and preferred activities in which to promote natural interactions among peers. Activities should also have properties that tap into motivation by supporting emotional regulation, as children are more likely to seek out activities that they know keep them well regulated. For example, a child may benefit from activities that have a clear beginning and end to ensure task completion and motivation, such as a puzzle, which has a clear beginning and end, in contrast to playing with Legos or blocks, in which the activity is more open ended and may not have an obvious end point. This structure may encourage the child to see the activity through to its completion especially when a peer is involved. Other motivational and organizing properties may include regular opportunities for movement, such as obstacle courses and other sensory-motor activities, if movement is an organizing factor for that child, or use of high-interest topics such as science for an older child at the Conversational Partner stage. Over time, a child develops positive emotional memories of these LAPP activities due to the awareness that such activities support motivation and emotional regulation.

7. *Expressing a range of social-communicative intentions and functions:* LAPP activities should be designed to target natural opportunities for a child to understand and use a variety of social-communicative acts for a variety of functions, including 1) behavioral regulation (e.g., requesting objects, assistance, making choices), 2) social interaction (e.g., requesting social games or routines, calling, greeting, showing off), and 3) joint attention (e.g., commenting, sharing and requesting information). Learning supports may be used to support communication for a wider variety of functions. For example, visual supports can be provided as word retrieval cues for the child to make appropriate comments and/or requests (e.g., "Puzzle is all done," "Julie, paint with me"). Use of such visual supports promotes a child's independence in peer interactions and decreases reliance on the verbal cues of adults. In LAPP activities, multiple opportunities also are presented for the child to increase his or her persistence in maintaining routines or for repairing social-communicative breakdowns with peers using conventional communicative means to do so, with appropriate supports as needed.

8. *Enhancing skills of peer partners:* As noted, in the SCERTS Model, the focus is not solely on the child with ASD. Considerable attention is given to enhancing the ability of all partners, including peers, to have successful experiences with the child with ASD. Goals for peers may include learning successful strategies and using interpersonal supports noted for all partners, including offering bids for social interaction, waiting for the initiation of communication, reading the communicative attempts and specific intentions of the child with ASD, responding in a manner that encourages continued interaction, and supporting emotional regulation.

9. *Adult partner's role:* The adult partner's role in LAPP activities includes 1) creating natural and motivating social-communicative opportunities, 2) modeling appropriate means of social-communication based on a child's developmental level and intervention goals, 3) prompting (if necessary) to enable the child to achieve social-communicative success with peers, 4) repairing breakdowns when necessary, 5) offering repeated opportunities for predictable interactions as more conventional means of social communication are learned, 6) monitoring the child's emotional regulation, and 7) providing transactional supports as needed. The adult designs a learning environment and controls for novelty through the use of activities ranging from planned activity routines, to engineered activities, to modified natural activities, and eventually to natural activities. The adult may initially serve as the primary partner or one of the primary partners as the necessary social-communicative skills and the child's sense of the routine are first being learned. The role of the adult as a primary partner fades as the peers are systematically taught to replace the adult in these same, familiar routines.

SUMMARY

The SCERTS Model is a flexible and functional model because the focus is on enhancing abilities across partners and settings in natural activities and routines. However, careful consideration needs to be given to the transactional supports provided, including interpersonal and learning supports, to address the priority goals in the SCERTS Model: enhancing success in social communication and supporting emotional regulation. To achieve these goals, strategic implementation of interpersonal and learning supports plays a critical role for children, regardless of ability.

Chapter 3

Transactional Support
Support to Families and Support Among Professionals

SUPPORT TO FAMILIES

The SCERTS Model demands a commitment to collaborating with families in assessment and program development and implementation, and this commitment is put into action as part of the SAP and in the Transactional Support domain of the model. There are many potential benefits of parent-professional partnerships, and successful collaboration ultimately results in maximizing the potential for the most positive outcomes for a child with ASD. For example, with a collaborative approach, relationships between a child with ASD and family members are more likely to improve, due to family members developing increased sensitivity about how their own behavior (i.e., interpersonal support) fosters social communication and emotional regulation for their child. Active involvement by parents and siblings also provides a sense of ownership of a child's progress. That is, family members take pride in their contributions—it is not simply that the child is sent to professionals to fix problems. This fosters a sense of empowerment and encourages active problem solving for family members.

Research has demonstrated that family involvement is a major factor that supports more positive outcomes for children (National Research Council [NRC], 2001), likely because collaboration results in greater consistency in activities and routines across settings and partners. Such consistency supports generalization of new skills that make a meaningful difference in a child's life and reduces confusion for the child, thus supporting emotional regulation. Finally, productive relationships among professionals, paraprofessionals, and family members provide a sense of trust and shared priorities and goals. Mutually supportive relationships are more likely to develop when there is a sense that "we are all in this together" to improve the quality of life of a child, which in most cases, improves the quality of life for the family.

In the SCERTS Model, support to families and direct family involvement are explicit essential elements of a comprehensive service delivery plan, rather than elements that are considered optional, due to the fact that family involvement is a crucial factor related to a successful educational plan. Although this aspect of the SCERTS Model is categorized under support to families within the Transactional Support domain, we once again acknowledge the multifaceted interrelationships among the Social Communication, Emotional Regulation, and Transactional Support domains of the SCERTS Model. The mutual influences among social communication, emotional regulation, and learning occur in a variety of contexts, the most important of which is the family context, due to the pervasive and enduring influence of family experience on a child's development. For example, progress in emotional regulation engenders growth in relationships with family members, which then fuels growth in social-communicative abilities, which in turn supports a growing sense of family members' competence and further deepening of relationships with their child. In this manner, as a child progresses in development, there will be significant transactional influences on family members' perceptions of and interactions with the child. These changing perceptions may have significant influences on family routines and learning opportunities that are made available. The nature of such influences depend on a number of factors, including 1) the rate and degree of a child's progress in reference to family members' expectations for change, 2) parents and professionals' interpretation of observed changes, 3) family member's perceptions of their role in the change process, and 4) other supports or stressors affecting the family (e.g., extended family support, financial security, quality of the marital relationship, sibling relationships). To further add to this complexity, the transactional influences between the child and family are dynamic and ever-changing as families and children change and grow.

As discussed in Chapter 1 in Volumes I and II, two of the SCERTS Model Core Values and Guiding Principles directly address family support and provide the foundation for all efforts to support families:

> It is the primary responsibility of professionals to establish positive relationships with children and with family members. All children and family members are treated with dignity and respect.

> Family members are considered experts about their child. Assessment and educational efforts are viewed as collaborative processes with family members, and principles of family-centered practice are advocated to build consensus with the family and enhance the collaborative process.

Support to families within the SCERTS Model is designed to directly address the challenges most commonly faced by families. Some challenges are directly related to addressing difficulties in social communication and emotional regulation and supporting other aspects of a child's development including independence and adaptive living skills. Other challenges faced by families may be secondary to the immediate effects of the everyday challenges of a child's disability. Such secondary challenges include dealing with educational systems and developing collaborative, productive working relationships with professionals. In developing a plan to support families, professionals must be cognizant of the full range of issues that families are attempting to address.

Characteristics of the SCERTS Family Support Plan

In the SCERTS Model, it is important that a plan to support a family have the following characteristics:

1. *The plan addresses the challenges family members identify as their priorities, and the plan evolves as family priorities change.* Family support is a dynamic process, as challenges and priorities for families change over time. Family priorities may change for a number of reasons: 1) as a natural part of a child's growth and development; 2) due to transitions in school services or other services; 3) due to unexpected progress or increased difficulties that were not anticipated; 4) due to new educational or medical information presented to the family; and 5) due to factors not related directly to the youngster with ASD such as illness in the immediate or extended family, employment changes, birth of another child, and so forth.

2. *The plan has as its ultimate goal enhancing the family's ability to actively and independently problem-solve, cope with, and address the challenges they face.* Most professionals are involved with families only for relatively brief periods in a child's preschool and school years. It is most desirable for families to develop independent problem-

solving, decision-making, and coping skills. It is undesirable for families to develop too great a dependence on professional advice for making crucial decisions. Professional support should be used as needed when family members feel such support would be helpful. This requires that professionals collaborate in a nonjudgmental manner with family members, even when there may be differences of opinion. Professionals must remain cognizant of the fact that it is not possible to truly understand the experience of being a parent of a child with ASD without having that experience directly. Therefore, professionals need to encourage independent problem solving and decision making, maintain a nonjudgmental attitude, work hard to resolve differences of opinion, and develop a plan in partnership with family members.

3. *The plan must be individualized, taking into account the tremendous variability and differing values across families.* Variability across families may be due to factors such as 1) different cultural, ethnic, and religious beliefs and traditions; 2) differences in family structure (e.g., number of other children if any, single-parent families, two working parents); 3) socioeconomic factors; 4) existence or absence of natural or extended support systems (e.g., relatives who live nearby); and 5) the family's perception of the child and the child's disability. Due to the dynamic and ever-changing qualities of family systems, sensitivity, flexibility, and creativity are essential features of family-centered support services.

4. *When more natural informal supports are available to the family or are arranged by the family, these supports should be recognized as an essential part of the plan even if they do not involve direct professional support.* Informal supports may include support meetings organized by parents with no professional involvement; parent-organized play dates; support from relatives, friends, and neighbors; and so forth. It is highly desirable for families to derive support from a variety of sources, including informal supports. Informal supports can be of tremendous value because in most cases, they occur within the natural social life and routines of the family and help to extend and solidify the family's social network, rather than being arranged by and dependent on professionals and conducted in settings outside of a family's social network. Furthermore, when support services are arranged by professionals, there may be additional costs involved, and provision of services may be dependent on professionals' schedules and thus may be inconvenient for families, resulting in further stress.

5. *A plan to support families should distinguish between educational support and emotional support activities so that there is no confusion regarding expectations and goals for such support activities.* We recognize that educational support and emotional support are often not mutually exclusive, as educational support activities may have emotional support benefits and vice versa. However, there is the potential for confusion and even resentment when the two are confounded. For example, some professionals may be trained and experienced in giving educational support such as communication enhancement techniques and dealing with problem behaviors but not in providing emotional support such as family counseling for marital stress or individual counseling for depression. Professionals must understand that in some circumstances, challenges experienced by family members may be beyond the professionals' training and capabilities and that in those circumstances it is appropriate to refer families to family support agencies, to other professionals, or to other

sources of support. Professionals and other service providers must rely on their knowledge of professional boundaries and their judgment in knowing when they can be helpful and when a family's difficulties are beyond their abilities. Well-intentioned but ill-informed attempts at giving support may actually be harmful.

Core Challenges Revisited

Once again, we wish to emphasize that professional support is most helpful when it directly addresses challenges faced by families. Table 3.1 presents the core challenges faced by families that were discussed in Chapter 4 in Volume I. We now describe briefly how the SCERTS Model addresses these challenges.

How the SCERTS Model Addresses Challenges within the Family

The focus on natural activities and routines in the SCERTS Model makes it far more likely that the balance of family life can be supported, an issue that parents identify as a major stress that they and other family members experience. As noted in Chapter 1 in this volume, an activity-based approach to supporting social communication and emotional regulation is more conducive to including all family members than is an approach that relies primarily on isolated skill-based teaching sessions that occur outside of daily activities, often involving a number of different professionals or paraprofessionals who visit the home. The use of isolated skill-based teaching sessions and home visits from many different professionals have the potential to create further imbalance for a family unless services are well-integrated into family life and directly involve family members. Furthermore, functional as well as fun activities that already occur or that can be scheduled to occur in the life of the family are more desirable than an overreliance on isolated teaching sessions because they provide a child with many opportunities for learning and practicing new skills with a variety of partners.

The family-centered philosophy of the SCERTS Model is designed to support families in making crucial decisions affecting both the child and other family members. Due to the fact that the model focuses on encouraging active family decision making rather than dependence on professional prescription, it is less likely that there will be disagreements among parents or family members that are triggered by professionals who impose inflexible and externally chosen treatment agendas. Furthermore, in the SCERTS Model, we believe that for professionals to be effective, it is important for

Table 3.1. Challenges faced by families requiring transactional support

Challenges within the family
Finding the balance in family life
Challenges in family decision making
Differences in how family members respond to the disability of autism spectrum disorder (ASD)
Challenges in changes to the family system: roles, lifestyle, and routines
Challenges to brothers and sisters
Challenges related to future uncertainty

Challenges related to factors outside the immediate family
Feelings of isolation
How family members interface with their social community
Challenges in understanding ASD and explaining it to others

Challenges in service profession and professional–parent interaction
Challenges in dealing with service delivery systems
Challenges in dealing with professionals and other service providers
Confusion regarding available interventions and models

them to have some idea of how family members are coping with, adapting to, and making sense of the disability of ASD. In order to do so, family members should be encouraged to share their perceptions of the child's disability, including how perceptions have evolved over time. In the SAP, caregivers are asked to

- Share their perceptions of their child's strengths and difficulties
- Articulate their primary concerns
- Express their hopes and expectations regarding the child's development

Caregivers also are also provided with the opportunity to discuss

- Their understanding of their child's disability
- How the disability affects their interactions and relationship with the child
- How the child's disability affects family life

Caregivers also are asked to indicate the types of information and support that would be most helpful for them. Family members also may be asked about how family roles and routines have changed, about successful and unsuccessful strategies that have been employed to promote social and communicative interactions with family members, and about a child's emotional regulation. When appropriate, family members are encouraged to share their sense of competence as well as limitations in fostering their child's communicative, social, and emotional development and independence. It also is important to discuss with family members any positive effects that having a child with ASD may have on the family or family life. Another important aspect of family support is how brothers and sisters are affected by having a sibling with ASD, and this issue is explored as well (we return to this issue later in this chapter). Finally, caregivers are asked what their expectations are for educational services for their child and are asked about any supports that they may consider helpful for the family. Concerns about the child's future and future uncertainty for the family inevitably have a major impact on family members; therefore, family members may be asked to share their thoughts and feelings about these issues as well. The questionnaire on the next page, Family Expectations for Services and Helpful Supports, can be used to gather some of this information from parents and other family members.

Parents often look to professionals to validate their perceptions regarding their child's abilities and progress and their own abilities as parents and interactive partners. As part of the process of developing positive and productive relationships, professionals have a responsibility to provide feedback regarding parents' sense of themselves as competent caregivers, when parents ask for such feedback either directly or indirectly. Certainly, parents' self-appraisals are largely influenced by their abilities to communicate with and to help their child regulate emotionally. Thus, professional feedback to parents on their interpersonal support abilities and style and their ability to read and respond to their child, whether it is solicited or not, contributes to the parents' sense of efficacy and ability to make positive changes to foster a more positive relationship with their child. In turn, parents should be encouraged to provide feedback to professionals about their impressions of services that are provided and the professionals' developing relationships with their child. If feedback is less than positive, professionals can use the information as an opportunity for growth and reflection and as a demonstration to parents that the parents' input is valued.

Family Expectations for Services and Helpful Supports

Child's name: _____ Person(s) completing this form: _____ Date: _____

Please answer the following questions. Your answers will help us to be more effective in working with you to address concerns you have about your child's development and to address other related issues raised by family members. It may be helpful to read all questions before providing written answers.

1. What are the primary concerns you have about your child's development?

2. What are your expectations and primary goals for the services we provide directly for your child?

3. What are the major challenges and stresses experienced by members of your family related to your child's disability? Feel free to list these challenges specific to different family members, including your child's brothers and sisters.

4. In what areas do you feel most competent or successful with your child?

5. What are your expectations and primary goals for the services we provide in helping your family with the challenges and stresses faced by family members?

6. What types of support would be most helpful to you in addressing the challenges family members face with your child's development?

7. What types of support would be most helpful to you in addressing the challenges family members face with other related issues?

The SCERTS® Model: A Comprehensive Educational Approach for Children with Autism Spectrum Disorders
by Barry M. Prizant, Amy M. Wetherby, Emily Rubin, Amy C. Laurent, & Patrick J. Rydell
Copyright © 2006 by Paul H. Brookes Publishing Co. All rights reserved.

How the SCERTS Model Addresses Challenges Related to Factors Outside the Immediate Family

As noted, feelings of isolation can be very stressful for family members. In the SCERTS Model, family support activities and a support plan are designed to mitigate feelings of isolation by creating multiple and varied opportunities for family members to discuss their feelings and experiences with other parents or brothers and sisters of children with ASD and other family members. Furthermore, with a focus on activity-based learning, families are encouraged to include their child in age-appropriate activities within the social community, rather than limiting opportunities by scheduling the child to have primarily adult–child therapies. With a focus on social communication and emotional regulation, the skills needed to connect with others as well as to cope in challenging circumstances are of the highest priority, making it more likely that interfacing with the larger social community will be successful. Furthermore, when feelings of embarrassment in public are an issue for family members due to a child's problem behaviors, the emotional regulatory focus of the SCERTS Model directly addresses this challenge. Family members are better able to support a child in more difficult circumstances, by enhancing the child's capacity to maintain emotional regulation through mutual and self-regulatory strategies and transactional support.

Finally, the educational and emotional support aspects of the SCERTS Model provide many opportunities for family members to develop the knowledge and skills to be better able to enhance their own understanding of ASD; explain ASD to relatives and friends; and in general, be better prepared to educate others about the difficulties faced by their child and how such difficulties affect the family. Specific activities and forums for family members to develop these abilities are discussed later in this chapter.

How the SCERTS Model Addresses Challenges in Service Provision and Parent-Professional Interaction

As noted, the SCERTS Model is best implemented as a team process with family members being a critical and essential part of the team. Within this dynamic process, issues such as challenges in dealing with service delivery systems (e.g., schools), challenges in dealing with professionals and other service providers, and confusion regarding available interventions and educational models may be addressed directly and on an ongoing basis. Parents who are knowledgeable about educational approaches and about the rights of their child are more likely to make informed decisions than are parents with limited knowledge.

Types of Support

Support in the SCERTS Model is conceptualized in reference to two major categories: *educational support*, which involves providing families with the information, knowledge and skills to support their child's development, and *emotional support*, which encompasses enhancing family members' abilities to cope with the inevitable stresses and challenges of raising a child with ASD.

Educational Support

The general goals of educational support to families are introduced next, along with desired outcomes for families. The goals and desired outcomes of educational support are as follows:

Goal 1: **To provide family members with information and resources to understand the nature of their child's disability and how it specifically affects their child's development**

Desired outcome: *Family members will become knowledgeable about ASD and how it specifically affects their child's functional abilities in life. They will be able to use resources to find information and continue to actively learn as their child develops.*

Goal 2: To provide family members with the knowledge and skills to support their child's development in everyday activities and to address specific issues that are identified by parents as most stressful and challenging

Desired outcome: *Family members will feel confident in providing the necessary supports to foster their child's development across different situations and in everyday activities and in identifying and coping with the most significant difficulties they face at any point in time.*

Goal 3: To help parents and other family members see professionals as ongoing, relevant resources who can help to address questions about treatment and educational approaches, who can discuss confusing and often controversial accounts of ASD in the literature and public media, and who can offer families guidance and lessen their confusion on other topics

Desired outcome: *Parents and other family members will use professionals as resources in a manner that addresses family members' questions and concerns about their child's program, as well as any other relevant issues about ASD and their child that affect the family.*

Goal 4: To help parents provide brothers and sisters with accurate, age-appropriate information about ASD specific to the challenges that siblings face (e.g., why playing and interacting may be difficult)

Desired outcome: *Siblings will develop the knowledge and understanding of ASD specific to the everyday challenges they face in interactions with their brother or sister.*

Goal 5: To help parents in supporting positive sibling relationships by fostering more successful play and social interactive experiences

Desired outcome: *Siblings will have positive and emotionally satisfying experiences with their brother or sisters and, over the long term, will develop a foundation of positive relationships.*

Goal 6: To help parents understand the legal rights of their child and their family regarding services and the systems that are responsible for providing services (e.g., early intervention, school-based programs)

Desired outcome: *Parents will be knowledgeable about their legal rights and those of their child, will be able to collaborate and deal effectively with systems that are responsible for providing services to their child based on those rights, and will make informed decisions based on their knowledge.*

Emotional Support

The goals of emotional support to families are reviewed next, along with desired outcomes for families.

Goal 1: To enhance family members' abilities to cope with the stresses and challenges of raising a child with ASD

Desired outcome: *Family members will develop specific coping abilities to manage the inevitable stresses that they will experience directly due to or as a secondary effect of the child's having ASD.*

Goal 2: To help family members understand and gain access to the range of formal and informal emotional supports that may be available

Desired outcome: *Family members will gain access to formal and informal supports that best match the emotional needs of family members at specific points in time.*

Goal 3: To support parents' efforts to deal successfully with professionals, as well as with educational and health care systems

Desired outcome: Parents will develop specific strategies to foster positive parent–professional relationships and will deal with emotional challenges that may be due to difficult interactions or relationships with professionals or due to difficulties in dealing with educational and health care systems.

Goal 4: To help family members to identify their own priorities and develop appropriate expectations and realistic, achievable goals for their child's development and family life

Desired outcome: Family members will be clear about the most important issues they wish to address for their child and family, will develop realistic goals and expectations for their child, and will create a balance in family life consistent with their lifestyle and values.

Goal 5: To help parents support siblings with information about ASD when the siblings have questions or when they experience difficulties associated with having a brother or sister with ASD and to help siblings discuss their feelings about having a brother or sister with ASD

Desired outcome: Siblings will be able to acquire the information they need to have a better understanding of issues they encounter related to having a brother or sister with ASD and will be able to cope with difficulties they may experience by discussing their feelings.

Goal 6: To help siblings develop coping strategies for situations that may be stressful

Desired outcome: Siblings will be able to develop and use a variety of coping strategies related to having a brother or sister with ASD.

Educational and Emotional Support Must Be Appropriate to the Family's Developmental Stage

Families experience different challenges at different points in their journey in raising a child with ASD. This section addresses issues that are more specific to age-related challenges and transitions. We now consider four different families at different points in their journeys, to illustrate how support must be appropriate to where a family is in its journey. (In Chapters 5–7 of this volume, we revisit some of these challenges as we consider in much greater detail the issues faced by six children and their families and how these challenges are addressed by providing a comprehensive SCERTS Model plan for each of the children based on a comprehensive assessment of their strengths and needs.) After this section, we discuss specific recommended approaches for the educational and emotional support goals just noted.

Early Identification

Scenario 1: Parents are expressing concerns about their child's development before diagnosis or any formal assessment and are seeking information as to whether they should be concerned about their child, and if so, what they need to do.

Predominant Educational Support and Emotional Support Issues

Most parents of children with ASD first may be confused about their child's limited social engagement, and limited emotional responsivity. Depending on a child's arousal bias (i.e., hyper- versus hypoaroused), concerns may include a child's high activity level, frenetic motor and sensory exploration, and sleep problems, which are most common in children with a high arousal bias. For children with a low arousal bias, concerns may relate to lethargy, passivity, lack of motivation, and general lack of focus and emotional responsiveness. Parents may be confused as to what behaviors and milestones are developmentally appropriate and are to be expected, what behaviors may be red flags for a child in the first 1–2 years of life, and whether parents should be concerned in the first place. This is especially true with a first-born child, as parents may have no or few reference points for comparison. Before diagnosis, parents may question whether their child's confusing behaviors have to do with their parenting skills, a perceived lack of attention given to their child due to other factors (e.g., a new baby being born, illness in the family), or other factors. Once again, this is especially true for first-born children, due to a lack of experience in raising a child.

What Are the Most Common Challenges in This Period?

Drawing from the list of challenges in Table 3.1, the primary challenges faced by most families in this early period include the following:

- Challenges in family decision making
- Differences in how family members respond to the disability of ASD
- Challenges related to future uncertainty
- Challenges in understanding ASD and explaining it to others
- Challenges in dealing with professionals and other service providers

What Helps in This Early Period?

We have found that the following approaches provide families with the most direct assistance, and we therefore incorporate them as rules of thumb for supporting families in the SCERTS Model:

1. Provide parents with clear and honest information about whether there is a problem, the nature of the problem and a provisional or firm diagnosis, depending on the evidence gathered. A "let's wait and see" attitude is not appropriate or helpful, as it does not give families direction or help to clear the overwhelming confusion they may be experiencing.

2. Provide clear and understandable information about the child's developmental strengths and needs.

3. Emphasize the need for parents and professionals to develop a partnership to address the child's developmental needs and to develop a plan collaboratively.

4. Provide understandable, current information about ASD.

5. Begin to discuss the landscape of educational and treatment options. It is not helpful for parents to be told of only one approach to follow based on the bias of the professional. Parents can only make informed choices about approaches and strategies by being informed.

6. Emphasize the potential for growth and positive change for the child.

7. Ask parents if they wish to be put in touch with other parents who have young children with ASD, parent organizations, or support groups.

8. Most of all, *listen, listen, listen!* to parental questions and concerns throughout this process so that you are on target in addressing family needs.

Planning Initial Comprehensive Services	*Scenario 2: The parents have a child who has been diagnosed recently, and they are attempting to cope emotionally with this overwhelming news. They wish to understand their child's challenges better, may continue to struggle with what ASD means, and are in need of initial recommendations for approaches to support their child's development.*
Predominant Educational Support and Emotional Support Issues	Around the time following diagnosis, parents are desperately trying to come to some understanding of the implications of a diagnosis of ASD, both for the short term as well as for many years into the future. The uncertainty of what the future holds, along with the daily stresses of trying to support their child's development often creates an emotionally overwhelming situation. Furthermore, the often contradictory information about different treatment approaches and about whether ASD can be "cured" or whether it is a life-long disability may further add to the confusion and stress. With the diagnosis of ASD, however, many families can now focus their energies on beginning to collaborate with professionals in treatment, which provides the hope that positive growth and progressive change will occur.
What Are the Most Common Challenges in This Period?	The primary challenges faced by most families in the initial planning of services include the following: • Challenges in family decision making • Differences in how family members respond to the disability of ASD • Challenges in changes to the family system: roles, lifestyle, and routines • Challenges related to future uncertainty • Feelings of isolation • Challenges in understanding ASD and explaining it to others • Challenges in dealing with service delivery systems • Challenges in dealing with professionals and other service providers • Confusion regarding available interventions and models
What Helps at Diagnosis or Shortly After Diagnosis?	The following approaches may be helpful in working with families at or shortly after diagnosis: 1. Focus on planning for and securing local services. 2. Provide family members with information about supporting the child's development at home. 3. Provide more technical information about services and recommended practices, such as the book *Educating Children with Autism* (NRC, 2001) and practical but less technical books written for parents. 4. Continue to emphasize the potential for growth and change. 5. For children in the early intervention years (birth to three years), provide information about the transition to preschool services. 6. Continue to ***listen, listen, listen!*** to parental questions and concerns so that you are on target in addressing family needs.

Transition to Early Elementary School Grades

Scenario 3: A family with greater experience and knowledge has a child who was diagnosed 2½ years ago who has received early intervention and preschool services and is attending kindergarten. This family wishes to explore additional educational options, such as placement in a typical first-grade class, to support their child's development.

Predominant Educational Support and Emotional Support Issues

The transition from the preschool years to the early elementary school years can be particularly stressful for families. The focus of the school experience for a child entering elementary school is no longer on social and play experiences as it is in the preschool years and begins to shift more to academic concerns, as those are the expectations for most children.

Some parents may also have heard that the greatest potential for a child's progress is up to 5 years of age (the so-called "window of opportunity") and that unless certain milestones are achieved by this age (e.g., acquisition of functional speech, social interest with peers), there is little potential for further growth. This may cause significant anxiety for parents. (We do not agree with this often-stated assertion, as there is no research evidence to support it, and we know of many children who go on to make significant progress, with significant spurts in development even beyond the preschool years and throughout the school years.) For children with significant challenges in emotional regulation, embarrassment in public due to behavioral difficulties may be a more prominent issue for family members, for as a child looks older, he or she is expected to be better regulated, and parents are expected to "control" their child in public if there are difficulties. Furthermore, many school-based services seem less family friendly than preschool and early intervention services, as the goals for educators in most educational settings shift primarily to the child, with less or no attention given to supporting family members.

What Are the Most Common Challenges in This Period?

Common challenges for families during the transition to early elementary school include

- Finding the balance in family life
- Challenges in family decision making
- Differences in how family members respond to the disability of ASD
- Challenges in changes to the family system: roles, lifestyle, and routines
- Challenges to brothers and sisters
- Challenges related to future uncertainty
- Feelings of isolation
- How family members interface with their social community, including concerns about embarrassment in public
- Challenges in understanding ASD and explaining it to others
- Challenges in dealing with service delivery systems
- Challenges in dealing with professionals and other service providers

What Helps While Planning for Services in the Early Elementary School Years?

The following approaches may be helpful while working with families to plan services in the early elementary school years:

1. Focus on transition planning and transition options from preschool to the early school years.

2. Discuss the range of options that are available or that can be created to address child goals and parental priorities.

3. Develop a plan to shift from home- to school-based services (if services have had a major home-based component).

4. If a child will receive both school-based and non–school-based services (i.e., clinic- or home-based services), develop a plan for a collaborative approach between school and nonschool professionals to coordinate efforts and to meet the child and family needs in supplementing the school-based educational program.

5. Discuss the difficult issue of developing new relationships and shifting the family's trust to the school system and new staff while respecting the family's desire to maintain relationships that have already been established with other professionals or service providers.

6. To develop a future-oriented outlook for planning, discuss the likelihood that intensive services will be required for at least a number of years because in most cases ASD is a lifelong developmental disability.

7. Continue to *listen, listen, listen!* to parental questions and concerns so that you are on target in addressing family needs.

Transition to Later Elementary School Grades

Scenario 4: A family has a 10-year-old child who has been fully included in the general education classroom with support until third grade. However, a significant increase in anxiety related to the pressure of more advanced academics and more complex social expectations has resulted in an increase in behavioral difficulties and, possibly, a need to reconsider how educational services are provided.

Predominant Educational Support and Emotional Support Issues

For a child in the early elementary school years, age-related issues such as the development of friendships with peers, greater independence in daily living skills, and academic success come to play a greater role. Siblings may become more aware of the extent of their brother's or sister's disability, especially younger siblings who may catch up and surpass their brother's or sister's abilities in some areas. When siblings attend the same school, a greater burden is placed on the typical sibling in the school setting as other children come to know that sibling as the one who has a brother or sister with ASD. Parents have to continue to make important decisions about the relevance of their child's school program, especially when there has been an academic focus, to the everyday functional needs of the child and family. For a child previously educated primarily in environments with typical peers, the possible need to provide increased support in a pull-out environment, such as a resource room, may be seen as a step back by parents. Furthermore, parents may have differences of opinion with professionals about issues such as the types and intensity of support that the student needs.

What Are the Most Common Challenges in This Period?

Common challenges in this period include

- Finding the balance in family life
- Challenges in family decision making
- Challenges to brothers and sisters
- Challenges related to future uncertainty
- Feelings of isolation
- How family members interface with their social community, including concerns about embarrassment in public
- Challenges in dealing with service delivery systems
- Challenges in dealing with professionals and other service providers

What Helps While Planning for School Services in the Elementary School Years and Beyond?

The following approaches may be helpful when working with families with a child who is in the later elementary school grades:

1. Focus discussion on social expectations for school success and the types of academic and emotional supports that will be required.
2. Discuss the direction to be taken in school programming, such as a relatively greater focus on an academic curriculum versus a functional curriculum or a combination of elements of each.
3. Discuss and consider different options for the child to be educated with peers, such as full inclusion, partial inclusion, and so forth.
4. Develop a plan for ongoing support for emotional regulation given the new challenges at school and the increase in social and academic concerns.
5. Continue to focus on the development of friendships and community-based activities.
6. Continue to *listen, listen, listen!* to parental questions and concerns so that you are on target in addressing family needs.

THE SCERTS MODEL FAMILY SUPPORT PRINCIPLES IN ACTION

Assessment Practices for Supporting Families Used in the SCERTS Model

We now highlight assessment principles and practices underlying the SAP that are critical in supporting families.

1. Assessments need to yield useful information directly linked to educational programming, which is compatible and consistent with the needs expressed by the family. When parents play an active role and are satisfied with the assessment process and the information they receive, positive and trusting parent–professional relationships are supported. However, a major source of mistrust and tension between parents and professionals arises when families receive information that they feel is not helpful or is only marginally relevant, especially when they must expend considerable emotional energy and, in some cases, fiscal resources in pursuing assessments to answer questions they may have. Far too often, parents feel they do not receive honest and frank answers to their questions, even when they are clear about their primary reasons for seeking an assessment. In the SAP, all efforts are made to support parents in making assessment a meaningful and positive experience.

2. Assessments should always involve direct observation of a child in natural activities and settings. In the SCERTS Model, direct observation across activities and settings is incorporated as part of the SAP-O. Checklists and questionnaires (the SCERTS Assessment Process–Report, or SAP-R) completed by individuals familiar with the child in a variety of settings are also used as part of the SAP. Videotapes provided by parents may also provide an opportunity for the child to be observed in natural activities or different settings. The result of using multiple sources of information is a more accurate picture of a child and a clear message to parents that assessment practices are committed to developing a comprehensive understanding of the child's strengths and needs.

3. Parents and other family members must be recognized and supported in understanding that they are the experts about their child. The SAP acknowledges the expertise of family members, as they are asked to share in the SAP-R their observations of the child's strengths or assets, as well as their primary concerns. They are also asked to validate whether the assessment process captures an accurate picture of the child. Parents are requested to specify the information they wish to acquire from the assessments and the major concerns for the family. When parents are actively engaged in the assessment process, not only are they educated about the process itself, but there is also more of an opportunity to develop a consensus about a child's developmental strengths and needs based on a shared set of observations.

4. Following the assessment process, immediate feedback should be given and should directly address the strengths and needs of the child. In the SAP, primary concerns identified by the family are addressed directly, and ample time is provided for questions and discussion. The manner in which professionals provide assessment feedback has a profound effect on parents' perceptions of their child, of themselves as parents, and of the professionals involved in the assessment. Stated simply, the behavior of professionals directly contributes to parents' perceptions of professionals as being helpful or as an additional source of stress, and the SAP attempts to support positive relationships from the onset of the process.

5. To the extent possible, information presented throughout and subsequent to the assessment process should be free of professional jargon or should be fully explained to caregivers. ASD is an extremely complex spectrum of disabilities, for professionals as well as for family members. This complexity is exacerbated when families receive information that is difficult to decipher and use, whether it is received verbally or in written form. In general, to the extent possible, professionals should provide feedback and respond to questions at a level appropriate to family members' understanding. As it may be difficult for professionals to completely avoid technical jargon, parents should be offered detailed explanations and should be offered ample time to ask questions. The SAP attempts to minimize the use of jargon and to develop a profile of a child that is understood and validated by parents.

Special Considerations Regarding the Role of Siblings in Assessment

In the SAP, brothers and sisters are recognized as a unique source of information and as important partners. Therefore, to the extent possible, they should be actively included in assessment. Of course, the specific types of involvement depend on the ages and developmental abilities of the siblings, the nature of assessment activities (e.g., questionnaires versus direct assessment), and the location of assessment activities (e.g., home versus center based).

Depending on these factors, brothers and sisters may be involved in assessment in a variety of ways and play multiple assessment roles that are similar to the roles of caregivers. First, parents may be encouraged to ask brothers and sisters to provide information when filling out the SAP-R Form, which asks about a child's communication and play abilities. Siblings may have unique opportunities with, experiences with, and observations of their brother or sister that parents do not have. This strategy is consistent with the use of multiple informants in assessment, a SCERTS Model assessment strategy that we consider an important principle when working with children with ASD.

Second, brothers and sisters may be direct participants in assessment by engaging in play interactions either during a clinic- or home-based assessment or during other observations of natural routines. In such circumstances, it is helpful to observe everyday routines such as snack or mealtime and provide siblings with choices of play activities to encourage interactions to be as natural as possible. For clinic- or school-based assessments involving a brother or a sister, caregivers can be encouraged to bring favorite toys or activities used by the children in play interactions at home so that familiar routines may be observed. Alternatively, introduction of new toys or activities provides an opportunity to observe interactive patterns and whether and how a sibling may assume a teaching or supportive role. The types of communicative adjustments and successful strategies that brothers and sisters demonstrate to foster successful communication may be an important source of information in planning educational efforts. If there are significant interactive difficulties, however, these may also be observed and addressed directly in working with siblings and caregivers, especially when caregivers identify such concerns as a priority goal in education.

Third, brothers and sisters may also fulfill the role as interpreter of subtle, unconventional, or unintelligible language and communicative behavior or signals of dysregulation. This role is most relevant for a child with ASD who has limited conventional means to communicate, especially for a child at the Social Partner stage or even at an early Language Partner stage. It is striking how often parents report that brothers and sisters are better interpreters of the communication of their child with ASD than are adults. Therefore, siblings should be considered potential valuable resources in explaining what a child is attempting to communicate and in reading signals of dysregulation. Educators may encourage brothers and sisters to interpret communicative signals or signs of dysregulation during play interactions by asking the sibling what his or her brother or sister means or is attempting to communicate or how the sibling knows that his or her brother or sister is becoming upset.

Fourth, brothers and sisters may also play the role of validators of observations; that is, a sibling may provide information as to whether the child's behavior as observed is typical of what the sibling usually sees. Finally, an older sibling who has a more clear awareness and understanding of the child's disability may be asked to discuss situations in which the child has the greatest difficulty and strategies that are most successful in helping the child to communicate, stay well regulated emotionally, and participate successfully in social interaction.

A few notes of caution are in order when brothers and sisters are involved in the assessment process. First, they should be given an explanation as to why the assessment is occurring. Usually, a simple explanation for young children will suffice, such as, "We would like to see how you play with blocks with Justin so that we can get an idea of how Justin plays and communicates. Is that okay?" Second, siblings should always be voluntary participants in assessment activities and should be given the option to decline. Praise should be given to siblings for their participation; however, a child's discomfort or refusal should be accepted and respected with no negative consequences. In addition, siblings should be commended for specific aspects of their interpersonal behavior that supports the child's social communication and emotional regulation. For example, siblings may be praised for use of specific adjustments such as simplifying linguistic input, modeling, and encouraging communicative initiation and play by following the child's interests.

Working with Family Members in Supporting the Development of Children with Autism Spectrum Disorders

Meeting the Goals and Objectives of Educational Support for Family Members

As discussed previously, a child's experience within the family context and with individual family members provides the most enduring influences on the child's development. Family activities and routines are the contexts in which challenges in social communication and emotional regulation are best addressed and progress is best supported.

Consistent with the priorities in the SCERTS Model, caregiver-directed approaches are primarily concerned with helping family members understand their child's difficulties and supporting their child's development in social communication, emotional regulation, and other abilities they identify as priorities. Educational support must be based on family priorities. To ensure that educational activities are meaningful for a family or for a group of families, we ask family members families to identify their needs for information through informal discussion, interviews, and/or written surveys. As noted earlier, we have designed a questionnaire for this purpose (see Figure 3.1).

We now consider, in greater depth, the goals for educational support that were discussed earlier in this chapter (see Table 3.2 for a summary of goals, desired outcomes, and objectives).

Goal 1: To provide family members with information and resources to understand the nature of their child's disability and how it specifically affects their child's development

Desired outcome: Family members will become knowledgeable about ASD and how it specifically affects their child's functional abilities in life. They will be able to use resources to find information and continue to actively learn as their child develops.

To achieve this goal, professionals must work with parents so that the parents can recognize and understand their child's behavioral patterns that relate to common characteristics of ASD, their child's strengths and needs in social communication, their specific strategies in communicating, and the difficulties the child may face in emotional regulation and related areas. As part of this process, parents need to be educated about the sequences and processes of communication and language development and related social-emotional capacities that are relevant to their child so that parents may have appropriate expectations regarding their child's development. Parents can then be supported in developing interactive styles that are appropriate and responsive to their children and supportive of successful communicative interactions.

As discussed earlier, the SCERTS Model draws from the developmental research literature on caregiver-child interaction, social-communicative development, and emotional regulation, as well as from research on ASD. With this research-based foundation, caregivers are provided with support in using styles and strategies that have been found to be most highly correlated with optimal social-communicative develop-

Table 3.2. Summary of goals, desired outcomes, and specific objectives of educational support to families in the SCERTS Model

Goal 1: **To provide family members with information and resources to understand the nature of their child's disability and how it specifically affects their child's development**

Desired outcome: Family members will become knowledgeable about ASD and how it specifically affects their child's functional abilities in life. They will be able to use resources to find information and continue to actively learn as their child develops.

Specific objectives

a. Professionals will educate family members about their child's level of social communication, specific strategies in communicating, and specific difficulties their child faces in emotional regulation and related areas.
b. Professionals will educate family members about the sequences and processes of language, communication development, and social-emotional development relevant to their child so that they may have appropriate expectations regarding their child's development.
c. Professionals will help family members to develop interactive styles that are appropriate and responsive to their children and supportive of successful communicative interactions.

Goal 2: **To provide family members with the knowledge and skills to support their child's development in everyday activities, and to address specific issues that are identified by parents as most stressful and challenging**

Desired outcome: Family members will feel confident in providing the necessary supports to foster their child's development across different situations and in everyday activities and in identifying and coping with the most significant difficulties they face at any point in time.

Specific objectives

a. Professionals will help family members to identify and modify daily activities and routines (learning supports).
b. Professionals will help family members to develop new activities that will support social communication development and improve relationships between family members and the child.

Goal 3: **To help parents and other family members see professionals as ongoing, relevant resources who can help address questions about treatment and educational approaches, who can discuss confusing and often controversial accounts of ASD in the literature and public media, and who can offer families guidance and lessen their confusion on other topics**

Desired outcome: Parents and other family members will use professionals as resources in a manner that addresses family members' questions and concerns about their child's program, as well as any other relevant issues about ASD and their child that affect the family.

Specific objectives

a. Professionals will provide unbiased information about educational approaches and will clearly state their bias about educational issues when relevant.
b. Professionals will help family members deal with and develop a better understanding of the critical and often controversial information available about ASD.

Goal 4: **To help parents provide brothers and sisters with accurate, age-appropriate information about ASD specific to the challenges that siblings face (e.g., why playing and interacting may be difficult)**

Desired outcome: Siblings will develop the knowledge and understanding of ASD specific to the everyday challenges they face in interactions with their brother or sister.

Specific objectives

a. Parents and professionals will acknowledge and address issues raised by siblings.
b. Parents and professionals will directly explain how problems associated with ASD affect interactions and relationships with family members.

Goal 5: **To help parents in supporting positive sibling relationships by fostering more successful play and social interactive experiences**

Desired outcome: Siblings will have positive and emotionally satisfying experiences with their brothers or sisters and, over the long term, will develop a foundation of positive relationships.

Specific objectives

a. Professionals will help family members to improve and facilitate play and social interactions among siblings.
b. Professionals will help siblings to become competent in reading the communicative and emotional regulatory signals of their brother or sister and thereby be able to respond to subtle or unconventional behaviors in a supportive manner.
c. Professionals will help siblings develop the social-communicative skills and strategies to interact and play successfully with their brother or sister with ASD.

d. Professionals will help siblings to understand that their brother's or sister's emotional and/or behavioral difficulties, when present, may be due to communicative limitations and other causes of emotional dysregulation.
   e. Professionals will help siblings to develop successful strategies to engage and respond to their brother or sister in everyday social-communicative and play interactions.

Goal 6: **To help parents understand the legal rights of their child and their family regarding services and the systems that are responsible for providing services (e.g., early intervention, school-based programs)**
Desired outcome: Parents will be knowledgeable about their legal rights and those of their child, will be able to collaborate and deal effectively with systems that are responsible for providing services to their child based on those rights, and make informed decisions based on their knowledge.
Specific objectives
   a. Professionals will provide parents with the information and with additional resources regarding their legal rights and those of their child.
   b. Professionals will provide parents with the skills and strategies to develop collaborative relationships with people who are responsible for providing services.

---

ment. These are delineated in the SCERTS Model as Interpersonal Support and Learning Support, which are assessed and targeted under the Transactional Support domain. The rationale for this focus is that research has found that caregivers of children with social-communicative difficulties may develop excessively directive interactive styles, possibly due to the children's delays in responding, that are not most conducive to supporting the children's communication development. In such cases, caregivers may need direct support in developing more supportive, facilitative styles of interaction. Caregivers who are demonstrating supportive and appropriate interactions may primarily need external validation by being given specific positive feedback about their manner with their child and reassurance of their abilities. When professionals are willing listeners and provide helpful feedback, parents are better able to problem-solve and understand how to deal with the challenges they face.

Goal 2: **To provide family members with the knowledge and skills to support their child's development in everyday activities, and to address specific issues that are identified by parents as most stressful and challenging**

Desired outcome: *Family members will feel confident in providing the necessary supports to foster their child's development across different situations and in everyday activities and in identifying and coping with the most significant difficulties they face at any point in time.*

As noted, the family context is essential in supporting social communication and emotional regulation. Characteristics of family activities and routines can have a profound effect on a child's ability to participate actively and confidently in social activities and to be well regulated emotionally, so as to benefit maximally from learning experiences. Many caregivers are able to benefit from professional support in identifying and modifying daily activities and routines and in developing new activities that foster social-communicative development and improve relationships between caregivers and their children.

Goal 3: **To help parents and other family members see professionals as ongoing, relevant resources who can help to address questions about treatment and educational approaches, who can discuss confusing and often controversial accounts of ASD in the literature and public media, and who can offer families guidance and lessen their confusion on other topics**

Desired outcome: *Parents and other family members will use professionals as resources in a manner that addresses family members' questions and concerns about their child's program, as well as any other relevant issues about ASD and their child that affect the family.*

To meet this goal, professionals must be committed to providing unbiased information about educational approaches so that parents can make informed decisions with confidence. When clear biases exist, as they often do, it is incumbent on professionals to clearly state their biases about educational issues so that parents may put the discussion in an appropriate context. These same principles hold for helping parents deal with and develop a better understanding of the critical and often times controversial information available about ASD. Such information ranges from the potential causes of ASD, to nutritional and biomedical treatments, to how a child's behavioral patterns may be understood. Professionals should never attempt to convince parents to faithfully adopt or to adhere to the beliefs of the professional, as this approach is counterproductive to supporting autonomy and critical decision making.

Goal 4: **To help parents provide brothers and sisters with accurate, age-appropriate information about ASD specific to the challenges that siblings face (e.g., why playing and interacting may be difficult)**

Desired outcome: *Siblings will develop the knowledge and understanding of ASD specific to the everyday challenges they face in interactions with their brother or sister.*

To address this goal, parents and professionals must first acknowledge and address issues raised by brothers and sisters that may be confusing to the brothers and sisters. These may range from broader questions about whether a brother or sister with ASD will ever be "normal" or will ever learn to talk to more specific questions about behavior. Parents and professionals may then directly explain how problems associated with ASD do not go away in a short period of time and how such problems may affect the child's interactions and relationships with family members. Such discussions must occur at an appropriate level of understanding relative to the age of the brother or sister. When such information is provided, it may help to prevent the development of feelings of self-doubt or inadequacy or misinterpretations of behavior such as, "My brother doesn't like me, and that's why he won't play with me." Without such information, a brother or sister may naturally attribute inaccurate reasons to his or her difficulties in engaging the child with ASD.

Goal 5: **To help parents in supporting positive sibling relationships by fostering more successful play and social interactive experiences**

Desired outcome: *Siblings will have positive and emotionally satisfying experiences with their brothers or sisters and, over the long term, will develop a foundation of positive relationships.*

To address this goal, it is essential that parents and professionals support brothers and sisters in developing competence in reading the communicative and emotional regulatory signals of their brother or sister and thereby in being able to respond to subtle or unconventional behaviors in a supportive manner. This also entails developing an understanding that emotional and/or behavioral difficulties, when present, may be due to communicative limitations and other causes of emotional dysregulation. With this foundation of understanding, brothers and sisters may be supported in developing successful strategies to engage and respond to their brother or sister in everyday social-communicative and play interactions. More specific strategies are discussed in the next section.

Goal 6: To help parents understand the legal rights of their child and their family regarding services and the systems that are responsible for providing services (e.g., early intervention, school-based programs)

Desired outcome: *Parents will be knowledgeable about their legal rights and those of their child, will be able to collaborate and deal effectively with systems that are responsible for providing services to their child based on those rights, and will make informed decisions based on their knowledge.*

To meet this goal, professionals must provide parents with information about their rights, as well as information about additional resources regarding their legal rights and those of their child. For example, advocacy organizations, family support agencies, parent-to-parent networks, and organizations providing legal assistance may be invaluable resources.

Parents also benefit from developing the specific skills and strategies to develop collaborative relationships with people who are responsible for providing services. As it often is inevitable that there are some differences of opinion between parents and professionals about services provided to a child, it is essential that all efforts be made to maintain a sense of mutual respect and collaboration and prevent the development of adversarial relationships. Parents may benefit from direct support when differences of opinion exist, by understanding their rights and those of their child and by having the skills and expertise to deal with such situations.

Providing Educational Support to Family Members

As noted, there is no clear dichotomy between educational and emotional support, as these issues are often enmeshed when working with families. However, it may be helpful to identify activities as either educational, such as demonstrating and teaching educational techniques, use of transactional supports, and so forth, or emotionally supportive in nature, such as discussing strategies to cope with emotionally challenging situations such as resolving disagreements between parents or embarrassment in public related to a child's behavior.

The following principles should be considered in helping family members create opportunities for learning and participating in social activities.

1. To the extent possible, activities to enhance social communication and emotional regulation should be planned for and should occur primarily within naturally occurring activities in the family context, not primarily in isolated teaching sessions. The most critical social-communicative experiences for a child occur in his or her interactions with family members in everyday activities, both when the child is learning basic communication skills during the Social Partner stage and when the child's communicative mastery is expanding at the Language and Conversational Partner stages. Daily routines and family events provide the experiential opportunities for learning and practicing communicative abilities and learning to remain well regulated emotionally when faced with everyday challenges to emotional regulation. Given the prominence of the child's early family relationships and family activities, professionals need to work closely with the family to use these activities and routines for promoting social-communicative competence and emotional regulation and fostering positive social relationships. When supporting family members in these efforts, it is critical that recommendations be compatible with the family's belief systems and social-cultural preferences. If not, there is the danger that family members will see recommendations as not relevant to family life and not respectful of the family's values.

2. Professionals need to be able to recognize and support effective caregiver interpersonal supports, such as modifications of interactive styles, with respect to the individual child's needs. Chapter 4 in Volume I discussed the challenges that a child with ASD may present to family members that require interpersonal support from all partners. With unclear expectations and a limited understanding of their child's disability, caregivers may employ a wide range of adaptive strategies (e.g., modify language to better communicate, use a slower interactional pace) or maladaptive strategies (e.g., use of a highly directive interaction style) in interactions. The SAP directly assesses positive as well as problematic aspects of interpersonal support with a range of partners, leading to the identification of goals and outcomes in the Interpersonal Support component of the Transactional Support domain of the SCERTS Model, which then inform efforts to provide educational support to families. It is important to recognize, however, that appropriateness of interactive style cannot be determined by reference to the characteristics of the partner's interactional style alone (e.g., how a parent models language). Appropriateness must be considered in reference to if and how a partner's style supports successful social-communicative exchange and emotional regulation for the child. For example, a more directive style, such as frequent use of commands and physical direction within a more challenging activity, may not be inappropriate when the child needs additional structure and support to participate optimally. However, frequent use of a directive style, even when not needed, may be detrimental to a child's development. Professionals must work closely with caregivers in developing an awareness of appropriate interpersonal supports for social communication and emotional regulation.

3. Activities should be safe, predictable, and fun and thus should allow a child to expend greater energy on social communication, social engagement, exploration, and problem solving. In the SCERTS Model, we emphasize the importance of predictability in meaningful and purposeful activities for children and shared positive emotional experiences. The cognitive and emotional comfort afforded by familiar routines and heightened structure supports emotional regulation and fosters children's sense of security and thus contributes to social-communicative competence and social-emotional well-being. Predictability and heightened structure can be incorporated into the physical environment, into the activity schedule, and within interactive and communicative routines as needed to support a well-regulated state (see Chapter 2 in this volume for further discussion). However, it is always important to provide a balance between structure and flexibility, to avoid situation-specific and rote learning and to increase adaptability to and tolerance of change. Primary involvement of the caregiver and use of favorite and familiar games, toys, and security objects also help to foster a sense of safety. Adding an element of joyfulness and fun motivates children to engage and communicate more frequently and consistently.

4. Family activities should support children's development of mastery motivation, self-determination, and a proactive sense of self. The concept of *mastery motivation* comes from the child development literature and refers to a child's developing capacity to persist and succeed in mastering tasks and challenges in everyday activities. Mastery motivation may be enhanced by introducing activities that are challenging but that are within the child's developmental grasp or "zone of proximal development" (Vygotsky, 1986). Opportunities for choice making and decision making foster self-determination and development of a sense of self as the child comes to learn that his or her preferences can be communicated and respected. Therefore, frequent opportunities should be made available for the child to make choices, and activities should reflect the child's motivations and developmental strengths.

5. Preferred relationships with peers, siblings, and adults should be taken into account in planning activities. Children need to develop secure attachments and relationships to feel safe in participating in and exploring new activities, especially in situations that may create potential difficulties in emotional regulation. Family relationships and special friendships allow for activities in which emerging communication skills can be learned and practiced with responsive partners. The result of many positive experiences with people significant to a child is a cumulative history of positive emotional memories, which leads the child to seek further opportunities to engage in those activities again.

6. Activities should reflect caregiver and child preferences. To address child and family needs and encourage family relationships, activities or routines targeted within the family context should be meaningful and relevant to the caregivers and an integrated part of the child's and family's life. It is within everyday family events that relationships evolve and relationship problems are addressed, negotiated, and resolved. Similarly, for children in child care, preschool, or school settings, experiences with children who are good social models are important for fostering communication and social-emotional development in the context of developing friendships.

We now consider two general educational approaches in working with caregivers that focus specifically on enhancing children's communication abilities and emotional regulation and caregiver–child interaction and relationships: direct individual caregiver–child coaching and caregiver education programs. Support may be provided within the family's home (if the family indicates that such services are not intrusive) or at a child's school program, depending on the age of the child and how such support can be arranged by family members and professionals relative to the family's lifestyle and routines.

Direct Individual Caregiver–Child Coaching or Guidance

In this approach, professionals work directly with a caregiver and the child, often interacting directly with the child and asking caregivers to observe, participate, and eventually emulate the style modeled by the teacher or clinician. This approach attempts to foster caregiver responsiveness, balanced turn taking, and shared control, with the goal of both partners developing a sense of effectiveness, competence, and confidence, and to foster positive experiences and relationships for both the caregiver and the child. Educators or clinicians may work directly with caregivers and their children during play interactions with the goals of identifying and addressing 1) social-communicative skills needed by the child, 2) emotional regulatory issues that interfere with successful interaction and learning, and 3) strategies that caregivers can learn to support their child's development and resolve interactional difficulties. Caregivers are supported in creating activities in which they can motivate their child to engage, follow their child's attentional focus, respond to their child intentions at an appropriate level to support the learning of new skills, and take turns that support further reciprocal interaction.

For example, at the Social Partner stage, this may involve responding to subtle nonverbal communicative signals, responding to the child's intentions, and then providing slightly more advanced models. For a child at the Language Partner stage, it may involve expanding on one- or two-word utterances and modeling more social functions of communication, such as commenting for joint attention. For a child at a

Conversational Partner stage, it may involve discussing past events with reference to appropriate supports, such as a personal journal with photographs. Different interactional strategies are geared to promote preverbal communication; verbal communication; and, eventually, conversation, which parallel the Social Partner, Language Partner, and Conversational Partner stages.

In direct individual caregiver–child coaching, educators or clinicians provide guidance and/or literally join with parents and a child to engage the child in interactions appropriate to his or her developmental capacities. Goals and strategies are highly individualized and are developed based on results of the SAP and goals selected from the SCERTS curriculum, grounded in a child's developmental capacities in social communication and emotional regulation.

Interactive guidance (McDonough, 1998) is an additional strategy that is a variation of caregiver coaching and may be used to help achieve these same goals with caregivers in the SCERTS Model. This approach is typically less direct in teaching caregivers specific strategies and may not necessarily involve direct interaction between the professional and child. Interactive guidance was developed due to the belief that when professionals are the ones who primarily work with a child, with caregivers only observing, the professional may unintentionally disempower a caregiver who is observing because the caregiver may feel that only the professional has the ability to help the child learn. In interactive guidance, professionals may observe caregiver–child interactions during regular routines or play activities and make suggestions to caregivers to improve communicative and caregiving interactions that caregivers can implement immediately. Thus, the goal is to have caregivers experience more successful and rewarding interactions directly, rather than observing a professional "mediator."

Finally, another model of providing services to children and caregivers is caregiver–child groups, which may be designed to address many of the goals of educational support discussed in this chapter, but which are conducted in a group format and involve direct work with caregivers and children. Small groups (three to five caregiver–child pairs) may meet for one to three sessions a week. During a predictable schedule of activities appropriate for the children's abilities (e.g., music, circle time, snack time, gross motor), clinicians or educators model facilitative communicative interactions and strategies, as well as the use of transactional supports such as visual supports to foster each child's social-communicative and emotional regulatory capacities. Individual therapy and caregiver support meetings may occur in coordination with the groups to more specifically address challenges faced by each child and caregiver. The additional benefits of a group model include the opportunity for caregivers to observe other children with ASD or related developmental difficulties and learn strategies that may be helpful for their child. In addition, caregivers have the opportunity to develop a support network with other caregivers to preclude the feelings of isolation so often experienced by families of young children with developmental difficulties.

Caregiver Education Programs

Educational approaches may provide information and support to caregivers, often in a group format, without direct involvement between a professional and a child. Educational programs may focus on helping caregivers to understand principles of social-communicative and emotional regulatory development and the caregivers' potential role in facilitating their child's development of communicative competence.

For example, The Hanen Centre in Toronto developed a caregiver program, *More than Words* (Sussman, 1999), which is specifically designed for children with ASD and their families. *More than Words* uses a group format and adult learning principles (i.e., active involvement and participation, negotiated agenda) to help caregivers understand their child's learning style and needs, develop activities for enhancing social communication, and modify their interpersonal support styles to foster their child's development. The program typically involves evening meetings with caregivers from five to eight families and periodic home visits over a 3-month period. Caregivers are asked to keep home diaries and to openly discuss issues with the group. A mutually supportive atmosphere is crucial for caregivers to share their successes and challenges with others. One strategy that is recommended to create such an atmosphere is the use of parent graduates from previous programs to cofacilitate programs.

Including Siblings in Efforts to Enhance Social Communication and Emotional Regulation Abilities

I learned how to use my sister's communication book and some sign language with her, and I even helped teach my parents how to use them too!
SEVEN YEAR OLD BROTHER OF A THREE YEAR OLD GIRL WITH ASD

As noted previously, there are several goals in fostering positive sibling relationships as an aspect of educational support in the SCERTS Model. These include

1. Facilitating positive play and social interactions among siblings

2. Helping siblings develop the social-communicative skills and strategies to interact and play successfully

3. Helping siblings in the role of teacher

There are great individual differences among the experiences of siblings who have brothers or sisters with ASD; however, there also are common sibling needs and concerns that change with circumstances and age. These needs include 1) receiving understandable information about ASD; 2) having open communication within the family about the child's difficulties; 3) parental recognition of the typical siblings' own strengths and accomplishments; 4) having "quality time" for all brothers and sisters with their parents on an individual basis; 5) having opportunities for contact and support from other siblings and families; and 6) developing ways to cope with stressful events such as peer and public responses, unexpected disruptions to family plans, and extra home responsibilities.

Specific to children with more limited abilities, the siblings of these children also need the following: 1) an ability to read their brother or sister and thereby to respond to subtle or unconventional communicative behaviors; 2) an understanding that emotional and/or behavioral difficulties, when present, may be due to communicative limitations and other causes of emotional dysregulation; and 3) successful strategies to engage and respond to their brother or sister in social-communicative and play interactions.

In planning activities to support abilities at home, efforts should be made to directly involve siblings, as well as caregivers and playmates. As with assessment, the nature of the siblings' involvement may vary according to activity settings, the developmental abilities of the children, and the relationships between the children. Siblings' interest in and willingness to participate also will influence the type of involvement. It is to be expected that the roles siblings may play will vary according to the relative ages and abilities of the children and may change over time. For example, children with similar abilities may interact as playmates, whereas children who are significantly developmentally advanced may take on a teacher or helper role. Furthermore, it is conceivable that in some cases, the role of playmate may eventually evolve into the role of helper or caregiver over time.

Facilitating Play and Social Interactions Among Siblings

Play and family routines should be the primary contexts for supporting social communication and emotional regulation among brothers and sisters because the role of social and play partner is common for most children. Play is a natural part of sibling interaction and is a vital context for communicative, social, and cognitive development. In planning facilitative activities focused on improving play and social interactions, the transactional notion of *mutual efficacy* in social-communicative interactions is an important premise. That is, both partners must experience some sense of social control, enjoyment, and success (i.e., mutual efficacy) so that a foundation of positive interactions and positive emotional memories can be established, which should enhance motivation to interact and communicate, as well as provide the positive experiences that strengthen relationships. If play interactions between siblings are not of concern, direct intervention may not be necessary, other than to provide encouragement and praise to both children for their positive behavior. However, due to developmental differences and some of the challenges associated with ASD discussed earlier, professionals and parents may need to support siblings in developing specific strategies to facilitate more successful interactions (Chapter 2 in this volume also addresses ways caregivers can foster success when a child with ASD is learning and playing with peers.)

Helping Siblings Develop the Social-Communicative Skills and Strategies to Interact and Play Successfully

Approaches to supporting parents and caregivers may be adapted to help brothers and sisters have more successful interactions with their siblings. In these approaches, attention is focused on helping brothers and sisters to 1) understand the child's level of communication through observation; 2) modify their language and communicative behavior to an appropriate level; 3) develop skills for increasing the child's responsiveness, turn taking, and reciprocity by following a child's attentional focus and lead; 4) expand and elaborate on the child's communicative and play behavior; 5) use appropriate supports such as visual supports when appropriate; and 6) develop appropriate strategies for fostering emotional regulation. We once again emphasize the importance of using everyday family routines and events to foster development rather than relying primarily on contrived teaching sessions. Based on findings from the SAP, specific social-communicative skills may be targeted in such routines and events.

In working with a sibling and the child with ASD directly or with caregivers serving as mediators, it is important that professionals be cognizant of the following issues:

1. *Many siblings have already developed positive and successful strategies* for communicating and playing with their brother or sister and for supporting emotional regulation. It should not be assumed that there are problems that need to be targeted. If there are problems, parents' priorities for their children should be acknowledged and addressed.

2. *Parents may be in the best position to provide guidance and support to siblings.* Parents observe their children in everyday interactions and are typically aware of the successes and difficulties siblings experience in different contexts.

3. *Siblings' developmental level and meta-communicative abilities (i.e., ability to reflect on and talk about communication skills) should be major considerations* in interactive and communicative guidance, whether this guidance is provided by parents or professionals. For example, a younger child will learn best through observing others' models and through imitation, whereas for an older and more able child, a discussion of successful ways to support communication and play, in addition to more direct strategies, would be appropriate.

4. *Siblings should not be overly corrected,* as frequent corrective feedback may lead to a sense of inadequacy and reduced motivation to participate. Evaluative feedback should be given in a supportive manner, when appropriate, with a strong bias toward praise and encouragement. Modeling of alternative strategies to replace unsuccessful communicative or play overtures is preferable to direct negative or corrective feedback. When the behavior of a child with ASD is particularly challenging, it is especially important that others share their own difficulties in interacting and playing with the child, so that siblings can put their experience with their brother or sister in perspective.

Helping Siblings in the Role of Teacher

From a transactional perspective, the teacher role will be most effective when the child with ASD responds to teaching interactions in positive ways. Therefore, an obvious focus in using an approach designed to support siblings in the teacher role would be to provide information, modeling, and coaching (when needed) to help make teaching interactions successful. Some strategies include the following:

1. *Discuss and model appropriate expectations about the communicative behavior and responsiveness of the child with ASD so that siblings do not experience frustration because expectations are too high.* For example, siblings may be told that their brother or sister cannot yet ask for toys with words, but that vocalizations or gestures or using pictures are the ways he or she communicates (at least in the short term). For a child with difficulty maintaining interactions for extended turns, siblings may be prepared to expect only brief interactive episodes during play and can be told that engagement will improve. For a child who has unconventional means to communicate or who is using or is learning to use AAC devices, information should be shared with siblings and other family members openly so that the child's readability and thus his or her communicative competence will be enhanced for all family members.

2. *Suggest activities and games that are likely to result in successful interactions and communicative exchange.* For example, appropriate activities would include those that 1) the child with ASD enjoys and is familiar with, 2) have an obvious and predictable structure, 3) can be learned through physical demonstration and modeling and are within the physical capabilities of both children, 4) are likely to provide positive emotional experiences, and 5) can be or are likely to be experienced frequently in the life of the family. The need for repetition and routine, which are essential characteristics of activities for very young children with ASD, should also be considered to support recognition and mastery for children with ASD and their siblings alike. It should be emphasized that we are not advocating inflexibly programming all teaching interactions. The spontaneity and creativity of siblings should also be encouraged and praised when observed in teaching interactions. Finally, we believe that considerable effort must also be directed to helping siblings identify family routines, motivating activities, and facilitative contexts that are likely to result in positive outcomes when such support is needed.

3. *Suggest and model changes in interpersonal style that are known to support more successful interactions with a child.* Depending on the profile and needs of the child with ASD, these may include asking siblings to slow down their movements, exaggerate their positive emotional responses, offer choices verbally and nonverbally, reduce the rate and amount of talking during play, and so forth.

Seven Ways to Be Family Centered in Fostering Development

In addition to following the family support principles outlined thus far in this chapter, the following are seven specific ways to support family members' efforts to foster a child's growth in social communication and emotional regulation:

1. Parents should be asked to indicate their priorities for services provided to their child, and such priorities should always be taken into account in establishing goals for a child. This is accomplished systematically as part of the SAP.

2. For home-based services, parents, brothers and sisters, or other people (e.g., other relatives, child care workers) should be offered the opportunity to be directly involved in activities or, at the very least, should be encouraged to observe activities to maximize understanding of goals and strategies and to support carryover.

3. Parents should be asked at what level they are able to participate in developing activities and in modifying family activities to address goals agreed on by the team. It is unreasonable for professionals to expect that all parents are able to assume a role that extends beyond typical caregiving activities. Professionals need to respect the roles that parents are comfortable in assuming regarding the degree of their involvement, as well as the amount of time parents can realistically make available outside of regular family routines.

4. School- or center-based activities should be designed, and the goals targeted in the activities should be selected, based on the likelihood that they will be relevant to activities that already occur or can be scheduled to occur on a regular basis in the life of the family.

5. When educational transactional supports are developed for school activities (e.g., visual schedules, choice boards, organizational supports), duplicates should be made and given to the family with ongoing support on how to use them.

6. An efficient and effective system of communication should be established among parents and professionals so that parents can provide ongoing feedback about their questions, concerns, and observations of progress.

7. When significant changes in services provided to a child are forthcoming (e.g., change of school, staffing changes), professionals should collaborate with parents to discuss and develop a transition plan well in advance of the changes.

Meeting the Goals and Objectives of Emotional Support for Family Members

Parents and other family members who may benefit from emotional support may be experiencing overwhelming emotions due to the challenges directly related to parenting a child with ASD, including frustration and fatigue, the complicated issues related to sibling relationships, and other family issues such as creating a balance in family life. As noted, these difficulties may be related directly to a child's difficulties in social communication, emotional regulation, and development of positive relationships. Stressors may also be related to the secondary challenges outside of the family discussed earlier, such as interfacing with the public and dealing with professionals and service delivery systems. Regardless of the source of emotional distress, caregivers must be provided with or must be encouraged to seek support when stresses in daily life interfere significantly with caregivers' emotional well-being and family functioning and should be encouraged to be as available as possible for supporting their child's development. By directly addressing the following goals for emotional support, professionals can collaborate with family members in a manner that strengthens long-term relationships that will benefit both the child and family (see Table 3.3 for a summary of goals, desired outcomes, and objectives).

Table 3.3. Summary of goals, desired outcomes, and related objectives of emotional support to families in the SCERTS Model

Goal 1: To enhance family members' abilities to cope with the stresses and challenges of raising a child with ASD

Desired outcome: Family members will develop specific coping abilities to manage the inevitable stresses that will be experienced directly due to or as a secondary effect of the child's having ASD.

Specific objectives

a. Professionals will help family members identify and articulate the major sources of stress related to having a child with ASD.
b. Professionals will support families in developing coping strategies specific to the major sources of stress that are identified.

Goal 2: To help family members understand and gain access to the range of formal and informal emotional supports that may be available

Desired outcome: Family members will gain access to formal and informal supports that best match the emotional needs of family members at specific points in time.

Specific objectives

a. Professionals will help family members identify or develop the supports that could be helpful in addressing the emotional needs of the family.
b. Professionals will help family members use such supports in a manner that best addresses family members' priorities.

Goal 3: To support parents' efforts to deal successfully with professionals, as well as with educational and health care systems

Desired outcome: Parents will develop specific strategies to foster positive parent–professionals relationships and will deal with emotional challenges that may be due to difficult interactions or relationships with professionals or due to difficulties in dealing with educational and health care systems.

Specific objectives

a. Professionals will identify desirable characteristics of parent–professional relationships and collaboration and the means to develop and maintain such relationships.
b. Professionals will support parents in addressing difficult relationships.
c. Professionals will support parents in coping with stresses that arise in dealing with educational and health care systems.

Goal 4: To help family members to identify their own priorities and develop appropriate expectations and realistic, achievable goals for their child's development and family life

Desired outcome: Family members will be clear about the most important issues they wish to address for their child and family, develop realistic goals and expectations for their child, and will create a balance in family life consistent with their lifestyle and values.

Specific objectives

a. Professionals will engage in dialogues with parents to identify the most crucial issues for the child and family.
b. Professionals will collaborate with parents to develop realistic short-term goals and expectations for the child.
c. Professionals will provide opportunities to discuss and problem-solve the challenges of bringing a balance to family life by identifying ways to support the marital relationship and to support siblings and other family members (grandparents and other relatives).

Goal 5: To help parents support siblings with information about ASD when the siblings have questions or when they experience difficulties associated with having a brother or sister with ASD and to help siblings discuss their feelings about having a brother or sister with ASD

Desired outcome: Siblings will be able to acquire the information they need to have a better understanding of issues they encounter related to having a brother or sister with ASD and will be able to cope with difficulties they may experience by discussing their feelings.

Specific objectives

a. Parents will create an atmosphere of open communication so that siblings feel comfortable in raising questions about their brother or sister or about ASD.
b. Parents will be able to responds to siblings' questions about ASD in a manner that is appropriate to the siblings' level of understanding.
c. Parents and professionals will provide opportunities for siblings to openly share their feelings.

Goal 6: To help siblings develop coping strategies for situations that may be stressful

Desired outcome: Siblings will be able to develop and use a variety of coping strategies related to having a brother or sister with ASD

Specific objectives

a. Parents and/or professionals will provide opportunities to a brother or sister to practice explaining their brothers or sister's disability to others.
b. Parents and/or professionals will provide opportunities to discuss other ways to cope in stressful situations specific to the situations encountered by siblings.

Goal 1: To enhance family members' abilities to cope with the stresses and challenges of raising a child with ASD

Desired outcome: *Family members will develop specific coping abilities to manage the inevitable stresses that they will experience directly due to or as a secondary effect of the child's having ASD.*

Goal 2: To help family members understand and gain access to the range of formal and informal emotional supports that may be available

Desired outcome: *Family members will gain access to formal and informal supports that best match the emotional needs of family members at specific points in time.*

To accomplish these goals, professionals and/or other individuals in a family's support network must work with family members to help them identify and articulate the major sources of stress related to having a child with ASD. Once this process begins, families may be supported in developing coping strategies specific to the major sources of stress that are identified. Professionals may be helpful in identifying or developing the supports that potentially would be helpful in addressing the emotional needs of the family and may also help family members use such supports in a manner that best addresses family member's priorities.

Support may be arranged formally with professionals or may occur informally through a family's social network. When arranged formally, emotional support may be provided in a number of ways. The benefit of support groups is the opportunity to hear a variety of perspectives from a number of other parents and the great likelihood that new relationships may develop due to the common life experiences of group participants. Professionals may facilitate such support meetings, or alternatively, may provide resources (e.g., a room at a school, announcements to families) for parents to organize and facilitate their own meetings. Individual support may be appropriate for specific personal issues that a family member would not discuss in a group or for issues that may not be directly related to raising a child but that may be associated with the challenges of doing so, such as additional stresses on a marriage.

Outside of arranged support activities, professionals who work with a child on a regular basis may support families in a number of ways in daily contacts and interactions:

- *Be a good listener.* Parents of children with ASD often have a limited number of people to talk with who know their child well. Sharing personal experiences is one positive strategy that parents may use to cope emotionally with the challenges of raising a child with ASD. If a parent begins to seek emotional support at an inconvenient time (e.g., when children are getting off the school bus), suggest another time to talk in the near future, or set up a telephone meeting. Professionals must recognize that at times, the more extreme reactions of parents of children with ASD may be due to the experience of chronic stress and that the best reaction is to listen, attempt to understand, and respect the parent's perceptions.

- *Don't always try to fix problems.* Be a resource to help parents problem-solve and make decisions based on available information and what they perceive intuitively as the right thing to do (their gut reaction). Ultimately, parents need to feel confident about their decision making, as they will need to live with their choices. Furthermore, a parent's expression of concern, which may initially sound like a request for advice, may truly be a plea to share how difficult things are. In other words, it may be a plea for emotional support, not educational recommendations.

- *Respect the perspective of the parent without being judgmental.* Regardless of the nature or intensity of a parent's feelings, it is not helpful to dismiss or minimize what a parent is feeling as it is his or her own reality. If it is felt that particular feelings are misdirected or based on a misunderstanding, it is still possible to communicate respect for what the parent feels, but also indicate that there are other perspectives or points of view.

- *Be honest and direct.* Parents are very sensitive to situations in which professionals appear to be withholding information, even if it is done with good intentions (e.g., minimizing the difficulty of child's problem behavior to spare a parent's feelings). Identifying crucial needs that require attention will ultimately be beneficial for all. Conversely, openly celebrating a child's progress and expressing appreciation to family members for the unique personal qualities of the child or who the child is *as a person* fosters a sense of relationship and mutual respect.

- *Try to meet parents and other family members outside the context of the school or agency.* Arranging for home visits, family picnics, or other activities opens up the opportunity for professionals to get to know parents and other family members in a different manner. For families involved in other activities related to ASD (e.g., fundraising, awareness campaigns such as walks for ASD), professionals may demonstrate support by participating in such activities.

- *Be a resource.* Many professionals are very knowledgeable based on their knowledge of research and literature and years of experience with children and families. Professionals may share stories and anecdotes about successes, creative strategies that other families have used to support their child, and so forth.

Goal 3: **To support parents' efforts to deal successfully with professionals, as well as with educational and health care systems**

Desired outcome: *Parents will develop specific strategies to foster positive parent–professional relationships and will deal with emotional challenges that may be due to difficult interactions or relationships with professionals or due to difficulties in dealing with educational and health care systems.*

To address this goal, professionals need to work with parents and identify desirable characteristics of positive, collaborative parent–professional relationships and the means to develop and maintain such relationships. When appropriate, professionals can also support parents in addressing difficult relationships they may have with other professionals and can provide assistance in dealing with stresses that arise with educational and health care systems.

Goal 4: **To help family members to identify their own priorities and develop appropriate expectations and realistic, achievable goals for their child's development and family life**

Desired outcome: *Family members will be clear about the most important issues they wish to address for their child and family, will develop realistic goals and expectations for their child, and will create a balance in family life consistent with their lifestyle and values.*

To address this goal, professionals may engage in dialogues with parents to identify the most crucial issues for the child and family and collaborate with the parents to develop realistic short-term objectives and expectations for their child. This occurs as a part of the SAP. However, other issues, such as facing the challenges of bringing a balance to family life, supporting the marital relationship, and supporting siblings and other family members may be addressed if the parents wish to address these issues.

Goal 5: **To help parents support siblings with information about ASD when the siblings have questions or when they experience difficulties associated with having a brother or sister with ASD and to help siblings discuss their feelings about having a brother or sister with ASD**

Desired outcome: *Siblings will be able to acquire the information they need to have a better understanding of issues they encounter related to having a brother or sister with ASD and will be able to cope with difficulties they may experience by discussing their feelings.*

Siblings also have emotional needs, as is clear from this brief exchange between a 7-year-old child and a therapist.

Clinician: If you have a question about your (3-year-old) brother or you just wanted to ask somebody about autism, who would you ask?
Child: Nobody.
Clinician: Why not?
Child: I'm embarrassed.

It is important for parents to create an atmosphere of open communication so that siblings feel comfortable in raising questions about their brother or sister or questions related to ASD. When a level of trust and understanding is provided, parents must then be able to responds to sibling's questions about ASD in a manner that is appropriate to their level of understanding. Both parents and professionals who have contact with siblings must provide opportunities for siblings to openly share their feelings because when this is not occurring, there is great potential for misunderstanding and resentment.

Goal 6: **To help siblings develop coping strategies for situations that may be stressful**

Desired outcome: *Siblings will be able to develop and use a variety of coping strategies related to having a brother or sister with ASD.*

As discussed, siblings inevitably encounter stressful circumstances, with one of the most common being the need to explain or respond to questions about differences observed in their brother or sister (Prizant, Meyer, & Lobato, 1997). Parents and/or professionals need to provide opportunities to a brother or a sister to practice explaining their brothers or sister's disability to others so that the sibling develops a level of comfort in doing so. Parents and/or professionals will also need to provide opportunities to discuss other ways to cope in stressful situations encountered by siblings.

For example, siblings often find themselves in situations where they must fulfill the role of an intermediary between their brother and sister with ASD and other children or adults. Siblings often benefit from simple descriptions or scripts that they may readily use when asked questions such as "Why does your brother talk like that?" or "What's wrong with your sister?" It is helpful for siblings, as it is for their parents, to distinguish between those people for whom and settings in which a full explanation is necessary and those in which a brief response will suffice. Siblings should also know that they may defer questions and comments to their parents or other responsible adults and that needing adult help does not reflect negatively on them.

Siblings may benefit from programs, workshops, and support groups that are designed specifically to educate and to support them. Services that meet the needs of siblings are consonant with the family-centered philosophy, a cornerstone of the SCERTS Model. Some early intervention programs and schools may offer regular opportunities, such as Family Day or Sibling Day, for siblings to meet the staff, to participate in activities, and to learn about the services that are offered. Such programs welcome siblings and recognize their special status, educate children about various disabilities, demystify special education settings, and help children to cope with the inherent challenges of having a sibling with ASD. Siblings have opportunities to ask questions, to share their experiences and concerns, to participate in structured activities, to meet other children who also have brothers and sisters with disabilities, and to learn from children who share similar experiences.

Some siblings, however, may have adjustment difficulties that can not be adequately addressed in play-based programs or support groups alone and that warrant referral for individual or family therapy. If it becomes clear that a sibling is experiencing excessive stress, worry, or anger or that the sibling-child relationship is disturbed, then a referral to a specialist in family issues may be needed. In some cases, parents may initiate therapy for siblings due to their concerns. Educational professionals may play a role in helping to identify when a referral may be helpful, in supporting parents in their decision to pursue psychological support services, and in facilitating such referrals for professional services.

Providing Support to Caregivers Regarding Sibling Issues

Professionals can support caregivers by providing information regarding ways that they can help siblings adapt and cope with the challenges of having a brother or sister with a communication disability. Caregivers may need help in explaining their child's communication disability to siblings and in facilitating interactions between their children. It is important that caregivers understand that siblings be offered choices, flexibility, and support in their sibling roles. It is imperative that parental expectations for sibling help and caregiving be reasonable, realistic, and developmentally appropriate in order to minimize undue stress and role confusion (Prizant, Meyer, et al., 1997). Parents should be encouraged to provide positive attention to the typical sibling as a person, celebrating his or her own accomplishments. The sibling should not be viewed as a surrogate parent responsible for taking care of the brother or sister with ASD, as this may cause resentment. It is important for caregivers to provide special time for siblings apart from the child with ASD.

Clear and direct communication among family members is essential and should be encouraged, including permission for siblings to discuss ASD and its impact on all family members. As noted, parents should be encouraged to speak honestly about their own experiences and feelings relative to their child because children learn to express their feelings and share their thoughts by observing their parents. Well-delineated yet flexible family roles that reflect family members' abilities and, in the case of siblings, developmental capacities contribute to family adaptation. The opportunity for a family member to make an active contribution to the child's care can contribute to a sense of competence and can preclude overdependence on professionals. Adequate formal and informal social support and the ability to ask for help when it is needed are important to the family's overall coping and adaptation. It also must be recognized by professionals that the presence and direct involvement of siblings may normalize the family environment and to provide caregivers with the experience and gratification of raising typically developing children.

Table 3.4 provides a list of support activities designed to address goals for educational and emotional support to family members, and a SCERTS Family Support Planning Form appears on the pages following Table 3.4.

Table 3.4. Sample educational and emotional support activities for a SCERTS Family Support Plan

Activities that provide educational support

Provision of resources: Professionals provide families with a list of resources or access to a library of resources to foster greater awareness of the nature of autism spectrum disorders (ASD), the range of interpersonal and learning supports available, and resources to support siblings and grandparents. *Suggested frequency:* Ongoing

Communication system between contexts (school and home): A system of communication allows parents and educational team members to provide ongoing feedback about their questions, concerns, and observations of progress. This system can be essential for fostering a child's ability to communicate across contexts, as visual supports can be embedded in daily notes. *Suggested frequency:* Daily

Frequent and consistent team meetings: Specific interpersonal and learning supports should be discussed regularly with those who interact with the child to support active carryover and consistency of transactional supports across contexts and partners (i.e., educational team members and family members). *Suggested frequency:* Biweekly or monthly, depending on the needs of the child and family

Direct individual caregiver–child coaching or guidance: A professional works directly with a caregiver and the child, within the family's home (if the family indicates that such services are not intrusive) or at a child's school program, depending on the age of the child and how such support can be arranged by family members and professionals relative to the family's lifestyle and routines. *Suggested frequency:* Determined by the family and team

Interactive guidance: A professional observes caregiver–child interactions during regular routines or play activities (perhaps through review of a videotape) and makes suggestions to caregivers to modify and improve communicative and caregiving interactions. *Suggested frequency:* Determined by the family and team

Caregiver–child groups: A small group (three to five caregiver–child pairs) is led by professionals who work directly with caregivers and their children. Individual educational services and caregiver support meetings may occur in coordination with the groups to more specifically address challenges faced by each child and caregiver. *Suggested frequency:* Determined by the family and team

Caregiver education programs: Caregivers participate in an education program that consists of presentations by outside speakers or school staff, with questions and discussion. Parents are encouraged to recommend topics and speakers. *Suggestion frequency:* Quarterly in the late afternoon or evening

Caregiver development day: A full day is devoted to providing information and discussing resources available for parents and family members. *Suggested frequency:* Annually

Classroom visits: Parents, siblings, and grandparents are invited to participate in visits to classrooms to observe students' programs. *Suggested frequency:* Determined by the family and team

Visual support "make and take" sessions: Parents and older siblings are invited to participate in an overview session at the beginning of the school year as an introduction to this resource that is available to parents throughout the school year. *Suggested frequency:* An initial overview session, followed by scheduled appointments

Book club: A nontechnical article or book is distributed to parents (for articles) or purchased by or loaned to parents (for books). Selections focus on primary issues that parents wish to discuss or on popular books related to ASD. Parents and staff meet in a group to discuss each selection and how it relates to the children. *Suggested frequency:* Triennially

Activities that provide emotional support

Support groups: Caregivers may come and meet informally with caregivers of other children. Discussion topics are chosen by participants, who are encouraged to share experiences, thoughts, and ideas or to just come and listen. *Suggested frequency:* Determined by the family and team

One-to-one support meetings: A family member is given the opportunity to meet with a staff member who knows the child and family to discuss specific acute issues or challenges that have arisen. These meetings are not intended to be used for ongoing professional support or for counseling that may be provided outside of the educational agency (appropriate referrals should be made when necessary). *Suggested frequency:* Determined by the family and team

Family fun events: Social events are organized for students, siblings, and other family members and staff to enjoy activities at the school or in the community on a weekend day (e.g., picnics, movies, bowling, crafts, drumming, music). *Suggested frequency:* Biannually

Parents' night out: A night scheduled for parents only to get together and enjoy a night of information, socialization, and networking. *Suggested frequency:* Annually

Drop-off night: Child care is offered for children with ASD as well as their siblings to allow parents to enjoy a worry-free and fun night out. If not feasible through an educational center or a school, referrals to community agencies and funding sources for respite would be an appropriate consideration. *Suggested frequency:* Annually

Sibling summer camp: A week-long, small-group camp session may be devoted to siblings of children with ASD. In an activity-based program, siblings are encouraged have fun and to share their thoughts and ideas regarding having a brother or sister with a disability. *Suggested frequency:* Annually

Adapted from Peck, C. (2003–2004). *Parent and family events.* Trumbull, CT: Cooperative Educational Services.

Note: As educational and emotional support must be based on family priorities as well as adapted to match unique cultural differences and expectations, families and educational team members are encouraged to implement, adapt, and augment these activities to address concerns and needs in an appropriate manner.

Furthermore, it is recognized that emotional support and educational support are not mutually exclusive; however, the goal of activities may be conceived of as primarily emotional or educational.

Family Support Planning Form (page 1)

Child's name: _____ Date: _____

GOALS OF EDUCATIONAL SUPPORT TO FAMILIES

1. To provide family members with information and resources to understand the nature of their child's disability and how it specifically affects their child's development

2. To provide family members with the knowledge and skills to support their child's development in everyday activities and to address specific issues that are identified by parents as most stressful and challenging

3. To help parents and other family members see professionals as ongoing, relevant resources who can help address questions about treatment and educational approaches, who can discuss confusing and often controversial accounts of ASD in the literature and public media, and who can offer families guidance and can lessen their confusion on other topics

4. To help parents provide brothers and sisters with accurate, age-appropriate information about ASD specific to the challenges that siblings face (e.g., why playing and interacting may be difficult)

5. To help parents in supporting positive sibling relationships by fostering more successful play and social interactive experiences

6. To help parents understand the legal rights of their child and their family regarding services and the systems that are responsible for providing services (e.g., early intervention, school-based programs)

Educational support requested by family members	How will educational support be provided?

The SCERTS® Model: A Comprehensive Educational Approach for Children with Autism Spectrum Disorders
by Barry M. Prizant, Amy M. Wetherby, Emily Rubin, Amy C. Laurent, & Patrick J. Rydell
Copyright © 2006 by Paul H. Brookes Publishing Co. All rights reserved.

Family Support Planning Form (page 2)

GOALS OF EMOTIONAL SUPPORT TO FAMILIES

1. To enhance family members' abilities to cope with the stresses and challenges of raising a child with ASD
2. To help family members understand and gain access to the range of formal and informal supports that may be available
3. To support parents' efforts to deal successfully with professionals, as well as educational and health care systems
4. To help family members to identify their own priorities and develop appropriate expectations and realistic, achievable goals for their child's development and family life
5. To help parents support siblings with information about ASD when the siblings have questions or when they experience difficulties associated with having a brother or sister with ASD and to help siblings discuss their feelings about having a brother or sister with ASD
6. To help siblings develop coping strategies for situations that may be stressful

Emotional support requested by family members	How will emotional support be provided?

The SCERTS® Model: A Comprehensive Educational Approach for Children with Autism Spectrum Disorders
by Barry M. Prizant, Amy M. Wetherby, Emily Rubin, Amy C. Laurent, & Patrick J. Rydell
Copyright © 2006 by Paul H. Brookes Publishing Co. All rights reserved.

Many of these activities could be offered by programs, and families may be encouraged to choose from the menu of available options in order to participate in activities that best fit their lifestyle and best address their concerns and needs.

SUPPORT AMONG PROFESSIONALS

Up to now, we have given much attention to the challenges faced by children with ASD, as well as to those faced by parents and other family members. Professionals and other service providers also face considerable challenges that receive too little attention in the educational and research literature. In the SCERTS Model, we believe that there must be direct and explicit recognition of such challenges, and a plan to mitigate challenges for professionals and other service providers so these individuals may be as effective as possible in supporting children and families. In this section we briefly reiterate major challenges and discuss ways in which support among professionals may be addressed as part of a comprehensive SCERTS Model plan.

Challenges Faced by Professionals and Other Service Providers

Once again, we must emphasize that the SCERTS Model works best as a team approach. In the SCERTS Model, our concept of a team approach is one in which family members; all professionals and service providers; and, when appropriate, the child with ASD plan and work together to develop a comprehensive plan to support the child's development and quality of life. A team approach is not simply a process that involves a group of people who make decisions. It also is an attitude or mindset that should allow each team member to feel part of a comprehensive network or community of support, rather than as isolated elements. When professionals and caregivers view themselves as part of a support network, the whole is greater than the sum of the parts.

A team approach offers many benefits, including 1) a range of expertise offered by providers from different disciplines as well as by family members, 2) the opportunity to actively problem-solve with others as positive or negative changes occur in a child's and a family's development, and 3) the opportunity for ongoing educational support when new information and innovations in techniques and approaches are shared by team members. Last, but certainly not least, a team approach offers the opportunity for developing a system and a safety net of emotional support, based on mutual respect and shared goals.

Unfortunately, there often are many challenges to implementing a team approach effectively, which include but are not limited to 1) lack of support from administrators and lack of an overall plan that supports team practice, 2) limited time for meeting and planning, 3) large class size and caseloads, 4) service providers who put their energy into protecting their "turf" rather than into fostering collaboration, 5) differences in educational philosophy and teaching practices across providers and/or family members, and 6) staff shortages and frequent staff turnover. The underlying causes of these problems are numerous and vary greatly across settings. However, without a team approach, secondary problems such as difficulties in ensuring continuity in programming across settings and problems in developing mutual respect and positive working relationships and support among service provider and parents become pervasive and interfering factors. We believe it is critical that administrators and all potential team members recognize that the investment in a true team approach will result in less stress for all and fewer difficulties in implementing a plan in a consistent and comprehensive manner. With a team approach, there are many possibilities for developing a system of support activities to allow service providers to be most effective and to be most energized to serve children and families.

As with providing support to families, providing support among professionals can be conceptualized in two major categories: 1) providing informal and planned opportunities for enhancing educational and therapeutic skills and 2) providing informal and planned opportunities for emotional support. Table 3.5 provides a listing of activities that have the potential to address the need for support among professionals and other service providers.

Educational Support

New approaches and educational strategies are constantly being developed and tested for children with ASD, based on empirical research; new technology; and the efforts of talented and creative educators, therapists, and parents. When professionals and service providers are given the opportunities to learn, grow, and be at the cutting edge, this freedom to learn fosters a sense of pride and achievement among the professionals, especially when there is a cohesive team process in place. Educational support can be provided informally or formally in a variety of formats.

Table 3.5. Sample educational and emotional support activities in a SCERTS Support Plan for Professionals and Service Providers

Activities that provide educational support

Mentoring arrangements: Based on observations and regularly scheduled meetings, less experienced staff can be given reflective feedback and recommendations to support their development. Mentoring arrangements can also provide opportunities for emotional support as well. *Suggested frequency:* Ongoing

Supervision meetings: Specific meetings are arranged with a designated supervisor for ongoing feedback regarding job performance. These meetings are important for identifying areas in need of improvement or development. *Suggested frequency:* Set by supervisor depending on experience and performance of professional

Team meetings: Meetings are conducted to review a child's progress and consider needed changes in a child's program. *Suggested frequency:* Monthly or bimonthly, depending on a child's age and progress

Consultation time for professional-to-professional exchange of ideas: Consultation time allows professionals to share new information to enhance services for a child or at a programmatic level. *Suggested frequency:* Weekly or bimonthly

Regularly scheduled staff in-service training sessions or professional development days: Professional development days provide more formal in-house professional development opportunities. *Suggested frequency:* 2–3 days per year

Consultant visits by specialists in autism spectrum disorders (ASD): Ongoing visits by specialists support the efforts of educational staff. *Suggested frequency:* Monthly

Attendance at regional or national conferences, workshops, and other continuing education activities outside of the school setting: Staff members may bring back new information to present to the team and to school personnel. *Suggested frequency:* 2–3 times per year

Involvement in research projects conducted in collaboration with university-based or university affiliated researchers: As projects allow

Activities that provide emotional support

Informal discussion during scheduled breaks (over lunch, during recess time): Suggested frequency: ongoing

Scheduled sharing opportunities at the end of the school day: Scheduled time at the end of the day allows professionals to share child-specific difficult issues or other emotional challenges or just to reflect on the day. *Suggested frequency:* Whenever possible

Brown bag lunches: Over lunch, professionals can share child-specific difficult issues or other emotional challenges. *Suggested frequency:* Weekly

Crisis meetings: Crisis meetings address urgent, critical issues that require immediate attention. *Suggested frequency:* As needed

Regularly scheduled staff retreats outside the school setting: Staff spend a day or a half-day away from the work setting to focus on ongoing topics related to emotional support issues and the educational program. *Suggested frequency:* Biannually

In school settings, mentoring arrangements may be made by pairing senior staff (e.g., more experienced teachers, occupational therapists, speech-language pathologists, or paraprofessionals) with less experienced staff. Through observations by and regularly scheduled meetings with senior staff, less experienced staff can be given reflective feedback and recommendations to support their development. Mentoring arrangements can also provide opportunities for emotional support as well.

Regular supervisory meetings, scheduled staff in-service training sessions, and consultant visits by specialists in ASD can also support the expertise of staff. Specific topics may be identified by staff to prioritize areas in need of development. Depending on the topics and time of such training sessions, parents and other caregivers may also be invited. The focus of such meetings may also be child specific, with a regular alternating schedule so that all children are discussed within a regular time frame to review progress.

Service providers also benefit greatly by attending regional or national conferences, workshops, and other continuing education activities outside of the school setting. Staff members may then bring back new information to present to the team and to school personnel. Whenever possible, involvement in research projects conducted in collaboration with university-based or university-affiliated researchers are great opportunities for professional growth.

Emotional Support

To be most effective, professionals and other service providers must be provided with a working context that recognizes and allows for open discussion about the emotional challenges and rewards in working with children with ASD. Open discussion may occur informally during scheduled breaks (e.g., over lunch, during recess). It may also occur during scheduled sharing opportunities at the end of the school day or over weekly brown bag lunches. Staff should also be given the opportunity to call crisis meetings when sudden changes in a child's behavior or when a personal difficulty experienced by a service provider warrants an urgent call for staff to address specific issues. Regularly scheduled staff retreats away from the school setting may also provide opportunities for emotional support. Regardless of the number and types of support activities that are available, the ultimate goal must be to reduce the factors that create stress for service providers and to foster a sense of personal growth and competence as one member of a network of concerned people who can direct their energies toward supporting children and families.

SUMMARY

Creating an atmosphere of support to families and among service providers is an extremely complex endeavor that often is a back-burner issue when so much energy is focused on providing education and treatment for a child with ASD. However, in the SCERTS Model, it is recognized that the time and effort put into support activities have a profound impact on the development of children, due to the complex transactional relationships among children, their families, and professionals and other service providers who support the children's development. Thus, support activities are essential components of a comprehensive SCERTS plan. We have developed two SCERTS Assessment Program–Quality Indicators (SAP-Q) scales—the SCERTS Program Quality Indicator Rating Scale: Support to Families and the SCERTS Program Quality Indicator Rating Scale: Support Among Professionals—for programs to evaluate how effective they are in addressing support goals for families and professionals. These two SAP-Q Forms, as well as a third SAP-O Form, appear in the appendix in this volume.

Chapter 4

Linking Transactional Support Goals to Social Communication and Emotional Regulation Goals

In this chapter, we address the integrated nature of the SCERTS Model in specific reference to how Transactional Support goals must be linked to goals in Social Communication and Emotional Regulation. Nevertheless, it is important to emphasize once again that although we have identified the primary domains of the model in reference to Social Communication, Emotional Regulation, and Transactional Support, we do not mean to imply that these domains are separate and distinct. On the contrary, in child development, and therefore in our assessment and educational programming approaches in the SCERTS Model, these domains are intimately interrelated and interwoven. Therefore, in practice, a child's abilities as well as potential in social communication and emotional regulation cannot be viewed apart from the transactional supports that are influencing a child's behavior and how the child's behavior is influencing partner behavior. More specifically, we now address the process of how interpersonal supports and learning supports are assessed and targeted when implementing the SCERTS Model.

IMPORTANCE OF ADDRESSING CHILD AND PARTNER GOALS

Transactional Nature of Developmental Challenges

Developmental challenges are transactional in nature. That is, such challenges are dynamic and are determined by child-specific factors, factors external to the child, and the interaction among these factors. If this were not the case, one would assume that a child's difficulties and progress would be determined solely by the type and severity of a child's developmental difficulties. For example, one would assume that a child's sensory, motor, cognitive, and social disabilities and so forth are fixed and that there is no potential for affecting such difficulties. When professionals work with caregivers to develop programs that will have a positive impact on a child's development and learning, they are working under the assumptions that such difficulties are not fixed and that there is tremendous potential for growth and change.

In the SCERTS Model, the transactional nature of development is addressed in two primary ways. First, relationships among different aspects of development, such as social communication, emotional regulation, and learning, are viewed as fluid and inseparable. Therefore, we expect that improvements in one domain, such as emotional regulation, will positively influence social communication and learning. Second, the role of a child's partners, including family members, peers, educators, and other caregivers will have a significant and long-term impact on the child's development. This impact occurs through interpersonal and learning supports provided by those partners, including how environments and everyday activities are arranged to support active participation and learning. We now summarize those aspects of child development, partner style, and the environment that influence a child's developmental achievements in social communication and emotional regulation.

1. *There is a strong relationship between a child's achievements in social communication and a child's achievements in emotional regulation.* Again, relationships among different aspects of development, such as social communication, emotional regulation, and learning, are viewed as fluid and inseparable. Therefore, we expect that improvements in one domain, such as emotional regulation, will positively influence social communication and learning. When a child develops a greater capacity to regulate arousal in social activities, for example, gains will likely be observed in that child's capacity to engage in reciprocal interaction with adults and peers.

2. *There is a strong relationship between a partner's implementation of interpersonal supports and a child's achievements in social communication and emotional regulation.* As noted, the role of a child's partners will have a significant and long-term impact on a child's development. Interpersonal supports such as being responsive to the child, fostering the child's initiation, respecting the child's independence, and modeling appropriate behaviors will directly support the child's development of social-communicative and emotional regulatory abilities. Additional interpersonal supports include the partner's ability to set the stage for active engagement, provide developmental support, and adjust language input based on the child's unique learning style and needs.

3. *There is a strong relationship between a partner's implementation of learning supports and a child's achievements in social communication and emotional regulation.* Learning supports provided by sensitive partners, including how environments and everyday activities are arranged to support active participation and learning (e.g., environmental arrangements, visual supports, activity modifications), have a significant impact on a child's development.

Child Progress or Lack of Progress Is Determined by Multiple Factors

Factors that influence a child's progress or lack of progress may be conceptualized in three major categories: within-child factors, partner factors, and environmental factors. These risk and protective factors were discussed and presented in Chapter 3 of Volume I. We briefly consider such factors, keeping in mind that they are not fixed and may be influenced by factors from other categories.

Within-Child Factors

It is now accepted that factors specific to a child's developmental and neuropsychological profile may have a significant impact on the child's abilities and development in social communication and emotional regulation. For example, impairments in a wide variety of developmental domains, such as sensory processing and motor, cognitive, and social development, put a child at increased risk for experiencing difficulties in social communication and emotional regulation. Other factors such as general health, allergies, and sleeping and other regulatory problems also may affect a child. Such factors are typically referred to as *biological* or *constitutional risk factors.* Many, but not all, of these within-child factors are not directly under the control of caregivers and professionals.

However, if these risk factors were the sole or primary determinants of children's developmental outcomes, we would expect that children with very similar factors associated with their development such as similar neurological impairments, genetic syndromes, or sensory profiles would be very much the same and develop the same. Research has demonstrated that this is not the case. For example, seminal research on early intervention outcomes (Shonkoff, Hauser-Cram, Krauss, & Upshur, 1992) demonstrated that factors outside of the child, such as family factors, are better predictors of the developmental outcomes of children with neurological and developmental disabilities than are within-child factors. Furthermore, it is now understood that neurological development is also transactional. That is, neurological development, and therefore a child's functional potential, is greatly affected by the types of stimulation and learning experiences provided by caregivers and the environment. Therefore, other factors must help provide an understanding of how caregivers and professionals may have positive influences on supporting a child's development.

Partner Factors   A basic premise of the SCERTS Model is that partners play the most critical role in supporting a child's development. Furthermore, this role goes well beyond the implementation of teaching strategies in structured or semistructured learning lessons to help the child learn new skills. It includes how partners teach skills in social communication and emotional regulation and support their use in everyday activities through the incidental interactions that occur in such activities. As discussed in Chapter 3 of Volume I, when a child experiences activities and interactions as successful and emotionally satisfying over time, and thus associates positive emotional memories with such activities and interactions as well as with the people involved with those activities, the child is more likely to want to be with and remain engaged with partners and seek out similar experiences. Conversely, if a child experiences activities and interactions as confusing, disorganizing, unmotivating, and stressful, the child is more likely to attempt to cope rather than learn by putting considerable energy into avoiding people and activities associated with those negative feelings. In the SCERTS Model, the history of positive interactions with partners who are able to support social communication and emotional regulation in everyday activities is the foundation of the development of positive and trusting relationships.

The importance of interpersonal support was eloquently described by Ros Blackburn (2005), a 35-year-old woman with autism. In discussing what was helpful to her during states of extreme dysregulation, she noted that the very presence of people she trusted and with whom she had a positive history could be the most important regulating factors. In fact, she recommended that during more extreme states of dysregulation, she is best supported "in silence, and through the presence of another person," rather than through active physical or verbal attempts to help her regulate.

In the SCERTS Model, specific interpersonal supports, extracted from more than 30 years of developmental research and clinical experience, are assessed in partner behavior as part of the SAP and are targeted in educational programming by linking child goals in Social Communication and Emotional Regulation to Interpersonal Support goals for partners. Therefore, we view learning as a mutually influential partnership, in which a child and his or her partners must collaborate to create positive and emotionally satisfying activities for learning and mutual enjoyment. Whenever necessary, partners must provide guided participation to support the child in being successful, rather than imposing their will on the child to coerce him or her to learn skills or to behave in a certain manner. Thus, partners guide and facilitate in the teaching and learning process to maximize motivation and self-determination rather than direct and control, which is more likely to result in passivity and, in some cases, refusal and resistance.

A critical component for such a partnership is knowledge of a child's developmental capacities so that learning can be targeted within the child's zone of proximal development. In other words, partners need to be highly sensitive to ensuring developmentally appropriateness, in reference to the child goals that are targeted as well as to the partners' behavior in supporting development.

Environmental Factors

The third category of factors is how environments are arranged and learning supports are used in educational programming and in everyday activities to support children's social communication and emotional regulation. Research, clinical experience, and firsthand accounts of people with ASD clearly indicate that environments and activities that are overly stimulating on a sensory level, visually disorganized, and/or unpredictable tend to be confusing and stressful, resulting in increased dysregulation and therefore reduced capacities in social communication and learning. In contrast, environments that have levels of stimulation that are organizing, that are within a person's processing capabilities, and that have predictable qualities tend to support emotional regulation. Whenever necessary and possible, sensitive partners attempt to control or modify environmental factors, such as by lessening noise or by reducing visual clutter in such a manner as to support emotional regulation. Furthermore, activities may be designed to create the motivation, opportunities, and needs to communicate.

In many cases, specific environmental supports may be designed and infused in activities throughout the day to support social communication and emotional regulation. It is now well known that the use of visual supports is very effective for children with ASD in clearly delineating many aspects of daily routines such as time schedules, steps within activities, time left to complete activities, and so forth. Modifications to academic curricula and activity adaptations (e.g., adjusting the social complexity of an activity, infusing an activity with motivating materials and topics, modifying the sensory properties of an activity) are also important factors in supporting children with ASD. Environmental factors that are delineated in the SCERTS Model and educational and learning supports that clearly are under the control of partners have been shown to have a major positive impact on children's success, as children spend more time actively learning rather than simply coping.

HOW TRANSACTIONAL SUPPORT GOALS ARE IDENTIFIED AND LINKED TO SOCIAL COMMUNICATION AND EMOTIONAL REGULATION GOALS

We now discuss some basic considerations in operationalizing how the Social Communication, Emotional Regulation, and Transactional Support domains of the SCERTS Model and the specific goals across these domains become interrelated when designing activities for a specific child's educational plan. The following considerations are offered as general guidelines and are followed by a more in-depth review organized by Social Communication and Emotional Regulation goals with examples of relevant transactional support at different developmental levels.

1. *There is no one-to-one correspondence between individual Social Communication or Emotional Regulation goals and Transactional Support goals, as multiple transactional support factors may affect progress in social communication and emotional regulation.* It would be overly simplistic to attempt to identify a specific Transactional Support goal that is most relevant for each Social Communication or Emotional Regulation goal for a specific child. To do so would deny the great individual differences across chil-

dren and their partners. For example, for the Conversational Partner Symbol Use goal *Learns by imitation, observation, instruction, and collaboration,* it is conceivable that a number of Transactional Support goals may be relevant and effective. For example, under the Learning Support goals in the Transactional Support domain, it may be necessary to target the goals *Partner structures activity for active participation* and/or *Partner uses visual and organizational support.* To determine the appropriate Learning Support goal for the Symbol Use goal just noted, it would be necessary to refer to the SAP-O Form to determine which supports are already in place and a child's response to such supports. As will be expanded on in the following sections, this is a dynamic process in which Transactional Support goal linkages to Social Communication and Emotional Regulation goals must be problem-solved in team meetings.

2. *Relevant transactional support factors for a child may vary depending on child-specific factors (e.g., learning style, arousal bias) and child-specific challenges in social communication and emotional regulation.* Another important consideration is the specific child factors that are most relevant in determining how transactional supports are linked to Social Communication and Emotional Regulation goals. For example, when addressing the Joint Attention goal *Shares emotion* with a child who is a strong visual learner, there may be greater emphasis placed on the Transactional Support goal *Partner uses augmentative communication support to encourage development* than for a child who is more adept at learning language and understanding language concepts through the auditory modality.

   Therefore, Transactional Support goals are identified by addressing those supports that are most likely linked to Social Communication and Emotional Regulation goals, based on assessment of Transactional Support in the SAP-O, a child's current abilities and weaknesses as determined by the SAP, and hypothesized challenges to the child's development discussed by the team.

3. *Because no one transactional support factor determines progress for each Social Communication and Emotional Regulation goal, the team must identify the most likely factors in transactional support in determining goals, affect change in those factors, and assess the impact on a child's development.* Once the likely factors in transactional supports are addressed in the child's educational programming by setting specific goals in interpersonal and learning supports, the child's progress in achieving the designated Social Communication and Emotional Regulation goals must be monitored carefully. This must be done to assess the impact of the supports on the child's development, whether it be positive or negative. If it is determined that progress is occurring more slowly than expected toward specific goals, appropriate changes may be made in Transactional Support goals to continue efforts to support the child's development.

DETERMINING TRANSACTIONAL SUPPORT GOALS AT EACH DEVELOPMENTAL STAGE

The remainder of this chapter is intended to be used as a resource for a child's educational team to support discussions regarding the development of appropriate interpersonal and learning supports for an individual child. Appropriate sections may be referred to when developing a child's program, specific to linking Social Communication and Emotional Regulation goals with Transactional Support goals.

We now address the process of determining appropriate Transactional Support goals more specifically by reviewing the Social Communication and Emotional Regulation goals for children at the Social Partner, Language Partner, and Conversational Partner stages of development and considering the role of Transactional Support goals for the partner in helping a child reach these goals. As natural routines across home, school, and community environments provide the educational and treatment contexts for learning and for supporting the development of positive relationships, the SCERTS Model uses a continuum of learning contexts in these settings, from planned activity routines to naturally occurring activities, as discussed in Chapter 1 of this volume. Along this continuum, Transactional Support goals for Interpersonal Support and Learning Support allow partners to encourage a child to progress in specific Social Communication and Emotional Regulation objectives.

As discussed in Chapter 1 of this volume, the SCERTS Model incorporates activity-based learning as a primary method to support the development of children with ASD. A MA & PA approach is used in which meaningful and purposeful activities are developed based on the goals for and developmental capacities of a child and are provided systematically throughout the child's daily routines. Chapter 1 of this volume includes guidelines for selecting appropriate activities for the child and determining the activity structure based on the continuum of naturalness. As noted previously, as many as two to five goals for the child may be embedded into a given activity-based learning context. Thus, the careful implementation of transactional supports within that activity will support a child's developmental achievements toward Social Communication and Emotional Regulation goals. The SAP Activity Planning Form, provided in Appendix A of Volume I, is an essential tool for planning the child's daily activities, the targeted Social Communication and Emotional Regulation objectives, and the critical Transactional Support goals that will be considered.

As interpersonal supports and learning supports are embedded across a number of natural activities, they will differ based on what is considered appropriate and natural for that activity context. For example, when implementing the Learning Support goal *Partner uses visual and organizational support* at the Language Partner stage, the supports that will be infused in a circle time activity in the classroom, such as the use of carpet squares and a picture schedule to denote the sequence of stories and songs, will most likely be different than the supports that will be used on the playground. Supports on the playground may include a choice board to remind the child of cooperative games that could be initiated and footprints in a line to denote where to line up at the end of recess. The potential range of variation in the implementation of a specific Transactional Support goal is highlighted later in this chapter.

Ongoing assessment of the effectiveness of transactional supports and partner goals is essential, particularly if a child is having difficulty in an activity. Increased rehearsal and practice may be needed to help a child become more familiar with the activity. For example, a planned activity routine, in contrast to a modified natural activity, might be most appropriate to provide the practice needed, and/or it may be appropriate to infuse more intensive transactional supports such as visual supports and environmental modifications to support the child's emotional regulation in the relatively unfamiliar activity. Such determinations are not the result of a static, "one-shot" process that is decided at an initial team meeting. Rather, a child's partners need to continually evaluate the impact of their interpersonal style and/or provision of learning supports on the child's success or lack thereof in a given activity on a daily, weekly, and quarterly basis.

We now address special considerations in linking Transactional Support goals to Social Communication and Emotional Regulation goals relative to the Social Partner,

Language Partner, and Conversational Partner stages. Each table that follows lists a child goal in Social Communication or Emotional Regulation and related partner goals in Interpersonal Support and Learning Support. In addition, for the child goals, the tables list *linked goals/objectives,* which are identical or nearly identical to goals or objectives in other components of the SCERTS Model (marked on the SAP-O Forms with = and ≈), and *related goals/objectives,* which are related to goals or objectives in other components of the SCERTS Model and should be targeted together during intervention (marked on the SAP-O Forms with ↔).

SOCIAL PARTNER STAGE

At the Social Partner stage, a child's partners have a significant impact on supporting the child's ability to become a more active social and communicative partner, to communicate with purpose or intent for a range of communicative functions, and to acquire and use conventional gestures and vocalizations within social-communicative exchanges. Likewise, the child's partners have a significant impact on the child's ability to be available for learning, to use effective behavioral strategies for self-regulation, and to request partner assistance to achieve and maintain a well-regulated state. As outlined earlier, there are a number of essential considerations when determining how to prioritize specific Transactional Support goals for the child's partners. The charts included for each goal area may be referred to as a resource for educational teams as they determine which Transactional Support goals should be considered when addressing specific Social Communication and Emotional Regulation goals for a child at the Social Partner stage. *Please note that the objectives related to the goal areas in each table are defined in Chapter 8 of Volume I.* Following each goal area, a "snapshot" example is provided of how each of the named Transactional Support goals might be modified based on the nature of the specific activity and child-specific factors (e.g., whether a child has a bias for a high state of arousal versus a low state of arousal, whether a child is a visual learner or an auditory learner).

Social Communication: Joint Attention

JA1 Engages in reciprocal interaction (Social Partner stage)

Child goal	Related partner goals	
Joint Attention JA1 Engages in reciprocal interaction	**Interpersonal Support** IS1 Partner is responsive to child IS2 Partner fosters initiation IS4 Partner sets stage for engagement	**Learning Support** LS1 Partner structures activity for active participation LS4 Partner modifies goals, activities, and learning environment
JA1 is linked to SR1. **Linked objectives** JA1.1 Responds to bids for interaction (= MR2.3) JA1.2 Initiates bids for interaction (= SR1.4) JA1.3 Engages in brief reciprocal interaction (= SR1.5) JA1.4 Engages in extended reciprocal interaction (= SR1.6)	A child's ability to respond to bids for interaction (JA1.1) and initiate bids for interaction (JA1.2) relies on a partner's ability to be responsive to the child's focus of attention (IS1.1), respond to the child's signals to foster a sense of communicative competence (IS1.3), offer choices nonverbally and verbally (IS2.1), and wait for and encourage child initiations (IS2.2).	A child's ability to engage in both brief and extended reciprocal interactions (JA1.3, JA1.4) relies on a partner's ability to modify the environment to create turn-taking opportunities and leave spaces for the child to fill in (LS1.2), provide a predictable sequence to an activity (LS1.3), and arrange the learning environment to promote child initiation (LS4.5).

Snapshot of Kendra

Kendra is a 2-year-old Social Partner who is working on initiating bids for interaction (JA1.2). She is described as a somewhat aloof, self-directed child who appears to fulfill her needs on her own. She may reach for a desired object but is not yet coordinating these gestures with gaze to ensure shared attention with a partner. Her partners discussed the need to achieve greater consistency with responding to her signals to foster her sense of communicative competence (IS1.3), wait for and encourage her initiations with others (IS2.2), and arrange learning environments to promote a higher frequency of initiation (LS4.5).

Playtime at home: Kendra's team discussed that during playtime at home, Kendra often engages in solitary play with preferred toys (e.g., music boxes, cause–effect pop-up toys). Her partners have found it challenging to encourage Kendra to communicate in this context. As Kendra's current goals include initiating bids for interaction, her partners discussed the need to modify playtime to promote a higher frequency of initiation from Kendra by *capturing her interest with toys requiring adult assistance* (i.e., by using communicative temptations). Providing toys such as wind-up toys and bubbles with a tight lid would provide more frequent opportunities for Kendra to practice communication with adult caregivers. Initially, her partners would need to *respond to each of Kendra's communicative bids, regardless of their subtle nature,* to foster her sense of competence. Her partners discussed that the next step, after she is more comfortable with the interactions, would be to *pause or delay before offering assistance* to encourage use of a gesture or vocalization to request.

Bedtime: As part of her bedtime routine, Kendra enjoys gathering her favorite toys from preferred videos (e.g., Teletubbies figurines) and lining them up along the headboard of her bed. Her team members noted that her partners could arrange this environment to promote a higher frequency of initiation by *placing these desired objects out of reach or in sealed see-through containers that would require partner assistance to be opened.* Rather than having all of her toys accessible, opportunities to communicate can be created by her partners. In addition, Kendra's team discussed the need for her partners to wait expectantly by standing in close proximity while looking up at a figurine to encourage her initiations for assistance.

JA2 Shares attention (Social Partner stage)

Child goal	Related partner goals	
Joint Attention JA2 Shares attention	**Interpersonal Support** IS1 Partner is responsive to child IS2 Partner fosters initiation IS4 Partner sets stage for engagement	**Learning Support** LS1 Partner structures activity for active participation LS4 Partner modifies goals, activities, and learning environment
JA2 is linked to SU2. **Linked objectives** JA2.3 Follows contact point (= SU2.4) JA2.4 Follows distal point (= SU2.5)	A child's ability to look toward people (JA2.1) and shift gaze between people and objects (JA2.2) relies on a partner's ability to respond to the child's focus of attention (IS1.1), wait for and encourage the child's initiations (IS2.2), and use appropriate proximity and nonverbal behavior to encourage interaction (IS4.3).	A child's ability to shift gaze between people and objects (JA2.2) and follow both contact and distal points (JA2.3, JA2.4) relies on a partner's ability to offer varied learning opportunities (LS1.5) and arrange the learning environment to enhance attention and motivation (LS4.5).

Snapshot of David

David is a 3-year-old Social Partner who is working on shifting gaze between people and objects (JA2.2). Although he is described as a curious child, with a keen interest in Thomas the Tank Engine trains and the alphabet, he is not yet sharing this interest with his partners. His partners discussed the need to respond to his focus of attention (IS1.1), use appropriate proximity and nonverbal behavior to encourage interaction (IS4.3), and arrange the learning environment to enhance David's attention and motivation (LS4.5).

Book time at home: David's team discussed that while reading stories at home, David often sits on a parent's lap. Although he is interested in the pictures, particularly in his alphabet books and Thomas the Tank Engine books, he is not yet shifting gaze between his caregiver and the pictures to share this interest. His team discussed the need for partners to consistently modify the learning environment to enhance David's ability to share attention by *maintaining a face-to-face position* when looking at picture books. Likewise, by *pointing to his favorite pictures* and *waiting with one's hands held out in anticipation,* partners may elicit a three-point gaze shift to share these pictures.

Arts and crafts center at preschool: At preschool, one of David's favorite activities is the arts and crafts center, as his teachers have already arranged the learning environment by including motivating materials in this activity. Cut-out pictures of Thomas the Tank Engine are often provided in a basket, along with a stamp kit with letters of the alphabet. To elicit David's shared attention, his partners discussed *the redesign of this center by using a semicircular table* so that a teacher could be directly in front of David as he sorts through the materials. Each teacher in the classroom would then be encouraged to respond to his focus of attention by *commenting on those items that David picks up* and by *using an animated facial expression* to catch his attention.

JA3 Shares emotion (Social Partner stage)

Child goal	Related partner goals	
Joint Attention JA3 Shares emotion	**Interpersonal Support** IS1 Partner is responsive to child IS2 Partner fosters initiation IS6 Partner adjusts language input IS7 Partner models appropriate behaviors	**Learning Support** LS2 Partner uses augmentative communication support to foster development LS4 Partner modifies goals, activities, and learning environment
JA3 is linked to MR2. **Linked objectives** JA3.1 Shares negative emotion using facial expressions or vocalizations (≈ MR3.1) JA3.2 Shares positive emotion using facial expressions or vocalizations (≈ MR3.2) JA3.3 Responds to changes in partners' expression of emotion (= MR2.4, SU2.7) JA3.4 Attunes to changes in partners' expression of emotion (= MR2.5)	A child's ability to share negative and positive emotion using facial expressions or vocalizations (JA3.1, JA3.2) and attune to changes in partners' expression of emotion (JA3.4) relies on a partner's ability to respond to the child's emotion and pace (IS1.2), wait for and encourage initiations from the child (IS2.2), use nonverbal cues to support understanding (IS6.1), and model appropriate nonverbal communication and emotional expressions (IS7.1).	A child's ability to share negative and positive emotion using facial expressions or vocalizations (JA3.1, JA3.2) and respond to changes in partners' expression of emotion (JA3.3) relies on a partner's ability to use an augmentative communication support to enhance the child's expression and understanding of emotion (LS2.3) and modify activities to be developmentally appropriate (LS4.6).

Snapshot of Bridget

Bridget is a 5-year-old Social Partner who is developing her ability to share positive emotions using clear facial expressions or vocalizations (JA3.2). Although she is described as a happy child, she is not yet sharing her states of emotion with her partners using clear facial expressions paired with gaze to ensure shared attention. Her partners discussed the need to more consistently respond to her emotion and pace (IS1.2), model appropriate nonverbal communication and emotional expressions (IS7.1), and use augmentative communication support to enhance her expression and understanding of emotion (LS2.3).

Music: In her kindergarten classroom, Bridget clearly displays the most positive emotion during music time. During her preferred songs, she may clap her hands together and jump up on her toes. Her team suggested that in these instances, her partners *provide very clear models of nonverbal emotional expressions* (e.g., smiling and laughing to indicate pleasure) while using an augmentative support (i.e., the sign for *happy*) to enhance her ability to express her emotions in a more conventional manner.

Occupational therapy: As Bridget clearly enjoys movement activities such as swinging and being "squished," her team members recognized that a one-to-one occupational therapy session was an appropriate context to establish planned activity routines to provide Bridget with practice in sharing her positive emotions. In doing so, her partner in this context, her occupational therapist, planned to work on her ability to *provide more sustained or static models of emotional expressions* (e.g., a happy face, clapping) while Bridget is on the swing or being squished in the ball pit. In addition, her occupational therapist would carry over the augmentative communication support discussed for the classroom context (i.e., the sign HAPPY) to heighten Bridget's understanding of her emotional state.

JA4 Shares intentions to regulate the behavior of others (Social Partner stage)

Child goal	Related partner goals	
Joint Attention JA4 Shares intentions to regulate the behavior of others	**Interpersonal Support** IS1 Partner is responsive to child IS2 Partner fosters initiation IS3 Partner respects child's independence IS7 Partner models appropriate behaviors	**Learning Support** LS2 Partner uses augmentative communication support to foster development LS4 Partner modifies goals, activities, and learning environment
JA4 is linked to MR2 and MR3. *Linked objectives* JA4.1 Requests desired food or objects (≈ MR2.6) JA4.2 Protests/refuses undesired food or objects (≈ MR3.4) JA4.3 Requests help or other actions (≈ MR3.3) JA4.4 Protests undesired actions or activities (≈ MR3.4)	A child's ability to request or protest food or objects (JA4.1, JA4.2), request help or other actions (JA4.3), and protest undesired actions or activities (JA4.4) relies on a partner's ability to respond appropriately to the child's signals to foster a sense of communicative competence (IS1.3); offer choices nonverbally or verbally (IS2.1); allow the child to initiate and terminate activities (IS2.4); honor protests, rejections, or refusals when appropriate (IS3.4); and model a range of communicative functions (IS7.2).	A child's ability to request or protest food or objects (JA4.1, JA4.2), request help or other actions (JA4.3), and protest undesired actions or activities (JA4.4) also relies on a partner's ability to use augmentative communication support to enhance the child's communication and expressive language (LS2.1) and arrange the learning environment to promote child initiation (LS4.5).
Related goals/objectives Achievements in JA4 are related to achievements in JA7.2, JA7.3, and SU4–SU5.		

Snapshot of Caleb

Caleb is a 6-year-old Social Partner who is developing his ability to share intentions to regulate another's behavior. In particular, he is developing his ability to request *and* protest food or objects (JA4.1, JA4.2). Although he has strong preferences, he continues to have difficulty communicating these to other people. Rather than pointing to a snack container and looking up at a caregiver, for example, he is more likely to attempt to remove the lid independently and/or to bang the container on the table. Likewise, when he is not interested in an item, he will clearly display this disinterest by dropping the item on the floor or by walking away. Although Caleb is clearly goal directed, his methods of achieving his goals do not yet consistently involve a social component or a bid for shared attention. His partners discussed the need to more consistently offer choices nonverbally or verbally (IS2.1), model a range of communicative functions (IS7.2), and arrange the learning environment to promote his initiation (LS4.5).

Snack time: In the classroom, Caleb's teachers discussed that snack time would provide an appropriate context to foster his ability to both request and protest desired snack items. As Caleb is typically provided with several preferred snack items, his team members recognized the need to *provide a choice of both preferred and nonpreferred snack items* to increase the frequency of opportunities for requesting *and* protesting. By providing both a preferred and nonpreferred snack item, Caleb would be less likely to walk away to reject the nonpreferred snack. Likewise, modifications to the learning environment were also considered critical for facilitating more conventional requests. Preferred items could be placed in *sealed see-through containers that will require assistance to be opened,* a modification to facilitate a give gesture for requesting. *A red basket would be also provided for Caleb to discard nonpreferred items* to discourage Caleb from tossing these items on the floor. The use of *a push-away gesture would be modeled* by team members.

Watching videos at home: After school, one of Caleb's preferred activities is watching a videotape at home before dinner. Typically, Caleb indicates his preferences by tapping a specific videotape that may be laying on the floor until one of his older siblings and/or parents places it in the VCR. His team members recognized this activity as an opportunity to support Caleb's ability to share his intentions for the purpose of requesting and/or protesting. His team discussed the need for partners to modify the learning environment by *placing all of Caleb's videotapes in a locked cabinet* out of his reach. Choices of available videotapes, both preferred and nonpreferred, could be indicated *using laminated portions of the videotape covers on the outside of the cabinet* (either in a choice binder or a folder). A partner would then be able to *model a request for a preferred videotape* by giving a picture to a partner when Caleb is standing near the video cabinet.

JA5 **Shares intentions for social interaction (Social Partner stage)**	Child goal	Related partner goals	
	Joint Attention JA5 Shares intentions for social interaction	*Interpersonal Support* IS1 Partner is responsive to child IS2 Partner fosters initiation IS7 Partner models appropriate behaviors	*Learning Support* LS1 Partner structures activity for active participation LS2 Partner uses augmentative communication support to foster development LS4 Partner modifies goals, activities, and learning environment
	JA5 is linked to MR3. **Linked objective** JA5.1 Requests comfort (≈ MR3.1) **Related goals/objectives** Achievements in JA4 are related to achievements in JA7.2, JA7.3, and SU4–SU5.	A child's ability to request social games (JA5.2), take turns (JA5.3), and show off (JA5.6) relies on a partner's ability to imitate the child (IS1.6), provide a balance of initiated and respondent turns (IS2.3), and model a range of communicative functions (IS7.2).	A child's ability to request social games (JA5.2) and greet others (JA5.4) relies on a partner's ability to create turn-taking opportunities and leave spaces for the child to fill in (LS1.2), use augmentative communication support to enhance the child's communication and expressive language (LS2.1), and arrange the learning environment to promote child initiation (LS4.5).

Snapshot of Rebecca

Rebecca is a 3-year-old Social Partner who is developing her ability to share intentions for social interaction. In particular, she is developing her ability to request social games (JA5.2). She clearly enjoys music (e.g., the song "If You're Happy and You Know It") and social games (e.g., Peekaboo) but seems to wait for adults to start these games rather than requesting them herself. Her partners discussed the need to provide a balance of initiated and respondent turns (IS2.3) to encourage Rebecca to both request social games and request that they be continued once they have started and use augmentative communication support to enhance Rebecca's communication for this social function (LS2.1).

Music at home: Songs such as "Five Little Monkeys" are quite motivating for Rebecca, who loves the predictability of the phrases and the sensory-motor input from the movement. Nevertheless, she has not yet initiated a request for this song despite her apparent interest when it is initiated by others. Her partners discussed that having an augmentative support would be a helpful visual cue to remind her to ask for this social game. A *"Five Little Monkeys" song board* would be made and placed in her playroom to encourage this request. To encourage active participation, *five picture icons representing monkeys* would be attached to the board with Velcro so that Rebecca could take one off at each phrase to provide a balance between caregiver- and child-initiated requests during the song.

Circle time at preschool: In her preschool classroom, Rebecca's teacher often sings familiar songs to the children to foster their attention and social engagement. These songs (e.g., "Old MacDonald," "Itsy Bitsy Spider," "The Hokey Pokey") are often initiated in a sequence as the first circle time routine. To encourage Rebecca's ability to request social games, her team discussed the need to provide a balance between teacher- and child-initiated requests. Therefore, following the first two songs, a child would be provided with *an opportunity to make a request for a preferred song.* An easel could be used to remind the children of their options. This *easel could display three or four different picture symbols denoting these songs.*

JA6 Shares intentions for joint attention (Social Partner stage)

Child goal	Related partner goals	
Joint Attention JA6 Shares intentions for joint attention	**Interpersonal Support** IS1 Partner is responsive to child IS2 Partner fosters initiation IS4 Partner sets stage for engagement IS7 Partner models appropriate behaviors	**Learning Support** LS1 Partner structures activity for active participation LS4 Partner modifies goals, activities, and learning environment
JA6 is not directly linked to SU, MR, or SR. *Related goals/objectives* Achievements in JA6 are related to achievements in JA7.2, JA7.3, and SU4–SU5.	A child's ability to comment on an object (JA6.1) and on an action or an event (JA6.2) relies on a partner's ability to respond to the child's focus of attention (IS1.1), wait for and encourage his or her initiations (IS2.2), use appropriate proximity and nonverbal behavior to encourage interaction (IS4.3), and model a range of communicative functions (IS7.2).	A child's ability to comment on an object (JA6.1) and on an action or an event (JA6.2) also relies on a partner's ability to offer varied learning opportunities (LS1.5), arrange the learning environment to promote child initiation (LS4.5), and infuse motivating materials and topics in activities (LS4.7).

Snapshot of Brett

Brett is a 2-year-old Social Partner who is developing his ability to share intentions for joint attention. Although he demonstrates interest in a variety of toys (e.g., toy animals, cartoon figurines), enjoys looking at pictures in photograph books, and often takes interest in events he observes (e.g., a wind-up toy hopping along the table), he is not yet sharing these interests with others by using gestures paired with gaze to indicate his focus of attention. Thus, his current goals include fostering his ability to use presymbolic communicative means such as gestures to comment on an object (JA6.1) and on an action or an event (JA6.2). His partners discussed the need to model a range of communicative means to serve the more social functions of commenting on objects (IS7.2), use appropriate proximity and nonverbal behavior to encourage this interaction (IS4.3), and offer varied learning opportunities (LS1.5) to entice Brett to share his focus of attention.

Lunch: Brett's team discussed that activities that involve the frequent introduction of novel toys or objects (e.g., drawing objects out a bag, hanging interesting items from the ceiling) are useful for fostering communicative acts for joint attention. Because Brett has shown an interest in holding and exploring his preferred figurines and animal toys while sitting in his high chair, his team decided to modify this activity by increasing novelty to entice Brett's curiosity and interest in sharing. A familiar routine of *presenting a "surprise can" would be introduced at the end of lunch*. This routine involves opening a familiar tin filled with novel and interesting toys that could be taken out one at a time. His partners would then encourage Brett to initiate a comment using a nonverbal gesture such as *a showing gesture,* by using appropriate proximity (i.e., *a face-to-face orientation at Brett's level*) and nonverbal behavior (i.e., *holding out one's hands to show a mutual interest in the toys*). The team further discussed that verbal prompts such as "What is it?" would be avoided in this activity to entice Brett to initiate a show gesture paired with gaze on his own so that he can *actively learn* to initiate to bring his partners' attention to what he is attending to.

Dressing: Brett's parents discussed that making the transition to his bedroom to change into pajamas would be another useful activity context for eliciting joint attention. When Brett enters his room, he always seems to seek out a preferred item to hold while his parents encourage him to dress. Thus, in this predictable context, his partners could vary one aspect of the activity to provide novelty to entice commenting bids. They discussed *hanging a mobile from the bedroom ceiling*. On this mobile, his parents could *hang a different picture each night* with some of Brett's favorite animals and cartoon characters to draw his attention (e.g., Winnie-the-Pooh characters, farm animals). On entering the room, his parents could then model the communicative function of commenting for joint attention by standing near the mobile, *pointing at the picture,* and smiling in anticipation. Through the addition of something novel each day, Brett will likely begin to anticipate this event with greater interest and excitement.

**JA7
Persists
and repairs
communication
breakdowns
(Social Partner
stage)**

Child goal	Related partner goals	
Joint Attention JA7 Persists and repairs communication breakdowns	**Interpersonal Support** IS1 Partner is responsive to child IS3 Partner respects child's independence IS5 Partner provides developmental support	**Learning Support** LS2 Partner uses augmentative communication support to foster development LS4 Partner modifies goals, activities, and learning environment
JA7 is not directly linked to SU, MR, or SR. **Related goals** Achievements in JA7 are related to achievements in JA4–JA6.	A child's ability to use an appropriate rate of communication for context (JA7.1) and to repeat and modify communication to repair communicative breakdowns (JA7.2, JA7.3) relies on a partner's ability to respond appropriately to the child's signals to foster a sense of communicative competence (IS1.3), provide time for the child to solve problems or complete activities at his or her own pace (IS3.2), attempt to repair breakdowns verbally or nonverbally (IS5.3), and give guidance and feedback as needed for success in activities (IS5.4)	A child's ability to use an appropriate rate of communication for context (JA7.1) and to repeat and modify communication to repair communicative breakdowns (JA7.2, JA7.3) also relies on a partner's ability to use augmentative communication support to enhance the child's communication and expressive language (LS2.1), adjust task difficulty for child success (LS4.2), provide activities to promote initiation and extended interactions (LS4.8), and increase expectations appropriately (LS4.10).

Snapshot of Isaac

Isaac is a 3-year-old Social Partner who has made great progress in his ability to share his intentions with those around him. Nevertheless, he continues to rely on adults' verbal cues and support to initiate bids for communication across contexts. In fact, Isaac often is a passive communicator, initiating only one or two communicative acts before appearing to lose interest or, in some cases, becoming increasingly dysregulated if his original communicative attempt was unsuccessful. By fostering Isaac's ability to share his goals with others more frequently and supporting his ability to acquire the means necessary to repair communication breakdowns and therefore experience greater success, his partners hoped to increase his active learning and self-confidence. Thus, his current goals include fostering his ability to repeat communicative acts to repair breakdowns (JA7.2). His partners discussed the need to attempt to repair breakdowns verbally or nonverbally (IS5.3), provide time for Isaac to solve problems or complete activities at his own pace (IS3.2), use augmentative communication support to enhance Isaac's communication and expressive language (LS2.1), and "up the ante" by increasing expectations appropriately (LS4.10).

Play at home: Isaac's team recognized that within each play session at home, the environment could be arranged to *include several activities that involve clear and predictable endpoints* and *visual supports to support Isaac's clarity.* For example, Isaac enjoys scavenger hunts for his favorite toys (e.g., magnetic letters, little people figurines) in which a visual map is provided to indicate which items need to be found. Team members recognized that Isaac's problem-solving skills would be more successful when Isaac is engaged in these types of activities, as he is in a more optimal state of arousal. In these contexts, his partners can "up the ante" more readily by *holding out for more sophisticated communication,* with modeling or prompting as needed (e.g., pointing to the desired items). Likewise, his *partners can attempt to repair breakdowns* either verbally or nonverbally by clarifying the meaning of the signal using the scavenger hunt map. Finally, his partners discussed the need to *give Isaac adequate time to actively solve problems on his own,* to build his self-confidence and sense of competence.

Play centers at preschool: Isaac's team indicated that Isaac is most comfortable and persistent while engaged in the constructive play center at preschool (e.g., completing puzzles, building block towers). Nevertheless, he has a low rate of communication and a tendency to lose interest in a play set if his original bids for a missing piece are not successful. His team felt that to provide Isaac with adequate time to actively solve problems on his own, it would require that *an adult caregiver be consistently present* during this activity to respond and/or attempt to repair to his unsuccessful communicative bids. An instructional assistant, for example, could be present to model basic signs (e.g., ALL DONE, HELP, OPEN) and "up the ante" *for more sophisticated communication.*

Social Communication: Symbol Use

SU1 Learns by imitation of familiar actions and sounds (Social Partner stage)

Child goal	Related partner goals	
Symbol Use SU1 Learns by imitation of familiar actions and sounds	**Interpersonal Support** IS1 Partner is responsive to child IS2 Partner fosters initiation IS5 Partner provides developmental support	**Learning Support** LS1 Partner structures activity for active participation LS4 Partner modifies goals, activities, and learning environment
SU1 is not directly linked to JA, MR, or SR.	A child's ability to take turns by repeating his or her own actions or sounds (SU1.1) and to imitate familiar actions or sounds when elicited immediately after a model (SU1.2) relies on a partner's ability to imitate the child (IS1.6), provide a balance of initiated and respondent turns (IS2.3), and encourage imitation (IS5.1).	A child's ability to spontaneously imitate familiar actions or sounds when elicited immediately after a model (SU1.2) and at a later time (SU1.4) relies on a partner's ability to create turn-taking opportunities and leave spaces for the child to fill in (LS1.2), offer repeated learning opportunities (LS1.4), and design and modify activities to be developmentally appropriate (LS4.6).

Snapshot of Brian

Brian is a 2-year-old Social Partner who is not yet imitating familiar actions by taking turns repeating his or her own actions or sounds (SU1.1). His parents describe him as an independent and curious toddler who tries to figure things out on his own. Rather than watching his father show him how to play with a preferred toy, a car spiral ramp, he plays with it on his own, learning primarily through observation of cause and effect whether his actions are successful in making interesting events happen. Currently, much of his play involves sensory-motor exploration, such as spinning the wheels of the cars and tapping on the lever of the car ramp to make a sound, rather than learning how to place and release the car down the spiraling track to get it to come out at the bottom. His partners recognized the need to imitate Brian's actions (IS1.6), create turn-taking opportunities and leave spaces for Brian to fill in (LS1.2), and modify activities to be developmentally appropriate (LS4.6) to encourage imitative learning to use the car ramp and engage in other activities in a developmentally appropriate manner.

Bath time: Modifying activities to be developmentally appropriate is an important first step for eliciting imitation. Although Brian enjoys the car spiral ramp, for example, *early imitation attempts would likely involve simple one-step actions* (e.g., smiling, cooing, banging objects together, stomping) rather than two-step actions (e.g., placing the car at the top of the spiral ramp and pushing the lever). Thus, his partners recognized the need to capitalize on simple motor actions that Brian already does successfully to address this objective. His partners recognized the need at bath time to more consistently imitate Brian's actions. *Duplicate sets of play materials would be made available.* When Brian splashed a truck in the water, so would his caregiver. If Brian made a sound or vocalization in this context, so would his caregiver. After his caregiver finished an imitative movement, he or she would *wait in an expectant posture for Brian to fill his turn* by repeating the same action.

Sandbox: One of Brian's favorite activities is playing in his backyard sandbox. He enjoys sensory-motor play such as watching the sand sift through his fingers and dragging his toy shovel through the sand to make a pattern. *Duplicate sets of play materials would be made available* in this context so that *Brian's caregivers could imitate these simple actions.* His team members discussed that by imitating the same action that Brian had found interesting, this would likely capture his focus of attention and entice his continued participation. His partners then discussed the need to modify this learning environment to create turn-taking opportunities by *pausing before imitating his action for the second time.*

SU2 Understands nonverbal cues in familiar activities (Social Partner stage)

Child goal	Related partner goals	
Symbol Use SU2 Understands nonverbal cues in familiar activities	**Interpersonal Support** IS4 Partner sets stage for engagement IS6 Partner adjusts language input	**Learning Support** LS1 Partner structures activity for active participation LS2 Partner uses augmentative communication support to foster development
SU2 is linked to JA2, JA3, and SR3. **Linked objectives** SU2.1 Anticipates another person's actions in familiar routines (= SR3.1) SU2.4 Follows a contact point (= JA2.3) SU2.5 Follows a distal point (= JA2.4) SU2.7 Responds to facial expression and intonation cues (≈ JA3.3)	A child's ability to anticipate another person's actions in familiar routines (SU2.1), follow situational cues in familiar activities (SU2.2), and follow contact and distal points (SU2.4, SU2.5) relies on a partner's ability to use appropriate proximity and nonverbal behavior to encourage interaction (IS4.3) and use nonverbal cues to support understanding (IS6.1).	A child's ability to anticipate another person's actions in familiar routines (SU2.1), follow gestural cues other than a point (SU2.3), and respond to visual cues (photographs or pictures) (SU2.6) relies on a partner's ability to provide a predictable sequence to an activity (LS1.3) and use augmentative communication support to enhance the child's understanding of language and behavior (LS2.2).

Snapshot of Amy

Amy is an 8-year-old Social Partner who has learned to anticipate another person's actions in familiar routines and follow situational cues. Nevertheless, she continues to work on her ability to respond to visual cues (photographs or pictures) (SU2.6) to aid her understanding of familiar routines. Her partners recognized the need to use nonverbal cues to support understanding (IS6.1), provide a predictable sequence to activities (LS1.3), and use augmentative communication support to enhance Amy's understanding of language and behavior (LS2.2).

Greetings at home: Amy has a strong attachment to all of her family members, including her mother, father, and older brother. However, when they arrive home from work, an errand, or school, she does not yet call attention to herself by greeting them as they enter the door. Her partners discussed that by *being shown a photograph of a famil-*

iar family member just prior to their arrival home, Amy may develop a greater understanding of this social ritual. Likewise, her partners at home discussed emphasizing the predictable steps in this routine by *pointing to the family member's car out the window; cupping one's ear to hear the keys;* and *saying, "Let's listen,"* or by *knocking on the door and modeling a wave gesture when the door opens.*

Bathroom at school: Within the past few years, Amy has developed a greater awareness of familiar routines at school and follows situational cues such as following her classmates to the bathroom, standing in line at the sink, and putting her hand under the faucet. Her independence in this routine, however, is not yet consistent across the many steps of the activity, as she continues to rely on frequent repetitions of verbal cues. Thus, her team members discussed the need to increase the predictability of this activity by *emphasizing the three critical steps* (i.e., washing hands, drying hands, and throwing out the paper towel), *use gestures to model each step on a consistent basis,* and *use photographs of each step, in sequence, to support her understanding of the verbal directions.*

SU3 Uses familiar objects conventionally in play (Social Partner stage)

Child goal	Related partner goals	
Symbol Use SU3 Uses familiar objects conventionally in play	**Interpersonal Support** IS5 Partner provides developmental support IS7 Partner models appropriate behaviors	**Learning Support** LS1 Partner structures activity for active participation LS4 Partner modifies goals, activities, and learning environment
SU3 is not directly linked to JA, MR, or SR. **Related goals/objectives** Early achievements in SU3 are related to achievements in SR2.1.	A child's ability to use familiar objects in constructive play (SU3.2) and use familiar objects conventionally toward him- or herself and others (SU3.3, SU3.4) relies on a partner's ability to encourage imitation (IS5.1), expand on the child's play and nonverbal communication (IS5.5), and model appropriate play (IS7.3).	A child's ability to use familiar objects in constructive play (SU3.2) and use familiar objects conventionally toward him- or herself and others (SU3.3, SU3.4) also relies on a partner's ability to provide a predictable sequence to the activity (LS1.3), offer repeated learning opportunities (LS1.4), and design and modify activities to be developmentally appropriate (LS4.6).

Snapshot of Luke

Luke is a 6-year-old Social Partner who has developed an ability to use familiar objects in constructive play. Although he occasionally still mouths objects and taps them on the table, particularly when he is tired and in a low arousal state, he has learned to stack blocks into tall towers and has taken an interest in completing simple insert puzzles. He is currently working on using familiar objects conventionally toward himself (SU3.3). His partners recognized that these early imaginative play schemes begin with actions that are most familiar to a child because they are experienced frequently in everyday routines (e.g., drinking with a bottle or cup, putting a hat on, brushing hair, putting a telephone to one's ear). In addition, Luke's partners recognized the need on their part to encourage imitation (IS5.1), model appropriate play (IS7.3), and offer repeated learning opportunities (LS1.4).

Centers at school: Luke recently began to take interest in the dress-up center of his kindergarten classroom. He enjoys looking at himself in the mirror and will put a rain hat on his head. His teachers recognized the need to encourage this emerging interest. To enhance predictability, *the use of a familiar song was introduced to encourage simple play schemes* (e.g., a song about getting dressed to go and play in the rain). Next, imitation of these basic play schemes would be encouraged using *duplicate sets of play materials. Also,* Luke's classmates would be encouraged to sing the song to provide additional repetition of these models and predictable activity structure.

Morning meeting: Luke's kindergarten teacher has developed a morning routine of having the children sing several songs, discuss the daily calendar, the weather, and do a show-and-tell activity. Frequent repetition of this routine would provide a useful context for addressing Luke's ability to using familiar objects conventionally toward himself, as his *peers could provide clear, repeated models of basic play schemes.* For example, after identifying the day of the week, a routine could be established in which *familiar objects are passed from one child to the next to model basic one-step play schemes* that occur each day (e.g., a pretend toothbrush could be passed around to mimic brushing teeth, a pretend spoon could be passed around to mimic eating breakfast, a pretend backpack could be passed around to mimic getting ready for school).

SU4
Uses gestures and nonverbal means to share intentions (Social Partner stage)

Child goal		Related partner goals	
Symbol Use SU4 Uses gestures and nonverbal means to share intentions		*Interpersonal Support* IS5 Partner provides developmental support S7 Partner models appropriate behaviors	*Learning Support* LS2 Partner uses augmentative communication support to foster development LS4 Partner modifies goals, activities, and learning environment
SU4 is not directly linked to JA, MR, or SR. *Related goals/objectives* Achievements in SU4 are related to achievements in JA4–JA6, MR1, MR3.3, and MR3.4.		A child's ability to use simple motor actions (SU4.3), conventional contact gestures and distal gestures (SU4.4, SU4.5) to share intentions relies on a partner's ability to expand on the child's play and nonverbal communication (IS5.5); model appropriate nonverbal communication and emotional expressions (IS7.1); and, in some situations, model appropriate behavior when the child uses inappropriate behavior (IS7.4).	A child's ability to use conventional contact gestures and distal gestures (SU4.4, SU4.5), use a sequence of gestures or nonverbal means (SU4.7), and coordinate these gestures and gaze (SU4.8), relies on a partner's ability to encourage the use of augmentative communication support to enhance the child's communication and expressive language (LS2.1), arrange the learning environment to promote child initiation (LS4.5), and "up the ante" to increase expectations appropriately (LS4.10).

Snapshot of Ernesto

Ernesto is a 2-year-old Social Partner who currently communicates using a range of early developing gestures. He may use proximity (e.g., standing close to the refrigerator while briefly glancing at a caregiver for a desired snack), physical manipulation gestures (e.g., pulling a caregiver's hand toward the door to request going outside), or reenactment gestures (e.g., spinning in place next to his caregiver to request "Ring Around the Rosy"). He currently is working on using conventional contact gestures (SU4.4) such as giving, pushing away, and pointing and coordinating these gestures with shared attention (SU4.8). His partners recognized their need to work on modeling appropriate nonverbal communication and emotional expressions (IS7.1), arrange the learning environment to promote child initiation (LS4.5), and "up the ante" to increase expectations appropriately (LS4.10).

Blowing bubbles: One of Ernesto's most preferred activities is blowing bubbles with his mom. He enjoys both popping the bubbles as well as playing with the bubble liquid on his high chair tray. He tends to request this activity by pulling his mother's hand toward the lid on the bubble jar or attempting to bite the lid off with his teeth. As this activity involves a natural opportunity for adult assistance (e.g., the need to open a bubble jar with a tight lid), Ernesto's mother and other partners discussed that it would be appropriate to *model a give gesture* in this type of activity and "up the ante" to *elicit this more sophisticated gesture once Ernesto is motivated to continue the activity.* Although the goal is to encourage higher level gestures, Ernesto's partners discussed the need to use exaggerated affect and social praise, limit high-level demands, and respond to Ernesto's early and later gestural forms of communication, as these strategies will be critical for promoting his self-esteem and encouraging his efforts as a communicator.

Outside play: Ernesto enjoys outside play with his father and older brothers. He always enjoys rolling and bouncing on a big beach ball and playing in the sandbox. His family mentioned that when it rains he "adores splashing in the puddles." To provide more frequent opportunities to model nonverbal conventional gestures such as giving, pushing away, and pointing, his team members discussed the need for partners to modify the activities with new steps to extend the interactions. They discussed *placing the beach ball just out of Ernesto's reach* but at the right height for him to use a contact point and look at a caregiver for help. In addition, they discussed *providing a container of water for Ernesto to play with* on the patio on sunny days. As the water would be in a sealed see-through container, caregivers would have the opportunity to *model a give gesture* and "up the ante" for this more sophisticated gesture of giving, given his intense motivation and interest in this activity.

SU5 Uses vocalizations to share intentions (Social Partner stage)

Child goal	Related partner goals	
Symbol Use SU5 Uses vocalizations to share intentions	**Interpersonal Support** IS1 Partner is responsive to child IS5 Partner provides developmental support	**Learning Support** LS1 Partner structures activity for active participation
SU5 is not directly linked to JA, MR, or SR. **Related goals** Achievements in SU5 are related to achievements in JA4–JA6, MR1, MR3.3, and MR3.4	A child's ability to use differentiated vocalizations (SU5.1), words bound to routines (SU5.3), and coordinate vocalizations with gaze and gestures (SU5.4) relies, in part, on a partner's ability to respond appropriately to the child's signals to foster a sense of communicative competence (IS1.3), imitate the child (IS1.6), and encourage imitation (IS5.1).	A child's ability to use a variety of consonant + vowel combinations (SU5.2), words bound to routines (SU5.3), and coordinate vocalizations with gaze and gestures (SU5.4) also relies on a partner's ability to create turn-taking opportunities and leave spaces for the child to fill in (LS1.2) and on the partner's ability to offer repeated learning opportunities (LS1.4).

Snapshot of Juan

Juan is a 3-year-old Social Partner who clearly uses sounds to communicate pleasure with an activity as well as discomfort or frustration. Therefore, his awareness of vocalizations as a means to express communicative intent is emerging. Juan's ability to pair his gestural forms of communication with vocalizations is not yet consistent. He uses a limited range of differentiated vocalizations. For example, he may use the open vowel sound "eh" to accompany the animal sound "neigh" during the "Old MacDonald" song, and he may use the open vowel sound "uh" as an attempt to say "up" when requesting to be lifted by his mother. He currently is working on coordinating vocalizations with gaze and gestures (SU5.4). As a result, the team discussed the need for Juan's partners to continue to respond appropriately to Juan's signals to foster a sense of communicative competence (IS1.3), increase turn-taking opportunities with spaces left for

Juan to fill in (LS1.2), and more consistently offer repeated learning opportunities (LS1.4), as practice is critical for ensuring growth in oral-motor planning and word retrieval.

Speech-language therapy: In his full day preschool program, Juan participates in three to four one-to-one speech-language sessions per week, as his difficulties with both oral-motor development and word retrieval warrant frequent motor practice coupled with efforts to foster his communicative competence using multimodal communication (e.g., gestures, signs, visual supports). His therapist has *designed the one-to-one sessions to mirror circle time in the classroom* so that Juan has additional practice for upcoming songs and storybooks. Planned activity routines for singing often involve *singing the same song several times in a row.* Likewise, his therapist is working on creating spaces for Juan to fill his turn vocally by pausing before key words (e.g., "If you're happy and you know it, shout . . . ") and to elicit gestures paired with vocalizations (e.g., pairing "ay" in "hooray" with arm movements).

Snack time: Juan enjoys crunchy snacks and often munches on pretzels during snack time. His team recognized that opportunities to increase turn-taking opportunities in which spaces are left for Juan to fill in (LS1.2) could be increased if the pretzels were *passed back and forth between Juan and a teacher in a sealed see-through container.* This accommodation would provide more consistent and repeated learning opportunities (LS1.4) for Juan to practice pairing gestures (i.e., a give gesture) with vocalizations (e.g., "oh" for "open"). His team discussed, however, that given Juan's challenges in expressing communicative intent through vocal means, it will continue to be important to *continue to respond quickly to his nonverbal attempts* to maintain his self-confidence as an effective communicator.

SU6 Understands a few familiar words (Social Partner stage)

Child goal	Related partner goals	
Symbol Use SU6 Understands a few familiar words	*Interpersonal Support* IS4 Partner sets the stage for engagement IS6 Partner adjusts language input	*Learning Support* LS2 Partner uses augmentative communication support to foster development LS3 Partner uses visual and organizational support
SU6 is not directly linked to JA, MR, or SR.	A child's ability to respond to his or her name (SU6.1), respond to a few words in familiar social games (SU6.2), and respond to a few frequently used phrases in familiar routines (SU6.4) relies on a partner's ability to secure the child's attention before communicating (IS4.2), use nonverbal cues to support understanding (IS6.1), and adjust complexity of language input to the child's developmental level (IS6.2).	A child's ability to respond to a few words in familiar social games (SU6.2); respond to a few familiar person, body part, or object names (SU6.3); and respond to a few frequently used phrases in familiar routines (SU6.4) relies on a partner's ability to use augmentative communication support to enhance the child's understanding of language and behavior (LS2.2) and use visual support to foster active involvement in group activities (LS3.6).

Snapshot of Rosa

Rosa is a 6-year-old Social Partner who attends an inclusive kindergarten and is working on responding to a few frequently used phrases in familiar routines (SU6.4). Within the past 6 months, she has improved her ability to respond to her name (SU6.1) and has learned several words in familiar social games (e.g., "Ready, set, ... *go*"). She has greater difficulty responding to phrases within familiar routines (e.g., "Let's go for a ride.... Go get your coat," "Time for night-night.... Let's brush your teeth"), as the auditory information coupled with the anticipatory excitement about these upcoming events often leads to high arousal that can be dysregulating and that can reduce her ability to process oral language. Therefore, her partners recognized the need to adjust complexity of their language input to Rosa's developmental level (IS6.2) and use augmentative communication support to enhance her understanding of language and behavior (LS2.2).

Recess at school: Rosa enjoys recess with her classmates but appears to rely on her teachers to help her make the transition to the playground and to become engaged in activities that she may enjoy with her peers (e.g., swinging on the swings, climbing the slide). Although they may use familiar phrases (e.g., "Time for recess.... Get your coat," "Do you want to ride the swings?" "The slide looks fun"), Rosa often needs physical guidance to become engaged. Her team discussed *adjusting the complexity of their language* to include simple one- and two-word phrases (e.g., "Recess.... Coat on," "Rosa swing?" "Slide?") and pairing their verbal language with an augmentative communication support to support her understanding. *A key chain with photographs of her coat, the swing, the slide, and a symbol for "all done"* was developed as an augmentative aid for this activity.

Lunch: After lunch, Rosa may get up from the table to indicate completion but requires both repetitions of familiar phrases (e.g., "Clean up your trash") and physical guidance to complete this activity. Her team discussed *adjusting their language input* (e.g., "Rosa all done.... Clean up") and providing her with an augmentative aid to support her understanding, *a place card with her name, that when flipped over, includes a photograph of the trash can* to support Rosa's understanding of the phrase "clean up."

Emotional Regulation: Mutual Regulation

MR1 Expresses range of emotions (Social Partner stage)

Child goal	Related partner goals	
Mutual Regulation MR1 Expresses range of emotions	**Interpersonal Support** IS4 Partner sets stage for engagement IS5 Partner provides developmental support IS7 Partner models appropriate behaviors	**Learning Support** LS1 Partner structures activity for active participation LS2 Partner uses augmentative support communication to foster development LS4 Partner modifies goals, activities, and learning environment
MR1 is not directly linked to JA, SU, or SR. **Related goals** Achievements in MR1 are related to achievements in SU4–SU5.	A child's ability to express happiness (MR1.1), sadness (MR1.2), anger (MR1.3), and fear (MR1.4) relies on a partner's ability to use appropriate proximity and nonverbal behavior to encourage interaction (IS4.3), expand on the child's play and nonverbal communication (IS5.5), and model appropriate nonverbal communication and emotional expressions (IS7.1).	A child's ability to express happiness (MR1.1), sadness (MR1.2), anger (MR1.3), and fear (MR1.4) also relies on a partner's ability to offer varied learning opportunities (LS1.5), use augmentative communication support to enhance the child's expression and understanding of emotion (LS2.3), and arrange the learning environment to enhance attention and motivation (LS4.4).

Snapshot of Mark

Mark is a 4-year-old Social Partner in a preschool program who demonstrates variable arousal levels and difficulty conveying his emotional state in a conventional manner. When he experiences more intense emotional extremes, he jumps up and down while looking off to the side (peripheral gaze). His objectives include expressing happiness (MR1.1) and anger (MR1.3). His partners are striving to model appropriate nonverbal communication and emotional expressions (IS7.1) and use augmentative communication support to enhance his understanding of emotion (LS2.3).

Choice time at preschool: During choice time, Mark is typically drawn to the garage and vehicle toy area. He truly enjoys playing with cars but does not yet use conventional means to express his joy, as he is often observed to express his excitement through jumping and peripheral gaze. His team recognized the need to provide more consistency with modeling appropriate nonverbal communication and emotional expressions by using *exaggerated gestures and facial expressions* to demonstrate their own excitement during Mark's play. Likewise, the use of an augmentative communication support was implemented, as team members discussed the importance of providing Mark with *a picture icon for "happy"* when he is using less conventional strategies for this expression.

Dinner at home: Mark's partners discussed that Mark's tendency to jump and use peripheral gaze has an entirely different meaning when making the transition away from a preferred video to dinner, a common transition each afternoon. In this activity, his team members recognized that these behaviors were a sign of extreme anger, although quite unconventional. As a result, they discussed the need to increase their use of *models for conventional expressions of "mad" such as stomping feet and shaking one's head.* In addition, to support his emotional understanding, the use of an augmentative support was implemented to *label Mark's emotional state by showing a picture icon of "mad."* It should also be noted that Mark's team members thought that a proactive support such as *an across-activity picture schedule* may be helpful for alleviating his anxiety during this transition.

MR2 Responds to assistance offered by partners (Social Partner stage)

Child goal	Related partner goals	
Mutual Regulation MR2 Responds to assistance offered by partners	**Interpersonal Support** IS1 Partner is responsive to child IS2 Partner fosters initiation IS4 Partner sets stage for engagement	**Learning Support** LS2 Partner uses augmentative communication support to foster development LS4 Partner modifies goals, activities, and learning environment
MR2 is linked to JA1, JA3, and JA4. **Linked objectives** MR2.3 Responds to bids for interaction (= JA1.1) MR2.4 Responds to changes in partners' expression of emotion (= JA3.3) MR2.5 Attunes to changes in partners' expression of emotion (= JA3.4) MR2.6 Makes choices when offered by partners (≈ JA4.1)	A child's ability to soothe when comforted by partners (MR2.1), engage when alerted by a partner (MR2.2), respond to bids for interaction (MR2.3), and attune to changes in partners' expression of emotion relies on a partner's ability to respond to the child's emotion and pace (IS1.2), offer choices nonverbally and verbally (IS2.1), get down on the child's level when communicating (IS4.1), and use appropriate words/intonation to support optimal arousal and engagement (IS4.4).	A child's ability to respond to changes in partners' expression of emotion (MR2.4) and make choices when offered by partners (MR2.6) relies on a partner's ability to use augmentative communication support to enhance the child's understanding of language and behavior (LS2.2) and design and modify activities to be developmentally appropriate (LS4.6)

Snapshot of Sally

Sally is a recently diagnosed 3-year-old Social Partner who tends to withdraw by spending hours looking out the window and watching the leaves blow on the trees outside. She experiences highs and lows in her arousal level throughout her day and often appears to not register the regulatory support that her partners attempt to offer her. Her objectives include engaging when alerted by partners (MR2.2) and making choices when offered by partners (MR2.6). A number of interpersonal supports and learning supports were reviewed, and her partners recognized the need to develop consistency with getting down on Sally's level when communicating (IS4.1), provide Sally with nonverbal or verbal choices to entice her attention (IS2.1), and design and modify activities to be developmentally appropriate (LS4.6).

Circle time: In her preschool program, Sally's team members discussed how to improve their ability to get down on her level when communicating. For example, the teacher suggested that she will try *sitting on the floor in front of the children,* particularly when addressing Sally to secure her attention. Next, the team discussed strategies for improving their consistency by *offering Sally choices during song time by introducing the props for two songs into her visual field* (i.e., a toy bus for "Wheels on the Bus" and rhythm sticks for a drumming song). Strategies for modifying story time to be more developmentally appropriate for Sally were also discussed. Several of Sally's favorite books (e.g., *Goodnight Moon; Brown Bear, Brown Bear*) were placed in the teacher's story basket to provide her with stories that included repetitive phrases and simplified language.

Snack at child care: Sally's team members discussed strategies for getting down on her level during snack time at her child care program. Modifications included having an adult caregiver *sit across from Sally during snack* (in a face-to-face position) while providing her with *choices of snack items* to facilitate her engagement in the activity. Next, they discussed the need to modify the developmental level of the activity to support Sally's ability to respond to assistance offered by partners. Specifically, they discussed *incorporating a familiar and predictable song to mark each portion of the routine* (e.g., washing hands, pouring juice, eating, cleaning up) to help her actively make the transition between activity segments.

MR3 Requests partners' assistance to regulate state (Social Partner stage)	Child goal	Related partner goals	
	Mutual Regulation	*Interpersonal Support*	*Learning Support*
	MR3 Requests partners' assistance to regulate state	IS1 Partner is responsive to child IS2 Partner fosters initiation IS5 Partner provides developmental support IS7 Partner models appropriate behaviors	LS1 Partner structures activity for active participation LS2 Partner uses augmentative communication support to foster development LS4 Partner modifies goals, activities, and learning environment
	MR3 is linked to JA3, JA4, JA5. **Linked objectives** MR3.1 Shares negative emotion to seek comfort (≈ JA3.1) MR3.2 Shares positive emotion to seek interaction (≈ JA3.2) MR3.3 Requests help when frustrated (≈ JA4.3) MR3.4 Protests when distressed (≈ JA4.2, JA4.4) **Related goals/objectives** Achievements in MR3 are related to achievements in JA5.1 and SU4–SU5.	A child's ability to share negative emotion to seek comfort (MR3.1), share positive emotion to seek interaction (MR3.2), request help when frustrated (MR3.3), and protest when distressed (MR3.4) relies on a partner's ability to respond appropriately to the child's signals to foster a sense of communicative competence (IS1.3), wait for and encourage initiations (IS2.2), expand on the child's play and nonverbal communication (IS5.5), and model appropriate nonverbal communication and emotional expressions (IS7.1).	A child's ability to share negative emotion to seek comfort (MR3.1), share positive emotion to seek interaction (MR3.2), request help when frustrated (MR3.3), and protest when distressed (MR3.4) also relies on a partner's ability to offer repeated learning opportunities (LS1.4), use augmentative communication support to enhance the child's communication and expressive language (LS2.1), use augmentative communication support to enhance the child's expression and understanding of emotion (LS2.3), and "up the ante" or increase expectations appropriately (LS4.10).

Snapshot of Kevin Kevin is a 4-year-old Social Partner who attends preschool and who demonstrates differentiated emotional expression yet has a difficult time using facial expression, gaze, and vocalizations to engage his caregivers. His objectives include shares positive emotions to seek interaction (MR3.2) and requests help when frustrated (MR3.3). His partners are working on achieving greater consistency with waiting for and encouraging initiations (IS2.2) and offering repeated learning opportunities (LS1.4).

Haircut: In addition to providing Kevin a behavioral support for regulation (i.e., *giving him access to his blanket*), his partners discussed the need to stay in *close proximity* to Kevin and *respond to any subtle attempts he may be using to engage them,* such as glancing at or reaching toward them. The goal is to encourage his initiations for help when frustrated with an activity. In these instances, his team discussed that providing more conventional and effective behavioral strategies such as *having a chewy candy or gum* might elicit additional and repeated requests for assistance while providing him with a regulating support.

Swimming pool: Kevin often plays by himself in the pool until others approach him. In these instances, he readily joins his peers in simple social games. They discussed the importance of encouraging Kevin's peers to *position themselves in close proximity to Kevin* in the pool while he is playing with his favorite beach ball. They also discussed the importance of encouraging his peers to *wait for a sufficient period of time before asking Kevin if he would like to play,* to give him ample time to initiate a positive emotional expression in response to the ball and to his peers' bids for interaction.

MR4 Recovers from extreme dysregulation with support from partners (Social Partner stage)

Child goal	Related partner goals	
Mutual Regulation MR4 Recovers from extreme dysregulation with support from partners	**Interpersonal Support** IS1 Partner is responsive to child IS3 Partner respects child's independence IS7 Partner models appropriate behaviors	**Learning Support** LS1 Partner structures activity for active participation LS2 Partner uses augmentative communication support to foster development LS3 Partner uses visual and organizational support
MR4 is not directly linked to JA, SU, or SR.	A child's ability to respond to partners' efforts to assist with recovery by moving away from an activity (MR4.1), respond to partners' use of behavioral strategies (MR4.2), and decrease the intensity of dysregulated state due to support from partners (MR4.5) relies on a partner's ability to ability to recognize signs of dysregulation and offer support (IS1.5); honor protests, rejections, or refusals when appropriate (IS3.4); and model appropriate nonverbal communication and emotional expressions (IS7.1).	A child's ability to respond to partners' attempts to reengage in interaction or activity (MR4.3) and decrease the amount of time needed to recover from extreme dysregulation due to support from partners (MR4.4) relies on a partner's ability to use augmentative communication support to enhance the child's expression and understanding of emotion (LS2.3), use visual support to foster active involvement in group activities (LS3.6), and modify sensory properties of the learning environment (LS4.3).

Snapshot of Tyrell Tyrell is a 2-year-old Social Partner who easily becomes distressed. His dysregulation often escalates to prolonged periods of crying and screaming. His partners note that when they attempt to console him, his dysregulation may continue to escalate. His objectives include responding to partners' efforts to assist with recovery by moving away from an activity (MR4.1) and decreasing amount of time to recover from extreme dysregulation due to support from partners (MR4.4). Tyrell's partners are striving to recognize his signals of dysregulation and to offer support (IS1.5) and modify the sensory properties of his learning environments (LS4.3).

Dressing: Tyrell's team discussed that dressing often causes Tyrell extreme dysregulation. The team agreed that changes to the routine itself were needed, by providing a consistent visual schedule of the steps within the activity, and that strategies were needed in the event that Tyrell becomes distressed while dressing. His team members agreed that when they observed Tyrell continually echoing portions of his favorite videotapes, one of Tyrell's reliable signs of dysregulation, they would *provide him with a brief break* and then *show him the next piece of clothing* to be put on. His team also agreed in the event of extreme dysregulation, they would help Tyrell regroup by *sitting quietly in close proximity to Tyrell, without making any demands,* which was observed to be helpful for him.

Outdoor play with his brother: Tyrell's team discussed that the unpredictable nature of Tyrell's older brother's actions frequently is a trigger for Tyrell's distress. Therefore, they decided to modify the sensory properties of the environment by creating *brief structured play opportunities* (e.g., taking turns on a slide) for Tyrell and his brother. Next, they discussed the need to closely observe Tyrell for signals of dysregulation, such as video talk, and to respond by offering Tyrell *time on the swing.* In addition, his team agreed to set up *a small tent in the backyard to provide a getaway spot* for Tyrell to support him when he becomes dysregulated.

Emotional Regulation: Self-Regulation

SR1 Demonstrates availability for learning and interacting (Social Partner stage)

Child goal	Related partner goals	
Self-Regulation SR1 Demonstrates availability for learning and interacting	**Interpersonal Support** IS1 Partner is responsive to child IS2 Partner fosters initiation IS4 Partner sets stage for engagement	**Learning Support** LS1 Partner structures activity for active participation LS3 Partner uses visual and organizational support LS4 Partner modifies goals, activities, and learning environment
SR1 is linked to JA1. **Linked objectives** SR1.4 Initiates bids for interaction (= JA1.2) SR1.5 Engages in brief reciprocal interaction (= JA1.3) SR1.6 Engages in extended reciprocal interaction (= JA1.4)	A child's ability to notice people and things in the environment (SR1.1), show interest in a variety of sensory and social experiences (SR1.2), and initiate bids for interaction (SR1.4) relies on a partner's ability to be responsive to the child's attempts to communicate (IS1.3) and/or to signs of dysregulation (IS1.5), as well as on the partner's ability to secure the child's attention before communicating (IS4.2).	A child's ability to seek and tolerate a variety of sensory experiences (SR1.3) and engage in both brief and extended reciprocal interactions (SR1.5, SR1.6) relies on a partner's ability to modify the environment to provide a clear beginning and ending to an activity (LS1.1), offer repeated learning opportunities to enhance familiarity (LS1.4), and use visual support to support smooth transitions between activities (LS3.3).

Snapshot of Michael

Michael, a 3-year-old Social Partner currently enrolled in a full-day preschool, demonstrates a bias toward a low state of arousal and a passive interaction style. His objectives include noticing people and things in the environment (SR1.1) and seeking and tolerating a variety of sensory experiences (SR1.3). His partners have prioritized the need to secure Michael's attention before communicating to him (IS4.2) and use visual support to foster smooth transitions between activities (LS3.3).

Bath time: Given Michael's arousal bias, his partners discussed that attempts to secure his attention would require *exaggerated affect* and the use of *familiar songs* embedded as part of this routine. A familiar rubber duckie would also be presented consistently as part of the routine so that it would come to serve as *a visual cue to indicate a transition to bath time.*

Circle time during preschool: His team members decided that efforts to secure Michael's attention during circle time would be enhanced by *consistently using his name to call his attention.* In addition, smooth transitions from one activity to the next would be facilitated by *using an object schedule to represent activity sequence* and by *using an "all done" bucket in which Michael could place the objects to convey activity completion.*

SR2
Uses behavioral strategies to regulate arousal level during familiar activities (Social Partner stage)

Child goal		Related partner goals
Self-Regulation SR2 Uses behavioral strategies to regulate arousal level during familiar activities	**Interpersonal Support** IS1 Partner is responsive to child IS3 Partner respects child's independence IS7 Partner models appropriate behavior	**Learning Support** LS1 Partner structures activity for active participation LS4 Partner modifies goals, activities, and learning environment
SR2 is not directly linked to JA, SU, or MR. **Related goals** Achievements in SR2 are related to achievements in SU3.1.	A child's ability to use behavioral strategies to increase and decrease arousal level during social interaction (SR2.2), as well as his or her ability to use behavioral strategies modeled by partners to regulate arousal level (SR2.3), relies on a partner's ability to recognize and support the child's behavioral strategies to regulate arousal level (IS1.4), interpret problem behaviors as communicative and/or regulatory (IS3.3), and model appropriate behavior when the child uses inappropriate behavior (IS7.4)	A child's ability to use behavioral strategies to regulate arousal level during solitary activity (SR2.1) as well as to engage productively in an extended activity (SR2.4) relies on a partner's ability to offer repeated learning opportunities (LS1.4), modify the sensory properties of the learning environment (LS4.3), and infuse motivating materials and topics into activities (LS4.7).

Snapshot of Jessica

Jessica is a 5-year-old Social Partner about to make the transition to kindergarten who demonstrates a bias toward a high state of arousal, due in part, to tactile defensiveness. She often attempts to avoid interactions with others. Her objectives include using behavioral strategies to increase and decrease arousal level during solitary activities (SR2.1) and using behavioral strategies to increase and decrease arousal level during social interactions (SR2.2). Her partners have prioritized their need to recognize and support Jessica's behavioral strategies to regulate arousal (IS1.4) and modify sensory properties of learning environment to support Jessica's ability to self-regulate (LS4.3).

Playground at school: Jessica's team members discussed her behavior on the playground. They *created a list of her actions that signal dysregulation and/or her early attempts at self-regulation* to facilitate the team's efforts to recognize her behavioral strategies and *created a list of organizing activities* that can be encouraged during these times to facilitate efforts to support her regulation. In addition, they agreed to modify the sensory properties of the environment by *having tricycles available* on the playground, as the sensory input of this activity has been consistently regulating for Jessica.

Arts and crafts: Jessica's team members determined that her tendency to escalate to extreme dysregulation and tantrum during arts and crafts was due, in part, to overarousal, her tactile defensiveness, and the lack of regulatory support that she needed as signaled by more subtle signals of dysregulation. Therefore, they *compiled a list of her behavioral signals indicating Jessica's increasing arousal, along with corresponding supportive sensory-motor strategies that could be modeled* for her. They also agreed to provide *alternative art materials* that required less tactile exploration, to minimize the risk for high arousal.

SR3 Regulates emotion during new and changing situations (Social Partner stage)

Child goal		Related partner goals
Self-Regulation SR3 Regulates emotion in new and changing situations	*Interpersonal Support* IS1 Partner is responsive to child IS2 Partner fosters initiation IS4 Partner sets stage for engagement	*Learning Support* LS1 Partner structures activity for active participation LS2 Partner uses augmentative communication support to foster development LS3 Partner uses visual and organizational support
SR3 is linked to SU2. **Linked objective** SR3.1 Anticipates another person's actions in familiar routines (= SU2.1)	A child's ability to participate in new and changing situations (SR3.2) relies on a partner's ability to offer breaks from interaction or activities as needed (IS1.7), allow the child to initiate and terminate activities (IS2.4), and use appropriate words/intonation to support optimal arousal level and engagement (IS4.4).	A child's ability to use behavioral strategies to regulate arousal level in new and changing situations (SR3.3) and use behavioral strategies to regulate arousal level during transitions (SR3.4) relies on a partner's ability to offer varied learning opportunities (LS1.5), use augmentative communication support to enhance the child's emotional regulation (LS2.4), and use support to organize segments of time across the day (LS3.4)

Snapshot of Tyler

Tyler is a 2½-year-old Social Partner receiving home-based services who demonstrates a variable arousal level and becomes easily upset when his routine is violated. His objectives include participating in new and changing activities (SR3.2) and using behavioral strategies to regulate arousal level during transitions (SR3.4). His partners are working on their ability to offer breaks from interactions and activities when needed (IS1.7) and use support to organize segments of time across the day (LS3.4).

Bedtime: Tyler's team recognized that even within a consistent bedtime routine, Tyler becomes disorganized across the various sudden transitions involved in preparing for bedtime. Therefore, in their effort to help Tyler with this challenge, they created a visual support to organize and indicate segments of time and upcoming transitions by implementing *a photograph schedule board* to indicate the sequence of steps and to prepare Tyler for transitions involved within this daily routine. In addition, his team discussed the need for each partner involved in this activity *to offer Tyler a break* when he persists in attempting to bite his hand, one of his most reliable signals of escalation to more extreme dysregulation. The photograph schedule board could then be used to heighten Tyler's awareness of the next step and the number of steps to completion when he is able to reengage in the bedtime routine.

Shopping and family errands: Again, Tyler's team discussed the need to prepare him for transitions by organizing segments of time using visual supports. During shopping trips and family errands, sequential information should be provided in a manner that is clear and explicit for Tyler. *A photograph book with interchangeable pictures* was discussed and designed. In this book, the photographs would be inserted to reflect the different stores that would be visited during that day's shopping trip. *A vibrating stuffed animal, known to provide regulating sensory input, was provided as a means for partners to offer Tyler a break.* As this was one of Tyler's favorite toys, the team felt that it would be useful for capturing and holding Tyler's attention during community outings.

SR4 Recovers from extreme dysregulation by self (Social Partner stage)

Child goal	Related partner goals	
Self-Regulation SR4 Recovers from extreme dysregulation by self	*Interpersonal Support* IS1 Partner is responsive to child IS3 Partner respects child's independence IS7 Partner models appropriate behaviors	*Learning Support* LS2 Partner uses augmentative communication support to foster development LS3 Partner uses visual and organizational support LS4 Partner modifies goals, activities, and learning environment
SR4 is not directly linked to JA, SU, or MR.	A child's ability to remove him- or herself from overstimulating or undesired activity (SR4.1), use behavioral strategies to recover from extreme dysregulation (SR4.2), and decrease the intensity of his or her dysregulated state (SR4.5) relies on a partner's ability to recognize and support the child's behavioral strategies to regulate arousal (IS1.4); honor protests, rejections, or refusals when appropriate (IS3.4); and model appropriate nonverbal communication and emotional expressions (IS7.1).	A child's ability to reengage in interactions and activities after recovering from extreme dysregulation (SR4.3) and decrease the amount of time to recover from incidences of extreme dysregulation (SR4.4) relies on a partner's ability to use augmentative communication support to enhance the child's expression and understanding of emotion (LS2.3), use visual support to foster active involvement in group activities (LS3.6), and modify sensory properties of the learning environment (LS4.3).

Snapshot of Kia

Kia is an 8-year-old Social Partner in a partially inclusive second-grade program who has frequent tantrums associated with transitions and busy environments. Her objectives include removing herself from overstimulating or undesired activities (SR4.1) and reengaging in interactions or activities after recovery from extreme dysregulation (SR4.3). Her partners have recognized the need to improve efforts to honor protests, rejections, or refusals when appropriate (IS3.4) and modify sensory properties in the learning environment (LS4.3) to support Kia's ability to rejoin developmentally appropriate activities (LS4.3).

Adapted physical education (APE): Although Kia's APE class was a small-group setting, her team members recognized that the setting, a large gym environment, was challenging for her due to both the noise level and the visual overload of the fluorescent lighting. After observing Kia for several weeks, the team noted that her tantrums consistently appeared to be attempts to refuse (i.e., protest) entering this setting and activity. The team discussed the need for Kia's partners to improve their efforts to *honor her protest behaviors used as attempts to refuse the activity* by helping her take a break on the stage, which was hidden behind a curtain at one end of the gym. They also discussed the need for partners to *decrease the sensory stimuli* in the gym by *turning off the fluorescent lights* and encouraging all present to *decrease vocal volume* (i.e., using "inside voices"), as these modifications to the environment would likely facilitate Kia's ability to reengage in the group activity.

Language arts: In the team's efforts to honor Kia's protests, team members recognized that her screeching during sedentary language arts were attempts to protest lessons that exceeded her perceived abilities. Thus, they discussed the importance of encouraging Kia to *remove herself to a "cozy corner"* in these situations. Next, they agreed that *supplementing the language lesson with organizing sensory information* (e.g., textured materials that Kia can manipulate) would increase the likelihood that she would rejoin the activity.

LANGUAGE PARTNER STAGE

At the Language Partner stage, a child's partners have a significant impact on supporting the child's ability to become more persistent in communicating for a range of intentions including requesting assistance, greeting others, showing off, taking turns, and commenting about actions or events. Partners also have a significant influence on a child's ability to use symbolic means to communicate, to use and understand words and word combinations to refer to objects and events, to imitate new behaviors, and to pretend with objects in play. Likewise, at the Language Partner stage, a child's partners have a significant impact on that child's ability to use both behavioral *and* language-based strategies for self-regulation; to regulate arousal level in new and changing situations; to use partner feedback as a means to refine emotional expression, develop more conventional strategies for regulation, and reengage in more challenging activities.

As outlined earlier in this chapter, a number of considerations must be taken into account when determining how to prioritize specific Transactional Support goals for a child's partners. The following charts are provided as a resource for educational teams as they determine which Transactional Support goals should be considered when addressing specific Social Communication and Emotional Regulation goals for a child at the Language Partner stage. *Please note that objectives related to the goal areas in each table are defined in Chapter 8 of Volume I.* Following each goal area, "snapshot" examples of how each of the named Transactional Support goals might be modified based on the nature of a specific activity and child-specific factors (e.g., whether a child has a bias for a high state of arousal versus a low state of arousal, whether a child has visual or auditory learning strengths) are provided.

Social Communication: Joint Attention

JA1 Engages in reciprocal interaction (Language Partner stage)

Child goal	Related partner goals	
Joint Attention JA1 Engages in reciprocal interaction	**Interpersonal Support** IS1 Partner is responsive to child IS2 Partner fosters initiation IS4 Partner sets stage for engagement	**Learning Support** LS1 Partner structures activity for active participation LS4 Partner modifies goals, activities, and learning environment
JA1 is linked to SR1. **Linked objectives** JA1.1 Initiates bids for interaction (= SR1.1) JA1.2 Engages in brief reciprocal interaction (= SR1.2) JA1.3 Engages in extended reciprocal interaction (= SR1.3)	A child's ability to initiate bids for interaction (JA1.1) and engage in brief and extended reciprocal interactions (JA1.2, JA1.3) relies on a partner's ability to be responsive to the child's signals to foster a sense of communicative competence (IS1.3), wait for and encourage child initiations (IS2.2), and provide a balance of initiated and respondent turns (IS2.3).	A child's ability to engage in both brief and extended reciprocal interactions (JA1.2, JA1.3) also relies on a partner's ability to modify the environment to create turn-taking opportunities and leave spaces for the child to fill in (LS1.2), arrange learning environments to promote child initiation (LS4.5), and provide activities to promote initiation and extended interaction (LS4.8).

Snapshot of Matthew

Matthew is a 4-year-old Language Partner who recently started his second year in an inclusive preschool program. He is a curious little boy who is beginning to seek out his social partners more frequently, particularly if he needs help with a preferred toy or would like a preferred snack. In fact, Matthew's parents often remark on his keen memory for words and scripted phrases associated with these toys and snacks. For example, he may use the gestalt phrase, "Touch a word and listen," to request his toddler laptop device, a favorite toy. Although he may initiate and respond to bids for interaction for brief exchanges with familiar partners, he is working on engaging in more extended reciprocal interactions (JA1.3). As his adult partners often elicit interaction by asking him questions, Matthew's team discussed the need to achieve greater consistency with providing a balance of initiated and respondent turns (IS2.3) and providing activities that promote initiation and extended interaction (LS4.8).

Playtime at home: Matthew's team discussed that during playtime at home, Matthew may request a preferred toy such as his car garage or vehicle puzzles but then plays with that toy independently. Thus, opportunities for reciprocal exchanges are limited. Currently, his parents find themselves asking Matthew many questions (e.g., "What do you see?" "What is it?). Matthew attends to these questions but typically responds through immediate echolalia by repeating the question rather than by providing an answer. To foster more extended interactions, his parents and the rest of the educational team discussed the need to achieve greater consistency with providing a balance of initiated and respondent turns by *modeling developmentally appropriate one- or two-word comments that Matthew might make* (e.g., "open garage," "drive car," "fire truck) and by *waiting to encourage his initiations.* Extended opportunities for requesting could also be encouraged through environmental arrangements such as *having the parts of these toy sets (e.g., cars, gas pump, people) placed in sealed see-through containers* to encourage a higher frequency of requests.

Choice time at preschool: On first arriving at preschool, Matthew is typically drawn to the area of the classroom where the toy garage and vehicles are available. He is beginning to take interest in his classmates as they join him in his play, but his interactions are limited to either simply observing their actions with the cars or, on occasion, protesting their intrusions in his play. His team members discussed the need to *have an instructional assistant present to model simple comments* about both Matthew's play and the actions of his peers (e.g., "Joey drive," "Brian push") to encourage more balance between initiated and respondent turns. Next, the team members discussed several environmental modifications to promote more extended interactions and a clear structure for turn taking. These included *designing a predictable race path for the children* to follow on the car table, with a clear starting line (e.g., the top of a ramp) and finish line (e.g., having the cars tap into a bell). As the race path would include a motivating end point, the children would be apt to take turns and extend interactions beyond one or two exchanges.

Linking Goals

JA2 Shares attention (Language Partner stage)

Child goal	Related partner goals	
Joint Attention JA2 Shares attention	*Interpersonal Support* IS2 Partner fosters initiation IS4 Partner sets stage for engagement	*Learning Support* LS1 Partner structures activity for active participation LS2 Partner uses augmentative communication support to foster development LS4 Partner modifies goals, activities, and learning environment
JA2 is linked to JA5 and SU2. *Linked objectives* JA2.2 Follows contact and distal point (= SU2.2) JA2.4 Secures attention to oneself prior to expressing intentions (≈ JA5.5)	A child's ability to shift gaze between people and objects (JA2.1), monitor the attentional focus of a social partner (JA2.3), and secure attention to oneself prior to expressing intentions (JA2.4) relies on a partner's ability to wait for and encourage the child's initiations (IS2.2) and use appropriate proximity and nonverbal behavior to encourage interaction (IS4.3).	A child's ability to monitor the attentional focus of a social partner (JA2.3) and secure attention to oneself prior to expressing intentions (JA2.4) also relies on a partner's ability to offer varied learning opportunities (LS1.5), use augmentative communication support to enhance the child's communication and expressive language (LS2.1), and arrange the learning environment to promote child initiation (LS4.5).

Snapshot of Monique

Monique is a 6-year-old Language Partner who participates in a small resource first-grade classroom with four other children. Her educational team and parents have observed her communication and language blossoming in the past few months, as she is more apt to use words to share her intentions. She has developed a range of single words for preferred snacks (e.g., "cookies," "milk," "nana" for "banana") and favorite toys (e.g., "video," "book," "marker"), and she typically pairs single words with photographic representations of familiar objects and people. Although she is becoming more persistent, she is not yet securing the attention of her parents, teachers, and/or peers when making a verbal request by calling out their name or tapping on their shoulder. Thus, she is working on securing attention to herself prior to expressing intentions (JA2.4). Her partners discussed the need to use appropriate proximity and nonverbal behavior to encourage interaction (IS4.3) and provide augmentative communication support to enhance her communication and expressive language (LS2.1).

Arts and crafts center: At school, one of Monique's favorite activities is the arts and crafts center, and she independently seeks this activity out during choice times and indoor recess. This activity center has already been designed to elicit requests for assistance and specific objects, as all of the paint brushes, paints, crayons, and stamps are in separate sealed containers. Monique typically makes a request by looking at the desired item and using a word or brief phrase (e.g., "paints, please"). She occasionally even makes this request when a teacher is not immediately present. To address Monique's goals, her partners discussed the need to *redesign this center to include a table that faces the center of the classroom,* as this will increase the likelihood of an adult's presence and *encourage a face-to-face orientation.* Next, her team discussed the need to provide an augmentative communication support to enhance her ability to call attention using her teacher's names. By placing *a menu of photographs of her teaching staff* on the arts and crafts table, Monique will have access to visual reminders of what to say and will be more likely to pair her request with her teacher's name.

Cooperative games in adaptive physical education (APE): Monique's team discussed that while playing APE games with her classmates, she may make a request of her peers but rarely uses their name to call their attention and/or rarely pairs her requests with gaze to ensure that they have attended to her request. For example, in one of her preferred games, she and her classmates are asked to take turns running under a parachute. Monique may use the phrase, "Ready . . . go," to encourage her classmates to take a turn, but these requests are not directed to a specific classmate. Thus, her team discussed the need for partners to consistently modify the learning environment to ensure more appropriate proximity with another peer by *having the classmates situated directly across from one another in a circle* under the parachute. Next, they discussed the need for an augmentative support to encourage the classmates to use each other's names in a modified Red Rover game. They designed *a photographic turn-taking dial using a game board spinner,* where each child's photograph and written name would be illustrated on a section of the spinner. Each child would be asked to use the spinner, which would land on a specific child's name and photograph, encouraging the calling out of another child's name to continue the game.

JA3 Shares emotion (Language Partner stage)

Child goal	Related partner goals	
Joint Attention JA3 Shares emotion	**Interpersonal Support** IS1 Partner is responsive to child IS2 Partner fosters initiation IS6 Partner adjusts language input IS7 Partner models appropriate behaviors	**Learning Support** LS2 Partner uses augmentative communication support to foster development LS4 Partner modifies goals, activities, and learning environment
JA3 is linked to MR1, MR2, SU2, and SR3. **Linked objectives** JA3.1 Shares negative and positive emotion (= MR1.1; ≈ MR3.1, MR3.2) JA3.2 Understands and uses symbols to express a range of emotions (≈ MR1.2, SR3.5) JA3.3 Attunes to changes in partners' expression of emotion (≈ SU2.4; = MR2.5)	A child's ability to share negative and positive emotion (JA3.1) and attune to changes in partners' expression of emotion (JA3.3) relies on a partner's ability to respond to the child's emotion and pace (IS1.2), wait for and encourage initiations (IS2.2), use nonverbal cues to support understanding (IS6.1), and model appropriate nonverbal communication and emotional expressions (IS7.1).	A child's ability to understand and use symbols to express a range of emotions (JA3.2) and describe the emotional state of another person (JA3.4) relies on a partner's ability to use augmentative communication support to enhance the child's expression and understanding of emotion (LS2.3) and adjust the social complexity to support organization and interaction (LS4.1).
Related objective Achievements in JA3 are related to achievement in SU5.6.		

Snapshot of Jamie

Jamie is a 4-year-old Language Partner in an inclusive preschool program who is developing his ability to understand and use symbols to express a range of emotions (JA3.2). Jamie is described as an easygoing child who has recently begun to share his states of emotion with his partners using clear facial expressions and gestures. He may smile after a preferred snack is provided for him and may grimace, tense his upper body, and clench his hands into fists when a favorite toy is removed. Although he uses quite a few signs and picture symbols to request these toys and activities, he continues to rely on facial expressions and gestures to share his emotions. His partners discussed the need to more consistently model appropriate nonverbal communication and emotional expressions (IS7.1) and use augmentative communication support to enhance his expression and understanding of emotion (LS2.3).

Circle time: During circle time, Jamie has been known to display distinct emotional reactions such as jumping up and down and smiling when a preferred song starts. On occasion, he clenches his hands into fists, becomes tense, and displays a more negative emotion if a teacher tries to physically prompt him to dance or participate in finger movements. Jamie's educational team recognized these opportunities as an appropriate context for address his use of symbols to express emotion. They discussed the need to *more consistently model simple emotion words* (e.g., "Jamie's happy," "Jamie's mad") in these instances to acknowledge and validate his emotional reactions. In addition, the circle time leader would have access to *an emotion chart* and photographs of each classmate. Thus, when a child is feeling happy, his or her photograph can be placed on the "happy" side of the chart (denoted with a large happy picture symbol) and when a child is feeling mad, his or her photograph can be placed on the "mad" side of the chart (denoted with a large mad picture symbol).

Playground: Jamie is generally very content on the playground; his enjoyment for gross motor activities (e.g., swinging and riding the stationary bouncy horses) is evident by his facial expressions and laughing. Nevertheless, he does occasionally display sadness when the swings are all occupied. Although he may use the sign for "more" when enjoying himself and the sign for "all done" when his classmates continue to use a piece of equipment, his use of the symbols for "happy" and "sad" have not yet emerged. His educational team recognized the need to *more consistently model simple emotion words* (e.g., "Jamie's happy," "Jamie's sad") in these instances to validate his emotional reactions in the context in which they occur. In addition, team members discussed using an augmentative support for Jamie to communicate his emotional state in this context. The playground monitor would wear *a key chain with picture symbols for "happy," "sad," and "mad,"* which could be used to model these emotion words when they occur as well as give Jamie an opportunity to use them to clarify his emotional state.

	Child goal	Related partner goals	
JA4 Shares intentions to regulate the behavior of others (Language Partner stage)	*Joint Attention* JA4 Shares intentions to regulate the behavior of others	*Interpersonal Support* IS1 Partner is responsive to child IS2 Partner fosters initiation IS3 Partner respects child's independence IS7 Partner models appropriate behaviors	*Learning Support* LS2 Partner uses augmentative communication support to foster development LS4 Partner modifies goals, activities, and learning environment
	JA4 is linked to MR2 and MR3. *Linked objectives* JA4.1 Requests desired food or objects (≈ MR2.6) JA4.2 Protests/refuses undesired food or objects ≈ MR3.4) JA4.3 Requests help or other actions (≈ MR3.3) JA4.4 Protests undesired actions or activities (≈ MR3.4) *Related goals* Achievements in JA4 are related to achievements in JA7.2, JA8.2, SU4–SU5, and MR3.7.	A child's ability to request and protest food or objects (JA4.1, JA4.2), request help or other actions (JA4.3), and protest undesired actions or activities (JA4.4) relies on a partner's ability to respond appropriately to the child's signals to foster a sense of communicative competence (IS1.3); offer choices nonverbally or verbally (IS2.1); allow the child to initiate and terminate activities (IS2.4); honor protests, rejections, or refusals when appropriate (IS3.4); and model a range of communicative functions (IS7.2).	A child's ability to request or protest food or objects (JA4.1, JA4.2), request help or other actions (JA4.3), and protest undesired actions or activities (JA4.4) also relies on a partner's ability to use augmentative communication support to enhance the child's communication and expressive language (LS2.1) and arrange the learning environment to promote child initiation (LS4.5).

Snapshot of Leo

Leo is an 8-year-old Language Partner who participates in a partially inclusive third-grade educational program. He communicates using a range of gestures and single words and is described by his new educational team as spirited and energetic. Although he has strong preferences, he is working on his ability to protest undesired actions or activities (JA4.4) using single words and early word combinations. Rather than saying "all done" or using a push away gesture paired with "stop" to reject an undesired action, Leo may turn his back, walk away, and/or cover his ears. Because these nonverbal acts are not always paired with gaze or verbal means, his effectiveness at "sharing" his intent to reject or protest the current activity is often compromised. His partners discussed the need to more consistently offer choices nonverbally or verbally (IS2.1) and use augmentative communication support to enhance Leo's communication and expressive language (LS2.1).

Lunch: In the cafeteria, Leo's instructional assistant often points toward Leo's preferred lunch items as Leo progresses through the lunch line, to support his success in this daily activity. He typically requests these items while simply looking away from undesired items on the cafeteria line. As the lunch line is a busy environment, adapting this context would be challenging. Thus, his team members recognized the need to *provide more explicit choices of both preferred and nonpreferred food items* before making the transition to the lunch line. In the classroom, *a picture-based lunch list* would be created to help Leo make choices between favorite and undesired food items from a cafeteria menu. Rejected items would be placed on a fill-in-the-blank card that reads "no _____." By presenting picture symbols of both preferred and nonpreferred items, the instructional assistant would encourage Leo to reject undesired food by using simple word combinations rather than by simply walking away. Leo could then bring his lunch list to the cafeteria as a within-task schedule for this activity.

Library: During independent reading in the library, the librarian often has the children sit together in small groups at a table to read. Leo occasionally becomes distressed in this context and may cover his ears and/or turn his back to his classmates, particularly if they are leaning against him, reading out loud, or playing with his clothing. His team recognized this activity as an opportunity to support Leo's ability to share his intentions for the purpose of protesting. *A picture symbol for "all done" paired with a symbol for "group"* would be available to Leo at the table. This phrase would be modeled for Leo when he shows signs of distress. Then, *a choice of group reading versus quiet reading could be offered* to Leo to clarify his intentions. If Leo chooses quiet reading, a table at which Leo could sit by himself could be offered.

JA5 Shares intentions for social interaction (Language Partner stage)	Child goal	Related partner goals	
	Joint Attention JA5 Shares intentions for social interaction	**Interpersonal Support** IS1 Partner is responsive to child IS2 Partner fosters initiation IS7 Partner models appropriate behaviors	**Learning Support** LS1 Partner structures activity for active participation LS3 Partner uses visual and organizational support LS4 Partner modifies goals, activities, and learning environment
	JA5 is linked to JA2 and MR3. **Linked objectives** JA5.1 Requests comfort (≈ MR3.1) JA5.5 Calls (≈ JA2.4) **Related goals/objectives** Achievements in JA5 are related to achievements in JA7.2, JA8.2, and SU4–SU5.	A child's ability to request social games (JA5.2), take turns (JA5.3), show off (JA5.6), and request permission (JA5.7) relies on a partner's ability to respond appropriately to the child's signals to foster a sense of competence (IS1.3), provide a balance of initiated and respondent turns (IS2.3), and model a range of communicative functions (IS7.2).	A child's ability to request social games (JA5.2), greet others (JA5.4), and call another's attention (JA5.5) relies on a partner's ability to create turn-taking opportunities and leave spaces for the child to fill in (LS1.2), use visual support to foster active involvement in group activities (LS3.6), and arrange the learning initiation (LS4.5).

Snapshot of Alexis Alexis is a 5-year-old Language Partner who spends half of her classroom time in an inclusive kindergarten setting. She is a talkative little girl who is known for reciting favorite parts of movie scenes and storybooks throughout her day (i.e., delayed echolalia). She enjoys engaging in social routines (e.g., "If you're happy, and you know it . . . clap your hands") and activities that have a very clear and predictable turn-taking structure (e.g., Barnyard Bingo). At this time, however, she often waits for her classmates to tell her that it is her turn or simply takes a turn when she would like to participate. Thus, she is working on her ability to share her intentions for the function of taking turns (JA5.3). Her partners discussed the need to model a range of communicative functions (IS7.2), including turn taking, and use visual support to foster active involvement in group activities (LS3.6).

Choice time in kindergarten: Games that involve a clear and predictable end point and clear turn-taking structure have always been the most successful for Alexis. For example, she has enjoyed Barnyard Bingo, which involves matching picture tokens on game boards with three pictures until a child or all of the children complete their boards. Nevertheless, Alexis has not yet initiated a request for turn taking despite her apparent interest in the activity and her peers. Her partners discussed that having an augmentative support would provide a helpful visual cue to remind her to ask for her turn and/or to comment that it is another child's turn. A teacher or paraprofessional would be available to model the use of this board by playing the game alongside Alexis and one or two classmates. Each child's photograph would be placed on *a turn-taking dial.* After a child's turn, the teacher would model turning the wheel and *using simple word combinations requesting that the next child take his or her turn* (e.g., "Sarah's turn," "Alexis's turn," "Jason's turn.").

Morning meeting: In her resource room, Alexis's special education teacher reviews the calendar, days of the week, the weather, and the daily schedule. She assigns a class member to help with each activity. Alexis enjoys being a leader, as each activity is paired with a song that is used to capture the group's attention (e.g., a "days of the week" song, a "what's the weather" song). Her teacher typically calls on several different children each day to lead these various activities. Her educational team recognized the need to *model word combinations for turn taking* during this activity (e.g., "Alexis's turn," "Nathan's turn") so that each of the children could begin using these phrases. In addition, an augmentative support would be reviewed at the beginning of morning meeting. This *visual support would include a list of jobs* (e.g., calendar helper, weekday helper, weather helper) in the sequence in which they occur. *A photograph of the specific child assigned to the job* would be placed on this visual support so that each child, including Alexis, can pass it to the next child in line and use a turn-taking phrase, such as "Joey's turn."

**JA6
Shares intentions
for joint attention
(Language Partner
stage)**

	Child goal	Related partner goals	
	Joint Attention JA6 Shares intentions for joint attention	*Interpersonal Support* IS1 Partner is responsive to child IS2 Partner fosters initiation IS4 Partner sets stage for engagement IS7 Partner models appropriate behaviors	*Learning Support* LS1 Partner structures activity for active participation LS2 Partner uses augmentative communication support to foster development LS4 Partner modifies goals, activities, and learning environment
	JA6 is not directly linked to SU, MR, or SR. *Related goals* Achievements in JA6 are related to achievements in JA7.2, JA8.2, and SU4–SU5.	A child's ability to comment on an object (JA6.1), comment on an action or an event (JA6.2), and request information about things of interest (JA6.3) relies on a partner's ability to respond to the child's focus of attention (IS1.1), wait for and encourage his or her initiations (IS2.2), use appropriate proximity and nonverbal behavior to encourage interaction (IS4.3), and model a range of communicative functions (IS7.2).	A child's ability to comment on an object (JA6.1), comment on an action or an event (JA6.2), and request information about things of interest (JA6.3) also relies on a partner's ability to offer varied learning opportunities (LS1.5), use augmentative communication support to enhance the child's communication and expressive language (LS2.1), and infuse motivating materials and topics in activities (LS4.7).

Snapshot of Warren

Warren is a 9-year-old Language Partner who is developing his ability to share intentions for joint attention. Although his exposure to picture communication supports have supported his ability to request and protest using a range of word combinations (e.g., "I want water," "bathroom please," "all done music"), he is not yet using language to comment about events in the immediate environment or pictures in a book. His partners, however, realized that their efforts to help Warren not yet placed an emphasis on this function of communication, as the majority of learning supports have been designed to encourage requesting. Thus, current goals for Warren include fostering his ability to comment on an action or an event (JA6.2). His partners discussed the need to model a range of communicative functions (IS7.2), such as commenting on actions and events; infuse motivating materials and topics in activities (LS4.7); and use augmentative communication support to enhance Warren's communication and expressive language (LS2.1).

Independent reading: Warren's elementary school encourages reading by having all of the school children participate in independent reading each morning. This has been a challenge for Warren, as his reading skills remain challenged by his language processing difficulties. Nevertheless, he does seem to take the greatest interest in *books that include pictures of himself and/or his family members.* Therefore, his educational team discussed that by infusing these motivating elements into this activity, both his participation and motivation to share could be fostered. *A series of photograph journals could be created* in partnership with Warren's parents, who would provide the photographs of recent family vacations and typical family activities at home. *Each photograph can be paired with picture symbols highlighting developmentally appropriate single words and word combinations* (e.g., "pajamas," "Warren dress," "Daddy hug," "Mommy read," "Warren sleep").

Group games: Warren typically has a difficult time engaging in small-group games in his resource classroom, despite the fact that the games have been selected based on his developmental level and interests (e.g., matching lotto games). As his bids for communication are primarily limited to requesting and protesting, commenting about his turn has not yet been observed. His educational team discussed the need to include motivating materials in this activity by *creating a matching lotto game that includes photographs of Warren and his classmates* engaging in familiar actions. The children could then be encouraged to match the appropriate comment to the picture (e.g., "Warren read," "Jason eat," "Allison drink") by providing *simple word combinations using picture symbols on index cards.*

JA7 Persists and repairs communication breakdowns (Language Partner stage)

Child goal	Related partner goals	
Joint Attention	*Interpersonal Support*	*Learning Support*
JA7 Persists and repairs communication breakdowns	IS1 Partner is responsive to child IS3 Partner respects child's independence IS5 Partner provides developmental support	LS2 Partner uses augmentative communication support to foster development LS4 Partner modifies goals, activities, and learning environment
JA7 is not directly linked to SU, MR, or SR. *Related goals* Achievements in JA7 are related to achievements in JA4–JA6.	A child's ability to use an appropriate rate of communication for the context (JA7.1) and recognize breakdowns in communication (JA7.3) relies on a partner's ability to respond appropriately to the child's signals to foster a sense of communicative competence (IS1.3), provide time for the child to solve problems or complete activities at his or her own pace (IS3.2), attempt to repair breakdowns verbally or nonverbally (IS5.3), and give guidance and feedback as needed for success in activities (IS5.4)	A child's ability to repeat and modify communication to repair communicative breakdowns (JA7.2) relies on a partner's ability to use augmentative communication support to enhance the child's communication and expressive language (LS2.1), adjust task difficulty for child success (LS4.2), provide activities to promote initiation and extended interactions (LS4.8), and increase expectations appropriately (LS4.10).

Snapshot of Jocelyn

Jocelyn is a 6-year-old Language Partner in an inclusive kindergarten class who has made great progress in her ability to share her intentions with those around her using both words and early word combinations. Nevertheless, in larger group activities, she continues to rely on an adult's verbal cues and support to initiate bids for communication. In circle time, for example, she may even "get lost" and spend lengthy periods of time reading the calendar on the wall behind her teacher. This occurs even when the teacher specifically poses a question or comment that Jocelyn would understand and would typically respond to. Her more active peers often jump in and fill this turn. This passivity is noticeable, and the kindergarten teacher is struggling to support Jocelyn's efforts to participate in circle time more independently and at a rate consistent for the context (e.g., once every 5–10 minutes). Thus, her current goals include using an appropriate rate of communication for the context (JA7.1). Her partners discussed the need to provide time for Jocelyn to solve problems or complete activities at her own pace (IS3.2) and use augmentative communication support to enhance her communication and expressive language (LS2.1).

Circle time: One of Jocelyn's relative strengths is her ability to process simple written language paired with simple graphic depictions of items or activities. Therefore, she is often drawn to the written information on the wall during more challenging group lessons and may drift off by reading the calendar and/or days of the week as her class is discussing a book that has just been read. This tendency, paired with her classmates' more active learning styles, compromises her ability to initiate responses to her teacher's inquiries, given the hastened pace. To support Jocelyn's rate of spontaneously initiated communication for this context, her team recognized the need to *use a written cue card to indicate who is the current teacher's helper.* This card would be passed to the student who should respond to the question or comment posed by the teacher, which would ensure Jocelyn more time to participate in the discussion, as her classmates would be more aware of who is supposed to be talking. Next, an instructional assistant would provide Jocelyn with *a written schedule of the activities of circle time* as well as *written ideas for "what to say"* to build Jocelyn's self-confidence in participating in this large-group setting.

Centers: During small-group learning contexts in her kindergarten classroom, Jocelyn tends to focus more on the activity than on her peers. An appropriate rate of communication in this context would typically entail approximately one bid for communication every 3 minutes. Her team observed, however, that the challenge of the activity itself limited her availability for engaging with her peers, leading to minimal time to process the language of her peers and formulate communicative bids. Therefore, team members recognized the need to *preteach the activities in a one-to-one planned activity routine* so that Jocelyn would not be challenged by the activity and the interaction. In addition, they recognized the need for augmentative communication supports at each center. Given Jocelyn's early reading abilities, simple word combinations were written at each center to encourage peer requests and comments (e.g., "Pass the _____," "I made a _____," "Look at _____"). *An instructional assistant would be present* to point to and model the use of these cards.

JA8 Shares experiences in reciprocal interaction (Language Partner stage)	Child goal	Related partner goals	
	Joint Attention JA8 Shares experiences in reciprocal interaction	*Interpersonal Support* IS1 Partner is responsive to child IS2 Partner fosters initiation IS4 Partner sets stage for engagement	*Learning Support* LS1 Partner structures activity for active participation LS2 Partner uses augmentative communication support to foster development LS3 Partner uses visual and organizational support LS4 Partner modifies goals, activities, and learning environment
	JA8 is not directly linked to SU, MR, or SR. *Related goals* Achievements in JA8 are related to achievements in JA4–JA6.	A child's ability to coordinate attention, emotion, and intentions to share experiences (JA8.1) and show reciprocity in speaker and listener roles to share experiences (JA8.2) relies on a partner's ability to be responsive to the child's signals to foster a sense of communicative competence (IS1.3), wait for and encourage child initiations (IS2.2), and provide a balance of initiated and respondent turns (IS2.3).	A child's ability to initiate interaction and share experiences with a friend (JA8.3) relies on a partner's ability to modify the environment to create turn-taking opportunities and leave spaces for the child to fill in (LS1.2), use augmentative communication support to enhance the child's communication and expressive language (LS2.1), use visual support to foster active involvement in group activities (LS3.6), and provide activities to promote initiation and extended interaction (LS4.8).

Snapshot of Harrison

Harrison is a 7-year-old Language Partner who has recently been blossoming in his second-grade classroom, which he attends for several hours a day outside of his resource classroom. He uses a range of early word combinations and has expanded the functions of his communication to include not only requesting and protesting but also commenting about events in the immediate environment. His teacher has noticed, however, that Harrison continues to have difficulty sharing experiences across contexts. When she inquires about his weekend or a recent family vacation, Harrison often smiles and may comment about something that occurred using a one- to two-word utterance if a visual reminder happens to be present (e.g., a new T-shirt with Mickey Mouse on the front). His ability to share experiences across contexts has not yet consistently emerged. Thus, his current goals include coordinating attention, emotion, and intentions to share experiences (JA8.1). His partners are striving to be responsive to Harrison's communicative signals to foster a sense of competence (IS1.3) and use visual support to foster active involvement in group activities (LS3.6).

Lunch: Harrison enjoys eating lunch with his second-grade classmates. However, his ability to participate in reciprocal interaction is limited to comments about the immediate environment (e.g., "I have a cheese sandwich," "This is good!"). His classmates are supportive and have been encouraged to be responsive to these more concrete topics but seem to have less confidence following Harrison's lead when he mentions events outside of the immediate context. He may, for example, use a single word (e.g., "violin") without any further elaboration, and his peers may neglect to encourage these comments. His educational team recognizes the need to *provide additional peer training* so that his classmates can be more responsive to Harrison's attempts to communicate across contexts. In addition, a visual support would be helpful for reminding Harrison what to say. Given the context, Harrison's classmates were asked what visual would work most effectively, and they suggested *a lunchbox postcard,* as this would fit in to the cafeteria scene and also provide Harrison with a photograph of a special event (e.g., a violin recital) with specific notes provided by his parents and/or a teacher (e.g., "I played violin. . . . I had a recital").

Dinner: At home, Harrison eats dinner with his parents and two older brothers. In a similar manner to his conversations at school, his ability to participate in reciprocal interaction is limited to comments about the immediate environment (e.g., "I like chicken," "This is sticky"). His educational team and parents discussed the need to *provide guidance to his siblings* so that they can be responsive to Harrison's attempts to communicate across contexts. In addition, a visual support would be needed to provide Harrison with support for what to say. His teachers at school noted that they would provide *a daily journal* that would include simple written reminders of special events that had occurred that day.

Social Communication: Symbol Use

SU1 Learns by observation and imitation of familiar and unfamiliar actions and words (Language Partner stage)

Child goal	Related partner goals	
Symbol Use	*Interpersonal Support*	*Learning Support*
SU1 Learns by observation and imitation of familiar and unfamiliar actions and words	IS1 Partner is responsive to child IS2 Partner fosters initiation IS4 Partner sets stage for engagement IS5 Partner provides developmental support	LS1 Partner structures activity for active participation LS3 Partner uses visual and organizational support LS4 Partner modifies goals, activities, and learning environment
SU1 is not directly linked to JA, MR, or SR.	A child's ability to spontaneously imitate familiar and unfamiliar actions or words immediately after a model (SU1.1, SU1.2) relies on a partner's ability to imitate the child (IS1.6), provide a balance of initiated and respondent turns (IS2.3), use appropriate proximity and nonverbal behavior to encourage interaction (IS4.3), and encourage imitation (IS5.1).	A child's ability to spontaneously imitate actions or words and add a different behavior (SU1.3) and spontaneously imitate a variety of behaviors later in a different context (SU1.4) relies on a partner's ability to offer repeated learning opportunities (LS1.4), use support to define steps within a task (LS3.1), and design and modify activities to be developmentally appropriate (LS4.6).

Snapshot of Nathan

Nathan is a 7-year-old Language Partner in a small self-contained educational program. He is described as a self-directed child who has difficulty monitoring the actions of others and learning through imitation and direct modeling. Learning daily living activities such as preparing lemonade can be challenging, as he relies on his visual memory of where items should be placed, as opposed to his memory of another's actions in relation to the items (e.g., how to stir, how to pour). Thus, he is currently working on imitating unfamiliar actions by closely approximating this action or word spontaneously (i.e., without direction to do so) immediately after a partner models the behavior (SU1.2). His partners recognized the need to achieve greater consistency with encouraging imitation (IS5.1), providing repeated learning opportunities (LS1.4), and using visual supports to define steps within a task (LS3.1).

Cooking: In Nathan's special education resource room, the teacher has set up a specific time each day for the children to practice cooking preferred meals and snacks. As Nathan has difficulty monitoring his teacher during this activity, his ability to imitate unfamiliar actions remains vulnerable and he often relies on both physical and verbal cues (e.g., "squeeze the lemon," "pour the water," "pour the sugar," "stir the lemonade"). Thus, his partners recognized the need to encourage imitation by *gaining his attention before modeling a specific action using a simple and rhythmic song lyric* (e.g., "This is the way we squeeze the lemons, squeeze the lemons . . ."). Next, they discussed the need to *provide frequent repetitions of the same actions* (e.g., having each of his classmates model the action following the teacher's model). Finally, *a within-task picture schedule* could be used to highlight each action word in sequence (e.g., "squeeze," "pour," "stir").

Music class: Nathan participates in music class twice per week along with typically developing peers in his second-grade class. In this context, Nathan easily becomes disorganized as he may shift from observing each of the 25 children to looking at the instruments at the front of the room. His educational team members discussed the need to encourage imitation by *ensuring that Nathan is situated immediately in front of the teacher.* Next, they discussed the need to provide repetitions of targeted actions by *preteaching fingerplays and/or simple actions on a music instrument before class. A picture action board* could also be used to highlight each of the unfamiliar actions (e.g., stomp, hum, tap feet) when they occur.

SU2 Understands nonverbal cues in familiar and unfamiliar activities (Language Partner stage)

Child goal	Related partner goals	
Symbol Use	*Interpersonal Support*	*Learning Support*
SU2 Understands nonverbal cues in familiar and unfamiliar activities	IS4 Partner sets stage for engagement IS6 Partner adjusts language input IS7 Partner models appropriate behaviors	LS1 Partner structures activity for active participation LS2 Partner uses augmentative communication support to foster development
SU2 is linked to JA2, JA3, and SR4. *Linked objectives* SU2.1 Follows situational and gestural cues in familiar and unfamiliar activities (= SR4.2) SU2.2 Follows contact and distal point (= JA2.2) SU2.4 Responds to facial expression and intonation cues (≈ JA3.3)	A child's ability to follow situational and gestural cues in familiar and unfamiliar activities (SU2.1), follow contact and distal points (SU2.2), and respond to facial expression and intonation cues (SU2.4) relies on a partner's ability to use appropriate proximity and nonverbal behavior to encourage interaction (IS4.3), use appropriate words/intonation to support optimal arousal level and engagement (IS4.4), use nonverbal cues to support understanding (IS6.1), and model appropriate nonverbal communication and emotional expressions (IS7.1).	A child's ability to follow situational and gestural cues in familiar and unfamiliar activities (SU2.1) and follow instructions with visual cues (photographs or pictures) (SU2.3) relies on a partner's ability to provide a predictable sequence to activity (LS1.3) and use augmentative communication support to enhance the child's understanding of language and behavior (LS2.2).

Snapshot of Anita

Anita is a 3-year-old Language Partner who recently made the transition into an inclusive preschool classroom. In the classroom, she has learned to anticipate another person's actions in familiar routines and follow situational cues. She responds to simple language (e.g., "wash hands," "put in trash") as long as it is part of a classroom routine (e.g., bathroom time, snack time). In less familiar activities, such as going the school library or going on a trip to the zoo, Anita has more difficulty following situational and gestural cues. Thus, she is currently working on following situational and gestural cues in familiar and unfamiliar activities (SU2.1). Her partners recognize the need to use appropriate proximity and nonverbal behavior to encourage interaction (IS4.3) and use augmentative communication support to enhance Anita's understanding of language and behavior (LS2.2).

Library: When making the transition to a new activity, Anita is often in a high state of arousal and appears to be less responsive to the available gestural and situational cues. As a result, she is not yet responding to directions such as "Everybody get in line" and "Everybody sit down" without physical guidance and support. Her partners discussed the need to prepare Anita for these transitions using augmentative communication supports. For example, *simple signs can be used to emphasize verbal language* in unfamiliar activities (e.g., using the sign for SIT to reinforce the action of "Everybody sit down," using the sign for BOOK to represent "Teacher's reading"). As Anita will likely be somewhat disorganized in this novel activity, her partners also recognized that efforts would need to be made to *provide gestural cues in close proximity and in face-to-face orientation* with Anita.

Family outings: Anita has two older sisters, and the family often enjoys opportunities to visit the zoo, the aquarium, and the children's museum. Although Anita often follows her sisters' leads when eating and brushing her teeth, she is less responsive to their cues when on a special family outing. Her parents and educational team recognized the need to prepare Anita for these unfamiliar activities using augmentative communication supports. For example, *photographs of the setting can be used to emphasize situational cues.* When going to the zoo, Anita's parents can provide her with photographs of the zoo entrance, some of the animals that might be seen, the popcorn stand, and so forth. As Anita will likely be in a high arousal state in this novel activity, her partners also recognized that efforts would need to be made to *provide gestural cues in close proximity and in face-to-face orientation* before entering a crowded exhibit to enable her to process these nonverbal signals.

SU3 Uses familiar objects conventionally in play (Language Partner stage)

Child goal	Related partner goals	
Symbol Use SU3 Uses familiar objects conventionally in play	**Interpersonal Support** IS5 Partner provides developmental support IS7 Partner models appropriate behaviors	**Learning Support** LS1 Partner structures activity for active participation LS2 Partner uses augmentative communication support to foster development LS4 Partner modifies goals, activities, and learning environment
SU3 is not directly linked to JA, MR, or SR.	A child's ability to use a variety of objects in constructive play (SU3.1), use familiar objects conventionally toward him- or herself and others (SU3.2, SU3.3), and combine a variety of actions with objects in play (SU3.4) relies on a partner's ability to encourage imitation (IS5.1) and model appropriate constructive and symbolic play (IS7.3).	A child's ability to use a variety of objects in constructive play (SU3.1), use familiar objects conventionally toward him- or herself and others (SU3.2, SU3.3), and combine a variety of actions with objects in play (SU3.4) also relies on a partner's ability to provide a predictable sequence to the activity (LS1.3), use augmentative communication support to enhance the child's understanding of language and behavior (LS2.2), and design and modify activities to be developmentally appropriate (LS4.6).

Snapshot of Eric

Eric is a 2½-year-old Language Partner who participates in a home-based early intervention program. He has recently developed a passion for his favorite video characters, the Teletubbies, and often carries the stuffed characters around with him. Although he may occasionally hug the characters and pretend to dance with them, his ability to elaborate on these play schemes has not yet emerged. In fact, he occasionally uses them for sensory-motor exploration (e.g., sucking on their tags, flicking the dolls side to side in his peripheral vision). Because encouraging more appropriate and symbolic play is a priority for Eric's parents, Eric's current goals include combining a variety of actions with objects in play (SU3.4). His educational team and parents recognize the need to improve their consistency with modeling appropriate constructive and symbolic play

(IS7.3) and use augmentative communication support to enhance Eric's understanding of language and behavior (LS2.2).

Play with parents: Eric's parents had recently removed the majority of his Teletubbies toys from his playroom, due to concern about his preference to engage in sensory-motor play with these items. However, his team members recognized that to address his ability to combine a variety of actions, they would need to incorporate motivating and familiar materials. The team also discussed the need to model higher level symbolic play schemes that are appropriate for Eric's developmental level more consistently. Thus, with each Teletubbies character they would *model a logical sequence of actions related to daily living routines that are familiar to Eric (e.g., getting dressed, taking a bath, eating a meal).* Next, team members discussed the need to provide Eric with augmentative supports so that he could recall these actions in sequence. They designed *a Teletubbies play book* that would include a series of simple actions using photographs of each of the characters (i.e., Po, Laa-Laa, Tinky-Winky, and Dipsy) paired with simple picture symbols for actions (e.g., "Po turn on bath," "Po get undressed," "Po take bath").

Reading: Eric's interest in the Teletubbies is not limited to the stuffed dolls or videos. In fact, his interest in reading Teletubbies books with his parents has recently blossomed as his familiarity with these characters has grown. To address his current goals of combining a variety of actions in play, his educational team recognized that these reading activities would provide additional opportunities for practice. Thus, when reading simple picture books with these characters, his parents would make an effort to *have the dolls available to model symbolic play schemes with each page of the story.* Next, they discussed the need to provide consistency with the use of augmentative supports. Therefore, they *attached simple symbols in the book* that would highlight the series of targeted actions using photographs of the characters paired with simple picture symbols for the actions (e.g., "Laa-Laa dance," "Laa-Laa hug," "Laa-Laa wave good-bye").

	Child goal	Related partner goals	
SU4 Uses gestures and nonverbal means to share intentions (Language Partner stage)	*Symbol Use* SU4 Uses gestures and nonverbal means to share intentions	*Interpersonal Support* IS5 Partner provides developmental support IS7 Partner models appropriate behaviors	*Learning Support* LS2 Partner uses augmentative communication support to foster development LS4 Partner modifies goals, activities, and learning environment
	SU4 is not directly linked to JA, MR, or SR. *Related goals/objectives* Achievements in SU4 are related to achievements in JA4–JA6, MR3.3, and MR3.4.	A child's ability to use a variety of conventional and symbolic gestures (SU4.1) and use a sequence of gestures or nonverbal means in coordination with gaze (SU4.2) relies on a partner's ability to give guidance and feedback as needed for success in activities (IS5.4); model appropriate nonverbal communication and emotional expressions (IS7.1); and, in some situations, model appropriate behavior when child uses inappropriate behavior (IS7.4).	A child's ability to use a variety of conventional and symbolic gestures (SU4.1) and use a sequence of gestures or nonverbal means in coordination with gaze (SU4.2) also relies on a partner's ability to encourage the use of augmentative communication support to enhance the child's communication and expressive language (LS2.1), arrange the learning environment to promote child initiation (LS4.5), and "up the ante" to increase expectations appropriately (LS4.10).

Snapshot of Casey Casey is a 3-year-old Language Partner attending a preschool special education classroom who currently communicates using simple echolalic phrases (e.g., "go for a ride," "Okay . . . let's go," "You want a drink?," "uh-oh"). He also uses a range of early developing gestures such as physical manipulation gestures (e.g., pulling a caregiver toward a high shelf for a desired toy) or reenactment gestures (e.g., putting his shoes on to ask to go outside). Recently, he has also started using conventional contact gestures such as giving, pushing away, and pointing to pictures in a book. When items are further out of his reach and/or when he is asked to respond to simple questions (e.g., "Do you want _____?"), his gestural repertoire remains limited. He has not yet, for example, started to use a distal point, a head nod, or a head shake. Thus, his current objectives include using a variety of conventional and symbolic gestures (SU4.1). His partners recognized their need to work on modeling appropriate nonverbal communication and emotional expressions (IS7.1), 2) arranging the learning environment to promote child initiation (LS4.5), and 3) "upping the ante" to increase expectations appropriately (LS4.10).

Backyard play: One of Casey's most preferred activities is playing outside with his older brother. He enjoys swinging on the swings, using the climbing structure, and digging in the sandbox. Although he often simply follows his brother around, he occasionally requests new activities or assistance by pulling his brother's hand toward the area of the yard where he would like to play. Occasionally, his brother mistakes his intentions by sitting in the sandbox as opposed to getting on the swings. His educational team recognized the need to arrange the learning environment to promote more effective communicative signals. They discussed that it would be simple to *move the sandbox to a separate corner of the yard,* as this would allow for a clearer distinction when Casey is attempting to request this activity from a distance. Next, they recognized the need to *encourage Casey's brother to provide more consistent models* for nonverbal communicative means (e.g., a distal point) and "up the ante" by modeling and *waiting for this gesture* when his brother pulls on him.

Snack time at preschool: In his special education preschool classroom, Casey is often provided with a preferred snack when returning from the playground after recess. As he clearly has strong preferences regarding food, his educational team recognized this activity as an opportunity to provide more frequent opportunities to *model nonverbal conventional gestures* such as a head shake and a head nod. In addition, they discussed the need to *arrange the learning environment to include both preferred and nonpreferred items* so that Casey could learn to use a head nod for those items he desired and a head shake for undesired snacks. His team reflected that because Casey is just learning these more sophisticated gestures, *"upping the ante" would need to be carefully monitored,* as the ultimate goal is to promote his self-confidence, not to impart frustration should these gestures be challenging to use.

Linking Goals

**SU5
Uses words and word combinations to express meanings (Language Partner stage)**

Child goal	Related partner goals	
Symbol Use	*Interpersonal Support*	*Learning Support*
SU5 Uses words and word combinations to express meanings	IS1 Partner is responsive to child IS6 Partner adjusts language input IS7 Partner models appropriate behaviors	LS2 Partner uses augmentative communication support to foster development LS4 Partner modifies goals, activities, and learning environment
SU5 is not directly linked to JA, MR, or SR. *Related goals/objectives* Achievements in SU5 are related to achievements in JA3.4, JA4–JA6, MR3.3, and MR3.4.	A child's ability to use at least 5–10 words or echolalic phrases as symbols (SU5.2), use early relational words (SU5.3), and use a variety of advanced relational words (SU5.5) relies on a partner's ability to respond appropriately to the child's vocal and verbal signals to foster a sense of communicative competence (IS1.3), adjust the complexity of language input to the child's developmental level (IS6.2), and model "child-perspective" language (IS7.5).	A child's ability to use a variety of names for objects, body parts, and agents (SU5.4) and use a variety of relational meanings in word combinations also relies on a partner's ability to encourage the use of augmentative communication support to enhance the child's communication and expressive language (LS2.1), arrange the learning environment to promote child initiation (LS4.5), and "up the ante" to increase expectations appropriately (LS4.10).

Snapshot of Myles Myles is a 12-year-old Language Partner recently enrolled in a specialized day program for young adolescents. His family and educational team are excited about his recent burst in spoken language. Although he has always used a range of gestures, signs, and pictures to communicate, he is now using simple words and brief echolalic phrases that are associated with specific contexts (e.g., "Take a break," "Let's chase," "Go to pool"). His former education program had emphasized his use of picture symbols specifically for the purposes of requesting (i.e., behavior regulation), and Myles can now use symbols to communicate for a wide range of nouns (e.g., "milk," "cookies," "pool"). Although he uses a limited number action words (e.g., "open," "help," "go") and the names of familiar people (e.g., "Mom," "Dad"), he is not yet combining these words to form relational meanings in word combinations appropriate to his developmental level (e.g., "Mom open," "Daddy help"). In fact, his use of these words depends on rote associations he has made between words and specific contexts or verbal cues, such as highly practiced questions. Thus, his current objectives are geared to increase language flexibility and sophistication and include using a variety of relational meanings in word combinations (SU5.6) across contexts and partners. As a result, his educational team members are working on their ability to adjust the complexity of language input to Myles's developmental level (IS6.2) and encourage the use of augmentative communication support to enhance Myles's communication and expressive language (LS2.1).

Lunch: At school, Myles eats in his classroom with four other students. Each student is required to make his or her own meal by following a picture schedule board for assembling a sandwich and pouring a drink before sitting down at the table. Myles enjoys this activity, as cheese sandwiches are a desired food item. Nevertheless, he often gets stuck and needs assistance with opening the package of cheese slices and cutting the sandwich in half. As he is currently working on using relational meanings in word combinations, his educational team recognized the need to *adjust their language models to include agent + action phrases* (e.g., "Ms. Jones help," "Ms. Jones open," "Ms. Smith cut"). To foster Myles' independence with formulating these developmentally appropriate word combinations, the team discussed the use of *color-coded picture symbols*. Using the Boardmaker software program, which contains colorful clear clip art images and symbol boxes, photographic representations of agents (e.g., "Ms. Jones," "Ms. Smith," "Myles") were copied into a symbol box and highlighted using a thick red border and action clip art symbols (e.g., "open," "help," "cut," "eat") were highlighted using a thick green border. A sentence strip was then designed with a blank box with a red border and a blank box with a green border to elicit an agent + action word combination. Myles could then match the appropriate symbols to their appropriate location on the board to make a request for assistance (e.g., "Ms. Jones" + "open").

Journal: In his educational program, Myles and his classmates are required to complete a daily journal to reflect on a special activity of the day. This activity has always been challenging for Myles, given his difficulties with formulating language for sharing intentions for joint attention across context. As Myles is currently working on using relational meanings in word combinations, his educational team recognized this activity as an appropriate context for his partners to *adjust their language models to include developmentally appropriate relational meanings such as agent + action phrases* (e.g., "Myles swim," "Myles jump," "Myles eat"). To foster Myles' independence with formulating these developmentally appropriate word combinations during journaling, the team discussed the use of *color-coded picture symbols within a photo-journal containing digital photographs of events that have occurred.* Using the Boardmaker software program, photographic representations of agents (e.g., Myles, teachers, classmates) were copied into a symbol box and highlighted using a thick red border, and clip art symbols for actions (e.g., "swim," "jump," "eat") were highlighted using a thick green border. A sentence strip was then designed with a blank box with a red border and a blank box with a green border to elicit an agent + action word combination in his journal. Myles could then match the appropriate symbols to their appropriate location on the board to make comments about the photograph.

SU6 Understands a variety of words and word combinations without contextual cues (Language Partner stage)	Child goal	Related partner goals	
	Symbol Use SU6 Understands a variety of words and word combinations without contextual cues	**Interpersonal Support** IS4 Partner sets stage for IS4 Partner sets stage for engagement IS6 Partner adjusts language input	**Learning Support** LS1 Partner structures activity for active participation LS2 Partner uses augmentative communication support to foster development LS4 Partner modifies goals, activities, and learning environment
	SU6 is linked to SR1. **Linked objectives** SU6.2 Responds to a variety of familiar words and phrases (= SR1.6)	A child's ability to respond to his or her name (SU6.1) and respond to a variety of familiar words and phrases (SU6.2) relies on a partner's ability to secure the child's attention before communicating (IS4.2), use nonverbal cues to support understanding (IS6.1), and adjust the complexity of language input to the child's developmental level (IS6.2).	A child's ability to understand a variety of names, relational words, and relational meanings in word combinations without contextual cues (SU6.3–SU6.5) relies on a partner's ability to offer repeated learning opportunities (LS1.4), use augmentative communication support to enhance the child's understanding of language and behavior (LS2.2), and design and modify activities to be developmentally appropriate (LS4.6).

Snapshot of Aaron   Aaron is a 4½-year-old Language Partner who attends an inclusive preschool classroom. He has learned to anticipate another person's actions in familiar routines, follow situational cues, and even respond to early relational words involving basic actions (e.g., "jump," "clap," "stand," "sit") and modifiers (e.g., colors, size differences). He clearly has a preference for visual over auditory information, as he tends to rely on his visual memory to figure out where things go and what to do. Thus, he is less apt to respond to spoken directions that contain multiple pieces of information (e.g., an action and an object, a modifier and an object) and is currently working on responding to relational meanings in word combinations without contextual cues (SU6.5). His partners recognized the need to adjust the complexity of language input to Aaron's developmental level (IS6.2) and increase use of augmentative communication support to enhance his understanding of language and behavior (LS2.2).

Arts and crafts: Aaron typically requires physical guidance and repetition of verbal directions to complete simple art projects involving basic action words such as "cutting," "gluing," and "coloring" and nouns such as "heart," "star," and "circle," despite his knowledge of these word concepts. As a result, his educational team recognized the need to adjust the complexity of their language input during this activity to match his current objectives. Thus, their *language models would include two-word combinations of action + object* (e.g., "cut circle," "glue circle") as opposed to more lengthy directions (e.g., "Aaron, it's time to cut the circle with the scissors," "Now, glue the circle on the paper," "Color the circle with your yellow marker"). Next, they discussed Aaron's learning style and his preference for visual information over auditory information and recognized the need for an augmentative support in this activity. They provided *index cards with color-coded picture symbols* to denote the action + the object in each direction. Using the Boardmaker software program, clip art symbols for actions (e.g., "cut," "glue," "color") were highlighted using a thick green border and symbols for objects (e.g., "circle," "star," "paper") were highlighted using a thick yellow border.

Alphabet worksheets: Aaron is currently working on writing his name and tracing letters of the alphabet. An instructional assistant has provided both physical guidance and repetition of verbal directions to complete these projects, and Aaron has not progressed with respect to his understanding of the oral language. Thus, his educational team recognized the need to ensure that his teaching staff is consistently adjusting the complexity of their language input to match his current objectives. Thus, their *language models would include two-word combinations of action + object* (e.g., "write name," "trace letter") as opposed to more lengthy directions (e.g., "Aaron, write your name at the top of the paper," "Trace the letter *B* with your crayon. It is in your desk"). Next, they discussed Aaron's learning style and his preference for visual information over auditory information and recognized the need for an augmentative support in this alphabet activity. They provided *a within-task schedule with color-coded picture symbols indicated in a series of three steps* to denote the action + the object in each direction (e.g., "write name," "trace letter," "turn in paper").

Emotional Regulation: Mutual Regulation

MR1 Expresses range of emotions (Language Partner stage)

Child goal	Related partner goals	
Mutual Regulation	**Interpersonal Support**	**Learning Support**
MR1 Expresses range of emotions	IS1 Partner is responsive to child IS2 Partner fosters initiation IS5 Partner provides developmental support IS7 Partner models appropriate behaviors	LS1 Partner structures activity for active participation LS2 Partner uses augmentative communication support to foster development LS4 Partner modifies goals, activities, and learning environment
MR1 is linked to JA3 and SR3. *Linked objectives* MR1.1 Shares negative and positive emotion (= JA3.1) MR1.2 Understands and uses symbols to express a range of emotions (≈ JA3.2; = SR3.5) *Related goals* Achievements in MR1 are related to achievements in SU4–SU5.	A child's ability to share negative and positive emotion (MR1.1), respond to assistance offered by partners (MR1.2), and change emotional expression in familiar activities based on partner feedback (MR1.3) relies on a partner's ability to attune to the child's emotion and pace (IS1.2), wait for and encourage initiation (IS2.2), provide guidance on expressing emotions and understanding the cause of emotion (IS5.5), and model appropriate nonverbal communication and emotional expressions (IS7.1).	A child's ability to share negative and positive emotion (MR1.1) and understand and use symbols to express a range of emotions (MR1.2) also relies on a partner's ability to offer varied learning opportunities (LS1.5), use augmentative communication support to enhance the child's expression and understanding of emotion (LS2.3), and arrange the learning environment to enhance attention (LS4.4).

Snapshot of Joseph

Joseph is a 3-year-old Language Partner who demonstrates variable arousal states and often uses unconventional means to express his emotions. When he experiences emotional extremes, Joseph frenetically rocks his tense body back and forth while rapidly flapping his hands on either side of his head. His objectives include sharing negative and positive emotion (MR1.1) and understanding and using symbols to express a range of emotions (MR1.2). His partners are attempting to provide guidance on expressing emotions and understanding the cause of emotion (IS5.5) and offer varied learning opportunities (LS1.5).

Snack: His partners recognize that Joseph is having a difficult time expressing his emotions conventionally through the use of gestures, facial expressions, and gaze. To facilitate these abilities, his partners discussed the need to *offer a variety food options during snack,* to elicit a variety of strong emotional reactions from Joseph, as he has a very distinct set of food preferences. Therefore, by offering both preferred and nonpreferred items, his partners would have opportunity to *model positive and negative emotional reactions, both verbally and nonverbally,* and Joseph would be *encouraged to imitate these emotional reactions,* with the ultimate goal of spontaneously expressing these emotions using more conventional means.

Playground: After carefully observing Joseph on the playground, his team agreed that Joseph's rocking and flapping behaviors on the playground were associated with extreme joy and excitement. The following supports were discussed as appropriate measures for helping Joseph to express this emotion in a more conventional way. First, Joseph's *playground buddy would be encouraged to help provide guidance with expressing emotion* by commenting about his friend's emotions (e.g., "Joseph looks excited. Joseph's happy"). Next, Joseph's *playground buddy would be encouraged to invite Joseph to play a "chase" game,* which Joseph typically enjoys. Joseph's teachers also discussed the need to increase the availability of *picture icons representing positive emotions* during natural breaks in the play.

MR2 Responds to assistance offered by partners (Language Partner stage)

Child goal	Related partner goals	
Mutual Regulation	**Interpersonal Support**	**Learning Support**
MR2 Responds to assistance offered by partners	IS1 Partner is responsive to child IS2 Partner fosters initiation IS4 Partner sets stage for engagement	LS2 Partner uses augmentative communication support to foster development LS4 Partner modifies goals, activities, and learning environment
MR2 is linked to JA3. **Linked objectives** MR2.5 Attunes to changes in partners' expression of emotion (= JA3.3) MR2.6 Makes choices when offered by partners (≈ JA4.1)	A child's ability to soothe when comforted by partners (MR2.1), engage when alerted by partners (MR2.2), respond to bids for interaction (MR2.3), and attune to changes in partners' expression of emotion (MR2.5) relies on a partner's ability to respond to the child's emotion and pace (IS1.2), offer choices nonverbally and verbally (IS2.1), get down on the child's level when communicating (IS4.1), and use appropriate words and intonation to support optimal arousal level and engagement (IS4.4).	A child's ability to respond to changes in a partner's expression of emotion (MR2.4), make choices when offered by partners (MR2.6), and make changes to regulatory strategies based on partner feedback in familiar activities (MR2.7) relies on a partner's ability to use augmentative communication support to enhance the child's understanding of language and behavior (LS2.2), adjust the social complexity to support organization and interaction (LS4.1), and design and modify activities to be developmentally appropriate (LS4.6).

Snapshot of Andrew

Andrew is a 7-year-old Language Partner who often has a difficult time attending in large-group activities. His partners feel that their persistent attempts to verbally cue him to attend in such activities are often in vain. His objectives include responding to bids for interaction (MR2.3) and changing regulatory strategies based on partner feedback in familiar activities (MR2.7). His partners are attempting to use appropriate words and intonation to support optimal arousal and engagement (IS4.4) and adjust the social complexity to support Andrew's organization and interaction (LS4.1).

Swimming class: Andrew's team discussed several supports that would ensure his successful participation in his swimming class. First, they agreed that *an instructional assistant would be assigned to Andrew and one other peer in large-group activities.* This instructional assistant would be able to provide *individualized attention;* adjust his or her *use of proximity, affect, and language* to elicit Andrew's response to directions; and constantly monitor Andrew's arousal state. They felt that these supports would decrease the complexity of the group activity. Next, the team discussed the need for Andrew to have access to visual supports. They discussed having *an instructional assistant wear a elastic cord bracelet with several important icons* attached (e.g., STOP, ALL DONE, MORE, SWIM), which could be used in the event that Andrew is not consistent in responding to verbal instructions due to an increase in his arousal level resulting in dysregulation.

Lunch: In the cafeteria, Andrew's team discussed that his ability to respond to assistance offered by partners remains inconsistent due to his tendency to be socially disengaged (i.e., shut down) in this busy environment. As a result, they discussed the need to create a "quiet zone" and have Andrew *eat lunch at a small round table in the corner of the cafeteria with only a few of his classmates*. Next, they discussed the need to encourage Andrew's *classmates to support his engagement in regulatory strategies* when they observe him becoming unfocused. Specifically, when Andrew begins to shut down, his classmates can encourage him to begin *a familiar turn-taking memory game related to lunch* (e.g., "I'm going on a picnic, and my mom packed me a _____") in an effort to refocus his attention and keep him engaged.

MR3 Requests partners' assistance to regulate state (Language Partner stage)

Child goal	Related partner goals	
Mutual Regulation MR3 Requests partners' assistance to regulate state	**Interpersonal Support** IS2 Partner fosters initiation IS4 Partner sets stage for engagement IS7 Partner models appropriate behaviors	**Learning Support** LS1 Partner structures activity for active participation LS2 Partner uses augmentative communication support to foster development LS4 Partner modifies goals, activities, and learning environment
MR3 is linked to JA3–JA4. *Linked objectives* MR3.1 Shares negative emotion to seek comfort (≈ JA3.1) MR3.2 Shares positive emotion to seek interaction (≈ JA3.1) MR3.3 Requests help when frustrated (≈ JA4.3) MR3.4 Protests when distressed (≈ JA4.2, JA4.4) *Related goals/objectives* Achievements in MR3 are related to achievements in JA4, JA5.1, and SU4–SU5.	A child's ability to share negative emotion to seek comfort (MR3.1), share positive emotion to seek interaction (MR3.2), request help when frustrated (MR3.3), protest when distressed (MR3.4), and use language strategies to request a break (MR3.5) relies on a partner's ability to wait for and encourage initiation (IS2.2), use appropriate proximity and nonverbal behavior to encourage interaction (IS4.3), model appropriate non-verbal communication and emotional expressions (IS7.1), and model "child-perspective" language (IS7.5).	A child's ability to use language strategies to request a break (MR3.5), use language strategies to request a regulating activity or input (MR3.6), and use language strategies to exert social control (MR3.7) relies on a partner's ability to offer repeated learning opportunities (LS1.4), use augmentative communication support to enhance the child's expression and understanding of emotion (LS2.3), use augmentative communication support to enhance the child's emotional regulation (LS2.4), and arrange the learning environment to promote child initiation (LS4.5).

Snapshot of Fredrick

Fredrick is a 4-year-old Language Partner who consistently responds to experiences, both positive and negative, with differentiated emotional expressions. However, his partners have observed that he has difficulty directing these expressions to others to request their assistance with regulation. His partners are most concerned about Fredrick's poor frustration tolerance. His objectives include requesting help when frustrated (MR3.3) and using a language strategy to request a break (MR3.5). His partners acknowledge the need to use appropriate proximity and nonverbal behavior to encourage interaction (IS4.3) and arrange the learning environment to promote child initiation (LS4.5).

Puzzle center: Fredrick's team agreed that the following modifications were essential to help Fredrick to request assistance appropriately during center time within his preschool environment. First, they decided that the classroom teacher would supervise the puzzle center. While supervising this center, *she would sit on the floor close to Fredrick, making sure that she was facing his general direction and was within his field of vision*. Next, they discussed *having a few puzzles available* that were of interest to Fredrick but that *slightly exceeded his skill level* so that he would be motivated to request assistance. Finally,

Linking Goals | Language Partner Stage | 133

his team discussed the need to *raise their hands to gesture "What?" or "Where?"* after gaining his attention when he appeared to be becoming overwhelmed by a task. His team had observed that these gestures were frequently useful for triggering Fredrick's language strategies.

Drawing: Despite Fredrick's love of drawing, he frequently becomes distressed when he is unable to produce "perfect" artwork. He is, however, very willing to have his partners help him complete drawings. Both at school and at home, his partners recognized the need for a number of transactional supports. First, *two icons would be positioned at the upper corner of Fredrick's paper, one depicting "help" and the other depicting "break."* Next, the team members discussed that to encourage Fredrick's independent use of these icons, either through exchange or with a verbal production, *they would need to be encourage his efforts by responding quickly.* However, if Fredrick becomes frustrated and does not access the icons, his partners discussed the need to *direct his attention to them.* Finally, strategies to *request help and a break would be modeled verbally.*

MR4 Recovers from extreme dysregulation with support from partners (Language Partner stage)	Child goal	Related partner goals	
	Mutual Regulation MR4 Recovers form extreme dysregulation with support from partners	**Interpersonal Support** IS1 Partner is responsive to child IS3 Partner respects child's independence IS6 Partner adjusts language input IS7 Partner models appropriate behaviors	**Learning Support** LS2 Partner uses augmentative communication support to foster development LS3 Partner uses visual and organizational support LS4 Partner modifies goals, activities, and learning environment
	MR4 is not directly linked to JA, SU, or SR.	A child's ability to respond to partners' efforts to assist with recovery by moving away from an activity (MR4.1), respond to partners' use of behavioral strategies (MR4.2), respond to partners' use of simple language strategies (MR4.3), and decrease the intensity of dysregulated state due to support from partners (MR4.6) relies on a partner's ability to recognize signs of dysregulation and offer support (IS1.5); honor protests, rejections, or refusals when appropriate (IS3.4); adjust the quality of language input to the child's arousal level (IS6.3); and model appropriate nonverbal communication and emotional expressions (IS7.1).	A child's ability to respond to partners' use of simple language strategies (MR4.3), respond to partners' attempts to reengage in interaction or activity (MR4.4) and decrease the amount of time needed to recover from extreme dysregulation due to support from partners (MR4.5) relies on a partner's ability to use augmentative communication support to enhance the child's understanding of language and behavior (LS2.2), use augmentative communication support to enhance the child's expression and understanding of emotion (LS2.3), and modify the sensory properties of the learning environment (LS4.3).

Snapshot of Kerri

Kerri is a 2-year-old Language Partner who often experiences high arousal levels associated with extreme joy as well as extreme anger. During these instances, Kerri typically becomes very unfocused and her activity level becomes frenetic. Her objectives include responding to partners' use of behavioral strategies (MR4.2) and decreasing the amount of time to recover due to support from partners (MR4.5). Her partners are striving to adjust the quality of their language input to her arousal level (IS6.3) and modify the sensory properties of the learning environment (LS4.3).

Playground play: The playground environment is often overwhelming for Kerri. Kerri's partners discussed that to attempt to prevent extreme dysregulation, they often take Kerri to the playground early in the day, when it is less crowded. However, dysregulation continues to occur, as the environment is quite exciting for her. They discussed the need to use *simplified language (e.g., speaking in early word combinations)* to help Kerri anticipate the sequence of events at the playground. They also discussed the need to provide frequent opportunities for *climbing and jumping activities,* interspersed with swinging and sliding, as the former activities are consistently organizing for her.

Diapering: Her parents asked the team to help identify and develop mutual regulatory transactional supports for diapering, as they consistently have difficulty managing Kerri's activity level during this routine. The following recommendations were made. Her parents could *pair simple language, such as "Time for diaper," while showing Kerri a clean diaper.* Next, they could help her *"bunny jump" to the changing area,* in an effort to provide organizing movement and proprioceptive input before the activity. During the diaper change itself, they discussed the need to provide Kerri with her *pacifier, a soothing behavioral strategy for regulation* and *sing a rhythmic toddler song that Kerri could clap along to.* After the diaper change, they discussed the need to provide more opportunities for jumping during social routines (e.g., monkeys jumping on the bed).

Emotional Regulation: Self-Regulation

SR1 Demonstrates availability for learning and interacting (Language Partner stage)

Child goal	Related partner goals	
Self-Regulation	**Interpersonal Support**	**Learning Support**
SR1 Demonstrates availability for learning and interacting	IS1 Partner is responsive to child IS4 Partner sets stage for engagement IS5 Partner provides developmental support	LS1 Partner structures activity for active participation LS2 Partner uses augmentative communication support to foster development LS4 Partner modifies goals, activities, and learning environment
SR1 is linked to JA1 and SU6. *Linked objectives* SR1.1 Initiates bids for interaction (= JA1.1) SR1.2 Engages in brief reciprocal interaction (= JA1.2) SR1.3 Engages in extended reciprocal interaction (= JA1.3) SR1.6 Responds to a variety of familiar words and phrases (= SU6.2)	A child's ability to initiate bids for interaction (SR1.1), engage in brief and extended reciprocal interactions (SR1.2, SR1.3), inhibit actions and behaviors (SR1.5), and demonstrate emotional expression appropriate to the context (SR1.8) relies on a partner's ability to attune to the child's emotion and pace (IS1.2), use appropriate words/intonation to support optimal arousal level and engagement (IS4.4), and provide guidance on expressing emotions and understanding the cause of emotion (IS5.5).	A child's ability to respond to social and sensory experiences with differentiated emotions (SR1.4), respond to a variety of familiar words and phrases (SR1.6), and persist in tasks with reasonable demands (SR1.7) relies on a partner's ability to provide a predictable sequence to activities (LS1.3), offer repeated learning opportunities (LS1.4), use augmentative communication support to enhance the child's understanding of language and behavior (LS2.2), and design and modify activities to be developmentally appropriate (LS4.6).

Snapshot of Kyara

Kyara is a 4-year-old Language Partner in an inclusive preschool who demonstrates a bias toward a high arousal state. Her partners have noticed that when Kyara experiences a spike in her arousal level, regardless of whether it is associated with a positive or negative emotion, Kyara may seek out objects to spin. Her partners also discussed that she rarely laughs when experiencing a positive emotion. Her objectives include responding to social and sensory experiences with differentiated emotions (SR1.4) and responding to a variety of familiar words and phrases (SR1.6). Her partners are prioritizing their need to provide support in expressing emotions and understanding the cause of emotion (IS5.5) and using augmentative communication support to enhance her understanding of language and behavior (LS2.2).

Waking up: Kyara's parents noted that when Kyara wakes up, she is often bright and alert. They also recognized that she tends to be very interactive and less likely to be overwhelmed by social interactions. Based on these factors, Kyara's team agreed that using *social games,* such as *Peekaboo and tickle routines,* while Kyara is still in her bed would provide a face-to-face activity-based context to help Kyara differentiate her emotional expression. Her parents discussed the need to provide more consistent *models of nonverbal emotional expressions* as well as to provide *simple language models* that match Kyara's emotional state (e.g., "Kyara is happy") during these games.

Free play at preschool. Kyara's team discussed Kyara's persistent difficulty responding to the teacher's directive to choose a free-play activity at the end of circle time. This routine was familiar to Kyara, but she often waited for physical prompting to move to another area of the room. Kyara's team discussed the need to *implement a visual choice board to be presented along with the teacher's spoken directions* to help Kyara respond to her teacher's language. They also discussed the need to include *picture icons representing "happy," "sad," and "mad"* to provide a visual cue for Kyara when she experiences an increase in arousal associated with a strong emotion and begins to spin objects.

SR2
Uses behavioral strategies to regulate arousal level during familiar activities (Language Partner stage)

Child goals	Related partner goals	
Self-Regulation	*Interpersonal Support*	*Learning Support*
SR2 Uses behavioral strategies to regulate arousal level during familiar activities	IS1 Partner is responsive to the child IS3 Partner respects child's independence IS7 Partner models appropriate behaviors	LS1 Partner structures activity for active participation LS2 Partner uses augmentative communication support to enhance development LS4 Partner modifies goals, activities, and learning environment
SR2 is not directly linked to JA, SU, or MR.	A child's ability to use behavioral strategies to regulate arousal level during solitary and social activities (SR2.1), use behavioral strategies modeled by partners to regulate arousal level (SR2.2), and use behavioral strategies to engage productively in an extended activity (SR2.3) relies on a partner's ability to recognize and support the child's behavioral and language strategies to regulate arousal level (IS1.4); honor protests, rejections, or refusals when appropriate (IS3.4); and model appropriate behavior when the child uses inappropriate behavior (IS7.4).	A child's ability to use behavioral strategies to regulate arousal level during solitary and social activities (SR2.1), use behavioral strategies modeled by partners to regulate arousal level (SR2.2), and use behavioral strategies to engage productively in an extended activity (SR2.3) also relies on a partner's ability to offer repeated learning opportunities (LS1.4), use augmentative communication support to enhance the child's emotional regulation (LS2.4), and adjust the social complexity to support the child's organization and interaction (LS4.1).

Snapshot of Jeff

Jeff is a 5-year-old Language Partner who easily becomes overwhelmed, particularly when he is outdoors. He has limited behavioral strategies for self-regulation and often looks to adults to help him to maintain engagement in ongoing activities. He does this by crashing his body into an adult and burying his face in the adult's lap. His objectives include using behavioral strategies to regulate arousal level during solitary and social activities (SR2.1) and using behavioral strategies modeled by partners to regulate arousal level (SR2.2). His partners are striving to model appropriate nonverbal communication and emotional expressions when Jeff uses inappropriate behavior (IS7.1) and offer repeated learning opportunities for Jeff so that he can practice these strategies (LS1.4).

Playground at school: Jeff's team acknowledges that the playground is a particularly challenging environment for Jeff. He clearly feels insecure on the playground and often keeps in close proximity to adults. When other children approach him, Jeff runs full steam ahead into the closest adult. His team discussed the need to make environmental and activity modifications on the playground to set the stage for Jeff's success. Specifically, the team members discussed the need to *create an area of the playground for small-group quiet play* (e.g., drawing with sidewalk chalk, painting with water) that would be facilitated by a teacher. Next, they discussed that *proactively offering Jeff hugs paired with the phrase "want hug"* when they notice him becoming agitated and disengaged would be helpful. The team also decided to keep *a body sock* on the playground and facilitate Jeff's use of this support independently during those times he is seeking out intense sensory supports. A body sock is a Lycra tube that a child can crawl into that provides both pressure and a cocoon-like private place.

Waiting for the bus: This activity was considered a high priority by Jeff's educational team and family, as he clearly experiences great difficulty waiting for the bus and providing effective transactional supports on a busy street corner has been challenging for Jeff's partners. A number of interpersonal and learning supports were considered to support Jeff's development of effective behavioral strategies for self-regulation. First, his team agreed to proactively provide Jeff with *a transition object on the way to the bus stop*. Next, they decided to encourage Jeff to wear *headphones playing preferred music* during his wait. Finally, they decided to have his partners *carry picture icons on a key chain depicting other behavioral strategies* (e.g., jump, hug, squeeze hands, have a chewy snack). As these supports emphasize self-regulation, Jeff may ultimately use them with minimal encouragement from his adult partners and achieve more independence with this transition to school.

SR3 Uses language strategies to regulate arousal level during familiar activities (Language Partner stage)	Child goals	Related partner goals	
	Self-Regulation SR3 Uses language strategies to regulate arousal level during familiar activities	*Interpersonal Support* IS3 Partner respects child's independence IS6 Partner adjusts language input IS7 Partner models appropriate behaviors	*Learning Support* LS1 Partner structures activity for active participation LS2 Partner uses augmentative communication support to foster development LS4 Partner modifies goals, activities, and learning environment
	SR3 is linked to JA3 and MR1. *Linked objective* SR3.5 Uses symbols to express a range of emotions (≈ JA3.2, = MR1.2)	A child's ability to use language strategies to regulate arousal level during solitary activities (SR3.1), use language strategies modeled by partners to regulate arousal level (SR3.3), and use symbols to express a range of emotions (SR3.5) relies on a partner's ability to interpret problem behavior as communicative and/or regulatory (IS3.3), adjust the quality of language input to the child's arousal level (IS6.3), and model appropriate nonverbal communication and emotional expressions (IS7.1).	A child's ability to use language strategies to regulate arousal level during social interactions (SR3.2), use language strategies to engage productively in an extended activity (SR3.4), and use symbols to express a range of emotions (SR3.5) relies on a partner's ability to offer repeated learning opportunities (LS1.4), use augmentative communication support to enhance the child's expression and understanding of emotion (LS2.3), and adjust the social complexity to support organization and interaction (LS4.1).

Linking Goals   Language Partner Stage | 137

Snapshot of Seth   Seth is a 2½-year-old Language Partner who demonstrates a wide range of behavioral strategies for regulation (e.g., holding favorite objects, using his pacifier, jumping in place); however, he is not yet using his expanding vocabulary to assist with his emotional regulation. His objectives include using language strategies to regulate arousal level during social interactions (SR3.2) and using symbols to express a range of emotions (SR3.5). His partners are attempting to adjust the quality of their language input to his arousal level (IS6.3) and use augmentative communication support to enhance his expression and understanding of emotion (LS2.3).

Parent–toddler music class: Seth enjoys his music class, especially when the class gets to use the drums or play music games with a large parachute; however, there are many transitions both to and from favorite activities that cause him to experience relatively strong emotions. When these transitions occur, Seth immediately reaches for his pacifier. The team members recognized the value of this behavioral strategy, but they feel that helping Seth to expand his repertoire of regulatory strategies to include his use of emerging language would be appropriate at this time. To help Seth meet this objective, the team members discussed the need to *provide simple labels, both auditory and visual (i.e., picture symbols), to mark changes in his emotional state.* For example, they discussed using comments appropriate to his emotional states, such as "Seth is happy" when the parachute appears and "Seth is mad" when the drums are put away.

Play with older sibling: Seth adores his brother, Timothy, and the two boys frequently play together; therefore, the team agreed that facilitating Timothy's ability to model appropriate language strategies for Seth would be a critical priority in helping Seth to achieve his self-regulatory objectives. With some guided play experiences, Timothy will be encouraged to use *simplified language while taking Seth's perspective* to help Seth soothe himself when he becomes upset (e.g., "I'm okay"). In addition, Timothy will also be encouraged to *show Seth picture icons* that can help Seth to recall language strategies and labels to express his emotional state (e.g., HAPPY, MAD).

SR4 Regulates emotion during new and changing situations (Language Partner stage)	Child goals	Related partner goals	
	Self-Regulation SR4 Regulates emotion during new and changing situations	*Interpersonal Support* IS4 Partner sets stage for engagement IS5 Partner provides developmental support IS7 Partner models appropriate behaviors	*Learning Support* LS3 Partner uses visual and organizational support LS4 Partner modifies goals, activities, and learning environment
	SR4 is linked to SU2. *Linked objective* SR4.2 Follows situational and gestural cues in unfamiliar activities (= SU2.1)	A child's ability to participate in new and changing situations (SR4.1), use language strategies to regulate arousal level in new and changing situations (SR4.4), use language strategies to regulate arousal level during transitions (SR4.6), and use behavioral strategies to regulate arousal level during transitions (SR4.5) relies on a partner's ability to use appropriate proximity and nonverbal behavior to encourage interactions (IS4.3), give guidance and feedback as needed for success in activities (IS5.4), and model "child-perspective" language (IS7.5).	A child's ability to follow situational and gestural cues in unfamiliar activities (SR4.2) and use behavioral strategies to regulate arousal level in new and changing situations (SR4.3) relies on a partner's ability to use visual support to enhance smooth transitions between activities (LS3.3), arrange the learning environment to enhance attention (LS4.4), and alternate between movement and sedentary activities as needed (LS4.9).

Snapshot of Kristen

Kristen is a 6-year-old Language Partner attending kindergarten who continues to be challenged by transitions and new environments. Her team has observed that Kristen has difficulty utilizing effective regulatory strategies in these instances and often resorts to reciting scripts from her favorite cartoons and playing with strings on her clothing. They acknowledged that once Kristen is engaged in these behaviors to self-regulate, it is very difficult to reengage her. Her objectives include participating in new and changing situations (SR4.1) and using language strategies to regulate arousal level during transitions (SR4.6). Her partners are striving to model "child-perspective" language (IS7.5) and alternate between movement and sedentary activities as needed (LS4.9).

Music class: Kristen's team observed that Kristen spends the majority of her music class looking for and playing with strings. After careful consideration, her team agreed that several factors appeared to be contributing to her difficulties participating in music class. These included that the components of this activity did not follow any predictable pattern; that there were many transitions within this single activity; and that due to scheduling constraints, music class followed reading group, another sedentary activity. Her team agreed that the following transactional supports were needed to improve Kristen's participation. They discussed the need to incorporate increased opportunities for movement into each activity such as having Kristen *help the teacher set up the classroom (e.g., pushing the chairs into place)* before class, *march during songs,* and *pass out musical instruments* to her peers. They also discussed the need to capitalize on Kristen's strong rote auditory memory by modeling regulatory language for her and encouraging her to use it herself. Specifically, they agreed to *model the phrase "first . . . then . . . "* to help Kristen anticipate and cope with transitions.

Signing in: In Kristen's kindergarten classroom, the first activity of the day involves signing in (i.e., tracing the letters of one's name on a class roster). This activity remains quite challenging for Kristen, as the classroom is quite busy during this transition and appears to be overwhelming for her. Capitalizing on her language learning style, her team discussed the need to improve the predictability of this activity by *creating a rhyme about the routine* for Kristen to repeat to herself as she completed the various portions of her sign in process. They also decided to *move the sign-in easel* from the middle of the room to the entry area so that it was in a less congested area. Finally, they agreed to *affix colorful footprints on the floor* to provide Kristen with a clear visual path to follow (i.e., from the easel area to the cubby area and from the cubby area to the book area).

Linking Goals

SR5 Recovers from extreme dysregulation by self (Language Partner stage)

	Child goals	Related partner goals	
	Self-Regulation	*Interpersonal Support*	*Learning Support*
	SR5 Recovers from extreme dysregulation by self	IS1 Partner is responsive to child IS3 Partner respects child's independence IS7 Partner models appropriate behaviors	LS2 Partner uses augmentative communication support to foster development LS3 Partner uses visual and organizational support LS4 Partner modifies goals, activities, and learning environment
	SR5 is not directly linked to JA, SU, or MR.	A child's ability to remove him- or herself from overstimulating or undesired activity (SR5.1), use behavioral strategies to recover from extreme dysregulation (SR5.2), and use language strategies to recover from extreme dysregulation (SR5.3) relies on a partner's ability to recognize signs of dysregulation and offer support (IS1.5), offer breaks from interaction or activity as needed (IS1.7), allow the child to take breaks and to move about as needed (IS3.1), and model "child-perspective language" (IS7.5).	A child's ability to reengage in interaction or activity after recovery from extreme dysregulation (SR5.4), decrease the amount of time needed to recover from extreme dysregulation (SR5.5), and decrease the intensity of dysregulated state (SR5.6) relies on a partner's ability to use augmentative communication support to enhance the child's emotional regulation (LS2.4), use visual support to foster active involvement in group activities (LS3.6), and modify the sensory properties of the learning environment (LS4.3).

Snapshot of Melissa

Melissa is a 9-year-old Language Partner who is at risk for experiencing periods of dysregulation when her partners use complicated language and when she is required to share her preferred items. At these times, Melissa often attempts to strike out at children and adults who are in close proximity to her, which has led many peers to be wary of her. Her objectives include removing herself from overstimulating or undesired activity (SR5.1) and decreasing the intensity of her dysregulated state (SR5.6). Her partners are striving to recognize signs of dysregulation and offer support (IS1.5) and modify sensory properties of the learning environment (LS4.3).

Math class: Melissa's math class is currently using unit cubes in their math lesson. Melissa loves these brightly colored interlocking blocks and becomes very upset when other children in her desk cluster attempt to use them. Her team discussed the need to provide Melissa with *her own set of materials for this activity.* Her team also *compiled a list of behaviors that Melissa typically engages in before striking out at others* and discussed the need to encourage Melissa to *take a break to go to the water fountain* when they observe this sequence beginning to occur. Finally, the classroom staff agreed to make a concerted effort to *decrease the complexity of directions for her assignments,* as complex language can be challenging for Melissa to follow.

Weekly cooking activity: Melissa frequently strikes out at others during cooking group. Some of her dysregulation stems from the fact that she must alternate turns with her classmates when using the mixer. Her staff discussed this issue and determined that because other children needed to learn how to run the mixer, increased support was needed to help Melissa cope with sharing this preferred activity. Her team decided to implement *a visual support* to help Melissa understand job assignments. This support consisted of *a vertical display of photographs of the various equipment in the kitchen with adjacent and corresponding blank boxes in which the children's pictures could be mounted with Velcro.* Next, the team discussed Melissa's signals of dysregulation specific to the cooking class and agreed that when Melissa begins to grab at specific utensils and cover her ears that she should be encouraged to take *a break to go to the water fountain.* In addition, team members agreed to monitor Melissa for the other signals of escalating dysregulation that they had previously discussed and offer support when these signals are observed.

CONVERSATIONAL PARTNER STAGE

At the Conversational Partner stage, a child's partners have a significant impact on the child's ability to develop more advanced language abilities and social awareness of others, which allows for extended sequences of communicative exchanges and greater sensitivity to others' perspectives and emotional states. Through transactional supports, partners play a critical role in facilitating the transition to sentence grammar and the transition to conversational discourse. Partners, for example, help to foster more sophisticated language forms, as well as the requirements and social conventions for appropriate behavior in different social situations. Likewise, partners play a critical role in facilitating a child's ability to use emotional memories to assist with emotional regulation, to plan and prepare for experiences and interactions, and to negotiate with both adults and peers.

Ultimately, a child at this stage begins to develop a greater awareness that successful social exchange is achieved only through a cooperative effort with one's partner or partners and that the rules of social appropriateness vary across contexts. Accomplishments of both the child and his or her partners naturally lead to a greater frequency of successful and mutually satisfying exchanges across partners, both adults and peers. This growth has a bidirectional transactional impact, as the ability to engage in conversational discourse tailored to a specific partner contributes to greater enjoyment for the partner and, consequently, that partner's motivation to maintain and seek out engagement with the child in the future. As partners are increasingly experiencing pleasure during social interactions with the child, the child's social network expands through the development of relationships and friendships.

As outlined earlier, a number of considerations are essential when determining how to prioritize specific Transactional Support goals for the child's partners. The following charts are provided as a resource for educational teams as they determine which Transactional Support goals should be considered when addressing specific Social Communication and Emotional Regulation goals for a child at the Conversational Partner stage. *Please note that the objectives related to the goal areas in each table are defined in Chapter 8 of Volume I.* Following each goal area, "snapshot" examples of how each of the named Transactional Support goals might be modified based on the nature of a specific activity and child-specific factors (e.g., whether a child has a bias for a high state of arousal versus a low state of arousal, whether a child has relative strengths in visual or auditory learning) are provided.

Linking Goals | Conversational Partner Stage | 141

Social Communication: Joint Attention

JA1 Shares attention (Conversational Partner stage)

Child goal	Related partner goals	
Joint Attention JA1 Shares attention	**Interpersonal Support** IS4 Partner sets stage for engagement	**Learning Support** LS2 Partner uses augmentative communication support to foster development LS4 Partner modifies goals, activities, and learning environment
JA1 is linked to SR1. *Linked objective* JA1.1 Monitors attentional focus of a social partner (= SR1.2)	A child's ability to monitor the attentional focus of a social partner (JA1.1), secure attention to oneself prior to expressing intentions (JA1.2), understand nonverbal cues of shifts in attentional focus (JA1.3), and modify language based on what partners have seen or heard (JA1.4) relies on a partner's ability to use appropriate proximity and nonverbal behavior to encourage interaction (IS4.2) and explicitly share emotions, internal states, and mental plans with the child (IS4.4).	A child's ability to modify language based on what partners have seen or heard (JA1.4) and share internal thoughts or mental plans with partners (JA1.5) relies on a partner's ability to use augmentative communication support to enhance the child's understanding of language and behavior (LS2.2) and arrange the learning environment to enhance attention (LS4.4).

Snapshot of Reed

Reed is an 8-year-old Conversational Partner who is in a general education second-grade classroom with comprehensive supports to foster his success. His expressive language has progressed remarkably in the past year and he is now using a variety of sentence constructions including declaratives (e.g., "The boy is riding a bike") and early conjunctions (e.g., "There is a cow and he is eating the grass"). His ability to recognize that more information is needed when his listener has not seen an event has not yet emerged, as he may come home from school and report to his parents, "Look at my scratch," without elaborating with a comment such as "I fell on the playground" to clarify this event for his parents, who had not seen him fall. Thus, he is currently working on modifying his language forms based on what partners have seen or heard (JA1.4). His educational team recognized that to address this objective, his partners need to explicitly share emotions, internal states, and mental plans with Reed (IS4.4); arrange the learning environment to enhance attention and motivation (LS4.4); and provide augmentative communication support to enhance Reed's understanding of language and behavior (LS2.2).

Choice time: At the end of each lunch period, Reed and his classmates have the opportunity to play interactive games and/or engage in independent leisure activities in the classroom. Typically, Reed uses this time to read a book or to attempt to engage a peer in simple and routine interactive games. His team recognized that this learning environment could be modified to enhance Reed's attention and motivation by *introducing barrier games,* games that are typically played by two children in which each child can see something that the other child cannot. Each child would be required to share his or her perceptions by *providing an explicit verbal description* of a picture or an object that he or she can see behind his or her side of the barrier. Games would be selected to highlight situations that might lend themselves to multiple interpretations or plausible inferences and *a teacher would be present to model* how what someone sees affects what they know. For example, in the *Where's Waldo* books, which have large illustrations of very detailed scenes, sentence structures would need to be quite specific if Reed would like his friend to locate a character on the page without having to point (e.g., "The man is standing next to the ice cream stand," "The girl who is wearing a blue shirt is swimming in the lake"). Both the descriptions and the interpretation need to be accurate to attain a successful match. Likewise, discussion related to misinterpretations may be useful for illustrating different visual perspectives.

Language arts: As part of Reed's language arts curriculum, he is currently working on creating simple oral and written narratives. He has made great gains in this activity and is beginning to use simple sentences to describe the actions of the characters (e.g., "The boy is catching the frog," "The frog jumped out of the water," "The boy missed the frog"). Nevertheless, he is not yet recognizing the impact of perception or lack thereof on what a character knows, and he has a tendency to focus on concrete sequences of actions to the exclusion of consideration of character intents. His educational team recognized the need to achieve more consistency with sharing emotions, internal states, and mental plans by *augmenting the stories with Comic Strip Conversations* (Gray 1994a). These augmentative supports are designed to visually illustrate what a character might be seeing and thinking and, therefore, what they may say in a given social situation.

JA2 Shares emotion (Conversational Partner stage)

Child goal	Related partner goals	
Joint Attention JA2 Shares emotion	*Interpersonal Support* IS4 Partner sets stage for engagement IS5 Partner provides developmental support IS7 Partner models appropriate behaviors	*Learning Support* LS2 Partner uses augmentative communication support to foster development LS4 Partner modifies goals, activities, and learning environment
JA2 is linked to SU2, MR1, and SR3. **Linked objectives** JA2.1 Understands and uses early emotion words (= MR1.1, SR3.1) JA2.3 Understands and uses advanced emotion words (= MR1.2, SR3.2) JA2.5 Understands and uses graded emotions (= MR1.3, SR3.3) JA2.6 Understands nonverbal cues of emotional expression (= SU2.2)	A child's ability to use early and advanced emotion words (JA2.1, JA2.3), understand and use graded emotions (JA2.5), understand nonverbal cues of emotional expression (JA2.6), and describe plausible causal factors for the emotions of oneself and others (JA2.7) relies on a partner's ability to share emotions, internal states, and mental plans with the child (IS4.4); provide guidance on expressing emotions and understanding the cause of emotions (IS5.4); provide guidance for interpreting others' feelings and opinions (IS5.5); and model appropriate nonverbal communication and emotional expressions (IS7.1).	A child's ability to use early and advanced emotion words (JA2.1, JA2.3), describe others' emotional states with early and advanced emotion words (JA2.2, JA2.4), understand and use graded emotions (JA2.5), and describe plausible causal factors for the emotions of oneself and others (JA2.7) relies on a partner's ability to use augmentative communication support to enhance the child's expression and understanding of emotion (LS2.3) and adjust the social complexity to support organization and interaction (LS4.1).

Snapshot of Julia

Julia is a 5-year-old Conversational Partner who just finished her second year of an inclusive preschool program. She is a talkative child who is described as having an exceptional vocabulary and a broad range of sentence constructions. Her parents, however, have noticed that Julia often displays only extreme, all-or-nothing emotional expressions. Although she has developed a range of early emotion words (e.g., "happy," "mad," "sad") as well as more advanced emotion words (e.g. "silly" "scared," "bored"), she has not yet achieved the ability to understand and express emotions with regard to their relative intensity. When she is mad, for example, she displays an extreme emotional state of very angered. Thus, her current objectives include understanding and using graded emotions (JA2.5). Her partners, therefore, are striving to provide guidance on expressing emotions and understanding the cause of emotions (IS5.4) and to use augmentative communication support to enhance Julia's expression and understanding of emotion (LS2.3).

Summer camp games: Because Julia is preparing for kindergarten, her educational program during the summer months includes an opportunity to develop reciprocal relationships with peers in a small group context. The first activity of camp typically involves a cooperative game such as an obstacle course, follow the leader, and/or completing a large floor puzzle as a group. Although Julia enjoys and succeeds in these activities, she may experience an extreme shift to a high state of arousal should her expectations be violated (e.g., a friend takes a longer turn, a piece of the puzzle is missing). Although she may use a language strategy to express that she is "mad," this emotional expression does not seem to guide her coping behaviors to match the intensity of the relatively mild causal factor. Thus, she can be inconsolable, use an extremely loud vocal volume, and lash out at her peers. Her educational team members recognized that greater consistency in supporting Julia to express graded emotions would be needed. Staff members would be encouraged to *model language of graded emotions using the vocal volume and nonverbal behavior* one might expect at this lesser intensity (e.g., "Julie, I'd be a bit *bothered* by that, too . . . "). Next, they discussed the need to implement an augmentative support that would help Julia measure the intensity of an emotion state by *providing a visual to represent different emotional degrees associated with a numeric or color-coded scale.* With this support, the camp staff could begin modeling statements such as "I feel a 2 happy right now," and "Now, I am a 4 happy," or "I am as mad as bright red!"

Bedtime story: Julia enjoys reading stories with her mother and father and often asks her parents to read something new. Typically, this is a positive time of the day for Julia and her parents to connect emotionally. Nevertheless, when a story includes a frightening element, she may quickly become dysregulated as she shifts from a content to terrified state in a matter of seconds, even if the story does not involve an event that would warrant an intense reaction. She appears to have a strong rote associative emotional memory with the concept of *scared* and the dramatic emotional display. Thus, her educational team helped Julia's parents to create an augmentative support, *a "scared" meter bookmark* that could be used as *a visual means to help Julia measure the intensity of her emotional state by representing different emotional degrees* (e.g., a scale of 1–5). In addition, time could be spent before reading the story to discuss different events associated with each graded numeric rating on the meter to foster Julia's understanding of these gradations.

**JA3
Shares intentions
for a variety
of purposes
(Conversational
Partner stage)**

Child goal	Related partner goals	
Joint Attention JA3 Shares intentions for a variety of purposes	**Interpersonal Support** IS1 Partner is responsive to child IS2 Partner fosters initiation IS3 Partner respects child's independence IS7 Partner models appropriate behaviors	**Learning Support** LS2 Partner uses augmentative communication support to foster development LS4 Partner modifies goals, activities, and learning environment
JA3 is linked to MR4. **Linked objectives** JA3.1 Shares intentions to regulate the behavior of others (= MR4.3) JA3.2 Shares intentions for social interaction (= MR4.4) JA3.3 Shares intentions for joint attention (= MR4.5) **Related goals/objectives** Achievements in JA3 are related to achievements in JA5.2 and SU4–SU5.	A child's ability to share intentions to regulate the behavior of others (JA3.1), for social interaction (JA3.2), and for joint attention (JA3.3) relies on a partner's ability to respond appropriately to the child's signals to foster a sense of competence (IS1.3), provide a balance of initiated and respondent turns (IS2.3), and model a range of communicative functions (IS7.2).	A child's ability to share intentions to regulate the behavior of others (JA3.1), for social interaction (JA3.2), and for joint attention (JA3.3) also relies on a partner's ability to use augmentative communication support to enhance the child's communication and expressive language (LS2.1) and provide activities to promote initiation and extended interaction (LS4.8).

Snapshot of Jun

Jun is a 9-year-old Conversational Partner who is participating in a partially inclusive third-grade classroom. He is an outgoing and curious young boy who has stated that he "wants to have friends" among his classmates and peers. The frequency of his spontaneous bids for communication has increased significantly in the past year, and he is now more likely to share intentions for social interaction. For example, he may verbally greet his peers on arriving at school (e.g., "Hey, everyone!"), he may call to gain the attention of another person (e.g., "Jason, can I play?"), and he may regulate interactions to keep turn-taking going (e.g., "Hey, Sarah, it's your turn"). He is not yet praising partners who have succeeded at a game or an activity and he is not yet expressing empathy about a positive or negative experience of a partner. Thus, his current objectives include sharing intentions for social interaction (JA3.2). His educational team recognizes that Jun's partners, both adults and peers, need to achieve greater consistency with modeling a range of communicative functions and rules of conversation (IS7.2) and providing augmentative communication support to enhance Jun's communication and expressive language for these functions (LS2.1).

Gym class: In the gymnasium, Jun is excited to engage in cooperative play with his third-grade classmates and will greet his peers and request to take turns in the games (e.g., basketball, relays). He is not yet praising them for their successes and/or commenting if they are disappointed (i.e., expressing empathy). His educational team discussed that *peer training* is a critical support. If *the gym teacher provides an explicit reminder for the students to praise each other* after taking turns in an activity, this will increase the frequency of models for Jun. Next, his special education resource teacher suggested an augmentative support for fostering these functions of communication in this activity. *A teammate banner* could be developed and placed in a visible location on the gymnasium wall. The banner could include a written model (e.g., *Teammates let each other know when they do a good job*) and an area for gold stars (i.e., a praise chart). Every time a student praises another peer, a star could be placed on the banner.

Social skills group: Jun participates in a small social skills group with three other children his age, which is led by a speech-language pathologist and an occupational therapist. In each session, the children decide a game to play, practice conversations, and prepare for social events that are scheduled to occur in the classroom in upcoming weeks. The session is videotaped so that *the videotape can be replayed to illustrate models* of specific objectives such as a child succeeding at a targeted behavior (e.g., taking turns with a peer, playing a game suggested by a peer). Jun's education team recognized the need in this context to provide explicit models for praising each other and expressing empathy. Next, *a helper card* could be used as an augmentative support to remind each student to praise another (e.g., "If I see a friend do a good job, I can say, 'That's cool!'").

JA4 Shares experiences in reciprocal interaction (Conversational Partner stage)

Child goal	Related partner goals	
Joint Attention JA4 Shares experiences in reciprocal interaction	**Interpersonal Support** IS1 Partner is responsive to child IS2 Partner fosters initiation IS5 Partner provides developmental support IS7 Partner models appropriate behaviors	**Learning Support** LS1 Partner structures activity for active participation LS2 Partner uses augmentative communication support to foster development LS3 Partner uses visual and organizational support LS4 Partner modifies goals, activities, and learning environment
JA4 is linked to SR1. **Linked objective** JA4.1 Shows reciprocity in speaker and listener roles to share experiences (= SR1.3)	A child's ability initiate a variety of conversational topics (JA4.2), gauge length and content of conversational turns based on his or her partners (JA4.6), and develop friendships with partners who share interests (JA4.8) relies on a partner's ability to be responsive to the child's communicative signals to foster a sense of competence (IS1.3), provide a balance of initiated and respondent turns (IS2.3), provide guidance for success in interaction with peers (IS5.1), and model a range of communicative functions and rules of conversation (IS7.2).	A child's ability to initiate interaction and share experiences with a friend (JA8.3) relies on a partner's ability to modify the environment to create turn-taking opportunities and leave spaces for the child to fill in (LS1.2), use augmentative communication support to enhance the child's communication and expressive language (LS2.1), use visual and organizational support to foster active involvement in group activities (LS3.6), and adjust the social complexity to support organization and interaction (LS4.1).

Snapshot of Trent

Trent is a 9-year-old Conversational Partner who is described as the teacher's pet in his third-grade classroom. This reputation has developed as a result of his strong desire to please adults and his interest in a range of academic subjects. His conversational topics have expanded within the past year to include school-related topics (e.g., how flowers grow), family-related topics (e.g., his pet hamster), as well as subject-related topics (e.g., natural disasters, the solar system). Trent continues to have difficulty forming peer relationships; however, he has not yet developed a sense of the topics of conversation that are of interest to his peers. This has led to an increased rift between Trent and his classmates, who are beginning to be put off by Trent's preference for discussing topics that they have heard countless times. Thus, his current objectives include initiating and maintaining conversations that relate to a partner's interests (JA4.3). His educational team recognizes that team members need to achieve greater consistency in providing guidance for success in interaction with peers (IS5.1) and using visual and organizational supports to foster Trent's active involvement in group activities (LS3.6).

Snack: In Trent's classroom, the students look forward to their morning snack break, as this is their first opportunity to chat with their friends about the events of the day before. Trent clearly recognizes this opportunity as a chance to connect with his classmates but has slowly been losing his friends' interest over the past couple of months due to his unusual selection and limited range of topics. His educational team discussed the need for Trent to have more explicit guidance for success in interaction with peers, as he typically has not had adult support in this area. Thus, *an instructional aide would remain present during this activity to monitor and, when necessary, provide strategic support to foster more successful and positive interactions.* Next, Trent's special education resource teacher suggested a visual and organizational support to foster Trent's active involvement in his peer's conversations. *A conversation map* could be created as an art project or a language arts activity. On this map, each student would be asked to draw a picture of themselves and list favorite topics related to their family (e.g., recent vacations), favorite topics related to school (e.g., favorite recess games, favorite snacks, upcoming holidays), and favorite subjects (e.g., Harry Potter movies, Captain Underpants books). These maps could then be placed in a visible location on the classroom wall so that Trent could refer to them during snack time to expand his range of topics related to a peer's interests.

Recess: As Trent would not have access to conversation maps at recess, his educational team recognized the need for explicit modifications to this activity to foster Trent's success in tailoring his conversational topics to his peers. The team decided that before recess, Trent's *special education resource teacher would meet with Trent to review the conversation maps* to prepare him for recess. A visual and organizational support to foster Trent's active involvement in his peer's conversations at recess could then be developed by creating *a pocket pal.* This pocket pal, a small pocket-size notebook, could list each of his classmates' names and several of their favorite recess activities and conversational topics. Trent could then glance at this pocket pal during recess.

JA5 Persists and repairs communication breakdowns (Conversational Partner stage)	Child goal	Related partner goals	
	Joint Attention JA5 Persists and repairs communication breakdowns	*Interpersonal Support* IS4 Partner sets stage for engagement IS5 Partner provides developmental support	*Learning Support* LS2 Partner uses augmentative communication support to foster development LS4 Partner modifies goals, activities, and learning environment
	JA5 is not directly linked to SU, MR, or SR. *Related objective* Achievements in JA5 are related to achievements in JA4.3.	A child's ability to recognize breakdowns in communication and request clarification (JA5.3) and modify language and behavior based on a partner's change in agenda and/or emotional reaction (JA5.4, JA5.5) relies on a partner's ability to share emotions, internal states, and mental plans with the child (IS4.4); attempt to repair breakdowns verbally or nonverbally (IS5.2); and provide guidance for interpreting others' feelings and opinions (IS5.5).	A child's ability to recognize breakdowns in communication and request clarification (JA5.3) and experience feelings of success and confidence during interactions (JA5.6) relies on a partner's ability to use visual support to foster active involvement in group activities (LS3.6) and adjust the social complexity to support organization and interaction (LS4.1).

Snapshot of Shannon

Shannon is an 8-year-old Conversational Partner who is described as a talkative and boisterous student in her second-grade program. She is a persistent communicator, who uses a range of sentence constructions to tell a story and engage in a conversational topic with a friend. Her range of topics remains somewhat limited, however, and she often initiates the same topic over and over again (e.g., favorite scenes in a Dr. Seuss movie). Her peers occasionally lose interest with these topics and express their frustration or boredom using facial expressions (e.g., rolling their eyes) and/or gestures (e.g., putting their chin on their hand). Shannon does not recognize these nonverbal cues, so she is likely to continue droning on about a topic despite the absence of interested listeners. Her current objectives include modifying language and behavior based on a partner's emotional reaction (JA5.5). Her educational team recognizes that Shannon's partners, both adults and peers, need to achieve greater consistency in explicitly sharing their emotions, internal states, and mental plans with Shannon (IS4.4) through verbal as opposed to nonverbal means and providing visual support to foster active involvement in these group activities (LS3.6).

Speech-language therapy: Shannon participates in small-group speech-language therapy to practice activities that she may have difficulty with in more complex social contexts. These sessions typically are designed as planned activity routines to practice for larger group activities that will occur in upcoming weeks in her educational programming such as recess games, conversations, and cooperative group work. Shannon is outgoing in this setting and enjoys "snack-n-chat," an activity designed to enhance her success in social conversations. Shannon's speech-language pathologist discussed the need for *peer training* to support Shannon's ability to modify language and behavior based on her partner's emotional reaction. *Each child would be encouraged to share his or her emotional state in relation to a topic verbally* so that the child speaking would have a clearer sense of his or her success with a given topic. Next, Shannon's speech-language pathologist discussed developing a visual and organizational support for this group activity. *A conversation helper* could be developed and placed in a visible location on the floor in between the children. This visual could include a written model (e.g., "I can let my friend know how I feel about this topic").

Cooperative group work: In her second-grade classroom, Shannon typically participates in at least one cooperative group work activity per day. Although the topic in these activities is typically predetermined (e.g., taking turns gluing on the parts of a flower), Shannon occasionally drifts off topic and initiates a discussion about the characters in a Dr. Seuss movie and their various antics. Although Shannon's classmates may communicate annoyance with facial expressions (e.g., looking away from Shannon) and/or gestures (e.g., making a stopping motion), Shannon typically misses these cues and continues on her current train of thought. Her special education resource teacher discussed the need for *peer training* to support Shannon's ability to modify language and behavior based on her partner's emotional reaction. *Each student would be encouraged to share his or her emotional state in relation to a topic verbally* so that Shannon would not have to rely on her interpretation of their nonverbal social cues. Next, a visual and organizational support for this group activity would be developed. *A cooperative group conversation starter board* could be developed and placed in a visible location on the table in between the students. Conversation starters would include a list of appropriate topics and comments such as praising a classmate (e.g., "I like what you did"), requesting permission (e.g., "Can I use the glue after you're done?"), and commenting about immediate events (e.g., "This project is so cool!").

Social Communication: Symbol Use

SU1 Learns by imitation, observation, instruction, and collaboration (Conversational Partner stage)

Child goal	Related partner goals	
Symbol Use SU1 Learns by imitation, observation, instruction, and collaboration	**Interpersonal Support** IS5 Partner provides developmental support IS7 Partner models appropriate behaviors	**Learning Support** LS1 Partner structures activity for active participation LS2 Partner uses augmentative communication support to foster development LS3 Partner uses visual and organizational support LS4 Partner modifies goals, activities, and learning environment
SU1 is linked to MR3 and SR4. *Linked objectives* SU1.2 Uses behaviors modeled by partners to guide behavior (= MR3.3) SU1.3 Uses internalized rules modeled by adult instruction to guide behavior (= SR4.1) SU1.4 Uses self-monitoring and self-talk to guide behavior (= SR4.3) SU1.5 Collaborates and negotiates with peers in problem solving (= MR3.4)	A child's ability to use behaviors modeled by partners to guide social behavior (SU1.2), use internalized rules modeled by adult instruction to guide behavior (SU1.3), and use self-monitoring and self-talk to guide behavior (SU1.4) relies on a partner's ability to provide guidance and feedback as needed for success in activities (IS5.3), model appropriate behavior when the child uses inappropriate behavior (IS7.4), and model "child-perspective" language and the use of self-talk (IS7.5).	A child's ability to use internalized rules modeled by adult instruction to guide behavior (SU1.3), use self-monitoring and self-talk to guide behavior (SU1.4), and collaborate and negotiate with peers in problem solving (SU1.5) relies on a partner's ability to provide a predictable sequence to activities (LS1.3), use augmentative communication support to enhance the child's understanding of language and behavior (LS2.2), use visual support to foster active involvement in group activities (LS3.6), and adjust the social complexity to support organization and interaction (LS4.1).

Snapshot of Carlos

Carlos, a 5-year-old Conversational Partner, just entered kindergarten several months ago. He communicates through a range of early sentence constructions and is an early reader. In his first couple of months in kindergarten, he has developed a strong relationship with his general education teacher and has begun to respond to direct instruction for specific classroom rules, particularly because each rule is written down near the area of the room where it should be applied. For example, near the snack tables, a sign says, "Wash hands before eating," and near the circle time area, a sign says, "Raise your hand before talking." Outside of these familiar classroom routines and basic rules, Carlos has not yet developed his use of inner language, or self-talk, to guide his behavior through more stressful activities such as a fire drill. When this occurred for the first time, for example, Carlos screeched, covered his ears, and pulled away from his teacher when she attempted to redirect him. There was no improvement the second time, as Carlos bolted out of the classroom ahead of the group and ran outside without supervision. His actions did not appear to be guided and thoughtful and suggested the need to support Carlos's ability to use self-monitoring and self-talk to guide his behavior (SU1.4). His educational team discussed the need to model "child-perspective" language and the use of self-talk (IS7.5) and use augmentative communication support to enhance Carlos' understanding of language and behavior in this novel context (LS2.2).

Fire drill: Responding to the fire drill has been challenging for Carlos, and he appears to be reacting to the alarm using unconventional behavioral strategies for self-regulation (e.g., bolting, screeching) as well as more conventional behavioral strategies for self-regulation (e.g., covering his ears). Although his use of simple sentence constructions has emerged, Carlos has not yet recognized how language can help him through these stressful circumstances. His general education teacher discussed the need to *model self-talk to all of the children before the next fire drill.* An augmentative support such as *a Social Story* (Gray, 1994a, 1994b) about *reaching safety during a fire* could be developed to emphasize positive self-talk (e.g., "Sometimes the fire alarm goes off and makes a loud sound. Sometimes I am scared, but this helps let us know we should go outside to safety. I can cover my ears and line up with my class. When we are outside, the alarm will not be so loud").

Circle time: A number of social scenarios seem to come up during circle time. Carlos may blow in his peers' ears to get their attention while the teacher is talking. He may lean against a classmate despite the classmate's expression of discomfort with this, and he may chew on his clothing while listening to a story. His teacher discussed the need to provide more consistent *models of self-talk from Carlos' perspective during these instances* to direct Carlos to use more conventional strategies for communicating with others and for regulating his arousal (e.g., "I can talk to my friends *after* circle time," "I can ask to sit in a chair if I am tired," "I can ask for a chewy tube when I am listening to stories"). To remind Carlos of this language, the teacher and instructional assistants could develop *a key chain of helper cards* to provide these models in writing and show them to Carlos when the need arises.

SU2 Understands nonverbal cues and nonliteral meanings in reciprocal interactions (Conversational Partner stage)

Child goal	Related partner goals	
Symbol Use SU2 Understands nonverbal cues and nonliteral meanings in reciprocal interactions	**Interpersonal Support** IS4 Partner sets stage for engagement IS7 Partner models appropriate behaviors	**Learning Support** LS1 Partner structures activity for active participation LS2 Partner uses augmentative communication support to foster development LS4 Partner modifies goals, activities, and learning environment
SU2 is linked to JA2. **Linked objective** SU2.2 Understands nonverbal cues of emotional expression (= JA2.6)	A child's ability to understand nonverbal cues of turn taking and topic change (SU2.1) and understand nonverbal cues of emotional expression (SU2.2) relies on a partner's ability to use appropriate words and intonation to support optimal arousal level and engagement (IS4.3); share emotions, internal states, and mental plans with the child (IS4.4); and model appropriate nonverbal communication and emotional expression (IS7.1).	A child's ability to understand nonverbal cues and nonliteral meanings of humor and figures of speech, teasing, sarcasm, and deception (SU2.3, SU2.4) relies on a partner's ability to offer varied learning opportunities (LS1.5), use augmentative communication support to enhance the child's understanding of language and behavior (LS2.2), and design and modify activities to be developmentally appropriate (LS4.6).

Snapshot of Chantel

Chantel is an 8-year-old second grader who is described as an expert mimic. One of her favorite activities involves reciting lines from her favorite movies and/or storybooks while looking at her body movements, facial expressions, and gestures in the mirror.

When she displays her emotional state, she tends to form a rote association with an entire package of accompanying nonverbal cues. For example, when she is mad, she displays this emotion by using a dramatic display that includes exaggerated gestures (i.e., hands on her hips paired with stomping her feet), vocal volume (i.e., a loud and sharp voice), and facial expressions (i.e., an exaggerated angered expression). Similarly, when a peer or an adult attempts to convey an emotional state, Chantel relies on the full package of gestures, facial expressions, and intonation to interpret their state. Thus, her educational team recognizes the need to prioritize her understanding of nonverbal cues of emotional expressions (SU2.2) by explicitly sharing emotional states that are paired with nonverbal cues (IS4.4) and using augmentative communication support to enhance Chantel's understanding of language and behavior (LS2.2).

Reading group: Chantel has typically enjoyed reading activities, particularly those storybooks that have elaborate illustrations paired with simple dialogue that she can mimic. Nevertheless, the stories in her second-grade reading group have significantly fewer pictures paired with the text and her ability to mimic or role play the actions, intentions, and emotional states of the characters in these stories is therefore limited. Her educational team recognized this activity as an opportunity to support Chantel's understanding of nonverbal cues such as gestures and intonation, as the children are often asked to read dialogue to one another. The children could be asked to *role play specific characters* in the stories using only one type of nonverbal cue (i.e., a gesture, a facial expression, and a voice) so that the other students could guess the emotional state. An augmentative support could be developed to foster Chantel's understanding that specific gestures and/or a specific voice give clues as to a character's emotions. The team discussed creating *a clue chart for reading group* with an answer key under the following categories: gestures (movements we make with our hands and body), faces (movements we make with our eyes, nose, and mouth), and voices (sounds that we make when we talk). With each category, the child can add new concepts that have been learned (e.g., a mad gesture is hands on hips, an excited face has raised eyebrows, a sad voice is shaky).

Recess: Chantel's educational team recognized recess as another critical activity for supporting her interpretation of nonverbal cues such as gestures, faces, and voices, as frequent communication breakdowns occur when Chantel requests to play with a child or group of children and misreads their cues. First, *peer training would be used to encourage classmates to pair their gestures and/or faces with a verbal discussion* of their emotional state. For example, if a child is happy and would like Chantel to join her, she might smile broadly and state, "I'd be happy to play with you." In contrast, if a group of children are playing an established game and are disinterested, they might use an extended hand gesture paired with the statement, "We're busy right now." Next, an augmentative support could be encouraged to foster Chantel's understanding that specific gestures and/or a specific voice give clues as to her classmates' emotions, *as each classmate could be taught simple signs* for emotions to pair a visual cue with their use of emotion words (e.g., "happy," "mad," "sad," "bored").

Linking Goals | Conversational Partner Stage | 151

SU3 Participates conventionally in dramatic play and recreation (Conversational Partner stage)

Child goal	Related partner goals	
Symbol Use	*Interpersonal Support*	*Learning Support*
SU3 Participates conventionally in dramatic play and recreation	IS5 Partner provides developmental support IS7 Partner models appropriate behaviors	LS1 Partner structures activity for active participation LS3 Partner uses visual and organizational support LS4 Partner modifies goals, activities, and learning environment
SU3 is not directly linked to JA, MR, or SR.	A child's ability to take on a role and engage in dramatic play (SU3.4), play in a common activity with other children (SU3.5), and take on a role and cooperate with peers in dramatic play (SU3.6) relies on a partner's ability to provide guidance for success in interaction with peers (IS5.1), provide guidance for interpreting others' feelings and opinions (IS5.5), and model appropriate dramatic play and recreation (IS7.3).	A child's ability to use logical sequences of actions in play about less familiar events (SU3.3), take on a role and cooperate with peers in dramatic play (SU3.6), and participate in rule-based group recreation (SU3.7) relies on a partner's ability to provide a predictable sequence to activities (LS1.3), use visual support to foster active involvement in group activities (LS3.6), adjust the social complexity to support organization and interaction (LS4.1), and design and modify activities to be developmentally appropriate (LS4.6).

Snapshot of John

John is a 10-year-old Conversational Partner who recently entered an inclusive educational program as a fourth grader. He is very interested in his new classmates and wishes to join them in after-school recreation activities such as soccer and Little League. At school, however, John struggles to keep up with his peers during playground games and in gym class. He has a difficult time learning the rules, and when he finally does learn them, he can quickly become distressed if rules are not followed precisely during a game, as is often the case. He has a temper that flares quickly and easily when he feels a rule has been broken or when he feels another student has done something he perceives as violating appropriate behavior. Although he desperately wants to fit in, his tendency to melt down and become overwhelmed due to the complexity of the rules and competition makes him stand out. Due to this vulnerability, he is beginning to be the target of teasing and bullying, especially by one student who knows the triggers to set him off. His parents and educational team recognize that supporting John's success in recreational activities should be prioritized, as he so wants to engage in these activities with his peers, but his self-esteem is currently quite fragile due to his challenges. As a result, his current objectives include a focus on participating in rule-based group recreation (SU3.7). His partners, therefore, are striving to model appropriate dramatic play and recreation (IS7.3) and design and modify activities to be developmentally appropriate (LS4.6).

Adaptive physical education (APE): John's limited success in his general education gym class has been a concern to his educational team members since his transition to the fourth grade. They discussed the need to modify the social complexity of this environment by reducing the group size and exposing him to games and activities that are more developmentally appropriate. Thus, the team met to discuss *having John participate in APE in addition to his general education gym class* to preteach specific games and boost his self-confidence in a smaller and more supportive setting. Games would be selected to ensure success by *focusing predominantly on cooperative play with limited competitive elements.* In addition, his peer group in both APE and his general education gym class would be provided with *peer training to model appropriate play and sportsmanlike conduct and to communicate to other children that bullying behavior is unacceptable.*

After-school recreation: John's desire to participate in after-school recreation is quite strong and his parents and educational team feel that supporting this desire is a critical priority to bolster his self-confidence. They recognized the need to *provide John with more frequent opportunities to engage in noncompetitive after-school recreation activities* such as Rollerblading, skiing, and snowboarding. An educational team member would *provide a handout for the instructors* that would emphasize the need to have John's peers provide appropriate models and encourage his efforts.

SU4 Uses appropriate gestures and nonverbal behavior for the context (Conversational Partner stage)

Child goal	Related partner goals	
Symbol Use SU4 Uses appropriate gestures and nonverbal behavior for the context	**Interpersonal Support** IS4 Partner sets stage for engagement IS5 Partner provides developmental support IS7 Partner models appropriate behaviors	**Learning Support** LS1 Partner structures activity for active participation LS2 Partner uses augmentative communication support to foster development
SU4 is not directly linked to JA, MR, or SR. **Related goals** Achievements in SU4 are related to achievements in JA3 and MR1.	A child's ability to use appropriate facial expressions, gestures, body posture, proximity, volume, and intonation for the context and partner (SU4.1–SU4.4) relies on a partner's ability to use appropriate proximity and nonverbal behavior to encourage interaction (IS4.2), provide guidance on expressing emotions and understanding the cause of emotions (IS5.4), and model appropriate nonverbal communication and emotional expressions (IS7.1).	A child's ability to use appropriate facial expressions, gestures, body posture, proximity, volume and intonation for the context and partner (SU4.1–SU4.4) also relies on a partner's ability to offer varied learning opportunities (LS1.5) and use augmentative communication support to enhance the child's expression and understanding of emotion (LS2.3).

Snapshot of Hope

Hope is a 7-year-old Conversational Partner who is participating in an inclusive first-grade classroom. Although she historically has been a more passive learner who rarely initiated interactions with her peers, Hope's recent gains in language have contributed to greater self-confidence and she is beginning to initiate more readily in both group activities and with one or two preferred peers on the playground. Although her facial expressions are usually appropriate for the context, her use of gestures can be unconventional and appear strange to her peers. For example, she has learned to raise her hand before speaking in morning meeting but may use this same gesture to call her peers' attention on the playground despite its inappropriateness in that context. As her educational team members recognize the importance of maintaining a strong social network, her objectives currently include supporting her to use appropriate gestures for a given context and partner (SU4.2). To support Hope, her partners are striving to model appropriate nonverbal communication and emotional expressions (IS7.1) and use augmentative communication support to enhance her expression and understanding of emotion (LS2.3).

Language arts worksheets: When completing language arts worksheets, Hope often attempts to solicit her peers' attention to request assistance and/or request materials.

She may, however, intrude on her classmates' personal space and mess up their materials by reaching across their papers or projects to point at a desired item (e.g., a colored pencil or scissors). If she is in a high state of arousal, she may even solicit her deskmate's attention by repeatedly rubbing on his arm, a gesture perceived as intrusive and bothersome. To foster Hope's awareness of more socially appropriate gestures for this context, her educational team discussed the need for more explicit modeling of gestures to solicit attention (e.g., tapping on a peer's shoulder). Each of *the instructional assistants and general education teacher would model and discuss these gestures when presenting directions for the lesson.* Next, her special education resource teacher suggested an augmentative support for fostering conventional gestures. *A helper card* could be developed and placed in a visible location on Hope's desk. The card could include a written model for self-talk (e.g., "If I need help, I can tap on my deskmate's shoulder").

Recess: Recognizing that gestures have a significantly different meaning depending on the social context, Hope's educational team members recognized the need to provide explicit support for her on the playground. As she is continuing to solicit her classmates' attention by raising her hand, the team members discussed the need to prepare Hope for this activity by providing an augmentative support before making the transition to the playground. A Social Story would be written to indicate strategies for securing peers' attention in a context-specific manner (e.g., tapping on their shoulder if their back is turned; simply saying, "Hey, what are you guys doing?") and *a peer buddy would be encouraged to explicitly model these strategies* for her during recess.

	Child goal	Related partner goals	
SU5 Understands and uses generative language to express meanings (Conversational Partner stage)	*Symbol Use* SU5 Understands and uses generative language to express meanings	*Interpersonal Support* IS6 Partner adjusts language input IS7 Partner models appropriate behaviors	*Learning Support* LS2 Partner uses augmentative communication support to foster development LS4 Partner modifies goals, activities, and learning environment
	SU5 is not directly linked to JA, MR, or SR. *Related goals* Achievements in SU5 are related to achievements in JA3 and MR1.	A child's ability to understand and use a variety of advanced relational meanings, reference to things, verb phrases, and sentence constructions (SU5.1–SU5.4) relies on a partner's ability to adjust complexity of language input to the child's developmental level (IS6.2) and model "child-perspective" language and the use of self-talk (IS7.5).	A child's ability to understand and use a variety of advanced relational meanings, reference to things, verb phrases, and sentence constructions (SU5.1–SU5.4) and understand and use connected sentences in oral and written discourse (SU5.5) relies on a partner's ability to use augmentative communication support to enhance the child's communication and expressive language (LS2.1) and adjust task difficulty for the child's success (LS4.2).

Snapshot of Devon Devon is a 6-year-old Conversational Partner who is in an inclusive first-grade classroom. His creative and generative language had been slow to develop, as he remained for a long while primarily a gestalt processor and relied on the use of borrowed language forms (delayed echolalia) and immediate echolalia to communicate and fill his turns in conversation. Over the past 18 months, however, his expressive language has progressed remarkably, and he is now generating a variety of creative sentence constructions, including declaratives (e.g., "My dad is fixing the lawn mower") and negatives (e.g., "We can't play outside in the rain"), with emerging production of complex sentence forms, specifically, simple conjoined sentences involving the conjunction *and* (e.g., "I have a pet dog *and* his name is Lucky"). Thus, he currently is working on understanding and producing a variety of sentence constructions (SU5.4). His educational team recognized that to address this objective, his partners would need to adjust the complexity of their language input to Devon's developmental level (IS6.2) and use augmentative communication supports to facilitate Devon's communication and expressive language (LS2.1).

Reading group: After completing an assigned reading, Devon and his classmates are asked to complete a comprehension worksheet to reinforce story grammar elements (e.g., where the story takes place, who the characters are, what events take place). Typically, Devon provides simple sentences such as "The boy was walking," as opposed to using more complex sentences to illustrate the causal and temporal (i.e., time) relationships in the story (e.g., "The boy was trying to catch a frog, *but* the frog was too fast," "The frog followed the boy *after* he went home"). Without these complex sentence structures, Devon's discussion of the story clearly misses essential elements that help to specify the full meaning. Thus, his special education resource teacher recognized the need to provide a written augmentative support to provide Devon with the support he needs to produce more complex sentences. His reading *comprehension worksheets would be modified to include a list of written choices* (paired with picture graphics) for Devon to insert into existing sentences. For example, several choices could be inserted into the sentence "The boy was trying to catch the frog, but _____." These might include "he was too fast," "he hid under the car," or "he fell and landed on his head." The most appropriate choice would be selected based on the context of the story and the picture cues provided.

Circle time: In whole-class discussions about stories read in reading group, Devon has difficulty formulating creative responses to questions posed by his teacher. To facilitate his competence in this activity, his educational team recognized the need to adjust the complexity of their language input to include *clear and explicit models of early conjoined sentences* by preparing several questions tailored to Devon's developmental level before the discussion. Next, they discussed the need to provide an augmentative support to enhance Devon's ability to combine sentence structures with conjunctions. When asked a question posed by his teacher (e.g., "Why did the boy feel sad at the end of the story?"), *written choices could be provided on a dry erase board* for Devon to choose from (e.g., *The boy felt sad because* _____ *a) he lost Lucky, b) he found a pet kitten, or c) he couldn't catch the frog*).

**SU6
Follows rules
of conversation
(Conversational
Partner stage)**

Child goal	Related partner goals	
Symbol Use SU6 Follows rules of conversation	*Interpersonal Support* IS5 Partner provides developmental support IS7 Partner models appropriate behaviors	*Learning Support* LS2 Partner uses augmentative communication support to foster development LS3 Partner uses visual and organizational support LS4 Partner modifies goals, activities, and learning environment
SU6 is not directly linked to JA, MR, or SR.	A child's ability to follow conventions for initiating, taking turns, and shifting topics in conversation (SU6.1, SU6.2) relies on a partner's ability to provide guidance and feedback for success in activities (IS5.3), model a range of communicative functions (IS7.2), and model appropriate behavior when the child uses inappropriate behavior (IS7.4).	A child's ability to follow conventions for initiating, taking turns, and shifting topics in conversation (SU6.1, SU6.2) also relies on a partner's ability to use augmentative communication support to enhance a child's communication and expressive language (LS2.1), use visual support to foster active involvement in group activities (LS3.6), and provide activities to promote initiation and extended interaction (LS4.8).

Snapshot of Anna

Anna is an 8½-year-old Conversational Partner who has been described as both precocious and articulate. Her expressive language skills have always been a relative strength, as her vocabulary far exceeds the expectations for her chronological age. Her parents, however, have noticed that Anna appears to have difficulty understanding the reciprocal nature of a conversation. She often interrupts people she is engaged with, tends to monopolize the conversation, and has a tendency to drift off topic. Her educational team recognizes the critical impact of these social-communicative difficulties on her achievement in an academic setting as well as on the formation of peer relationships. Therefore, she is currently working on following verbal conventions for initiating conversations and taking turns (SU6.1). Her partners are striving to model a range of communicative functions and rules of conversation (IS7.2) and use visual support to foster active involvement in group activities (LS3.6).

Lunch bunch: Anna greatly enjoys the opportunity to participate in "lunch bunch," a small-group activity designed to provide students with explicit support in engaging in mutually satisfying social conversations with adult support. Anna's speech-language pathologist leads this group and has noticed Anna's ongoing challenges in responding appropriately to cues for turn taking in conversation. Anna is eager to engage and typically leads the conversation by providing a series of comments about her preferred topics (e.g., Harry Potter novels). She tends, however, to dominate the conversation and not exchange turns with others. Her educational team discussed the need to use a visual *conversation board* to foster active involvement in this group activity. For each comment, the speech-language pathologist could place a small visual cue (e.g., a ball of playdough) under the "I can make a comment" side of the conversation board. With each question posed by a child, the speech-language pathologist could place a larger visual cue (e.g., a larger ball of playdough) under the "I can ask a question" side of the conversation board. These visual supports may highlight the notion that asking a question is more valuable, as it turns the conversation over to a partner.

Cooperative learning in science: As science is a preferred subject as well as a relative strength of Anna's, she is quite verbose in this context. Thus, when her teacher divides the students into groups, her peers occasionally are not pleased to be being paired with Anna, knowing that she may be overly directive and consequently act like a "little teacher." Her educational team recognized this activity as a priority and discussed the need to *have the science teacher model appropriate group leadership and turn taking* to the whole class before forming the groups. Next, a visual support to foster more active involvement would be needed to encourage Anna to shift the conversational turn to a classmate. Thus, they provided a squishy *talking ball* to provide a concrete visual cue to indicate who was speaking and to serve as a reminder to pass the conversational turn to another student. Interruptions are more obvious and marked more clearly—the student who is being interrupted can simply hold up the talking ball as a visual cue to mark his or her turn.

Emotional Regulation: Mutual Regulation

MR1 Expresses range of emotions (Conversational Partner stage)

Child goals	Related partner goals	
Mutual Regulation MR1 Expresses range of emotions	**Interpersonal Support** IS4 Partner sets stage for engagement IS5 Partner provides developmental support IS7 Partner models appropriate behaviors	**Learning Support** LS1 Partner structures active participation LS2 Partner uses augmentative communication support to foster development
MR1 is linked to JA2, and SR3. **Linked objectives** MR1.1 Understands and uses early emotion words (= JA2.1, SR3.1) MR1.2 Understands and uses advanced emotion words (= JA2.3, SR3.2) MR1.3 Understands and uses graded emotions (= JA2.5, SR3.3) **Related goals** Achievements in MR1 are related to achievements in SU4–SU5.	A child's ability to understand and use early emotion words, advanced emotion words, and graded emotions (MR1.1–MR1.3); change emotional expression based on partners' feedback (MR1.4); and use nonverbal cues of emotional expression (MR1.5) relies on a partner's ability to share emotions, internal states, and mental plans with child (IS4.4); attempt to repair breakdowns verbally or nonverbally (IS5.2); and model appropriate nonverbal communication and emotional expressions (IS7.1).	A child's ability to understand and use early emotion words, advanced emotion words, and graded emotions (MR1.1–MR1.3) also relies on a partner's ability to offer varied learning opportunities (LS1.5), use augmentative communication support to enhance the child's expression and understanding of emotion (LS2.3), and use augmentative communication support to enhance the child's emotional regulation (LS2.4).

Snapshot of Liam

Liam is a 7-year-old Conversational Partner who participates in an inclusive second-grade classroom. Although he uses a wide range of sentence constructions to communicate his intentions, he currently uses only early emotion words such as "happy," "sad," and "mad" to convey his emotional state. He is not yet using more advanced emotion words across activity contexts. His partners have also noted that his emotional display seems to have little to do with the emotional states of his partners or to the general mood of a social environment. Thus, his objectives currently include understanding and using advanced emotion words (MR1.2) and changing emotional expression based on partner feedback (MR1.4). His partners are striving to share emotions, internal states, and mental plans with Liam (IS4.4) and use augmentative communication support to enhance Liam's expression and understanding of emotion (LS2.3).

Lunch: Liam currently eats lunch with a small group of classmates in the school cafeteria with an instructional assistant to foster successful interactions. His teachers have observed that Liam often gets lost when his friends engage in heated debates or disagreements about the best parts of recent movies or video games. His educational team discussed that efforts needed to be made to help Liam's classmates share their emotions and opinions more explicitly and provide an augmentative support to emphasize the emotional states of those involved. Therefore, the instructional assistant will work on providing Liam's classmates with support to use more explicit *emotion words in their conversations,* in an effort to help Liam differentiate and comprehend more advanced emotional concepts. Next, the children would be encouraged to *play a "freeze game."* This game would entail the instructional assistant raising his/her hand when an emotionally charged interaction (positive or negative) occurs between the children. Group members would then freeze and talk out the interaction so that the children could reflect on the emotional states and intentions of others. The staff member could then *use a wipe-off board to provide a graphic depiction* of the discussion and each of the classmates' emotions/opinions.

Reading group: In reading group, Liam often has difficulty comprehending text that involves more advanced emotion words, due, in part, to his limited ability to role play the emotional display associated with these more challenging concepts (e.g., "interested," "frustrated," "worried," "stressed"). Therefore, his educational team discussed the need to highlight the emotional states of the characters more explicitly by *initiating a charades portion of reading group* so that the students could practice enacting the characters' emotional expression. In addition, they discussed the potential benefit of creating *a word wall using a bulletin board that lists emotion words and their definitions.* Liam and his classmates would be encouraged to actively use this wall to support their emotional expression both during reading group and across the day.

MR2 Responds to assistance offered by partners (Conversational Partner stage)	Child goals	Related partner goals	
	Mutual Regulation MR2 Responds to assistance offered by partners	**Interpersonal Support** IS1 Partner is responsive to child IS4 Partner sets stage for engagement IS6 Partner adjusts language input	**Learning Support** LS1 Partner structures activity for active participation LS2 Partner uses augmentative communication support to foster development LS4 Partner modifies goals, activities, and learning environment
	MR2 is not directly linked to JA, SU, or SR.	A child's ability to soothe when comforted by partners (MR2.1), engage when alerted by partners (MR2.2), respond to bids for interaction (MR2.3), and attune to changes in partners' expression of emotion (MR2.5) relies on a partner's ability to attune to the child's emotion and pace (IS1.2), secure the child's attention before communicating (IS4.1), and adjust the quality of the language input to the child's arousal level (IS6.3).	A child's ability to respond to changes in partners' expression of emotion (MR2.4), attune to changes in partners' expression of emotion (MR2.5), and respond to information or strategies offered by partners (MR2.6) relies on a partner's ability to provide a predictable sequence to activity (LS1.3), use augmentative communication support to enhance the child's understanding of language and behavior (LS2.2), and adjust task difficulty for child success (LS4.2).

Snapshot of Keith   Keith is a 6½-year-old Conversational Partner attending a kindergarten class who has been described as precocious with respect to his language abilities, as he has a strong vocabulary and sophisticated grammar and articulation given his age. Despite these relative strengths, he continues to experience significant difficulties with emotional regulation and is frequently in a high state of arousal throughout the day. In these instances, he often tunes out when his partners, both adults and peers, use complex language in their effort to support his ability to regroup. Keith is therefore not yet responding consistently to the strategies that his partners use an effort to help him decrease his arousal state. His objectives include attuning to changes in partners' expression of emotions (MR2.5) and responding to information or strategies offered by partners (MR2.6). His partners are supporting Keith by adjusting the quality of the language input to his arousal level (IS6.3) and adjusting task difficulty for Keith's success (LS4.2).

Play with parents: Keith's educational team recognizes the need to improve consistency across all partners' attempts to support his regulation, as their current attempts, which are predominantly verbal in nature, often result in heightening his dysregulation. During play at home, for example, the team members discussed that when Keith is in a high state of arousal, he has difficulty processing his parent's requests to settle down and he may lash out by grabbing at his mother's hair as she persists in speaking to him. Thus, they discussed the need to adjust their language input by *modeling a soothing tone of voice and neutral emotion* and *using very simple and positive language (e.g., "I'm frustrated, I just need to take a break")*. As language strategies for regulation are only emerging for Keith, the team members also discussed the need to *model behavioral strategies* such as walking away to take a break, or squeezing a fidget toy such as a stress ball. Finally, Keith's team discussed the need to adjust playtime activities to foster greater success such as *limiting the competitive element in the games* that he might play with his parents and siblings.

Journal at school: Keith's educational team also discussed the need to improve the consistency with their current attempts to support his regulation when Keith is writing in his journal at school. As handwriting has been a challenge for Keith, he often anticipates this activity with anxiety and may become quite dysregulated. His teachers' current attempts to help Keith settle are predominantly verbal in nature and often result in further disorganization. Thus, his team members discussed the need to *model a soothing tone of voice and neutral emotional state,* while *using very simple and positive language (e.g., "This is hard. I need some help")*. As handwriting clearly poses a compromising factor, Keith's team also discussed the need to adjust journal time to foster greater success by *having him use a computer to provide his responses.*

| Linking Goals | | | Conversational Partner Stage | 159 |

MR3 Responds to feedback and guidance regarding behavior (Conversational Partner stage)

Child goals	Related partner goals	
Mutual Regulation	*Interpersonal Support*	*Learning Support*
MR3 Responds to feedback and guidance regarding behavior	IS1 Partner is responsive to child IS5 Partner provides developmental support	LS2 Partner uses augmentative communication support to foster development LS4 Partner modifies goals, activities, and learning environment
MR3 is linked to SU1. *Linked objectives* MR3.3 Uses behaviors modeled by partners to guide behavior (= SU1.2) MR3.4 Collaborates and negotiates with peers in problem solving (= SU1.5)	A child's ability respond to feedback regarding the appropriateness of emotional display and regulatory strategies (MR3.1, MR3.2), use behaviors modeled by partners to guide behavior (MR3.3), collaborate and negotiate with peers in problem solving (MR3.4), and accept ideas from partners during negotiation to reach compromise (MR3.5) relies on a partner's ability to provide information or assistance to regulate state (IS1.6), provide guidance for success in interactions with peers (IS5.1), provide guidance on expressing emotions and understanding the cause of emotions (IS5.4), and provide guidance for interpreting others' feelings and opinions (IS5.5).	A child's ability to respond to feedback regarding the appropriateness of regulatory strategies (MR3.2) and accept ideas from partners during negotiation to reach compromise (MR3.5) relies on a partner's ability to use augmentative communication support to enhance the child's understanding of language and behavior (LS2.2), arrange the learning environment to enhance attention (LS4.4), and "up the ante" to increase expectations appropriately (LS4.10).

Snapshot of Shawna

Shawna is an 8-year-old Conversational Partner in second grade who is described by her parents and educational team members as a very bright girl with strong opinions and a stubborn streak. When engaged in cooperative play or group work with her peers, she is more comfortable setting and enforcing the rules than creating them with her peers. In fact, she has significant difficulty accommodating to the ideas or opinions of her classmates and may become quite bossy and/or distraught if not in control. Her current objectives include collaborating and negotiating with peers in problem solving (MR3.4) and accepting ideas from partners during negotiations to reach compromise (MR3.5). Her partners are striving to provide guidance for success in interactions with peers (IS5.1) and "up the ante" to increase expectations appropriately (LS4.10).

Playground games: Shawna is clearly interested in playing with her classmates and frequently attempts to engage in play with her peers by calling out their names and telling them what games she would like to play. Her success, however, is currently limited due to her difficulty with accepting the ideas of others. Her educational team recognizes a need to provide more explicit guidance for success in interactions with her peers and would like to improve their efforts to encourage her to follow her peers' leads without lessening her interest. Her team discussed the potential benefit of *reviewing expectations for recess with the class before the transition* to the playground. Next, team members discussed the need for a visual support on the playground to foster success with peer negotiations. *A pipe cleaner would be used as a "meter of flexibility" on the playground for all of the children.* When Shawna is having a difficult time accepting her peers' ideas, for example, the pipe cleaner would be held straight and rigid. However, if she accepts the ideas of others, it would be bent to represent her ability to negotiate. The team also discussed the need to *preteach Shawna and her classmates a variety of strategies for coopera-*

tive decision making (e.g., "Rock, paper, scissors"; "Eeny, meaney, miney, mo") to use for deciding who has control or the next turn.

Cooperative work in science: Shawna's participation in group work is also compromised by her apparent need to be in control and provide directives to her classmates. Therefore, her team discussed the need to support Shawna's awareness of *the rules of the classroom community*. This written support would explicitly lay out strategies for successful group negotiations. For example, the support would illustrate that each child has an idea of what to do first, how to finish the project, and what materials are valid to use. Therefore, in group projects, a child may need to change his or her idea to come up with the group idea. Next, Shawna's educational team discussed that an instructional assistant or resource teacher would need to be present to foster success. This staff member *would list each group member's ideas on a wipe-off board*, leaving time for group discussion. Successful compromise would be strongly encouraged. A *"talking ball"* would be passed to each child as he or she takes a turn.

MR4 Requests partners' assistance to regulate state (Conversational Partner stage)	Child goals	Related partner goals	
	Mutual Regulation MR4 Requests partners' assistance to regulate state	*Interpersonal Support* IS2 Partner fosters initiation IS3 Partner respects child's independence IS7 Partner models appropriate behaviors	*Learning Support* LS2 Partner uses augmentative communication support to foster development LS4 Partner modifies goals, activities, and learning environment
	MR4 is linked to JA3. *Linked objectives* MR4.3 Shares intentions to regulate the behavior of others (= JA3.1) MR4.4 Shares intentions for social interaction (= JA3.2) MR4.5 Shares intentions for joint attention (= JA3.3)	A child's ability to share negative emotion to seek comfort (MR4.1), share positive emotion to seek interaction (MR4.2), share intentions to regulate behavior of others (MR4.3), and request assistance to resolve conflict and problem-solve situations (MR4.6) relies on a partner's ability to wait for and encourage initiations (IS2.2), interpret problem behaviors as communicative and/or regulatory (IS3.3), and model a range of communicative functions (IS7.2).	A child's ability to share intentions to regulate the behavior of others (MR4.3) and for social interactions and joint attention (MR4.4, MR4.5) and request assistance to resolve conflict and problem-solve situations (MR4.6) relies on a partner's ability to use augmentative communication support to enhance the child's communication and expressive language (LS2.1), use augmentative communication support to enhance the child's expression and understanding of emotion (LS2.3), and arrange the learning environment to promote child initiation (LS4.5).

Snapshot of Dougie

Dougie is a 4-year-old Conversational Partner in a special education preschool classroom and home-based program. His language abilities have blossomed in recent months, as he is using more creative sentences and sharing more of his experiences with familiar partners. His educational team, however, noticed that his communicative functions remain limited, particularly with respect to requesting support for mutual regulation. His objectives include sharing intention to regulate behavior of others (MR4.3) and sharing intentions for joint attention (MR4.5). His partners are supporting Dougie by modeling a range of communicative functions and rules of conversation (IS7.2) and arranging the learning environment to promote child initiation (LS4.5).

Blocks: Dougie loves to play with blocks in both his home and school environments. Therefore, his team agreed that this activity would provide an excellent context for facilitating Dougie's ability to ask for assistance from others. Specifically, they discussed the need for his partners to *model a variety of language structures during his play*. They agreed to *model directives* (e.g., "Dad put the block under the bridge"), *comments* (e.g., "This is a big tower"), *and sharing of intentions/plans* (e.g., "I'm gonna crash the fort") *from Dougie's perspective*. They also discussed the need to ensure that *specific blocks that were preferred by Dougie were out of his reach and/or sight* so that he would need to request assistance to complete his constructions, as this would provide a natural opportunity to foster his initiations.

Bathing: Bathing is another preferred activity for Dougie. Thus, his family raised the possibility of *embedding supports within this routine* to encourage him to initiate more frequent bids for behavior regulation and joint attention. Team members discussed the need to model a range of communicative functions by *commenting on his play* to encourage more frequent commenting (e.g., "I'm playing with the duck") and the need to arrange the learning environment to promote his requests for assistance (e.g., *placing desired bath toys in an out of reach wall basket*).

MR5 Recovers from extreme dysregulation with support from partners (Conversational Partner stage)

Child goals	Related partner goals	
Mutual Regulation	*Interpersonal Support*	*Learning Support*
MR5 Recovers form extreme dysregulation with support from partners	IS1 Partner is responsive to child IS3 Partner respects child's independence IS6 Partner adjusts language input IS7 Partner models appropriate behaviors	LS2 Partner uses augmentative communication support to foster development LS4 Partner modifies goals, activities, and learning environment
MR5 is not directly linked to JA, SU, or SR.	A child's ability to respond to partners' efforts to assist with recovery by moving away from an activity (MR5.1), respond to partners' use of behavioral strategies and language strategies (MR5.2, MR5.3), and decrease the intensity of dysregulated state due to support from partners (MR5.6) relies on a partner's ability to recognize signs of dysregulation and offer support (IS1.5); honor protests, rejections, or refusals when appropriate (IS3.4); adjust the quality of language input to the child's arousal level (IS6.3); and model appropriate nonverbal communication and emotional expressions (IS7.1).	A child's ability to respond to partners' use of simple language strategies (MR5.3), respond to partners' attempts to reengage in interaction or activity (MR5.4) and decrease the amount of time needed to recover from extreme dysregulation due to support from partners (MR5.5) relies on a partner's ability to use augmentative communication support to enhance the child's understanding of language and behavior (LS2.2), use augmentative communication support to enhance the child's expression and understanding of emotion (LS2.3), and modify the sensory properties of the learning environment (LS4.3).

Snapshot of Christopher

Christopher is a 9-year-old Conversational Partner who recently made the transition into the fourth grade. His language abilities have always been a relative strength, and his vocabulary and grammar are often described as precocious, particularly in his areas of special interest, automobile designs. However, when Christopher is distressed, his parents and educational team notice a remarkable decline in his ability to use language to either communicate and/or engage in self-talk for emotional regulation. In his first few months of fourth grade, Christopher has been having significant emotional outbursts. His outbursts, in fact, have increased in frequency, and his mother has been called to take him home from school due to his extreme episodes of dysregulation resulting, in some instances, in damage to his desk and the classroom furniture. In addition to increasing efforts to modify the curriculum and social environment as preventative strategies to decrease anxiety and frustration, his educational team discussed the need to support Christopher's ability to recover more quickly from incidences of extreme dysregulation. His objectives include responds to partners' efforts to assist with recovery by moving away from an activity (MR5.1) and responds to partners' use of behavioral strategies to recover from extreme dysregulation (MR5.2). His partners are striving to adjust the quality of language input to Christopher's arousal level (IS6.3), use augmentative communication support to enhance his understanding of language and behavior (LS2.2), and modify the sensory properties of the learning environment (LS4.3).

Math worksheets: During independent math work using worksheets in the classroom, Christopher has been observed to become visibly frustrated when he gets stuck on a word problem and is unable to complete the task independently. His increased motoric disorganization and anger often lead to his swiping the materials off his desk and pushing his desk over. His educational team discussed the need to improve strategies to support Christopher in recovering from extreme dysregulation. First, they discussed the need to *provide a safe "break spot" for Christopher within the classroom,* such as a quiet corner with bean bag chairs, partitioned off with stable bookcases. *Access to preferred audio books* was also considered, as this strategy would help Christopher block out classroom noise and could be tied into his special interest (e.g., automobile makes and models). Next, his team discussed the need to *provide Christopher with break cards* that he could keep in his pockets and at his desk, as his ability to request a break verbally would likely be compromised in the event of extreme dysregulation.

Cooperative games in gym class: By their very nature, negotiations with peers during gym class are often quite challenging for Christopher due to visual motor difficulties and challenges with accepting another's idea. Thus, gym activities often lead to extreme dysregulation. His educational team discussed the need to decrease the complexity of the language involved in these discussions by *using a wipe-off board to help the classmates plan out the games.* They also discussed the need for Christopher to have access to *his break cards* for use during gym class. Finally, they discussed the need to provide him with *visual choices* (e.g., walking laps in the gym, sorting books in the library, helping the janitor) when Christopher's arousal level begins to escalate.

Linking Goals

Emotional Regulation: Self-Regulation

SR1 Demonstrates availability for learning and interacting (Conversational Partner stage)

Child goals	Related partner goals	
Self-Regulation	*Interpersonal Support*	*Learning Support*
SR1 Demonstrates availability for learning and interacting	IS4 Partner sets stage for engagement IS5 Partner provides developmental support IS7 Partner models appropriate behaviors	LS1 Partner structures activity for active participation LS3 Partner uses visual and organizational support LS4 Partner modifies goals, activities, and learning environment
SR1 is linked to JA1 and JA4. *Linked objectives* SR1.2 Monitors attentional focus of a social partner (= JA1.1) SR1.3 Shows reciprocity in speaker and listener roles to share experiences (= JA4.1)	A child's ability to monitor the attentional focus of a social partner (SR1.2), show reciprocity in the speaker and listener roles to share experiences (SR1.3), and express emotions appropriately to context (SR1.6) relies on a partner's ability to use appropriate proximity and nonverbal behavior to encourage interaction (IS4.2), provide guidance for success in interaction with peers (IS5.1), and model appropriate nonverbal communication and emotional expressions (IS7.1).	A child's ability to respond to sensory and social experiences with differentiated emotions (SR1.1), demonstrate the ability to inhibit actions and behaviors (SR1.4), and persist during tasks with reasonable demands (SR1.5) relies on a partner's ability to offer varied learning opportunities (LS1.5), use supports to define the steps and time for completion of activities (LS3.2), and design and modify activities to be developmentally appropriate (LS4.6).

Snapshot of Sam

Sam is a 5-year-old Conversational Partner in an inclusive kindergarten setting. Sam most often is focused and attentive during interactions with adults; however, he has a tendency to tune out during interactions with peers. His objectives include monitoring the attentional focus of a social partner (SR1.2) and persisting during tasks with reasonable demands (SR1.5). His partners are providing guidance for success in interaction with peers (IS5.1) and using visual supports to define the steps and time for completion of activities (LS3.2).

Morning greeting: Sam's kindergarten class participates in a morning greeting routine everyday. As Sam's engagement in this activity is variable, his partners recognize the need to provide more explicit guidance to his peers to encourage success. In particular, they discussed the need to encourage each of the children to *use gestures to augment their verbal greetings (e.g., a wave or a hand shake)* to foster Sam's understanding. Next, they discussed the importance of using a visual support to detail the sequence of events involved in the greeting routine by reading a brief *Social Story to the class and sending the story home* with Sam for him to read and practice the ritual before its occurrence. In addition, Sam's team discussed several environmental modifications such as *providing carpet squares in a semicircle* to visually arrange the layout of the class, which would help organize the flow of the morning greeting.

Group games: During cooperative games, Sam has difficulty attending to the flow of interaction across his classmates' turns and recognizing steps toward the completion of his own turn. Sam's team discussed the need to provide more explicit visual supports to indicate the steps within the games as well as the specific goals of each child's turn. The team members discussed the need to create *rule charts that would correspond to each game that Sam may play with his peers.* These *charts could then be reviewed with Sam* before the initiation of each game to remind him how many players would be involved, how to take turns, what the sequence of steps within a turn is, and how the game is completed. Sam's team also discussed the need to provide more explicit guidance to encourage success with his peers both at school and with his neighborhood friends. For example, team members discussed the need to have *Sam's peers tap on Sam's shoulder or call out his name* when he is having difficulty attending to them while they are talking.

SR2 Uses behavioral strategies to regulate arousal level during familiar activities (Conversational Partner stage)

Child goals	Related partner goals	
Self-Regulation	Interpersonal Support	Learning Support
SR2 Uses behavioral strategies to regulate arousal level during familiar activities	IS1 Partner is responsive the child IS3 Partner respects child's independence IS7 Partner models appropriate behaviors	LS1 Partner structures activity for active participation LS2 Partner uses augmentative communication support to foster development LS4 Partner modifies goals, activities, and learning environment
SR2 is not directly linked to JA, SU, or SR.	A child's ability to use behavioral strategies to regulate arousal level during solitary and social activities (SR2.1), use behavioral strategies modeled by partners to regulate arousal level (SR2.2), and use behavioral strategies to engage productively in an extended activity (SR2.3) relies on a partner's ability to recognize and support the child's strategies to regulate arousal (IS1.4), allow the child to take breaks to move about as needed (IS3.1), and model appropriate behavior when the child uses inappropriate behavior (IS7.4).	A child's ability to use behavioral strategies to regulate arousal level during solitary and social activities (SR2.1), use behavioral strategies modeled by partners to regulate arousal level (SR2.2), and use behavioral strategies to engage productively in an extended activity (SR2.3) also relies on a partner's ability to offer repeated learning opportunities (LS1.4), use augmentative communication support to enhance the child's emotional regulation (LS2.4), and alternate between movement and sedentary activities as needed (LS4.9).

Snapshot of Tom

Tom is a 4-year-old Conversational Partner who does not yet consistently use behavioral strategies to regulate his own arousal. Rather, he relies on adults in close proximity to cope with dysregulation during stressful social interactions or when he is exposed to disorganizing environmental stimuli. On occasion, Tom does use behavioral strategies when prompted by caregivers that appear to be regulating for him. Therefore, Tom's educational team members have prioritized Tom's independent ability to use these strategies. His objectives include using behavioral strategies to regulate arousal level during solitary and social activities (SR2.1) and using behavioral strategies modeled by partners to regulate arousal level (SR2.2). His partners are supporting him by modeling appropriate behaviors when Tom uses inappropriate behaviors (IS7.1) and alternating between movement and sedentary activities as needed (LS4.9).

Play with train set: Tom frequently chooses to play with a train set in both his home and school environments. Although this is clearly a preferred activity, Tom finds it to be very exciting and often becomes increasingly disorganized when engaged with the train cars. After several minutes, Tom typically lies on the floor and begins to focus his attention only on the spinning wheels of the train cars. Members of his educational team recognize that their efforts to redirect Tom's attention and facilitate his organization are clearly an area of need. Therefore, they discussed the need to implement the following modifications to assist Tom in his self-regulatory efforts during this activity, as this would, in turn, support his ability to play more productively and be more available for engagement. Lastly, they identified the need to increase the consistency by which they model appropriate self-regulatory behaviors. For example, they discussed the importance of *saying "time to jump" while showing him a photograph of the trampoline* when Tom shows signs of dysregulation (e.g., remaining disengaged by studying the trains' wheels to an excessive degree).

Ring Around the Rosy with peers: Although Tom enjoys engaging with his peers, his arousal often becomes heightened in these activities, and he may flap his hands and suddenly bolt from the activity. This pattern, coupled with limited self-regulatory strategies, leads to increased disorganization as the activity progresses. Thus, Tom's educational team discussed the need to balance these more intense movement activities with more sedentary actions to reduce his extreme high arousal state, while modeling more appropriate self-regulatory behaviors. As jumping provides an organizing input for Tom when he becomes distressed or exciting, team members discussed the importance of encouraging Tom to *jump along to the rhythm of the song rather than to walk or run* when in a state of high arousal. In addition, Tom's partners agreed to *model squeezing his hands together tightly and drinking from a sports bottle* in between turns during interaction with peers to provide Tom with alternative behavioral strategies for regulation.

SR3
Uses language strategies to regulate arousal level during familiar activities (Conversational Partner stage)

Child goals	Related partner goals	
Self-Regulation SR3 Uses language strategies to regulate arousal level during familiar activities	*Interpersonal Support* IS1 Partner is responsive to child IS5 Partner provides developmental support IS7 Partner models appropriate behaviors	*Learning Support* LS1 Partner structures activity for active participation LS2 Partner uses augmentative communication support to foster development LS4 Partner modifies goals, activities, and learning environment
SR3 is linked to JA2 and MR1. **Linked objectives** SR3.1 Understands and uses early emotion words (= JA2.1, MR1.1) SR3.2 Understands and uses advanced emotion words (= JA2.3, MR1.2) SR3.3 Understands and uses graded emotions (= JA2.5, MR1.3)	A child's ability to understand and use early emotion and advanced emotional words (SR3.1, SR3.2), understand and use graded emotions (SR3.3), and use language strategies modeled by partners to regulate arousal level (SR3.5) relies on a partner's ability to respond appropriately to the child's signals to foster a sense of competence (IS1.3), provide guidance as needed for success in activities (IS5.3), and model "child-perspective" language and the use of self talk (IS7.5).	A child's ability to understand and use early emotion and advanced emotional words (SR3.1, SR3.2), understand and use graded emotions (SR3.3), use language strategies to regulate arousal level during solitary and social activities (SR3.4), and use language strategies to engage productively in an extended activity (SR3.6) relies on a partner's ability to provide a predictable sequence to activity (LS1.3), use augmentative communication support to enhance the child's expression and understanding of emotion (LS2.3), and "up the ante" to increase expectations appropriately (LS4.10).

Snapshot of Maria

Maria is a 7-year-old Conversational Partner fully included in the second grade. When Maria becomes dysregulated, she primarily uses behavioral strategies for self-regulation. However, she is often able to correctly identify her general emotional state (e.g., "I feel mad," "I am happy," "That made me sad") when questioned by an adult partner. She is not yet, however, expressing more graded emotions. Her objectives include understanding and using graded emotions (SR3.3) and using language strategies modeled by partners to regulate arousal level (SR3.5). Her partners are helping Maria achieve these objectives by modeling "child-perspective" language and the use of self-talk (IS7.5) and using augmentative communication to enhance her expression and understanding of emotion (LS2.3).

Math group: Maria frequently becomes frustrated during her math group. Her escalation to extreme dysregulation, in fact, can be quite sudden and extreme. During these periods, she uses behavioral strategies to cope with these emotional spikes (e.g., chewing on her pencil, darting about the room). Her partners are concerned that Maria is missing out on valuable learning opportunities and that the darting behavior is sometimes disruptive to the classroom. They would like to support Maria's use of language strategies within the group to foster more sustained engagement and self-regulation. Her partners' ability to provide transactional supports to foster these objectives; however, remains inconsistent. Thus, her team members discussed the need to achieve greater consistency with modeling "child-perspective" language and the use of self-talk by incorporating augmentative communication supports to foster more graded emotional expression. First, they discussed *implementing an emotion wheel* that depicts eight different emotions that Maria may experience. Maria would then be encouraged to use this wheel to identify both positive and negative emotional states, as her partners would model accompanying language (e.g., "I feel frustrated when . . . "). Next, they discussed using *an emotion meter* to help Maria begin to understand the grading of these emotions while modeling appropriate self-talk (e.g., "When I am a little bit mad, I can ask for help. When I am really frustrated, I can ask for a break").

Gymnastics class: Maria is clearly interested in her community gymnastics class; however, she often becomes frightened due to loud noises and unanticipated movement. In this context, her partners have had more difficulty modeling self-talk and using augmentative supports. They discussed the need, therefore, for achieving greater consistency with use of transactional supports across settings. First, her partners discussed the need to create *a miniature version of the emotion wheel* used during her math group for her gymnastics instructor to keep in his pocket and make available to Maria as needed. Next, her partners discussed strategies for providing *language models that reflect different degrees of "scared,"* as appropriate. Finally, her partners discussed additional augmentative supports for this activity context. For example, they will encourage Maria to keep *a journal of her emotional experiences,* by writing down their intensity, how they are related to different events and experiences at gymnastics, and matching them with digital photographs. This journal can then be reviewed before class to help Maria prepare for these situations more explicitly.

Linking Goals

SR4 Uses metacognitive strategies to regulate arousal level during familiar activities (Conversational Partner stage)

Child goals	Related partner goals	
Self-Regulation	*Interpersonal Support*	*Learning Support*
SR4 Uses metacognitive strategies to regulate arousal level during familiar activities	IS1 Partner is responsive to child IS4 Partner sets stage for engagement IS5 Partner provides developmental support IS7 Partner models appropriate behavior	LS1 Partner structures activity for active participation LS2 Partner uses augmentative communication support to foster development LS3 Partner uses visual and organizational support
SR4 is linked to SU1. *Linked objectives* SR4.1 Uses internalized rules modeled by adult instruction to guide behavior (= SU1.3) SR4.3 Uses self-monitoring and self-talk to guide behavior (= SU1.4)	A child's ability to use internalized rules modeled by adult instruction to guide behavior (SR4.1), use self-monitoring and self-talk to guide behavior (SR4.3), and identify and reflect on strategies to support regulation (SR4.5) relies on a partner's ability to provide information or assistance to regulate state (IS1.6); share emotions, internal state, and mental plans with the child (IS4.4); provide guidance on expressing emotions and understanding the cause of emotions (IS5.4); and model "child-perspective" language and the use of self talk (IS7.5).	A child's ability to use metacognitive strategies to plan and complete activities (SR4.2) and to use emotional memory to assist with emotional regulation (SR4.4) relies on a partner's ability to define clear beginnings and endings to activities (LS1.1), use augmentative communication support to enhance the child's emotional regulation (LS2.4), and use support to define the steps and time for completion of activities (LS3.2).

Snapshot of Rob

Rob is a 10-year-old Conversational Partner attending a general education fourth-grade class with support of an aide. He uses a range of behavioral and language strategies to maintain a well-regulated state. His partners have observed recently that Rob is just beginning to use classroom rules to guide his behavior without prompting from his aide, such as requesting a break before taking one and talking himself through challenging situations. Given this, his partners prioritized the following objectives for him: using internalized rules modeled by adult instruction to guide behavior (SR4.1) and using self-monitoring and self-talk to guide behavior (SR4.3). His partners are attempting to support him by providing information or assistance to regulate state (IS1.6) and using supports to define steps and time for completion of activities (LS3.2).

Library: Rob's team discussed that because going to the school library is one of Rob's favorite activities, he would likely be invested in learning and using supports and strategies that would increase his success during this activity. Greater consistency, however, would be needed in providing Rob with information or assistance for self-regulation and with implementing supports to define the steps and time for completion of library activities. His team members discussed the need to create *a pocket-size written schedule that indicted the sequence of activities during a library visit.* Rob would be encouraged to review this schedule before making the transition and also refer to it during the activity. Next, his team discussed the need to place *a digital clock* on the librarian's desk so that Rob would be able to independently monitor the time that has elapsed and anticipate the transition back to the classroom. Finally, his educational team discussed the use of *Comic Strip Conversations* (Gray, 1994a) as a means to help Rob understand how his ability to follow the rules has a positive impact on his teachers and classmates.

Transition from school to home: At the end of the day, Rob often has difficulty organizing himself and can become quite dysregulated as the classroom becomes busier and noisier when his classmates and teachers begin to pack up before students go to the school bus or are picked up by their parents. His team members discussed that providing Rob with information or assistance for self-regulation and with implementing supports to define the steps and time for completion of these tasks at the end of the school day has not yet been consistent across his adult partners. Therefore, they discussed the need to help Rob by creating *a check-off system listing all of the steps requiring completion for a successful transition.* They also discussed the need to have Rob *begin packing up his belongings just before the other children do* so that he would encounter less distraction. In case that these strategies are not successful, the team also discussed having Rob pack up early and leave the hectic classroom to do an organizing activity with the speech-language pathologist in her therapy room. This activity, *typing a daily review story using the Writing with Symbols word processing program* with both written narrative text and icons, would be a very focusing activity, providing a finished product for Rob that he could then print, take home, and share with his parents.

SR5 Regulates emotion during new and changing situations (Conversational Partner stage)

Child goals		Related partner goals
Self-Regulation SR5 Regulates emotion during new and changing situations	*Interpersonal Support* IS1 Partner is responsive to child IS7 Partner models appropriate behaviors	*Learning Support* LS1 Partner structures activity for active participation LS2 Partner uses augmentative communication support to foster development LS4 Partner modifies goals, activities, and learning environment
SR5 is not directly linked to JA, SU, or MR.	A child's ability to use language strategies and metacognitive strategies to regulate arousal level in new and changing situations (SR5.2, SR5.3) and use language strategies and metacognitive strategies to regulate arousal level during transitions (SR5.5, SR5.6) relies on a partner's ability to recognize and support the child's behavioral, language, and metacognitive strategies to regulate arousal (IS1.4), provide information or assistance to regulate state (IS1.6), and model "child-perspective" language and the use of self-talk (IS7.5).	A child's ability to use behavioral strategies to regulate arousal level during new and changing situations (SR5.1) and use behavioral strategies to regulate arousal level during transitions (SR5.4) relies on a partner's ability to offer repeated learning opportunities (LS1.4), use augmentative communication support to enhance the child's emotional regulation (LS2.4), and modify the sensory properties of learning environment (LS4.3).

Snapshot of Myra

Myra is a 6-year-old Conversational Partner who continues to become disorganized and upset during transitions. Therefore, her partners are seeking to help her cope with transitions by increasing her use of a variety of self-regulatory strategies. Her objectives include using behavioral strategies to regulate arousal level during transitions (SR5.4) and using metacognitive strategies to regulate arousal level during transitions (SR5.6). Her partners are attempting to recognize and support Myra's strategies to regulate arousal (IS1.4) and use augmentative communication support to enhance Myra's emotional regulation (LS2.4).

Transition from recess to classroom: Despite the predictability of the routine, Myra consistently becomes distressed when she must make the transition from the playground to the school building after recess. Her partners noted, however, that they have not consistently recognized and supported Myra's strategies to regulate her arousal nor have they used an augmentative communication support to support her emotional regulation during this transition. Myra's team discussed the need to *compile a list of Myra's signals of dysregulation* as this would help with achieving consistency across staff members (e.g., teachers, playground monitors, instructional assistants, therapists). They agreed that this was essential, as some of Myra's signals were less obvious than others (e.g., gritting teeth) and not all partners on the playground are familiar with Myra. Next, they discussed providing *a feelings book* for Myra to use before her transition from recess to the classroom. This book would contain *visual supports for helping Myra with emotional identification, emotional understanding, and emotional regulation* (e.g., "I feel sad when I leave the playground. It's okay—I can think about what I will play the next time"). Finally, the team discussed that movement-based activities and "heavy work" tend to be organizing for Myra, so providing her with *the job of carrying a large, heavy bag of balls* off the playground may be helpful.

Transition to tae kwon do: Myra's parents reported that Myra's transitions from one activity to the next in community settings are also challenging, particularly the transition from home to tae kwon do. Given the importance of addressing these capacities across contexts, her educational team emphasized the need to educate Myra's parents and partners to recognize and support Myra's strategies to regulate arousal and use an augmentative communication support to help Myra's self-regulation. Therefore, team members discussed the need to implement the following supports to achieve consistency across contexts. First, they discussed the need to *compile a list of signals of dysregulation for her tae kwon do instructor.* Next, they discussed the importance of having Myra's parents *review the sequence of the lesson with Myra during their drive* to the class. *A written schedule paired with photographs of tae kwon do* could be provided and mounted on the back of the driver's seat for Myra to review during this discussion. Finally, they discussed the need for *simple, consistent cuing to help Myra use behavioral regulatory strategies* (e.g., deep breathing) for relaxation during class (Cautela & Groden, 1981).

	Child goals	Related partner goals	
SR6 Recovers from extreme dysregulation by self (Conversational Partner stage)	*Self-Regulation* SR6 Recovers from extreme dysregulation by self	*Interpersonal Support* IS1 Partner is responsive to child IS3 Partner respects child's independence IS7 Partner models appropriate behaviors	*Learning Support* LS2 Partner uses augmentative communication support to foster development LS3 Partner uses visual and organizational support LS4 Partner modifies goals, activities, and learning environment
	SR6 is not directly linked to JA, SU, or MR.	A child's ability to remove him- or herself from overstimulating or undesired activity (SR6.1), use behavioral strategies and language strategies to recover from extreme dysregulation (SR6.2, SR6.3), and decrease intensity of dysregulated state (SR6.6) relies on a partner's ability to attune to the child's emotion and pace (IS1.2); recognize and support the child's behavioral, language, and metacognitive strategies to regulate arousal (IS1.4); honor protests, rejections, or refusals when appropriate (IS3.4); and model "child-perspective" language and the use of self-talk (IS7.5).	A child's ability to remove him- or herself from overstimulating or undesired activity (SR6.1), reengage in interaction or activity after recovery from extreme dysregulation (SR6.4), and decrease the amount of time needed to recover from extreme dysregulation (SR6.5) relies on a partner's ability to use augmentative communication support to enhance the child's emotional regulation (LS2.4), use visual support to foster active involvement in group activities (LS3.6), and modify the sensory properties of the learning environment (LS4.3).

Snapshot of Brent   Brent is a 7-year-old Conversational Partner in first grade who experiences extreme distress when his expectations are violated, particularly if an adult partner simply uses the verbal instruction "no." His team discussed that to prevent or reduce the incidence of these episodes, they would need to make a concerted effort to provide Brent with more information about task demands by using turn-taking supports and within-task schedules before a given activity. However, they recognized that despite their preventative efforts, Brent was still at high risk for having these episodes of extreme dysregulation, given his development level and sensitivities. Therefore, they prioritized the following objectives for Brent: using language strategies to recover from extreme dysregulation (SR6.3) and reengaging in interaction or activity after recovery from extreme dysregulation (SR6.4). His partners are attempting to support Brent by modeling "child-perspective" language and the use of self-talk (IS7.5) and modifying the sensory properties of the learning environment (LS4.3).

Arts and crafts: Brent's participation in arts and crafts is often compromised by his strong desire to follow his preconceived notion of the sequence of activities based on his preferences. Therefore, when activities presented in class do not match Brent's expectations, he often becomes quite distressed and may shout, cover his ears, and bolt around the room. His partners in this context recognize their need to provide visual supports and modify the sensory properties of the art room to foster Brent's success and to provide more consistent models for self-talk. For example, they discussed a need to consistently provide *visual support depicting the sequence of activities for each art class* and to *review this list with Brent before the transition.* In addition to this proactive support, the team members discussed the need to consider supports during the activities themselves to support Brent when he may become dysregulated. His *visual schedule would always be made available in his visual field* (e.g., placed next to him on the table) so that he could refer to it, and *opportunities for a break would be granted when appropriate.* They also agreed that once Brent began to deescalate, they would *model language strategies* (e.g., "Today, I use crayons in art. I'm mad. I wanted to finger paint. Maybe, next time we will paint. Today, crayons"). Modifying Brent's seating arrangement was also considered critical, as *positioning his seat near the doorway would allow for more effective departure from the classroom if a break supervised by an instructional assistant is needed.*

Outdoor play at child care: As Brent is less able to regroup in a heightened state of arousal, his team discussed the importance of sharing information with Brent up front in an effort to prevent these periods of extreme dysregulation. In their effort to achieve consistency across contexts, the team members recognize the need to modify the sensory properties of the child care setting to foster Brent's success and to encourage child care staff to provide more consistent models for self-talk. In this context, they discussed creating *a Social Story* to provide Brent with an augmentative support to illustrate those social behaviors and interactions that are encouraged on the playground such as taking turns, waiting for playground equipment, and asking adults for help. Next, they discussed the use of *key words* as a means to help trigger Brent's *verbal scripts of self-regulatory language* (e.g., saying "turns" to mean "After [child's name] swings, I will get a turn"). Finally, they discussed several environmental modifications to foster Brent's success. For example, they agreed to keep *a large container of bubbles* on the playground, as they had discovered that blowing bubbles consistently reengaged Brent in play with his peers.

Chapter 5

Enhancing Social Communication, Emotional Regulation, and Transactional Support at the Social Partner Stage

From Assessment to Program Implementation

To develop a comprehensive educational program or to modify an existing program for a child at the Social Partner stage, the SCERTS Model prioritizes those developmental capacities that support a child's communicative competence across people, places, and circumstances. As delineated in Chapter 7 of Volume I, this process begins by identifying goals and objectives in the areas of social communication and emotional regulation based on a child's current developmental capacities in these domains and is followed by determining the most applicable transactional supports for the child and family. This must be a flexible process based on the child's learning strengths and needs, the family's priorities, and the challenges of activities in daily routines and ongoing educational programming.

In this chapter, we describe the development and implementation of educational programs for two children at the Social Partner stage, one at the novice level and one at the advanced level of this stage. These two children demonstrate very different levels of ability and therefore allow us to consider the range of issues that must be addressed for programming at the Social Partner stage. We must emphasize that the goals and activities described in this chapter are not being offered as a "prescription" to follow for all children at this stage, as each child's program should be individualized based on his or her unique social communication and emotional regulation needs and learning strengths and weaknesses. As discussed in Chapter 1 of this volume, educational priority goals for a child are based on the following criteria: 1) Goals target the most *functional* abilities in social communication and emotional regulation (i.e., abilities that support a child's active engagement in natural activities in daily routines), 2) goals directly *address family priorities* (i.e., goals are consistent with the values of parents and other family members), and 3) goals are *developmentally appropriate* (i.e., goals are consistent with the child's performance on the SAP-O). By following these criteria, the focus remains on fostering a child's ability to understand how and when to use acquired skills as independently as possible and apply these abilities consistently and in a functional manner in activities that are prioritized by the family and the many partners in the child's daily life.

Furthermore, as discussed in Chapter 1 of this volume, a SCERTS Model program should include *at least* 25 hours per week on a year-round basis of planned learning opportunities with sufficient individualized attention for the child to remain actively engaged. Thus, designing a comprehensive and intensive educational program for a child at the Social Partner stage requires an effort to 1) establish a blueprint for meaningful and purposeful activities in daily routines, 2) determine the current challenges posed in these settings, and 3) determine the complexity of the social contexts (i.e., one-to-one, small-group, or large-group settings) that would be appropriate depending on the child's unique social-communicative and emotional regulatory capacities. In addition, it is critical to keep in mind the importance of providing opportunities for the child to learn with typically developing children and other children who can provide good language and social models when social communication objectives are identified as part of the child's educational program (refer to the section in Chapter 2 of this volume called Successful Inclusion and Learning and Playing with Peers).

A child's increasing success in more natural contexts often requires a deliberate effort by family and educational team members to implement planned activity routines, engineered activities, and modified natural activities. As noted in Chapter 1 of this volume, the SCERTS Model does not advocate a strict hierarchical sequence when considering this continuum of naturalness. Rather, planned activity routines and engineered and modified activities may be incorporated at different times of the day depending on the complexity of the various activities and the child's variability across the day. In some cases, one-to-one planned activity routines may be provided as an opportunity for increased practice or rehearsal for achieving specific goals. This is because practice and rehearsal is most effective in the context that the child will eventually use the targeted capacities and skills, to support an understanding of the natural cues of how and when to use the skills being addressed.

In addition, as discussed in Chapter 3 of this volume, the SCERTS Model recognizes that the successful provision of a comprehensive educational program for a child at the Social Partner stage is not dependent solely on the determination of objectives and supports for the child. A SCERTS Family Support Plan is needed to address the provision of both educational and emotional support to family members, and a SCERTS Support Plan for Professionals and Service Providers is needed to address the need for ongoing training, continuing education, and team collaboration. Embedded in a network of support, a child's partners can collaborate in a coordinated manner in fostering social communication and emotional regulation and implementing appropriate transactional supports. These support plans should be sensitive to the changing needs of the child, the family, and the service providers and tailored to meet the unique challenges faced by children at the Social Partner stage.

As discussed in Chapter 2 of Volume I, the Social Partner stage encompasses two major developmental transitions that enable a child to become a more active social and communicative partner: 1) the ability to communicate with purpose or intent for a range of communicative functions and 2) the acquisition and use of *conventional* gestures and vocalizations in emotionally satisfying and reciprocal social communicative exchanges. Intentional or purposeful communication refers to one's ability to *share* desired goals with others. This early communicative milestone is achieved as a child learns how to initiate a communicative signal (e.g., gestures and/or vocalizations) *and directs this signal toward another person* with either eye gaze or physical contact to ensure a partner's attention. In doing so, the child demonstrates an awareness of some of the earliest strategies for establishing shared or joint attention as well as an awareness of those gestures and vocal strategies that most effectively convey communicative intent.

In addition, as a child acquires these necessary skills for engaging in social communication, he or she develops a sense of both competence and confidence, which contributes to the child's emerging sense of self, and will typically begin to more actively seek interaction as a context for learning language and problem solving (also referred to as *active learning*). This latter accomplishment supports an ability to persist and repair communicative breakdowns that occur and to seek out others not only as sources of assistance but also as sources of social engagement, information, and comfort and joy.

In the Social Communication domain of the SCERTS Model, these achievements typically develop as a result of a child's accomplishments in both joint attention and symbol use. In the Emotional Regulation domain of the SCERTS Model, these achievements rely on the child's accomplishments in mutual regulation and self-regulation.

PRIORITIZING GOALS FOR JOINT ATTENTION AT THE SOCIAL PARTNER STAGE

A number of critical milestones in joint attention contribute to a child's transition from the Social Partner stage to the Language Partner stage and to the development of socially conventional and purposeful communication. These milestones provide the framework for prioritizing goal areas for a child with ASD as he or she progresses through the Social Partner stage. They include the child's ability to 1) engage in reciprocal interaction, 2) share attention with partners, 3) share emotion, 4) share (express) intentions to regulate behavior, 5) share intentions for social interaction, 6) share intentions for joint attention, and 7) persist and repair communicative breakdowns. These abilities contribute to the child's capacity to share attention with partners in communicative exchanges and participate as a true social partner. Specific milestones along this developmental trajectory provide developmental benchmarks that guide the determination of weekly objectives for a child at the Social Partner stage. These include the following:

1. The child *engages in reciprocal interaction* by

    a. Responding to bids for interaction

    b. Initiating bids for interaction

    c. Engaging in brief reciprocal interaction

    d. Engaging in extended reciprocal interaction

2. The child *shares attention* by

    a. Looking toward people

    b. Shifting gaze between people and objects

    c. Following another person's contact point

    d. Following another person's distal point

3. The child *shares emotion* by

    a. Directing negative emotion using facial expressions or vocalizations

    b. Directing positive emotion using facial expressions or vocalizations

    c. Responding to changes in partners' expression of emotion

    d. Attuning to changes in partners' expression of emotion

4. The child *shares intentions to regulate the behavior of others* by
   a. Requesting desired food or objects
   b. Protesting/refusing undesired food or objects
   c. Requesting help or other actions
   d. Protesting undesired actions or activities
5. The child *shares intentions for social interaction* by
   a. Requesting comfort
   b. Requesting social games
   c. Taking turns
   d. Greeting others
   e. Calling others
   f. Showing off
6. The child *shares intentions for joint attention* by
   a. Commenting on objects
   b. Commenting on actions or events
7. The child *persists and repairs communication breakdowns* by
   a. Using an appropriate rate of communication for the context
   b. Repeats communication to repair breakdowns
   c. Modifies communication to repair breakdowns

As discussed in Chapter 2 of Volume I, children with ASD at the Social Partner stage typically show difficulties with these early achievements in shared attention, as evidenced by a limited ability to orient to (i.e., turn to and focus on) people, to follow their focus of attention, to use gaze shifts, to share emotion, and/or to follow what others are pointing to or looking at (i.e., gaze/point following). Therefore, these children's ability to consider what another person may be trying to communicate or what another person may be attending to often is quite compromised, as is their ability to communicate for more social purposes, such as social interaction and joint attention.

PRIORITIZING GOALS FOR SYMBOL USE AT THE SOCIAL PARTNER STAGE

A number of critical milestones in symbol use contribute to a child's transition from the Social Partner stage to the Language Partner stage and to the development of socially conventional and purposeful communication. As the child first begins to communicate with intent, many gestures and vocalizations will initially be unconventional or idiosyncratic. Partners other than the child's immediate caregivers may have difficulty interpreting these signals. Early gestures often involve manipulating another's hand (i.e., physical manipulation) or recreating part of the desired event (i.e., reenactment). These types of gestures develop early and are typically followed in development by more conventional or easily understood gestures such as a give gesture, a push-away gesture, index finger pointing, head nodding, and so forth. The transition to more conventional gestures typically occurs before the emergence of first words.

Knowledge of how typically developing children make this transition, and current research related to the social communication patterns of children with ASD, contribute to a team's ability to prioritize critical goal areas in Symbol Use. As a child progresses through the Social Partner stage, a number of critical abilities contribute to the capacity to use more conventional means or behaviors to communicate intentions by communicating with purpose using gestures and vocalizations that are easily readable and have shared meanings with partners. These include the ability to 1) learn by imitation of familiar actions and sounds, 2) understand nonverbal cues in familiar activities, 3) use familiar objects conventionally in play, 4) use gestures and nonverbal means to share intentions, 5) use vocalizations to share intentions, and 6) understand a few familiar words. Specific milestones along this developmental trajectory provide benchmarks that guide the determination of weekly objectives for a child at this stage. These include the following:

1. The child *learns by imitation of familiar actions and sounds* by

    a. Taking turns by repeating his or her own actions or sounds

    b. Imitating familiar actions or sounds when elicited immediately after a model

    c. Spontaneously imitating familiar actions or sounds immediately after a model

    d. Spontaneously imitating familiar actions or sounds at a later time

2. The child *understands nonverbal cues in familiar activities* by

    a. Anticipating another person's actions in familiar routines

    b. Following situational cues in familiar activities

    c. Following gestural cues other than a point

    d. Following another person's contact point

    e. Following another person's distal point

    f. Responding to visual cues (photographs or pictures)

    g. Responding to facial expression and intonation cues

3. The child *uses familiar objects conventionally in play* by

    a. Using exploratory actions on objects

    b. Using familiar objects in constructive play

    c. Using familiar objects conventionally toward self

    d. Using familiar objects conventionally toward others

4. The child *uses gestures and nonverbal means to share intentions* by

    a. Using proximity

    b. Using facial expressions

    c. Using simple motor actions

    d. Using conventional contact gestures such as giving, pushing away, showing, reaching/touching, and pointing/touching

e. Using conventional distal gestures such as waving, distal reaching, distal pointing, clapping, head shaking, and head nodding

   f. Using reenactment or symbolic distal gestures

   g. Using a sequence of gestures or nonverbal means

   h. Coordinating gestures and gaze

5. The child *uses vocalizations to share intentions* by

   a. Using differentiated vocalizations

   b. Using a variety of consonant + vowel combinations

   c. Using words bound to routines

   d. Coordinating vocalizations with gestures and gaze

6. The child *understands a few familiar words* by

   a. Responding to his or her own name

   b. Responding to a few words in familiar social games

   c. Responding to a few familiar person, body part, or object names

   d. Responding to a few frequently used phrases in familiar routines

As discussed in Chapter 2 of Volume I, children with ASD at the Social Partner stage typically show difficulties with these early achievements in symbol use, as evidenced by limited range of conventional gestures and vocalizations in the early stages of communication development. Children with ASD may, in fact, communicate through the use of 1) presymbolic motoric gestures, including contact gestures such as leading, pulling, or physically manipulating another's hand, often without eye gaze, or 2) reenactment strategies, involving replicating an event or part of an event to request that the event happen. These unconventional means of communication may be used for an extended period of time in lieu of using conventional gestures such as showing, waving, pointing, and shaking or nodding one's head. Furthermore, challenges in visually orienting to a partner contribute to the difficulties that children with ASD have when performing on elicited imitation tasks using both actions of their body without objects and actions with objects. Likewise, children with ASD who are very young or who are nonverbal/presymbolic typically have very limited use of functional actions with objects as well as relative weaknesses in comprehension of others' nonverbal communication.

As discussed in Chapter 3 of Volume I, some children with ASD may develop unconventional and socially undesirable behaviors to communicate, such as screaming, aggression, self-injurious behavior, tantrums, going limp, or dropping to the ground to avoid or to escape from activities. The use of such problem behaviors for communication may be a direct consequence of limitations in acquiring conventional and more symbolic means to communicate, as they are often used in lieu of more conventional gestures for protesting or establishing social control. Therefore, it is imperative to consider the use of problem behaviors for communication relative to a child's available repertoire of other verbal and nonverbal communicative behaviors, as the presence of problem behaviors may reflect limitations in symbolic capacity that should be addressed when determining Symbol Use goals.

PRIORITIZING GOALS FOR MUTUAL REGULATION AT THE SOCIAL PARTNER STAGE

A number of critical milestones in mutual regulation support a child's transition from the Social Partner stage to the Language Partner stage and to the development of effective and efficient emotional regulation strategies that support the child's ability to be an active and attentive communicative partner. An important distinction in the process of mutual regulation is whether a partner *responds* to the child's signals of dysregulation or whether the child *initiates* and intentionally directs signals to others, resulting in regulatory support. Early in the Social Partner stage, a child has not yet developed the communicative capacity and social awareness to intentionally signal to a partner that he or she needs assistance for emotional regulation; however, signs of dysregulation may be readily observable. Communicative partners' ability to read and respond to these signals of dysregulation, which may include facial expressions, vocalizations, bodily tension, activity level, and so forth, contributes to a process referred to as *respondent mutual regulation.* As a child's social communicative abilities develop throughout the Social Partner stage, so does the child's ability to initiate requests for assistance for emotional regulation. This process is referred to as *initiated mutual regulation,* as the child actively seeks assistance from partners. Initiated mutual regulation may occur initially through the use of unconventional means, such as idiosyncratic gestures, and eventually through the use of more conventional gestures, and vocalizations, a process that reflects increasing abilities in social communication.

Critical goal areas in the Mutual Regulation component are prioritized based on two primary sources: 1) a team's knowledge of how typically developing children make the transition to becoming more active social partners who are increasingly able to seek assistance from others and 2) current research related to the mutual regulatory challenges faced by children with ASD. Priority goals in Mutual Regulation include the ability to 1) express a range of emotions, 2) respond to assistance offered by partners, 3) request partners' assistance to regulate emotional state, and 4) recover from extreme dysregulation with support from partners. Specific milestones along this developmental trajectory provide benchmarks that guide the determination of weekly objectives for a child at this stage. These include the following:

1. The child *expresses a range of emotions* by
    a. Expressing happiness
    b. Expressing sadness
    c. Expressing anger
    d. Expressing fear

2. The child *responds to assistance offered by partners* by
    a. Soothing when comforted by partners
    b. Engaging when alerted by partners
    c. Responding to bids for interaction
    d. Responding to changes in partners' expression of emotion
    e. Attuning to changes in partners' expression of emotion
    f. Making choices when offered by partners

3. The child *requests partners' assistance to regulate state* by
   a. Sharing negative emotion to seek comfort
   b. Sharing positive emotion to seek interaction
   c. Requesting help when frustrated
   d. Protesting when distressed
4. The child *recovers from extreme dysregulation with support from partners* by
   a. Responding to partners' efforts to assist with recovery by moving away from activity
   b. Responding to partners' use of behavioral strategies
   c. Responding to partners' attempts to reengage in interaction or activity
   d. Decreasing amount of time to recover from extreme dysregulation due to support from partners
   e. Decreasing intensity of dysregulated state due to support from partners

As discussed in Chapter 3 of Volume I, a child with ASD at the Social Partner stage typically shows difficulties with mutual regulation, as evidenced by challenges in expressing emotion due to limitations in the ability use of gestures, facial expressions, and body language. In turn, communicative partners often have difficulty interpreting the child's emotional and arousal states, resulting in the use of respondent mutual regulatory strategies that do not always facilitate organization. In addition to accurately interpreting a child's idiosyncratic signs of dysregulation, it is critical that a partner consider the child's arousal bias and emotional reactions to activities and events to design and implement effective mutual regulatory strategies that facilitate the child's organization. For example, to support a dysregulated hyperreactive child with auditory sensitivities, a partner must recognize the need to reduce the intensity of environmental stimulation, such as the humming of an air conditioner, to help the child achieve a better regulated state. In contrast, to support a dysregulated hyporeactive child during a transition, a partner must recognize the need to increase the use of movement and rhythm to help increase his or her attention and engagement during the transition. When partners are unable to read signs of dysregulation relative to a child's arousal bias, respondent regulatory strategies may be applied haphazardly and therefore may be unsuccessful or may even result in more extreme dysregulation.

Challenges in social communication further affect a child's ability to recognize a communicative partner as a potential source of assistance and therefore the ability to direct readable signals to others to request for emotional regulatory support. Collectively, these difficulties exacerbate a child's difficulties in using or responding to mutual regulatory strategies.

PRIORITIZING GOALS FOR SELF-REGULATION AT THE SOCIAL PARTNER STAGE

A number of critical milestones in self-regulation contribute to a child's transition from the Social Partner stage to the Language Partner stage and to the child's development of effective and efficient regulation strategies that support the ability to be an active and attentive communicative partner. Early in the Social Partner stage, a child's primary drive is to use simple behavioral means (e.g., sensory and motor actions) with biologically determined protective mechanisms to achieve a state of homeostasis. In turn, a well-regulated state supports a child's ability to interact, explore, and engage. In early stages, there is a clear interdependence between mutual and self-regulatory capacities, as the presence of responsive partners helps to foster the development of effective behavioral strategies used for self-regulation. Environmental supports, such as the availability of comfort objects and organizing stimulation, also support the development of self-regulatory abilities that enable a child to respond to new and changing situations and recover from extreme dysregulation.

Critical goal areas in the Self-Regulation component are prioritized based on two sources of information: 1) how typically developing children acquire and expand their self-regulation abilities and 2) the difficulties children with ASD have in self-regulation. Priority goals for self-regulation include the ability to 1) demonstrate availability for learning and interacting, 2) use behavioral strategies to regulate arousal level during familiar activities, 3) regulate emotion during new and changing situations, and 4) recover from extreme dysregulation by oneself. Specific milestones along this developmental trajectory provide benchmarks that guide the determination of weekly objectives for a child at this stage. These include the following:

1. The child *demonstrates availability for learning and interacting* by
    a. Noticing people and things in the environment
    b. Showing interest in variety of sensory and social experiences
    c. Seeking and tolerating a variety of sensory experiences
    d. Initiating bids for interaction
    e. Engaging in brief reciprocal interaction
    f. Engaging in extended reciprocal interaction
    g. Responding to social and sensory experiences with differentiated emotions

2. The child *uses behavioral strategies to regulate arousal level during familiar activities* by
    a. Using behavioral strategies to regulate arousal level during solitary activities
    b. Using behavioral strategies to regulate arousal level during social interactions
    c. Using behavioral strategies modeled by partners to regulate arousal level
    d. Using behavioral strategies to engage productively in an extended activity

3. The child *regulates emotion in new and changing situations* by
    a. Anticipating another person's actions in familiar routines
    b. Participating in new and changing situations
    c. Using behavioral strategies to regulate arousal in new and changing situations
    d. Using behavioral strategies to regulate arousal level during transitions

4. The child *recovers from extreme dysregulation by him- or herself* by
    a. Removing him- or herself from overstimulating or undesired activity
    b. Using behavioral strategies to recover from extreme dysregulation
    c. Reengaging in interaction or activity after recovery from extreme dysregulation
    d. Decreasing amount of time to recover from extreme dysregulation
    e. Decreasing intensity of dysregulated state

As discussed in Chapter 3 of Volume I, children with ASD at the Social Partner stage typically show difficulties in these early self-regulation milestones, as evidenced by challenges sustaining attention during social interactions, displaying strong and sudden emotional reactions, and having difficulty tolerating transitions. Factors associated with ASD that contribute to these challenges include 1) atypical responses to stimulation that result in arousal biases (e.g., hypersensitivity to sensation and stimulation resulting in a bias for a high state of arousal, hyposensitivity resulting in a bias for a low state of arousal), 2) challenges perceiving physiological changes in arousal state, and 3) difficulties expressing emotions.

Social communicative challenges further affect self-regulatory abilities. In particular, these challenges affect a child's ability to express changes in emotion that are readable and socially acceptable and to employ emotional regulatory strategies that have been modeled for the child. In addition, children with ASD at the Social Partner stage often use self-regulatory strategies that appear to be idiosyncratic; unconventional; and, in some cases, socially stigmatizing (e.g., flapping hands, walking on toes, mouthing, biting, rocking). These idiosyncratic self-regulatory behaviors may be viewed as problem behaviors and targeted for elimination in some educational approaches. It is important to consider that these behaviors may be a direct consequence of a limited repertoire of socially appropriate and effective self-regulatory and social communicative strategies. In the SCERTS Model, considering the emotional regulatory functions of such behavioral patterns is considered critical when determining appropriate goals in Self-Regulation.

PRIORITIZING GOALS FOR INTERPERSONAL SUPPORT AT THE SOCIAL PARTNER STAGE

Although we have focused primarily on a child's abilities and behavior in social communication and emotional regulation at the Social Partner stage, it is critical to emphasize, once again, the overriding influence of the behaviors of partners on a child's development and success in interpersonal interaction. Achievements in the developmental capacities of social communication and emotional regulation at the Social Partner stage are dependent on a successful history of predictable and supportive interactions with partners who have fostered social engagement, communicative initiation, and the attainment of a well-regulated state. Such interpersonal accommodations are referred to as *interpersonal supports* in the SCERTS Model and are considered critical when prioritizing partner goals in the domain of Transactional Support.

The following dimensions of the Interpersonal Support component of Transactional Support are viewed as essential for supporting a child's ability to engage as a true social partner. The partner 1) is responsive to the child, 2) fosters initiation, 3) respects the child's independence, 4) sets the stage for engagement, 5) provides developmental support, 6) adjusts language input, and 7) models appropriate behaviors. Specific objectives in these dimensions provide benchmarks that guide the development of individualized interpersonal supports and the identification of weekly objectives not only for the child but also for the child's partners. These include the following:

1. The *partner is responsive to the child* by

    a. Following the child's focus of attention

    b. Attuning to the child's emotion and pace

    c. Responding appropriately to the child's signals to foster a sense of communicative competence

d. Recognizing and supporting the child's behavioral strategies to regulate arousal level

e. Recognizing signs of dysregulation and offering support

f. Imitating child

g. Offering breaks from interaction or activity as needed

h. Facilitating reengagement in interactions and activities following breaks

2. The *partner fosters initiation* by

    a. Offering choices nonverbally or verbally

    b. Waiting for and encouraging initiations

    c. Providing a balance of initiated and respondent turns

    d. Allowing the child to initiate and terminate activities

3. The partner *respects the child's independence* by

    a. Allowing the child to take breaks to move about as needed

    b. Providing time for the child to solve problems or complete activities at own pace

    c. Interpreting problem behavior as communicative and/or regulatory

    d. Honoring protests, rejections, or refusals when appropriate

4. The *partner sets stage for engagement* by

    a. Getting down on the child's level when communicating

    b. Securing the child's attention before communicating

    c. Using appropriate proximity and nonverbal behavior to encourage interaction

    d. Using appropriate words and intonation to support optimal arousal level and engagement

5. The *partner provides developmental support* by

    a. Encouraging imitation

    b. Encouraging interaction with peers

    c. Attempting to repair breakdowns verbally or nonverbally

    d. Giving guidance and feedback as needed for success in activities

    e. Expanding on a child's play and nonverbal communication

6. The *partner adjusts language input* by

    a. Using nonverbal cues to support understanding

    b. Adjusting complexity of language input to the child's developmental level

    c. Adjusting quality of language input to the child's arousal level

7. The partner *models appropriate behaviors* by

    a. Modeling appropriate nonverbal communication and emotional expressions

    b. Modeling a range of communicative functions

c. Modeling appropriate play

　　d. Modeling appropriate behavior when the child uses inappropriate behavior

　　e. Modeling "child-perspective" language

Social interactions are transactional in nature; therefore, the child's communicative partners must respond flexibly and in a supportive manner to foster the child's development of communicative and regulatory abilities. As described in Chapter 4 of Volume I, some children with ASD are at risk for developing a sense of interpersonal interaction as overwhelming, confusing, and stressful based on a history of repeated unsuccessful experiences. Other children with ASD are at risk for limited engagement and low motivation to participate in social interactions due to language and sensory processing difficulties and/or a hyporesponsive bias toward interpersonal events. A child's partners are also at risk for experiencing interactions with the child as challenging, especially in reference to supporting the child's communicative intent and in reading the child's subtle signs of dysregulation.

At the Social Partner stage, a child's developmental vulnerabilities and learning style differences have a transactional influence on the child's partners. For example, a child's difficulties processing language often results in a lack of, or inconsistent, responses to a partner's verbal bids for interaction. Therefore, a partner may view the child as difficult to reach and/or difficult to engage with. Similarly, a partner may have difficulty reading a child's bids for communication or signals of dysregulation due to their unconventional and/or subtle nature. This challenge limits the partner's ability to respond to the child's intent, which in turn would build the child's sense of communicative competence. Likewise, a child's difficulties in understanding emotional cues, gestures, and facial expression often results in lack of, inconsistent, or inappropriate responses to a partner's nonverbal and emotional communication. In some situations, children may shut down or tune out in the face of difficult-to-process information, resulting in lack of or inconsistent response to a partner who is genuinely invested in connecting with the child and maintaining engagement.

Last, a child's sensory processing difficulties (e.g., patterns of hypo- or hyperreactivity) may result in inconsistent reactions to sensory input and fluctuating states of arousal, which is a challenging pattern for the child's partners to read and respond to successfully. These dimensions of interpersonal interaction contribute to the child's ability to communicate with intent, and a partner's ability to model conventional means of communicating.

PRIORITIZING GOALS FOR LEARNING SUPPORT AT THE SOCIAL PARTNER STAGE

Achievements in social communication and emotional regulation are facilitated, in part, by the effective use of learning supports. Learning supports are accommodations that include a range of environmental modifications, visual supports, and other relevant learning and instructional strategies that may be used to facilitate a child's communication and expressive language, understanding of language and social expectations, activity structure (e.g., the sequence of steps and end goal of an activity), emotional expression, and emotional regulation. It is critical that the child's partners use such accommodations to modify activities and learning environments in a manner that supports organization, provides opportunities for active learning, and promotes child initiation and participation.

The following dimensions of the Learning Support component are viewed as essential for supporting a child's ability to engage as a competent Social Partner. The partner 1) structures an activity for active participation; 2) uses augmentative communication support to foster development; 3) uses visual and organizational support; and 4) modifies goals, activities, and the learning environment to suit the child's specific developmental level and learning style differences. Specific objectives in these dimensions provide benchmarks that guide the development of individualized learning supports and the identification of weekly objectives not just for the child but also for that child's partners. These include the following:

1. The *partner structures an activity for active participation* by
    a. Defining a clear beginning and ending to an activity
    b. Creating turn-taking opportunities and leaving spaces for the child to fill in
    c. Providing a predictable sequence to an activity
    d. Offering repeated learning opportunities
    e. Offering varied learning opportunities

2. The *partner uses augmentative communication support to foster development* by
    a. Using augmentative communication support to enhance the child's communication and expressive language
    b. Using augmentative communication support to enhance the child's understanding of language and behavior
    c. Using augmentative communication support to enhance the child's expression and understanding of emotion
    d. Using augmentative communication support to enhance the child's emotional regulation

3. The *partner uses visual and organizational support* by
    a. Using support to define steps within a task
    b. Using support to define steps and time for completion of activities
    c. Using visual support to enhance smooth transitions between activities
    d. Using support to organize segments of time across the day
    e. Using visual support to enhance attention in group activities
    f. Using visual support to foster active involvement in group activities

4. The *partner modifies goals, activities, and the learning environment* by
    a. Adjusting social complexity to support organization and interaction
    b. Adjusting task difficulty for child success
    c. Modifying sensory properties of the learning environment
    d. Arranging the learning environment to enhance attention

e. Arranging the learning environment to promote child initiation

f. Designing and modifying activities to be developmentally appropriate

g. Infusing motivating materials and topics in activities

h. Providing activities to promote initiation and extended interactions

i. Alternating between movement and sedentary activities as needed

j. "Upping the ante" or increasing expectations appropriately

As discussed in Chapter 4 of Volume I, children with ASD at the Social Partner stage demonstrate unique patterns of learning preferences and weaknesses, which requires that individualized learning supports be implemented to foster both social communication and emotional regulation. A greater understanding of the learning and cognitive styles of children with ASD has led to the development of a wide range of effective visual, organizational, and learning supports. A number of these supports fall under the umbrella term *augmentative and alternative communication,* or *AAC.* Although there are clear individual variations among children with ASD, a child with ASD may demonstrate a strong preference for nontransient visual information. This refers to information that remains static or fixed in place over time, such as pictures, visual-spatial patterns, and objects. Thus, the SCERTS Model emphasizes the role of partners in capitalizing on a child's preference for static visual information as a means to help the child compensate for difficulties processing information that is more transient or fleeting in nature, such as the spoken word or nonverbal social cues. In the SCERTS Model, partners are encouraged to use visual and organizational supports to define steps within a task, to define steps and time for completion of activities, and to support smooth transitions between activities. Likewise, partners are encouraged to implement augmentative communication supports, such as gestures, signs, and pictures, to foster a child's expressive communication and language development, understanding of language, and emotional regulation.

Children at the Social Partner stage also may have a tendency to rely on context-specific conditions to communicate with intent and/or to use more conventional means of communicating. This may be a reflection of a preference for static environmental cues and/or strengths in gestalt, episodic memory and rote, associative memory. Thus, the SCERTS Model encourages a child's partners to develop an understanding of this unique learning style and encourages the incorporation of learning supports to define a clear beginning and end to natural activities, to provide predictable learning opportunities, and to offer both repeated *and* varied learning opportunities.

Because these learning supports contribute to a child's ability to remain actively engaged in natural routines and to develop those developmental capacities essential to being a social partner, the SCERTS Model prioritizes systematic goals for partner behavior. These goals are designed to enhance environmental and activity modifications, the implementation of visual supports, and the use of highly predictable and repetitive learning opportunities when developing a comprehensive program or modifying an existing program for a child with ASD at the Social Partner stage.

Chapter 4 in this volume provides many examples of how the implementation of learning supports fosters 1) a child's ability to communicate with purpose or intent for a range of communicative functions and 2) the acquisition and use of *conventional* gestures and vocalizations in social communicative exchanges. We now shift to a more in-depth and comprehensive look at the development of SCERTS Model programs for two children at the Social Partner stage.

SPOTLIGHTS ON CHILDREN AT THE SOCIAL PARTNER STAGE

In the following sections, two children and families are spotlighted to illustrate the process of identifying and prioritizing goals for a child at the novice Social Partner stage and a child at the advanced Social Partner stage. The term *spotlight* is used because each of these vignettes is reflective of a child and family at a specific intersection on their developmental journey. The SCERTS Model recognizes the dynamic processes involved in assessment and program planning. Following the criteria for goal selection, ongoing assessment will be necessary to identify goals and objectives that are considered 1) functional, 2) a family's priorities, and 3) developmentally appropriate. It is expected that goals may need to be modified as a child's program evolves.

A number of other decisions should be reassessed regularly (i.e., every 3 months) to determine any necessary program adjustments and modifications. These include 1) the choice of meaningful and purposeful activities to focus on in a child's daily routines; 2) the intensity of social support, such as the ratio of adult to child support in social groupings; and 3) the range of naturalness of activities (e.g., planned activity routines, engineered activities, modified natural activities). These spotlights are provided to illustrate the processes involved in implementing the SCERTS Model from assessment through implementation of a program addressing social communication, emotional regulation, and transactional support for children with ASD at the Social Partner stage. (Chapters 6 and 7 in this volume present spotlights on children at the Language Partner and Conversational Partner stages, respectively.) Blank versions of the assessment forms mentioned in the spotlights can be found in Appendix A of Volume I.

SPOTLIGHT ON JASON, A NOVICE SOCIAL PARTNER

Jason, the first child whom we spotlight, is at the novice level of the Social Partner stage. Jason is a sweet and bright-eyed boy who is 2 years and 3 months old. He has an infectious smile and an enthusiasm for both music and gross motor play. He is an easygoing child who rarely becomes upset. Although an only child, Jason often visits his cousin Amy, who is also 2 years old. As his parents watched the two children grow and develop, they became concerned about Jason's development, particularly over the past 3–4 months. Although he enjoys watching his parents blow bubbles and sing his favorite songs, he often takes care of his needs on his own and prefers to play by himself even when his cousin is in the same room.

Jason's parents also became concerned because Jason is not yet using words, and they worry about his limited ability to form relationships with his aunt and uncle, Amy's parents. Because his aunt and uncle visit frequently and often have him and his parents over to their home, they are very familiar to him. Nevertheless, he does not typically greet or interact with them. When Jason enters his aunt and uncle's home, for example, he will, without exception, make his way to the pantry and begin to play with the swinging doors.

During Jason's second-year check up, Jason's parents had raised their concerns with his pediatrician, and Jason was subsequently referred to a diagnostic evaluation at 2 years and 2 months of age. Members of his evaluation team indicated that Jason's behavior and his developmental profile were consistent with the criteria for ASD, and a referral was made to regional early intervention providers. Although Jason's parents had been concerned about his development before this evaluation, the diagnosis only escalated their anxiety. The evaluation had, in fact, led to more questions than answers. His parents had questions regarding the nature of ASD and the rationale for the diagnosis, they had questions regarding Jason's future and whether he would be ready for preschool, and they had questions about the most appropriate course of action to take. It was their focus on this latter question that brought them to early intervention for a treatment planning assessment. They hoped that with an appropriate therapeutic and educational program, Jason would improve his ability communicate, would form more secure relationships with his aunt and uncle, and would develop a greater interest in playing with his cousin.

During Jason's initial visits with the early intervention program staff, Jason participated in the SAP. Thus, this spotlight illustrates the steps that Jason's family and his service providers took as part of this assessment process. As discussed in Chapter 7 of Volume I, the SAP was implemented to 1) establish Jason's current profile of developmental strengths and needs; 2) determine meaningful, purposeful, and motivating goals to address; 3) select the most appropriate learning contexts and complexity of social support based on Jason's natural routines and activities; and 4) determine the necessary transactional supports to foster Jason's development and his relationships with his family and peers. Because a comprehensive SCERTS Model program also includes explicit plans for support to families and support among professionals, information from the SAP was also used to ensure that Jason's early intervention program is compatible and consistent with the needs expressed by his family. In addition, the assessment team determined the specific educational supports and emotional supports that would be provided for Jason's family members and the professionals who would be involved in the implementation of Jason's program.

SAP Step 1: Determining Jason's Communication Stage

Based on a review of Jason's developmental history and information obtained through an initial telephone interview, the early intervention service coordinator determined that the appropriate SAP forms to use for the assessment would be those designated for the Social Partner stage. This was based on the completion of the Worksheet for Determining Communication Stage and a review of the criteria used to determine a child's communication stage in the SAP, as Jason is not yet using referential words or symbols to communicate with intent on a regular basis.

SAP Step 2: Gathering Information with the Social Partner SAP-R Form

Following the telephone interview, the SAP-R Form for the Social Partner Stage was mailed to Jason's parents. They completed this form and returned it to Jason's service coordinator before their initial appointment with the early intervention program. This questionnaire identified 1) the primary concerns and stresses faced by Jason's parents, 2) Jason's primary strengths and his parents' concerns about his development, 3) the activities in which both Jason's strengths and areas of need would likely be seen, 4) Jason's typical partners, and 5) the natural contexts in Jason's life. The information gathered from Jason's SAP-R is summarized next:

1. The primary concerns and stresses faced by Jason's parents included

    - "The accuracy of the diagnosis"
    - "How best to support him"
    - "Why he is not talking yet"
    - "His limited engagement with family members, in particular, his cousin Amy"

2. Jason's parents identified the following strengths and needs in his current profile:

Strengths	Needs
"Jason is an easygoing toddler." "He enjoys music." "He is very independent."	"Jason is not talking yet. He needs to develop more effective communication." "He is not yet listening and following simple directions. He needs to pay attention to the social environment." "He appears to be preoccupied with his toys and difficult to reach. He needs to develop a greater interest in social routines."

3. The activities in which both Jason's strengths and areas of need would likely be seen included

   - Feeding routines (e.g., breakfast, snack, lunch)
   - Play routines with his mom and dad (e.g., bubbles, dancing/singing, puzzles)
   - Visiting his cousin Amy and his aunt and uncle

4. Jason's typical partners

   - Mom
   - Dad
   - Amy (2-year-old cousin)
   - Aunt
   - Uncle

5. Natural contexts in Jason's life include the following:

   - Caregiving routines at home
   - Play routines at home
   - Visits to Amy's house
   - Occasional trips to the neighborhood playground

SAP Step 3: Identifying Assessment Team Members and Planning the SAP-O

On receiving the completed SAP-R, Jason's early intervention service coordinator began completing the SAP Map for Planning the SAP-Observation. This form was used to help determine the appropriate members of Jason's assessment team, their roles and responsibilities, and whether any outside referrals would need to take place. In addition, as part of planning the administration of the SAP-O, the following variables were considered to ensure a sample of observations that would provide the most typical picture of Jason, and the most useful information: 1) the *location* (i.e., natural contexts) where the observations would take place, 2) the specific *length* of the observations, 3) the *partners* who would be present, 4) the *group size* of the social contexts during the observations, 5) the nature of the *activities,* and 6) the number of *transitions* during each observation (please refer to Chapter 7 in Volume I for a more detailed discussion of these variables).

After reviewing the information provided in the SAP-R and each of these variables, Jason's early intervention service coordinator was able to plan the upcoming observations to ensure a more representative sample. First, given that Jason is a Social

Partner, the minimum length of total observation time was identified as 2 hours. However, given that young children clearly vary from one day to the next, this allotted time was split across 2 separate days (i.e., 1 hour per observation day). Next, because Jason is a young child at the Social Partner stage, Jason's early intervention service coordinator recognized that the range of social contexts and partners in his daily life remains quite limited, similar to that of other children his age. Thus, observation of Jason engaged with only familiar partners, as opposed to both familiar and unfamiliar partners, was considered an appropriate plan. Likewise, representative group sizes (i.e., group sizes natural to Jason's natural environment) were identified and included one to one (e.g., Jason with his mother and Jason with his father) and small group (Jason with his aunt, uncle, and cousin Amy). Given that Jason's parents had expressed concern about Jason's behavior at home as well as at his aunt and uncle's house, these two contexts were identified as the primary locations for the observations. Although Jason's parents had reported that he occasionally visits the neighborhood playground, his service coordinator noted that these visits, because of their occasional nature, might not have provided as representative a sample of Jason's behavior.

After determining the specific contexts for the observations, Jason's service coordinator carefully reviewed the primary concerns of Jason's parents and those activities that they felt would provide a sample of Jason's strengths and areas of need. Additional variables were considered to ensure that the assessment team would gain an accurate picture. For example, it was evident that Jason's behavior may be different when Jason is engaged in a must-do caregiving activity versus a play-based activity, a motor-based activity versus a sedentary activity, a social activity versus a solitary activity, and a preferred activity versus a nonpreferred activity. With this information, three activities were identified for his home-based observation. These included 1) a motor-based play routine (i.e., familiar songs and dancing) with his mom and/or his dad as a partner, 2) a must-do caregiving activity (i.e., snack), and 3) a sedentary play activity (i.e., bubbles and/or puzzles) with his mom and/or dad. An additional three activities were identified for his community-based observation at his cousin's house. These included 1) a social activity involving a greeting ritual with his aunt and uncle; 2) a sedentary and solitary play-based activity at his aunt and uncle's house (e.g., physical exploration, such as playing with the swinging doors); and 3) a nonpreferred social activity with his cousin Amy (e.g., "Ring Around the Rosy").

Because all children who participate in the SAP should be observed across at least three transitions, at least two transitions per observation day were planned for Jason. On the first day, for example, the service coordinator planned to observe Jason making the transition from motor-based play activities to his highchair for snack time and then observe him making the transition from snack to a sedentary play activity (e.g., blowing bubbles) in the family's play room. On the second day of observation, Jason would be observed making the transition from the car to his aunt and uncle's house and then making the transition from a solitary preferred activity to a social play-based activity with his cousin Amy.

A review of Jason's SAP-R and his recent diagnostic evaluation revealed that an audiological evaluation had not yet been completed. Given that parental concerns included limited use of words and difficulty listening and following simple directions, an audiological evaluation was recommended to rule out the presence of a hearing loss. Thus, a referral to a pediatric audiologist was made. Information included in Jason's SAP Map is provided in Figure 5.1A to illustrate the outcome of this planning process. After Jason's SAP Map was created, the service coordinator transferred relevant information to the cover sheet of the SAP-O Form (see Figure 5.1B).

Figure 5.1A. Jason's SAP Map.

Figure 5.1B. Cover sheet (p. 1) of Jason's SAP-O Form.

SAP Step 4: Completing the SAP-O Form

Jason's assessment team (i.e., his service coordinator, speech-language pathologist, and occupational therapist) used the SAP-O Form for the Social Partner stage to gather information across their two observations (see Chapter 7 of Volume I for specific administration instructions). Information was gathered across three domains, two of which focused on assessing Jason's strengths and needs (i.e., Social Communication and Emotional Regulation) and one that addressed the strengths and needs of his partners in various environments (i.e., Transactional Support). Jason's early interventionists adopted a team approach at gathering and documenting information across contexts, partners, and observation days. Because his service coordinator, a licensed social worker, was present at both observations, she elected to gather the majority of the information on the Transactional Support domain (i.e., Interpersonal Support and Learning Support). This included information related to those supports already present in these contexts as well as those that would be beneficial for fostering Jason's development. Jason's speech-language pathologist elected to document information related to the Social Communication domain, and the occupational therapist elected to document Jason's behavior in the Emotional Regulation domain. However, information related to the Social Communication domain was augmented by Jason's occupational therapist, as she was present across both days of the observation.

SAP Step 5: Conducting Behavior Sampling

Toward the completion of Jason's second observation at his cousin's home, his early intervention team members briefly reviewed his SAP-O Form. They agreed that although they had gathered a wealth of information from observing his interactions in his natural environments and activities, there were a number of unanswered questions remaining related to his abilities in the Social Communication and Emotional Regulation domains. They felt that this had occurred due to Jason's passive communication style, which limited the number of opportunities to observe his current repertoire of communicative means, and the nature of the activities observed, which primarily involved preferred and familiar activities with only a few exceptions (e.g., making the transition to play "Ring Around the Rosy" with his cousin Amy). The areas for which they desired more information included

- JA4.3 and SU4.4—Jason's use of conventional contact gestures for requesting (e.g., a give gesture),
- JA3.1, JA4.4, SU4.2, and SU4.4—his ability to protest and/or share negative emotions when his expectations were violated (e.g., a push-away gesture, facial expressions),
- JA3.4 and MR2.5—his ability to attune his emotions to his caregivers' expressions
- SR3.2—his ability to participate in new and changing situations

With these remaining questions, Jason's early intervention team agreed that an additional session in the familiar context of the home environment would provide information necessary to address these questions related to his developmental profile and help guide the development and implementation of a more appropriate educational program. In this subsequent session, the team members asked Jason's parents if they would be comfortable introducing and participating in several structured situations designed to illustrate Jason's competence and abilities in the areas just outlined. For example, to observe and document Jason's use of conventional contact gestures for requesting (JA4.3 and SU4.4), a series of communicative temptations (i.e., highly motivating activities that require adult assistance such as blowing bubbles, playing with wind-up toys, and inflating balloons), were administered (see Chapter 7 of Volume I for more detailed instructions for implementing communicative temptations). Next, Jason's reactions to new and changing situations (SR3.2) were sampled by tempting him to engage in a novel but highly appealing activity for him (i.e., a colorful parachute) and playing a variety of games associated with this item (e.g., "The parachute goes up . . . up . . . up . . . *and down,*" Peekaboo, "Shake it fast, shake it slow").

Additional behavior sampling strategies were discussed by Jason's team members. These included those that involved artificially staging situations that would not typically occur in the natural environment. For example, Jason's ability to protest when his expectations were violated was observed by staging a situation in which a preferred activity was brought to an end before its completion (JA3.1, JA4.4, SU4.2, and SU4.4). Because his parents had mentioned that Jason had a particular affinity for toddler videos, his early intervention team capitalized on this preference by asking the family to invite Jason to watch a favorite video and then having them turn the video off after a few moments. In addition, Jason's parents were asked to engage Jason in building a block tower and to display exaggerated sadness when the structure crashed. This staged situation was an attempt to secure information related to his ability to attune his emotion to the expressions of his caregivers (JA3.4 and MR2.5). (Please note that these staged situations are meant primarily for an assessment situation and would not typically be recommended as part of a child's education/intervention program.)

SAP Step 6: Compiling and Integrating Information with the SAP Summary Form

Following the completion of the two observation days, Jason's audiological evaluation at the children's hospital audiology unit, and the follow-up behavior sampling session at Jason's home, his service coordinator held a meeting with his parents, his speech-language pathologist, and his occupational therapist to compile and integrate information, a step that involves two key information sources: 1) summarizing strengths and needs from the SAP-O and 2) documenting family perception of the SAP-O results.

Key Information Source 1: Summarizing Strengths and Needs

Social Communication: Joint Attention

During their team meeting, Jason's parents and early intervention providers initially focused on determining Jason's strengths and challenges in joint attention. Based on information obtained through the SAP-O, his parents and service providers agreed that Jason had a limited ability to share his intentions and emotions with others, as his ability to shift attention and direct communicative signals toward others appeared to be more of an emerging rather than a solidly established capacity. Although he clearly demonstrated activity preferences (e.g., playing with bubbles, watching videos, visually exploring toys), he most often expressed his interests by focusing solely on the activities without shifting his gaze between his parents and the desired activity to determine if they were engaged in and/or interested in the same activity.

His speech-language pathologist noted that Jason did not consistently observe whether his partners responded when his signals were not clearly directed to others. For example, during the home-based observation, Jason had placed his mother's hand on a bubble container to request continuation of this preferred bubble activity. This *intentional* request stood in contrast to Jason's less clear request for a snack just a few minutes later. Rather than pointing to a box of crackers on the counter and/or shifting his gaze between the box and his mother, he walked over to the counter and stared intently at the cracker box. The team and his parents agreed that although Jason was clearly goal directed in his desire to get the crackers, his method of achieving his goal did not involve social communication involving a request or a bid for shared attention.

During their discussions, it became evident to the team and Jason's parents that Jason's primary means for requesting or protesting were not shared with others due to his limited use of gaze and/or physical contact gestures to gain his listener's attention. Therefore, it was determined that the majority of his communicative signals were *preintentional,* in that they were not directed to others with a clear purpose or goal. Jason's occupational therapist supported this conclusion by contributing an additional example that occurred in the context of his aunt and uncle's home. She explained that when his aunt had attempted to engage Jason in "Ring Around the Rosy" with his cousin Amy, Jason dropped Amy's hand and attempted to walk away from the activity without pairing this signal with communicative gaze to *share* his protest or refusal with his family members.

Overall, Jason's parents and team members concluded that Jason demonstrated primarily a passive interactive style in both of his familiar environments, as he demonstrated a limited capacity to *initiate* requests for toys, snacks, and social routines (e.g., greetings, familiar songs, social games). While the early intervention team was reviewing the SAP-O Forms, it became evident that Jason's ability to initiate requests for continuing familiar social routines was influenced by the nature of the activity. Jason demonstrated an increased rate of initiation as well as an improved capacity to share positive emotion, for example, when familiar activities were infused with high emotion (e.g., a partner displayed joy and excitement) and motor-based play. His preferred social routines, in fact, tended to be those with a predictable sequence of actions and exaggerated emotion (e.g., "If You're Happy and You Know It," "Five Little Monkeys"). A complete summary of Jason's current profile of strengths and areas of need in the Joint Attention component is included in a sample SAP-O Form and a sample SAP Summary Form (SAP Sum) (see Figures 5.2 and 5.8).

Social Communication: Symbol Use

After establishing Jason's baseline in joint attention, his team and parents turned their attention toward determining Jason's strengths and challenges with respect to his abilities in symbol use. As the team discussed both observation days, it became evident that during Jason's interactions with his family members, he relied heavily on unconventional means to convey his intentions (e.g., physical proximity, physical manipulation gestures). The team members also noted that Jason's imitation skills were quite limited and that he primarily used objects in an exploratory manner by mouthing and banging them.

Jason's parents highlighted Jason's consistent use of proximity to indicate an interest or desire to obtain an item or assistance while playing (e.g., staring intently at a bubble wand, touching a specific puzzle). Jason's use of physical proximity was also observed with respect to his intent to protest/refuse during administration of the SAP-O. When less preferred activities were introduced (e.g., "Ring Around the Rosy" with his cousin Amy), Jason frequently sought to distance himself from the activity as a means to express his disinterest. His parents considered Jason's use of physical proximity to be his most effective means of communication. They further stated that their ability to

SAP-OBSERVATION FORM: Social Partner Stage
Social Communication (page 2)

Child's name: __Jason__

Qtr 1	Qtr 2	Qtr 3	Qtr 4	JOINT ATTENTION
				1 Engages in reciprocal interaction
1				JA1.1 Responds to bids for interaction (= MR2.3)
1				JA1.2 Initiates bids for interaction (= SR1.4)
1				JA1.3 Engages in brief reciprocal interaction (= SR1.5)
0				JA1.4 Engages in extended reciprocal interaction (= SR1.6)
				2 Shares attention
1				JA2.1 Looks toward people
0				JA2.2 Shifts gaze between people and objects
0				JA2.3 Follows contact point (= SU2.4)
0				JA2.4 Follows distal point (= SU2.5)
				3 Shares emotion
0				JA3.1 Shares negative emotion using facial expressions or vocalizations (= MR3.1)
1				JA3.2 Shares positive emotion using facial expressions or vocalizations (= MR3.2)
0				JA3.3 Responds to changes in partners' expression of emotion (= MR2.4, SU2.7)
0				JA3.4 Attunes to changes in partners' expression of emotion (= MR2.5)
				4 Shares intentions to regulate the behavior of others (↔ JA7.2, JA7.3, SU4–SU5)
1				JA4.1 Requests desired food or objects (= MR2.6)
1				JA4.2 Protests/refuses undesired food or objects (= MR3.4)
1				JA4.3 Requests help or other actions (= MR3.3)
0				JA4.4 Protests undesired actions or activities (= MR3.4)
				5 Shares intentions for social interaction (↔ JA7.2, JA7.3, SU4–SU5)
1				JA5.1 Requests comfort (= MR3.1)
0				JA5.2 Requests social game
0				JA5.3 Takes turns
0				JA5.4 Greets
0				JA5.5 Calls
0				JA5.6 Shows off
				6 Shares intentions for joint attention (↔ JA7.2, JA7.3, SU4–SU5)
0				JA6.1 Comments on object
0				JA6.2 Comments on action or event
				7 Persists and repairs communication breakdowns
0				JA7.1 Uses appropriate rate of communication for context
0				JA7.2 Repeats communication to repair breakdowns (↔ JA4–JA6)
0				JA7.3 Modifies communication to repair breakdowns (↔ JA4–JA6)

SCORING KEY: 2, criterion met consistently (across two partners in two contexts); **1,** criterion met inconsistently or with assistance; **0,** criterion not met

Figure 5.2. Jason's SAP-O Form (Joint Attention component).

SAP-OBSERVATION FORM: Social Partner Stage
Social Communication (page 3)

Child's name: __Jason__

Qtr 1	Qtr 2	Qtr 3	Qtr 4	SYMBOL USE
				1 Learns by imitation of familiar actions and sounds
0				SU1.1 Takes turns by repeating own actions or sounds
0				SU1.2 Imitates familiar actions or sounds when elicited immediately after a model
0				SU1.3 Spontaneously imitates familiar actions or sounds immediately after a model
0				SU1.4 Spontaneously imitates familiar actions or sounds at a later time
				2 Understands nonverbal cues in familiar activities
1				SU2.1 Anticipates another person's actions in familiar routines (= SR3.1)
0				SU2.2 Follows situational cues in familiar activities
0				SU2.3 Follows gestural cues other than a point
0				SU2.4 Follows a contact point (= JA2.3)
0				SU2.5 Follows a distal point (= JA2.4)
0				SU2.6 Responds to visual cues (photographs or pictures)
0				SU2.7 Responds to facial expression and intonation cues (= JA3.3)
				3 Uses familiar objects conventionally in play
2				SU3.1 Uses exploratory actions on objects (↔ SR2.1)
1				SU3.2 Uses familiar objects in constructive play
0				SU3.3 Uses familiar objects conventionally toward self
0				SU3.4 Uses familiar objects conventionally toward other
				4 Uses gestures and nonverbal means to share intentions (↔ JA4–JA6, MR1, MR3.3, MR3.4)
2				SU4.1 Uses proximity
1				SU4.2 Uses facial expressions
2				SU4.3 Uses simple motor actions
0				SU4.4 Uses conventional contact gestures ☐ give ☐ push away ☐ show ☐ reach/touch ☐ point/touch
0				SU4.5 Uses conventional distal gestures ☐ wave ☐ distal reach ☐ distal point ☐ clap ☐ head shake ☐ head nod
0				SU4.6 Uses reenactment or symbolic distal gestures
0				SU4.7 Uses sequence of gestures or nonverbal means
0				SU4.8 Coordinates gestures and gaze
				5 Uses vocalizations to share intentions (↔ JA4–JA6, MR1, MR3.3, MR3.4)
0				SU5.1 Uses differentiated vocalizations (↔ MR1)
0				SU5.2 Uses a variety of consonant + vowel combinations
0				SU5.3 Uses words bound to routines
0				SU5.4 Coordinates vocalizations with gaze and gestures
				6 Understands a few familiar words
0				SU6.1 Responds to own name
0				SU6.2 Responds to a few words in familiar social games
0				SU6.3 Responds to a few familiar person, body part, or object names
0				SU6.4 Responds to a few frequently used phrases in familiar routines

SCORING KEY: 2, criterion met consistently (across two partners in two contexts); **1,** criterion met inconsistently or with assistance; **0,** criterion not met

Figure 5.3. Jason's SAP-O Form (Symbol Use component).

interpret this particular aspect of Jason's behavior has provided them with a sense of his communicative goals and has resulted in a greater sense of efficacy in their interactions with meeting Jason's needs.

Frequent communicative breakdowns, however, were evident throughout the SAP-O. This appeared to be related to Jason's idiosyncratic strategies of communicating his preferences and needs. Although proximity was evidently his primary mode of communication, Jason's early developing gestures also consisted of either *physical manipulation gestures* or *reenactment gestures*. His physical manipulation gestures included requests for assistance (e.g., pulling his mother's hand toward a container of bubbles), and his reenactment gestures included requests for comfort (e.g., crawling into his father's lap) and requests for actions (e.g., leaning toward his mother to communicate that he wanted to pop bubbles on his face).

Although Jason's emerging ability to use early developing gestures in purposeful communicative exchanges was evident, his limited capacity for joint attention clearly compromised his ability to use gaze, vocalizations, and higher level gestures to repair less successful communicative attempts. As noted previously, Jason's parents have observed that his ability to share positive emotion by looking up and smiling during familiar social games has emerged; however, Jason is reportedly quite passive in his attempts to initiate these routines. Conventional gestures were not noted on the SAP-R Form, were not observed during an administration of the SAP-O, and were not elicited during behavior sampling (i.e., communicative temptations). A complete summary of Jason's current profile of strengths and areas of need in the Symbol Use component is included in a sample SAP-O Form and a sample SAP Sum (see Figures 5.3 and 5.8).

Emotional Regulation: Mutual Regulation

At this point in the meeting, Jason's team members and parents shifted their discussion to the SAP-O findings related to Jason's strengths and challenges in mutual regulation. The team initially reflected on their previous discussions of Jason's social communication abilities and their impact on his emotional regulatory abilities. Both his parents and his team recognized that Jason's limited ability to share his intentions and emotions with others, as well as his reliance on early developing gestures to communicate, contributed significantly to his challenges in mutual regulation, as documented during the SAP-O.

Jason's easygoing temperament and ability to go with the flow had been reported before the SAP-O in the SAP-R, the parent questionnaire. His parents had reported that "Jason tends to be a happy child who rarely becomes upset." The service coordinator offered an example to corroborate his parents' perceptions. She indicated that during one of the SAP-O visits, Jason's cousin Amy grabbed a manipulative toy from Jason. When this occurred, he showed no outward display of negative emotion and quietly drifted away from this activity. His parents commented that this was typical for Jason and that they could not recall the last time he appeared to be truly mad or sad. Based on this information, his parents and team members felt that Jason's ability to express a range of basic emotions (e.g., sadness, fear, anger) was quite limited. In addition, behavior sampling designed to observe and document Jason's ability to attune his emotions to the expressions of his caregivers also revealed significant challenges, as he continued smiling when his caregivers staged emotional distress.

Despite these difficulties expressing and attuning his emotions conventionally through vocalizations, gestures, and facial expressions, his occupational therapist documented several instances throughout the SAP-O when Jason exhibited signs of dysregulation (e.g., difficulty attending in his environment and engaging with others). These signals, however, were less conventional. For example, during a greeting routine with his aunt and uncle, Jason was observed to be dysregulated in that his state of arousal was too low for the demands of the activity. He was seemingly unaware of this social event, as he was observed to maintain his visual focus on the edge of the pages in a board book that he was holding. Other signals of dysregulation observed over the course of the 2-day observation included Jason's tendency to seek out visual information in his environment that involved straight or connecting lines (e.g., examining his aunt and uncle's swinging doors), maintaining an unfocused gaze, and mouthing non-food objects.

Last, it was evident that Jason's passive interaction style limited his ability to actively request assistance from others to help him attain a regulated state using conventional means. Therefore, with the exception of an occasional reenactment gesture (e.g., climbing into his father's lap to request comfort), Jason rarely directed his requests for assistance to his partners using gaze or gestures. In contrast to his difficulty with initiating these requests, Jason was, on several occasions, observed to use a smile as a signal of his readiness for continued interaction during a social game. For the most part, the team determined that his partners needed to be sensitive readers of his subtle and unconventional signals to help him attain and maintain a regulated state to promote his active engagement. Strategies that appeared most effective to support his engagement included use of high emotion, motor-based play, and song routines with heightened sensory-motor properties. A complete summary of Jason's current profile of strengths and areas of need in the Mutual Regulation component is included in a sample SAP-O Form and a sample SAP Sum (see Figures 5.4 and 5.8).

Emotional Regulation: Self-Regulation

Next, Jason's parents and team members discussed Jason's abilities and challenges in self-regulation. Based on information obtained through the SAP-R and the SAP-O, the team felt that Jason's repertoire of self-regulatory strategies was extremely limited. Jason's team and parents concluded that Jason demonstrates a bias toward a low state of arousal and often appears to be passive. He demonstrated clear signs of dysregulation (i.e., an arousal level too low for the demands of the environment) throughout the observation sessions, including maintaining an unfocused gaze and seeking out visually stimulating activities; however, these behavioral strategies were not effective in helping him to increase his arousal level to be more available to engage in activities.

This was clearly observed during the SAP-O, during solitary play activities, and during greeting routines with his family members. At these times, Jason's visual strategies to increase stimulation became the focus of his attention and he had difficulty independently shifting his attention to attend to the important features of ongoing activities. In the SAP-R, his parents had reported that it is often difficult to break into Jason's inefficient behavioral self-regulatory strategies and reengage him in an activity.

Jason's limited repertoire of effective self-regulatory strategies results in his limited availability for learning and interacting. The team agreed that although Jason shows a relative interest in his physical surroundings, he often appears unaware of his partners as they come and go in his environment. These difficulties compound his challenges with participating in new and changing situations. Although Jason does not become observably upset in these situations, his arousal level is often too low and he has difficulty orienting to novel stimuli and activities unless they incorporate movement and music. A complete summary of Jason's current profile of strengths and areas of

SAP-OBSERVATION FORM: Social Partner Stage
Emotional Regulation
(page 4)

Child's name: Jason

Qtr 1	Qtr 2	Qtr 3	Qtr 4	MUTUAL REGULATION
				1 Expresses range of emotions (↔ SU4–SU5)
1				MR1.1 Expresses happiness
0				MR1.2 Expresses sadness
0				MR1.3 Expresses anger
0				MR1.4 Expresses fear
				2 Responds to assistance offered by partners
0				MR2.1 Soothes when comforted by partners
1				MR2.2 Engages when alerted by partners
0				MR2.3 Responds to bids for interaction (= JA1.1)
1				MR2.4 Responds to changes in partners' expression of emotion (= JA3.3)
0				MR2.5 Attunes to changes in partners' expression of emotion (= JA3.4)
0				MR2.6 Makes choices when offered by partners (= JA4.1)
				3 Requests partners' assistance to regulate state
0				MR3.1 Shares negative emotion to seek comfort (= JA3.1; ↔ JA5.1)
1				MR3.2 Shares positive emotion to seek interaction (= JA3.2)
0				MR3.3 Requests help when frustrated (= JA4.3; ↔ SU4–SU5)
1				MR3.4 Protests when distressed (= JA4.2, JA4.4; ↔ SU4–SU5)
				4 Recovers from extreme dysregulation with support from partners
0				MR4.1 Responds to partners' efforts to assist with recovery by moving away from activity
1				MR4.2 Responds to partners' use of behavioral strategies
0				MR4.3 Responds to partners' attempts to reengage in interaction or activity
0				MR4.4 Decreases amount of time to recover from extreme dysregulation due to support from partners
0				MR4.5 Decreases intensity of dysregulated state due to support from partners

SCORING KEY: 2, criterion met consistently (across two partners in two contexts); **1**, criterion met inconsistently or with assistance; **0**, criterion not met

Figure 5.4. Jason's SAP-O Form (Mutual Regulation component).

SAP-OBSERVATION FORM: Social Partner Stage
Emotional Regulation
(page 5)

Child's name: Jason

Qtr 1	Qtr 2	Qtr 3	Qtr 4	SELF-REGULATION
				1 Demonstrates availability for learning and interacting
1				SR1.1 Notices people and things in the environment
1				SR1.2 Shows interest in a variety of sensory and social experiences
0				SR1.3 Seeks and tolerates a variety of sensory experiences
1				SR1.4 Initiates bids for interaction (= JA1.2)
1				SR1.5 Engages in brief reciprocal interaction (= JA1.3)
0				SR1.6 Engages in extended reciprocal interaction (= JA1.4)
1				SR1.7 Responds to sensory and social experiences with differentiated emotions
				2 Uses behavioral strategies to regulate arousal level during familiar activities
1				SR2.1 Uses behavioral strategies to regulate arousal level during solitary activities (↔ SU3.1)
1				SR2.2 Uses behavioral strategies to regulate arousal level during social interactions
0				SR2.3 Uses behavioral strategies modeled by partners to regulate arousal level
0				SR2.4 Uses behavioral strategies to engage productively in an extended activity
				3 Regulates emotion in new and changing situations
1				SR3.1 Anticipates another person's actions in familiar routines (= SU2.1)
1				SR3.2 Participates in new and changing situations
0				SR3.3 Uses behavioral strategies to regulate arousal level in new and changing situations
0				SR3.4 Uses behavioral strategies to regulate arousal level during transitions
				4 Recovers from extreme dysregulation by self
0				SR4.1 Removes self from overstimulating or undesired activity
1				SR4.2 Uses behavioral strategies to recover from extreme dysregulation
0				SR4.3 Reengages in interaction or activity after recovery from extreme dysregulation
0				SR4.4 Decreases amount of time to recover from extreme dysregulation
0				SR4.5 Decreases intensity of dysregulated state

SCORING KEY: 2, criterion met consistently (across two partners in two contexts); **1**, criterion met inconsistently or with assistance; **0**, criterion not met

Figure 5.5. Jason's SAP-O Form (Self-Regulation component).

Transactional Support: Interpersonal Support

need in the Self-Regulation component is included in a sample SAP-O Form and a sample SAP Sum (see Figures 5.5 and 5.8).

When discussing Interpersonal Support, Jason's parents indicated that they often feel ineffective at reaching Jason when he is either in a low arousal state and too unfocused to be engaged socially or is overly focused when looking at objects or toys. His aunt and uncle have also experienced the same difficulty with engaging Jason. In the SAP-R, Jason's parents had revealed that Jason "appears preoccupied with his toys and is difficult to reach." In the SAP-O, this was observed when Jason arrived at his cousin's home. In this context, his aunt and uncle appeared frustrated when they had difficulty redirecting Jason's visual attention from the pages of a book when they were attempting to greet him. The SAP-R Form revealed that "Jason is not yet listening and following simple directions." Thus, effective communicative exchanges do not yet occur on a consistent basis.

Despite these challenges, Jason's service coordinator recognized unique interpersonal strengths in Jason's social network that were clearly fostering more competent social communication and emotional regulation and, as such, should continue to be encouraged. In particular, she noted that Jason's parents were occasionally able to read Jason's more subtle forms of communication, such as his use of physical proximity to indicate his interest in an item and his use of physical distance to indicate his disinterest. These interpersonal supports have led to an emerging sense of competence between Jason and his parents, as he appears to be using physical proximity more readily in recent months. His aunt and uncle, however, admitted that they felt less comfortable with interpreting Jason's subtle signals and requested guidance with understanding his intent and signs of dysregulation.

By reviewing the SAP-R and SAP-O results, Jason's parents and early intervention team members were able to identify a number of interpersonal supports that were emerging as areas of strength in his social network and those that were considered critical areas of need. The following chart provides examples of several of these areas.

Interpersonal Support

Strengths	Needs
Jason's parents are learning to respond to Jason's focus of attention and to his use of proximity to request preferred activities and/or snacks (IS1.1, IS1.3).	His parents feel confident that they know when Jason would like a specific item or snack but are less certain as to how to foster his initiation of a request and what form of communication to model (IS1.3, IS2.2, IS7.1).
All of Jason's partners are beginning to recognize when Jason is dysregulated or disengaged with his cousin and familiar adults (IS1.5).	Jason's parents and his aunt and uncle notice and are able to identify his focus of attention; however, they often feel ineffective at determining how to encourage an interaction (IS2.1, IS4.3, IS5.1).
	All of Jason's partners have difficulty offering support when Jason is not attending or when he is disengaged (IS1.5, IS4.3).

A complete summary of the use of various interpersonal supports by Jason's social network is provided in a sample SAP-O Form and a sample SAP Sum (see Figures 5.6 and 5.8).

Transactional Support: Learning Support

A final component of Jason's team meeting included a discussion of those learning supports that have already been implemented in his daily routines and activities and those that should be considered to foster his competence with social communication and

SAP-OBSERVATION FORM: Social Partner Stage
Transactional Support (page 6)

Child's name: Jason

Qtr 1	Qtr 2	Qtr 3	Qtr 4	INTERPERSONAL SUPPORT
				1 Partner is responsive to child
1				IS1.1 Follows child's focus of attention
1				IS1.2 Attunes to child's emotion and pace
1				IS1.3 Responds appropriately to child's signals to foster a sense of communicative competence
1				IS1.4 Recognizes and supports child's behavioral strategies to regulate arousal level
1				IS1.5 Recognizes signs of dysregulation and offers support
0				IS1.6 Imitates child
1				IS1.7 Offers breaks from interaction or activity as needed
1				IS1.8 Facilitates reengagement in interactions and activities following breaks
				2 Partner fosters initiation
0				IS2.1 Offers choices nonverbally or verbally
1				IS2.2 Waits for and encourages initiations
0				IS2.3 Provides a balance of initiated and respondent turns
1				IS2.4 Allows child to initiate and terminate activities
				3 Partner respects child's independence
1				IS3.1 Allows child to take breaks to move about as needed
1				IS3.2 Provides time for child to solve problems or complete activities at own pace
0				IS3.3 Interprets problem behavior as communicative and/or regulatory
2				IS3.4 Honors protests, rejections, or refusals when appropriate
				4 Partner sets stage for engagement
1				IS4.1 Gets down on child's level when communicating
1				IS4.2 Secures child's attention before communicating
1				IS4.3 Uses appropriate proximity and nonverbal behavior to encourage interaction
1				IS4.4 Uses appropriate words and intonation to support optimal arousal level and engagement
				5 Partner provides developmental support
1				IS5.1 Encourages imitation
0				IS5.2 Encourages interaction with peers
1				IS5.3 Attempts to repair breakdowns verbally or nonverbally
1				IS5.4 Provides guidance and feedback as needed for success in activities
1				IS5.5 Expands on child's play and nonverbal communication
				6 Partner adjusts language input
0				IS6.1 Uses nonverbal cues to support understanding
0				IS6.2 Adjusts complexity of language input to child's developmental level
0				IS6.3 Adjusts quality of language input to child's arousal level
				7 Partner models appropriate behaviors
1				IS7.1 Models appropriate nonverbal communication and emotional expressions
0				IS7.2 Models a range of communicative functions □ a. behavior regulation □ b. social interaction □ c. joint attention
1				IS7.3 Models appropriate play
0				IS7.4 Models appropriate behavior when child uses inappropriate behavior
0				IS7.5 Models "child-perspective" language

SCORING KEY: 2, criterion met consistently (across two partners in two contexts); **1**, criterion met inconsistently or with assistance; **0**, criterion not met

The SCERTS® Model: A Comprehensive Educational Approach for Children with Autism Spectrum Disorders
Copyright © 2006 by Paul H. Brookes Publishing Co. All rights reserved.

Figure 5.6. Jason's SAP-O Form (Interpersonal Support component).

SAP-OBSERVATION FORM: Social Partner Stage
Transactional Support (page 7)

Child's name: Jason

Qtr 1	Qtr 2	Qtr 3	Qtr 4	LEARNING SUPPORT
				1 Partner structures activity for active participation
0				LS1.1 Defines clear beginning and ending to activity
0				LS1.2 Creates turn-taking opportunities and leaves spaces for child to fill in
1				LS1.3 Provides predictable sequence to activity
1				LS1.4 Offers repeated learning opportunities
1				LS1.5 Offers varied learning opportunities
				2 Partner uses augmentative communication support to foster development
0				LS2.1 Uses augmentative communication support to enhance child's communication and expressive language
0				LS2.2 Uses augmentative communication support to enhance child's understanding of language and behavior
0				LS2.3 Uses augmentative communication support to enhance child's expression and understanding of emotion
0				LS2.4 Uses augmentative communication support to enhance child's emotional regulation
				3 Partner uses visual and organizational support
0				LS3.1 Uses support to define steps within a task
0				LS3.2 Uses support to define steps and time for completion of activities
0				LS3.3 Uses visual support to enhance smooth transitions between activities
0				LS3.4 Uses support to organize segments of time across the day
0				LS3.5 Uses visual support to enhance attention in group activities
0				LS3.6 Uses visual support to foster active involvement in group activities
				4 Partner modifies goals, activities, and learning environment
1				LS4.1 Adjusts social complexity to support organization and interaction
0				LS4.2 Adjusts task difficulty for child success
1				LS4.3 Modifies sensory properties of learning environment
0				LS4.4 Arranges learning environment to enhance attention
0				LS4.5 Arranges learning environment to promote child initiation
1				LS4.6 Designs and modifies activities to be developmentally appropriate
0				LS4.7 Infuses motivating materials and topics in activities
1				LS4.8 Provides activities to promote initiation and extended interaction
1				LS4.9 Alternates between movement and sedentary activities as needed
1				LS4.10 "Ups the ante" or increases expectations appropriately

SCORING KEY: 2, criterion met consistently (across two partners in two contexts); **1**, criterion met inconsistently or with assistance; **0**, criterion not met

The SCERTS® Model: A Comprehensive Educational Approach for Children with Autism Spectrum Disorders
Copyright © 2006 by Paul H. Brookes Publishing Co. All rights reserved.

Figure 5.7. Jason's SAP-O Form (Learning Support component).

emotional regulation. His service coordinator, who had observed both days of the SAP-O and the behavior sampling session noted that a number of learning supports already appeared to be effective in supporting Jason's social engagement and communication. These included his parents' ability to structure activities for active participation and modify the sensory properties of activities and the environment to foster his success. His service coordinator had been impressed by Jason's ability to remain engaged in a social routine that his parents had initiated and structured (e.g., "If You're Happy and You Know It"). They clearly recognized that this activity had a predictable sequence of actions that Jason could anticipate. They also had modified the motivating sensory properties of the environment by using routines with movement and music, two variables that often enhanced Jason's social engagement.

Thus, by reviewing the SAP-R and SAP-O results, Jason's parents and early intervention team members were able to identify a number of learning supports that were emerging as areas of strength in his social network and those that were considered critical areas of need. The following chart provides examples of several of these areas.

Learning Support	
Strengths	Needs
Jason's parents are learning how to provide a predictable sequence of actions in an activity (LS1.3).	Because Jason rarely initiates social routines, the team discussed the importance of defining a clear beginning and ending to a given activity (LS1.1).
Jason's parents occasionally initiate social routines that involve both movement and music to enhance his attention and entice him to communicate (LS4.4, LS4.5).	Jason's parents were quite skilled at initiating and maintaining Jason's engagement in a routine; however, they felt less effective at creating turn-taking opportunities and leaving spaces for Jason to participate more frequently (LS1.2).

A complete summary of the use of various learning supports by Jason's social network is provided in a sample SAP-O Form and a sample SAP Sum (see Figures 5.7 and 5.8).

Social-Emotional Growth Indicators: Results and Impressions

Next, Jason's team turned its attention to calculating his baseline composite scores for his Social-Emotional Growth Indicators. Jason's parents expressed considerable interest in these indicators, recognizing that his scores would provide benchmarks against which to measure future gains in Jason's general qualities of behavior. The general qualities of behavior measured by the Social-Emotional Growth Indicators include 1) Happiness, 2) Sense of Self, 3) Sense of Other, 4) Active Learning and Organization, 5) Flexibility and Resilience, 6) Cooperation and Appropriateness of Behavior, 7) Independence, and 8) Social Membership and Friendships (see Chapter 7 in Volume I for further discussion of the Social-Emotional Growth Indicators). Jason's Social-Emotional Growth Indicators revealed relative strengths in the areas of Happiness, and Social Membership and Friendships. Areas of relative weakness, which were consistent with the concerns of Jason's family and educational team included Active Learning and Organization, and Sense of Self.

Key Information Source 2: Family Perception of SAP-O Results and Priorities

Before identifying the specific goals and objectives for Jason's educational program, the early intervention team asked Jason's parents to share their perceptions of the 2 days of observation, behavior sampling, and recent audiological evaluation; whether representative samples of his behavior were obtained; and whether Jason's strengths and difficulties were accurately captured in the SAP Sum. Next, they were invited to reiterate their primary concerns and to discuss their hopes and expectations regarding Jason's development. This opportunity provided critical baseline information for Jason's early intervention team, as an understanding of how Jason's difficulties affect family interactions and family life will provide a critical measure of the family's progress over time. In addition, his parents were also asked to indicate the types of information and support that would be most helpful for them. These family perceptions were included on Jason's SAP Sum (see Figure 5.8).

SAP Step 7: Prioritizing Goals and Objectives

Based on the information compiled throughout the SAP from the SAP-R, SAP-O, behavior sampling, audiological evaluation, and SAP Sum, Jason's parents and early intervention team members worked together to prioritize goals and objectives 1) that were the most *functional,* 2) that directly *addressed family priorities,* and 3) that matched the *developmental areas of need* revealed on the SAP Sum for both Jason and his partners. His performance on the SAP-O was not the sole factor for selecting weekly objectives, as equal consideration was given to those objectives that would be the most functional and those that most closely matched family priorities. Although this occasionally results in selection of objectives that might appear out of sequence in reference to the structure of goals and objectives in the SAP, this flexibility and individualization is actually considered critical for successful implementation of a SCERTS Model program.

As recommended in Chapter 7 of Volume I, objectives in Joint Attention and Symbol Use were often paired so that Jason would learn to communicate his intentions with more sophisticated symbolic means. Likewise, a number of Interpersonal Support and Learning Support objectives were combined so that Jason's partners could learn to modify their interactive style as well as incorporate learning and environmental accommodations in a given activity. Please refer to Jason's SAP Sum for a listing of objectives identified by Jason's team (see Figure 5.8).

SAP Step 8: Recommending Further Assessment if Needed

When reviewing the SAP Sum, Jason's early intervention team recommended an additional audiological evaluation to address concerns about the accuracy of Jason's recent testing, as a hearing loss had not yet been ruled out. In the Family Perception and Priorities section of the SAP Sum, his parents reported that Jason was, in fact, fairly uncooperative during several of the procedures attempted. In one of the activities, Jason was asked to sit on his father's lap and the audiologist attempted to observe if Jason shifted his focus of attention toward musical teddy bears placed in different corners of the room, a procedure referred to as *sound field audiometry.* Although Jason occasionally responded to these various stimuli, the audiologist indicated that this procedure did not adequately rule out more subtle forms of hearing loss, such as a hearing loss in only one ear (i.e., unilateral hearing loss). A more definitive test would involve headphones, as this procedure can rule out hearing loss in both ears (i.e., bilateral hearing loss) as well as hearing loss in one ear. His parents noted that Jason quickly removed the headphones and retreated from the testing environment when this procedure was attempted.

Hearing testing in young children is challenging. When social-communicative and emotional regulatory difficulties are present, however, this challenge can often provide quite an obstacle to more traditional forms of audiological testing. Therefore, Jason's team members agreed that a referral for an otoacoustic emissions screening would be appropriate. In this procedure, Jason would not be required to provide a behavioral response such as shifting his head toward a sound or raising his hand. Rather, the procedure would objectively measure the function of his inner ear. If difficulties were to be noted with this screening, a more comprehensive test referred to as the *brainstem auditory evoked response* would then be recommended. In this procedure, Jason's auditory nerve response would be measured directly, once again requiring very little cooperation on his part. Given the significant nature of Jason's social and communication difficulties, this referral was considered an essential aspect of his programming to ensure that adequate learning supports would be provided for him.

SAP Step 9: Design a SCERTS Educational Program for Jason, His Parents, and His Service Providers

Step 9 of the SAP involved identifying a number of key meaningful and purposeful activities, the levels of social support in these activities (i.e., the roles and responsibilities of educational team members), and familiar partners who would play a critical role in service provision. In an early intervention setting, Jason's service coordinator took the primary role of organizing an educational and supportive program for Jason and his family. With an awareness of the critical features that are characteristic of effective interventions, she led a discussion about the need for early and intensive educational programming and *at least* 25 hours per week on a year-round basis of planned and developmentally appropriate learning opportunities. In addition, she indicated that sufficient individualized attention and opportunities for a low ratio of children to adults would be needed for Jason to remain actively engaged during his programming.

This step of the SAP culminated in the development of two SAP Activity Planning Forms (as discussed in Chapter 7 of Volume I and Chapter 1 of this volume), each of which incorporated approximately 3 hours of meaningful and purposeful activities in Jason's natural routines. The first form outlined Jason's typical morning routines (see Figure 5.9), and the second form outlined Jason's typical afternoon routines (see Figure 5.10). Therefore, a plan was established for approximately 6 hours per day, for a total of 30 hours per week, of SCERTS Model programming.

Jason's SAP Activity Planning Forms included the specific goals that would be addressed in these activities, the complexity of social context (i.e., the degree of naturalness and the amount and frequency of one-to-one support) that would be appropriate depending on Jason's unique social-communicative and emotional regulatory capacities, and the partners that would be present throughout the day. In addition, the SAP Activity Planning Forms identified the partner objectives and specific transactional supports (e.g., interpersonal supports, learning supports) that would be embedded in each activity (see Figures 5.9 and 5.10).

Next, Jason's service coordinator reported information provided by his parents on the SAP-R as well as information obtained through the Transactional Support domain of the SAP-O, to lead a discussion with the team regarding the provision of a SCERTS Family Support Plan. As discussed in Chapter 3 of this volume, the provision of both educational and emotional support to a child's immediate and extended family is a critical priority in the SCERTS Model, rather than being considered optional. Thus, Jason's service coordinator noted that the development of Jason's educational program would not be complete without this crucial step.

Educational Support for Jason's Family

As noted previously, primary educational concerns expressed by Jason's parents included 1) the accuracy of his diagnosis, 2) how best to support him, 3) the factors that are preventing his use of words to communicate, and 4) and how to address his limited engagement with his family members, in particular, his cousin Amy. Thus, educational support appeared to be needed to address the following general goals.

SAP Summary Form
Social Partner Stage

Child's name: Jason

Quarterly start date of observation: 11-3-05 Child's age: 2 years, 3 months

SCERTS Profile

SOCIAL COMMUNICATION

Joint Attention
- JA1 Engages in reciprocal interaction
- JA2 Shares attention
- JA3 Shares emotion
- JA4 Shares intentions to regulate the behavior of others
- JA5 Shares intentions for social interaction
- JA6 Shares intentions for joint attention
- JA7 Persists and repairs communication breakdowns

Symbol Use
- SU1 Learns by imitation of familiar actions and sounds
- SU2 Understands nonverbal cues in familiar activities
- SU3 Uses familiar objects conventionally in play
- SU4 Uses gestures and nonverbal means to share intentions
- SU5 Uses vocalizations to share intentions
- SU6 Understands a few familiar words

EMOTIONAL REGULATION

Mutual Regulation
- MR1 Expresses range of emotions
- MR2 Responds to assistance offered by partners
- MR3 Requests partners' assistance to regulate state
- MR4 Recovers from extreme dysregulation with support from partners

Self-Regulation
- SR1 Demonstrates availability for learning and interacting
- SR2 Uses behavioral strategies to regulate arousal level during familiar activities
- SR3 Regulates emotion during new and changing situations
- SR4 Recovers from extreme dysregulation by self

SCERTS Profile (continued)

TRANSACTIONAL SUPPORT

Interpersonal Support
- IS1 Partner is responsive to child
- IS2 Partner fosters initiation
- IS3 Partner respects child's independence
- IS4 Partner sets stage for engagement
- IS5 Partner provides developmental support
- IS6 Partner adjusts language input
- IS7 Partner models appropriate behaviors

Learning Support
- LS1 Partner structures activity for active participation
- LS2 Partner uses augmentative communication support to foster development
- LS3 Partner uses visual and organizational support
- LS4 Partner modifies goals, activities, and learning environment

Social-Emotional Growth Indicators Profile

1. Happiness
2. Sense of Self
3. Sense of Other
4. Active Learning and Organization
5. Flexibility and Resilience
6. Cooperation and Appropriateness of Behavior
7. Independence
8. Social Membership and Friendships

Family Perception and Priorities

Is this profile an accurate picture of your child? If not, explain.

This is an accurate picture of Jason's strengths and needs, with the exception of the audiological test results.

Is there any additional information that is needed to develop your child's educational plan?

Not at this time

If you were to focus your energies on one thing for your child, what would that be?

We would like help with communicating with Jason and helping him play with his cousin.

What skills would you like your child to learn in the next 3 months?
- The ability to initiate social routines and play activities
- The ability to recover from dysregulation with support from partners
- The ability to use gestures to communicate

Figure 5.8. Jason's SAP Sum.

Prioritize Weekly SCERTS Objectives

Child Social Communication and Emotional Regulation objectives	Partner Transactional Support objectives
1. Jason will respond to bids for interaction (JA1.1).	1. Partner will follow Jason's focus of attention (IS1.1).
2. Jason will request desired food or objects (JA4.1).	2. Partner will attune to Jason's emotion and pace (IS1.2).
3. Jason will request social games (JA5.2).	3. Partner will recognize signs of dysregulation and offer support (IS1.5).
4. Jason will use conventional contact gestures (SU4.4).	4. Partner will offer choices nonverbally or verbally (IS2.1).
5. Jason will engage when alerted by partners (MR2.2).	5. Partner will use appropriate proximity and nonverbal behavior to encourage interaction (IS4.3).
6. Jason will respond to partners' use of behavioral strategies (MR4.2).	6. Partner will define a clear beginning and ending to activities (LS1.1).
7. Jason will notice people and things in the environment (SR1.1).	7. Partner will create turn-taking opportunities and leave spaces for Jason to fill in (LS1.2).
8. Jason will seek and tolerate a variety of sensory experiences (SR1.3).	8. Partner will modify sensory properties of learning environment (LS4.3).

Further Assessment—Key Results or Additional Recommendations

Results of Jason's audiological testing were not conclusive. Therefore, further testing of Jason's hearing abilities through an otoacoustic emissions test is recommended.

SAP Activity Planning

Identify key activities using the SAP Activity Planning Form for
☒ Morning schedule ☒ Afternoon schedule

SCERTS Family Support Plan

Educational Support		Emotional Support	
Activity	How often	Activity	How often
Provision of educational resources	Ongoing	Parent support group	Monthly
Direct individual child–caregiver coaching	Weekly	One-to-one support meetings	Monthly
Interactive guidance	Weekly		
Team meeting	Biweekly		
Caregiver education program	Weekly		

SCERTS Support Plan for Professionals and Service Providers

Educational Support		Emotional Support	
Activity	How often	Activity	How often
Mentoring for paraprofessional staff	5 hrs/week	Supervision meetings	Biweekly
Supervision meetings	Biweekly	Team meetings	Monthly
Team meetings	Monthly		
In-service training	Monthly		

Figure 5.8. (continued)

					SAP Activity Planning Form												
Child's name: Jason						Communication stage: Social Partner						Date: 11-14-05			Page #: 1 (A.M.)		
Activity/time	Social complexity	Group size	Team members and partners	Jason will respond to bids for interaction.	Jason will request desired food or objects.	Jason will request social games.	Jason will use conventional contact gestures.	Jason will engage when alerted by partners.	Jason will respond to partners' use of behavioral strategies.	Jason will notice people and things in the environment.	Jason will seek and tolerate a variety of sensory experiences.	Partner will follow Jason's focus of attention.	Partner will attune to Jason's emotion and pace.	Partner will recognize signs of dysregulation and offer support.	Partner will offer choices nonverbally or verbally.	Partner will define a clear beginning and ending to activities.	Partner will create turn-taking opportunities and leave spaces for Jason to fill in.	Partner will modify sensory properties of learning environment.	Team members and partners / Sample transactional supports
				Weekly child objectives								Weekly partner objectives							Social worker (SW), occupational therapist (OT), speech-language pathologist (SLP), paraprofessional (P), mom (M), dad (D), aunt (A), uncle (U), cousin (C)
Breakfast (MOD) 9:00 A.M.–9:30 A.M.	1:1	3–4	M, P, SLP/OT		X		X					X	X		X				(LS) While seated in a highchair, food items will be offered in see-through containers that are difficult to open.
Morning play (PAR, ENG) 9:30 A.M.–10:15 A.M.	1:1	3–4	M, P, SLP/OT	X		X		X	X					X			X	X	(IS) Partners will offer frequent choices of toys and will pair play routines with songs.
Diaper change (NAT) 10:15 A.M.–10:30 A.M.	1:1	2–3	M, SW				X		X				X			X		X	(IS) Sensory-motor play and singing will be incorporated during the diaper change.
Morning play (PAR & ENG) 10:30 A.M.–11:15 A.M.	1:1	3–4	M, P, SW		X	X			X						X				(LS) In Jason's backyard, a see-through bin will be placed in the sandbox to entice Jason's interest in preferred cause–effect toys.
Lunch (MOD) 11:15 A.M.–12:00 A.M.	1:1	2–3	M, P				X	X				X	X						(LS) At a child-size table, choices of food items will be offered in see-through containers that are difficult to open.

Instructions: Write the weekly Social Communication and Emotional Regulation objectives for the child and the Transactional Support objectives for the partner in the vertical boxes across the top. In the far right vertical box at the upper right-hand corner, list the team members and the child's partners and numbers or initials for each team member or partner. In each row below the column headings, write a brief description of the activity and the time, the ratio for social complexity, the group size, and the number or initials of the team members or partners participating in that activity. Then check off all of the objectives that will be targeted in each activity. Write in a brief description of sample transactional support used in each activity.

Figure 5.9. Jason's SAP Activity Planning Form (morning activities) (*Key:* PAR, planned activity routine; ENG, engineered activity; MOD, modified natural activity; NAT, naturally occurring event; LS, learning support; IS, interpersonal support).

Goal 1: To provide Jason's family with information and resources to understand the nature of Jason's disability and how it specifically affects his development. For Jason's family, areas of need included 1) understanding Jason's level of social communication, his current strategies for communicating, and his current difficulties with emotional regulation and 2) understanding the sequences and processes of language, communication, and social-emotional development relevant for Jason so that family members may develop appropriate expectations regarding his development.

Desired outcome: Jason's family members will become knowledgeable about ASD and how it specifically affects Jason's functional abilities in life, particularly regarding 1) understanding Jason's level of social communication and 2) understanding the sequences and processes of language, communication, and social-emotional development. They will be able to use resources to find information and continue to actively learn as Jason develops.

Goal 2: To provide Jason's family with the knowledge and skills to support Jason's development in everyday activities, and to address specific issues that are identified as most stressful and challenging. For Jason's family, these issues include

Assessment to Implementation: Social Partner Stage

SAP Activity Planning Form

Child's name: Jason **Communication stage:** Social Partner **Date:** 11-14-05 **Page #:** 2 (P.M.)

Activity/time	Social complexity	Group size	Team members and partners	Jason will respond to bids for interaction.	Jason will request desired food or objects.	Jason will request social games.	Jason will use conventional contact gestures.	Jason will engage when alerted by partners.	Jason will respond to partners' use of behavioral strategies.	Jason will notice people and things in the environment.	Jason will seek and tolerate a variety of sensory experiences.	Partner will follow Jason's focus of attention.	Partner will attune to Jason's emotion and pace.	Partner will recognize signs of dysregulation and offer support.	Partner will offer choices nonverbally or verbally.	Partner will use appropriate proximity and nonverbal behavior to encourage interaction.	Partner will define a clear beginning and ending to activities.	Partner will create turn-taking opportunities and leave spaces for Jason to fill in.	Partner will modify sensory properties of learning environment.	Team members and partners / Sample transactional supports
				Weekly child objectives								Weekly partner objectives								Sample transactional supports
Transition to aunt and uncle's house (MOD) 1:00 P.M.–1:30 P.M.	1:1	5	M, P, A, U					X	X									X	X	(IS) Greeting song will be initiated in car, and A and U will wait at front door with a choice of preferred toys.
Afternoon play (PAR and ENG) 1:30 P.M.–2:15 P.M.	1:1	5–6	P, A, U, C			X	X					X	X							(IS) A list of signals of dysregulation will be created to enhance the ability of A, U, and C to respond appropriately.
Diaper change (NAT) 2:15 P.M.–2:30 P.M.	1:1	2	A				X					X		X					X	(IS) Sensory-motor play and singing will be incorporated by A.
Afternoon snack (MOD) 2:30 P.M.–3:00 P.M.	1:1	5	P, A, C, SW		X	X										X	X			(LS) At child-size table, food choices will be offered nonverbally in see-through containers that are difficult to open, first to C and then to Jason.
Afternoon play (PAR and ENG) 3:00 P.M.–4:00 P.M.	1:1	5	P, A, U, C, SW	X	X											X		X		(IS) A, U, and C will be encouraged to pause before predictable phrases in familiar songs for Jason to fill in his turn.

Team members and partners: Social worker (SW), occupational therapist (OT), speech-language pathologist (SLP), paraprofessional (P), mom (M), dad (D), aunt (A), uncle (U), cousin (C)

Instructions: Write the weekly Social Communication and Emotional Regulation objectives for the child and the Transactional Support objectives for the partner in the vertical boxes across the top. In the far right vertical box at the upper right-hand corner, list the team members and the child's partners and numbers or initials for each team member or partner. In each row below the column headings, write a brief description of the activity and the time, the ratio for social complexity, the group size, and the number or initials of the team members or partners participating in that activity. Then check off all of the objectives that will be targeted in each activity. Write in a brief description of sample transactional support used in each activity.

Figure 5.10. Jason's SAP Activity Planning Form (afternoon activities) (*Key:* PAR, planned activity routine; ENG, engineered activity; MOD, modified natural activity; NAT, naturally occurring event; LS, learning support; IS, interpersonal support).

1) developing interactive styles that are appropriate and responsive to Jason and supportive of successful communicative interactions and 2) identifying and modifying daily activities and routines (learning supports) that will support social communication development and improve relationships between Jason and his caregivers and Jason and his cousin.

Desired outcome: *Jason's family members will feel confident in providing the necessary supports to foster Jason's development across different situations and in everyday activities and in identifying and coping with the most significant difficulties they face at any point in time. In particular, they will develop confidence with 1) developing interactive styles that are appropriate and responsive to Jason and 2) identifying and modifying daily activities and routines (learning supports) that will support development and relationships.*

Given that Jason was recently diagnosed and his family was actively gathering information about the diagnosis, the first step of the SCERTS Family Support Plan included *provision of educational resources.* Taking into account the tremendous variability and differing values across families, Jason's service coordinator provided an individualized list of books written for parents of children with ASD, web sites, and support agencies that would provide essential information about Jason's development, the nature of ASD, and recommendations for appropriate educational programming. The next step of the family support plan included both *direct individual caregiver–child coaching or guidance* (i.e., opportunities for early intervention staff to join with Jason and his caregivers in developmentally appropriate activities) and *interactive guidance* (e.g., opportunities for early intervention service providers to observe Jason's interactions with caregivers and to provide suggestions and recommendations for immediate implementation) to focus on the current partner objectives identified in the SAP-O. Partner objectives such as *Responds appropriately to child's signals to foster a sense of competence* (IS1.3), *Waits for and encourages initiation* (IS2.2), and *Recognizes signs of dysregulation and offers support* (IS1.5) would be addressed.

Jason's service coordinator, speech-language pathologist, and occupational therapist would alternate in leading a *team meeting* with the family on a semimonthly basis (2 hours per month) specifically to provide educational support. Because Jason's aunt and uncle clearly provide an informal support network for the family, they were encouraged to participate in these sessions as much as possible. Last, because Jason's parents were interested in meeting other families, the service coordinator recommended a *caregiver education program* following the Hanen Centre's *More than Words* curriculum (Sussman, 1999), which is specifically designed for children with ASD and their families. A group session would be beginning in 3 weeks, and Jason's parents agreed, with great interest, to participate.

Emotional Support for Jason's Family

Although Jason's parents had been concerned about their son's development before his initial diagnostic evaluation, the diagnosis only escalated their anxiety. Their involvement in the SAP was, however, a first step in working through many of the questions related to Jason's diagnosis. Nevertheless, Jason's family appeared to need emotional support in the following areas.

Goal 1: To support Jason's family members in their ability to cope with the stresses and challenges of raising a child with ASD

Desired outcome: *Jason's family will develop specific coping abilities to manage the inevitable stresses that they will experience directly due to or as a secondary effect of Jason's having ASD.*

Goal 2: To help Jason's family understand and gain access to the range of formal and informal emotional supports that may be available

Desired outcome: *Jason's family will gain access to formal and informal supports that best match their emotional needs at specific points in time.*

Goal 3: To support Jason's family members in their efforts to deal successfully with professionals, as well as with educational and health care systems

Desired outcome: *Jason's family will develop specific strategies to foster positive parent–professional relationships and deal with emotional challenges that may be due to difficult interactions or relationships with professionals or due to difficulties in dealing with educational and health care systems.*

Goal 4: **To help Jason's family members identify their own priorities and develop appropriate expectations and realistic, achievable goals for Jason's development and family life**

Desired outcome: *Jason's family members will be clear about the most important issues they wish to address for Jason and the family, will develop realistic goals and expectations for Jason, and will create a balance in family life consistent with their lifestyle and values.*

A range of options was discussed with Jason's parents regarding emotional supports in the early intervention program. These included formal supports such as a parent *support group* held once a month at the center, parent support groups in the larger community, and *one-to-one support meetings* with a psychologist on staff at the early intervention center. During the meeting, Jason's parents expressed a strong desire to have the opportunity for private guidance and support and requested to meet with the psychologist as an additional resource on a monthly basis.

Support Among Professionals

As a final step in planning and designing Jason's educational program, Jason's service coordinator discussed how the SCERTS Model recognizes that professionals and other service providers face considerable challenges when implementing an intensive educational program. For professionals and other service providers (e.g., paraprofessionals) to be as effective as possible in supporting children and families, a SCERTS Support Plan for Professionals and Service Providers would need to be developed. Because Jason's team, as described in the SAP Activity Planning Form, includes not only professionals but also paraprofessionals, *mentoring arrangements* were scheduled on a daily basis for at least 5 hours per week of paraprofessional supervision provided by Jason's speech-language pathologist, occupational therapist, and/or social worker. Supervision would involve both direct educational and interactive guidance as well as one-to-one emotional support in biweekly *supervision meetings.*

Next, Jason's service coordinator indicated that each month, Jason's team members would arrange a *team meeting* to discuss his progress and the need for consistency with both interactive and learning supports. His speech-language pathologist was also asked to provide an *in-service training session* to provide specific guidance on social communicative development, interpersonal supports, and learning supports for a child at the novice Social Partner stage.

SAP Step 10: Performing Ongoing Tracking

Following the identification of Jason's and his partners' weekly objectives, the team members discussed the need to track his ongoing progress in his educational program. They decided that the second version of the SAP Daily Tracking Log (discussed in Chapter 7 of Volume I) would be best suited for this purpose, given Jason's age and his limited engagement in more varied activities. His team recognized that although it would not be feasible to take data on every objective in every activity, it would be critical to track Jason's progress to inform decision making about the effectiveness of his program's implementation. Thus, the team members discussed the need to track Jason's performance with each objective on a daily basis in approximately two activities. Primary responsibility for data collection during Jason's morning activity routine would be assigned to his service coordinator and occupational therapist. They would specifically track his progress as it related to four of Jason's Social Communication and Emotional Regulation objectives (JA1.1, SU4.4, MR2.2, and SR 1.3) and their own progress related to four of the Transactional Support objectives (IS1.2, IS2.1, IS4.3, and LS4.3) that were identified as weekly priorities on the SAP Sum. Next, Jason's parents and the paraprofessional agreed to assume responsibility for data collection during Jason's afternoon activity routines. Specifically, they would be tracking Jason' performance on the other four Social Communication and Emotional Regulation objectives (JA4.1, JA5.2, MR4.2, and SR1.1) and their performance on the other four Transactional Support objectives (IS1.1, IS1.5, LS1.1, and LS1.2) targeted on the SAP Sum as weekly priorities.

Next, Jason's team formulated a plan for using the information documented on the SAP Daily Tracking Log in order to complete the SAP Weekly Tracking Log. The team members decided that his service coordinator would be responsible for compiling this information and sharing it with the team and that it would be critical to track Jason's progress from week to week to inform decision making about the effectiveness of program implementation. They decided that it would be critical to revisit programming decisions if Jason were to achieve a score of 0 for 3 weeks in a row. Finally, they discussed the need to complete a new SAP Form each quarter for Jason to determine if targeted objectives had been achieved and whether new objectives would be needed. The quarterly assessment would be used to determine if limited progress would warrant a change in Jason's targeted objectives.

SPOTLIGHT ON SARAH, AN ADVANCED SOCIAL PARTNER

Sarah is at the advanced level of the Social Partner stage. Sarah is a petite and energetic 5-year-old girl who is participating in a full-day integrated preschool program in her local public school district. At 23 months of age, Sarah was diagnosed with ASD and has benefited from approximately 3 years of therapeutic and educational programming. Her mother and father describe her as a sensitive and shy child who until recently only rarely initiated social interactions. According to her parents, this sensitivity has significantly limited the development of relationships with her preschool classmates and with her older brother, Zachary, who is 7 years old.

Over the past 6 months, however, Sarah has begun to blossom, and she is more focused and goal-directed and more interested in engaging others. She now more readily initiates bids for communication and social interaction, particularly with familiar caregivers and other familiar adults. She has also begun to take an interest in observing other children. From a distance, she now occasionally watches Zachary when he is playing with his train set, and she stays in closer proximity while observing her classmates when they are either singing songs in the classroom or playing on the swings on the playground. Sarah is now beginning to use more conventional gestures such as giving items to her caregivers and pointing to a desired toy, sometimes pairing her gestures with vocalizations, particularly when her initial attempts at communicating are unsuccessful. In familiar routines, she has been observed to use two different word approximations. For example, she occasionally fills in the word "go," following her teacher's use of the carrier phrase, "Ready, set . . . ," and she occasionally uses "Mo . . . mo" as an approximation for the word "Elmo" when requesting a preferred videotape at home. In addition to these emerging word approximations, Sarah has recently begun to use a picture symbol for the first time, albeit inconsistently, to request her favorite silky blanket both at home and in her preschool classroom.

Although her parents and teachers are encouraged to observe Sarah initiating more frequently and using word approximations, they noted that the words often come and go. Her communicative exchanges remain quite brief and inconsistent, depending on the context and the familiarity of her partner. When communication breakdowns occur, they are a source of frustration for Sarah and contribute to extreme dysregulation in the form of frequent tantrums. Several other factors that also appear to contribute to Sarah's frequent dysregulation include her strong emotional reactions and her distress during unpredictable and unfamiliar activities.

In particular, she demonstrates heightened sensitivity or hyperreactivity to environmental stimuli, especially to unexpected touch and environmental noises, and has difficulty understanding the expectations of social situations. These challenges appear to lead to increased anxiety and prolonged periods of social disengagement marked either by tuning out and shutting down or by screeching and having tantrums when others attempt to keep her engaged. Her preschool teachers, for example, report an average of six to eight tantrums per day, which range from 2 to 10 minutes in length. In these instances, she may cry and scream inconsolably. Based on the changes in Sarah's social communicative profile and her continued challenges in emotional regulation, Sarah's parents and educational team members agreed that it would be timely to review her current educational programming to make the necessary program adjustments and modifications to her goals and objectives.

As part of this review of Sarah's educational program, the SAP was administered. Thus, this spotlight illustrates the steps that Sarah's family and her educational team took in implementing the SAP. The SAP was implemented to 1) establish Sarah's current profile of developmental strengths and needs; 2) determine meaningful, purposeful, and motivating goals to address; 3) select the most appropriate learning contexts and complexity of social support based on Sarah's natural routines and activities; and 4) determine the necessary transactional supports to foster Sarah's development and her relationships with her family, peers, and teaching staff. Because a comprehensive SCERTS Model program also includes explicit plans for support to families and support among professionals, information from the SAP was also used to ensure that Sarah's educational program is compatible and consistent with the needs expressed by her family. In addition, the assessment team determined the specific educational and emotional supports that would be provided for Sarah's family members and the professionals who would be involved in implementing Sarah's program.

SAP Step 1: Determining Sarah's Communication Stage

After a review of Sarah's current behavior in her home and school environments, her preschool special education team leader determined that the appropriate SAP forms to use for the assessment would be those designated for the Social Partner stage. This was based on the completion of the Worksheet for Determining Communication Stage and a review of the criteria used to determine a child's communication stage in the SAP. Although Sarah is beginning to use symbols to communicate (i.e., two different word approximations and one picture symbol), her use of these "words" remains quite inconsistent. Thus, she is using fewer than three symbols consistently, referentially, and with intent.

SAP Step 2: Gathering Information with the Social Partner SAP-R Form

Prior to a monthly team meeting attended by Sarah's parents and her educational team, Sarah's parents were asked to complete the SAP-R Form to provide additional information regarding Sarah's behavior in her home and community environments. This questionnaire identified 1) the primary concerns and stresses faced by Sarah's parents, 2) the primary strengths they see in Sarah and their primary concerns regarding her development, 3) the activities in which both Sarah's strengths and areas of need would likely be observed in her home and community environments, 4) Sarah's typical partners in the home and community, and 5) the typical contexts in Sarah's life outside of school. Sarah's educational team also completed a separate copy of the SAP-R Form to identify similarities and discrepancies with respect to Sarah's behavior in the classroom and school versus her behavior in other natural environments. The information gathered from Sarah's SAP-R is summarized next:

1. The primary concerns and stresses faced by Sarah's parents included

    - "Her frequent and intense tantrums"
    - "Her limited and inconsistent use of words"
    - "Her difficulty handling changes in routine"
    - "How to encourage more extended interactions with her brother Zachary"

2. Sarah's parents and educational team identified and agreed on the following strengths and needs in her current profile:

Strengths	Needs
"Sarah is beginning to use words and pictures to communicate." "She learns routines quickly." "She is beginning to take an interest in her brother and her classmates."	"Sarah frequently has tantrums. She needs to learn more effective strategies for coping with her emotions." "Her use of words and/or pictures seems to come and go. She needs to improve her recall of words." "Her interactions with others are so brief. She needs to remain engaged for longer periods of time."

3. The activities in which both Sarah's strengths and areas of need would likely be seen included

    - Activity center time in her preschool classroom; this includes small-group activities such as playdough, art, and blocks
    - Circle time activities following a consistent classroom routine
    - Playing with her brother on the school playground after school

4. Sarah's typical partners

    - Mom
    - Dad
    - Zachary (her 7-year-old brother)
    - Preschool classmates (eight children)
    - Special education preschool teacher
    - Classroom instructional assistants (two different adults)
    - Speech-language pathologist
    - Occupational therapist

Assessment to Implementation: Social Partner Stage   211

5. Natural contexts in Sarah's life include
    - Caregiving routines at home
    - Play routines at home
    - Classroom routine at school
    - School playground
    - School bus

SAP Step 3: Identifying Assessment Team Members and Planning the SAP-O

After collecting the completed SAP-R Forms from Sarah's parents and educational team members, Sarah's special education preschool teacher began completing the SAP Map for Planning the SAP-Observation. This form was used to help determine members of Sarah's assessment team, their roles and responsibilities, and whether any outside referrals would need to take place. In addition, as part of planning the administration of the SAP-O, the following variables were considered to ensure a representative sample: 1) the *location* (i.e., natural contexts) where the observations would take place, 2) the specific *length* of the observations, 3) the *partners* who would be present, 4) the *group size* of the social contexts during the observations, 5) the nature of the *activities*, and 6) the number of *transitions* during each observation (see Chapter 7 in Volume I for a more detailed discussion of these variables).

After reviewing the information provided in the SAP-R and each of these variables, Sarah's educational team was able to plan the observations to ensure a representative sample of Sarah's abilities and challenges. First, given that Sarah is a Social Partner, the minimum length of total observation time was identified as 2 hours. However, given that Sarah's abilities vary greatly depending on the context and her partners, the team decided that it would be best to split the observation between two distinct environments, observing 1 hour in each environment and incorporating both familiar and less familiar partners. To guide the activities to be observed, group sizes typical to Sarah's daily environments and activities were identified as one to one (e.g., Sarah with her teacher) and small group (e.g., Sarah with her classmates, Sarah with her family).

Given that Sarah's team had expressed concern about Sarah's behavior in the classroom as well as in less structured environments such as the playground, these two contexts were identified as the primary locations for the observations. After determining the specific contexts for the observations, Sarah's special education preschool teacher carefully reviewed the primary concerns of Sarah's parents and educational team, as well as those activities that they felt would provide a sample of Sarah's strengths and areas of need. Additional variables were also considered to ensure that Sarah's assessment team would gain an accurate picture. For example, it was evident that Sarah would behave differently when engaged in an unstructured versus a structured activity, a busy environment versus a quiet environment, a social activity versus a solitary activity, and a language-based versus a non-language-based or visually supported task.

With this information, three activities were identified for her school-based observation. These included 1) her morning routine (i.e., making the transition to the classroom with one-to-one assistance), 2) circle time with her special education preschool teacher and eight peers, and 3) a loosely structured free-play period (i.e., activity center time). Two additional activities were identified for her as part of an after-school community-based observation. This observation was conducted on the school playground with her parents and her brother Zachary. These activities included 1) a solitary play-based activity (e.g., riding the slide) and 2) a chase game with her parents and brother, which was a social routine typical for the family.

As noted, children who participate in the SCERTS Assessment Process should be observed across at least three transitions. Because handling changes in routine and making transitions were identified as an area of concern for Sarah, multiple transitions per observation were planned by her educational team members to ensure that a sufficient amount of information would be gathered about these challenges. During the first observation, for example, Sarah's occupational therapist planned to observe Sarah making the transition from the bus to the classroom as well as from circle time to free play. During the second observation, Sarah's special education preschool teacher and speech-language pathologist would be observing during her transition from school to the playground and from a preferred solitary activity to a familiar social routine with her family. The information on the planned transitions would be summarized in the SAP Map.

SAP Step 4: Completing the SAP-O Form

Sarah's assessment team, which included her special education preschool teacher, her speech-language pathologist, and her occupational therapist, used the SAP-O Form for the Social Partner stage to gather information across their two observations (see Chapter 7 of Volume I for specific administration instructions). Information was gathered for the Social Communication and Emotional Regulation domains, which focused on assessing Sarah's strengths and needs, and for the Transactional Support domain, which addressed the strengths and needs of her partners in various environments. Responsibilities for observing Sarah during the assessment were divided among the team members, to capture a detailed and representative sample of Sarah's behavior and strategies used by her partners for supporting Sarah.

Because her speech-language pathologist would be present at both observations, the team agreed that she should gather the majority of the information related to the Social Communication and Emotional Regulation domains. Sarah's occupational therapist and special education preschool teacher therefore were assigned to gather the majority of the information related to the Transactional Support domain (i.e., Interpersonal Support and Learning Support components) and to supplement the observations of the speech-language pathologist as appropriate.

SAP Step 5: Conducting Behavior Sampling

Toward the completion of Sarah's second observation on the playground, her educational team members briefly reviewed her SAP-O Form. They agreed that although they had gathered much of the information they needed by observing her in carefully selected activities and environments, there were two unanswered questions remaining related to her abilities in the Social Communication and Emotional Regulation domains. The nature of the activities did not allow for observation of low-frequency behaviors that may only occur in specific types of circumstances (e.g., a partner using a gesture to call Sarah's attention). The observation involved primarily familiar and predictable activities with only a few exceptions. Thus, the areas about which the team members desired more information included

- JA2.3 and JA2.4—Sarah's ability to follow both contact and distal pointing across partners and activities (e.g., by directing her gaze where her partner is pointing)

- SR3.3—Sarah's ability to uses behavioral strategies to regulate arousal in new and changing situations

With these remaining questions in mind, Sarah's team agreed that a brief additional observation of Sarah during her adaptive physical education (APE) session would contribute to a more comprehensive developmental profile and help guide the development and implementation of a more appropriate educational program. Sarah attends her APE session once per week with three of her classmates and a classroom instructional assistant; thus, there is typically a ratio of one teacher to two students. Sarah's educational team felt that this environment would be the most appropriate for the additional observation, as it incorporates a relatively unfamiliar partner, the APE teacher, whom Sarah only sees once per week. In addition, the APE teacher often introduces novel activities in her sessions and frequently encourages Sarah and her classmates to participate in setting up by retrieving materials.

Sarah's special education preschool teacher met with the APE teacher before this additional observation to ensure that the session would address the educational team's remaining questions by staging and facilitating specific interactions between Sarah and her peers. For example, to observe and document Sarah's ability to follow contact pointing (JA2.3), Sarah's APE teacher indicated that she would encourage Sarah to look at a therapy ball by pointing directly to a ball in front of her. Her APE teacher indicated that she would stage an opportunity for Sarah to follow a distal point (JA2.4), by asking her to retrieve the parachute for a group play routine by placing the item at a distance, pointing, and asking, "Sarah, get me that, please." Next, Sarah's ability to use behavioral strategies to regulate her arousal in new and changing situations (SR3.3) would be sampled, with the APE teacher encouraging her to engage in a visually supported game of Red Light, Green Light, with her peers.

SAP Step 6: Compiling and Integrating Information with the SAP Summary Form

Following the completion of the two observations and the additional brief observation of Sarah in her APE class, Sarah's educational team and parents met to compile and integrate information, a step that involves two key information sources: 1) summarizing strengths and needs from the SAP-O and 2) documenting family perception of the SAP-O results.

Key Information Source 1: Summarizing Strengths and Needs

Social Communication: Joint Attention

During their team meeting, Sarah's parents and educational team initially focused on determining Sarah's strengths and challenges with respect to her current profile in joint attention. Based on information obtained through the SAP, her educational team members and parents agreed that Sarah's overall ability to share her desired goals or communicative intentions with familiar adults had improved remarkably over the past 6 months. Her special education preschool teacher and parents both indicated that overall, "She appears to have a stronger motivation to interact and communicate." During her classroom observations, this was evidenced by more consistent responses from Sarah to her partners' efforts to interact with her. Sarah participated in several different social routines initiated by her teacher during circle time, and she used more varied strategies to initiate social interactions, particularly with familiar adults.

In fact, during the transition into her preschool classroom, Sarah was noted to spontaneously request assistance with opening her backpack by using a conventional give gesture and looking up toward the instructional assistant. She then immediately followed this request for assistance with an additional request for a preferred Elmo board book. The instructional assistant had, in this instance, removed two books from the backpack and had offered a choice for Sarah. Sarah quickly responded using a contact point paired with a word approximation, "Mo . . . mo," for "Elmo" to indicate her desire to have access to the book. Information gathered from the SAP-R completed by her educational team also confirmed this progress, as Sarah's therapists and instructional assistants observed Sarah persisting to a much greater extent when her initial communicative attempts were unsuccessful. On some occasions, Sarah remained engaged for approximately two communicative exchanges. Before these social-communicative accomplishments, Sarah had been more likely to move from activity to activity, more likely to attempt to gain access to items on her own, and less able to persist and/or repair communication breakdowns when she was unsuccessful.

Despite this progress, both caregiver report and direct observation revealed that Sarah's range of communicative functions were restricted based on the expectations for a child making the transition to the early Language Partner Stage. Although she was noted to communicate for the purpose of requesting preferred snacks and toys and requesting assistance during self-care routines, she was less apt to remain well regulated and share her protests or expressions of negative emotion with others. For example, when Sarah was encouraged to participate in the unfamiliar game of Red Light, Green Light, in her APE session, she did not use conventional means to protest/refuse. Rather, she dropped to the floor and produced a piercing scream. Thus, her sudden escalation to extreme dysregulation as a form of protest/refusal behavior remains a significant concern, as she is not able to secure another's attention and use conventional means to communicate protest or refusal.

The team also agreed that Sarah's range of strategies for expressing more social-communicative functions remained limited; however, her capacity for communicating for the purpose of social interaction appeared to be emerging. In particular, team members noted her emerging ability to draw attention to herself through the initiation of social routines or by requesting continuation of routines, requesting comfort, greeting, calling, and/or showing off. Sarah clearly has, in fact, demonstrated a number of relative strengths with respect to her ability to share positive emotions. During activity center time, Sarah initiated communicative bids for the following purposes: 1) to show off and express her pleasure at successfully operating a See 'n Say toy (i.e., she activated the toy, looked up at a familiar adult, and smiled), 2) to request the continuation of pleasurable social routines, and 3) to request comfort from her mother after a fall during the family's chase game on the school playground.

Of these more social functions, her ability to share her joy and excitement during familiar social games and songs was highlighted as a significant developmental achievement by her team members during their discussion. The speech-language pathologist took this opportunity to explain to the team the critical nature of this capacity. She explained that the ability to share a positive response to an event implies an understanding that others may also be delighted in that same experience. Thus, when one communicates about pleasurable events, the pleasure becomes shared and leads to the development of relationships and, eventually, friendships. For Sarah, it was evident, however, that these exchanges of shared positive emotion were primarily limited to familiar adults as opposed to her peers in the classroom, a critical area of need. A complete summary of Sarah's current profile of strengths and areas of need in the Joint Attention component would be recorded on her SAP-O Form and SAP Sum.

Social Communication: Symbol Use

After establishing Sarah's baseline in joint attention, her educational team and parents turned their attention toward determining Sarah's strengths and challenges in symbol use. Based on the SAP-R completed by Sarah's parents and by Sarah's educational team, it was evident that Sarah's repertoire of more conventional contact gestures such as giving items to her caregivers and touching or pointing to a desired toy, along with the use of more distal gestures, had clearly expanded in the past 6 months. At home, for example, Sarah reportedly has begun to use both contact conventional gestures (e.g., give, reach/touch, push away, point/touch) as well as more distal gestures such as a wave to greet her father on his arrival home from work, a reach paired with gaze to request a videotape from a high shelf, and a clapping gesture to show off after singing a familiar song with her brother Zachary. Because these more sophisticated gestures emerge in reciprocal interactions with partners and through nonverbal imitation, Sarah's educational team noted that the use of these more conventional gestures reflects a very positive shift in her social awareness, as she is sharing more easily readable forms of communication.

Sarah's parents also noted that she is beginning to pair her gestures with vocalizations (e.g., "ah," "oh") more frequently, particularly when her initial attempts at communicating are unsuccessful. In familiar routines, she has been observed to use two different word approximations. For example, she reportedly fills in the word "go" following her mother's use of the carrier phrase, "Ready, set . . . ," and she occasionally uses, "Mo . . . mo," as an approximation for the word, "Elmo," when requesting a preferred videotape at home. This latter word approximation was also observed during the administration of the SAP-O when requesting an Elmo board book. In addition to these emerging word approximations, Sarah has reportedly begun to use a picture symbol to request her favorite silky blanket during down time in the classroom when the symbol is made available to her. Her family noted that when they observe Sarah using this symbol to request her blanket at home, the symbol has to be in close proximity to her and her attention needs to be drawn to it. Thus, she is not yet independently seeking out the symbol and/or spontaneously exchanging it with an adult.

Despite her remarkable progress, information gathered during the SAP-O suggested that Sarah continues to have several significant patterns of vulnerability in regard to her coordination of gaze with her gestural and vocal communicative means. First, Sarah's use of gaze appears to depend strongly on the familiarity of the activity and her comfort level with her communicative partner. In addition, Sarah tends to use gaze in coordination with her gestures more frequently when her conversational partner holds out and delays before responding. Although the emerging use of gaze is reflective of Sarah's developing awareness of another's perspective, the limited use of gaze in more novel activities and with partners who facilitate its use perpetuates her difficulties in expressing intent across partners and settings and in reading another's nonverbal social cues to guide her behavior (e.g., others' facial expressions and emotions).

Next, it was noted that Sarah's limited use of conventional gestures or vocalizations to communicate for the purpose of refusing an activity and/or protesting was in stark contrast to her emerging use of gestures for requesting assistance. In fact, rather than use conventional means to protest and refuse, Sarah quickly became dysregulated due to anxiety or frustration, and she was more likely to screech, have a tantrum, and drop to the floor. Although Sarah was observed to use a push-away gesture to reject several items during activity center time, her use of a head shake to indicate "no" was not observed. Additional gestures that were neither reported nor observed included a distal index finger point paired with gaze to comment about an interesting item or event, a head nod to indicate affirmation, a wave gesture to greet, and a show gesture to call attention to items of mutual interest.

During the administration of the SAP-O, it became evident that the sophistication of Sarah's communication was dependent on several variables. These included the familiarity of her partner, the predictability of the activity, and her overall arousal level and emotional regulation. For example, during highly predictable activities with familiar partners (e.g., playing chase with family members, singing songs during circle time with her teacher), Sarah was able to use conventional gestures and, on occasion, the word "go" to communicate within the routine. These abilities stood in contrast to her communicative strategies when her arousal state was heightened due to the presence of unpredictable partners, including her brother and peers; new and changing activities; and/or busier or more stimulating environments. In these instances, she frequently relied on early developing strategies such as physical manipulation gestures or reenactment gestures. Her physical manipulation gestures included requests for assistance with the parachute (e.g., pulling her APE teacher's hand toward the parachute) and her reenactment gestures included requests for assistance with emotional regulation. For example, during the SAP-O, Sarah was noted to cover her head with her hands when the noise level in the classroom became overwhelming for her. This action was a reenactment of a strategy often employed by one of the classroom instructional assistants (e.g., placing her hands firmly on Sarah's head in a soothing manner when she is distressed). A complete summary of Sarah's current profile of strengths and areas of need in Symbol Use would be included on the SAP-O Form and SAP Sum.

Emotional Regulation: Mutual Regulation

At this point in the meeting, Sarah's team members and parents shifted their discussion to the SAP-O findings related to her strengths and challenges in mutual regulation. The team initially reflected on their previous discussions of Sarah's social-communicative abilities and their impact on her emotional regulatory abilities. Both her parents and her team recognized that Sarah's recent gains in her capacities for joint attention and symbol use, as recorded on the SAP-O, were related to concurrent gains in mutual regulation. The combination of Sarah's increased motivation and her more sophisticated means to communicate, which now included conventional gestures, vocalizations, and several words, have contributed to her emerging ability to direct requests for comfort and assistance to others. This has, in turn, supported her ability to maintain a more regulated state across contexts. This was clearly seen during the recent administration of the SAP-O. For example, while Sarah was playing a chase game with her parents, she fell down and was observed to become quickly distressed. However, she then walked over to her mother and reached her arms up to request comfort, an apparent bid for mutual regulation, as she appeared to have a sense that her mother could help her attain a more regulated state. When her mother responded by bending down and hugging Sarah tightly (i.e., a behavioral strategy to support regulation), Sarah calmed within a few minutes. This capacity for initiated mutual regulation is newly emerging; therefore, her ability to use such strategies to support emotional regulation remains inconsistent, particular with less familiar and trusted partners.

Sarah's educational team members noted that Sarah had used a similar strategy to request comfort from her special education preschool teacher but did not direct similar requests to other classroom staff or her APE teacher. Therefore, when Sarah became distressed in the classroom in the absence of her teacher, she was noted to reach the point of extreme dysregulation more quickly, as there was not a person present with whom she had the same trusting and secure relationship. In these instances, she often cried inconsolably. During the team meeting, both Sarah's mother and her teacher agreed that these extreme instances of dysregulation were more likely to occur if a partner had difficulty reading her request for assistance; if the partner was not able to respond to Sarah's request right away; and most significantly, if there was not a partner present with whom she had a secure and trusting relationship.

Sarah was also observed to have made gains in her ability to express her emotional state. She was, in fact, observed to use differentiated facial expressions and vocalizations to convey happiness, sadness, anger, and fear. Her expressions, however, tended to be exaggerated and their intensity was not always reflective of what her caregivers felt was socially appropriate given the routine or activity in which she was engaged. In particular, when Sarah entered states of heightened arousal precipitated by unfamiliar activities, violated expectations, and/or busier environments, her emotional expressions were often difficult to read particularly for less familiar partners. Her occupational therapist offered the following example. When Sarah was running with her father, she grinned and let out what appeared to be a delighted screech as she anticipated continuation of the game. However, when her brother was encouraged to join them in play and brushed up against her and then grabbed her arm, she again grinned and screeched but also showed increasing signs of being quite tense and anxious. Her mother commented that in this latter instance Sarah became upset and she quickly moved to intervene and comfort her. Sarah's surface behavior in the two instances appeared very similar; however, on closer examination, her underlying emotional states were very different. Therefore, an unfamiliar or less sensitive partner may have misinterpreted the second instance as one of joy and may have reacted in a manner that resulted in escalation to extreme dysregulation.

Overall, information gathered from both the SAP-R and the SAP-O suggested that Sarah's ability to respond to and employ mutual regulatory strategies to help recover from periods of extreme dysregulation appears to be emerging. Nevertheless, a number of critical vulnerabilities were evident. In fact, when Sarah experienced periods of extreme dysregulation, she was no longer able to use her most sophisticated means of communication to request assistance, such as through conventional gestures and vocalizations, and her ability to attain and maintain a regulated state depended on the skill of her partners in reading her signals. Her mother and teacher agreed that when a skilled partner is with her and intervenes quickly, either by decreasing stimulation in the environment or by hugging her tightly, Sarah occasionally regroups and recovers with relative ease. In contrast, if a partner is unfamiliar with Sarah's signs of dysregulation or if he or she cannot intervene quickly enough, Sarah's dysregulation occasionally escalates to an extreme state. In these latter instances, she has been observed to be unresponsive to mutual regulatory strategies and has melted down for lengthy periods of time, throwing things, screaming, and crying herself into a state of exhaustion.

A complete summary of Sarah's current profile of strengths and areas of need in the Mutual Regulation component would be included on her SAP-O Form and SAP Sum.

Emotional Regulation: Self-Regulation

Next, Sarah's parents and team members focused the discussion on Sarah's behavior with respect to her abilities and challenges in self-regulation. Based on information obtained through the SAP-R and SAP-O, Sarah's educational team felt that Sarah's repertoire of self-regulatory strategies remains extremely limited, as evidenced by her frequent periods of extreme dysregulation and tantrums. Sarah's team and parents concluded that Sarah demonstrates a bias toward a high state of arousal and often appears to be on guard. According to information reported in her parent's SAP-R, Sarah demonstrates strong emotional reactions to events and activities in her environment. Her parents commented, in fact, that the intensity of her reactions is often concerning and it occasionally appears as if Sarah's nervous system is continuously raw and exposed, as she often can not tolerate the level of stimulation encountered throughout her day. In addition, her father reported that Sarah handles unfamiliar activities and interactions with her brother only in small doses. Otherwise, she is likely to become overwhelmed and, in turn, extremely dysregulated.

During the SAP-O, her educational team members observed a similar pattern. During her APE session, Sarah engaged briefly in a parachute game with three of her classmates. She appeared to be happy and content, as evidenced by her engagement and use of reenactment gestures to request that the routine continue; however, as the activity progressed, Sarah was observed to become restless and disengaged, flapping her hands and averting her gaze. From this point, Sarah's arousal quickly escalated and she was observed to run from the activity screeching and covering her ears. These signals of dysregulation clearly show signs of Sarah's attempts to employ behavioral strategies to assist with self-regulation of arousal and emotion. Therefore, information gathered during Sarah's SAP-O suggested that Sarah occasionally attempts to use simple motor actions (e.g., visual strategies, movement strategies) to support emotional regulation during social interactions.

Last, Sarah's parents as well as educational team members noted that Sarah's limited self-regulatory strategies were particularly evident during new and changing activities. Her parents reported, in fact, that they attempt to keep her daily routine as consistent and predictable as possible and try to avoid stimulating social situations, to avoid tantrums. During the administration of the SAP-O, Sarah was observed to have significant difficulty during all transitions, particularly from a preferred and soothing activity to a more stressful activity, such as making the transition to circle time. As noted, her protests were often demonstrated through unconventional means such as screeching, dropping to the ground, and/or bolting from the new activity.

In light of these behavioral patterns, it was evident during the SAP-O that Sarah frequently experiences periods of extreme dysregulation. Behaviors consistent with extreme dysregulation consisted of Sarah's throwing objects in her environment, covering her ears, and running and crying to the point of exhaustion. On more than one occasion, Sarah was observed to try to remove herself from an undesired activity before engaging in behaviors indicating extreme dysregulation. Her parents commented that this pattern had only appeared recently and that they were encouraged by it. Team members acknowledged that this was a positive self-regulatory strategy and was an area that warranted support and intervention. Sarah's team members, including her parents, added that several predictable circumstances and cumulative factors would put her at risk for escalating to dysregulation involving extreme problem behaviors and/or disengagement or shut-down. These included busier environments, unpredictable noises in her environment, unexpected touch, activities that exceeded her developmental skill level, and the presence of adults of whom she had negative emotional memories.

A complete summary of Sarah's current profile of strengths and areas of need in the Self-Regulation component would be included on her SAP-O Form and SAP Sum.

Transactional Support: Interpersonal Support

Both the SAP-R and the SAP-O were reviewed to determine the strengths and needs of Sarah's social network and to identify interpersonal supports that could be implemented to facilitate Sarah's social communication and emotional regulation. In this discussion, her parents and educational team members discussed how Sarah's developmental vulnerabilities are likely to have a transactional influence on partners. For example, Sarah's difficulties with processing language may result in a lack of, or inconsistent, response to a partner's verbal bids for interaction. Therefore, a partner may view her as difficult to reach and/or difficult to engage with. An interpersonal support in this instance would involve *focused change* on the part of Sarah's partner, as those partners who can adjust the complexity of their language input to Sarah's developmental level by using gestures, single words, or routinized phrases, would likely elicit more consistent reciprocity.

In addition, Sarah's team noted that those partners who provide time for Sarah to solve problems or complete activities at her own pace are often rewarded with better engagement and cooperation, in contrast to those partners who are more physically directive in guiding Sarah through an activity using hand-over-hand assistance or other direct cues. Sarah's sensory processing difficulties, including her sensory hyperreactivity, may result in inconsistent reaction to sensory input and inconsistent states of arousal, which, in turn, may lead to tantrums and screeching, a challenging pattern for her partners to respond to with success. Partners who are better able to interpret her escalating signals either as communicative bids and/or as signals of dysregulation will likely be more effective at both preventing and addressing extreme instances of dysregulation.

By reviewing the SAP-R and SAP-O results, Sarah's parents and educational team members were able to identify a number of interpersonal supports that were emerging as areas of strength in her social network and those that were considered critical areas of need. The following chart provides examples.

Interpersonal Support

Strengths	Needs
Sarah's parents are often able to recognize when Sarah is dysregulated or is about to become disengaged in a given social situation, and they may accommodate Sarah by giving her breaks as needed and adjusting the quality of their language to her arousal level (IS1.5, IS3.1, IS6.3).	Sarah's partners are beginning to recognize that when Sarah is becoming dysregulated, it is critical to allow her to solve problems or complete activities at her own pace. Intervening when she is already upset and at higher levels of dysregulation can further exacerbate the problem (IS3.2).
Sarah's classroom staff (e.g., teachers, instructional assistants, therapists) are beginning to develop a range of interpersonal supports that are being used fairly consistently across activities. These include offering choices of play materials and waiting for and encouraging initiation (IS2.1, IS2.2).	Reading and efficiently responding to bids for mutual regulation and/or communicative exchanges is a critical area of need (IS1.3, IS1.5). Sarah's partners could benefit from support in adjusting the complexity of language input to Sarah's developmental level (e.g., using gestures, single words, or phrases that are part of a routine) (IS6.2).

Transactional Support: Learning Support

A complete summary of the use of various interpersonal supports by Sarah's social network would be included in Sarah's SAP-O Form and SAP Sum.

A final component of Sarah's team meeting included a discussion of those learning supports that have already been implemented as transactional supports in her daily routines and activities and those that should be considered to foster her competence with social communication and emotional regulation. Her occupational therapist and special education preschool teacher had noted a number of learning supports that already appeared to be supporting Sarah's social engagement and communication. These included her parents' ability to structure activities for active participation and modify the sensory properties of activities and the environment to foster her success, by decreasing stimulation in more overstimulating environments. In addition, Sarah's occupational therapist noted that Sarah's teacher developed a predictable sequence of actions in a large-group circle time activity and has used visual supports to foster Sarah's attention and engagement across various songs, games, and activities.

Finally, Sarah's parents and educational team members discussed the need to capitalize on her preference for static, unchanging, and predictable visual information, as this may help Sarah compensate for difficulties processing information that is more transient or fleeting in nature, such as speech. Her positive response to predictable environmental cues, such as carrier phrases, "Ready, set . . . ," and static visual cues, such as a picture of Elmo, to support retrieval of words further suggests the potential benefit of increasing the use of visual supports and other AAC supports in Sarah's educational programming. Thus, all partners were encouraged to use visual and organizational supports to define steps within a task, to define steps and time for completion of activities, and to support smooth transitions between activities. Likewise, partners were encouraged to implement AAC supports, such as gestures, signs, and pictures, to foster Sarah's expressive communication.

By reviewing the SAP-R and SAP-O results, Sarah's parents and other team members were able to identify a number of learning supports that were emerging as areas of strength in her social network and those that were considered critical areas of need. The following chart provides examples.

Learning Support	
Strengths	Needs
Sarah's parents have developed the ability to structure activities for active participation and modify the sensory properties of activities and the environment to foster her success (e.g., decreasing stimulation in more overstimulating environments) (LS1.3, LS4.2).	Because Sarah's words come and go depending on whether predictable carrier phrases (e.g., "Ready, set . . . ") or visual cues (e.g., a picture of Elmo) are used by her partners, it is essential that the use of an augmentative communication support be increased (LS2.3).
Sarah's special education preschool teacher has developed a predictable sequence of actions in a large-group circle time activity and has used visual support to encourage Sarah's awareness of the steps within this activity. These supports have subsequently fostered Sarah's attention and engagement (LS1.3, LS3.1)	The use of visual supports to define steps within a task, to define the steps and time for completion of activities, and to support smooth transitions between activities will need to be implemented across a greater range of partners and activities (LS3.1–LS3.3).

A complete summary of the use of various learning supports by Sarah's social network would be included in SAP-O Form and SAP Sum.

Social-Emotional Growth Indicators: Results and Impressions

Next, Sarah's team turned their attention to calculating her baseline composite scores for her Social-Emotional Growth Indicators. Her entire team expressed considerable interest in these indicators, recognizing that Sarah's scores would provide benchmarks against which to measure future gains in her general qualities of behavior. The general qualities of behavior measured by the Social-Emotional Growth Indicators include 1) Happiness, 2) Sense of Self, 3) Sense of Other, 4) Active Learning and Organization, 5) Flexibility and Resilience, 6) Cooperation and Appropriateness of Behavior, 7) Independence, and 8) Social Membership and Friendships (see Chapter 7 in Volume I for further discussion of these indicators). Calculation of Sarah's Social-Emotional Growth Indicators revealed relative strengths in the areas of Active Learning and Organization, and Sense of Self. Areas of need included Flexibility and Resilience, and Cooperation and Appropriateness of Behavior.

Key Information Source 2: Family Perception of SAP-O Results and Priorities

Before identifying the specific goals and objectives for Sarah's educational program, her parents were asked to share their perceptions of her SAP-Observations and the behavior sampling session, whether representative samples were obtained, and whether Sarah's strengths and difficulties were accurately captured in the SAP Sum. Next, they were invited to reiterate their primary concerns and to discuss their hopes and expectations regarding Sarah's development. This opportunity provided critical baseline information for Sarah's educational team, as understanding of how Sarah's difficulties affect family interactions and family life provides a critical measure of the family's progress over time. In addition, her parents were also asked to indicate the types of information and support that would be most helpful for them. Family perceptions would be recorded on the SAP Sum.

SAP Step 7: Prioritizing Goals and Objectives

Based on the information compiled throughout the SAP from the SAP-R, SAP-O, behavior sampling, and SAP Sum, Sarah's parents and educational team members worked together to prioritize goals and objectives that were 1) the most *functional,* 2) directly *addressed family priorities,* and 3) matched the *developmental areas of need* revealed on the SAP Sum for both Sarah and her partners. Her performance on the SAP-O was not the sole factor for selecting weekly objectives, as equal consideration was given to those objectives that would be the most functional and those that most closely matched family priorities. Although this occasionally results in selection of objectives that might appear out of sequence, this flexibility and individualization is actually considered critical for successful implementation of a SCERTS Model program.

As noted in Chapter 7 of Volume I, objectives in Joint Attention and Symbol Use were paired so that Sarah would learn to communicate her intentions using increasingly sophisticated symbolic means. Likewise, a number of Interpersonal Support and Learning Support objectives were combined so that Sarah's partners can learn to modify their interactive style as well as incorporate learning and environmental accommodations in a given activity.

SAP Step 8: Recommending Further Assessment if Needed

When reviewing the SAP Sum, Sarah's parents felt that a representative sample of Sarah's social communication and emotional regulation challenges was obtained along with information regarding the most appropriate transactional supports. Aside from systematic reassessment at 3-month intervals, additional testing was not recommended by Sarah's team.

SAP Step 9: Designing a SCERTS Educational Program for Sarah, Her Parents, and Her Service Providers

Step 9 of the SAP involved identifying a number of key meaningful and purposeful activities, the complexity of social support in these activities (i.e., the roles and responsibilities of educational team members), and familiar partners who will play a critical role in service provision. In an integrated preschool setting, Sarah's team leader, her special education preschool teacher, took the primary role of organizing an educational and support program for Sarah and her family. This teacher led a discussion about the continued need for intensive educational programming and *at least* 25 hours per week on a year-round basis of planned and developmentally appropriate learning opportunities. In addition, she indicated that sufficient individualized attention would be needed for Sarah to remain actively engaged during her programming. A plan to provide educational support to her family would need to be developed in collaboration with Sarah's parents to address their ongoing anxiety regarding her emotional regulation at home and in the community.

This step of the SAP culminated in the development of two SAP Activity Planning Forms, each of which incorporated approximately 3 hours of meaningful and purposeful activities in Sarah's natural routines in the morning and afternoon, respectively. Therefore, a plan was established for approximately 6 hours per day, for a total of 30 hours per week, of SCERTS Model programming. The SAP Activity Planning Forms included the specific goals that would be addressed in these activities and the complexity of social context (i.e., the degree of naturalness and the amount and frequency of one-to-one support) that would be appropriate depending on Sarah's unique social-communicative and emotional regulatory capacities. In addition, the SAP Activity Planning Forms were completed to identify the Transactional Support partner objectives and specific transactional supports (e.g., interpersonal supports and learning supports) that would be embedded in each activity.

Next, Sarah's team leader reported information provided by Sarah's parents on the SAP-R as well as information obtained through the Transactional Support domain of the SAP-O, to lead a discussion with the team regarding the provision of a SCERTS Family Support Plan. As discussed in Chapter 3 of this volume, the provision of both educational support and emotional support to a child's immediate and extended family is a critical priority in a comprehensive service delivery program, rather than being considered optional. Thus, Sarah's team leader noted that the development of Sarah's educational program would not be complete without this crucial step.

Educational Support for Sarah's Family

As noted previously, primary educational concerns expressed by Sarah's parents included 1) the presence of persistent emotional regulatory challenges, exemplified by Sarah's frequent, intense tantrums and difficulty handling changes in routine; 2) the factors contributing to Sarah's limited and inconsistent use of words to communicate; and 3) how best to support her in playful interactions with her brother Zachary. Thus, educational support appeared to be needed in the following general areas.

Goal 1: **To provide Sarah's family with information and resources to understand the nature of Sarah's disability and how it specifically affects her development.** For Sarah's family members, areas of need included 1) understanding Sarah's current difficulties with emotional regulation and the mutual and self-regulatory strategies that she currently employs; 2) understanding Sarah's level of social communication and her current strategies for communicating; and 3) understanding the sequences and processes of social-emotional, language, and communication development relevant for Sarah, so that they may develop appropriate expectations regarding her development.

Desired outcome: Sarah's family members will become knowledgeable about the characteristics of ASD and how these characteristics specifically affect Sarah's functional abilities in life, particularly regarding 1) understanding Sarah's current difficulties with emotional regulation; 2) understanding Sarah's level of social communication; and 3) understanding the sequences and processes of social-emotional, language, and communication development relevant for Sarah's development. They will be able to use resources to find information and continue to learn as Sarah develops.

Goal 2: **To provide Sarah's family with the knowledge and skills to support Sarah's development in everyday activities, and to address specific issues that are identified as most stressful and challenging.** For Sarah's family, these issues include 1) identifying safe and predictable daily activities and routines that are supportive of Sarah's engagement in interactions with her brother Zachary and 2) facilitating and supporting Zachary's ability to use interpersonal supports and learning supports effectively.

Desired outcome: Sarah's family members will feel confident in providing the necessary supports to foster Sarah's development across different situations and in everyday activities and in identifying and coping with the most significant difficulties they face at any point in time. In particular, they will develop confidence with 1) identifying safe and predictable daily activities and routines that are supportive of Sarah's engagement in interactions with her brother Zachary and 2) facilitating and supporting Zachary's ability to use interpersonal supports and learning supports effectively.

The first step of the SCERTS Family Support Plan for Sarah's family included *provision of resources*. Taking into account the tremendous variability and differing values across families, Sarah's team leader offered an individualized list of recently published books, videotapes, and articles written for parents of children with ASD that provided recommendations for appropriate educational programming and information related to the social-emotional and communication development of young children. The next step of the family support plan included *interactive guidance*. This component was included to ensure a consistent and collaborative focus between home and school on the current partner objectives identified in the SAP-O. The following partner objectives would be addressed: *Recognizes signs of dysregulation and offers support* (IS1.5), *Uses augmentative communication support to enhance child's communication and expressive language* (LS2.1), and *Uses visual support to enhance smooth transitions between activities* (LS3.3).

The team, including Sarah's parents, determined that Sarah's special education preschool teacher would make a home/community visit on a monthly basis (1.5 hours per month) to hold a *team meeting* specifically to provide educational support targeting these objectives. Because Sarah's family prioritized her emerging interest in interacting with her brother, the team agreed that Zachary should participate in these sessions as much as possible. Time would be set aside during each visit help Zachary use visual supports while playing with his sister and to help him to recognize his sister's signs of dysregulation.

In addition to monthly educational visits, Sarah's team recognized the need to devise an efficient, daily *system of communication* as a means to problem-solve challenges that were likely to arise due to Sarah's regulatory challenges, as well as to celebrate her accomplishments. The team agreed on the use of a form divided into comment blocks for social communication, emotional regulation, and transactional support for this purpose. Finally, because Sarah's parents were interested in learning how to promote friendships between Sarah and her classmates, the team leader recommended that Sarah and her mother participate in a *caregiver–child group* (i.e., a "Mommy and Me" lunch) that was scheduled on a weekly basis and facilitated by Sarah's speech-language pathologist at school. Sarah's parents expressed excitement about this educational and networking opportunity and her mother agreed to participate.

Emotional Support for Sarah's Family

Although Sarah's parents thoroughly enjoy their daughter and have been proactively involved in supporting her development and planning her educational programming since the time of her diagnosis, it became clear through the SAP that emotional support appeared to be needed in the following areas.

Goal 1: To support Sarah's family members in their ability to cope with the stresses and challenges of raising a child with ASD

Desired outcome: *Sarah's family will develop specific coping abilities to manage the inevitable stresses that they will experience directly due to or as a secondary effect of Sarah's having ASD.*

Goal 2: To help Sarah's family members understand and gain access to the range of formal and informal emotional supports that may be available

Desired outcome: *Sarah's family members will gain access to formal and informal supports that best match their emotional needs at specific points in time.*

Goal 3: To help Sarah's family members identify their own priorities and develop appropriate expectations and realistic, achievable goals for Sarah's development and family life

Desired outcome: *Sarah's family members will be clear about the most important issues they wish to address for Sarah and the family, will develop realistic goals and expectations for Sarah, and will create a balance in family life consistent with their lifestyle and values.*

A range of options was discussed with Sarah's parents regarding emotional supports in the community. These included formal supports such as a districtwide parent *support group* held once a month at the school district's administration building, parent support groups in the larger community, and resources for *one-to-one support meetings*. During the meeting, Sarah's parents expressed a strong desire to have the opportunity to connect with the local community and to join in the monthly districtwide support meeting offered by the school system.

Support Among Professionals

As a final step in planning and designing Sarah's educational program, her team leader discussed how the SCERTS Model recognizes that professionals and other service providers face considerable challenges when implementing an intensive educational program. For professionals and other service providers (e.g., paraprofessionals) to be as effective as possible in supporting children and families, a SCERTS Support Plan for Professionals and Service Providers would need to be developed. Because Sarah's team, as described in the SAP Activity Planning Form, included not only professionals but also paraprofessionals, *mentoring arrangements* were scheduled on a daily basis for at least 5 hours per week of paraprofessional supervision provided by her special education preschool teacher, her speech-language pathologist, and/or her occupational therapist. Supervision would involve both direct educational and interactive guidance as well as one-to-one emotional support in bimonthly *supervision meetings*. Next, her team leader indicated that each month, Sarah's team members would arrange a *team meeting* to discuss her progress and the need for consistency with both interactive and learning supports. Her occupational therapist was also asked to provide an *in-service training session* geared at providing specific guidance related to Sarah's emotional regulatory development and related to the effective, individualized interpersonal supports and learning supports designed to facilitate her arousal level and emotional expression.

SAP Step 10: Performing Ongoing Tracking

Following the identification of weekly objectives for Sarah and her partners, her team discussed the need to track her ongoing progress in her educational program. They discussed that the second version of the SAP Daily Tracking Log would be best suited for this purpose given Sarah's age and her continued difficulties with persisting during challenging activities. During their discussion, her team recognized that although it would not be feasible to take data on every objective in every activity, it would be critical to track Sarah's progress to inform decision making about the effectiveness of her program's implementation. As a result, progress with each objective would be monitored on a daily basis in one or two activities. Primary responsibility for data collection during Sarah's morning activity and school routines would be assigned to her educator and paraprofessional. They would specifically track her progress as it related to half of Sarah's Social Communication and Emotional Regulation objectives, as well as half of the Transactional Support objectives for her partners. Her parents and the paraprofessional would then be responsible for data collection during her afternoon activity routines.

Sarah's team formulated a plan for using the information documented on the SAP Daily Tracking Log to complete a SAP Weekly Tracking Log. Her speech-language pathologist would compile this information each week and take responsibility for sharing it with the team. Her team also discussed that it would be critical to track Sarah's progress from week to week to inform decision making about the effectiveness of program implementation. Finally, they discussed the need to complete a new SAP for Sarah each quarter to determine if targeted objectives had been achieved and whether new objectives would be needed. This quarterly assessment will also determine if limited progress should warrant a change in her targeted objectives.

Chapter 6

Enhancing Social Communication, Emotional Regulation, and Transactional Support at the Language Partner Stage

From Assessment to Program Implementation

To develop a comprehensive educational program or to modify an existing program for a child at the Language Partner stage, the SCERTS Model prioritizes those developmental capacities that support a child's communicative competence across people, places, and circumstances. As delineated in Chapter 7 of Volume I, this process begins by identifying goals and objectives in the areas of social communication and emotional regulation based on a child's current developmental capacities in these domains and is followed by determining the most applicable transactional supports for the child and family. This must be a flexible process that is dependent on the child's learning strengths and needs, the family's priorities, and the demands of the child's natural routines and ongoing educational programming.

In this chapter, we describe the development and implementation of educational programs for two children at the Language Partner stage, one at the novice level and one at the advanced level of this stage. These two children demonstrate very different levels of ability and therefore allow us to consider the range of issues that must be addressed for programming at the Language Partner stage. Again, we must emphasize that the goals and activities described in this chapter are not being offered as a "prescription" to follow for all children at this stage, as each child's program should be individualized based on his or her unique social-communicative and emotional regulatory needs and learning strengths and weaknesses. As discussed in Chapter 1 of this volume, educational priority goals for a child are based on the following criteria: 1) Goals target the most *functional* abilities in social communication and emotional regulation (i.e., abilities that support the child's active engagement in natural activities in daily routines), 2) goals directly *address family priorities* (i.e., goals are consistent with the values of parents and other family members), and 3) goals are *developmentally appropriate* (i.e., goals are consistent with the child's performance on the SAP-O). By following these criteria, the focus remains on fostering a child's ability to understand how and when to use acquired skills as independently as possible and apply these abilities consistently and in a functional manner in activities that are prioritized by the family and the many partners in that child's daily life.

Furthermore, as discussed in Chapter 1 of this volume, a SCERTS Model program should include *at least* 25 hours per week on a year-round basis of planned learning opportunities with sufficient individualized attention for the child to remain actively engaged. Thus, designing a comprehensive and intensive educational program for a child at the Language Partner stage requires an effort to 1) establish a blueprint for meaningful and purposeful activities in daily routines, 2) determine the current challenges posed in these settings, and 3) determine the complexity of the social contexts (i.e., one-to-one, small-group, or large-group settings) that would be appropriate depending on the child's unique social-communicative and emotional regulatory capacities. In addition, it is critical to keep in mind the importance of providing opportunities for the child to learn with typically developing children and other children who can provide good language and social models when such social communication objectives are identified as part of the child's educational program (refer to the section in Chapter 2 of this volume called Successful Inclusion and Learning and Playing with Peers).

A child's increasing success in more natural contexts often requires a deliberate effort by family and educational team members to implement planned activity routines, engineered activities, and modified natural activities. As noted in Chapter 1 of this volume, the SCERTS Model does not advocate a strict hierarchical sequence when considering this continuum of naturalness. Rather, planned activity routines and engineered and modified activities may be incorporated at different times of the day depending on the complexity of the various activities and the child's variability across the day. In some cases, one-to-one planned activity routines may be provided as an opportunity for increased practice or rehearsal for achieving specific goals. In using planned activity routines at the Language Partner stage, it is important to use the same or similar materials that are available in the natural learning environments. At the Language Partner stage, however, coping with variability and flexibility becomes increasingly important for children who have greater developmental capacities. Practice and rehearsal continue to be most effective in the context that a child will eventually use the targeted capacities to support an understanding of the natural cues of how and when to use the skills being addressed. However, as compared with the Social Partner stage, introduction of increased flexibility to support active problem solving in dealing with new experiences also comes to play a more significant role in educational programming.

In addition, as discussed in Chapter 3 of this volume, the SCERTS Model recognizes that the successful provision of a comprehensive educational program for a child at the Language Partner stage is not dependent solely on the determination of objectives and supports for the child. A SCERTS Family Support Plan is needed to address the provision of both educational and emotional support to family members, and a SCERTS Support Plan for Professionals and Service Providers is needed to address the need for ongoing training, continuing education, and team collaboration. Embedded in a network of support, a child's partners can begin to develop competencies in fostering social communication and emotional regulation and implementing appropriate transactional supports. These support plans should be sensitive to the changing needs of the child, the family, and service providers and tailored to meet the unique challenges faced by children at the Language Partner stage.

As discussed in Chapter 2 of Volume I, the Language Partner stage encompasses two major developmental transitions that enable a child to become a more active social and communicative partner: 1) the transition to *first words* and 2) the transition to *word combinations*. A child entering this stage is showing greater evidence of intentionality than a child at the Social Partner stage. In fact, a child at this stage has clearly become more persistent in communicating for specific social (e.g., requesting comfort) as well as nonsocial goals (e.g., requesting and protesting). In addition, a child at the Language Partner stage uses a larger repertoire of *active learning strategies* to develop the capacity to symbolize, as evident in the ability to use and understand words to refer to objects and events, to imitate new behaviors, and to pretend with objects in play. In this stage, the child is developing an increased awareness of his or her effectiveness in communicating intentions to partners and the need to use more explicit communicative signals to convey a message. The acquisition of an initial repertoire of words, followed by a rapid expansion of vocabulary and combinations of words, enables the child to share a greater variety of intentions, emotions, and personal experiences.

Likewise, during the Language Partner stage, the child expands his or her ability to share attention, as evidenced in an emerging capacity to deduce the underlying intentions of others' verbal and nonverbal communication by noticing what a partner is attending to and by considering ongoing activities of others. More sophisticated joint attention capacities enable a child to use additional strategies for securing another's attention by calling out a caregiver's name, to greet a greater number of partners, to request permission, and to comment about interesting items and events.

In the Social Communication domain of the SCERTS Model, these achievements typically develop as a result of a child's accomplishments in both joint attention and symbol use. In the Emotional Regulation domain, these achievements rely on the child's accomplishments in mutual regulation and self-regulation.

PRIORITIZING GOALS FOR JOINT ATTENTION AT THE LANGUAGE PARTNER STAGE

A number of critical milestones in joint attention contribute to a child's transition from the Language Partner stage to the Conversational Partner stage and to the development of more effective and explicit communicative exchanges in reciprocal interactions. These milestones provide the framework for prioritizing goal areas for a child with ASD as he or she progresses through the Language Partner stage. They include the child's ability to 1) engage in reciprocal interaction, 2) share attention, 3) share emotion, 4) share intentions to regulate behavior, 5) share intentions for social interaction, 6) share intentions for joint attention, 7) persist and repair communicative breakdowns, and 8) share experiences in reciprocal interaction.

At the Language Partner stage, growth in Joint Attention underlies a child's mastery of the foundations for engaging in reciprocal communication and involves the coordination of abilities mastered in the Social Partner stage. Thus, a child at the Language Partner stage is developing the capacity to coordinate attention, emotion, *and* intentions not only to comment on objects or events but also to share experiences in early social conversations. Integration of these abilities contributes to the child's expanding repertoire of communicative functions and the child's capacity to engage in more extended reciprocal interactions (i.e., by showing reciprocity in both speaker and listener roles). Specific milestones along this developmental trajectory provide developmental benchmarks that guide the determination of weekly objectives for a child at this stage. These include the following:

1. The child *engages in reciprocal interaction* by
    a. Initiating bids for interaction
    b. Engaging in brief reciprocal interaction
    c. Engaging in extended reciprocal interaction

2. The child *shares attention* by
   a. Shifting gaze between people and objects
   b. Following contact and distal points
   c. Monitoring the attentional focus of a social partner
   d. Securing attention to him- or herself prior to expressing intentions

3. The child *shares emotion* by
   a. Sharing negative and positive emotion
   b. Understanding and using symbols to express a range of emotions
   c. Attuning to changes in partners' expression of emotion
   d. Describing the emotional state of another person

4. The child *shares intentions to regulate behavior of others* by
   a. Requesting desired food or objects
   b. Protesting undesired food or objects
   c. Requesting help or other actions
   d. Protesting undesired actions or activities

5. The child *shares intentions for social interaction* by
   a. Requesting comfort
   b. Requesting social games
   c. Taking turns
   d. Greeting
   e. Calling
   f. Showing off
   g. Requesting permission

6. The child *shares intentions for joint attention* by
   a. Commenting on objects
   b. Commenting on actions or events
   c. Requesting information about things of interest

7. The child *persists and repairs communication breakdowns* by
   a. Using an appropriate rate of communication for the context
   b. Repeating and modifying communication to repair
   c. Recognizing breakdowns in communication

8. The child *shares experiences in reciprocal interaction* by
   a. Coordinating attention, emotion, and intentions to share experiences
   b. Showing reciprocity in speaker and listener roles to share experiences
   c. Initiating interaction and sharing experiences with a friend

A child with ASD at the Language Partner stage may have achieved some of the basic developmental milestones of intentional communication, but challenges in joint attention continue and compromise important foundational abilities for further social-communicative growth. As discussed in Chapter 2 of Volume I, a child with ASD at this stage often demonstrates limitations in the following abilities: 1) visually observing partners and using more sophisticated strategies to secure their attention; 2) monitoring the attentional focus of a partner by looking at and/or commenting on what the partner is paying attention to; 3) interpreting others' nonverbal social cues to both infer and describe their emotional states; and 4) communicating for a variety of social purposes (e.g., expressing emotions, commenting, requesting permission) to maintain more extended reciprocal exchanges (e.g., requesting social games, taking turns, sharing experiences).

At this stage, these limitations are particularly evident as a child with ASD begins to interact with more varied partners and in more varied contexts. Although variability in different settings is often observed in typically developing children, especially when the children are first exposed to unfamiliar contexts, the degree of this discrepancy is typically so great and so prolonged in a child with ASD that the term *situation-specific learning* has been used to describe these differences (see Chapter 2 in Volume I for further discussion). Thus, at the Language Partner stage, a child with ASD often shows a strong bias toward familiar partners and familiar routines. Therefore, in the SAP, the expectations for determining whether a child has met criterion for a specific skill increase from those at the Social Partner stage. This shift, which is evident in the SAP-O scoring key for this stage, has been implemented to ensure that specific objectives are met across at least two different activities (e.g., caregiving routine, play) or contexts (e.g., school, home) and at least three different partners.

PRIORITIZING GOALS FOR SYMBOL USE AT THE LANGUAGE PARTNER STAGE

A number of critical milestones in Symbol Use contribute to a child's transition from the Language Partner stage to the Conversational Partner stage and to the development of more effective and explicit communicative exchanges in reciprocal interactions. Symbol Use achievements at this stage also include the development of more creative and generative language use. As a child enters the Language Partner stage, a range of more conventional or easily understood gestures such as giving and pushing away objects, showing objects, index finger pointing, and head nodding have already emerged and have become reliable means to communicate along with the emergence of early symbolic communicative forms such as signs, pictures, and words bound to routines. The acquisition of an initial repertoire of word forms or early symbolic language is then typically followed by a rapid expansion of vocabulary and combinations of words, enabling a child to share a greater variety of intentions, emotions, and personal experiences.

Knowledge of how typically developing children make this transition to the Language Partner stage, and current research related to the social-communicative patterns of children with ASD, contribute to a team's ability to prioritize critical goal areas in Symbol Use. These include the ability to 1) learn by observation and imitation of familiar and unfamiliar actions and words, 2) understand nonverbal cues in familiar and unfamiliar activities, 3) use familiar objects conventionally in play, 4) use gestures and nonverbal means to share intentions, 5) use words and word combinations to express meanings, and 6) understand a variety of words and word combinations without contextual cues. Specific milestones along this developmental trajectory provide benchmarks that guide the determination of weekly objectives for a child at this stage. These include the following:

1. The child *learns by observation and imitation of familiar and unfamiliar actions and words* by
    a. Spontaneously imitating familiar actions or words immediately after a model
    b. Spontaneously imitating unfamiliar actions or words immediately after a model
    c. Spontaneously imitating actions or words and adding a different behavior
    d. Spontaneously imitating a variety of behaviors later in a different context

2. The child *understands nonverbal cues in familiar and unfamiliar activities* by
    a. Following situational and gestural cues in familiar and unfamiliar activities
    b. Following contact and distal points
    c. Following instructions with visual cues (photographs or pictures)
    d. Responding to facial expression and intonation cues

3. The child *uses familiar objects conventionally in play* by
    a. Using a variety of objects in constructive play
    b. Using a variety of familiar objects conventionally toward him- or herself
    c. Using a variety of familiar objects conventionally toward another
    d. Combining a variety of actions with objects in play

4. The child *uses gestures and nonverbal means to share intentions* by
    a. Using a variety of conventional and symbolic gestures such as a show, a wave, a distal reach/point, a clap, a head shake, and a head nod
    b. Using a sequence of gestures or nonverbal means in coordination with gaze

5. The child *uses words and word combinations to express meanings* by
    a. Coordinating sounds/words with gaze and gestures
    b. Using at least 5-10 words or echolalic phrases as symbols
    c. Using early relational words, such as for existence, nonexistence/disappearance, recurrence, and rejection
    d. Using a variety of names for objects, body parts, and agents
    e. Using a variety of advanced relational words such as personal-social words, action words, modifiers, and *wh-* words
    f. Using a variety of relational meanings in word combinations, such as modifier + object, negation + object, and agent + action + object

6. The child *understands a variety of words and word combinations without contextual cues* by
    a. Responding to his or her name
    b. Responding to a variety of familiar words and phrases
    c. Understanding a variety of names without contextual clues

d. Understanding a variety of relational words without contextual clues, such as words for actions, modifiers, and *wh-* words.

e. Understanding a variety of relational meanings in word combinations without contextual clues, such as modifier + object, negation + object, and agent + action + object

A child with ASD at the Language Partner stage typically shows difficulties with these achievements in symbol use, as evidenced by challenges with making the transition to first words as well as challenges with making the transition from single words to a flexible, rule-governed language system. Thus, the ability to form a range of creative word combinations including people as agents, a range of actions, and a range of objects (e.g., agent + action + object sentences) is often quite compromised. These challenges limit the child's effectiveness with sharing a greater variety of intentions, emotions, and personal experiences, which are hallmark achievements of this stage.

A number of developmental vulnerabilities and learning style differences contribute to these challenges in symbol use at the Language Partner stage for a child with ASD. These include but are not necessarily limited to the following: 1) difficulties with learning through social observation, which affects the development of action words and symbolic play; 2) difficulties with recalling words outside of the specific contexts in which they were learned (i.e., difficulties with word retrieval); 3) a reliance on gestalt language processing, as evidenced by a high proportion of echolalia; and for a significant proportion of children, 4) difficulties with vocal and speech communication due to problems in oral-motor and motor speech production. It is critical to recognize these potential challenges when developing a comprehensive educational program or modifying an existing program for a child with ASD at the Language Partner stage.

A child with ASD may demonstrate significant challenges learning through social observation and therefore may have difficulty following an adult's focus of attention. As a result, vocabulary development at the Language Partner stage often remains constrained to those word forms that are modeled by an adult partner who is following the *child's* attentional focus, such as nouns or object labels of preferred toys or snacks. Symbolic word forms for referents other than nouns, such as action words and modifiers, are therefore later developing in a child with ASD, as these forms require an ability to determine the focus of an adult's attention and observe the adult's actions and intents while processing language models. Likewise, the development of spontaneous make-believe and functional play, which are also learned through observation of social activities, is often quite constrained at this stage due to the social underpinnings of these capacities.

The development of symbol use in a child with ASD may be further compromised by a prolonged reliance on episodic associations, a learning strategy observed in very young children at earlier stages of development. With a strong preference for static environmental or visual cues and/or relative strengths in rote memory, a child may hear and remember a word or a chunk of language as part of an episode. Thus, it is the situation-specific learning conditions of that episode (e.g., the visual cues in the environment, the verbal cues of a partner, the physical cues of a teacher) that supports word recall rather than true concept knowledge (i.e., semantics). This reliance on episodic memory may compromise word retrieval when a child with ASD is using single words at the novice Language Partner stage as well as when beginning to combine words at the advanced Language Partner stage. Once again, this is more likely to occur with action words as opposed to object labels. Action words, unlike objects, involve constantly changing episodes or conditions. For example, the word "open" can encompass many distinct and unique actions, as the action looks different with a door than with a jar of bubbles. In contrast, nouns often have nontransient referents that are defined by similarities in perceptual attributes (e.g., roundness for balls). Thus, word retrieval challenges are often more apparent as a child begins to develop action words and more conceptual language.

In addition, a child with ASD at the Language Partner stage may learn to talk using a gestalt style of language learning. As discussed previously, this refers to the process of learning language, at least initially, by memorizing phrases or sentences with limited understanding of the components of language (i.e., the meaning of the individual words). Thus, a child may go through a period of using chunks of language or echolalia, the immediate repetition (i.e., immediate echolalia) or delayed repetition (i.e., delayed echolalia) of the speech of others. Although a child with ASD may learn to use these gestalt forms to express communicative intentions with greater relevance and meaning in communicative interactions, objectives at the Language Partner stage have been designed to support an ability to break down these echolalic chunks into smaller meaningful units corresponding to the words or constituents in the chunk. The process of segmenting echolalic utterances is critical to the process of making the transition to a rule-governed, generative language system, which is the pinnacle achievement of this stage.

Finally, the transition to first words and the transition to word combinations at the Language Partner stage may be further compromised by the remarkable variability in the ability to use vocal communication or speech observed in children with ASD. As discussed in Chapter 2 of Volume I, it is estimated that one third to one half of children and adults with ASD have significant difficulty using speech as a functional and effective means of communication. Although core challenges in joint attention and symbol use are clearly the most universal factors to consider when addressing a child's social and communicative competence, some children with ASD have a very limited inventory of consonant sounds and use less complex syllabic structure due to oral-motor planning difficulties and/or delays in phonological development (Bryson, 1996; Lord & Paul, 1997; NRC, 2001). These individual variations clearly need to be considered when prioritizing critical goals and objectives for a child as well as when developing appropriate interpersonal supports and learning supports.

PRIORITIZING GOALS FOR MUTUAL REGULATION AT THE LANGUAGE PARTNER STAGE

A number of critical milestones in Mutual Regulation support a child's transition from the Language Partner stage to the Conversational Partner stage and to the development of more effective and language-based strategies for regulation in reciprocal interactions. To understand the process of mutual regulation for a child at the Language Partner stage, it must be determined whether partners are primarily responding to the child's signals of dysregulation (i.e., *respondent mutual regulation*), or whether a child initiates and intentionally directs signals to others (i.e., *initiated mutual regulation*). Early in the Language Partner stage, a child's developing social awareness and social-communicative abilities should support the ability to use initiated mutual regulatory strategies to regulate his or her emotions; however, the process of respondent mutual regulation remains important. This is particularly true when a child's social-communicative abilities vary as a result of fluctuations in arousal state. For instance, a child at the Language Partner stage who is experiencing extreme dysregulation may not be able to efficiently direct a request for assistance to a partner but may benefit from respondent mutual regulation or partner initiated support, which is dependent on a partner's ability to both recognize signs of dysregulation and offer support.

As a child progresses through the Language Partner stage, the sophistication of initiated mutual regulatory strategies also develops. This is due, in part, to the child's greater awareness of the need to obtain regulatory assistance and increased ability to communicate this need through a more explicit repertoire of both nonverbal and verbal communicative means characteristic of this stage (e.g., gestures, words, word combinations). The child's requests may be aimed at securing either behavioral or language-based assistance. During this stage, the child's increased social referencing, along with feedback and guidance from partners, helps to shape and guide the child's emotional responses and behavior.

Critical goal areas in Mutual Regulation are prioritized based on two primary sources: 1) a team's knowledge of how typically developing children make the transition to the Language Partner stage and thus are increasingly able to use symbolic means seek assistance from others and 2) current research related to the mutual regulatory challenges faced by children with ASD. Priority goals in Mutual Regulation include the ability to 1) express a range of emotions, 2) respond to assistance offered by caregivers, 3) request caregiver assistance to regulate emotional state, and 4) recover from extreme dysregulation with support from partners. Specific milestones along this developmental trajectory provide benchmarks that guide the determination of weekly objectives for a child at this stage. These include the following:

1. The child *expresses a range of emotions* by
    a. Sharing negative and positive emotions
    b. Understanding and using symbols to express a range of emotions
    c. Changing emotional expression in familiar activities based on partners' feedback

2. The child *responds to assistance offered by partners* by
    a. Soothing when comforted by partners
    b. Engaging with alerted by partners
    c. Responding to bids for interaction
    d. Responding to changes in partners' expression of emotion
    e. Attuning to changes in partners' expression of emotion
    f. Making choices when offered by partners
    g. Changing regulatory strategies based on partners' feedback in familiar activities

3. The child *requests a partner's assistance to regulate state* by
    a. Sharing negative emotion to seek comfort
    b. Sharing positive emotion to seek interaction
    c. Requesting help when frustrated
    d. Protesting when distressed
    e. Using language strategies to request a break

    f. Using language strategies to request regulating activity or input

    g. Using language strategies to exert social control

4. The child *recovers from extreme dysregulation with support from partners* by

    a. Responding to partners' efforts to assist with recovery by moving away from activity

    b. Responding to partners' use of behavioral strategies

    c. Responding to partners' use of simple language strategies

    d. Responding to partners' attempts to reengage in interaction or activity

    e. Decreasing amount of time to recover from extreme dysregulation due to support from partners

    f. Decreasing intensity of dysregulated state due to support from partners

As discussed in Chapter 3 of Volume I, a child with ASD at the Language Partner stage often exhibits difficulties in mutual regulation. These challenges are due, in part, to a restricted range of emotional expression (e.g., limited use of gestures, facial expressions, body language) and/or extreme emotional reactions (e.g., emotional expression perceived as excessive for the context). Other variations in communication of emotional state often observed in Language Partners with ASD, such as immature patterns of behavior (e.g., crashing into others, hitting, biting), also affect the ability to secure appropriate and supportive assistance from partners. These unconventional behaviors clearly have a transactional influence, as a child's partners perceive them as problem behaviors rather than as signs of dysregulation. In these unfortunate circumstances, the child's attempts at securing assistance from others may lead to further isolation and/or emotional distress, as the partner's reaction (e.g., punishing or ignoring the behaviors) may not address the child's need for support.

It also is worth noting that challenges with accurately interpreting a child's emotional expression and signs of dysregulation are further compounded by arousal bias, as a child with a hyporeactive bias often sends remarkably different signals than a child with a hyperreactive bias. Accurate assessment of these factors is essential to the design and implementation of mutual regulation strategies that facilitate a child's organization. For example, one might need to recognize the benefit of reducing the intensity of environmental stimulation to help a child who is hyperreactive to achieve a more regulated state, such as by closing the classroom door while another group of students gathers noisily in the hallway. In contrast, one might need to recognize the benefit of increasing the use of visual supports to help a child who is hyporeactive maintain his engagement and focus during a transition or a multistep activity. If these factors are not considered, respondent strategies may be attempted but may not succeed at supporting a child's unique needs.

Challenges in the developmental capacities of social communication and arousal state regulation further affect a child's ability to recognize a communicative partner as a potential source of assistance and therefore the ability to direct readable signals to others for assistance with emotional regulation. For example, when a child with ASD experiences a strong emotion and a corresponding extreme change in emotional state, the child's ability to respond adaptively to a situation may be compromised. Thus, a child who, when well regulated, can verbally request assistance from a partner who is present in the room may not be able to do so when dysregulated. Collectively, these difficulties exacerbate a child's difficulties in using or responding to mutual regulatory strategies.

PRIORITIZING GOALS FOR SELF-REGULATION AT THE LANGUAGE PARTNER STAGE

A number of critical milestones in Self-Regulation contribute to a child's transition from the Language Partner stage to the Conversational Partner stage and to the development of more effective and language-based strategies for regulation in reciprocal interactions. Early in the Language Partner stage, a child is primarily dependent on *behavioral strategies* as a means to self-regulate; these strategies are either biologically driven (e.g., shutting down to tune out background noise) or have been fostered by responsive partners (e.g., covering one's ears during a fire alarm).

As symbolic capacities expand, the child is also able to employ *language strategies* for these same purposes. Language strategies are words or other symbols (e.g., signs, pictures) that the child uses to self-regulate arousal level. For example, a child who is sensitive to noise may prepare for a recital in the auditorium by using self-talk (e.g., "Three songs, then all done"). The collective use of behavioral strategies and language strategies contributes to a child's competence with attaining a well-regulated state and therefore supports a child's ability to develop more explicit forms of communication and engage in extended reciprocal interactions. Hallmarks of these expanding regulatory abilities at the Language Partner stage include a child's increasing ability to tolerate transitions, manage changes in routine, and control behavioral impulses.

A team's knowledge of typical development and current research related to the self-regulatory challenges faced by children with ASD contribute to the team's ability to prioritize critical goal areas in Self-Regulation. These priority goals include the ability to 1) demonstrate availability for learning and interacting, 2) use behavioral strategies to regulate arousal level during familiar activities, 3) use language strategies to regulate arousal during familiar activities, 4) regulate emotion during new and changing situations, and 4) recover from extreme dysregulation on one's own. Specific milestones along this developmental trajectory provide benchmarks that guide the determination of weekly objectives for a child at this stage. These include the following:

1. The child *demonstrates availability for learning and interacting* by
   a. Initiating bids for interaction
   b. Engaging in brief reciprocal interaction
   c. Engaging in extended reciprocal interaction
   d. Responding to social and sensory experiences with differentiated emotions
   e. Demonstrating the ability to inhibit actions and behaviors
   f. Responding to a variety of familiar words and phrases
   g. Persisting during tasks with reasonable demands
   h. Demonstrating emotional expression appropriate to the context

2. The child *uses behavioral strategies to regulate level of arousal during familiar activities* by
   a. Using behavioral strategies to regulate arousal level during solitary and social activities

b. Using behavioral strategies modeled by partners to regulate arousal level

c. Using behavioral strategies to engage productively in an extended activity

3. The child *uses language strategies to regulate level of arousal during familiar activities* by

    a. Using language strategies to regulate arousal level during solitary activities

    b. Using language strategies to regulate arousal level during social interactions

    c. Using language strategies modeled by partners to regulate arousal level

    d. Using language strategies to engage productively in an extended activity

    e. Using symbols to express a range of emotions

4. The child *regulates emotion during new and changing situations* by

    a. Participating in new and changing situations

    b. Following situational and gestural cues in unfamiliar activities

    c. Using behavioral strategies to regulate arousal level in new and changing situations

    d. Using language strategies to regulate arousal level in new and changing situations

    e. Using behavioral strategies to regulate arousal level during transitions

    f. Using language strategies to regulate arousal level during transitions

5. The child *recovers from extreme dysregulation by him- or herself* by

    a. Removing him- or herself from overstimulating or undesired activity

    b. Using behavioral strategies to recover from extreme dysregulation

    c. Using language strategies to recover from extreme dysregulation

    d. Reengaging in interaction or activity after recovery from extreme dysregulation

    e. Decreasing amount of time to recover from extreme dysregulation

    f. Decreasing intensity of dysregulated state

As discussed in Chapter 3 of Volume I, children with ASD at the Language Partner stage typically show difficulties in these self-regulation milestones, as evidenced by limitations in the ability to sustain attention during social interactions, a tendency to display strong and sudden emotional reactions, and challenges with tolerating transitions. Factors associated with ASD that contribute to these challenges include 1) atypical responses to stimulation resulting in arousal biases (e.g., hypersensitivity resulting in a bias for a high state of arousal, hyposensitivity resulting in a bias for a low state of arousal), 2) challenges perceiving physiological changes in arousal state, and 3) difficulties expressing emotions.

Social-communicative challenges can further compromise a child's development of self-regulatory abilities. In particular, at the Language Partner stage, challenges in joint attention affect a child's ability to respond to social feedback regarding the acceptability of his or her behavior as well as a child's ability to employ emotional regulatory strategies that have been modeled by others. In turn, children with ASD at the Language Partner stage may continue to display extreme emotional reactions and use self-regulatory strategies that appear to be idiosyncratic; unconventional; and, in some cases, socially stigmatizing (e.g., flapping hands, walking on toes, biting, rocking). As discussed in Chapter 5 of this volume, these idiosyncratic self-regulatory behaviors may inadvertently be viewed as problem behaviors and may be targeted for elimination. Because these behaviors may be a direct consequence of a child's limited repertoire of socially appropriate and effective self-regulatory strategies, the emotional regulatory functions of such behavioral patterns should be considered when determining appropriate goals in Self-Regulation.

PRIORITIZING GOALS FOR INTERPERSONAL SUPPORT AT THE LANGUAGE PARTNER STAGE

It is critical to again emphasize the transactional impact of the behaviors of partners, and the relationships with partners on a child's development and sense of competence and confidence at the Language Partner stage. Achievements in the developmental capacities of social communication and emotional regulation at the Language Partner stage are dependent on a successful history of predictable and supportive interactions with a range of partners who have fostered social engagement, communicative initiation, and the attainment of a well-regulated state. Interpersonal accommodations (referred to as *interpersonal supports* in the SCERTS Model) are considered to be essential when prioritizing partner goals in the domain of Transactional Support.

The following dimensions of the Interpersonal Support component of Transactional Support are viewed as critical for supporting a child's ability to engage as a competent Language Partner. The partner 1) is responsive to the child, 2) fosters initiation, 3) respects the child's independence, 4) sets the stage for engagement, 5) provides developmental support, 6) adjusts language input, and 7) models appropriate behaviors. Specific objectives in these dimensions provide benchmarks that guide the development of individualized interpersonal supports and the identification of weekly objectives not only for the child but also for the child's partners. These include the following:

1. The *partner is responsive to the child* by

    a. Following the child's focus of attention

    b. Attuning to the child's emotion and pace

    c. Responding appropriately to the child's signals to foster a sense of communicative competence

    d. Recognizing and supporting the child's behavioral and language strategies to regulate arousal level

    e. Recognizing signs of dysregulation and offering support

    f. Imitating the child

    g. Offering breaks from interaction or activity as needed

    h. Facilitating reengagement in interactions and activities following breaks

2. The *partner fosters initiation* by

    a. Offering choices nonverbally or verbally

    b. Waiting for and encouraging initiations

    c. Providing a balance of initiated and respondent turns

    d. Allowing the child to initiate and terminate activities

3. The partner *respects the child's independence* by
   a. Allowing the child to take breaks to move about as needed
   b. Providing time for the child to solve problems or complete activities at his or her own pace
   c. Interpreting problem behavior as communicative and/or regulatory
   d. Honoring protests, rejections, or refusals when appropriate

4. The *partner sets stage for engagement* by
   a. Getting down on the child's level when communicating
   b. Securing the child's attention before communicating
   c. Using appropriate proximity and nonverbal behavior to encourage interaction
   d. Using appropriate words and intonation to support optimal arousal and engagement

5. The *partner provides developmental support* by
   a. Encouraging imitation
   b. Encouraging interaction with peers
   c. Attempting to repair breakdowns verbally and nonverbally
   d. Giving guidance and feedback as needed for success in activities
   e. Providing guidance on expressing emotions and understanding the cause of emotion

6. The *partner adjusts language input* by
   a. Using nonverbal cues to support understanding
   b. Adjusting the complexity of language input to the child's developmental level
   c. Adjusting quality of language input to the child's arousal level

7. The partner *models appropriate behaviors* by
   a. Modeling appropriate nonverbal communication and emotional expressions
   b. Modeling a range of communicative functions such as behavior regulation, social interaction, and joint attention
   c. Modeling appropriate constructive and symbolic play
   d. Modeling appropriate behavior when the child uses inappropriate behavior
   e. Modeling "child-perspective" language

Social interactions are transactional in nature; therefore, the child's communicative partners must respond flexibly and in a supportive manner to foster the child's development of communicative and regulatory abilities. As described in Chapter 4 of Volume I, some children with ASD are at risk for developing a sense of interpersonal interaction as overwhelming, confusing, and stressful based on a history of repeated unsuccessful experiences. Other children with ASD are at risk for limited engagement and low motivation to participate in social interactions due to language and sensory processing difficulties and/or a hyporesponsive bias toward interpersonal events. A child's partners also are at risk for experiencing interactions with the child as challenging, especially in reference to supporting the child's reciprocal engagement and the child's attainment of a well-regulated state.

At the Language Partner stage, a child's developmental vulnerabilities and learning style differences have a transactional influence on the child's partners. For example, a child at the Language Partner stage may have difficulties comprehending and processing language, resulting in the child's avoidance of childhood activities that are typical for a Language Partner (e.g., activities that are dependent on an ability to understand words and word combinations without the use of contextual cues). Therefore, both adults and peers may view the child as aloof, unresponsive, and/or difficult to engage. Similarly, difficulties comprehending and processing language at the Language Partner stage may evoke anxiety in the child, a pattern that can contribute to a partner's perception of the child as problematic or, in some cases, noncompliant. Expressive communication difficulties can further exacerbate interactional difficulties between a child and a partner. As noted previously, a child with ASD at the Language Partner stage may use a limited range of vocabulary, may have difficulty with word retrieval, may use unconventional verbal means such as echolalia to convey a range of intentions, and/or may have difficulties producing intelligible speech as an efficient mode of communication. These challenges significantly affect a partner's ability to understand the child and therefore may further contribute to the partner's impression of a child that as difficult to engage.

In addition to these language-based challenges, interactions between a child and a partner can be compromised by the child's difficulties in understanding emotional cues, gestures, and facial expressions, resulting in a lack of, inconsistent, or inappropriate responses to a partner's nonverbal and emotional communication. In some situations, a child may shut down or tune out when faced with difficult-to-process information, such as words and word combinations, nonverbal gestures, and emotional expression, resulting in the child's being unavailable for interaction due to extreme dysregulation. In addition, the child's peers and/or siblings may develop a sense of frustration during interactions, as their emotional signals might be missed by the child with ASD.

Last, a child's sensory processing difficulties (e.g., patterns of hypo- or hyperreactivity) may result in inconsistent reactions to sensory input and inconsistent states of arousal, which is a challenging pattern for the child's partners to read and respond to successfully. Thus, a critical priority at the Language Partner stage is to systematically address goals for partner behavior with respect to interactive style.

A partner's implementation of interpersonal supports fosters a child's attainment of critical Language Partner milestones, including the child's development of 1) more reciprocal communicative exchanges, 2) creative and generative language use, and 3) more effective and efficient regulation strategies.

PRIORITIZING GOALS FOR LEARNING SUPPORT AT THE LANGUAGE PARTNER STAGE

Achievements in social communication and emotional regulation are facilitated, in part, by the effective use of learning supports. Learning supports are accommodations that include a range of environmental modifications, visual supports, and other relevant learning and instructional strategies that may be used to facilitate a child's communication and expressive language, understanding of language and social expectations, activity structure (e.g., the sequence of steps and end goal of an activity), emotional expression, and emotional regulation. It is critical that the child's partners use such accommodations to modify activities and learning environments in a manner that supports organization, provides opportunities for active learning, and promotes child initiation.

The following dimensions of Learning Support are viewed as essential for supporting a child's ability to engage as a competent Language Partner. The partner 1) structures an activity for active participation; 2) uses augmentative communication support to foster development; 3) uses visual and organizational support; and 4) modifies goals, activities, and the learning environment to suit a child's developmental level and learning style differences. Specific objectives in these dimensions provide benchmarks that guide the development of individualized learning supports and the identification of weekly objectives not just for the child but also for that child's partners. These include the following:

1. The *partner structures activity for active participation* by
    a. Defining clear beginnings and endings to an activity
    b. Creating turn-taking opportunities and leaving spaces for the child to fill in
    c. Providing a predictable sequence to an activity
    d. Offering repeated learning opportunities
    e. Offering varied learning opportunities

2. The *partner uses augmentative communication support to foster development* by
    a. Using augmentative communication support to enhance the child's communication and expressive language
    b. Using augmentative communication support to enhance the child's understanding of language and behavior
    c. Using augmentative communication support to enhance the child's expression and understanding of emotion
    d. Using augmentative communication support to enhance the child's emotional regulation

3. The *partner uses visual and organizational support* by
    a. Using support to define steps within a task
    b. Using support to define steps and time for completion of activities
    c. Using visual support to enhance smooth transitions between activities
    d. Using support to organize segments of time across the day
    e. Using visual support to enhance attention in group activities
    f. Using visual support to foster active involvement in group activities

4. The *partner modifies goals, activities, and the learning environment* by
    a. Adjusting social complexity to support organization and interaction
    b. Adjusting task difficulty for child success
    c. Modifying sensory properties of the learning environment
    d. Arranging the learning environment to enhance attention
    e. Arranging the learning environment to promote child initiation

Assessment to Implementation: Language Partner Stage

f. Designing and modifying activities to be developmentally appropriate

g. Infusing motivating materials and topics in activities

h. Providing activities to promote initiations and extended interactions

i. Alternating between movement and sedentary activities as needed

j. "Upping the ante" or increasing expectations appropriately

As discussed in Chapter 4 of Volume I, children with ASD at the Language Partner stage demonstrate unique patterns of learning preferences and weaknesses, which requires that individualized learning supports be implemented to foster both social communication and emotional regulation. A greater understanding of the learning and cognitive styles of children with ASD has led to the development of a wide range of effective visual, organizational, and learning supports. A number of these supports fall under the umbrella term *AAC*. Although there are clear individual variations among children with ASD, a child with ASD may demonstrate a strong preference for nontransient visual information. This refers to information that remains static or fixed in place over time, such as pictures, visual-spatial patterns, and objects. With this in mind, the SCERTS Model emphasizes the role of partners in capitalizing on a child's preference for static visual information as a means to help the child compensate for difficulties processing information that is more transient or fleeting in nature, such as the spoken word or nonverbal social cues. In the SCERTS Model, partners are encouraged to use visual and organizational supports to define steps within a task, to define time for completion of activities, and to support smooth transitions between activities. Likewise, partners of a child with ASD at the Language Partner stage are encouraged to implement AAC supports, such as gestures, signs, pictures, and words, to foster a child's transition from predominantly echolalic language forms to more creative and generative combinations of words and, eventually, the formulation of more complex word combinations. Furthermore, AAC supports may be used to facilitate a child's use of more sophisticated language when oral-motor and/or word retrieval difficulties compromise language recall.

In addition, a child at the Language Partner stage may have difficulty maintaining active engagement in social interactions and activities due to language processing and emotional regulatory difficulties. Thus, the SCERTS Model encourages a child's partners to develop an understanding of these challenges and encourages the partners' incorporation of learning supports to define a clear beginning and end to natural activities, to provide predictable learning opportunities, and to offer both repeated *and* varied learning opportunities. Learning supports designed to modify activities and learning environments also are considered critical to the facilitation of a child's ability to maintain active engagement. Therefore, consideration is given to how the social complexity, physical properties, and sensory characteristics of a given activity can be modified to promote active engagement for the child.

An additional learning support consideration at the Language Partner stage relates to the tendency for a child with ASD to rely on episodic associations that result in situation-specific learning. To deal with this challenge, AAC supports can serve as visual bridges across contexts, demonstrating commonalities across experiences and promoting generalization and spontaneity in new and changing environments. For example, a child may learn to associate a picture symbol for a bathroom with many bathrooms across settings and may use it when needed to ask to go to the bathroom, rather than thinking of each bathroom as a totally different place requiring a separate learning process. These learning supports may also enable a child with ASD to determine how and when to use a targeted learning objective more independently across settings and partners.

Learning supports contribute to a child's ability to remain actively engaged in natural routines. Therefore, the SCERTS Model prioritizes systematic goals for partner behavior. These goals are designed to enhance environmental and activity modifications, the implementation of visual supports, the implementation of AAC systems to foster communicative development, and the use of highly predictable and repetitive learning opportunities when developing a comprehensive program or modifying an existing program for a child with ASD at the Language Partner stage.

SPOTLIGHTS ON CHILDREN AT THE LANGUAGE PARTNER STAGE

In the following sections, two children and families are spotlighted to illustrate the process of identifying and prioritizing goals for a child at the novice Language Partner stage and a child at the advanced Language Partner stage. The term *spotlight* is used because each of these vignettes is reflective of a child and family at a specific intersection on their developmental journey. The SCERTS Model recognizes the dynamic processes involved in assessment and program planning. Following the criteria for goal selection, ongoing assessment will be necessary to identify goals and objectives that are considered 1) functional, 2) a family's priorities, and 3) developmentally appropriate. It is expected that initial goals will need to be modified as a child's program evolves.

A number of other decisions should be reassessed regularly (i.e., every 3 months) to determine any necessary program adjustments and modifications. These include 1) the choice of meaningful and purposeful activities to focus on in a child's daily routines; 2) the intensity of social support, such as the ratio of adult to child support in social groupings; and 3) the range of naturalness of activities (e.g., planned activity routines, engineered activities, modified natural activities). These spotlights are provided to illustrate the processes involved in implementing the SCERTS Model from assessment to implementation of a program addressing social communication, emotional regulation, and transactional supports for children with ASD at the Language Partner stage. (Chapters 5 and 7 in this volume present spotlights on children at the Social Partner and Conversational Partner stages, respectively.) Blank versions of the assessment forms mentioned in the spotlights can be found in Appendix A of Volume I.

SPOTLIGHT ON GREGORY, A NOVICE LANGUAGE PARTNER

Gregory is at the novice level of the Language Partner stage. Gregory is a sweet and gentle 9-year-old boy who lives at home with his mother, who is a single parent. He is participating in a full-day educational program in his local public school district and participates in both horseback riding and swimming lessons during several after-school programs. At 2 years of age, Gregory was diagnosed with Autistic Disorder, which falls under the generic category of ASD. Following Gregory's diagnosis, Gregory's mother actively searched for and obtained a variety of early intervention services, including an intensive home-based educational program following a traditional applied behavior analysis (ABA) approach and speech-language therapy. Gregory participated in these services until his third birthday, when his school district assumed responsibility for the provision of his educational program.

Gregory's current program consists of attending a full-day self-contained special education classroom with three other children with ASD, with daily opportunities for inclusion in a general education third-grade classroom; speech-language therapy; occupational therapy; and adaptive physical education. Although his early intervention program had followed a more traditional ABA model, his current IEP pulls from a number of philosophies and approaches. The curriculum in his special education classroom, for example, is largely based on ABA techniques and is facilitated by his special education teacher or an instructional assistant in isolation from the other children in his class. Several other educational approaches, however, are also evident in his self-contained learning environment. These include the use of structured workstations and environmental arrangements consistent with the Structured Teaching approach in the TEACCH curriculum (Schopler et al., 1995), instruction in the Picture Exchange Communication System (PECS), and oral-motor therapy.

Although Gregory has developed many skills as a result of his current educational program, his educational team and his mother have expressed concerns about Gregory's persistent difficulties with *spontaneously* initiating engagement with both adults *and* peers and engaging in more *reciprocal* interactions. He tends to communicate primarily for instrumental functions such as requesting and protesting and continues to have difficulty greeting others, requesting social games, and commenting about his experiences. Likewise, his mother and the team have expressed concerns about Gregory's ability to remain actively engaged across his daily routines at school and at home, as he can be easily distracted or disengaged.

As a result of these concerns, Gregory's mother requested a meeting with his educational team to clarify the priorities of his educational program. Although she has been quite pleased with the eclectic nature of his program, she feels that his learning has remained fixed to specific contexts and people and that more consistency addressing his needs across settings and partners may be helpful. For example, his team members agreed that although Gregory appears to be interested in peers in his inclusive classroom and has developed relationships with a number of the adult staff members at school, he has not yet developed a friend among his peers.

Gregory's team members and his mother felt that several factors continue to contribute to these challenges. First, Gregory's difficulties with social communication appear to be a major factor. In addition to having difficulties in establishing shared attention (i.e., joint attention) and developing language (i.e., symbol use), Gregory clearly has significant oral-motor planning difficulties, resulting in limited use of recognizable speech. Familiar adult partners are able to understand his frequently used word approximations (e.g., "buh" for "book," "weh" for "swing," and "Deh . . . eee" for "Gregory"), but his peers in the third grade rarely notice and/or respond to these utterances during large-group interactions. Gregory's pace of interaction is slow and he often attempts to use physical proximity and gestures to communicate with peers, means that are easily overlooked in his busy third-grade classroom.

Gregory's team members further acknowledged that the introduction of the PECS has greatly expanded Gregory's ability to request objects and familiar social routines. However, because his use of this AAC approach is linked to specific activities (e.g., snack, breaktime, lunch), Gregory's opportunities to use PECS to communicate with his peers are very limited, as are his opportunities to use PECS for more social functions (e.g., sharing his experiences). Despite these shortcomings, his team members noted that they are generally impressed that the introduction of picture symbols has resulted in an expanded symbolic vocabulary of approximately 20 words that Gregory uses consistently with intent. His vocabulary, which had been primarily limited to object labels for preferred foods and toys, has recently expanded to include colors of objects and a word to reject activities (i.e., a symbol for "no"). At times, Gregory does require verbal cues (e.g., "What do you want?"; "Need help?") to initiate requests using his picture symbols. This is primarily evident when Gregory is in a low state of arousal and is having difficulty attending.

Gregory's mother and team members agreed that Gregory's arousal level is often too low for the demands of his social and physical environment and that they often feel the need to get him up and going through the use of physical activity and predictable routines. Without support from caregivers, Gregory often appears unfocused and distracted. In fact, his mother and team members agree that Gregory would likely choose to spend the majority of his day looking out the window out of the corner of his eye (e.g., watching the tree branches sway in the wind). Clearly this low arousal bias also affects his ability to interact successfully with his peers.

Based on these persistent challenges in Gregory's social-communicative profile and his continued challenges in emotional regulation, Gregory's mother and educational team members agreed that it would be timely to review his current educational programming to make the necessary program adjustments and modifications to his goals and objectives to facilitate his development in these areas. Because of his mother's concern regarding a mechanism to prioritize critical developmental objectives for Gregory in his eclectic educational program as well as the need for consistency in the implementation of learning accommodations across settings and partners, the SAP was administered. Thus, we now illustrate the steps that Gregory's mother and his educational team members took in implementing this process.

The SAP was implemented to 1) establish Gregory's current profile of developmental strengths and needs; 2) determine meaningful, purposeful, and motivating goals to address; 3) select the most appropriate learning contexts and complexity of social support based on Gregory's natural routines and activities; and 4) determine the necessary transactional supports to foster Gregory's development and his relationships with his mother, peers, and teaching staff. Because a comprehensive SCERTS Model program also includes explicit plans for support to families and support among professionals, information from the SAP was also used to ensure that Gregory's educational program would be compatible and consistent with the needs expressed by his mother. In addition, the assessment team determined the specific educational supports and emotional supports that would be provided for Gregory's mother and the professionals who would be involved in the implementation of Gregory's program.

SAP Step 1: Determining Gregory's Communication Stage

During an initial SAP team meeting, Gregory's special education teacher led the team in a discussion of Gregory's current behavior in his home and school environments. Based on their discussion, his team determined that the appropriate SAP forms to use for the assessment would be those designated for the Language Partner stage. This decision was based on the completion of the Worksheet for Determining Communication Stage and the criteria for determining a child's communication stage in the SAP. Gregory uses approximately 20 symbols (i.e., picture symbols and word approximations) to make requests of his partners consistently and in goal-directed communicative bids. The team also noted that Gregory was not yet independently using creative word combinations to communicate and that the functions of his communication were restricted to basic requests and protests; therefore, he did not yet meet the criteria for the Conversational Partner stage.

SAP Step 2: Gathering Information with the Language Partner SAP-R Form

During a monthly team meeting attended by Gregory's mother and his educational team, Gregory's mother was asked to complete the SAP-R Form to provide additional information regarding Gregory's behavior in his home and community environments. This questionnaire identified 1) the primary concerns and stresses faced by Gregory's mother, 2) Gregory's primary strengths and his mother's concerns about his development, 3) the activities in which both Gregory's strengths and areas of need would likely be seen in his home and community environments, 4) Gregory's typical partners in the home and community, and 5) the natural contexts in Gregory's life outside of school. Gregory's educational team also completed a separate version of the SAP R Form to identify similarities and discrepancies with respect to Gregory's behavior in school versus his behavior in other natural environments. The information gathered from both of Gregory's SAP-R Forms is summarized next:

1. The primary concerns and stresses faced by Gregory's mother included

    - "His reliance on others to help him stay focused"
    - "His limited reasons for communicating"
    - "His articulation difficulties"
    - "His limited friendships"
    - "The amount of time spent trying to keep him engaged"

2. Gregory's mother and educational team identified the following strengths and needs in his current profile:

Strengths	Needs
"Gregory uses word, approximations, gestures, and picture symbols to communicate."	"Gregory needs to have greater success when attempting to interact with peers."
"He is interested in his peers."	"He needs to maintain his focus during activities and interactions."
"He enjoys physical activity."	"He needs to communicate for more social functions such as playing or sharing."

3. The activities in which both Gregory's strengths and areas of need would likely be observed included

    - Snack, an activity that follows a consistent classroom routine and incorporates the use of augmentative communication supports
    - Inclusion with peers in the third-grade classroom
    - Swimming lessons during an after-school program

4. Gregory's typical partners include

    - Mom
    - Special education teacher
    - General education teacher

- Classroom instructional assistant
- Speech-language pathologist
- Occupational therapist
- Adaptive physical education teacher
- Special education classmates (3 children)
- Third-grade classmates (23 children)
- Peers at swim class (3 children)

5. Natural contexts in Gregory's life include
    - Caregiving routines at home
    - Play routines at home
    - Classroom routines in special education classroom
    - Classroom routines in general education classroom
    - School playground
    - Community indoor swimming pool
    - Therapeutic horseback riding stables

SAP Step 3: Identifying Assessment Team Members and Planning the SAP-O

After collecting both of the completed SAP-R Forms from Gregory's mother and his educational team members, Gregory's special education teacher began completing the SAP Map for Planning the SAP-Observation. This form was used to help identify appropriate members of Gregory's assessment team and their roles and responsibilities. Consideration was given to whether any referrals to outside professionals would need to be made. In addition, as part of planning the administration of the SAP-O, the following variables were considered to ensure that a representative sample of Gregory's abilities and needs would be documented: 1) the *location* (i.e., natural contexts) where the observations would take place, 2) the specific *length* of the observations, 3) the *partners* who would be present, 4) the *group size* of the social contexts during the observations, 5) the nature of the *activities,* and 6) the number of *transitions* during each observation (see Chapter 7 in Volume I for a more detailed discussion of these variables).

After reviewing the information provided in the SAP-R and each of these variables, Gregory's educational team was able to plan the upcoming observations to document a representative sample of Gregory's abilities and challenges. First, given that Gregory is at Language Partner stage, the minimum length of total observation time was identified as 2 hours. However, given that Gregory's abilities vary greatly depending on the context and his partners, the team decided that it would be best to split the observation among three environments (i.e., 1 hour per environment), incorporating both adults and peers as his communicative partners. Likewise, representative group sizes (i.e., group sizes typical to Gregory's natural environment) were identified and considered: one to one (e.g., Gregory with the instructional assistant), small group (e.g., Gregory with his mother, swim instructor, and three peers at swim class), and large group (e.g., Gregory in his third-grade inclusive classroom). Given that Gregory's team had expressed concern regarding inconsistencies in Gregory's behavior based on environmental and social variables, these three locations and group sizes were identified as the primary contexts for the observations.

After determining the specific contexts for the observations, Gregory's special education teacher carefully reviewed the primary concerns of Gregory's mother and educational team, as well as those activities that they felt would provide a sample of Gregory's strengths and areas of need. Additional variables were considered to ensure that the assessment team would gain an accurate picture. For example, it was evident that Gregory would behave differently when engaged in an unstructured versus a structured activity, a busy environment versus a quiet environment, a motor-based versus a sedentary activity, and a language-based versus a non-language-based or a visually supported task. With this information, four activities were identified for his school-based observation. These included 1) participation in snack with the instructional assistant and classmates in his special education classroom, 2) participation in an individual work session with his special educator, 3) participation in an art activity in his inclusive third-grade classroom, and 4) participation in a group reading activity in his inclusive third-grade classroom. One additional activity, participation in swimming lessons, was identified as part of an after-school community-based observation. Due to scheduling difficulties with staff members, it was determined that this activity would be videotaped and that the team would review the videotape during a team meeting.

As noted in Chapter 7 of Volume I, children who participate in the SAP-O should be observed across at least three transitions. Therefore, Gregory's special educator planned for transitions to be a part of each observation to ensure a representative sampling of Gregory's behavior in new and changing situations. During the first observation, for example, team members planned to observe Gregory preparing his snack and making the transition to eating with his classmates, as well as making the transition from snack to independent work. During the second observation, Gregory's team members would observe Gregory's transitions from his self-contained classroom to his inclusive third-grade classroom and, in this context, from an art activity to a group reading activity. Finally, during the third observation, Gregory's team members would observe his transition in and out of the pool during his swimming lesson. Information included in Gregory's SAP Map is provided in Figure 6.1A to illustrate the outcome of this planning process. After Gregory's SAP Map was created, the service coordinator transferred relevant information to the cover sheet of the SAP-O Form (see Figure 6.1B).

SAP Step 4: Completing the SAP-O Form

Gregory's SAP team (i.e., his special education teacher, his speech-language pathologist, and his occupational therapist) used the SAP-O Form for the Language Partner stage to gather information across their three observations (see Chapter 7 in Volume I for specific administration instructions). Information was gathered under three domains, two of which focused on assessing Gregory's strengths and needs (i.e., Social Communication and Emotional Regulation) and one that addressed the strengths and needs of his partners in various environments (i.e., Transactional Support).

Gregory's team members agreed that to capture a detailed and representative sample of Gregory's profile and the strategies used by his partners supporting him, they would need to divide observation responsibilities during the assessment. Because his speech-language pathologist would be present at both observations and would be viewing the videotape, the team agreed that she should gather the majority of the information related to Social Communication and Emotional Regulation, as these two domains are central to Gregory's current challenges, as identified by his mother and the team. His occupational therapist and special education teacher therefore were assigned to gather the majority of the information related to the components in the Transactional Support domain (i.e., Interpersonal Support and Learning Support) and to supplement the observations made by the speech-language pathologist as appropriate.

Figure 6.1A. Gregory's SAP Map.

Figure 6.1B. Cover sheet (p. 1) of Gregory's SAP-O Form.

Assessment to Implementation: Language Partner Stage

SAP Step 5: Conducting Behavior Sampling

Following the completion of the three scheduled observations, including the team's review of Gregory's videotaped swim class, the team members briefly reviewed Gregory's SAP-O Form. They agreed that although they had gathered a wealth of information from observing his interactions in his natural environments and activities, there were a number of questions remaining related primarily to Gregory's abilities in the Social Communication domain. They felt that these questions remained, in part, due to the nature of the activities observed. During social interactions in the majority of the activities, Gregory was primarily in a passive, respondent role and therefore his opportunities to initiate communication to spontaneously share his intentions for the purposes of social interaction and joint attention were limited. His team members observed that due to Gregory's tendency to remain in a passive, respondent role, they were often waiting for his response to their prompts and initiations and noted that he rarely needed to *persist and repair* to clarify his spontaneous intents. With this in mind, the areas they desired more information, including

- JA5.4—Gregory's ability to share intentions for social interaction by greeting others

- JA6.2—Gregory's ability to share intentions for joint attention by commenting on actions or events

- JA7.2—Gregory's ability to persist and repair communication breakdowns by repeating and modifying communication

With these remaining questions, Gregory's educational team agreed that an additional observation in the familiar context of his special education classroom would provide needed information to guide the development and implementation of an appropriate educational program. In this subsequent session, his team members structured several brief activities designed to illustrate Gregory's competence and abilities in the areas just outlined. For example, to document Gregory's use of conventional communicative means (e.g., gestures, picture symbols, words) to greet partners (JA5.4), the team observed Gregory when his special education teacher entered the room and stood in close proximity to Gregory, but Gregory did not initiate a greeting.

Next, Gregory's ability to share information related to actions and events (JA6.2) was sampled through the introduction of a photograph journal from home with accompanying picture symbols for agents (people) and actions using color coding (i.e., a red border indicating an agent and a green border indicating an action word) to support his ability to place the pictures in the proper sequence. Gregory's speech-language pathologist first demonstrated how to construct an early developing word combination (e.g., an agent + an action) using picture symbols and then encouraged Gregory to do the same (e.g., "Gregory swim").

Finally, the team turned their attention to Gregory's ability to persist and repair communication breakdowns (JA7.2). To do so, team members staged or created situations that did not typically occur in Gregory's natural environments. For example, when Gregory handed a picture symbol of a preferred book to the instructional assistant, she paused before responding to his communicative attempt to see if he would persist and, if so, what means he would use to repair the breakdown. Several other situations that required Gregory's ability to persist and repair communicative breakdowns through the use of verbal, gestural, and picture symbol means were also staged. During this sampling, Gregory's speech-language pathologist paid special attention to Gregory's use of word approximations in his efforts to establish shared attention, as well as the sophistication of his speech production and oral-motor movements, as this was a primary concern of his mother and clearly was affecting his ability to communicate effectively with his peers.

SAP Step 6: Compiling and Integrating Information with the SAP Summary Form

Following the completion of the initial observations and the follow-up behavior sampling session in Gregory's special education classroom, Gregory's educational team and his mother met to compile and integrate information, a step that involves two key information sources: 1) summarizing strengths and needs from the SAP-O and 2) documenting family perception of the SAP-O results.

Key Information Source 1: Summarizing Strengths and Needs

Social Communication: Joint Attention

During the team meeting, Gregory's mother and educational team members initially focused on determining Gregory's strengths and needs in joint attention. Based on information obtained through the SAP-O, Gregory's mother and service providers agreed that Gregory is truly a Language Partner in that he is able to use a variety of gestures, pictures, and word approximations to share attention, emotion, and intentions. His speech-language pathologist remarked that when Gregory is well regulated and engaged in social interactions, his ability to share his intentions to regulate the behavior of others appears solidly established. In other words, his ability to request and refuse has emerged as an area of relative strength. The speech-language pathologist offered the following example. During his snack routine at school, Gregory was able to use picture symbols consistently to request desired foods and assistance as well as to refuse undesired foods. His occupational therapist added that in reviewing the videotape of Gregory in his swimming class, this ability to share intentions was also evident, despite the fact that Gregory did not have access to picture symbols. In this setting, for example, he used gestures, gaze, and word approximations for the same function (e.g., clapping and saying "ma" while looking at his mother to indicate that he wanted to continue using the kickboard).

The team agreed that these examples represented Gregory's abilities at their peak and that when Gregory was not as well regulated, he often relied on less sophisticated or symbolic means to secure his partners' attention and share his intentions. In his inclusive third-grade classroom, which is a relatively complex social environment, Gregory relied primarily on physical contact (e.g., touching the instructional assistant's arm) and/or more subtle means of gaining another person's attention (e.g., standing in close proximity). For example, when he desired a drink of water, he stood near the water fountain rather than pointing and/or using a word approximation to make this request. His special educator commented that these presymbolic means of gaining a partner's attention were more likely to be seen during prolonged sedentary activities. She had observed Gregory repeatedly touching the instructional assistant's arm during an art activity; however, Gregory waited for the assistant to ask him, "What do you want?" before using a picture symbol to request help.

Next, the team turned their attention to Gregory's ability to share a variety of intentions from requesting and protesting to greeting and commenting. They all agreed that he is, for the most part, consistent in his ability to use pictures, gestures, and word approximations to communicate his basic needs by requesting objects, food, comfort, and familiar social games with a range of preferred partners, including his mother, his special education teacher, and the instructional assistant. He also is beginning to comment on objects with picture symbols. For example, while completing a matching task during his individual work time with his special educator, Gregory independently selected his picture symbols representing *blue* and *red* to comment on the color of the objects with which he was working. However, Gregory was not yet able to *independently* comment on actions and events or to request information about upcoming events or things that he found interesting.

During the behavior sampling session, Gregory had taken an interest in the color-coded picture supports used for commenting in his photograph journal, but he required considerable assistance to construct the basic agent + action word combinations. The team agreed that because Gregory's current educational program frequently places him in a respondent role in activities requiring few varied needs to communicate, his ability to share his intentions for social interaction, including taking turns, greeting, calling, showing off, and requesting permission, remains limited.

Next, the team turned their attention to how Gregory's passive nature affected his ability to persist and repair during communicative breakdowns. Because this was not observed in the natural activities selected for the SAP-O, information was gathered primarily during the behavior sampling session. It was observed that Gregory had significant difficulty repeating and modifying his communication strategies to repair communicative breakdowns. During the behavior sampling, when Gregory's initial attempts to communicate by handing a picture to the instructional assistant had failed, he repeated the same strategy before attempting a new strategy. Similarly when Gregory's attempt to request to play on the swings using the word approximation "weh," paired with communicative gaze was not effective, Gregory tried once more and then stood next to the swing set to clarify this request. In part, his team felt that his difficulty persisting and repairing was due to his variable arousal level and difficulty sustaining attention; however, the team members also recognized that several other factors were contributing to this pattern. In particular, they commented on how his inconsistent ability to secure another's attention before communicating, his persistent oral-motor challenges, and challenges with persistence and repair of breakdowns adversely affected his ability to sustain interactions with peers.

A complete summary of Gregory's current profile of strengths and areas of need in the Joint Attention component is included in a sample SAP-O Form and a sample SAP Sum (see Figures 6.1 and 6.8).

Social Communication: Symbol Use

After establishing Gregory's baseline in joint attention, his educational team determined Gregory's strengths and needs in symbol use. Based on both initial observations, it became evident that Gregory communicates using a variety of early developing and later developing gestures, a variety of single-word approximations, and a variety of picture symbols. In his special education classroom and his swimming lessons, he was noted to consistently use a give gesture to request assistance, a reach gesture and a push-away gesture to indicate his preference for various activities, and a contact index finger point to request specific items. Despite his effective use of these gestures, his ability to consistently pair gestures with gaze as a means of securing attention to himself prior to expressing his intentions remains limited when he is dysregulated. His

SAP-OBSERVATION FORM: Language Partner Stage
Social Communication (page 2)

Child's name: _Gregory_

JOINT ATTENTION

Qtr 1	Qtr 2	Qtr 3	Qtr 4	
				1 Engages in reciprocal interaction
2				JA1.1 Initiates bids for interaction (= SR1.1)
1				JA1.2 Engages in brief reciprocal interaction (= SR1.2)
1				JA1.3 Engages in extended reciprocal interaction (= SR1.3)
				2 Shares attention
2				JA2.1 Shifts gaze between people and objects
1				JA2.2 Follows contact and distal point (= SU2.2)
1				JA2.3 Monitors attentional focus of a social partner
0				JA2.4 Secures attention to oneself prior to expressing intentions (= JA5.5)
				3 Shares emotion
2				JA3.1 Shares negative and positive emotion (= MR1.1; = MR3.1, MR3.2)
0				JA3.2 Understands and uses symbols to express a range of emotions (= MR1.2, SR3.5)
1				JA3.3 Attunes to changes in partners' expression of emotion (= SU2.4; = MR2.5)
0				JA3.4 Describes the emotional state of another person (↔ SU5.6)
				4 Shares intentions to regulate the behavior of others (↔ JA7.2, JA8.2, SU4–SU5, MR3.7)
2				JA4.1 Requests desired food or objects (= MR2.6)
2				JA4.2 Protests/refuses undesired food or objects (= MR3.4)
2				JA4.3 Requests help or other actions (= MR3.3)
2				JA4.4 Protests undesired actions or activities (= MR3.4)
				5 Shares intentions for social interaction (↔ JA7.2, JA8.2, SU4–SU5)
2				JA5.1 Requests comfort (= MR3.1)
2				JA5.2 Requests social game
0				JA5.3 Takes turns
0				JA5.4 Greets
0				JA5.5 Calls (= JA2.4)
0				JA5.6 Shows off
0				JA5.7 Requests permission
				6 Shares intentions for joint attention (↔ JA7.2, JA8.2, SU4–SU5)
1				JA6.1 Comments on object
0				JA6.2 Comments on action or event
0				JA6.3 Requests information about things of interest
				7 Persists and repairs communication breakdowns
1				JA7.1 Uses appropriate rate of communication for context
1				JA7.2 Repeats and modifies communication to repair (= JA4–JA6)
0				JA7.3 Recognizes breakdowns in communication
				8 Shares experiences in reciprocal interaction
0				JA8.1 Coordinates attention, emotion, and intentions to share experiences
0				JA8.2 Shows reciprocity in speaker and listener roles to share experiences (↔ JA4–JA6)
0				JA8.3 Initiates interaction and shares experiences with a friend

SCORING KEY: **2**, criterion met consistently (across three partners in two contexts); **1**, criterion met inconsistently or with assistance; **0**, criterion not met

Figure 6.2. Gregory's SAP-O Form (Joint Attention component).

SAP-OBSERVATION FORM: Language Partner Stage
Social Communication (page 3)

Child's name: _____

SYMBOL USE

Qtr 1	Qtr 2	Qtr 3	Qtr 4	
				1 Learns by observation and imitation of familiar and unfamiliar actions and words
				SU1.1 Spontaneously imitates familiar actions or words immediately after a model
				SU1.2 Spontaneously imitates unfamiliar actions or words immediately after a model
				SU1.3 Spontaneously imitates actions or words and adds a different behavior
				SU1.4 Spontaneously imitates a variety of behaviors later in a different context
				2 Understands nonverbal cues in familiar and unfamiliar activities
				SU2.1 Follows situational and gestural cues in familiar and unfamiliar activities (= SR4.2)
				SU2.2 Follows contact and distal point (= JA2.2)
				SU2.3 Follows instructions with visual cues (photographs or pictures)
				SU2.4 Responds to facial expression and intonation cues (= JA3.3)
				3 Uses familiar objects conventionally in play
				SU3.1 Uses a variety of objects in constructive play
				SU3.2 Uses a variety of familiar objects conventionally toward self
				SU3.3 Uses a variety of familiar objects conventionally toward other
				SU3.4 Combines a variety of actions with objects in play
				4 Uses gestures and nonverbal means to share intentions (↔ JA4–JA6, MR3.3, MR3.4)
				SU4.1 Uses a variety of conventional and symbolic gestures ☐ a. show ☐ d. clap ☐ f. head nod ☐ b. wave ☐ e. head shake ☐ g. other _____ ☐ c. distal reach/point
				SU4.2 Uses sequence of gestures or nonverbal means in coordination with gaze
				5 Uses words and word combinations to express meanings (↔ JA4–JA6, MR3.3, MR3.4)
				SU5.1 Coordinates sounds/words with gaze and gestures
				SU5.2 Uses at least 5–10 words or echolalic phrases as symbols
				SU5.3 Uses early relational words ☒ a. existence ☒ b. nonexistence/disappearance ☒ c. recurrence ☒ d. rejection
				SU5.4 Uses variety of names for objects, body parts, and agents
				SU5.5 Uses variety of advanced relational words ☐ a. personal-social ☐ b. action ☒ c. modifier ☐ d. wh- word
				SU5.6 Uses variety of relational meanings in word combinations (↔ JA3.4) ☐ a. modifier + object ☐ b. negation + object ☐ c. agent + action + object
				6 Understands a variety of words and word combinations without contextual cues
				SU6.1 Responds to own name
				SU6.2 Responds to a variety of familiar words and phrases (= SR1.6)
				SU6.3 Understands a variety of names without contextual cues
				SU6.4 Understands a variety of relational words without contextual cues ☐ a. action ☒ b. modifier ☐ c. wh- word
				SU6.5 Understands a variety of relational meanings in word combinations without contextual cues ☐ a. modifier + object ☐ b. negation + object ☐ c. agent + action + object

SCORING KEY: **2**, criterion met consistently (across three partners in two contexts); **1**, criterion met inconsistently or with assistance; **0**, criterion not met

Figure 6.3. Gregory's SAP-O Form (Symbol Use component).

speech-language pathologist commented that Gregory had not demonstrated the ability to use more sophisticated gestures such as a wave gesture, a head nod, and a head shake during the SAP-O. His mother agreed with these remarks, as these challenges are often observed at home.

In addition to these challenges with nonverbal communication, the team concluded that several other factors were limiting Gregory's symbolic communication skills. These included his oral-motor planning difficulties as well as his difficulties with word retrieval. Currently, Gregory's symbolic communication skills comprise a limited number of word approximations for familiar object labels (e.g., "buh" for "book," "weh" for "swing," "buh dee oh" for "video") and picture symbols for object labels, attributes (e.g., colors), words for recurrence (e.g., "more," "yes"), and words for rejection (e.g., "no"). In addition, based on the Worksheet for Word Meanings in the Language Partner Stage, his inventory of agent labels, action words, emotion words, and early word combinations (e.g., agents + actions, actions + objects) remains limited at this time either with or without the availability of picture symbols.

With respect to his understanding of language, his team noted that during his swimming lesson and his individual work session with the special educator, Gregory clearly demonstrated the ability to orient his body toward an object held in front of him; to respond to both gestural and verbal cues; and to discriminate among basic object words, action words, and early descriptive concepts (e.g., colors, letters, numbers). For example, Gregory's swim instructor held out a kickboard and motioned Gregory over to the stack of boards while asking him to pick up a red one. Gregory was able to following this direction without difficulty. His understanding of more advanced relational words, particularly in word combinations, had not yet been demonstrated consistently. During art time, Gregory had to rely on the instructional assistant's use of physical gestures (i.e., tactile cues) and visual models to follow steps in each activity. Gregory also had difficulty responding to word combinations of agents paired with actions during his individual work session (e.g., "horse run," "doggy jump"), as he tended to focus his attention on only one element of the directive. The team agreed that these difficulties may be due, in part, to Gregory's need to rely on visual memory or contextual cues when responding to directives, a characteristic of his situation-specific learning style. When these contextual cues are absent, Gregory's responses are much more inconsistent.

Gregory's mother agreed with this observation and offered the example of Gregory getting his shoes. She commented that if she was getting ready to go out and was gathering her coat and shoes and she requested that Gregory retrieve his own shoes, he often did so without hesitation. However, if she was sitting in the living room reading a book and made the same request, Gregory would likely not complete the action. Throughout the SAP-O it was evident that Gregory demonstrated a strong preference for information that is nontransient in nature, such as objects and picture cues that remain visible over time. The entire team agreed that Gregory clearly responds more efficiently to oral directions paired with visual information (e.g., pairing a request for "clean up" with a gesture toward a bag) and he benefits from the use of visual supports to organize his behavior (e.g., a between-task picture schedule). A complete summary of Gregory's current profile of strengths and areas of need in the Symbol Use component is included in a sample SAP-O Form and a sample SAP Sum (see Figures 6.3 and 6.8).

Emotional Regulation: Mutual Regulation

Gregory's team members then discussed the SAP-O findings related to his strengths and needs in mutual regulation. The team members reflected on their previous discussions of Gregory's social-communicative abilities and the impact of these areas on his emotional regulatory abilities. In doing so, Gregory's mother and other team members recognized that Gregory's increasing symbolic abilities and his capacity to share his intentions to regulate the behavior of others were both positively affecting his emerging abilities to use initiated mutual regulatory strategies, as documented during the SAP-O. This was particularly evident when he was actively engaged in a social interaction or an activity. In these instances, Gregory was able to protest when distressed, seek help when frustrated, and share positive and negative emotions through nonverbal means.

Gregory was beginning to seek assistance with emotional regulation from his partners by using the word approximation "huh" for "hug" with a picture symbol for the same action. Gregory used this strategy on several occasions throughout the SAP-O and seemed to do so when his attention was starting to wane, but he was still interested in the task. For instance, his occupational therapist documented his use of this request for regulatory assistance during the photograph journal behavior sampling activity as well as during his individual work sessions. Despite these encouraging examples, the team did not feel that Gregory's capacity to request assistance was solidly established, as he was not observed to use such requests when his arousal level was truly too low to maintain engagement in his current activity. They also expressed concern that he was not yet using emotion words to express his feelings.

Gregory's passive nature had been reported by both his mother and his educational team before the SAP-O was conducted, in their respective SAP-R Forms. In these forms, both his educational team members and his mother commented that Gregory often requires a great deal of support to maintain engagement in an ongoing activity. The team agreed that as a result of Gregory's bias toward a low state of arousal and his general hyporesponsive reactions toward environmental and social stimuli, his emotional expression was often restricted and his attention and actions were frequently more reflective of his emotional state and arousal level than were his facial expressions. For example, during snack, Gregory's facial expression was neutral, but he was attentive and actively engaged. In contrast, during group reading in his inclusive third-grade classroom, Gregory's facial expression again was neutral; however, the instructional assistant observed him to be gazing out the window and gently rocking himself. Based on her interpretation of the focus of his attention and his action, she determined that his arousal level had dropped and that he required assistance to regain a well-regulated state. She was observed to alert him by rubbing his back briskly and taking him for a short walk in the room. Given these supports, Gregory was able to reengage in the class. His team agreed that when partners offer organizing supports, such as visual structure, movement, exaggerated positive emotion, and deep pressure, Gregory is more consistently able to reengage in the activity at hand. His team also acknowledged that these types of supports were essential for helping Gregory to make transitions between activities.

Next, Gregory's team discussed the issue of extreme dysregulation, as they noted that he experiences extreme dysregulation when he is in both a low state of arousal and a high state of arousal. Thus, he may be unavailable for learning or social engagement when his arousal level is either too high or too low. Extremes of both of these arousal states significantly affect his ability to maintain engagement and benefit from naturally occurring learning opportunities in his environment. His team recognized his signals of extreme dysregulation associated with low arousal as 1) staring off into the distance, 2) vocalizing to himself, 3) gently rocking, 4) rapidly blinking his eyes, and 5) a significant reduction in the frequency and sophistication of his communication. Throughout the SAP-O, these signals were observed when Gregory had been engaged in a sedentary activity for an extended period or when there was no organizing visual information available to him such as a photograph schedule.

Gregory's speech-language pathologist had also documented several clear signals of extreme dysregulation associated with a high state of arousal. These were seen only on two occasions during the SAP-O process, during the transition from art to group reading and when he was required to leave the pool at the end of his swimming lessons. On both occasions, he averted his gaze and attempted to bang his head. His speech-language pathologist identified the common thread during these observation periods. On both occasions, Gregory was not well prepared for the transition as no visual supports were presented and the environments had become very busy with many people moving about, resulting in a flood of auditory and transient visual information.

A complete summary of Gregory's current profile of strengths and areas of need in the Mutual Regulation component is included in a sample SAP-O Form and a sample SAP Sum (see Figures 6.4 and 6.8).

Emotional Regulation: Self-Regulation

Next, Gregory's mother and team members discussed Gregory's abilities and challenges in self-regulation. Based on information attained through the SAP-R and the SAP-O, the team felt that a number of Gregory's behavioral strategies for self-regulation were supportive of his ability to learn and interact in his environment. Throughout the SAP-O, the team recorded several different behavioral strategies used by Gregory that seemed to support his ability to participate in activities. These included banging his hands on the table, shaking his head from side to side, and tapping his feet. Through the use of these strategies, Gregory was occasionally able to regulate his arousal level and, in turn, initiate and participate in more extended social interactions. These strategies, however, had the potential to leave a negative impression on his peers and were not always effective at achieving the most optimal state of arousal. As a result, Gregory was observed on a number of occasions to be in a state of arousal that was too low for the expectations of the social environment, a pattern suggesting a limited repertoire of self-regulatory strategies.

In some instances, Gregory's arousal state was so low that he was essentially unavailable for extended periods of time, a pattern that his team identified as periods of extreme dysregulation. When these periods were associated with a low state of arousal, Gregory exhibited clear signs of dysregulation, including rocking, staring off into the distance, making repetitive sounds, and rapidly blinking his eyes. As documented in the Mutual Regulation component, Gregory's team noted that he exhibited such behaviors during the group reading activity observed as part of the SAP-O. These behavioral strategies were not effective for helping him to increase his arousal level to support his availability for engagement. In fact, Gregory's visual and movement strategies, although aimed potentially at increasing his arousal level, appeared to keep him so preoccupied as to preclude his ability to independently shift his attention to the activity.

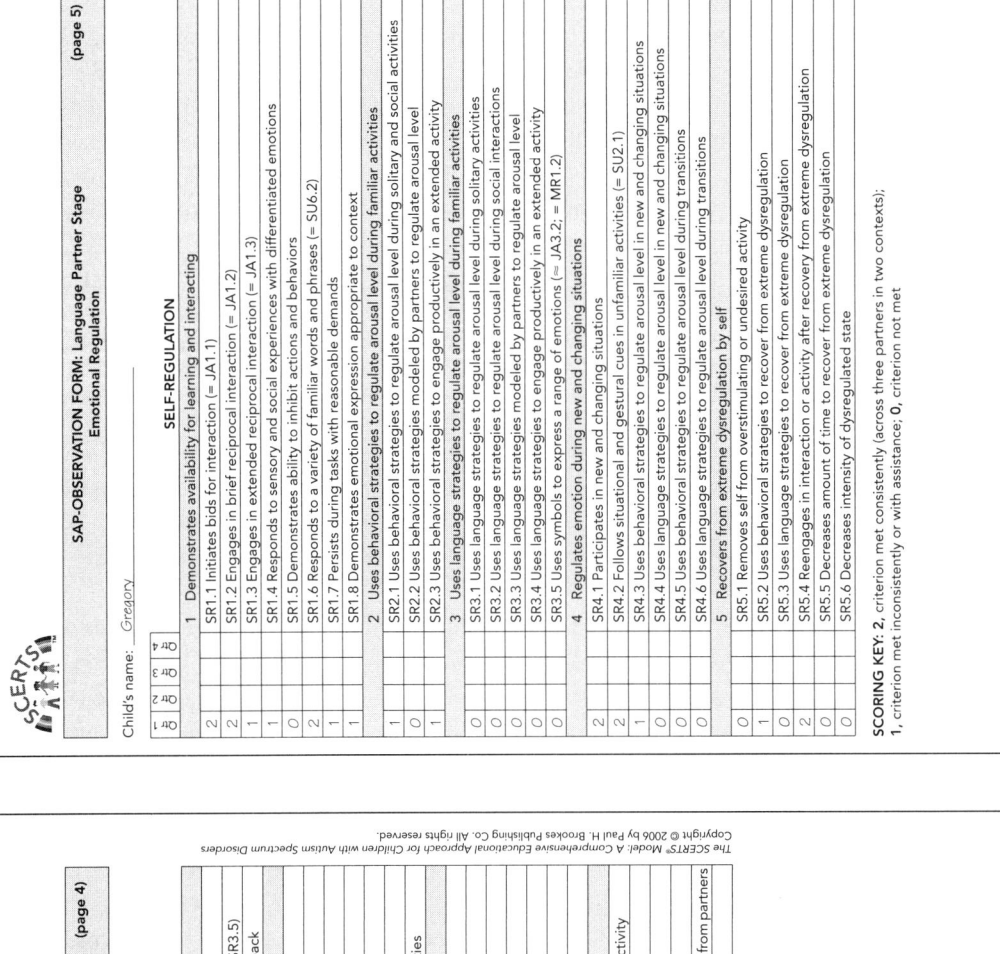

Figure 6.4. Gregory's SAP-O Form (Mutual Regulation component).

Figure 6.5. Gregory's SAP-O Form (Self-Regulation component).

Gregory's limited use of behavioral strategies also compromised his ability to self-regulate when experiencing periods of extreme dysregulation associated with high arousal. In his inclusive third-grade classroom and his swimming lesson, he attempted to use inefficient behavioral strategies such as head banging and gaze aversion with little success. From his team's discussion, it became evident that Gregory was not yet able to effectively use behavioral strategies to help with recovery from extreme dysregulation or to regulate his arousal level during new and changing situations. Gregory's occupational therapist also remarked that although Gregory is a symbolic communicator and a Language Partner, he was not yet able to use language-based strategies to help regulate his level of arousal during familiar activities, nor did he appear to be using strategies modeled by caregivers. A complete summary of Gregory's current profile of strengths and areas of need in the Self-Regulation component is included in a sample SAP-O Form and a sample SAP Sum (see Figures 6.5 and 6.8).

Transactional Support: Interpersonal Support

Both the SAP-R and the SAP-O were reviewed to determine the strengths and needs of Gregory's social network and the interpersonal supports needed to facilitate his abilities in social communication and emotional regulation. His mother and educational team members discussed how Gregory's developmental vulnerabilities are likely to have a transactional influence on his partners. For example, Gregory's emotional regulatory difficulties clearly contribute to inconsistent states of arousal and his frequent use of behavioral strategies for self-regulation (e.g., rapidly blinking his eyes, averting his gaze). During classroom observations, it was noted that these signals, due to their unconventional nature, were often challenging for unfamiliar partners to interpret, particularly peers. Nevertheless, when the instructional assistant encouraged interactions with his peers by supporting their ability to interpret these subtle signals, successful peer exchanges were more likely.

Gregory's bias toward a low state of arousal and restricted emotional expression often contributed to the perception that he is aloof, uninterested, or difficult to engage. Gregory's educational team felt this was particularly true for his third-grade peers in his inclusive classroom, as they were not observed to initiate greetings and/or play with Gregory without encouragement from an adult. The interpersonal supports that appeared to be helpful in these circumstances involved helping Gregory's peers understand his learning style and encouraging them to modify their interaction style to be more animated, to include more simplified language, and to provide more time for Gregory to solve problems or to complete activities at his own pace. The team agreed that the consistent use of these types of interpersonal supports by all of Gregory's partners would likely elicit more consistent responses from Gregory and therefore may change the perception that he is uninterested and difficult to engage. In addition, Gregory's educational team noted that those partners who provide extra time for Gregory to solve problems or complete activities at his own pace often are rewarded with increased engagement and cooperation than those who attempt to move Gregory passively through an activity.

By reviewing the SAP-R and SAP-O results, Gregory's mother and educational team members were able to identify a number of interpersonal supports that were emerging as areas of strength in his social network and those that were considered areas of need. The following chart provides examples of several of these areas.

Interpersonal Support	
Strengths	**Needs**
Gregory's mother consistently responds appropriately to Gregory's communicative signals to foster a sense of competence and, in turn, models a range of communicative functions (IS1.3, IS7.2). Gregory's adult partners at school (i.e., his teachers, instructional assistants, and therapists) are beginning to develop a range of interpersonal supports that are being used consistently across activities. These include recognizing signs of dysregulation and offering support (IS1.5), as well as securing Gregory's attention prior to communicating with him (IS4.2).	Gregory needs to initiate more often, as he is in a respondent role for much of his day. Thus, there is a great need for partners to wait for and encourage initiations, provide a balance of initiated and respondent turns, and allow Gregory to initiate and terminate activities (IS2.2–IS2.4). There is a need to encourage interactions with peers (IS5.2) by supporting an appreciation of Gregory's subtle signals of dysregulation and use of strategies that most effectively establish and maintain his attention. There is a need to facilitate Gregory's attempts to repair communicative breakdowns verbally and nonverbally across partners and settings (IS5.3).

A complete summary of the use of various interpersonal supports by Gregory's social network is provided in a sample SAP-O Form and a sample SAP Sum (see Figures 6.6 and 6.8).

Transactional Support: Learning Support

Gregory's team meeting continued with a discussion of learning supports that have already been implemented as transactional supports in his daily routines and those that should be considered. His therapists and special education teacher specified the learning supports that already were supporting Gregory's participation in the classroom and in the community. These included his mother's ability to structure activities for active participation by providing clear structure and movement opportunities; her ability to modify the sensory properties of activities; and her ability to modify the environment to foster his success, as exemplified by positioning Gregory with his back to a visually distracting wall of cluttered banners during his swim lesson. In addition, Gregory's occupational therapist noted that both Gregory's instructional assistant and his special education teacher effectively used a between-task visual schedule to help him prepare for transitions and upcoming activities. Gregory's mother and educational team members discussed the need to capitalize on his preference for visual information to help him comprehend expectations not just across tasks but also *within tasks* (e.g., through the use of within-task schedules, visual supports to foster participation in group activities, and visual supports to encourage turn taking with peers).

Gregory's mother and team members also discussed the importance of AAC strategies for fostering Gregory's abilities in the Social Communication domain. Although the team members acknowledged that they have used picture symbols with Gregory, they agreed that his AAC system could be used more consistently with a number of modifications that could be made to enhance his communication and expressive language, as well as his expression and understanding of emotion.

Thus, by reviewing the SAP-R and SAP-O results, Gregory's mother and educational team members were able to identify a number of learning supports that were emerging as areas of strength in Gregory's social network and those that were considered critical areas of need. The following chart provides examples of several of these areas.

SAP-OBSERVATION FORM: Language Partner Stage
Transactional Support (page 6)

Child's name: _____

Q1	Q2	Q3	Q4	INTERPERSONAL SUPPORT
				1 Partner is responsive to child
				IS1.1 Follows child's focus of attention
				IS1.2 Attunes to child's emotion and pace
				IS1.3 Responds appropriately to child's signals to foster a sense of communicative competence
				IS1.4 Recognizes and supports child's behavioral and language strategies to regulate arousal level
				IS1.5 Recognizes signs of dysregulation and offers support
				IS1.6 Imitates child
				IS1.7 Offers breaks from interaction or activity as needed
				IS1.8 Facilitates reengagement in interactions and activities following breaks
				2 Partner fosters initiation
				IS2.1 Offers choices nonverbally or verbally
				IS2.2 Waits for and encourages initiations
				IS2.3 Provides a balance of initiated and respondent turns
				IS2.4 Allows child to initiate and terminate activities
				3 Partner respects child's independence
				IS3.1 Allows child to take breaks to move about as needed
				IS3.2 Provides time for child to solve problems or complete activities at own pace
				IS3.3 Interprets problem behavior as communicative and/or regulatory
				IS3.4 Honors protests, rejections, or refusals when appropriate
				4 Partner sets stage for engagement
				IS4.1 Gets down on child's level when communicating
				IS4.2 Secures child's attention before communicating
				IS4.3 Uses appropriate proximity and nonverbal behavior to encourage interaction
				IS4.4 Uses appropriate words and intonation to support optimal arousal level and engagement
				5 Partner provides developmental support
				IS5.1 Encourages imitation
				IS5.2 Encourages interaction with peers
				IS5.3 Attempts to repair breakdowns verbally or nonverbally
				IS5.4 Provides guidance and feedback as needed for success in activities
				IS5.5 Provides guidance on expressing emotions and understanding the cause of emotions
				6 Partner adjusts language input
				IS6.1 Uses nonverbal cues to support understanding
				IS6.2 Adjusts complexity of language input to child's developmental level
				IS6.3 Adjusts quality of language input to child's arousal level
				7 Partner models appropriate behaviors
				IS7.1 Models appropriate nonverbal communication and emotional expressions
				IS7.2 Models a range of communicative functions
				☒ a. behavior regulation ☒ b. social interaction ☒ c. joint attention
				IS7.3 Models appropriate constructive and symbolic play
				IS7.4 Models appropriate behavior when child uses inappropriate behavior
				IS7.5 Models "child-perspective" language

SCORING KEY: 2, criterion met consistently (across three partners in two contexts); **1**, criterion met inconsistently or with assistance; **0**, criterion not met

Figure 6.6. Gregory's SAP-O Form (Interpersonal Support component).

SAP-OBSERVATION FORM: Language Partner Stage
Transactional Support (page 7)

Child's name: _Gregory_

Q1	Q2	Q3	Q4	LEARNING SUPPORT
				1 Partner structures activity for active participation
1				LS1.1 Defines clear beginning and ending to activity
2				LS1.2 Creates turn-taking opportunities and leaves spaces for child to fill in
1				LS1.3 Provides predictable sequence to activity
2				LS1.4 Offers repeated learning opportunities
2				LS1.5 Offers varied learning opportunities
				2 Partner uses augmentative communication support to foster development
1				LS2.1 Uses augmentative communication support to enhance child's communication and expressive language
1				LS2.2 Uses augmentative communication support to enhance child's understanding of language and behavior
0				LS2.3 Uses augmentative communication support to enhance child's expression and understanding of emotion
0				LS2.4 Uses augmentative communication support to enhance child's emotional regulation
				3 Partner uses visual and organizational support
0				LS3.1 Uses visual support to define steps within a task
0				LS3.2 Uses visual support to define steps and time for completion of activities
1				LS3.3 Uses visual support to enhance smooth transitions between activities
2				LS3.4 Uses visual support to organize segments of time across the day
0				LS3.5 Uses visual support to enhance attention in group activities
0				LS3.6 Uses visual support to foster active involvement in group activities
				4 Partner modifies goals, activities, and learning environment
1				LS4.1 Adjusts social complexity to support organization and interaction
1				LS4.2 Adjusts task difficulty for child success
1				LS4.3 Modifies sensory properties of learning environment
1				LS4.4 Arranges learning environment to enhance attention
1				LS4.5 Arranges learning environment to promote child initiation
1				LS4.6 Designs and modifies activities to be developmentally appropriate
1				LS4.7 Infuses motivating materials and topics in activities
1				LS4.8 Provides activities to promote initiation and extended interaction
1				LS4.9 Alternates between movement and sedentary activities as needed
1				LS4.10 "Ups the ante" or increases expectations appropriately

SCORING KEY: 2, criterion met consistently (across three partners in two contexts); **1**, criterion met inconsistently or with assistance; **0**, criterion not met

Figure 6.7. Gregory's SAP-O Form (Learning Support component).

Learning Support	
Strengths	Needs
Gregory's mother has developed the ability to adjust task difficulty for Gregory's success and offers repeated learning opportunities to capitalize on his need for repetition (LS4.2, LS1.4). Gregory's special education teacher and instructional assistant have developed a number of visual schedules to help Gregory anticipate transitions and upcoming activities (LS3.3).	Increased use of augmentative communication supports to enhance Gregory's communication and expressive language (LS2.1) is recommended, as Gregory continues to have difficulty producing intelligible speech, communicating for a variety of functions (e.g., greeting, calling, showing off, commenting), and repairing communicative breakdowns. There should be more consistent use of visual supports to define steps within a task, to define steps and time for completion of activities, and to enhance smooth transitions between activities, all of which would support his regulation across a greater range of partners and activities (LS3.1-LS3.3).

A complete summary of the use of various learning supports by Gregory's social network is provided in a sample SAP-O Form and a sample SAP Sum (see Figures 6.7 and 6.8).

Social-Emotional Growth Indicators: Results and Impressions

Next, Gregory's team computed his baseline composite scores for his Social-Emotional Growth Indicators. These indicators would provide useful benchmarks against which to measure future gains in Gregory's general qualities of behavior. The general qualities of behavior measured by the Social-Emotional Growth Indicators include 1) Happiness, 2) Sense of Self, 3) Sense of Other, 4) Active Learning and Organization, 5) Flexibility and Resilience, 6) Cooperation and Appropriateness of Behavior, 7) Independence, and 8) Social Membership and Friendships. Calculation of Gregory's Social-Emotional Growth Indicators revealed relative strengths in the areas of Happiness, and Flexibility and Resilience. Areas of relative weakness included Sense of Other, and Cooperation and Appropriateness of Behavior.

Key Information Source 2: Family Perception of SAP-O Results and Priorities

Before identifying the specific goals and objectives for Gregory's educational program, his mother was asked to share her perceptions of the SAP-O and the behavior sampling session. Specifically, did she believe that observations were representative of his behavior, and were Gregory's strengths and needs accurately captured on the SAP Sum? Gregory's mother indicated that the SAP-O had captured an accurate snapshot of her son at this time of year but informed the staff that she felt that his emotional regulatory challenges were not nearly as great in the late spring and summer. She commented that this was likely due to two factors: 1) the amount of daylight and 2) the increased opportunities for Gregory to play actively outdoors. It was evident that frequent reevaluation (every 3 months) would be appropriate for addressing Gregory's changing needs.

Following this discussion, Gregory's mother was invited to reiterate her primary concerns and to discuss her hopes and expectations regarding Gregory's development. This opportunity provided critical baseline information for Gregory's educational team, as an understanding of how Gregory's difficulties affect his mother and family life provides a critical measure of the family's progress over time. In addition, his mother was also asked to indicate the types of information and support that would be most helpful for her. Family perceptions are included on the sample SAP Sum shown in Figure 6.8.

SAP Step 7: Prioritizing Goals and Objectives

Based on the information compiled and integrated throughout the SAP, including the SAP-R, SAP-O, follow-up behavior sampling, and SAP Sum, Gregory's mother and educational team members worked together to prioritize goals and objectives 1) that were the most *functional,* 2) that directly *addressed family priorities,* and 3) that matched the *developmental areas of need* documented on the SAP Sum for both Gregory and his partners. His performance on the SAP-O was not the sole factor for selecting weekly objectives, as equal consideration was given to those objectives that would be the most functional and those that most closely matched his mother's priorities. Although this process occasionally results in selection of objectives that might appear out of sequence in reference to the structure of goals and objectives in the SAP, this flexibility and individualization is considered critical for successful implementation of a SCERTS Model program.

Objectives in Joint Attention and Symbol Use were paired so that Gregory would learn to communicate his intentions using increasingly sophisticated symbolic means. Likewise, a number of Interpersonal Support and Learning Support objectives were combined so that Gregory's partners could learn to modify their interactive style as well as incorporate learning and environmental accommodations in a given activity. Please refer to Gregory's SAP Sum for a listing of objectives identified by the team (see Figure 6.8).

SAP Step 8: Recommending Further Assessment if Needed

When reviewing the SAP Sum, Gregory's mother felt that a representative sample of Gregory's social-communicative and emotional regulatory challenges was obtained along with information regarding the most appropriate transactional supports. Aside from systematic reassessment at 3-month intervals, additional assessment was not recommended at this time.

SAP Step 9: Design a SCERTS Educational Program for Gregory, His Mother, and His Service Providers

Step 9 of the SAP involved identifying a number of key meaningful and purposeful activities, the social support to be provided in these activities (i.e., the roles and responsibilities of educational team members), and familiar partners who will play a critical role in service provision. In his educational program, Gregory's team leader, his special education teacher, took the primary role of organizing an educational and support program for Gregory and his mother. His special education teacher discussed the need for intensive educational programming and *at least* 25 hours per week on a year round basis of planned and developmentally appropriate learning opportunities. In addition, she indicated that sufficient individualized attention would be needed for Gregory to remain actively engaged during programming. A plan to provide educational and emotional support to his mother also was needed to address her ongoing concerns about the amount of support that Gregory requires at home and in the community.

This step of the SAP culminated in the development of two SAP Activity Planning Forms, each of which incorporated approximately 3 hours of meaningful and purposeful activities in Gregory's natural routines. The first form outlined Gregory's typical morning routines (see Figure 6.9), and the second form outlined Gregory's typical afternoon routines (see Figure 6.10). Therefore, a plan was established for approximately 6 hours per day, for a total of 30 hours per week, of educational programming. The SAP Activity Planning Forms included the specific goals that would be addressed in these activities and the complexity of the social context (i.e., the degree of naturalness and the amount and frequency of individualized support) that would be appropriate de-

SAP Summary Form
Language Partner Stage

Child's name: Gregory
Quarterly start date of observation: 2-3-2005   Child's age: 9 years

SCERTS Profile

SOCIAL COMMUNICATION

Joint Attention
- JA1 Engages in reciprocal interaction
- JA2 Shares attention
- JA3 Shares emotion
- JA4 Shares intentions to regulate the behavior of others
- JA5 Shares intentions for social interaction
- JA6 Shares intentions for joint attention
- JA7 Persists and repairs communication breakdowns
- JA8 Shares experiences in reciprocal interaction

Symbol Use
- SU1 Learns by observation and imitation of actions and words
- SU2 Understands nonverbal cues in familiar and unfamiliar activities
- SU3 Uses familiar objects conventionally in play
- SU4 Uses gestures and nonverbal means to share intentions
- SU5 Uses words and word combinations to express meanings
- SU6 Understands a variety of words and word combinations without contextual cues

EMOTIONAL REGULATION

Mutual Regulation
- MR1 Expresses range of emotions
- MR2 Responds to assistance offered by partners
- MR3 Requests partners' assistance to regulate state
- MR4 Recovers from extreme dysregulation with support from partners

Self-Regulation
- SR1 Demonstrates availability for learning and interacting
- SR2 Uses behavioral strategies to regulate arousal level during familiar activities
- SR3 Uses language strategies to regulate arousal level during familiar activities
- SR4 Regulates emotion during new and changing situations
- SR5 Recovers from extreme dysregulation by self

SCERTS Profile (continued)

TRANSACTIONAL SUPPORT

Interpersonal Support
- IS1 Partner is responsive to child
- IS2 Partner fosters initiation
- IS3 Partner respects child's independence
- IS4 Partner sets stage for engagement
- IS5 Partner provides developmental support
- IS6 Partner adjusts language input
- IS7 Partner models appropriate behaviors

Learning Support
- LS1 Partner structures activity for active participation
- LS2 Partner uses augmentative communication support to foster development
- LS3 Partner uses visual and organizational support
- LS4 Partner modifies goals, activities, and learning environment

Social-Emotional Growth Indicators Profile

1. Happiness
2. Sense of Self
3. Sense of Other
4. Active Learning and Organization
5. Flexibility and Resilience
6. Cooperation and Appropriateness of Behavior
7. Independence
8. Social Membership and Friendships

Family Perception and Priorities

Is this profile an accurate picture of your child? If not, explain.
Yes; however, his regulatory challenges are not as great in late spring and summer.

Is there any additional information that is needed to develop your child's educational plan?
Not at this time

If you were to focus your energies on one thing for your child, what would that be?
His ability to play with his peers and friends

What skills would you like your child to learn in the next 3 months?
The ability to initiate successful interactions with peers
Improved ability to maintain his attention
The ability to communicate for social reasons

Figure 6.8. Gregory's SAP Sum.

Prioritize Weekly SCERTS Objectives

Child Social Communication and Emotional Regulation objectives	Partner Transactional Support objectives
1. Gregory will engage in brief reciprocal interaction (JA1.2).	1. Partner will wait for and encourage initiations (IS2.2).
2. Gregory will comment on actions or events (JA6.2).	2. Partner will encourage interactions with peers (IS5.2).
3. Gregory will use a variety of conventional and symbolic gestures (SU4.1).	3. Partner will attempt to repair breakdowns verbally or nonverbally (IS5.3).
4. Gregory will use a variety of advanced relational words (SU5.5).	4. Partner will define a clear beginning and ending to activities (LS1.1).
5. Gregory will understand and use symbols to express a range of emotions (MR1.2).	5. Partner will use an augmentative communication support to enhance Gregory's communication and expressive language (LS2.1).
6. Gregory will respond to partners' use of language strategies (MR4.3).	6. Partner will use augmentative communication support to enhance Gregory's expression and understanding of emotion (LS2.3).
7. Gregory will use behavioral strategies modeled by partners to regulate arousal level (SR2.2).	7. Partner will use support to define steps within a task (LS3.1).
8. Gregory will use language strategies to regulate arousal level in new and changing situations (SR4.4).	8. Partner will use visual support to foster active involvement in group activities (LS3.6).

Figure 6.8. (continued)

Further Assessment—Key Results or Additional Recommendations

No additional testing was completed or recommended.

SAP Activity Planning

Identify key activities using the SAP Activity Planning Form for
☒ Morning schedule ☒ Afternoon schedule

SCERTS Family Support Plan

Educational Support		Emotional Support	
Activity	How often	Activity	How often
Provision of resources Classroom visits Caregiver education programs "Make and take" sessions Team meetings System of daily communication Family fun events	Ongoing Monthly Quarterly As needed Monthly Daily Monthly	One-to-one support: meetings with child care component	Monthly

SCERTS Support Plan for Professionals and Service Providers

Educational Support		Emotional Support	
Activity	How often	Activity	How often
Mentoring arrangements Supervision meetings Team meetings Crisis meetings	5 hours/week Biweekly Monthly As needed	Supervision meetings Crisis meetings	Biweekly As needed

Figure 6.9. Gregory's SAP Activity Planning Form (morning activities) (*Key:* PAR, planned activity routine; ENG, engineered activity; MOD, modified natural activity; NAT, naturally occurring event; LS, learning support; IS, interpersonal support).

pending on Gregory's unique social-communication and emotional regulatory capacities. In addition, the SAP Activity Planning Forms were completed to identify the partner objectives and specific transactional supports (i.e., interpersonal supports and learning supports) that would be embedded in each activity. See Figure 6.9 and 6.10 to review these two sample SAP Activity Planning Forms for Gregory and his educational team.

Next, Gregory's team leader reported information provided by Gregory's mother on the SAP-R as well as information obtained for the Transactional Support domain of the SAP-O to lead a discussion with the team regarding the provision of a SCERTS Family Support Plan. Gregory's team leader noted that the development of Gregory's educational program would not be complete without the provision of both educational support and emotional support to his mother.

Educational Support for Gregory's Mother

As noted previously, primary educational concerns expressed by Gregory's mother included Gregory's reliance on others to help him stay focused, his limited reasons for communicating (e.g., requests, refusals), his limited friendships, and the amount of time spent trying to keep him engaged. Thus, educational support appeared to be needed in the following general areas.

Assessment to Implementation: Language Partner Stage

SAP Activity Planning Form

Child's name: Gregory Communication stage: Language Partner Date: 2-21-2005 Page #: 2 (P.M.)

Activity/time	Social complexity	Group size	Team members and partners	Gregory will engage in brief reciprocal interaction.	Gregory will comment on actions or events.	Gregory will use a variety of conventional and symbolic gestures.	Gregory will use a variety of advanced relational words.	Gregory will understand and use symbols to express a range of emotions.	Gregory will respond to partners' use of language strategies.	Gregory will use behavioral strategies modeled by partners to regulate arousal level.	Gregory will use language strategies to regulate arousal level in new and changing situations.	Partner will wait for and encourage initiations.	Partner will encourage interactions with peers.	Partner will attempt to repair breakdowns verbally or nonverbally.	Partner will define a clear beginning and ending to activities.	Partner will use augmentative communication support to enhance Gregory's communication and expressive language.	Partner will use augmentative communication support to enhance Gregory's expression and understanding of emotion.	Partner will use supports to define steps within a task.	Partner will use visual support to foster active involvement in group activities.	Team members and partners / Sample transactional supports
Lunch Bunch (ENG) 12:00 P.M.–12:30 P.M.	1:3	3	IA, P	X	X							X	X							(IS) Third-grade peers will be encouraged to model one- to two-word comments, point to Gregory's lunch, and wait for his response.
Recess with third graders (MOD) 12:30 P.M.–1:00 P.M.	1:8	24	IA, OT, GET, P	X						X				X					X	(LS) A game spinner with photographs of Gregory's third-grade buddies will be used for turn-taking on motor equipment (e.g., swings).
Independent reading with third graders (MOD) 1:00 P.M.–1:30 P.M.	1:8	24	GET, IA, SLP, P				X		X	X				X	X					(LS) Photo albums will be used in lieu of third-grade books and paired with picture symbols for agents + actions. Partners will model walking to water fountain during periods of low arousal. A visual timer will be set for Gregory to refer to.
Independent work (MOD and PAR) 1:30 P.M.–3:00 P.M.	1:1	1	SET, IA, SLP				X	X										X	X	(LS) The emotion wheel used in adaptive physical education (see A.M. planning form) will be duplicated for his work space so that symbols to match Gregory's emotions are accessible.

Team members and partners: Special education teacher (SET), general education teacher (GET), occupational therapist (OT), speech-language pathologist (SLP), instructional assistants (IA), adaptive physical education teacher (APE), mom (M), peers (P)

Instructions: Write the weekly Social Communication and Emotional Regulation objectives for the child and the Transactional Support objectives for the partner in the vertical boxes across the top. In the far right vertical box at the upper right-hand corner, list the team members and the child's partners and numbers or initials for each team member or partner. In each row below the column headings, write a brief description of the activity and the time, the ratio for social complexity, the group size, and the number or initials of the team members or partners participating in that activity. Then check off all of the objectives that will be targeted in each activity. Write in a brief description of sample transactional support used in each activity.

Figure 6.10. Gregory's SAP Activity Planning Form (afternoon activities) (_Key:_ PAR, planned activity routine; ENG, engineered activity; MOD, modified natural activity; NAT, naturally occurring event; LS, learning support; IS, interpersonal support).

Goal 1: **To provide Gregory's mother with the knowledge and skills to support Gregory's development in everyday activities, and to address specific issues that she identified as most stressful and challenging.** For Gregory's mother, priorities related to this goal included 1) understanding Gregory's current difficulties with emotional regulation and developing an awareness of the self-regulation and mutual regulation strategies that he currently employs and 2) understanding AAC systems and their role in supporting Gregory's use of these strategies in everyday activities.

Desired outcome: *Gregory's mother will feel confident in providing the necessary supports to foster Gregory's development of 1) self-regulation and mutual regulation strategies and 2) augmentative communication.*

Goal 2: **To help Gregory's mother understand her legal rights and those of her child regarding services and the systems that are responsible for providing services.** For Gregory's mother, concerns included entitlement to state- and federally funded home-based therapeutic services that would increase Gregory's ability to remain engaged across home- and community-based routines.

Desired outcome: *Gregory's mother will be knowledgeable about her legal rights and those of her child, will be able to collaborate and deal effectively with systems that are responsible for providing services to her child based on those rights, and will make informed decisions based on that knowledge. Gregory's mother will become more knowledgeable about entitlement to state- and federally funded home-based therapeutic services.*

The first step of the SCERTS Family Support Plan included the *provision of educational resources*. First, Gregory's team leader informed Gregory's mother about the existence of programming for home-based therapeutic services that provide developmental support in home and community settings that would thereby support Gregory's mother in helping to maintain Gregory's engagement and active participation at home and in the community. This was a high-priority support given that Gregory's mother is a single parent. She was provided with a list of local agencies as well as brief descriptions of the type of services that each provides. Taking into account that Gregory's mother has limited time to research and educate herself about AAC, the team leader offered her a brief, individualized list of articles written in lay terminology for parents of children with ASD that discuss the implementation of AAC supports in home and community environments. The team leader also provided Gregory's mother with a handout that specifically describes effective and socially appropriate behavioral strategies for emotional regulation appropriate for a child with ASD at the Language Partner stage, and strategies for facilitating replacement of the more inefficient strategies that Gregory currently employs.

The next step of the family support plan included opportunities for Gregory's mother to observe school activities as part of regularly scheduled *classroom visits* and opportunities to participate in *caregiver education programs*. This component was included to ensure a consistent and collaborative focus between home and school. Partner objectives such as *Uses augmentative communication support to enhance child's communication and expressive language* (LS2.1), *Uses support to define steps within a task* (LS3.1), and *Uses visual support to enhance smooth transitions between activities* (LS3.3) would be addressed. The team also invited Gregory's mother to participate in visual support *"make and take"* sessions. This support activity would involve an initial training session arranged by Gregory's speech-language pathologist that would provide guidance on how to use the equipment in the school's parent library (e.g., clip art software, color printers, laminators) to design visual supports for use at home. Following this session, Gregory's mother could schedule an appointment with the librarian to use the equipment at her convenience. The team agreed that it also would be appropriate for Gregory's mother to participate in monthly *team meetings* to discuss updates and revisions to transactional supports used at home and at school.

In addition to these monthly educational support activities, Gregory's team recognized the need to devise an efficient *daily system of communication* as a means to problem-solve challenges that were likely to arise due to Gregory's social-communicative and emotional regulatory difficulties, as well as celebrate his accomplishments. For this purpose, the team agreed on the use of a form divided into comment blocks for the Social Communication, Emotional Regulation, and Transactional Support domains. Finally, because Gregory's mother was interested in learning how to promote friendships between Gregory and his classmates, his special education teacher recommended that Gregory and his mother participate in the *family fun events* held at Gregory's school. Each month, an evening was planned to explicitly address peer interaction and successful strategies for engaging children in cooperative and motivating activities.

Based on information obtained through the SAP-R completed by Gregory's mother and through an interview with her, it became clear that emotional support appeared to be needed in the following areas.

Emotional Support for Gregory's Mother

Goal 1: To enhance Gregory's mother's abilities to cope with the stresses and challenges of raising a child with ASD, particularly given that she is a single parent, as well as to cope with the amount of time and effort required on a daily basis to facilitate Gregory's engagement

Desired outcome: Gregory's mother will develop specific coping abilities to manage the inevitable stresses that she will experience directly due to or as a secondary effect of Gregory's having ASD.

Goal 2: To help Gregory's mother understand and gain access to the range of formal and informal emotional supports that may be available

Desired outcome: Gregory's mother will gain access to formal and informal supports that best match her emotional needs at specific points in time.

Goal 3: To support Gregory's mother in her efforts to deal successfully with professionals, as well as with educational and health care systems

Desired outcome: Gregory's mother will develop specific strategies to foster positive parent–professional relationships and deal with emotional challenges that may be due to difficult interactions or relationships with professionals or to difficulties in dealing with educational and health care systems.

A range of options was discussed with Gregory's mother regarding emotional supports in the community. These included formal supports such as a districtwide *parent support group* held once a month, parent support groups in the larger community, and resources for counseling. During the meeting, Gregory's mother expressed that she did not feel that she had time in her schedule to take advantage of these support options, in part due to her limited options for child care. As a result, the team offered an option for *one-to-one support meetings* on a monthly basis that would include a *child care component* (i.e., an individualized meeting with the school's social worker while Gregory participated in an extended school-day afternoon session). Recognizing that Gregory's mother had limited opportunities to do things for herself and to recharge her batteries, the team also encouraged her to take advantage of respite services offered through the county and state.

Support Among Professionals

As a final step in planning and designing Gregory's educational program, his special education teacher discussed how the SCERTS Model recognizes that professionals and other service providers face considerable challenges when implementing an intensive educational program. For professionals and other service providers (e.g., instructional assistants, paraprofessionals) to be as effective as possible in supporting children and families, a SCERTS Support Plan for Professionals and Service Providers would be needed. Because Gregory's team, as described in the SAP Activity Planning Form, included not only professionals but also paraprofessionals, *mentoring arrangements* were scheduled on a daily basis for at least 5 hours per week. Paraprofessional supervision would be provided by either Gregory's special education teacher, his speech-language pathologist, and/or his occupational therapist. The supervision would involve both direct educational and interactive guidance as well as one-to-one emotional support in bimonthly *supervision meetings*. Next, his special education teacher indicated that each month, Gregory's team members would arrange a *team meeting* to discuss his progress and the need for consistency with both interpersonal and learning supports. Last, it was agreed that the staff could call *crisis meetings* if Gregory exhibits sudden changes in his behavior or if a staff member is having a particularly difficult time successfully implementing transactional supports.

SAP Step 10: Performing Ongoing Tracking

Following the identification of weekly objectives for Gregory and his partners, his team discussed the need to track his ongoing progress in his educational program. During their discussion, his team recognized that although it would not be feasible to take data on every objective in every activity, it would be critical to track Gregory's progress to inform decision making about the effectiveness of his program's implementation. As a result, progress with each objective would be monitored on a daily basis in one or two activities. To share responsibility for data collection, his speech-language pathologist would assume primary responsibility for collecting data related to his Social Communication objectives, his occupational therapist would assume primary responsibility for collecting data related to his Emotional Regulation objectives, and his special educator would be responsible for monitoring Transactional Support objectives.

Next, Gregory's team formulated a plan for using the information documented on the SAP Daily Tracking Log to complete a SAP Weekly Tracking Log. His special education teacher would compile and integrate this information and take responsibility for sharing it with the team. These reviews would be essential for recognizing growth and/or lack of progress in specific objectives. The SAP would then be readministered quarterly.

SPOTLIGHT ON ETASH, AN ADVANCED LANGUAGE PARTNER

Etash is at the advanced level of the Language Partner stage. Etash is an active, vibrant, and alert 5-year-old boy who has a slight frame and large brown eyes. He lives at home with his parents, who are first-generation immigrants from India; his maternal grandmother; and his 28-month-old sister, Madhur. He is described as a persistent communicator who uses multiple ways of communicating with others, including gestures, gaze, facial expressions, words, and short phrases. He most often relies on repeating language modeled for him (i.e., immediate echolalia) or repetition of phrases that he has heard previously and essentially has borrowed from previous contexts (i.e., delayed echolalia). Although his parents describe him as an engaging child during predictable and preferred activities, he often becomes distressed and, at times, aggressive when he encounters new and changing situations.

Etash's strong preference for predictability and familiar routines significantly restricts his family's ability to include him in daily activities such as going to the grocery store, going out for dinner, and visiting family friends. His limited willingness to interact with unfamiliar people affects his family's ability to secure child care, a pattern that contributes to the family feeling trapped in their own home and bound to fixed routines. His family members note that when Etash is outside of the home, he can be quite anxious. Although he occasionally uses the phrase "all done," these protests quickly escalate into screaming and bolting, and his behavior often becomes inappropriate and frustrating to his family. If encouraged to enter a new setting, he often physically resists by pushing away from his parents' hands, dropping to the floor, and/or hitting when he is being held or touched. In addition, he may walk on his toes and flap his hands, which can attract even more embarrassing attention from people close by.

This familial stress is further compounded by several additional factors. First, Etash's grandmother has not yet developed an understanding of the significant nature of Etash's developmental challenges due, in part, to cultural and language-based differences. As a result, a tension has developed between her and Etash's parents, as she often equates Etash's difficulties with lenient caregiving and asserts that Etash is a child who needs to be disciplined with a firmer hand. Next, Etash's parents are continually worried about his behavior toward his sister. Etash frequently hits or lashes out at Madhur, often in response to her intrusions during play or when she cries. Therefore, instead of encouraging a relationship, Etash and Madhur's parents find themselves frequently trying to keep their two children away from one another to prevent such incidents. Finally, the parents are anxious about a recent recommendation that Madhur be referred for a developmental evaluation due to concerns about her language and motor skills.

At 3 years of age, Etash was diagnosed with pervasive developmental disorder-not otherwise specified, which falls under the generic category of ASD. At the direction of Etash's pediatrician, Etash's parents then contacted their local public school district. Through a series of educational planning meetings, it was agreed that Etash qualified for special education services, and an IEP was developed. During his first year of preschool, Etash participated in an inclusive half-day program in a language-based classroom with seven children with special needs, seven typically developing children, one teacher, and one instructional assistant. His peers were a diverse group of students with a range of abilities and disabilities. The schedule of the classroom included opportunities for extended periods of exploratory play and unstructured time.

In preparation for determining placement before Etash's second year of preschool at 4 years of age, Etash's educational team and parents reviewed his progress toward IEP objectives and agreed that he often appeared to be overwhelmed in the classroom environment. During choice time, for example, he typically sat in a corner and watched as others moved about the room, appearing defensive to intrusions by either adults or peers. They determined that a placement in a classroom with a more predictable schedule and reduced social complexity would be appropriate for Etash, as he was clearly not remaining actively engaged across his school day. As a result, Etash spent his second year of preschool participating in a self-contained classroom designed to support children with an ASD diagnosis, with six children, two teachers, and an instructional assistant.

Etash clearly benefited from the supports inherent in this self-contained program, as the classroom staff had been trained specifically to address the needs of students with ASD. Frequent consultations by specialists in the fields of ASD and AAC were provided as part of a pilot program initiated by the public school district to provide support to professionals and service providers. Visual supports had been incorporated to indicate the activity schedule throughout the day, the environment had been modified to foster Etash's attention and engagement, and the teacher-student ratio (one teacher for every two students) was much smaller than that of his previous year of preschool. Etash made remarkable gains in this environment, and it was clear to his parents and educational team that this type of learning environment would be appropriate as he made the transition to a kindergarten placement.

However, concerns were raised by his parents that no such classroom was currently available within the public school district. The district's pilot program for providing specialized educational programming for students with ASD had only been implemented at the preschool level. His school district was only prepared to offer half-day kindergarten programming (i.e., 15 hours per week), which was not consistent with an appropriate placement for Etash given the recommendations of the NRC (2001) for educating children with ASD. In considering a placement and educational program for Etash's kindergarten school year, Etash's educational team and parents agreed that it would be appropriate to collaborate with the Bayport Learning Center, a nearby private school specializing in the education of children with ASD.

The kindergarten program at Bayport offered a daily full-day, multidisciplinary program cotaught by a special educator and a speech-language pathologist. An occupational therapist would also be present for half of the day to consult with staff and supervise two instructional assistants. Etash's class at Bayport would consist of five other children with ASD. Opportunities for inclusion would be scheduled three afternoons per week in his kindergarten classroom at his public school with the support of instructional assistants from his Bayport program. His educational team and parents agreed that these opportunities for inclusion would be essential for supporting Etash's ability to remain connected to children from his neighborhood.

After an initial adjustment period of 6 weeks in this new program, the Bayport Learning Center staff administered the SAP to individualize Etash's learning program by prioritizing appropriate development goals and objectives and determining how best to support him and his family. Thus, this spotlight illustrates the steps that Etash's family and educational team members took in implementing this tool. The SAP was implemented to 1) establish Etash's current profile of developmental strengths and needs; 2) determine meaningful, purposeful, and motivating goals to address; 3) select the most appropriate learning contexts and complexity of social support based on Etash's natural routines and activities; and 4) determine the necessary transactional supports to foster Etash's development and his relationships with his family, peers, and teaching staff.

Because a comprehensive SCERTS Model program also includes explicit plans for support to families and support among professionals, information from the SAP was also used to ensure that Etash's educational program would be compatible and consistent with the needs expressed by his family. In addition, the assessment team determined the specific educational supports and emotional supports that would be provided for Etash's family and the professionals who would be involved in the implementation of Etash's program.

SAP Step 1: Determining Etash's Communication Stage

During an initial SAP team meeting, Etash's lead teacher at Bayport, a special educator, led a discussion of Etash's current behavior in his home and school environments. Based on their discussion, his team determined that the appropriate SAP Form to use for the assessment would be the one designated for the Language Partner stage. This was based on the completion of the Worksheet for Determining Communication Stage and the criteria for determining a child's communication stage in the SAP. Etash currently uses approximately 85 words referentially and a number of brief phrases to communicate his intent. Although Etash's ability to use simple phrases was viewed as a relative strength, his team noted that many of his phrases were echolalic (i.e., repetition of phrases previously heard) and that he was only just beginning to independently use creative word combinations to communicate. Given these abilities, the team agreed that Etash did not yet meet the criteria for the Conversational Partner stage.

SAP Step 2: Gathering Information with the Language Partner SAP-R Form

During this meeting, Etash's parents were asked to complete the SAP-R Form to provide additional information regarding Etash's behavior in his home and community environments. This questionnaire identified 1) the primary concerns and stresses faced by Etash's family, 2) Etash's primary strengths and the concerns that the family has about Etash's development, 3) the activities in which both Etash's strengths and areas of need would likely be seen in his home and community environments, 4) Etash's typical partners in the home and community, and 5) the typical contexts in Etash's life outside of school. Etash's educational team also completed a separate SAP-R Form to identify similarities and discrepancies with respect to Etash's behavior at school versus his behavior in other natural environments. The information gathered from both of Etash's SAP-R Forms is summarized next:

1. The primary concerns and stresses faced by Etash's family included

   - "The stress of raising two children with developmental delays"
   - "Etash's aggressive behavior directed toward his sister"
   - "Not being able to go out due to Etash's unpredictable behavior"
   - "Etash's withdrawal and avoidance of family activities"
   - "His odd habits—flapping his hands and walking on his toes—which attract attention"

2. Etash's parents and educational team identified and agreed on the following strengths and concerns in his current profile:

Strengths	Needs
"Etash is an observant child who is constantly aware of his physical and social environments."	"Etash needs to develop strategies to cope with changes in routines or violations of his expectations."
"Etash is able to use words, phrases, gestures, gaze, and facial expressions to communicate."	"He needs to learn more socially appropriate strategies for self-regulation when he is overwhelmed or upset."
"He is beginning to protest anxiety provoking activities in more acceptable ways (e.g., a push-away gesture; saying 'all done')."	"He needs to develop a greater ability to express himself using his own words."

3. The activities in which both Etash's strengths and areas of need would likely be seen included

   - Morning meeting in his Bayport Learning Center classroom
   - Inclusion in his public school afternoon kindergarten class
   - Play time at home with his sister (after school)

4. Etash's typical partners

   - Mom
   - Dad
   - His grandmother

- Madhur (his 28-month-old sister)
- Special education teacher at Bayport
- Two classroom instructional assistants
- General education teacher at the public school
- Speech-language pathologist at Bayport
- Occupational therapist at Bayport
- Music therapist at Bayport
- Five special education classmates at Bayport
- Eighteen kindergarten classmates at the public school

5. Natural contexts in Etash's life included
   - Caregiving routines at home
   - Play routines at home
   - Classroom routines in the special education classroom at Bayport
   - Classroom routines in the general education classroom at the public schools
   - Playground at Bayport and the public school

SAP Step 3: Identifying Assessment Team Members and Planning the SAP-O

After collecting the completed SAP-R Forms from both Etash's family and his educational team members at Bayport, Etash's lead teacher began completing the SAP Map for Planning the SAP-Observation. This form was used to help identify appropriate members of Etash's assessment team and their roles and responsibilities. Consideration was also given to whether any referrals to outside professionals would need to be made. In addition, as part of planning the administration of the SAP-O, the following variables were considered to ensure that a representative sample of Etash's abilities and needs would be documented: 1) the *location* (i.e., natural contexts) where the observations would take place, 2) the specific *length* of the observations, 3) the *partners* who would be present, 4) the *group size* of the social contexts during the observations, 5) the nature of the *activities*, and 6) the number of *transitions* during each observation (see Chapter 7 in Volume I for a more detailed discussion of these variables).

After reviewing the information provided in the SAP-R and each of these variables, the educational team planned the observations. First, given that Etash is a Language Partner, the minimum length of observation was identified as 2 hours. However, based on information gathered during the SAP-R, the team identified inconsistencies in Etash's behavior across various natural environments, presumably based on environmental and social factors. Given this information, the team decided that it would be best to split the observation among his three most frequently experienced environments: home, the special education classroom at Bayport Learning Center, and his inclusive kindergarten at his public school. These observations would each last 1 hour and would incorporate both adult and peer partners. Likewise, representative group sizes in Etash's typical environments were identified and considered. The following social groupings were selected: small group (i.e., Etash with his peers in his Bayport classroom and Etash with his family at home) and large group (i.e., Etash in his inclusive kindergarten classroom). These locations and group sizes were identified as the primary contexts for the observations, as they were common in Etash's daily experiences.

In considering the specific contexts for the observations, Etash's lead teacher carefully reviewed the primary concerns of Etash's family and educational team, as well as those activities that they felt would provide a sample of Etash's strengths and areas of need. Additional variables were also considered to ensure that his assessment team would gain an accurate picture. For example, it was evident that Etash would behave differently when engaged in an unstructured versus a structured activity, a busy environment versus a quiet environment, an adult-directed activity versus a child-directed activity, and a familiar versus an unfamiliar activity. With this information, four activities were identified for Etash's two school-based observations. These activities included 1) his participation in morning meeting (at Bayport), 2) his participation in a birthday celebration for a classmate (at Bayport), 3) his participation in free play (in the inclusive kindergarten classroom), and 4) his participation in an art activity (in the inclusive kindergarten classroom). One additional activity, Etash's participation in play with his sister at home, was identified as part of an after-school home-based observation. Due to family preference, it was determined that this activity would be videotaped and that the team would review the videotape during a team meeting.

As noted on the SAP Map, children who participate in the SAP should be observed across at least three transitions. Therefore, Etash's lead teacher planned for transitions to be a part of each observation to ensure a representative sampling of Etash's behavior during transitions. During the first observation (at Bayport), for example, his team members planned to observe him preparing for and making the transition to morning meeting, as well as to the birthday celebration. During the second observation (at the public school), Etash's team members would observe Etash making the transition from the school bus to his kindergarten classroom and from free play to an art activity. During the third observation, Etash's team members would have the opportunity to observe his transition between child- and adult-directed play in his home environment. This information would be summarized in a SAP Map.

SAP Step 4: Completing the SAP-O Form

Etash's SAP assessment team (i.e., his special education teacher, his speech-language pathologist, his school psychologist, and his occupational therapist) used the SAP-O Form for the Language Partner stage to gather information across their three observations (see Chapter 7 in Volume I for specific administration instructions). Information was gathered under three domains: Social Communication and Emotional Regulation, which focused on assessing Etash's developmental strengths and needs, and Transactional Support, which addressed the strengths and needs of his partners in various environments. Etash's team members agreed that to capture a detailed and representative sample of Etash's profile and the strategies used by his partners to support him, they would need to divide observation responsibilities during the assessment.

The team decided that Etash's speech-language pathologist should gather the majority of the information related to the Social Communication domain, as she would be present at both observations and would also be viewing the videotape. Etash's school psychologist and special educator agreed to share the responsibility for gathering the majority of information related to Emotional Regulation, as this domain was considered integral to Etash's challenges with maintaining social engagement and following social conventions of appropriate behavior in school. His occupational therapist and special educator were assigned to gather the majority of the information related to the Transactional Support domain (i.e., Interpersonal Support and Learning Support) and to supplement the observations made by the other team members.

SAP Step 5: Conducting Behavior Sampling

Following the completion of the three scheduled observations, including the team's review of Etash's videotaped play at home, the team members briefly reviewed his SAP-O Form. They agreed that although they had gathered a wealth of information, there were a number of questions remaining related to his abilities in the domains of Social Communication and Emotional Regulation. This had occurred, in part, due to the structure of the activities observed. During most observations, expectations for activities were clearly established and Etash was encouraged to participate in them; therefore, his need to request permission to participate in or to change activities was limited. His team members felt that the activities observed likely did not capture a true picture of Etash's play skills due to his heightened level of arousal during play observations in his inclusive kindergarten class and with his sister at home. Questions also remained about the range of regulatory strategies that Etash employs when engaged in solitary activities, as all of the observations occurred only in small- and large-group settings. Therefore, the areas for which his team desired more information included

- JA5.7—Etash's ability to share intentions for social interaction by requesting permission
- SU3.3—Etash's ability to use a variety of familiar objects conventionally toward another person
- SR2.1—Etash's ability to use behavioral strategies to regulate arousal during solitary and social activities

To collect this information, Etash's educational team agreed that an additional session in the familiar context of his Bayport special education classroom would provide the information needed to address these questions related to his developmental profile and therefore would assist in the development and implementation of a more appropriate and individualized educational program. In this subsequent session, his team members structured several brief activities designed to illustrate Etash's competence and abilities in the areas just outlined. For example, so that the team could observe Etash's use of behavioral strategies to self-regulate during solitary play (SR2.1), his favorite area of the classroom, vehicle play, was opened during a choice time period. This allowed team members to document Etash's attention and his actions, such as toe walking and hand flapping, in relation to changes in his arousal level in this type of activity.

Next, Etash's ability to use conventional communicative strategies, such as gestures, words, and phrases to request permission (JA5.7), was sampled during a transition to the playground. Etash and his classmates were encouraged to line up at the door, which was closed before each child's departure. This provided a motivating opportunity to require each student to request permission to independently open the door so that they could join their peers on the playground. Phrases such as "Open door?" and/or social referencing toward a teacher were desired outcomes of this sampling. Etash was encouraged to be close to the front of the line so that he would not become too dysregulated by the change in routine caused by the closing of the door after each child's departure.

Finally, the team turned their attention to Etash's play skills, namely the use of a variety of familiar objects conventionally toward a partner during play (SU3.3). Although Etash is comfortable in familiar play schemes of conventional play, such as putting a "driver" in a vehicle and pretending to drive, his play schemes tend not to involve the use of variety of agents or others, as is typically observed with evolving imaginative play. To determine Etash's capacity in this aspect of his development, his lead teacher provided a number of play materials in the sandbox during playground time at Bayport. Etash often spontaneously gravitated toward the sandbox, so this location was considered ideal. Three different sets of objects were provided. These included a preferred play set, the garage (i.e., with a garage, several cars, several drivers, and a gas pump), and additional sets included a kitchen set (i.e., with a table, eating utensils, a mom, a dad, and several children) and a farm set (i.e., with several animals, a farmer, and a tractor). The instructional assistant would be available in the sandbox area to model different play schemes in an attempt support this behavior sampling activity.

SAP Step 6: Compiling and Integrating Information with the SAP Summary Form

Following the completion of the three observations and the follow up behavior sampling session at Bayport, Etash's educational team and his parents met to compile and integrate information, a step that involves two key information sources: 1) summarizing strengths and needs from the SAP-O and 2) documenting family perception of the SAP-O results.

Key Information Source 1: Summarizing Strengths and Needs

Social Communication: Joint Attention

During the team meeting, Etash's family and educational team members initially focused on determining Etash's strengths and challenges in Joint Attention. His lead teacher discussed how at the Language Partner stage, children are typically developing the capacity to coordinate attention, emotion, *and* intentions to share experiences in early social conversations, a developmental advancement over commenting on objects or events in the immediate environment. Integration of these abilities contributes to a child's expanding repertoire of communicative functions and the child's capacity to engage in more extended reciprocal interactions by participating in both speaker and listener roles and engaging in early social conversations.

Based on information obtained through the SAP-O, Etash demonstrates relative strengths in his ability to coordinate attention with others when sharing his intentions in familiar and predictable situations. As noted, Etash can be a very persistent communicator when requesting preferred toys and activities, and his ability to engage in more extended reciprocal interactions has begun to blossom. At home, for example, he may initiate social interaction by requesting a familiar social routine such as singing the Barney fire truck song with his mother and sister and requesting the continuation of this routine for greater than four exchanges, even on those occasions when his sister has started a different phrase using the motions accompanying the song. He also has recently shown more persistence at school when requesting desired snacks and when requesting assistance with activities of daily living, such as hanging up his coat, putting on his shoes, and opening the door to the playground.

Etash's parents noted on the SAP-R Form that in the past few months, Etash has begun to call out to preferred partners to draw attention to himself either by saying their name or pulling on their arm. In familiar situations, this persistence and goal-directedness was also apparent when he protested/refused undesired activities and intrusions on his play in his classroom. Etash was observed to use a push-away gesture across a number of activities, such as pushing away a cupcake and pushing away his teacher when playing in the sandbox; a head shake to indicate "no"; and the phrase "all done." These communicative strategies have clearly increased his effectiveness when communicating his intent and have enhanced his overall ability to cope across different situations.

Etash's need for familiarity and routines, however, has limited his ability to adapt to and participate in more complex and less familiar social situations and those that involve small and large groups of children. Thus, his ability to remain socially engaged and to communicate varies greatly across different situations. In a novel activity with limited predictability (i.e., a classmate's birthday party), his educational team noted that he tended to withdraw or flee from interactions with his peers rather than to participate in social exchanges. Thus, his ability to persist and repair communicative breakdowns is more restricted in challenging situations. Likewise, when Etash was distressed, his ability to coordinate his bids for assistance and interaction with signals to establish shared attention, such as gaze shifts, tapping on a teacher's shoulder, and/or calling out another's name was quite limited. He often was left to recover from dysregulation on his own or wait until a responsive teacher or caregiver helped him regroup.

The different functions of Etash's communication, as documented through the SAP-O by his educational team, remain limited primarily to more instrumental functions, such as requesting objects; requesting assistance; protesting; and requesting social routines, such as requesting social games, greetings, showing off, and taking turns in clear and predictable games or songs. During the observations and the behavior sampling session, Etash was observed to comment on objects or actions that were within his focus of attention, such as by saying "Thomas" when referring to his favorite train and "car crash, uh-oh!" when referring to a car accident in toy garage. These comments, however, were typically related to his focus of attention, as Etash appeared to show a limited ability to follow another's visual perspective, such as noticing what someone else was looking at, and/or a limited ability to follow another's gestures, such as a friend's pointing to the block tower that he had just built. Thus, his ability to share experiences with a peer by exchanging comments in a reciprocal exchange was not yet observed nor was his ability to share an experience outside of the here and now. Etash only communicated about another person's actions if the toys had initially been part of his own play scheme. For example, he protested, "Don't do that!" when his sister took one of his trains out of a lineup that he had created with all of his Thomas the Tank Engine trains.

Challenges in consistently coordinating attention and communicative signals and limitations in communicating for more social purposes were compounded by the difficulties that Etash showed with sharing his emotions in a conventional or symbolic manner. His lead teacher and school psychologist had observed a fairly consistent pattern during play-based opportunities with his peers. Etash would experience a shift in his emotional state and arousal, becoming tense and excited, and his peers would move away from him because they became uncomfortable when he gave such signals indicative of high arousal. Without the tools to share his positive and negative emotions appropriately, his idiosyncratic means of coping with his changes in state, which included hand flapping, lashing out, and jumping up and down, led to his peers' wariness about staying in close proximity to him, resulting in further isolation for Etash. Thus, a serious concern was raised by his team members about the need to identify appropriate contexts for fostering success with his peers, to build his self-confidence and strengthen his social network. This was considered a crucial next step in developing an IEP for Etash.

Social Communication: Symbol Use

After establishing Etash's baseline on the SAP in joint attention, his team and family turned their attention toward determining Etash's strengths and challenges in symbol use. As noted previously, Etash's single-word vocabulary appears to be expanding, as he was both observed and has been reported to use approximately 85 single words. He is clearly a multimodal communicator who uses conventional gestures (e.g., reaching, pointing, head shaking, pushing away), gaze, facial expressions, words, and short phrases to communicate. Because he is quite persistent in certain contexts, as noted previously, his team observed that he often uses a combination of words, gaze, and gestures to clarify his message. These abilities have increased his competence and effectiveness at communicating for requesting, protesting, and initiating social routines. He has even used these abilities to make simple comments about his play and the objects with which he is currently engaged, saying, for example, "Thomas is a train!" and "car crash, uh-oh!"

Based on documentation in the SAP-O, Etash's challenges in Joint Attention appear to have a limited ability to learn through social observation and have, as a result, a compromised development of play schemes that involve the use of objects in a socially conventional manner (e.g., pretending to wash dishes in a kitchen set). Because Etash often does not attend to his partners' perspective by looking at what they are looking at, he often does not have a full sense of what his partners are doing or what their intentions are. His team members discussed that these limited social observation skills are clearly restricting his use of more varied play schemes, as he was only observed to enact play schemes that he has memorized from familiar videos and books, such as driving a Thomas the Tank Engine train or pretending to put Bob the Builder in his bulldozer.

Difficulties with learning through social observation were also noted to be influencing Etash's development of more varied action words. During the administration of the SAP-O, his speech-language pathologist used the Worksheet for Word Meanings in the Language Partner Stage. She noted that Etash's single-word vocabulary was primarily limited to early relational words (e.g., "no," "bye-bye," "more," "all done") and the names of objects (e.g., "train," "bubbles," "car," "balloon"), body parts (e.g., "head," "tummy," "nose"), and agents (e.g., "Mom," "dad," "Madhur," his lead teacher's name). His development of more advanced relational words (e.g., action words, modifiers, *wh-* words) was not observed with great frequency throughout the SAP. Etash did use high-frequency words that he was comfortable with from his frame of reference (e.g., "go," "crash," "open") rather than those that would arise from the perspective of another person (e.g., "*write* . . . name," "*light* . . . candles," "*turn on* . . . computer").

Perhaps the most apparent challenge that Etash's team observed in symbol use was Etash's reliance on echolalia when formulating utterances beyond the single-word level. Although Etash was observed to produce phrases with as many as four words (e.g., "Hang up coat, please"), these phrases were examples of delayed echolalia borrowed from language modeled by an adult in a previous context or immediate echolalia of language modeled for him. Etash's team members were struck by his remarkable ability to form episodic associations, as he often recalled words or chunks of language far after the initial model had been provided for him. His school psychologist gave an example to illustrate this remarkable recall. When Etash was observed making the transition from the school bus to his inclusive kindergarten classroom, he dropped his lunch box on the curb. Etash looked up at the instructional assistant and commented, "Get your bucket and sponge!" His school psychologist remarked that this phrase had been used in a video that the children had watched during their first week at the Bayport. In that video, a child had also dropped his lunch box and had made that exact same remark.

Etash's speech-language pathologist noted that although Etash's reliance on static environmental or visual cues to generate language is a relative strength, this tendency has led to difficulties with word retrieval. Thus, it was strongly recommended that the team implement AAC supports to foster Etash's ability to combine individual words to form creative word combinations such as agent + action + object, modifier + object, and negation + object. Although Etash was capable of producing four-word utterances, his speech-language pathologist referred back to the SAP-O and noted that these milestones should be addressed to enhance Etash's competence in creative language production.

Emotional Regulation: Mutual Regulation

At this point in the meeting, Etash's team members and parents began to discuss the SAP-O findings related to Etash's strengths and challenges in mutual regulation. The team initially reflected on their previous discussions of Etash's social-communicative abilities and the impact of these areas on his emotional regulatory abilities. In doing so, both his parents and his educational team recognized that Etash's gains in joint attention and symbol use were positively contributing to his repertoire of mutual regulatory strategies, as documented during the SAP-O.

First, the team noted that Etash's increased capacity to share his intentions to regulate the behavior of others using more readable or conventional gestures has led to improvements in his ability to request assistance from his caregivers and teachers to regulate his emotions. In fact, each team member could recall at least one instance during each observation where Etash had protested an anxiety-provoking activity through the use of a push-away gesture. The school psychologist discussed that during a peer's birthday celebration, Etash's newly developing strategies led to his increased participation in watching his friend blow out the candles, even though this was a potentially distracting event. When Etash's teacher attempted to give him a cupcake while he was closely watching his friend, he quickly used his hand to push her hand and the cupcake out of his space. Because this protest was both efficient and readable, his teacher honored his protest, which supported Etash's ability to remain engaged in the activity. She cleared off the area in front of his seat and walked away, allowing Etash to regroup and attend to his friend who was blowing out the candles. Before he had developed a push-away gesture, Etash might have lashed out at his teacher and/or begun to scream in protest of his teacher's intrusion and/or the undesired snack. These earlier patterns had affected both his own ability to remain engaged in an activity and his peers' ability to enjoy the activity.

In addition to Etash's increased ability to protest and have greater control in more anxiety-provoking activities, his communicative abilities were also beginning to allow him to request assistance and social interaction during routine social exchanges. Although emerging, these abilities were noted to be more robust with very familiar partners, such as with his mother during play routines at home and the instructional assistant during predictable classroom routines. For example, during his transition from the bus to his public school kindergarten classroom, Etash independently asked the instructional assistant for help with hanging up his coat. In doing so, he looked up and used the phrase, "Hang up coat, please," a phrase that he had borrowed from the instructional assistant, who often used that same phrase to familiarize Etash with the arrival routine. Once again, his ability to use this efficient and readable request for assistance supported his ability to maintain a well-regulated state despite the fact that he was entering the large-group social environment of his inclusive kindergarten classroom. Previously, Etash may have withdrawn from this challenging task by going limp in the instructional assistant's arms, bolting or fleeing from the environment, and/or crying.

Despite these encouraging changes, it was evident from the team discussion that Etash's development of mutual regulatory skills remained inconsistent, as such skills were only observed to be emerging predominantly in familiar routines and with familiar partners. He was not yet observed to use efficient and readable protests and requests in unfamiliar activities, with unfamiliar partners, or when his arousal level was truly too high to maintain an active state of engagement. For example, although his lead teacher at Bayport had observed Etash stating "all done" as a means of conveying a request for a break during morning meeting, his occupational therapist had observed Etash flee from his peer's birthday celebration once the children had sung "Happy Birthday" and the candles were blown out. Once these familiar routines were completed, Etash clearly was in need of assistance with regulating his arousal and emotional state. Fleeing or escaping from an activity is a behavioral strategy that Etash continues to use frequently and does not involve engaging a teacher or caregiver, as he has not yet learned to consistently secure the attention of his partner when protesting and/or seeking assistance for regrouping. Therefore, the team agreed that Etash's ability to share negative emotions, to request comfort, and to protest when distressed were emerging abilities that were not yet solidly established.

Even before the observations, both his parents and his educational team had reported Etash's unpredictable nature in their respective SAP-R Forms. Thus, this topic was raised in the team meeting to determine whether Etash's emotional signals are clear and readable signals to his partners, for this would allow his partners to monitor changes in his emotional state with greater consistency and accuracy. His parents and team members commented that although Etash's nonverbal emotional expression was easy to read due to its intense nature, his inability to symbolically identify his own emotional state using words or pictures did not help Etash to prevent escalation to higher levels of dysregulation by seeking emotional regulatory assistance from those around him. When he is upset, his ability to read the emotional cues of others, such as sad or mad facial expressions, and respond to language modeled to him (e.g., "You feel sad," "You look mad") creates situations in which caregiver assistance can lead to further emotional distress. In other words, efforts to help Etash can essentially backfire. He clearly is in need of support to enhance his ability to express himself in a more symbolic manner, using strategies such as visual supports (e.g., using picture symbols to represent emotions across task schedules and in within-task checklists), opportunities for shared control (e.g., being offered choices, participating in activity set up), clear and predictable routines, and the incorporation of music. These strategies need to be implemented consistently to facilitate Etash's ability to participate in activities. Without these supports, Etash will be prone to experience periods of high arousal and extreme dysregulation.

Finally, Etash's team turned their attention to a discussion of instances of extreme dysregulation, as information obtained through the observations suggested that he spends a significant portion of his day in an extremely dysregulated and unavailable state. The team agreed that several factors contribute to Etash's bias toward a high state of arousal. In particular, they highlighted his sensitivity to unanticipated stimulation (e.g., noises, dynamic visual information, touch), his rote learning style, his preference for limited change or novelty in his routines, and his need to be in control. Given the broad nature of these factors and the frequent swings in arousal state, it was evident to the team that Etash was spending a great deal of his day, both at home and at school, in extreme dysregulation and was not always benefiting from natural incidental learning opportunities in his environment. His school psychologist had documented several clear signals of extreme dysregulation associated with Etash's high arousal. These included 1) fleeing or escaping; 2) striking out; 3) jumping up and down while turning his back on his partners; and 4) shutting down, as evidenced by a significant reduction in the frequency and sophistication of his communication.

Throughout the observations, signals of extreme dysregulation were noted whenever Etash was challenged by a novel activity, the sequence of steps in an activity was not clear, and the social complexity of his environment increased (e.g., smaller to larger groups). Several examples were offered during the meeting. At home, Etash had been observed to flee from the room when his mother attempted to introduce a new game with his sister. He tried to hit his sister when she removed a train from his lineup and began to play with it. At school, he withdrew from the block area when two boisterous peers intruded and began to play with the blocks, and he ran off when his request to be finished with his art project was initially denied by the instructional assistant.

In each of these instances, it was clear that Etash recovered from extreme dysregulation only when caregivers and teachers introduced interpersonal and learning supports to foster his mutual regulation. These supports had several common elements. They were aimed at decreasing the complexity of the environment, providing predictable sequence of activities and steps in an activity, and fostering Etash's sense of competency and control. A complete summary of Etash's current profile of strengths and areas of need in the Mutual Regulation component would be included in his SAP-O Form and SAP Sum.

Emotional Regulation: Self-Regulation

Next, Etash's parents and team members discussed Etash's abilities and challenges in self-regulation. Based on information attained through the SAP-R and the SAP-O, the team noted how behavioral strategies such as toe-walking, hand-flapping, and jumping up and down were both signals of his dysregulation as well as beginning attempts at self-regulation. In fact, Etash often used these strategies to prevent escalation to extreme dysregulation. Nevertheless, these strategies only marginally supported his ability to learn and interact in his environment and, given that they were confusing to other children and appeared unconventional, they occasionally caused the other children to withdraw from or avoid Etash, thus limiting his opportunities for social engagement. The strategies also were becoming significantly distressing and increasingly embarrassing in public for his parents.

The team recorded several instances during the SAP-O when Etash employed a behavioral strategy such as hand flapping to decrease his arousal level during both solitary and social play. As noted, these attempts clearly only served as a starting point for self-regulation, as they were not sufficient to allow Etash to return to a state in which he was available for engagement. Instead, he was observed to become so preoccupied with the sensory and motor aspects of such behavior that he often had difficulty refocusing on the current task or social activity. Therefore, it was determined that Etash's ability to engage in extended reciprocal interactions and lengthy activities was much more dependent on the qualities of the activities that supported regulation (e.g., the structure of that activity, the predictability of the partner, the presence of organizing transactional supports) than on his own resources in maintain a well-regulated state. When considering Etash's availability for learning and interacting, the team also reflected on how the limited effectiveness of his current behavioral strategies affected his ability to persist during tasks with reasonable demands and his ability to inhibit his tendency to act impulsively.

As a result of Etash's needs in self-regulation, his team focused more specifically on his impulsive and unpredictable behavior in challenging situations. When his occupational therapist observed the videotape of Etash playing at home with his sister, the therapist noted how Etash's mother had attempted to establish a turn-taking structure to encourage the children to share a preferred train. When his mother indicated that it was Madhur's turn, Etash became distressed, began to cry, and attempted to grab the toy from her. When his mother modeled acceptable behavioral and language strategies for expressing his unhappiness, such as stomping one's feet and saying "I'm mad," Etash did not attend to his mother modeling these strategies, nor did he respond. Instead, he lashed out once again by grabbing at the toy and throwing his body backwards against the floor. Limited use of behavioral strategies to cope with this distress was evident, leading to a very impulsive and aggressive style.

Etash does appear to be beginning to use caregiver modeled language strategies to help him persist during preferred activities. For example, both his speech-language pathologist and his occupational therapist commented on Etash's use of language to help organize his play with cars during behavior sampling. Etash was observed to repeatedly say, "Car up," indicating that the car was riding up in the elevator in the play set, followed by "Car go down," indicating the car was driving down the ramp after it had reached the top. This self-talk clearly helped Etash sequence the activity and maintain active engagement.

Next, the team turned their attention to Etash's challenges dealing with new and changing situations. As indicated on the SAP-R Forms completed by Etash's family and educational team, this was an area of primary concern and was viewed as a factor that was limiting Etash's ability to participate successfully in various activities and environments typically experienced by children his age. During the observations, it was evident that unscheduled transitions and unanticipated events were extremely anxiety provoking for Etash. He often employed behavioral strategies such as toe walking and hand flapping at these times; however, due to the limited effectiveness of these strategies, he typically ended up disengaging or having a tantrum. In contrast, when Etash was clearly prepared for a change in an activity or routine, such as when partners used learning supports such as visual schedules and timers, he was often able to go with the flow. Again, this reliance on mutual regulatory supports suggested a need to focus on Etash's use of self-regulatory strategies to cope with new and changing situations to decrease his reliance on those around him.

Etash's limited repertoire of effective language and behavioral strategies also compromised his ability to self-regulate when experiencing periods of extreme dysregulation associated with high arousal. During an art activity, Etash was observed to become extremely dysregulated when his bid to end an activity was refused. In this instance, Etash fled the table and began to jump up and down while vocalizing loudly. However, it was not until the instructional assistant helped to direct Etash to a less stimulating environment (i.e., the "cozy corner") that he began to regroup. At this point in time, Etash was not yet able to effectively use behavioral strategies to help with recovery from extreme dysregulation. A complete summary of Etash's current profile of strengths and

Transactional Support: Interpersonal Support

areas of need in the Self-Regulation component would be included in his SAP-O Form and SAP Sum.

Both the SAP-R and the SAP-O were reviewed to gain a sense of the strengths and needs of Etash's social network and those interpersonal supports that could be implemented to facilitate social communication and emotional regulation. Etash's school psychologist focused on how Etash's developmental vulnerabilities are likely to have a transactional influence on his partners. For example, Etash's bias toward a high state of arousal and unpredictable emotional reactions may result in adults and peer partners perceiving him as volatile, aggressive, and even dangerous. Etash's team felt this was particularly true of partners who were less familiar with him, who interacted with him in less structured environments, and who were his age.

Interpersonal supports in this instance would involve helping Etash's partners to understand his learning style and his sensitivities to environmental stimuli, his signals of dysregulation, and effective mutual regulatory supports. The team agreed that the consistent use of these types of interpersonal supports by all of Etash's partners might elicit more consistent reciprocity and engagement. In addition, they noted that those partners who provide Etash opportunities to share social control through the offering of choices, the honoring of his desire to terminate activities, and the encouragement of his initiations are often rewarded with sustained engagement, a positive emotional response, and greater shared attention as compared with those partners who attempt to control Etash's behavior in a more reactive and directive manner. In fact, Etash sought out partners who provided opportunities for shared control and honored his refusals, and tended to avoid partners who were more controlling and directive.

By reviewing the SAP-R and SAP-O results, Etash's parents and educational team members were able to identify a number of interpersonal supports that were emerging as areas of strength in his social network and those that were considered critical areas of need. The following chart provides examples of each.

Interpersonal Support

Strengths	Needs
Etash's mother consistently offers choices verbally and nonverbally (IS2.1).	Etash's partners are beginning to recognize that Etash is better able to maintain engagement when he feels a sense of shared control. Therefore, they recognize the need to build in opportunities for him to make choices, complete activities at his own pace, solve problems, and reject activities when appropriate throughout his day (IS2.1, IS3.2–IS3.4).
Etash's educational team (e.g., teachers, instructional assistant, therapists) is beginning to develop a range of interpersonal supports that are being used fairly consistently across Etash's school day. These include recognizing signs of dysregulation and offering support, interpreting problem behaviors as communicative or regulatory, and adjusting the complexity of language input to Etash's arousal level (IS1.5, IS3.3, IS6.2).	Etash's partners have realized a need to provide developmental support that appropriately encourages and ensures success during Etash's interaction with peers, as his peers may be avoiding him due to his unpredictable emotions and unconventional self-regulatory strategies (IS5.2).
	Etash's partners recognized that modeling appropriate nonverbal communication and emotional expression remains a challenge, as this occasionally contributes to further emotional distress when Etash is upset (IS7.1).

A complete profile of the use of various interpersonal supports by Etash's social network would be included on his SAP-O Form and SAP Sum.

Transactional Support: Learning Support

A final component of Etash's team meeting included a discussion of those learning supports that have already been implemented as transactional supports in his daily routines and activities and those that should be considered to foster his competence with social communication and emotional regulation. His educational team noted that a number of learning supports were already supporting his participation in his two classrooms. These included his family's incorporation of motivating materials, such as vehicles cars, trucks, and trains, in daily activities, and their attempts to modify the sensory properties of the learning environment, such as keeping the majority of Etash and Madhur's toys organized in separate boxes and cleaned up after each use. In addition, Etash's occupational therapist noted that the educational staff often used a between-task visual schedule to help Etash prepare for transitions and upcoming activities. Etash's parents and educational team members discussed the need to use similar supports so that Etash would be able to comprehend a predictable sequence in activities and participate in varied learning opportunities without becoming distressed.

Etash's family and educational team also discussed the importance of AAC supports for Etash. This had not been addressed in his previous educational programming; however, because Etash continues to rely on echolalia, his use of creative word combinations remains limited. As noted, he has a strong tendency to borrow phrases that he has heard before as single units, due to his limited capacity to generate novel utterances and his limited understanding of the individual words and word relations in phrases and sentences that he hears. Because he has a strong preference for static visual information, the team discussed how picture symbols could be implemented to help Etash break down the distinct components or words in these multiword utterances and support his transition to more creative and generative language. Thus, by reviewing the SAP-R and SAP-O results, Etash's parents and educational team members were able to identify a number of learning supports that were emerging as areas of strength in his social network and those that were considered critical areas of need. The following chart provides examples of several of these areas.

Learning Support	
Strengths	**Needs**
Etash's parents have developed the ability to modify the sensory properties of the home environment and to incorporate motivating materials into activities (LS4.3, LS4.7). Etash's educational staff members have developed a number of visual schedules to help Etash anticipate transitions and upcoming activities (LS3.3).	Because Etash continues to rely on echolalia and single-word utterances to communicate, his team agreed that there is a need to implement the use of AAC supports to foster his expressive language and use more creative combinations of words (LS2.1). The use of learning supports to provide Etash with an understanding of the steps within a task needs to be consistently integrated across contexts and partners (LS3.1).

A complete summary of the use of various learning supports by Etash's social network would be included in his SAP-O Form and SAP Sum.

Social-Emotional Growth Indicators: Results and Impressions

Next, Etash's team computed his baseline composite scores for his Social-Emotional Growth Indicators. These indicators would provide useful benchmarks against which to measure future gains in Etash's general qualities of behavior. The general qualities of behavior measured by the Social-Emotional Growth Indicators include 1) Happiness, 2) Sense of Self, 3) Sense of Other, 4) Active Learning and Organization, 5) Flexibility and Resilience, 6) Cooperation and Appropriateness of Behavior, 7) Independence, and

8) Social Membership and Friendships. Calculation of Etash's Social-Emotional Growth Indicators revealed a relative strength in the area of Sense of Self. Areas of relative weakness included Happiness, Flexibility and Resilience, and Cooperation and Appropriateness of Behavior.

Key Information Source 2: Family Perception of SAP-O Results and Priorities

Before identifying the specific goals and objectives for Etash's educational program, his parents were asked to share their perceptions of his SAP-O and the behavior sampling session. In particular, they were asked to comment on whether representative samples of Etash's behavior had been obtained and whether Etash's strengths and difficulties were accurately captured on the SAP Sum. Etash's mother and father indicated that they felt that the SAP had captured an accurate "snapshot" of their son during a time of transition, referring to his recent move to a new educational program at Bayport. They commented that the team had seen how Etash responds to new situations, as he appeared to be somewhat more anxious and aggressive than he had been toward the end of his second year of preschool. His parents were looking forward to his next reassessment 3 months later, as this would be occurring after his school routine was more solidly established.

Following this discussion, Etash's parents were invited to reiterate their primary concerns and to discuss their hopes and expectations regarding Etash's development. They expressed appreciation that the Bayport staff had taken the time to acquaint themselves with the challenges his family faces with Etash at home and that these difficulties are being considered when determining goals for educational programming. Etash's lead teacher at Bayport reiterated the team's belief that it is essential to assess a child's strengths and needs across a variety of contexts to truly understand the child. Next, Etash's parents were asked to indicate the types of information and supports that would be most helpful for their family. Family perceptions would be included on Etash's SAP Sum.

SAP Step 7: Prioritizing Goals and Objectives

Based on the information compiled and integrated throughout the SAP, including the SAP-R, SAP-O, behavior sampling, and SAP Sum, Etash's parents and educational team members worked together to prioritize goals and objectives that were the most *functional,* directly *addressed family priorities,* and matched the *developmental areas of need* for both Etash and his partners. His performance on the SAP-O was not the sole factor for selecting weekly objectives, as equal consideration was given to those objectives that would be the most functional and those that most closely matched his parent's priorities. As noted, this occasionally results in selection of objectives that might appear out of sequence on the SAP; nevertheless this flexibility and individualization is actually considered critical for successful implementation of a SCERTS Model program. The ability of Etash's team to target objectives in Joint Attention and Symbol Use through the use of consistent interpersonal supports and learning supports will allow Etash to learn to communicate a range of intentions using increasingly sophisticated symbolic means. His weekly objectives would be included on his SAP Sum.

SAP Step 8: Recommending Further Assessment if Needed

When reviewing the SAP Sum, Etash's parents felt that a representative sample of Etash's social-communicative and emotional regulatory challenges was obtained along with information regarding the most appropriate transactional supports. Nevertheless, they also hoped to gain a better understanding of his learning style and cognitive abilities, as he has now entered kindergarten and will be facing the challenge of keeping up with his peers academically for the years ahead. As the school psychologist at Bayport had a great deal of experience and training in evaluating young children with ASD, she agreed that it would be an appropriate time to administer baseline measures and would begin psychoeducational testing in a series of small sessions in the next several months.

SAP Step 9: Design a SCERTS Educational Program for Etash, His Family, and His Service Providers

Step 9 of the SAP involved identifying a number of key meaningful and purposeful activities, the complexity of social support in these activities (i.e., the roles and responsibilities of educational team members), and familiar partners who will play a critical role in service provision. Etash's team leader, his special education teacher, took the primary role of organizing the educational and support program for Etash and his parents. With an awareness of the critical features that are characteristic of effective interventions, she led a discussion about the continued need for intensive educational programming and *at least* 25 hours per week on a year-round basis of planned and developmentally appropriate learning opportunities. In addition, she indicated that continued individualized attention would be needed for Etash to remain actively engaged during his programming. A plan to provide educational support to his family also needed to be developed in collaboration with them to address their ongoing concerns regarding his behavior in the home environment.

This step of the SAP culminated in the development of two SAP Activity Planning Forms, each of which incorporated approximately 3 hours of meaningful and purposeful activities in Etash's natural routines. The first form outlined Etash's typical morning routines at the Bayport Learning Center and the second form outlined Etash's typical afternoon routines at his public school inclusive kindergarten. Therefore, a plan was established for approximately 6 hours per day, for a total of 30 hours per week of educational programming.

The SAP Activity Planning Forms included the specific goals that would be addressed in these activities and the complexity of social context (i.e., the degree of naturalness and the amount and frequency of one-to-one support) that would be appropriate given Etash's unique social-communicative and emotional regulatory capacities. In addition, the SAP Activity Planning Forms were completed to identify the partner objectives and specific transactional supports (e.g., interpersonal supports, learning supports) that would be embedded in each activity.

Next, Etash's team leader reported information provided by his family on the SAP-R as well as information obtained through the SAP-O regarding the Transactional Support domain, to discuss the provision of a SCERTS Family Support Plan. As discussed in Chapter 3 of this volume, the provision of both educational support and emotional support to a child's immediate and extended family is a critical priority in a comprehensive service delivery program rather than being considered optional. Thus, Etash's team leader noted that the development of Etash's educational program would not be complete without this crucial step.

Educational Support for Etash's Family

As noted, primary educational concerns expressed by Etash's parents included the challenges they encountered due to Etash's unpredictable behavior (particularly with his sister), their limited strategies with helping him participate in family activities (both inside and outside of the home), and their difficulties explaining the nature of Etash's difficulties to his grandmother in terms that she could understand and accept. Thus, Educational Support appeared to be needed to address the following general goals.

Goal 1: **To provide Etash's family members with the knowledge and skills to support Etash's development in everyday activities, and to address specific is-**

sues that are identified as most stressful and challenging. For Etash's family, priorities related to this goal included 1) understanding Etash's current difficulties with emotional regulation and how to recognize signs of emotional distress and 2) implementing learning supports developed in the school environment in everyday activities at home and in the community (e.g., going to the grocery store, visiting family friends).

Desired outcome: Etash's family members will feel confident in providing the necessary supports to foster Etash's emotional regulation across different situations and in everyday activities and in identifying and coping with the most significant difficulties they face at any point in time.

Goal 2: To provide Etash's family members with information and resources to understand the nature of Etash's disability and how it specifically affects his development. In particular, the family needs educational materials that can be translated and shared with Etash's grandmother.

Desired outcome: Etash's members, including his grandmother, will become knowledgeable about ASD and how specifically it affects Etash's functional abilities in life. They will be able to use resources to find information and continue to actively learn as Etash develops.

The first step of the SCERTS Family Support Plan included provision of resources. First, Etash's team leader offered his parents several reprints of articles that discussed the nature of emotional regulatory difficulties frequently encountered by children with ASD. She also provided Etash's parents with a handout that specifically described effective and socially appropriate *behavioral strategies* for emotional regulation that would be suitable for a child with ASD at the Language Partner stage and strategies for facilitating replacement of the more inefficient strategies that Etash currently employs. The teacher warned that the list of strategies provided in the handout was general and that strategies more specific to Etash would be discussed at regular *team meetings* to be offered on a monthly basis. Last, a handout was provided specifically to support Etash's grandmother's understanding of ASD. These handouts contained basic information related to the ASD diagnosis and associated core challenges in social communication and emotional regulation.

The next step of the SCERTS Family Support Plan included ensuring that Etash's family had access to educational resources and consistency of approach could be achieved across home and school. Etash's parents and grandmother were encouraged to participate in *classroom visits* involving a weekly observation of Etash at school. Because the classroom at Bayport had been designed with a one-way mirror to facilitate these observations, Etash's distraction would be less significant than it would be were his parents and grandmother in the classroom with him. The school psychologist at Bayport would be present with his parents and grandmother at this time to narrate the sequence of events and highlight successful use of interpersonal and learning supports. Next, Bayport offered bimonthly *caregiver education programs* to supplement these observations. Partner objectives identified in the SAP-O would be targeted during these educational opportunities. Partner objectives such as *Uses an augmentative communication system to enhance child's communication and expressive language* (LS2.1) and *Uses support to define steps within a task* (LS3.1) would be addressed.

Next, the team offered the family the opportunity to participate in monthly home visits aimed at providing *interactive guidance* and modeling in natural activities in family routines. The family appreciated this offer and agreed to the potential benefit of such guidance; however, they were uncomfortable with school personnel visiting their home, so they requested that the sessions be completed at Bayport. The team agreed to this modification of the plan and established a monthly family session with the school psychologist and occupational therapist.

In addition to these monthly educational support activities, Etash's team recognized the need to devise an efficient, daily *system of communication* as a means to problem-solve challenges that were likely to arise due to Etash's social-communicative and emotional regulatory difficulties, as well as celebrate his accomplishments. For this purpose, the team agreed on the use of a form divided into comment blocks for Social Communication, Emotional Regulation, and Transactional Support domains.

Emotional Support for Etash's Family

Throughout the SAP, Etash's family had candidly discussed the stresses that they encountered on a daily basis. It was clear that these stresses had multiple origins and clearly affected the family's quality of life. Therefore it was apparent to the team that emotional support was also needed to address the following goals.

Goal 1: **To support Etash's family members in their ability to cope with the stresses and challenges of raising a child with ASD.** In particular, they identified as a priority coping with and managing Etash's unpredictable emotional reactions and challenging behaviors (e.g., aggression toward his sister).

Desired outcome: *Etash's family will develop specific coping abilities to manage the inevitable stresses that they will experience directly due to or as a secondary effect of Etash's having ASD, including Etash's unpredictable emotional reactions and challenging behaviors (e.g., aggression toward his sister).*

Goal 2: **To help Etash's family understand and gain access to the range of formal and informal emotional supports that may be available**

Desired outcome: *Etash's family will gain access to formal and informal supports that best match the emotional needs of family members at specific points in time.*

Goal 3: **To help Etash's family identify their own priorities and develop appropriate expectations and realistic, achievable goals for Etash's development and family life**

Desired outcome: *Etash's family will be clear about the most important issues they wish to address for Etash and the family, will develop realistic goals and expectations for Etash, and will create a balance in family life consistent with their lifestyle and values.*

A range of options was discussed with Etash's parents regarding emotional supports at Bayport, at the inclusive kindergarten, and in the community. These included formal supports such as a Bayport *support group* held one evening per month at the school, community-based parent support groups, and resources for individualized counseling services. Etash's family, however, expressed that they would feel uncomfortable in a group setting and preferred to discuss *individualized support meetings*. Etash's school psychologist proposed that due to the acute nature of the challenges they were experiencing, she would be available to meet with them on a biweekly basis for a 3-month period to support their needs and explore other avenues for support with them. The team then discussed Bayport's *family fun events*. These social events, organized for students and their families, would provide the family with opportunities for Etash's family to go out and play in a safe and nonjudgmental environment. The staff also encouraged Etash's parents to take advantage of the Bayport *drop-off nights* staffed by two lead teachers and four instructional assistants. These evenings were scheduled semiannually and were offered to provide parents with a child care solution and a chance to enjoy an event in the community that may not have been an option otherwise.

Support Among Professionals

For the final step in planning and designing Etash's educational program, his special education teacher discussed how the SCERTS Model recognizes that professionals and other service providers face considerable challenges when implementing an intensive educational program. For professionals and other service providers (e.g., instructional assistants, paraprofessionals) to be as effective as possible in supporting children and families, a well-established SCERTS Support Plan for Professionals and Service Providers would need to be developed. Because Etash's team, as described in the SAP Activity Planning Form, included not only professionals but also paraprofessionals, *mentoring arrangements* were scheduled on a daily basis for at least 5 hours per week of paraprofessional supervision provided by either Etash's special education teacher, his speech-language pathologist, and/or his occupational therapist. Supervision would involve both direct educational and interactive guidance as well as one-to-one emotional support in bimonthly *supervision meetings.* Next, his lead teacher indicated that each month, Etash's team members would arrange a *team meeting* (as discussed previously) to discuss Etash's progress and the need for consistency with both interpersonal and learning supports. It was agreed that the staff could call *crisis meetings* if Etash exhibits sudden changes in his behavior or if a staff member is having a particularly difficult time successfully implementing transactional supports.

SAP Step 10: Performing Ongoing Tracking

Following the identification of Etash's weekly objectives and the weekly objectives of his partners, his team discussed the need to track his ongoing progress in his educational program. During their discussion, his team recognized that although it would not be feasible to take data on every objective in every activity, it would be critical to track Etash's progress to inform decision making about the effectiveness of his program's implementation. As a result, progress with each objective would be monitored on a daily basis in one or two activities. To share responsibility for data collection, his speech-language pathologist would assume primary responsibility for collecting data related to his Social Communication objectives, his special educator and occupational therapist would assume primary responsibility for collecting data related to his Emotional Regulation objectives, and his school psychologist would be responsible for monitoring Transactional Support objectives.

Next, Etash's team formulated a plan for using the information documented on the SAP Daily Tracking Log to complete a SAP Weekly Tracking Log. They discussed having Etash's lead special education teacher compile and integrate this information and take responsibility for sharing it with the team. These reviews would be essential for recognizing growth and/or lack of progress in specific objectives. The SAP would then be readministered quarterly.

Chapter 7

Enhancing Social Communication, Emotional Regulation, and Transactional Support at the Conversational Partner Stage
From Assessment to Program Implementation

To develop a comprehensive educational program or to modify an existing program for a child at the Conversational Partner stage, the SCERTS Model prioritizes those developmental capacities that support a child's communicative competence across people, places, and circumstances. As delineated in Chapter 7 of Volume I, this process begins by identifying goals and objectives in the areas of social communication and emotional regulation based on a child's current developmental capacities in these domains and is followed by determining the most applicable transactional supports for the child and family. This must be a flexible process based on the child's learning strengths and needs, the family's priorities, and the demands of the child's natural routines and ongoing educational programming.

In this chapter, we describe the development and implementation of educational programs for two children at the Conversational Partner stage, one at the novice level and one at the advanced level of this stage. These two children demonstrate very different levels of ability and therefore allow us to consider the range of issues that must be addressed for programming at the Conversational Partner stage. We must once again emphasize that the goals and activities described in this chapter are not being offered as a "prescription" to follow for all children at this stage, as each child's program should be individualized based on his or her unique social-communicative and emotional regulatory needs, and learning strengths and weaknesses. As discussed in Chapter 1 of this volume, educational priority goals for a child are based on the following criteria: 1) goals target the most *functional* abilities in social communication and emotional regulation (i.e., abilities that support the child's active engagement in natural activities in daily routines), 2) goals directly *address family priorities* (i.e., goals are consistent with the values of parents and other family members), and 3) goals are *developmentally appropriate* (i.e., goals are consistent with the child's performance on the SAP-O). By following these criteria, the focus remains on fostering a child's ability to understand how and when to use acquired skills as independently as possible and apply these abilities consistently and in a functional manner in activities that are prioritized by the family and the many partners in that child's daily life.

Furthermore, as discussed in Chapter 1 of this volume, a SCERTS Model program should include *at least* 25 hours per week on a year-round basis of planned learning opportunities with sufficient individualized attention for the child to remain actively engaged. Thus, designing a comprehensive and intensive educational program for a child at the Conversational Partner stage requires an effort to 1) establish a blueprint for meaningful and purposeful activities in daily routines, 2) determine the current challenges posed in these settings, and 3) determine the complexity of the social contexts (i.e., one-to-one, small-group, or large-group settings) that would be appropriate depending on the child's unique social-communicative and emotional regulatory capacities. In addition, it is critical to keep in mind the importance of providing opportunities for the child to learn with typically developing children and other children who can provide good language and social models, as this is a strong emphasis at this stage (refer to the section in Chapter 2 of this volume called Successful Inclusion and Learning and Playing with Peers).

A child's increasing success in more natural contexts often requires a deliberate effort by family and educational team members to implement planned activity routines, engineered activities, and modified natural activities. As noted in Chapter 1 of this volume, the SCERTS Model does not advocate a strict hierarchical sequence when considering this continuum of naturalness. Rather, planned activity routines and engineered and modified activities may be incorporated at different times of the day depending on the complexity of the various activities and the child's variability across the day. In some cases, one-to-one planned activity routines may be provided as an opportunity for increased practice or rehearsal for achieving specific goals. In using planned activity routines, however, it always is important to use the same or similar materials that are available in the natural learning environments and activities. This is due to the fact that practice and rehearsal is most effective in the context that the child will eventually use the targeted capacities, to support an understanding of the natural cues of how and when to use the skills being addressed.

This emphasis in variables occurring in natural contexts is particularly relevant for a child at the Conversational Partner stage. In contrast to children at the Social Partner and Language Partner stages, a child at this stage ultimately begins to develop a greater awareness that successful social exchange is achieved only through cooperative effort with one's partner or partners and that the rules of social appropriateness vary across contexts. A child at the Conversational Partner stage is developing increased flexibility not only to new and changing situations but also to the perspective and opinions of others, both adults and peers. Thus, efforts to support gains in social communication and emotional regulation are not easily achieved outside of a child's natural social contexts and interactive partners. A strong emphasis on peer training is embedded in activity-based intervention planning at this stage. Peer training enables a child's companions to experience success and pleasure during social interactions with the child, thereby expanding the child's social network through the development of relationships and friendships.

In addition, as discussed in Chapter 3 of this volume, the SCERTS Model recognizes that the successful provision of a comprehensive educational program for a child at the Conversational Partner stage is not dependent solely on the determination of objectives and supports for the child. A SCERTS Family Support Plan is needed to address the provision of both educational support and emotional support to family members, and a SCERTS Support Plan for Professionals and Service Providers is needed to address the need for ongoing training, continuing education, and team collaboration. Embedded in a network of support, a child's partners can begin to develop competencies in fostering social communication and emotional regulation and implementing appropriate transactional supports. These support plans should be sensitive to the changing needs of the child, the family, and service providers and tailored to meet the unique challenges faced by children at the Conversational Partner stage.

As discussed in Chapter 2 of Volume I, a child at the Conversational Partner stage is acquiring more advanced language abilities and social awareness of others, which allow for extended sequences of communicative exchange, greater sensitivity to others' perspectives and emotional states, and therefore a deepening of relationships with partners. This stage encompasses two major developmental transitions that enable a child to become a more competent social and communicative partner: 1) the transition to *sentence grammar* and 2) the transition to *conversational discourse.* A child at the novice level of the Conversational Partner stage is moving from using early multiword utterances to constructing sentences based on rules of grammar and syntax. With an expanding knowledge of grammatical forms, syntax, and vocabulary, language becomes more precise, explicit, and descriptive. As a child develops a greater awareness of a social partner's perspective, by knowing whether a partner is paying attention, is interested, and is already familiar with a topic or an event, the use of language expands to more reciprocal conversations about abstract events outside of the immediate context. With this growth, a child develops the ability to communicate about future and past events, request information about others' thoughts and feelings, and share one's thoughts and emotional states.

At the advanced level of the Conversational Partner stage, a child begins to develop an even greater awareness of the experiential knowledge and preferences of a communicative partner, the conventions for social conversational exchanges, and the requirements and social conventions for appropriate behavior in different social situations. These achievements in Conversational Partner stage coincide with the development of a broader repertoire of learning strategies, referred to in Chapter 2 of Volume I as *instructed learning* strategies and *collaborative learning* strategies. As a child progresses through this stage, learning occurs not only through imitation but also through a process of internalizing a dialogue that requires coordinating different perspectives. The child's perspective of an event is now coupled with information gained from 1) a teacher's perspective through direct instruction or guidance and 2) a peer's perspective through the exchange of ideas, plans, and preferences. The child can now draw on this information in future situations, allowing for greater social problem solving, the ability to inhibit and judge one's behavior relative to social and moral rules, and the ability to monitor the perspectives of others using mental-state language (e.g., "He thinks that I think . . . ") and adjust one's behavior accordingly.

With these achievements, a child begins to develop the abilities 1) to use social experience and emotional memories to assist with emotional regulation, 2) to plan and prepare for experiences and interactions, and 3) to negotiate with both adults and peers. A child at this stage begins to develop a greater awareness that successful social exchange with partners underlies the development of positive relationships and is achieved only through cooperative and shared efforts with partners. With a greater understanding that social rules vary across contexts and partners, the child is more able to select topics based on a partner's interests, maintain a conversational exchange by considering the relevance of the information being shared, and gauge the length and content of a conversational turn. With increased awareness of one's own perspective as well as another's perspective, a child is increasingly drawn toward peers with common interests, allowing for greater capacity to both establish and *maintain* relationships with friends.

In the Social Communication domain of the SCERTS Model, these achievements typically develop as a result of more advanced developmental competencies in both joint attention and symbol use. In the Emotional Regulation domain, these achievements rely on more advanced developmental competencies in mutual regulation and self-regulation.

PRIORITIZING GOALS FOR JOINT ATTENTION AT THE CONVERSATIONAL PARTNER STAGE

A number of critical milestones in joint attention contribute to a child's growth at the Conversational Partner stage, resulting in greater ability to achieve successful communicative exchanges with a range of partners, both adults and peers, across contexts. These milestones provide the framework for prioritizing goal areas for a child with ASD as he or she progresses through the Conversational Partner stage. They include the child's ability to 1) share attention, 2) share emotion, 3) share intentions for a variety of purposes, 4) share experiences in reciprocal interaction, and 5) persist and repair communicative breakdowns.

A child who is making the transition from the Language Partner to the Conversational Partner stage has already had an extensive history of participating in a variety of social learning experiences, in which there were innumerable opportunities to use contextual information to consider another's perspective and modify one's use and interpretation of language based on the perspectives of those involved. With greater self-awareness and understanding of social conventions, the child begins to develop the capacity to monitor the appropriateness of his or her conversational discourse relative to a specific partner's needs and interests. The child learns to recognize whether a partner is paying attention and is interested and whether the partner needs more information about a given topic. These capacities lead to a greater awareness of the need to secure a partner's attention before starting a conversation, select topics of conversation that a specific partner enjoys, and gauge the amount of background information to provide for the partner. The child begins to understand how to modify language based on what a partner has seen or heard and, as a result, begins to share thoughts or internal states with others more readily.

These accomplishments in joint attention naturally lead to a greater frequency of successful and mutually satisfying exchanges across partners, both adults and peers. This growth has a bidirectional transactional impact, as the ability to engage in conversational discourse tailored to a specific partner contributes to greater enjoyment for the partner and consequently adds to that partner's motivation to maintain and seek out engagement with the child in the future. As partners are increasingly experiencing pleasure during social interactions with the child, the child's social network expands through the development of relationships and friendships. Although growth in joint attention continues to develop far beyond the early childhood years, specific milestones along this developmental trajectory provide developmental benchmarks that guide the determination of weekly objectives for supporting more sophisticated social perspective-taking and conversational abilities. These include the following:

1. The child *shares attention* by

    a. Monitoring the attentional focus of a social partner

    b. Securing attention to him- or herself prior to expressing intentions

    c. Understanding nonverbal cues of shifts in attentional focus

d. Modifying language based on what a partner has seen or heard

e. Sharing internal thoughts or mental plans with a partner

2. The child *shares emotion* by

    a. Understanding and using early emotion words

    b. Describing others' emotional states with early emotion words

    c. Understanding and using advanced emotion words

    d. Describing others' emotional states with advanced emotion words

    e. Understanding and using graded emotions

    f. Understanding nonverbal cues of emotional expression

    g. Describing plausible causal factors for emotions of oneself and others

3. The child *shares intentions for a variety of purposes* by

    a. Sharing intentions to regulate the behavior of others, such as by requesting desired objects and activities, requesting help, requesting a break, and protesting/refusing undesired activities

    b. Sharing intentions for social interaction, such as by greeting, calling, requesting comfort, regulating turns, requesting permission, praising a partner, expressing empathy, and sharing secrets

    c. Sharing intentions for joint attention, such as by commenting on immediate, past, and imagined events; providing requested information about immediate and past events; requesting information about immediate, past, and future events; expressing feelings and opinions; and anticipating and planning outcomes

4. The child *shares experiences in reciprocal interaction* by

    a. Showing reciprocity in speaker and listener roles to share experiences

    b. Initiating a variety of conversational topics

    c. Initiating and maintaining conversations that relate to a partner's interests

    d. Maintaining interaction by requesting or providing relevant information

    e. Providing needed information based on a partner's knowledge of a topic

    f. Gauging length and content of conversational turn based on the partner

    g. Preferring to be engaged with partners

    h. Having friendships with partners who share interests

5. The child *persists and repairs communication breakdowns* by

    a. Using appropriate rate of communication for context

    b. Repeating and modifying communication to repair breakdowns

    c. Recognizing breakdowns in communication and requesting clarification

    d. Modifying language and behavior based on a partner's change in agenda

e. Modifying language and behavior based on a partner's emotional reaction

f. Expressing feelings of success and confidence during interactions

Although a child with ASD at the Conversational Partner stage may be using increasingly sophisticated expressive language, challenges in joint attention often prevent the *use* of this language in truly effective communicative exchanges and reciprocal social interactions. These limitations often compromise the child's ability to 1) understand the communicative intentions of another (e.g., his or her attentional focus, interests, and opinions); 2) interpret and use nonverbal communicative signals as they relate to another's attention, emotional state, and intentions/thoughts; 3) modify topic selections and repair communicative breakdowns based on a listener's perspective (e.g., past experience with that topic, interest, emotional state); and 4) share internal thoughts or mental plans, experiences, and intentions.

In addition, whereas the social network of a typically developing child is naturally expanding at the Conversational Partner stage, for a child with ASD, challenges in joint attention may result in a more restricted social network. Opportunities to engage with adults and peers tend to decrease when there has been a longstanding history of communicative breakdowns and/or unsuccessful interactions. Initiating a conversation without establishing a partner's attentional focus, selecting and/or getting stuck on inappropriate topics of conversation or topics of little interest to a partner, and being nonresponsive to a partner's emotional cues of distress or boredom may be socially stigmatizing from the perspective of the child's adult communicative partners and the child's peers. Clearly, this creates an additional obstacle for the child with ASD as well as for the child's educational team and caregivers when they are attempting to develop a comprehensive educational program, as peers may either withdraw or respond to the child's communicative overtures in an unsupportive manner, such as with teasing or bullying.

The impact of challenges in joint attention are particularly evident outside of familiar contexts and partners, when there may be greater demands for deducing and adhering to social rules or when unfamiliar and therefore less predictable partners may have less tolerance for unconventional patterns of behavior and violations of social expectations. Therefore, in the SCERTS Model, our expectations for determining whether a child has met criterion for a specific objective increases from those at the Language Partner stage, as societal expectations for children at this developmental stage increase as well. This shift, which is evident in the SAP-O scoring key for this stage, has been implemented to ensure that specific objectives are met across at least two contexts (e.g., school, home, community) and at least three different partners (with at least one being a peer). Thus, at the Conversational Partner stage, a strong emphasis is placed on supporting a child's growth in joint attention to develop capacities across a range of partners and to gain experience and success across school, home, and community contexts.

PRIORITIZING GOALS FOR SYMBOL USE AT THE CONVERSATIONAL PARTNER STAGE

A number of critical milestones in Symbol Use contribute to a child's growth at the Conversational Partner stage, culminating in a greater ability to achieve successful communicative exchanges with a range of partners, both adults and peers, across contexts. These milestones provide the framework for prioritizing goal areas for a child with ASD as he or she progresses through the Conversational Partner stage. They include a child's ability to 1) learn by imitation, observation, instruction, and collaboration; 2) understand nonverbal cues and nonliteral meanings in reciprocal interactions; 3) participate conventionally in dramatic play and recreation; 4) use appropriate gestures and nonverbal behavior for the context; 5) understand and use generative language to express meaning; and 6) follow rules of conversation.

For a child at the novice level of the Conversational Partner stage, a primary accomplishment lies in progressing from using early multiword combinations to constructing different types of sentences, such as questions, statements, and negatives, following rules of grammar and syntax. With each grammatical form, syntactic structure, and language concept, the child acquires a new symbolic tool to more explicitly share or clarify a message to a communicative partner and gains a better understanding of language and stories told by others. Thus, the child is more able to communicate about past and future events, request information from and about others, and use and comprehend narrative discourse. Similarly, the child begins to learn in an explicit manner that nonverbal cues such as gestures, facial expressions, body orientation, and intonation have *shared meanings* that provide information about the exchange of turns in conversation and a partner's attentional focus, emotional state, and intentions. In fact, as the child progresses from the novice level to the advanced level of the Conversational Partner stage, a greater awareness of how nonverbal cues and behaviors can influence the meaning of a partner's message emerges, allowing for recognition of nonliteral meanings of language denoting humor, figurative expressions, sarcasm, and deception.

The understanding and use of nonverbal social cues and language provide a foundation for achieving success in sharing experiences and ideas with others. Nevertheless, a competent communicator also needs to grasp how the social rules influence the interpretation of a message that is shared in conversation. Thus, as the child reaches the advanced level of the Conversational Partner stage, greater use of newly developing learning strategies allows for more sophisticated social problem solving and negotiation, the ability to inhibit behavior based on social and moral rules, and the ability to follow the rules of conversation and social appropriateness across contexts. A child in this stage is learning, for example, to monitor the social reactions of others that may result from behavioral patterns that violate social expectations such as 1) using vocal volume inappropriate for a context (e.g., speaking too loudly in the library, speaking too quietly when reading a book aloud to the class), 2) initiating a topic in an inappropriate manner for a given context (e.g., starting a topic of conversation during a teacher's lecture without raising one's hand), or 3) speaking out of turn and/or walking away during a conversation with a peer.

Specific milestones in Symbol Use provide benchmarks along this developmental trajectory that guide the determination of weekly objectives for a child at this stage. These include the following:

1. The child *learns by imitation, observation, instruction, and collaboration* by

    a. Spontaneously imitating a variety of behaviors later in a different context

    b. Using behaviors modeled by partners to guide social behavior

    c. Using internalized rules modeled by adult instruction to guide behavior

    d. Using self-monitoring and self-talk to guide behavior

    e. Collaborating and negotiating with peers in problem solving

2. The child *understands nonverbal cues and nonliteral meanings in reciprocal interactions* by

    a. Understanding nonverbal cues of turn taking and topic change

b. Understanding nonverbal cues of emotional expression

c. Understanding nonverbal cues and nonliteral meanings of humor and figures of speech

d. Understanding nonverbal cues and nonliteral meanings of teasing, sarcasm, and deception

3. The child *participates conventionally in dramatic play and recreation* by

    a. Using logical sequences of actions in play about familiar events

    b. Using miniature or abstract objects as props

    c. Using logical sequences of actions in play about less familiar events

    d. Taking on a role and engaging in dramatic play

    e. Playing in a common activity with other children

    f. Taking on a role and cooperating with peers in dramatic play

    g. Participating in rule-based group recreation

4. The child *uses appropriate gestures and nonverbal behavior for the context* by

    a. Using appropriate facial expressions for the context and partner

    b. Using appropriate gestures for the context and partner

    c. Using appropriate body posture and proximity for the context and partner

    d. Using appropriate volume and intonation for the context and partner

5. The child *understands and uses generative language to express meanings* by

    a. Understanding and using a variety of advanced relational words, such as words denoting *wh-* concepts, temporal concepts, physical concepts, numerical concepts, location or spatial concepts, kinship concepts, and causality

    b. Understanding and using reference to things, such as subject pronouns, other pronouns, determiners, and plurals

    c. Understanding and using a variety of verb phrases, such as main verbs, tense markers, helping verbs, modals, and negation

    d. Understanding and using a variety of sentence constructions such as declaratives, imperatives, negations, interrogatives, embedded sentences, and conjoined sentences

    e. Understanding and using connected sentences in oral and written discourse

6. The child *follows rules of conversation* by

    a. Following conventions for initiating conversation and taking turns

    b. Following conventions for shifting topics in conversation

    c. Following conventions for ending conversation

    d. Following conventions of politeness and register

Although there is great heterogeneity among children with ASD at the Conversational Partner stage with respect to ability to understand and use generative language, there are a number of common challenges in symbol use that affect the ability to achieve communicative competence across a range of social partners and contexts. Consideration of these challenges is critical, as these limitations often compromise a child's ability to 1) develop more sophisticated learning strategies that allow for consideration of different perspectives when problem solving, self-monitoring, and negotiating; 2) understand and use nonverbal cues and nonliteral meanings that provide insight into a partner's emotional state and intentions; 3) participate conventionally in dramatic play and recreation by co-constructing play schemes in collaboration with peers and following the rules of more organized activities; 4) recognize the need to *use* more sophisticated grammatical and syntactic forms to provide information needed by a partner, 5) follow the rules of conversational discourse, and 6) understand the rules of different social contexts.

For a child with ASD, these challenges in symbol use clearly result from a number of developmental, cognitive, and social factors, including the cumulative impact of the decreased opportunities for social problem solving that result from a limited social network. As noted previously, a history of communicative breakdowns and ineffective social exchanges with both adults and peers often results in a child having a limited range of partners with whom to practice social-communicative skills and therefore acquire the rules of social conversational discourse. In addition, the presence of distinct learning style differences may compromise a child's ability to derive meaning from nonverbal social cues and situational cues, a pattern that limits an awareness of a partner's focus of attention, emotional state, and underlying intentions. As a result of these social and cognitive factors, a child with ASD may struggle on a daily basis to adapt strategies for initiating, maintaining, and terminating conversations depending on the social context (e.g., a friendly conversation during recess, a formal presentation to the class at school) and the status of the partner (e.g., a younger sibling, a teacher).

Children with ASD typically adhere to more specific and unchanging set of rules of social discourse that are applied faithfully and inflexibly regardless of a partner or context. This extreme literalness or social inflexibility compromises a child's competence at the Conversational Partner stage, as social-communicative success at this level is built on flexibility and sensitivity to changing requirements across partners and social contexts. Therefore, systematically addressing goals in Symbol Use is a critical priority when developing a comprehensive program or modifying an existing program for a child with ASD.

PRIORITIZING GOALS FOR MUTUAL REGULATION AT THE CONVERSATIONAL PARTNER STAGE

A number of critical milestones in Mutual Regulation support a child's growth at the Conversational Partner stage. These milestones support the child's expansion of effective, efficient, and socially appropriate regulation strategies that, in turn, culminate in a greater ability to achieve successful communicative exchanges with a range of partners, both adults and peers, across contexts. As the child progresses at the Conversational Partner stage, the development of more sophisticated *initiated mutual regulatory strategies* typically coincides with emergence of more explicit and precise language and nonverbal communicative strategies. With the use of more readable facial expressions, gestures, and symbolic language to express a range of emotions and request assistance from partners, the child is more able to initiate mutual regulation with greater efficiency. In addition, a child at the Conversational Partner stage is developing a greater awareness of the need for emotional regulatory assistance, based on the child's increased awareness and comprehension of his or her emotional and arousal states and of environmental factors contributing to dysregulation. Finally, a child's understanding of the rules of social appropriateness in different contexts and ability to respond to feedback and guidance provided by partners, referred to earlier as *instructed learning* and *collaborative learning,* enable the child to self-monitor emotional responses to different situations and communicate for assistance in a socially appropriate or conventional manner. In seeking mutual regulation, the child's requests may be aimed at securing behavioral, language-based, or metacognitive (i.e., cognitive/problem solving) assistance.

To understand the process of mutual regulation at the Conversational Partner stage, it continues to be important to discern the predominant patterns observed for a child. Is regulation achieved primarily because partners respond to the child's signals of dysregulation (i.e., *respondent mutual regulation*), or is the child able to initiate and intentionally direct signals to others to request support (i.e., *initiated mutual regulation*)? As the child progresses through the Conversational Partner stage, accomplishments in joint attention and symbol use clearly support an increased ability to employ conventional and more sophisticated initiated mutual regulatory strategies to regulate emotions; however, the process of respondent mutual regulation also remains important to consider. This is particularly true in those instances where a child's social-communicative abilities vary as a result of fluctuations in arousal state. For instance, at the Conversational Partner stage a child experiencing extreme dysregulation may not be able to efficiently direct a request for assistance to a partner but may benefit from partner initiated support. Thus, respondent mutual regulation, which relates to a partner's ability to both recognize signs of dysregulation and offer support, remains quite relevant at this stage.

Critical goal areas in Mutual Regulation are prioritized based on a team's knowledge of 1) how typically developing children acquire abilities in mutual regulation and 2) current research on the mutual regulatory challenges faced by children with ASD. These priority goals include the ability to 1) express a range of emotions, 2) respond to assistance offered by partners, 3) respond to feedback and guidance regarding behavior, 4) request partners' assistance to regulate state, and 5) recover from extreme dysregulation with support from partners. Specific milestones along this developmental trajectory provide benchmarks that guide the determination of weekly objectives for a child at this stage. These include the following:

1. The child *expresses a range of emotions* by
   a. Understanding and using early emotion words
   b. Understanding and using advanced emotion words
   c. Understanding and using graded emotions
   d. Changing emotional expression based on partner feedback
   e. Using nonverbal cues of emotional expression

2. The child *responds to assistance offered by partners* by
   a. Soothing when comforted by partners
   b. Engaging when alerted by partners
   c. Responding to bids for interaction
   d. Responding to changes in partners' expression of emotion
   e. Attuning to changes in partners' expression of emotion
   f. Responding to information or strategies offered by partners

3. The child *responds to feedback and guidance regarding behavior* by
    a. Responding to feedback regarding the appropriateness of emotional display
    b. Responding to feedback regarding the appropriateness of regulatory strategies
    c. Using behaviors modeled by partners to guide behavior
    d. Collaborating and negotiating with peers in problem solving
    e. Accepting ideas from partners during negotiation to reach compromise
4. The child *requests partners' assistance to regulate state* by
    a. Sharing negative emotion to seek comfort
    b. Sharing positive emotion to seek interaction
    c. Sharing intentions to regulate the behavior of others, such as by requesting desired objects and activities, requesting help, requesting a break, and protesting/refusing undesired activities
    d. Sharing intentions for social interaction, such as by greeting, calling, requesting comfort, regulating turns, requesting permission, praising partners, expressing empathy, and sharing secrets
    e. Sharing intentions for joint attention, such as by commenting on immediate, past, and imagined events; providing requested information about immediate and past events; requesting information about immediate, past, and future events; expressing feelings and opinions; and anticipating and planning outcomes
    f. Requesting assistance to resolve conflicts and problem-solve situations
5. The child *recovers from extreme dysregulation with support from partners* by
    a. Responding to partners' efforts to assist with recovery by moving away from activity
    b. Responding to partners' use of behavioral strategies
    c. Responding to partners' use of language strategies
    d. Responding to partners' attempts to reengage in interaction or activity
    e. Decreasing amount of time to recover from extreme dysregulation due to support from partners
    f. Decreasing intensity of dysregulated state due to support from partners

A child with ASD at the Conversational Partner stage typically exhibits difficulties in Mutual Regulation. These challenges are due, in part, to ongoing limitations in social communication, as evidenced by 1) a restricted range of nonverbal forms of emotional expression, 2) a restricted range of emotional vocabulary, 3) difficulty understanding and using graded emotions, and 4) difficulties sharing intentions for the purpose of securing regulatory assistance. Difficulties in mutual regulation are also due, in part, to the presence of variable arousal states, as evidenced by difficulties with maintaining a state of arousal that matches the social requirements of a given context.

The combination of these factors precludes the use of more sophisticated learning strategies such as instructed learning and collaborative learning, as these strategies require a child to remain engaged and attend to a partner's provision of direct guidance and feedback regarding behavior. In turn, a child's ability to acquire the rules of conversational discourse and more socially conventional strategies for emotional regulation is often compromised, particularly with respect to graded emotions. Therefore, a child with ASD at the Conversational Partner stage often lacks both range and refinement of expression and may exhibit no or only very subtle reactions or very extreme reactions when displaying emotions. At this stage, the impact of these social-communicative challenges is particularly evident when the child is learning emotional concepts that rely heavily on social norms or conventions (e.g., guilt, embarrassment, pride, jealousy). Because a child learns to map emotion words and concepts on internal states and experiences through interactions with others, difficulty understanding and interpreting social interactions translates into difficulties comprehending and using emotional concepts that reflect complex interpersonal experiences.

Immature patterns of behavior, such as chewing on clothing, having tantrums, and fleeing from the social setting are often observed, even at the Conversational Partner stage, particularly during extreme periods of dysregulation. This is due, in part, to the fact that a repertoire of conventional means to express emotions has not yet been established. A reliance on unconventional behaviors clearly has a transactional influence on a child's partners. These behaviors, although starting points for attempts at regulation, may not result in appropriate and supportive assistance from partners, as they may be perceived as problem behaviors rather than as signs of dysregulation. In these unfortunate circumstances, the child's attempts at securing assistance from others, or signals that should be read as indicating the need for assistance, may lead to further isolation and/or emotional distress, as a partner's reaction, such as punishing or ignoring the behaviors, may not address the child's need for support.

Furthermore, a partner's problems with accurately interpreting a child's emotional expression and signs of dysregulation are further compounded by arousal bias, as a child with a hyporeactive bias often sends remarkably different signals than a child with a hyperreactive bias. Accurate assessment of these factors is essential to the design and implementation of mutual regulatory strategies that facilitate a child's organization and maintenance of a well-regulated state. For example, a partner may need to recognize the benefit of increasing the use of language strategies to help a child who is hyperreactive to achieve a more regulated state (e.g., providing a within-task schedule to help the child prepare for a potentially overwhelming activity). In contrast, for a child with a hyporeactive bias, a partner may need to recognize the benefit of increasing the use of opportunities for movement and interaction during a sedentary, less preferred activity (e.g., having the child distribute materials to his classmates before a spelling test). If these factors of arousal state and arousal bias are not considered, a child may not receive the appropriate support to address his or her unique needs.

PRIORITIZING GOALS FOR SELF-REGULATION AT THE CONVERSATIONAL PARTNER STAGE

A number of critical milestones in Self-Regulation contribute to a child's growth at the Conversational Partner stage. These milestones support the child's expansion of effective, efficient, and socially appropriate emotional regulatory strategies that, in turn, support a greater ability to achieve successful communicative exchanges with a range of adults and peer partners across contexts. A child at the novice level of the Conversational Partner stage is likely to continue to use a variety of *behavioral strategies* and early *language strategies* as a means to self-regulate. The behavioral strategies employed by a child at this stage may either be biologically driven (e.g., bolting from a noisy activity) or fostered by responsive partners (e.g., stomping one's feet when mad). Language strategies typically exhibited at this stage include the use of words (i.e., saying, "I can do this") or other symbols (e.g., signs, pictures, the written word) that the child has learned to use for the purpose of self-regulation through various learning strategies, including imitation, instructed learning, and collaborative learning. For example, a child who is anxious about transitions may prepare for an impending change in activity by using self-talk, such as by saying, "First I finish math, then I eat lunch."

At the advanced level of the Conversational Partner stage, a child may begin to develop *metacognitive strategies* for the purpose of self-regulation. Metacognitive strategies consist of strategies that reflect a child's awareness of his or her abilities in relation to the demands of an activity, knowledge of which regulatory strategies to employ, and the ability to use this information to successfully engage in an activity. For example, a child who is faced with a challenging activity might reflect on his or her abilities and range of self-regulation strategies and subsequently may formulate a plan for completing the activity.

The collective use of behavioral strategies, language strategies, and metacognitive strategies contributes to a child's attainment of a well-regulated state and therefore supports the child's ability to interact, explore, and engage in social interaction across contexts and partners. The child's state of emotional regulation and arousal and the demands of the social environment contribute to the specific strategies or combinations of strategies that the child employs in any specific situation. Hallmarks of these expanding self-regulatory abilities at the Conversational Partner stage include the child's increasing ability to use emotional memories to assist with emotional regulation, the ability to plan and prepare for experiences and interactions, the ability to monitor the social environment to inform emotional reactions in a situation, and the ability to use language to negotiate with a partner or partners.

A team's knowledge of typical emotional self-regulatory development and current research related to the self-regulatory challenges faced by children with ASD at the Conversational Partner stage contribute to the team's ability to prioritize critical goal areas in Self-Regulation. These priority goals include the ability to 1) demonstrate availability for learning and interacting; use 2) behavioral strategies, 3) language strategies, and 4) metacognitive strategies to regulate arousal level during familiar activities; 5) regulate emotion during new and changing situations; and 6) recover from extreme dysregulation by oneself. Specific milestones along this developmental trajectory provide benchmarks that guide the determination of weekly objectives for a child at this stage. These include the following:

1. The child *demonstrates availability for learning and interacting* by

    a. Responding to sensory and social experiences with differentiated emotions

    b. Monitoring the attentional focus of a social partner

    c. Showing reciprocity in speaker and listener roles to share experiences

    d. Demonstrating ability to inhibit actions and behaviors

    e. Persisting during tasks with reasonable demands

    f. Demonstrating emotional expression appropriate to the context

2. The child *uses behavioral strategies to regulate arousal level during familiar activities* by

    a. Using behavioral strategies to regulate arousal level in solitary and social activities

b. Using behavioral strategies modeled by partners to regulate arousal level

c. Using behavioral strategies to engage productively in an extended activity

3. The child *uses language strategies to regulate arousal level during familiar activities* by

    a. Understanding and using early emotion words

    b. Understanding and using advanced emotion words

    c. Understanding and using graded emotions

    d. Using language strategies to regulate arousal level during solitary and social activities

    e. Using language strategies modeled by partners to regulate arousal level

    f. Using language strategies to engage productively in an extended activity

4. The child *uses metacognitive strategies to regulate arousal level during familiar activities* by

    a. Using internalized rules modeled by adult instruction to guide behavior

    b. Using metacognitive strategies to plan and complete activities

    c. Using self-monitoring and self-talk to guide behavior

    d. Using emotional memory to assist with emotional regulation

    e. Identifying and reflecting on strategies to support regulation

5. The child *regulates emotion during new and changing situations* by

    a. Using behavioral strategies to regulate arousal level during new and changing situations

    b. Using language strategies to regulate arousal level in new and changing situations

    c. Using metacognitive strategies to regulate arousal level in new and changing situations

    d. Using behavioral strategies to regulate arousal level during transitions

    e. Using language strategies to regulate arousal level during transitions

    f. Using metacognitive strategies to regulate arousal level during transitions

6. The child *recovers from extreme dysregulation by him- or herself* by

    a. Removing him- or herself from overstimulating or undesired activity

    b. Using behavioral strategies to recover from extreme dysregulation

    c. Using language strategies to recover from extreme dysregulation

    d. Reengaging in interaction or activity after recovery from extreme dysregulation

    e. Decreasing amount of time needed to recover from extreme dysregulation

    f. Decreasing intensity of dysregulated state

As discussed in Chapter 3 in Volume I, a child with ASD at the Conversational Partner stage often has difficulty achieving these self-regulation milestones and may, as a result, display strong and sudden emotional reactions or may be otherwise unavailable for learning and social engagement in everyday activities. These challenges are further evidenced by difficulties attending to relevant information in a social setting, delaying gratification, and controlling impulses. At this stage, factors contributing to these difficulties often include 1) atypical responses to stimulation resulting in a bias for either a high state of arousal or a low state of arousal; 2) limited self-perception of physiological changes in arousal state; 3) a restricted range of nonverbal and language-based strategies for emotional expression; 4) limited ability to use instructed and collaborative learning strategies to acquire socially conventional communication and regulatory strategies; and 5) difficulties with cognitive appraisal, which is the ability to self-reflect, make judgments about one's abilities, and predict one's own behavior or reactions through the use of metacognitive skills.

As discussed, social-communicative challenges at the Conversational Partner stage often compromise a child's development of self-regulatory abilities. In particular, challenges in joint attention affect a child's ability to respond to social feedback regarding the acceptability of his or her behavior and emotional expression, as well as the ability to employ emotional regulatory strategies that have been modeled by others. In turn, at the Conversational Partner stage, a child with ASD may continue to display extreme emotional reactions and may use self-regulatory strategies that appear to be idiosyncratic; unconventional; and, in some cases, socially stigmatizing (e.g., rocking intensively, flapping hands, walking on toes), especially when viewed in the context of more advanced language and academic skills. As discussed in Chapter 5 of this volume, these idiosyncratic self-regulatory behaviors may inadvertently be viewed as problem behaviors by a child's partners and may be targeted for elimination in some educational approaches. It is important to consider, however, that these behaviors may be a direct consequence of a child's limited repertoire of socially appropriate and effective self-regulatory strategies, as well as limited abilities in social communication. In the SCERTS Model, the emotional regulatory functions of such behavioral patterns are considered when determining appropriate goals in Self-Regulation.

A child's development of language strategies and metacognitive strategies to assist with emotional regulation is strongly influenced by joint attention and symbol use. A child not only needs to orient and observe partners in the social environment but also needs to be able to understand and use the language and metacognitive strategies that are being modeled. Therefore, challenges in social communication undermine the development of inner language, a necessary achievement for a child at this stage. Inner language allows a child to represent events in memory and to problem-solve through inner symbolic means. This ability serves to organize social experience and behaviors, allowing the child to use metacognitive strategies to think about and learn from past social events and therefore plan for future social events (i.e., plan for and adapt to new experiences based on previous experiences). This ability, coupled with instructed learning and collaborative learning, allows a child to consider multiple perspectives when anticipating and preparing for dysregulating events. With a limited ability to use inner language, reflecting on and learning from past events and experiences in a manner that supports active engagement and emotional regulation can be quite compromised.

PRIORITIZING GOALS FOR INTERPERSONAL SUPPORT AT THE CONVERSATIONAL PARTNER STAGE

It is critical to emphasize, once again, the overriding influence of the behaviors of partners on a child's development and success in interpersonal interaction at the Conversational Partner stage. Achievements in the developmental capacities of social communication and emotional regulation at the Conversational Partner stage are dependent on a successful history of predictable and supportive interactions with partners who have fostered social engagement, communicative initiation, and maintenance of a well-regulated state. Interpersonal accommodations (referred to as *interpersonal supports* in the SCERTS Model) are considered to be critical when prioritizing partner goals in the domain of Transactional Support.

The following dimensions of the Interpersonal Support component of Transactional Support are viewed as essential for supporting a child's ability to engage as a competent Conversational Partner. The partner 1) is responsive to the child, 2) fosters initiation, 3) respects the child's independence, 4) sets the stage for engagement, 5) provides developmental support, 6) adjusts language input, and 7) models appropriate behaviors. At the Conversational Partner stage, specific objectives in these dimensions provide benchmarks that guide the development of individualized interpersonal supports and the identification of weekly objectives not only for the child but also for the child's partners. These include the following:

1. The *partner is responsive to the child* by
   a. Following the child's focus of attention
   b. Responding to the child's emotion and pace
   c. Responding appropriately to the child's signals to foster a sense of competence
   d. Recognizing and supporting the child's behavioral, language, and metacognitive strategies to regulate arousal
   e. Recognizing signs of dysregulation and offering support
   f. Providing information and assistance to regulate state
   g. Offering breaks from interaction or activity as needed
   h. Facilitating reengagement in interactions and activities following breaks

2. The *partner fosters initiation* by
   a. Offering choices nonverbally or verbally
   b. Waiting for and encouraging initiations
   c. Providing a balance of initiated and respondent turns
   d. Allowing the child to initiate and terminate activities

3. The partner *respects the child's independence* by
   a. Allowing the child to take breaks to move about as needed
   b. Providing time for the child to solve problems or complete activities at his or her own pace
   c. Interpreting problem behavior as communicative and/or regulatory
   d. Honoring protests, rejections, or refusals when appropriate

4. The *partner sets stage for engagement* by
   a. Securing the child's attention before communicating
   b. Using appropriate proximity and nonverbal behavior to encourage interaction
   c. Using appropriate words and intonation to support optimal arousal level and engagement
   d. Sharing emotions, internal states, and mental plans with the child

5. The *partner provides developmental support* by
   a. Providing guidance for success in interaction with peers

b. Attempting to repair breakdowns verbally or nonverbally

  c. Providing guidance and feedback as needed for success in activities

  d. Providing guidance on expressing emotions and understanding the cause of emotions

  e. Providing guidance for interpreting others' feelings and opinions

6. The *partner adjusts language input* by

  a. Using nonverbal cues to support understanding

  b. Adjusting complexity of language input to the child's developmental level

  c. Adjusting quality of language input to the child's arousal level

7. The *partner models appropriate behaviors* by

  a. Modeling appropriate nonverbal communication and emotional expressions

  b. Modeling a range of communicative functions, including behavior regulation, social interaction, and joint attention

  c. Modeling appropriate dramatic play and recreation

  d. Modeling appropriate behavior when the child uses inappropriate behavior

  e. Modeling "child-perspective" language and the use of self-talk

Social interactions are transactional in nature; therefore, a child's communicative partners must respond flexibly and in a supportive manner to foster the child's development of communicative and regulatory abilities. As described in Chapter 4 of Volume I, some children with ASD at the Conversational Partner stage may be at risk for developing a sense of interpersonal interaction as overwhelming, confusing, and stressful based on a history of repeated unsuccessful experiences. Other children with ASD are at risk for limited engagement and low motivation to participate in social interactions secondary to language and sensory processing difficulties and/or a hyporesponsive bias toward interpersonal events. Equally important to consider is the notion that a child's partners are also at risk for experiencing interactions with the child as challenging, especially in reference to supporting the child's reciprocal engagement and the child's attainment of a well-regulated state. This may lead the child's peers to either inadvertently withdraw or react in a socially aggressive manner, such as with teasing or bullying.

At the Conversational Partner stage, a child's developmental vulnerabilities and learning style differences often have a transactional influence on his or her partners. For example, although a child at the Conversational Partner stage may have relatively strong expressive and receptive language abilities, he or she may have difficulty in using these skills in complex environments that demand rapid shifting of attention and selective focus on verbal information. This vulnerability may result in the child's avoidance of typical childhood activities (e.g., playground games such as Four Square or Kick the Can) that are dependent on an ability to engage with others in busy environments with intense and complex stimulation. Persistent challenges with higher level language abilities, such as comprehension of nonliteral forms of language (e.g., idioms, metaphors, cynicism, sarcasm) that require integration of linguistic information, situational cues, and nonverbal social cues, may also affect a child's motivation to engage with others when the child perceives such activities as stressful or confusing. Consequently, both adults and peers may view a child with ASD at the Conversational Partner stage as aloof, unavailable, and/or difficult to engage.

Similarly, difficulties comprehending these higher level language forms and/or processing language in complex environments may evoke anxiety in a child with ASD at the Conversational Partner stage, a pattern that can contribute to a partner's perception of the child as problematic or noncompliant. In some cases, this problematic behavior does not manifest itself as disengagement; rather, it takes the form of repeated attempts to control factors that are potentially dysregulating, such as engaging others in a topic of conversation revolving around an area of special interest; maintaining a specific visual-spatial order, such as keeping all cabinet doors closed; or needing to stay in the exact same position in line at school. Such patterns, often labeled as "obsessive-compulsive," may be attempts to create order and maintain some degree of control in otherwise confusing and overwhelming situations, with little regard for partners' preferences. This may contribute to partners' perception of a child as inflexible, odd, or obsessed with strange interests, leading to additional challenges establishing and maintaining friendships.

In addition to being affected by these language-based challenges, interactions with a child at the Conversational Partner stage can be compromised by the child's difficulties in understanding emotional cues, gestures, and facial expressions. These developmental vulnerabilities often result in a lack of response or inconsistent and inappropriate responses to partners' nonverbal and emotional communication. In some situations, a child may shut down or tune out in the face of this difficult-to-process information, such as complex verbal information, nonverbal social cues, and emotional expressions, resulting in the child's being unavailable for interaction due to extreme dysregulation. In addition, the child's peers and/or siblings may develop a sense of frustration during interactions, as the child with ASD might miss or misread their emotional signals.

Last, a child's sensory processing difficulties (e.g., patterns of hypo- or hyperreactivity) may result in inconsistent reactions to sensory input and inconsistent states of arousal, a challenging pattern for the child's partners to read and respond to successfully. Because these dimensions of interpersonal interactions contribute to a child's ability to experience successful communicative exchanges with a range of partners across contexts, a critical priority at the Conversational Partner stage is to systematically address goals for partner behavior with respect to interactive style when developing a comprehensive program or modifying an existing program for a child with ASD.

A partner's implementation of interpersonal support fosters a child's attainment of critical Conversational Partner milestones, including 1) the child's ability to understand nonverbal cues signaling shifts in attentional focus, 2) the child's ability to initiate conversations as they relate to a partner's interests, and 3) the child's development of effective and efficient regulation strategies.

PRIORITIZING GOALS FOR LEARNING SUPPORT AT THE CONVERSATIONAL PARTNER STAGE

Achievements in social communication and emotional regulation are facilitated, in part, by the effective use of learning supports. As noted in previous chapters, learning supports are accommodations that include a range of environmental modifications, visual supports, and other relevant learning strategies used by partners with a child. These supports may be used to facilitate a child's communication and expressive language, understanding of language and social expectations (e.g., the sequence of steps and end goal of an activity), emotional expression, and emotional regulation. It is critical that the child's partners use such accommodations to modify activities and learning environments in a manner that supports organization, provides opportunities for active learning, and promotes child initiation. Learning supports in the SCERTS Model are considered critical when prioritizing partner goals in the domain of Transactional Support.

The following dimensions of the Learning Support component of Transactional Support are essential for supporting a child's ability to engage as a competent Conversational Partner. The partner 1) structures an activity for active participation; 2) uses augmentative communication support to foster development; 3) uses visual and organizational support; and 4) modifies goals, activities, and the learning environment to suit the child's specific developmental level and learning style differences. Specific objectives in these dimensions provide benchmarks that guide the development of individualized learning supports and the identification of weekly objectives not just for the child but also for that child's partners. These include the following:

1. The *partner structures an activity for active participation* by
    a. Defining clear beginnings and endings to an activity
    b. Creating turn-taking opportunities and leaving spaces for the child to fill in
    c. Providing a predictable sequence to an activity
    d. Offering repeated learning opportunities
    e. Offering varied learning opportunities

2. The *partner uses augmentative communication support to foster development* by
    a. Using augmentative communication support to enhance the child's communication and expressive language
    b. Using augmentative communication support to enhance the child's understanding of language and behavior
    c. Using augmentative communication support to enhance the child's expression and understanding of emotion
    d. Using augmentative communication support to enhance the child's emotional regulation

3. The *partner uses visual and organizational support* by
    a. Using support to define steps within a task
    b. Using support to define steps and time for completion of activities
    c. Using visual support to enhance smooth transitions between activities
    d. Using support to organize segments of time across the day
    e. Using visual support to enhance attention in group activities
    f. Using visual support to foster active involvement in group activities

4. The *partner modifies goals, activities, and the learning environment* by
    a. Adjusting social complexity to support organization and interaction
    b. Adjusting task difficulty for child success

c. Modifying sensory properties of the learning environment

d. Arranging the learning environment to enhance attention

e. Arranging the learning environment to promote child initiation

f. Designing and modifying activities to be developmentally appropriate

g. Infusing motivating materials and topics in activities

h. Providing activities to promote initiations and extended interactions

i. Alternating between movement and sedentary activities as needed

j. "Upping the ante" or increasing expectations appropriately

As discussed, children with ASD at the Conversational Partner stage demonstrate unique patterns of learning preferences and weaknesses, which support the need for the implementation of learning supports to foster both social communication and emotional regulation. A greater understanding of the learning and cognitive styles of children with ASD has, in fact, led to the development of a wide range of useful visual, organizational, and learning supports. A number of these supports fall under the umbrella term of *AAC*. Although there are clear individual variations among children with ASD at this stage of development, particularly with respect to verbal versus visual learning styles, several well-documented patterns of learning contribute to the effective application of these supports. As discussed, children with ASD, regardless of whether they prefer verbal or visual information, seem to more effectively process and use information that remains static or fixed in place over time (e.g., objects, pictures, written words). The SCERTS Model emphasizes the role of partners in capitalizing on a child's preference for static information as a means to help the child compensate for difficulties processing information that is more transient or fleeting in nature, such as the spoken word or nonverbal social cues. In the SCERTS Model, partners are encouraged to use static and clear visual and organizational supports to define steps within a task, to define time for completion of activities, and to support smooth transitions between activities. Likewise, partners of a child with ASD at the Conversational Partner stage are encouraged to implement augmentative communication supports designed to match a child's unique preferences (e.g., gestures, signs, pictures, the written word) to foster a child's ability to recall words and to formulate and express thoughts in a conventional manner, particularly when that child is experiencing extreme dysregulation.

In addition, children at the Conversational Partner stage may have difficulty maintaining active engagement in social interactions and activities due to difficulties processing higher level or nonliteral language. Such language is typical of everyday conversation with adults and peers and discourse used by teachers in classroom settings. The complexity of such language may exacerbate difficulties with emotional regulation, particularly across transitions and new and changing situations. Thus, the SCERTS Model encourages a child's partners to develop an understanding of these challenges and encourages the partners' incorporation of learning supports to clearly mark beginnings and ends to activities, to provide predictable learning opportunities, and to offer both repeated and varied learning opportunities. Learning supports designed to modify activities and learning environments also are considered critical to the facilitation of a child's ability to learn and play with peers, as this is a critical emphasis in this stage (see Chapter 2 in this volume for a discussion of peer goals and activities used in learning and playing with peers, or LAPP). Therefore, consideration is given to how the social complexity, physical properties, and sensory characteristics of a given activity can be modified to create an environment that promotes active engagement for the child and his or her social network of peers.

Because these learning supports contribute to a child's ability to remain actively engaged in natural routines, and to develop those capacities essential to be a competent Conversational Partner, the SCERTS Model prioritizes systematic goals for partner behavior. These goals are designed to enhance environmental and activity modifications, the implementation of visual supports, the implementation of augmentative communication support to enhance communicative development, and the use of predictable and repetitive learning opportunities when developing a comprehensive program or modifying an existing program for a child with ASD at the Conversational Partner stage.

SPOTLIGHTS ON CHILDREN AT THE CONVERSATIONAL PARTNER STAGE

In the following sections, two children and families are spotlighted to illustrate the process of identifying and prioritizing goals for a child at the novice Conversational Partner stage and a child at the advanced Conversational Partner stage. The term *spotlight* is used because each of these vignettes is reflective of a child and family at a specific intersection on their developmental journey. The SCERTS Model recognizes the dynamic processes involved in ongoing assessment and program planning. Following the criteria for goal selection, ongoing assessment will be needed to identify goals that are 1) functional, 2) family priorities, and 3) developmentally appropriate. It is expected that initial goals will need to be modified as a child's program evolves.

A number of other decisions should be reassessed regularly (i.e., every 3 months) to determine any necessary program adjustments and modifications. These include 1) the choice of meaningful and purposeful activities to focus on in a child's daily routines; 2) the intensity of social support, such as the ratio of adult to child support in social groupings; and 3) the range of naturalness of activities (e.g., planned activity routines, engineered activities, modified natural activities). These spotlights are provided to illustrate the processes involved in implementing the SCERTS Model from assessment to practical implementation of a program addressing social communication, emotional regulation, and transactional support for children with ASD at the Conversational Partner stage. (Chapters 5 and 6 in this volume present spotlights on children at the Social Partner and Language Partner stages, respectively.) Blank versions of the assessment forms mentioned in the spotlights can be found in Appendix A of Volume I.

SPOTLIGHT ON KANEESHA, A NOVICE CONVERSATIONAL PARTNER

Kaneesha is at the novice level of the Conversational Partner stage. She is a charming and endearing 6-year-old girl with ASD who lives at home with her mother; father; and two sisters, Briana (9 years old) and Shanise (4 years old). She attends an inclusive first-grade classroom at the local public school and rides the bus each day with her older sister, Briana. She recently has developed stronger relationships with her sisters, who can now entice her to join their play, particularly when they are engaged in Kaneesha's preferred activities such as dancing along to favorite music CDs and riding bikes in the backyard. Kaneesha also enjoys helping her mother and father in the kitchen as they prepare family meals. In these situations, in fact, Kaneesha can be very persistent and opinionated. She makes specific requests about what should be included in a meal and expresses her distaste if something is not available.

In the past year, Kaneesha's ability to communicate with more precise and explicit language has begun to emerge, and her sentence length has increased from word combinations to simple sentences. She communicates through a wide range of gestures, a broad single-word vocabulary that includes functional words such as "more," "all done," "open," and "help," and a number of delayed echolalic phrases (e.g., "I want tickles, please"; "No thank you, I'm all done"). Recently, she has also been using more creative sentences to request social interaction with her family. These have included simple sentences such as "Shanise ride bikes, please," and "Briana play computer, please," as well as more complex sentences such as "Mommy, put the pizza in the oven," and "Where did Daddy go?"

Although she can be quite animated with familiar partners and routines, Kaneesha tends to disengage easily and is unavailable much of the time. This has been a persistent challenge in her first-grade class, which has 19 other children. When left alone in the classroom, Kaneesha is content to sing quietly, look out the window, and/or suck her thumb and rarely initiates interactions with others. Her teachers, in fact, feel that Kaneesha requires consistent one-to-one adult support to participate in large-group activities such as circle time and small-group activities such as playing a board game with classmates. This is particularly critical when there is a change in the routine and/or a preferred activity is not available during choice time or recess, as Kaneesha is occasionally prone to extreme dysregulation and can be difficult to console. In these instances, she often cries, sucks her thumb, and requires a lengthy period of time to recover before returning to classroom activities. Her use of emotion words to share her emotional state in these instances remains quite limited. In addition, her teachers remain concerned about her ability to maintain a conversation, as she often tunes out or only partially attends to the questions or comments directed to her. For example, she may repeat only the last word of a question rather than provide a relevant response. This is particularly noticeable when the topic is somewhat removed from the current activity, such as recalling what she has played during recess earlier in the day. Therefore, Kaneesha's conversations tend to remain limited to comments about the here and now, such as commenting about an art project, her snack, or a story being read during circle time.

Kaneesha's previous 3 years of educational programming through her public school district consisted of attending full-day self-contained classroom programs with five to seven other children with special needs. There also were opportunities for inclusion with typically developing children in the afternoons. In these programs, her family and educational team members had watched Kaneesha's social-communicative and emotional regulatory skills mature and now believe that that Kaneesha has clearly developed a stronger preference to engage with her peers as opposed to being on her own. This led to a greater ability for Kaneesha to monitor and recognize what her classmates are doing during recess, as she is beginning to show greater motivation to join their activities. Thus, as she made the transition to her inclusive first-grade classroom 3 months ago, a variety of learning accommodations and supports were designed to capitalize on her emerging social interest.

Because there are 19 other children in her classroom, including 3 other children with special needs, an inclusion specialist is in the classroom full time to support those students who have IEPs. The inclusion specialist coordinates her efforts with the general education teacher and provides supervision to the two full-time instructional assistants who support Kaneesha and her classmates throughout the day. In addition to her first-grade program, Kaneesha participates in daily one-to-one and small-group special education tutoring sessions in the Learning Center, speech-language therapy, occupational therapy, adapted physical education (APE), and friendship groups. In addition, given Kaneesha's special interest in art and drawing, her inclusion specialist has arranged for her to participate in an individual art project at the start of each school day, an accommodation that fosters Kaneesha's engagement and attention while she is making the transition from the bus to her first-grade classroom.

Although her family and educational team feel Kaneesha is benefiting from her first-grade setting, her educational team felt the need to address ongoing concerns regarding Kaneesha's tendency to disengage throughout the day. Therefore, the SAP was initiated to address these concerns. In addition to prioritizing objectives in both social communication and emotional regulation, the team was interested in ensuring that appropriate interpersonal supports and learning supports were identified and implemented to foster Kaneesha's active engagement throughout her school day and at home.

Thus, this spotlight illustrates the steps that Kaneesha's educational team and her family took in undertaking the SAP. The SAP was implemented to 1) establish Kaneesha's current profile of developmental strengths and needs; 2) determine meaningful, purposeful, and motivating goals to address; 3) select the most appropriate learning contexts and complexity of social support based on Kaneesha's natural routines and activities; and 4) determine the essential transactional supports to foster Kaneesha's development and her relationships with her family, peers, and teaching staff.

Because a comprehensive SCERTS Model program also includes explicit plans for support to families and support among professionals, information from the SAP also was used to ensure that Kaneesha's educational program was compatible and consistent with the needs expressed by her family. In addition, the assessment team determined the specific educational supports and emotional supports that would be provided for Kaneesha's family and the service providers who would be involved in the implementation of Kaneesha's program.

SAP Step 1: Determining Kaneesha's Communication Stage

During an initial team meeting, Kaneesha's inclusion specialist, a certified special education teacher, led a discussion of Kaneesha's behavior in her home and school environments. Her educational team determined that the appropriate SAP forms to use for the assessment would be those designated for the Conversational Partner stage. This was based on the completion of the Worksheet for Determining Communication Stage and the criteria for determining a child's communication stage in the SAP, as Kaneesha currently uses more than 100 words referentially and more than 20 spontaneous, creative phrases and sentences to communicate her intent. Unlike a child at the Language Partner stage, Kaneesha's use of language and emotional regulatory skills had been observed across home and school settings and across a range of partners. Although Kaneesha's ability to use word combinations was viewed as a relative strength, her team recognized that on some occasions, she did rely on either immediate echolalia, the immediate repetition of speech directed to her, or delayed echolalia, the delayed repetition of phrases that she heard in previous contexts. Echolalic patterns were particularly apparent when Kaneesha was in a low state of arousal and needed more processing time to understand a direction, when she was tuning out but still understood that she needed to respond, or when she was distressed. Thus, the educational team agreed that it would be important to observe Kaneesha's use of language across contexts and arousal states.

SAP Step 2: Gathering Information with the Conversational Partner SAP-R Form

Kaneesha's parents were asked to complete the SAP-R Form to provide additional information regarding Kaneesha's behavior in her home and community environments. This questionnaire identified 1) the primary concerns and stresses faced by Kaneesha's family, 2) Kaneesha's primary strengths and the families concerns about her development, 3) the activities in which both Kaneesha's strengths and areas of need would likely be seen in her home and community environments, 4) Kaneesha's typical partners in the home and community, and 5) the natural contexts in Kaneesha's life outside of school. Kaneesha's educational team also completed a separate SAP-R Form to identify similarities and discrepancies with respect to Kaneesha's behavior at school versus her behavior in other natural environments. The information gathered from both of Kaneesha's SAP-R Forms is summarized next:

1. The primary concerns and stresses faced by Kaneesha's family and educational team members included

   - "The amount of time and energy required to help Kaneesha participate in social activities"
   - "Her continued reliance on scripted phrases over more creative language"
   - "Her tendency to tune out or disengage throughout her day"
   - "Her limited use of language to communicate about past and future events"
   - "Her ongoing difficulties responding to language in the classroom"

2. Kaneesha's parents and educational team identified the following strengths and needs in her current profile:

Strengths	Needs
"Kaneesha is interested in a range of activities and contexts—dancing, riding bikes, drawing, and playing on the computer."	"Kaneesha needs to remain engaged with her siblings and classmates with less adult support."
"Kaneesha is using more explicit language to communicate."	"Kaneesha needs to develop words to express her emotional state."
"Kaneesha is beginning to participate in familiar routines with her siblings and her classmates more frequently."	"Kaneesha needs to improve her understanding of language and use of more creative language."

3. The activities in which both Kaneesha's strengths and areas of need would likely be seen included

   - Working on an art project when she arrives at school
   - Listening to stories during circle time
   - Completing worksheets during reading and math
   - Writing in her journal in the Learning Center
   - Participating in lunch and recess activities with her classmates
   - Playing at home with Briana and Shanise
   - Preparing snacks and meals at home with her mother and/or father

4. Kaneesha's typical partners included

   - Dad

- Mom
- Her sister Briana
- Her sister Shanise
- Inclusion specialist (special education teacher)
- Two instructional assistants
- First-grade general education teacher
- Speech-language pathologist
- Occupational therapist
- Adapted physical educational teacher
- First-grade classmates (19 children)

5. Natural contexts in Kaneesha's life included
   - Caregiving routines at home
   - Play routines at home
   - Academic classroom routines
   - Social classroom routines
   - Gymnastics class at the community center

SAP Step 3: Identifying Assessment Team Members and Planning the SAP-O

Kaneesha's inclusion specialist collected the completed SAP-R Forms from both Kaneesha's family and her educational team members and began completing the SAP Map for Planning the SAP-Observation. This form was used to help identify the appropriate members of Kaneesha's assessment team and their roles and responsibilities. Consideration was also given to whether any referrals to outside professionals would need to be made. In addition, as part of planning the administration of the SAP-O, the following variables were considered to ensure a representative sample: 1) the *location* (i.e., natural contexts) where the observations would take place, 2) the specific *length* of the observations, 3) the *partners* who would be present, 4) the *group size* of the social contexts during the observations, 5) the nature of the *activities,* and 6) the number of *transitions* during each context.

After reviewing the information provided in the SAP-R and each of these variables, the educational team planned the observations to ensure a representative sample of Kaneesha's abilities and needs. First, given that Kaneesha is at the Conversational Partner stage, the minimum length of total observation time was identified as 3–4 hours. Her team agreed that it would be best to divide the observation time between her school and home environments due to the number and variety of natural contexts that Kaneesha participates in on a weekly basis. At least 3 hours of initial observations in the school environment would be appropriate, due to the varied nature of the activities occurring throughout Kaneesha's school day, and observations would be scheduled to include both adult partners and peer partners. The team planned an additional hour of home-based observation, as Kaneesha's strengths and needs outside of the school context also would need to be assessed. Based on the scoring criteria for the Conversational Partner stage, Kaneesha needs to demonstrate a specific skill across at least two contexts (e.g., school, home, or community settings) and at least three different partners, with at least one being a peer, to show that a particular skill is a consistent and solid part of her repertoire.

When the educational team was planning the observations, representative group sizes (i.e., group sizes typical for Kaneesha's natural environments) were identified and considered. Her family and educational team members planned to observe activities representing a range of levels of social complexity: 1) one to one (i.e., supervised art time in the classroom and individualized tutoring in the Learning Center), 2) small group (i.e., Kaneesha in a math center in the classroom and Kaneesha with her family at home) and 3) large group (i.e., Kaneesha in her first-grade classroom). These group sizes and contexts were typical of Kaneesha's daily experiences.

Next, Kaneesha's inclusion specialist reviewed the primary concerns of Kaneesha's family and educational team, as well as those activities in which both Kaneesha's strengths and areas of need would likely be seen. Additional variables also were considered to ensure that the assessment team gained an accurate picture of Kaneesha. For example, it was evident that she would behave differently when engaged in an unstructured versus a structured activity, a preferred activity versus a nonpreferred activity, a busy environment versus a calm environment, and a language-based versus a non-language-based activity. With this information, six activities were identified for her school-based SAP-Observations. These included 1) working on an art project on arrival at school, 2) listening to stories during morning circle time with classmates, 3) completing a math worksheet in the math center in the classroom, 4) writing in a journal with an instructional assistant in the Learning Center, 5) having lunch in the cafeteria, and 6) going to recess with her classmates. Two additional activities, 1) preparing a snack with her mother and 2) playing at home with Briana and Shanise, were identified as part of an after-school home-based observation. Both Kaneesha's family and educational team members agreed that Kaneesha might be distracted if school staff were to come to her home. Therefore, her parents agreed to videotape these activities and share the videotape with the staff during a follow-up meeting.

As noted, children who participate in the SAP should be observed across at least three transitions. Therefore, Kaneesha's inclusion specialist planned for transitions to be a part of each observation to acquire a representative sampling of Kaneesha's behavior during transitions. During the first observation, her team members planned to observe her working on her art project and making the transition to morning circle time with her classmates. During that same observation, an additional transition from circle time to math centers would be observed. During the second observation, Kaneesha's team members would observe Kaneesha making the transition from writing in her journal in the Learning Center to having lunch in the cafeteria as well as from lunch to outdoor recess with her classmates. During her home-based videotaped observation, Kaneesha's team members would observe her make the transition from preparing an after-school snack to playing with her sisters. The decisions made during this planning process would be recorded on Kaneesha's SAP Map.

SAP Step 4: Completing the SAP-O Form

Kaneesha's educational team used the SAP-O Form for the Conversational Partner stage to gather information across their three observations. Information was gathered for assessing Kaneesha's strengths and needs for social communication and emotional regulation and the strengths and needs of her partners in transactional supports across various environments.

Team members agreed that to obtain a detailed and representative profile of Kaneesha's abilities and the strategies used by her partners, they would need to divide observational responsibilities. The speech-language pathologist and general education teacher agreed to focus their attention on gathering information about Kaneesha's social-communicative abilities. The inclusion specialist would gather the majority of the information related to emotional regulation because the specialist would be present at both observations and also would be viewing the videotape. Close observation of emotional regulatory abilities would be necessary for determining appropriate steps for supporting Kaneesha's active engagement throughout her day. Kaneesha's occupational therapist and an instructional assistant were assigned to gather the majority of the information related to transactional supports, specifically, interpersonal supports and learning supports, and to supplement the observations made by the other team members as appropriate.

SAP Step 5: Conducting Behavior Sampling

Following the completion of the three scheduled observations, including the team's review of Kaneesha's videotaped session at home, her team members briefly reviewed her SAP-O Form. A number of questions remained regarding specific Social Communication and Emotional Regulation objectives, even though the team had gathered a wealth of information from observing her interactions in typical environments and activities. This was particularly evident with respect to the use of a number of skills with less familiar partners in less familiar settings.

Thus, for the next step in the SAP, the team identified three areas in which behavior sampling would be required. The first related to Kaneesha's acquisition of creative and generative language. The team remarked that Kaneesha clearly continues to borrow language heard in previous contexts (i.e., delayed echolalia) and, on occasion, repeats the sentences modeled to her by her classmates (i.e., immediate echolalia). As a result, the team members agreed that during the observations it had been difficult to determine if Kaneesha had understood and/or used advanced relational words with a range of semantic meanings in her spontaneous language (SU5.1), as it had not always been possible to determine if utterances were creative or were instances of delayed echolalia. Therefore, sampling was considered essential to acquire a larger language sample, to ascertain whether Kaneesha was making the transition from predominantly echolalic language forms to more creative and generative language.

Next, Kaneesha's inclusion specialist remarked that she needed more opportunities to observe Kaneesha's ability to use internalized rules modeled by adult instruction to guide her behavior across contexts and partners (SR4.1). Although the specialist had noticed Kaneesha raising her hand before commenting during circle time, the team had only observed one other instance of this skill when she had stated "thank you" at home after her mother had handed her a slice of pizza. Therefore, the team realized that this skill needed to be documented with a different partner to confirm that it was an established part of her repertoire.

Kaneesha's educational team also decided that her ability to remain actively engaged across contexts without adult support and her ability to use strategies to regulate her own arousal level that have been taught and/or modeled by her teachers (MR2.6) needed additional scrutiny because these were primary concerns expressed by her family and team. During the first two observations, Kaneesha's response to behavioral or language-based mutual regulatory strategies (i.e., those offered by others) was inconsistent, as she often relied on her own attempts to self-regulate by sucking her thumb or by singing to herself. She often engaged in such strategies despite their ineffectiveness at supporting her. For example, during circle time, Kaneesha appeared to be drifting off and was in a state of arousal that was too low to ensure active engagement; thus, she began to suck her thumb. An instructional assistant recognized this as a signal of a decrease in arousal and offered her a "chewy tube" (i.e., a safe a resistive object to chew on); however, Kaneesha turned away, continued to suck her thumb, and did not accept this replacement strategy. While she was at the math center, she began to sing to herself, a signal that her teacher interpreted as a signal of dysregulation, as she had seen Kaneesha sing before when engaged with a talkative group of children. When the teacher modeled having Kaneesha raise her hand to request a break, Kaneesha turned away and apparently did not recognize that raising her hand could lead to an opportunity for a break.

With these areas of concern in mind, Kaneesha's educational team desired more information with respect to the following objectives:

- SU5.1—Kaneesha's understanding and use of a variety of advanced relational words, such as words denoting *wh-* concepts, temporal concepts, physical concepts, numerical concepts, location concepts, kinship concepts, and causality
- SR4.1—Kaneesha's use of internalized rules modeled by adult instruction to guide behavior
- MR2.6—Kaneesha's ability to respond to information or strategies offered by partners

After identifying these remaining questions, Kaneesha's educational team considered the use of activities set up specifically to address these questions through behavior sampling. With respect to Kaneesha's understanding and use of advanced relational words (SU5.1), an additional observation session was scheduled during a one-to-one speech-language therapy session. The inclusion specialist agreed to attend the session and would use the Worksheet for Language Elements in the Conversational Partner Stage to tally and list examples of each word category (e.g., temporal words, numerical words, location words) observed.

For this additional session, Kaneesha's speech-language pathologist planned three activities that were designed to elicit descriptive and precise language use. These included 1) an *oral narrative activity* using a wordless picture book to observe the language forms that Kaneesha uses to describe simple social scenes in the story; 2) a *scavenger hunt* with a map of Kaneesha's favorite items hidden around the room, an activity that would elicit the use of location words (e.g., "under," "behind," and "next to"), as Kaneesha would be required to describe where each item had been found to gain access to them; and 3) a *barrier game,* a turn-taking activity involving a visual barrier between Kaneesha and her speech-language pathologist, in which each player would have a magnetic castle scene and would have to describe where each item is going to be placed so that the partner could match that placement on their castle. Because the barrier game would provide an opportunity to observe Kaneesha comprehending another person's directions, specific words could be sampled directly if they had not been observed in her expressive language. For example, her speech-language pathologist could sample numeric concepts by indicating that "the princess is holding two magic wands" and providing Kaneesha with a chance to match that on her castle picture.

Next, Kaneesha's educational team planned another additional session to elicit information related to Kaneesha's ability to internalize rules modeled by adults to guide her behavior and her ability to respond to information or strategies offered by others to regulate her arousal level (SR4.1). Because Kaneesha's parents mentioned that Kaneesha had recently begun to participate in a gymnastics class at the local community center and had adjusted nicely to this context with particular respect to her engagement, the inclusion specialist felt that an additional videotape review would be helpful. Her parents were excited about this opportunity, as they had hoped to provide feedback to her gymnastics teacher on the use of transactional supports that might foster Kaneesha's engagement in gymnastics. Thus, her educational team could learn more about Kaneesha's current abilities and could offer strategies to foster greater consistency across partners and contexts, an important goal for a child and team members at the Conversational Partner stage.

In the context of the gymnastics class, her educational team felt that their would be ample opportunities for Kaneesha to demonstrate her ability to follow internalized rules such as taking off one's shoes before climbing on the mats and waiting in line before using the trampoline. In addition, there likely would be a number of opportunities to observe Kaneesha's ability to respond to her gymnastic teacher's attempts to support her engagement (MR2.6), such as how she responds to behaviors modeled by the teacher while waiting in line (e.g., standing on tiptoe, stretching one's arms).

SAP Step 6: Compiling and Integrating Information with the SAP Summary Form

Following the completion of the initial observations, the first videotape review, and the follow-up behavior sampling observations, Kaneesha's educational team and her parents met to compile and integrate information, a step that involves two key information sources: 1) summarizing strengths and needs from the SAP-O and 2) documenting family perception of the SAP-O results.

Key Information Source 1: Summarizing Strengths and Needs

Social Communication: Joint Attention

Kaneesha's family and educational team members initially focused on determining Kaneesha's strengths and challenges with respect to her current profile in joint attention. The inclusion specialist discussed how early in the Conversational Partner stage, a child's emerging social awareness supports the ability to recognize whether a partner is paying attention and is interested and whether the partner needs more information about a given topic. A child at this stage begins to understand how to modify language based on what a partner has seen or heard and, as a result, begins to share thoughts or emotions with others more readily.

Based on information obtained through the SAP-O, Kaneesha demonstrates relative strengths in her ability to establish shared attention across a range of partners and contexts, particularly when sharing intentions to regulate the behavior of others (e.g., requesting desired objects and actions, requesting help). In fact, as noted previously, Kaneesha can be a very persistent communicator in familiar routines at home. When making pizza with her mother for an afternoon snack, she clearly demonstrated an understanding of the nonverbal cues that indicate a shift in attentional focus, as she quickly followed her mother to the refrigerator when her mother turned to look in that direction. This social referencing allowed Kaneesha to infer that her mother was selecting toppings for the pizza. Kaneesha was then observed to use gaze and to tap on her mother's shoulder to secure her attention when her mother was preoccupied with gathering items out of the refrigerator. She made a specific request, "Let's put on mozzarella, cheddar cheese, and pepperoni!" and then protested when her mother indicated that there was no pepperoni left. She continued to persist by making additional requests, clearly recognizing her mother as a source of assistance. For example, Kaneesha used the phrase, "I need help, please," while she was trying to open the bag of shredded cheese. Thus, the team agreed that in familiar routines, her capacity for establishing shared attention has emerged as a relative strength.

At school, Kaneesha also was observed to monitor the attentional focus of her partners, a developmental capacity that leads to greater social problem solving (e.g., understanding what a person is doing) and greater attention to another's topic or interests (e.g., "Jessica is riding on the swings; maybe I can swing with Jessica"). During the observation of Kaneesha participating in circle time, she was observed to shift her gaze from her classmates to the teacher, recognizing that their attentional focus was on the story being read. At recess, she monitored the actions of her classmates and even made several comments suggesting her awareness of their actions and activities (e.g., "I see Jericha on the swings," "Justin's on the slide"). Both Kaneesha's parents and her educational team recognized that these emerging skills are leading to a higher frequency of social initiations that are related to a partner's interests. Nevertheless, they did note that Kaneesha's ability to recall her peers' interests outside of the context in which the children are playing remains limited. Thus, the discussion turned toward creating a learning support, such as an "All About Me and My Class" storybook. This book would include a picture of a classmate on each page, surrounded by picture symbols of his or her favorite recess games.

As noted on the SAP-R and the SAP-O, several joint attention limitations continue to compromise Kaneesha's competence in social interaction with both adults and peers and across home and school contexts. First, although she often uses nonverbal means to express her emotional state and may use words and phrases to protest, her use of emotion words to describe her emotional state and the emotional state of others remains dependent on the verbal cues of her parents and teachers. In addition to compromising her emotional regulatory skills, a limited vocabulary of emotion words was quite evident in Kaneesha's conversations with her peers, classroom lessons, and her first-grade journal. When she participates in reciprocal exchanges with her classmates, for example, she tends to focus on the concrete and visual aspects of her current activity rather than on her internal state (e.g., "I have a peanut butter and jelly sandwich"). Her classmates, on the other hand, are elaborating their comments with emotional expressions (e.g., "My cheese sandwich is kind of yucky. I wish my mom had made a bologna sandwich—those are really good!"). In her first-grade journal, she wrote, *I am jumping in the ball pit* rather than *I like jumping in the ball pit because it makes me feel happy.* Her limited use of emotion words clearly compromises her ability to provide her partners with information about her internal state. In a similar manner, her limited comprehension of emotion words compromises her ability to consider the impact of her actions on a classmate's emotional state. Thus, her educational team identified this aspect of her development as a critical area of need.

Kaneesha's parents also had reported that Kaneesha's limited ability to share intentions for joint attention by communicating about past, future, and imaginary events continues to compromise her competence in social interaction with both adults and peers and across home and school contexts and therefore affects her ability to form true friendships at school. Although Kaneesha is developing a greater ability to share immediate experiences (e.g., "I see Jericha riding the swings," "Justin's on the slide"), her reliance on visual cues in the environment to recall this language is quite evident. Information gained through the SAP-O also showed that Kaneesha's language is limited to the "here and now," with the exception of those activities that involve visual cues that foster her recall of language across contexts. For example, in her first-grade journaling activity, she was observed to have a more extended reciprocal interaction with an instructional assistant about an activity that she had already completed (i.e., jumping in the ball pit). The ball pit, however, was still in her visual field, suggesting the need to include more learning supports, such as a journal of digital photographs, to foster her recall of events and language over time and across contexts.

A complete summary of Kaneesha's current profile of strengths and areas of need in the Joint Attention component would be included on her SAP-O Form and SAP Sum.

Social Communication: Symbol Use

After establishing Kaneesha's baseline in the SAP in Joint Attention, her educational team and family determined Kaneesha's strengths and needs with respect to her abilities in symbol use. As noted previously, Kaneesha uses more than 100 words referentially and more than 20 spontaneous, creative phrases and sentences to communicate her intent. In the past year, her parents and educational team have observed the emergence of Kaneesha's ability to communicate with more precise and explicit language, as her sentence length has increased from early word combinations to simple sentences. As noted, one of her ongoing challenges has been her reliance on scripted language or echolalia (immediate or delayed) over more creative and generative language forms.

During the administration of the SAP-O, Kaneesha's educational team noted an apparent reliance on echolalia when using words and word concepts that she did not yet fully comprehend. During the behavior sampling session led by her speech-language pathologist and documented by her inclusion specialist, activities such as an oral narrative, scavenger hunt, and barrier game were helpful in identifying which aspects of language Kaneesha has not yet developed. The team reviewed the Worksheet for Language Elements in the Conversational Partner Stage to note specific examples of word categories that Kaneesha understands and uses. In the oral narrative activity, for example, Kaneesha told the story illustrated in *A Boy, a Dog, and a Frog* by Mercer Mayer. This wordless storybook elicited comments from Kaneesha such as "The boy is walking," "The frog is sitting on a leaf," "The boy fell in the water," "The boy is all wet," and "The frog is jumping." Thus, it was clear that Kaneesha is using a creative range of agents, actions, and objects, a hallmark accomplishment of the Language Partner stage. This pattern was, in fact, observed at home, as she had used simple sentences such as "Shanise ride bikes, please" and "Briana play computer, please."

Nevertheless, both her speech-language pathologist and her inclusion specialist were concerned about Kaneesha's limited use of more advanced relational meanings, typically an early Conversational Partner stage achievement. First, they noted a limited use of temporal relations (e.g., "now," "later," "after") to connect scenes in the story. In addition, Kaneesha used very few physical relations (e.g., "The boy is all wet") and those that were observed appeared to be somewhat echolalic in nature, as they appeared to have been borrowed from previous stories with similar scenes. Next, although clearly emerging, Kaneesha's use of location words (e.g., "in," "on," "under," "over," "to") was limited and appeared to be restricting her use of more descriptive language throughout a simple story (e.g., "The boy is walking to the pond," "The frog is jumping over the boy's head"). Last, Kaneesha was not yet observed to use causal words to establish relationships between the scenes of the story (e.g., "The boy was all wet *because* he fell in the water"). This skill often relies on achievements in joint attention, as a child's ability to monitor the attentional focus of another agent provides the context for determining causal relationships (e.g., the boy was looking at the branch he had just tripped on after falling in the water).

Next, the barrier game that was played during the behavior sampling session illustrated additional challenges with using and understanding advanced relational words, including *wh-* words and numerical concepts. For example, Kaneesha had difficulty using *wh-* words to ask questions about her speech-language pathologist's actions in the game, as she was only noted to use one question form during this activity (i.e., "Where did _____ go?"), a question she uses frequently across contexts by substituting only the object or noun phrase (e.g., "Where did Daddy go?"). Similarly, when her speech-language pathologist indicated that she had placed "three flowers in the castle," Kaneesha only placed one, perhaps showing a tendency to tune in to only the noun, the location word, and the object (i.e., "flower," "in, " "castle"). Thus, building her understanding of specific word concepts and understanding of relationships between words and sentences was considered a critical priority in her educational programming.

The implementation of picture symbols for sentence assembly was discussed to as a learning support for fostering Kaneesha's transition from more echolalic language forms to more creative and generative language. This AAC support could visually illustrate the individual units within language forms by providing a static cue for the specific components of a multiword utterance. Each portion of the sentence (e.g., subject, verb, preposition, object phrase) would be color coded and a sentence template would be provided to indicate the order of the words using color-coded sequences (i.e., the template contains color-coded dashed lines with a different color for each word to indicate where individual words would go, similar to a Hangman game). These cues would foster Kaneesha's ability to *independently* determine appropriate word order for more sophisticated simple sentences, thereby decreasing her reliance on her teacher's verbal cues (see Chapter 4 in this volume for other examples).

Despite these challenges in the understanding and use of generative language to express meaning, several emerging areas of competence were noted with respect to Kaneesha's Symbol Use, namely her expanding repertoire of learning strategies such as imitative learning and instructed learning. First, her educational team members observed her use of imitation to learn conventional play and adaptive behaviors both at home and at school. During her home-based observation, her educational team had been impressed by her ability to imitate her mother making a pizza for an after-school snack. This action had then also been observed at school during a break from classroom activities, as Kaneesha was observed to make a pizza in the playhouse at school by assembling the pretend dough, adding pretend cheese, and cooking it in the oven. Next, her ability to consider her perspective of an event as well as her teacher's guidance or instruction, appeared to be emerging as well. This learning strategy is evident by Kaneesha's use of internalized rules modeled by adult instruction to guide her behavior across contexts and partners (e.g., raising her hand before commenting during circle time, stating "thank you" after her mother handed her a slice of pizza). These learning strategies have clearly supported Kaneesha's development of both symbolic play as well as her ability to learn new sequences of actions as part of daily routines, such as hanging up her coat and hat in her cubby, and as part of transitions, such as taking off her shoes before climbing on the tumbling mat at gymnastics. A complete summary of Kaneesha's current profile of strengths and areas of need in the Symbol Use component would be included on her SAP-O Form and SAP Sum.

Emotional Regulation: Mutual Regulation

Kaneesha's educational team members and parents then discussed the SAP-O findings related to her strengths and needs in mutual regulation. The team reflected on their previous discussions of Kaneesha's social-communicative abilities and their impact on her emotional regulatory abilities. Kaneesha's gains in joint attention and in symbol use did appear to be having a positive impact on her ability to use initiated mutual regulatory strategies, as documented during the SAP-O. Specifically, the team members noted that Kaneesha's ability to secure attention to herself by looking up at a teacher, calling out another person's name, and tapping on another person's shoulder has supported her effectiveness in getting her needs met, particularly when Kaneesha requests assistance by stating, "I need help, please," and when she refuses dysregulating activities by stating, "No, thank you," or "I'm all done." Nevertheless, ongoing challenges in both joint attention and symbol use continue to limit Kaneesha's ability to use emotion words to share her emotional state with others and her ability to use behavior modeled by partners to self-regulate in a more conventional or socially appropriate manner. These later skills were observed to be emerging but not yet established across partners and contexts.

Kaneesha's ability to understand and use both early and advanced emotion words was identified as a primary area of concern both in the SAP-R and during the administration of the SAP-O, as these limitations compromised her partners' ability to recognize signs of dysregulation and therefore their ability to offer her support (i.e., respondent mutual regulation). Although she occasionally used emotion words when prompted by her parents and/or her teachers, she rarely used these words spontaneously and tended to communicate her emotional regulatory state through subtle nonverbal signals such as turning her head away, singing to herself, and sucking her thumb. Challenges in reading her signals were particularly evident when she was with less familiar partners and/or her peers. Her parents and therapists at school were occasionally able to respond to her nonverbal signals of dysregulation; however, unfamiliar partners were less likely to offer emotional regulatory assistance until she had become even more dysregulated, as signaled by her crying and disengaging for prolonged periods of time. In gymnastics class, for example, her teacher did not notice that Kaneesha became distressed when a series of complex instructions were given and the girls were expected to make the transition to a new area of the room. Although she initially showed signs of disengagement and anxiety by walking away from the group, sucking her thumb, and walking on her toes, Kaneesha did not use emotion words to express her distressed emotional state. Eventually, she began to sob, to the surprise of her teacher, who previously had been unaware of her distress.

In some instances, Kaneesha's nonverbal emotional expressions were more conventional or readable, allowing her partners' to respond by acknowledging her feelings and modeling emotion words for her. For example, as she completed a picture of a princess, Kaneesha appeared quite happy. She looked up toward an instructional assistant and clapped her hands to share her positive feeling, and she was observed to comment, "Feel happy," when an instructional assistant asked, "Do you feel happy?" Her parents also noted that on one occasion, Kaneesha indicated, "I feel happy," after receiving a new doll for her birthday, perhaps recalling a scene from a favorite storybook that illustrated this exact situation. Thus, Kaneesha's spontaneous ability to recall emotion words had not yet been observed across partners and settings, but she clearly was developing a greater capacity to use these phrases in appropriate situations.

Despite Kaneesha's difficulties in using emotion words, her inclusion specialist noted that Kaneesha's ability to ask for assistance appeared to be a relative strength, as this skill was demonstrated across multiple partners and contexts. At home, for example, Kaneesha had been observed to use the phrase, "I need help, please," while she was trying to open the bag of shredded cheese for a pizza. Similarly, at school, her general education teacher observed Kaneesha writing in her first-grade journal. In this activity, she had been attempting to draw a picture of herself in the ball pit, an activity that she liked to do in the Learning Center, but she had difficulty writing the sentence, *I am jumping in the ball pit.* She gradually became dysregulated as she had difficulty with the handwriting task, and she began to turn away from the table and started sucking on her thumb. However, she quickly turned back to an instructional assistant, looked up, and stated, "Ms. P., write *jumping.*"

Her team noted that Kaneesha's ability to request assistance is less consistent when she is in a low state of arousal, the state in which she was observed to experience her most extreme dysregulation. In these instances, she tended to rely on unconventional behavioral strategies to self-regulate and was minimally responsive to her partners' efforts to model regulatory strategies. Kaneesha's inclusion specialist observed several clear signals during periods of very low arousal and extreme dysregulation, when Kaneesha was most unavailable for engagement, as evidenced by not responding or only responding minimally. These signals included 1) looking away in a nonfocused manner, 2) singing to herself, 3) twirling her hair with her fingers, 4) walking on her toes, and 5) sucking her thumb. These signals typically were seen in busy social environments that did not have a clear and predictable sequence of events, visual structure, and/or opportunities for movement. For instance, during lunch in the cafeteria, Kaneesha was observed to tune out and stare out the window rather than eat her lunch or interact with her peers. In this and similar instances, Kaneesha typically responded to the persistent behavioral mutual regulatory strategies used by her partners, such as her teacher's providing her with a quick back rub as a means to alert her to engage with her classmates at the table.

Finally, Kaneesha's ability to respond to partner feedback regarding the appropriateness of regulatory strategies remains inconsistent but appears to be emerging. In circle time, she had not yet shifted from sucking her thumb to using a "chewy tube" or to using more language-based strategies such as raising her hand to request a break while at the math center. Nevertheless, during behavior sampling at gymnastics class, Kaneesha was observed to respond to her teacher's efforts to model strategies for reengagement while waiting in line for the trampoline. When Kaneesha started to drift off and began to sing to herself, her teacher modeled the behavioral strategy of stretching her arms out to the side and over her head. Kaneesha responded nicely to this movement-based strategy and continued using this until it was her turn on the trampoline. At school, Kaneesha has become more responsive to the rule that it is okay to suck her thumb at home but that while at her desk at school, it is preferable to use the "chewy tube" attached to her pencil, as this strategy is more socially appropriate and effective.

A complete summary of Kaneesha's current profile of strengths and areas of need in the Mutual Regulation component would be included on her SAP-O Form and SAP Sum.

Emotional Regulation: Self-Regulation

Next, Kaneesha's team members and parents discussed Kaneesha's abilities and needs in self-regulation. Based on information gathered through the SAP, the team discussed a number of relative strengths as well as emerging skills related to her overall availability for learning and interacting with others. Kaneesha's ability to monitor the attentional focus of her partners, for example, clearly had a positive impact on her availability for learning and social engagement. During the observation of Kaneesha participating in circle time, she shifted her gaze from her classmates to the teacher, recognizing that their attentional focus was on the story being read. At recess, she monitored the actions of her classmates and even made several comments suggesting her awareness of their actions and activities (e.g., "I see Jericha on the swings," "Justin's on the slide"). The team believed that as Kaneesha's ability to monitor her partners' attentional focus supports her ability to self-regulate, this growth will enhance her ability to join her peers on her own and follow their lead, an early aspect of collaborative learning.

Kaneesha's ability to persist during tasks with reasonable demands and to inhibit her actions and behaviors were also emerging skills that were contributing to her overall availability for learning and interacting. Kaneesha's speech-language pathologist had observed Kaneesha working on an art project and then joining her class in circle time. In the context of her art project, Kaneesha's persistence was quite noticeable, as she remained engaged and persisted in this activity until her drawing was complete. During the calendar and weather portions of circle time, Kaneesha raised her hand and waited to be called on rather than impulsively providing an answer when her teacher asked for a volunteer. This action was indicative of both her availability for engagement and her emerging ability to follow social conventions based on her internalized set of rules.

Information gathered during the SAP-R and SAP-O led to a discussion of Kaneesha's current self-regulatory abilities, including her behavioral, language, and metacognitive strategies. First, her team members read through a list of behavioral strategies that Kaneesha consistently employed. These included 1) sucking her thumb, 2) singing to herself, 3) walking on her toes, and 4) twirling her hair in her fingers. Her team agreed that these strategies served as early attempts at self-regulation, as well as signals to caregivers of her dysregulation. The team also agreed that the effectiveness of these strategies was variable, as the strategies were not always supportive of her ability to learn and interact with others. For example, sucking her thumb seemed to help her regroup while completing her first-grade journal; however, it did not appear to be effective on the playground, which was a less structured environment. In this setting, she became so engrossed with sucking her thumb that it interfered with her ability to participate in a follow-the-leader game, and in other activities with her peers. Thus, although Kaneesha's ability to use behavioral strategies to regulate her arousal is emerging, she is not yet using more effective and socially acceptable behavioral strategies modeled by her parents and teachers.

Next, Kaneesha's team identified her use of language strategies to regulate her arousal in both solitary and social activities. Her general education teacher commented that during transitions, Kaneesha often quietly vocalized to herself, such as by singing, "Journal time is all done; it's time for lunch," appropriately changing the names of the activities from her schedule to fit the situation. Her inclusion specialist observed that when Kaneesha was listening to music CDs with her siblings, she often repeated, "It's Briana's turn" or "It's Shanise's turn," as she waited for her turn to select a song for dancing. These examples were viewed as very positive; however, the team did agree that

Kaneesha was not yet understanding and using emotion words and graded emotions, limitations that would likely prevent her from developing self-talk for self-regulation of emotional states.

Next, the team noted apparent limitations in Kaneesha's ability to reflect on an upcoming activity, determine her own state of arousal, and use problem solving strategies to support her own organization and attention. Such limitations are not uncommon for a child at the early Conversational Partner stage who is not yet fully able to benefit from both instructed and collaborative learning strategies. One exception to these limitations appears to be Kaneesha's emerging ability to use internalized rules modeled by adults to guide her behavior. As noted, Kaneesha has learned to say "thank you" and "please" both at home and at school, and she also has learned to raise her hand during circle time when she would like to make a comment or answer a question. In a newer setting such as her gymnastics class, her ability to use internalized rules was also observed. This capacity demonstrates an emerging awareness of social conventions and the use of externalized language to guide and to monitor her behavior.

Finally, the team discussed Kaneesha's ability to recover from extreme dysregulation, which appeared to differ depending on whether she was in an extremely high or an extremely low arousal state. Her team felt that Kaneesha was often able to independently and efficiently recover from states of high arousal through the use of behavioral strategies, such as turning away from a distressing activity, and language strategies, such as talking herself through a transition. Her ability to recover from extreme dysregulation associated with low arousal states, however, was inconsistent. In fact, when Kaneesha drifted off into a state of low arousal, as evidenced by tuning out and being unavailable, she was only able to reengage with the direct assistance of an adult. For example, during the later part of circle time, Kaneesha shifted to a state of arousal that was too low to ensure active engagement, likely due to the sedentary nature of the activity and the complexity of her teacher's language. During this time, Kaneesha was allowed to attempt strategies to reengage on her own, such as sucking her thumb; however, when this was not effective, it was necessary for an instructional assistant to intervene by modeling more efficient and socially appropriate strategies. These included modeling a request for a short walking break and then returning to the circle when Kaneesha was more alert. A complete summary of Kaneesha's current profile of strengths and areas of need in the Self-Regulation component would be included on her SAP-O Form and SAP Sum.

Transactional Support: Interpersonal Support

Both the SAP-R and the SAP-O were reviewed to gain a sense of the strengths and needs of Kaneesha's social network and those interpersonal supports that might be useful for facilitating her social communication and emotional regulation. Kaneesha's inclusion specialist first focused on how Kaneesha's challenges in the areas of emotional regulation and social communication frequently had a transactional impact on her partners, particularly her peers. For example, Kaneesha's bias toward a low state of arousal and her difficulties using efficient emotional regulatory strategies often limited her ability to maintain an active alert state and thus her engagement in lengthy interactions with her peers. This was particularly true when the nature of the activity was unclear or when she was in an unstructured environment, such as on the playground during recess. In these types of settings and activities, Kaneesha's peer partners often perceived her as disinterested and distant. In turn, they appeared less inclined to invite her to play with them in unstructured settings.

The team considered a number of interpersonal supports to enable Kaneesha's classmates to achieve greater success in both initiating and successfully engaging Kaneesha in an interaction. She was more likely to initiate and participate in interactions with partners who recognized her signs of dysregulation and offered support. Therefore, it was determined that peers needed coaching to be able to use supportive strategies more consistently. For example, the inclusion specialist commented that Kaneesha's peers have not yet been coached in how to secure her attention before communicating with Kaneesha, such as by coming in close proximity, tapping her on her shoulder, and calling her name. They also needed support in using appropriate words and intonation patterns, such as using simple sentences with exaggerated positive emotion (e.g., "Kaneesha, come play Follow the Leader with us!") to set the stage for more successful exchanges. In addition, her team felt that an instructional assistant could play with Kaneesha on the playground before recess to model appropriate dramatic play and recreation activities that her classmates might want to play. During these planned activity routines, Kaneesha would be pretaught the rules of the games so that she would not be challenged both by the activity and the social interaction.

By reviewing the SAP-R and SAP-O results, Kaneesha's parents and educational team members were able to identify a number of interpersonal supports that were emerging as areas of strength in her social network and those that were considered critical areas of need. The following chart provides examples.

Interpersonal Support

Strengths	Needs
Kaneesha's partners (both at school and home) recognize her signs of dysregulation and offer her support, often by responding to her emotion and pace (IS1.5, IS1.2)	Kaneesha's partners (at home, school, and her community gymnastics class) need to model appropriate behavior (e.g., regulatory strategies) when Kaneesha uses inappropriate or socially unconventional strategies (IS7.4)
Kaneesha's educational team members allow Kaneesha time to solve problems and complete activities at her own pace (IS3.2)	There is an ongoing need to provide guidance for Kaneesha to express her emotions and to understand the cause of her emotions, to help facilitate her use of more explicit emotional expression (IS5.4)
The instructional assistants often are able to recognize when Kaneesha would benefit from a break to move about and are able to facilitate reengagement in interactions and activities these breaks (IS3.1, IS1.8)	Kaneesha's educational team need to provide guidance to her peers to support greater success in interactions, as her peers may be inadvertently excluding her from activities if she appears disinterested (IS5.1)
	The instructional assistants need to model appropriate dramatic play and recreation activities on the playground, to increase Kaneesha's successful participation in social interactions at recess (IS7.3)

A complete summary of the use of various interpersonal supports by Kaneesha's social network would be included on her SAP-O Form and SAP Sum.

Transactional Support: Learning Support

A final component of Kaneesha's team meeting included a discussion of those learning supports that have already been implemented as transactional supports in her daily routines and those that should be considered to augment her programming. Based on the SAP-O, the learning supports that appeared to be most effective in her home and school environments had either an element of predictability or provided static visual information. At home, these included her family's attempts to provide predictable sequences for familiar activities such as meal preparation and to offer repeated learning opportunities by repeating familiar activities such as riding bikes with her sisters and dancing along to favorite music CDs. At school, these included the use of a between-task schedule using picture symbols paired with written words to help Kaneesha prepare for transitions and upcoming activities, as well as visual supports for organizing the length and sequence of events across the day, such as using a timer with a fading visual cue to indicate the duration of lunch. These supports were presumed to be contributing to her emerging use of self-talk to prepare for transitions (e.g., "Journal time is all done; it's time for lunch").

Her team also recognized the need to use additional supports to encourage her use of 1) emotion words for emotional expression (e.g., using picture cues to support her recall of emotional vocabulary), 2) more creative expressive language (e.g., using picture-based sentence assembly supports), and 3) more socially appropriate emotional regulatory strategies (e.g., providing her with a visual menu of regulatory strategies that fit the social context of the classroom). She also needed support to follow language embedded in more complex tasks (e.g., using a within-task schedule that provides pictures and words to guide Kaneesha through a complicated math center lesson). Thus, the team agreed that it would be important to use an AAC system for supporting her understanding of language and behavior, her emotional expression, and her emotional regulation. Thus, by reviewing the SAP-R and SAP-O results, Kaneesha's parents and educational team members were able to identify the learning supports already being used that were emerging as areas of strength in her social network, as well as those that were considered critical areas of need. The following chart provides examples of several of these areas.

Learning Support	
Strengths	**Needs**
Kaneesha's family members provide predictable sequences for familiar activities and offer repeated learning opportunities (LS1.3, LS1.4)	Kaneesha's team members need to use augmentative communication support to enhance her communication and expressive language (LS2.1)
Kaneesha's educational team members provide between-task schedules to help her anticipate transitions and upcoming activities and organize segments of time across the day (LS3.3, LS3.4)	Kaneesha's team members need to use an augmentative communication support to foster her expression of emotion words and her emotional understanding (LS2.3) as well as her development of socially appropriate emotional regulation strategies (LS2.4)
	Kaneesha's team members need to provide Kaneesha with an augmentative communication support to foster her understanding of language and behavior as well as the steps within tasks (LS2.2, LS3.1)

A complete summary of the current use of various learning supports by Kaneesha's social network would be included on her SAP-O Form and SAP Sum.

Social-Emotional Growth Indicators: Results and Impressions

Next, Kaneesha's team calculated her baseline composite scores for her Social-Emotional Growth Indicators. These indicators would provide useful benchmarks against which to measure future gains in her general qualities of behavior. The general qualities of behavior measured by the Social-Emotional Growth Indicators include 1) Happiness, 2) Sense of Self, 3) Sense of Other, 4) Active Learning and Organization, 5) Flexibility and Resilience, 6) Cooperation and Appropriateness of Behavior, 7) Independence, and

8) Social Membership and Friendships. Tabulation of Kaneesha's Social-Emotional Growth Indicators revealed a relative strength in the area of Happiness and emerging strengths in Social Membership and Friendships. An area of relative weakness was Flexibility and Resilience.

Key Information Source 2: Family Perception of SAP-O Results and Priorities

Before identifying the specific goals and objectives for Kaneesha's educational program, the educational team asked her parents whether the initial observations and the behavior sampling sessions captured a representative sample of Kaneesha's behavior and whether Kaneesha's strengths and needs were accurately captured on the SAP Sum. Kaneesha's mother and father indicated they felt that the results were an accurate reflection of their daughter's current strengths and needs. They also indicated that the SAP had accurately captured the significant challenges faced by Kaneesha's partners when attempting to initiate and maintain engagement with her.

Kaneesha's parents were then asked to reiterate their primary concerns and to discuss their hopes and expectations regarding Kaneesha's development, to clarify goals and desired outcomes for a SCERTS Family Support Plan. Next, her parents were asked to indicate the types of information and support that would be most helpful for their family at home and in the community. Family perceptions would be included on Kaneesha's SAP Sum.

SAP Step 7: Prioritizing Goals and Objectives

Based on the information compiled and integrated throughout the SAP, including the SAP-R, the SAP-O, the behavior sampling, and the SAP Sum, Kaneesha's parents and educational team members prioritized goals and objectives that were 1) the most *functional,* 2) directly *addressed family priorities,* and 3) matched the *developmental areas of need* for both Kaneesha and her partners, and these were documented on the SAP Sum. Her performance on the SAP-O was not the sole factor for selecting weekly objectives, as equal consideration was given to those objectives that would be the most functional and those that most closely matched her family's priorities. Although this process occasionally results in selection of objectives that might appear out of sequence in reference to the structure of goals and objectives in the SAP, this flexibility and individualization is considered critical for successful implementation of a SCERTS Model program. This information would be included on Kaneesha's SAP Sum.

SAP Step 8: Recommending Further Assessment if Needed

When reviewing the SAP Sum, Kaneesha's parents felt that Kaneesha's social-communicative and emotional regulatory needs were documented accurately, as was information regarding the most appropriate transactional supports. Aside from systematic reassessment of the SAP at 3-month intervals, Kaneesha's team did not recommend additional assessment.

SAP Step 9: Designing a SCERTS Educational Program for Kaneesha, Her Parents, and Her Service Providers

Step 9 of the SAP involved identifying a number of key meaningful and purposeful activities, the complexity of social support in these activities (i.e., the roles and responsibilities of educational team members), and the familiar partners who will play a critical role in service provision. Kaneesha's team leader, her inclusion specialist, assumed the primary role of organizing the educational and support program for Kaneesha and her family. She discussed the continued need for intensive educational programming and *at least* 25 hours per week on a year-round basis of planned and developmentally appropriate learning opportunities. In addition, she indicated that continued individualized attention would be needed to support Kaneesha's active learning during her programming. There also was a need for the team and her family to develop a plan for educational and emotional support in a collaborative manner, to address their ongoing concerns about how best to facilitate her development in their home environment.

This step of the SAP culminated in the development of two SAP Activity Planning Forms, each of which incorporated approximately 3 hours of meaningful and purposeful activities in Kaneesha's natural routines. The first form outlined Kaneesha's typical morning routines in her first-grade classroom and the second form outlined Kaneesha's typical afternoon routines in the Learning Center, lunch, recess and her return to the first-grade classroom. Therefore, a plan was established for approximately 6 hours per day, for a total of 30 hours per week of educational programming.

The SAP Activity Planning Forms included the specific goals that would be addressed in these activities and the complexity of social context (i.e., the degree of naturalness and the amount and frequency of one-to-one support) that would be appropriate depending on Kaneesha's social-communicative and emotional regulatory capacities. In addition, the SAP Activity Planning Forms were completed to identify the partner objectives and specific transactional supports (i.e., interpersonal supports and learning supports) that would be embedded in each activity.

Next, Kaneesha's inclusion specialist reported information provided by her family on the SAP-R as well as information obtained through the Transactional Support domain of the SAP-O, for the team to develop and provide a SCERTS Family Support Plan. The provision of both educational support and emotional support to a child's immediate and extended family is a critical priority in a comprehensive program and thus the development of Kaneesha's educational program would not be complete without this crucial step. The purpose of educational support and emotional support is to foster her family's ability to actively and independently problem-solve and address the challenges they face, empowering them to cope with future challenges.

Educational Support for Kaneesha's Family

As noted previously, primary educational concerns expressed by Kaneesha's parents included the challenges they encountered due Kaneesha's low arousal bias, as her current repertoire of self-regulatory strategies remained inefficient and socially unconventional. They also had expressed concern about her continued reliance on scripted phrases over more creative language and limited ability to communicate about past events. Thus, educational support appeared to be needed in the following general areas.

Goal 1: **To provide Kaneesha's family members with the knowledge and skills to support Kaneesha's development in everyday activities and to address specific issues that are identified as most stressful and challenging.** For Kaneesha's family, these issues include supporting Kaneesha's development of 1) self-regulatory strategies, 2) creative language, and 3) communication about past events.

Desired outcome: *Kaneesha's family members will feel confident in providing the necessary supports to foster Kaneesha's development of 1) more conventional self-regulatory strategies, 2) more creative language, and 3) communication about past events across different situations and in everyday activities and will be able to identify and cope with the most significant difficulties they face at any point in time.*

Goal 2: **To help Kaneesha's parents provide Kaneesha's sisters, Briana and Shanise, with accurate, age-appropriate information about ASD specific to the challenges they face.** These include 1) finding activities that Briana and Shanise enjoy that will also be motivating for Kaneesha and 2) learning strategies to support Kaneesha's active engagement (e.g., simplifying language and exaggerating intonation to support processing).

Desired outcome: *Briana and Shanise will develop the knowledge and understanding of ASD specific to the everyday challenges they face in interactions with Kaneesha to help them 1) find activities that they enjoy playing with Kaneesha and 2) simplify language and use appropriate intonation to support her language processing and engagement.*

The first step of the SCERTS Family Support Plan included the *provision of resources* by educational team members. Given the primary concerns expressed by the family, the inclusion specialist offered Kaneesha's parents several handouts that discussed the use of visual supports that would be appropriate for supporting her development of creative language at home, as well as her ability to communicate about past events. Next, Kaneesha's parents were provided with a variety of resources from the school library specifically for Kaneesha's sisters, Briana and Shanise. For example, Briana was provided with a short book written for elementary and secondary school children that included a series of brief essays written by other siblings of children with ASD, whereas Shanise was provided with a picture book explaining, through both pictures and words, some of the unique ways children with ASD learn and activities that children with ASD often enjoy. These supports were provided to increase knowledge and understanding of ASD for young children.

The next step of the SCERTS Family Support Plan was to ensure that Kaneesha's family had access to educational resources and that a consistent approach could be achieved across home, community, and school. Kaneesha's parents were encouraged to participate in an upcoming *visual support "make and take" session* offered by the school. This support activity would involve an initial training session arranged by Kaneesha's speech-language pathologist that provides guidance on how to use the resources available in the school district's parent library (e.g., clip art software, color printers and laminators) to design visual supports for use at home. Following this session, Kaneesha's parents could schedule an appointment with the librarian to use the equipment at their convenience. In addition, her parents were informed about a *caregiver education program* offered one evening per month to support families in daily routines at home and in the community. Each session would be designed to focus on a particular area of the Interpersonal Support and Learning Support components of the SCERTS Model and would be led by a professional experienced in these areas, such as a speech-language pathologist, an occupational therapist, or an inclusion specialist. Kaneesha's parents and team members agreed that involvement in this ongoing educational series would enhance her parents' skills to address partner objectives such as *Uses augmentative communication support to enhance child's communication and expressive language* (LS2.1) and *Uses augmentative communication support to enhance child's expression and understanding of emotion* (LS2.3).

In addition to these monthly educational support activities, Kaneesha's educational team recognized the need to arrange a monthly *team meeting* and devise an *efficient system of daily communication* between home and school to convey information related to Kaneesha's successes and challenges in both environments. As one of the current concerns related to Kaneesha's family's ability to foster Kaneesha's communication about past events, her inclusion specialist discussed that it would be appropriate for an instructional assistant to include digital photographs of special events that had occurred during Kaneesha's school day, which would serve as learning supports to facilitate her use of language when her family was discussing school events at home with her.

Emotional Support for Kaneesha's Family

Kaneesha's family conveyed a general sense of satisfaction with their family life; however, they did mention several unique challenges that they encountered due to Kaneesha's difficulties. These challenges have included 1) the family's frustration related to limited spontaneity during family time due to Kaneesha's need for constant predictability, 2) concern regarding the emotional well-being of Briana and Shanise, and 3) parental fatigue and stress associated with juggling family life and Kaneesha's needs. Therefore, it was apparent to the team that emotional support was also needed in the following areas.

Goal 1: To help Kaneesha's family members understand and gain access to the range of formal and informal emotional supports that may be available

Desired outcome: Kaneesha's family members will gain access to formal and informal supports that best match their emotional needs at specific points in time.

Goal 2: To help Kaneesha's parents support her siblings with information about ASD when they have questions or when they experience difficulties associated with having a sister with ASD and to help Kaneesha's parents support her siblings in discussing their feelings about having a sister with ASD

Desired outcome: Briana and Shanise will be able to acquire the information they need to have a better understanding of issues they encounter related to having a sister with ASD and will be able to cope with difficulties they may experience by discussing their feelings.

A range of options was discussed with Kaneesha's parents regarding the available emotional supports and an appropriate plan for SCERTS Family Support (see Chapter 3 in this volume for a listing of supports). These included formal supports such as a *support group* held one evening per month at the school, community-based parent support groups, and community-based sibling support groups. During the meeting, Kaneesha's parents expressed that they were appreciative for the range of resources available; however, at this time, they felt that the supports provided by their informal social networks at work and through their religious organization were adequate. However, they felt that the community-based sibling support groups were worth exploring for Briana at this time, as she was beginning to be exposed to questions about her sister and teasing from classmates. Based on this discussion, the staff invited Briana to participate in a *classroom visit,* referred to as Sibling Day in Kaneesha's classroom. This day had been designed for siblings of students in the class to meet the staff, to participate in activities, and to learn about their brother's or sister's educational programs. Siblings have opportunities to ask questions, to share their experiences and concerns, and to meet other children who also have brothers and sisters with disabilities.

The team then discussed a community organization that sponsors *family fun events.* These social events, organized for children and their families, would provide the family with opportunities for Kaneesha's family to go out and play with families that faced challenges similar to theirs. Briana and Shanise would be able to meet other children their age in this context and feel connected to a larger network of siblings of children with disabilities.

Support Among Professionals

As a final step in planning and designing Kaneesha's educational program, her inclusion specialist discussed how the SCERTS Model recognizes that professionals and other service providers may face considerable challenges when implementing an intensive educational program. She also discussed the unique challenges of providing such a program in an inclusive setting, such as feeling isolated from other special education service providers. For professionals and other service providers such as instructional assistants to be as effective as possible in supporting a child and family, a SCERTS Support Plan for Professionals and Service Providers would need to be developed. Because Kaneesha's team, as described in the SAP Activity Planning Form, includes not only professionals but also two instructional assistants, *mentoring arrangements* were scheduled on a daily basis for at least 5 hours per week of paraprofessional supervision provided by either Kaneesha's inclusion specialist, her speech-language pathologist, and/or her occupational therapist. Supervision would involve both direct educational and interactive guidance as well as one-to-one emotional support in a bi-weekly supervision meeting. Additional time was included on a weekly basis for *consultation* between her speech-language pathologist and her occupational therapist to consult to her inclusion specialist and general education teacher. Next, her inclusion specialist indicated that each month, Kaneesha's team members, including her general education teacher, would arrange a *team meeting* to discuss her progress and the need for consistency with both interpersonal and learning supports. It was agreed that the staff could call *crisis meetings* if Kaneesha exhibits sudden changes in her behavior or if a staff member is having a particularly difficult time successfully implementing transactional supports.

SAP Step 10: Performing Ongoing Tracking

Following the identification of Kaneesha's weekly objectives and the weekly objectives of her partners, her team discussed the need to track her progress on an ongoing basis in her educational program. Her team recognized that although it would not be feasible to take data on every objective in every activity, it would be critical to track Kaneesha's progress to inform decision making about the effectiveness of her program's implementation. As a result, progress with each objective would be monitored on a daily basis in one or two activities. To share responsibility for data collection, her speech-language pathologist would assume primary responsibility for collecting data related to Kaneesha's Social Communication objectives, her occupational therapist would assume primary responsibility for collecting data related to her Emotional Regulation objectives, and her inclusion specialist would be responsible for monitoring Transactional Support objectives.

Next, Kaneesha's team formulated a plan for using the information documented on the SAP Daily Tracking Log to complete a SAP Weekly Tracking Log. They discussed having Kaneesha's inclusion specialist compile and integrate this information and take responsibility for sharing it with the team. These reviews would be essential to recognize growth and/or lack of progress in specific objectives. The SAP would then be readministered quarterly.

SPOTLIGHT ON ALAN, AN ADVANCED CONVERSATIONAL PARTNER

Alan, the final child whom we spotlight, is at the advanced level of the Conversational Partner stage. He is a bright and talkative 9½-year-old boy with Asperger syndrome who recently entered the third grade at his local elementary school. He lives at home with his mother and father and is an only child. His family has moved frequently in the past several years due to his father's military base transfers. With each move Alan's parents have noticed a striking change in Alan's anxiety and ability to control his temper. His mother and father further lament that Alan often spends his afternoons and weekends on his own, despite the fact that many children his age live nearby in his neighborhood.

Although Alan has a lot to say and can always strike up a conversation, he seems to be more successful with older children and/or adults. With children his age, interactions either lead to emotionally intense misunderstandings or inevitably come to a halt as he shifts the topic to his current passion about submarines. Although his special interests have changed from time to time, Alan is currently very enthusiastic about reading books about naval history and researching German U-boats through on-line searches. He has amassed quite an extensive knowledge of this subject area and enjoys challenging his father, a naval commander, to recall information about submarine missions and mechanical specifications.

On entering the second grade, Alan's educational team members at his previous school had recognized a number of challenges that appeared to be barriers to his academic and social success. Initially, they noticed that Alan was becoming more sensitive both in the classroom and at recess and that he seemed to misjudge the actions or nonverbal cues of his classmates quite frequently. For example, when a classmate would bump into him while waiting in line, Alan would occasionally act impulsively and either lash out or make a harsh comment. Similarly, they noticed that his ability to cope with changes in routine or expectations relied on the presence of an adult to coach him through more stressful circumstances by explicitly explaining each change, the reason for the occurrence of the change, and a coping strategy he could use. Without this support, he appeared to follow a rather black-and-white adherence to rules and was prone to reprimanding both his peers and his teachers if he felt that they were not following these guidelines.

Despite Alan's fairly sophisticated language skills and what appeared to be a sincere interest in establishing friendships, his second-grade educational team had felt that Alan's conversations were becoming increasingly one-sided. He rarely followed up on topics that his classmates had introduced in conversation, such as sports, movies, and birthday parties. Rather, his conversations always seemed to return to submarine talk regardless of his classmates' level of interest or knowledge of the topic. For example, his teacher observed Alan either walking away from classmates if a topic did not interest him or interrupting his classmates' ongoing discussions to provide information about a famous U-boat capture in World War II. On those infrequent occasions that Alan was able to find a peer interested in naval history, it was strikingly obvious that he rarely recognized opportunities for that classmate to participate in the conversation, as he preferred to be in the role of information provider, not allowing for shared control of the conversational flow. Thus, his educational team had become increasingly concerned about his social membership in his peer group, as he was becoming more vulnerable to being rejected and/or teased due to his unusual style and interests.

The concerns that had been raised by Alan's second-grade educational team, along with the longstanding concerns of his parents, had led to a referral for a specialized diagnostic evaluation, which had resulted in a diagnosis of Asperger syndrome when Alan was 8 years old. His mother and father felt that in some respects, the diagnosis provided them with greater clarity about Alan's unusual patterns of behavior and emotional lability. Nevertheless, they were unsure about the implications of this diagnosis in the long term and how they could use information related to this diagnosis to help Alan develop friendships, cope with his emotions in more appropriate ways, and succeed in school. These concerns were further exacerbated by their recent move and transition to a new elementary school. Alan's anxiety was so intense that he had refused to attend his first day of the third grade. Although he was quite angry and difficult to console, his parents were able to encourage him to join his new class by reminding him about their upcoming family vacation to the Museum of Science and Industry in Chicago. Alan had been talking about this museum for years, as he had wanted to see the U-505, which he noted was "the only maritime vessel of its type on display in the United States."

Alan's current educational program consists of his participation in a general education third-grade classroom, along with 21 peers. In his classroom setting, he is supported by an inclusion tutor who works in close collaboration with Alan's teacher to provide explicit instructions regarding the expectations of specific academic and social activities. Support is provided to the classroom teacher and inclusion tutor through ongoing consultations by a speech-language pathologist, resource teacher, and social worker. In addition, monthly clinics had been scheduled to coordinate services across school and home. In Alan's classroom, a variety of learning supports and accommodations are currently in place, including 1) within-task schedules to remind him to progress through an activity independently and 2) a between-task schedule to support smooth transitions between activities. In addition, Alan is provided with frequent opportunities to take a break and/or go for a walk, as it has been apparent that these breaks have supported his regulation throughout the day and that toward the end of the day, his level of fatigue put him at risk for greater impulsivity and communicative breakdowns.

Alan has also recently begun to participate in small-group learning opportunities for both academic and social support. First, a small-group learning opportunity has been designed in the school's resource room for 1 hour, twice a week, with two other children with similar abilities and needs. This learning context was provided to foster Alan's proficiency in those academic areas, reading comprehension and written expression, that had become increasingly challenging for him. His speech-language pathologist also has developed an opportunity for small-group learning for 30 minutes, three times per week. This social skills group opportunity was designed to help Alan develop a greater understanding of how to *use* his language when interacting with partners by adhering to the conventions for initiating, taking turns, and ending conversations. In addition, this context provides an opportunity for Alan to develop a greater awareness of his peers' preferences for topics and his ability to use nonverbal social cues to self-monitor his actions based on his peers' perspectives.

In addition, Alan's current programming includes a weekly visit with the school's social worker. Because children with Asperger syndrome are at an increased risk for emotional difficulties, particularly with respect to increased anxiety, anger, and depression, his educational team felt that it would be essential for Alan to have a "safe" person with whom to discuss ongoing social concerns, such as teasing, bullying, problems in social understanding, and so forth. The focus of these one-to-one sessions has been to promote self-reflection, positive self-esteem, a more accurate perception of social mishaps that occur, and more active planning and support for learning how to self-regulate in more stressful or dysregulating situations.

Although Alan had initially responded quite well to his new elementary school and third-grade educational program, his school staff observed more pronounced challenges in both social communication and emotional regulation following his return from Thanksgiving vacation. A recent shift in the classroom to more cooperative learning experiences and group projects has proven to be more difficult for Alan than the staff anticipated. Increased expectations regarding reading comprehension and writing associated with the third-grade curriculum have led to increased anxiety and frustration. Alan's teacher remarked that he is becoming explosive and unpredictable in the classroom. He often yells or attempts to clear off the table physically when his peers make suggestions during group projects that do not coincide with his expectations. In addition, he now appears more likely to retreat to submarine talk than at the beginning of the school year and now often disengages entirely by writing lists of submarines and comparing and contrasting their armament.

Based on these recent concerns both at home and in the classroom, the SAP was undertaken to prioritize objectives in both social communication and emotional regulation and to ensure that appropriate interpersonal supports and learning supports were identified to support Alan's active engagement throughout his school day and at home. Therefore, to foster Alan's development and his relationships with his parents, peers, and educational staff, the SAP was implemented to 1) establish Alan's current profile of developmental strengths and needs; 2) determine meaningful, purposeful, and motivating goals to address; 3) select the most appropriate learning contexts and complexity of social support based on Alan's natural routines and activities; and 4) determine essential transactional supports.

Because a comprehensive SCERTS Model program also includes explicit plans for support to families and support among professionals, information from the SAP also was used to ensure that Alan's educational program was compatible and consistent with the needs expressed by his family. In addition, the assessment team determined the specific educational supports and emotional supports that would be provided for Alan's family and the service providers who would be involved in the implementation of Alan's program.

SAP Step 1: Determining Alan's Communication Stage

During an initial SAP team meeting, Alan's team leader, a clinical social worker, led a discussion of Alan's current profile. His educational team and parents completed the Worksheet for Determining Communication Stage and determined that the appropriate SAP forms to use for the assessment would be the one designated for the Conversational Partner stage. This was based on the criteria for determining a child's communication stage, as Alan is currently using far more than 100 words referentially and far more than 20 spontaneous, creative phrases and sentences to communicate his intent. His expressive and receptive language skills (i.e., vocabulary, grammar, and syntax) have, in fact, reportedly been an area of relative strength since preschool. His ability to *use* these language skills reflects the achievements of the Conversational Partner stage. However, his abilities to 1) share experiences in reciprocal interaction, 2) follow the rules of conversation, 3) engage in collaborative learning with his peers, and 4) regulate his arousal level remain significant areas of need.

SAP Step 2: Gathering Information with the Conversational Partner SAP-R Form

Alan's parents were asked to complete the SAP-R Form to provide additional information about Alan's behavior in his home and community environments. This questionnaire identified 1) the primary concerns and stresses faced by Alan's family, 2) Alan's primary strengths and challenges observed by the family, 3) the activities in which both Alan's strengths and areas of need would likely be seen in his home and community environments, 4) Alan's typical partners in the home and community, and 5) the natural contexts in Alan's life outside of school. Alan's educational team also completed a separate SAP-R Form to identify similarities and discrepancies in Alan's behavior at school versus his behavior in other natural environments. The information gathered from both of Alan's SAP-R Forms is summarized next:

1. The primary concerns and stresses faced by Alan's family included

    - "Managing Alan's increasing anxiety"
    - "Coping with his tantrums and outbursts"

- "Supporting his ability to compromise and negotiate, particularly when he perceives that his rules are being broken"
- "Supporting his ability to develop friendships"
- "Uncertainty about the implications of his social difficulties in the future"

2. Alan's parents and educational team identified and agreed on the following strengths and needs in his current profile:

Strengths	Needs
"Alan's memory for factual information related to subjects that interest him is extraordinary." "During academic lessons suited to his interests, Alan is outgoing and eager to participate." "He continues to show a strong desire to develop friendships."	"Alan needs to develop a greater range of interests, as his tendency to become preoccupied limits his growth across academic subjects." "Alan needs to develop more appropriate coping strategies for regulating his emotions and inhibiting impulsivity, particularly when he perceives a task as challenging." "Alan needs to develop strategies for interpreting the actions of his peers, as his misunderstandings can contribute to problematic behaviors and further social isolation." "Alan needs to learn to follow conventions for initiating, taking turns, and ending conversations, as he has a tendency to be one-sided or domineering."

3. The activities in which both Alan's strengths and areas of need would likely be seen included:
   - Completing a worksheet related to a history or science lesson in his third-grade classroom
   - Participating in a cooperative art project in his third-grade classroom
   - Playing during recess on the playground with his classmates
   - Doing recreational activities during gym class
   - Participating in social skills group activities with his speech-language pathologist
   - Completing homework assignments at home with his mother
   - Doing typical leisure activities at home or on the weekend (e.g., researching naval history and submarines)
   - Playing with neighborhood peers on the playground

4. Alan's typical partners
   - Dad
   - Mom
   - General education teacher
   - Inclusion tutor (i.e., an instructional assistant)
   - Special education resource teacher

- Social worker
- Speech-language pathologist
- Physical education teacher
- Librarian
- Third-grade classmates (21 children)
- Neighborhood children

5. Natural contexts in Alan's life included
    - Activities of daily living at home
    - After-school routines at home
    - Neighborhood playground
    - Academic classroom routines
    - Social classroom routines
    - Speech-language therapy room
    - School cafeteria
    - School gymnasium
    - School library

SAP Step 3: Identifying Assessment Team Members and Planning the SAP-O

Alan's team leader collected the completed SAP-R Forms from both Alan's family and his educational team members and began completing the SAP Map for Planning the SAP-Observation. This form was used to help identify appropriate members of Alan's assessment team and their roles and responsibilities. Consideration was also given to whether any referrals to outside professionals would need to be made. In addition, as part of planning the administration of the SAP-O, the following variables were considered to obtain a representative sample of Alan's behavior: 1) the *location* (i.e., natural contexts) where the observations would take place, 2) the specific *length* of the observations, 3) the *partners* who would be present, 4) the *group size* of the social contexts during the observations, 5) the nature of the *activities,* and 6) the number of *transitions* during each context.

After reviewing the information provided in the SAP-R and each of these variables, the educational team planned the observations to ensure a representative sample of Alan's abilities and challenges. First, given that Alan is at the Conversational Partner stage, the minimum length of total observation time was identified as 3–4 hours. Therefore, the team agreed that at least 3 hours of initial observations would be gathered in the school environment, due to the varied nature of the activities occurring throughout his school day. Observations in this context would be scheduled to include both adult partners and peer partners. Next, the team planned an additional hour of observation in the home and neighborhood contexts, as Alan's strengths and needs outside of school would need to be assessed to address his parent's concerns and determine whether he has met the criteria for each objective in the SAP-O. Based on the scoring criteria for the Conversational Partner stage, Alan must demonstrate a specific skill across at least two contexts (e.g., school, home, or community settings) and at least three different partners, with at least one being a peer, to determine that a particular skill was a consistent and solid part of his repertoire.

When planning the specifics of the observations, representative group sizes typical to Alan's natural environment were identified and considered. The following social contexts were planned: one-to-one activity (i.e., Alan working on a homework assignment at home with his mother), small-group activity (i.e., doing a cooperative art activity with four classmates, participating in social skills group with two peers, and participating in interactive play at the playground with approximately four neighborhood children), and large-group activity (i.e., completing a worksheet related to a history lesson in his third-grade classroom). These group sizes and locations were identified as the primary contexts for the observations, as they were common in Alan's daily experiences.

Next, Alan's team leader reviewed the primary concerns of his parents and educational team, as well as those activities in which both Alan's strengths and areas of need would likely be seen. Additional variables also were considered to ensure that his assessment team gained an accurate picture. For example, it was evident that he would behave differently when engaged in an unstructured versus a structured activity, a preferred activity versus a nonpreferred activity, a busy environment versus a calm environment, and a social versus a solitary activity.

With this information, six activities were identified for Alan's school-based observations: 1) a cooperative art project in his third-grade classroom, 2) his social skills group, 3) lunch in the cafeteria, 4) recess activities on the playground, 5) a history lesson in which he needed to complete a worksheet in his third-grade classroom, and 6) recreational activities in gym class. Three additional activities were also planned as part of an after-school home- and neighborhood-based observation: 1) doing typical leisure activities at home, 2) completing a homework assignment with his mother, and 3) playing with his neighborhood peers on the playground. Both his parents and educational team members agreed that Alan's anxiety might unnecessarily increase if school staff were to come to his home and neighborhood. Therefore, Alan's mother agreed to videotape these activities and share the videotape with the staff during a follow-up meeting to obtain a representative sample of Alan's behavior during this portion of the SAP. Everyone agreed, however, that it would be essential that Alan be prepared to have the video camera set up during these activities.

Children who participate in the SAP should be observed across at least three transitions. Therefore, Alan's team leader planned for transitions to be a part of each observation to acquire a representative sample of Alan's behavior during transitions. During the first observation, for example, his team members planned to observe him doing a cooperative art project and making the transition to his social skills group. Next, he would be observed leaving his social skills group and making the transition to the cafeteria to eat lunch with his class. During the second observation, Alan's team members would observe Alan participating in recess, returning to the classroom for an academic lesson (i.e., completing a worksheet related to a history lesson), and then lining up with his classmates to go to gym class. During the home- and neighborhood-based observations, Alan's team members would have opportunity to observe his transitions between doing independent leisure activities at home, completing his homework, and playing with neighborhood children. Information included in Alan's SAP Map is provided in Figure 7.1A to illustrate the outcome of this planning process. After Alan's SAP Map was created, the service coordinator transferred relevant information to the cover sheet of the SAP-O Form (see Figure 7.1B).

SAP Step 4: Completing the SAP-O Form

Alan's educational team used the SAP-O Form for the Conversational Partner stage to gather information for their three observations. Information was gathered for assessing Alan's strengths and needs in social communication and emotional regulation and the strengths and needs of his partners in various environments (i.e., transactional sup-

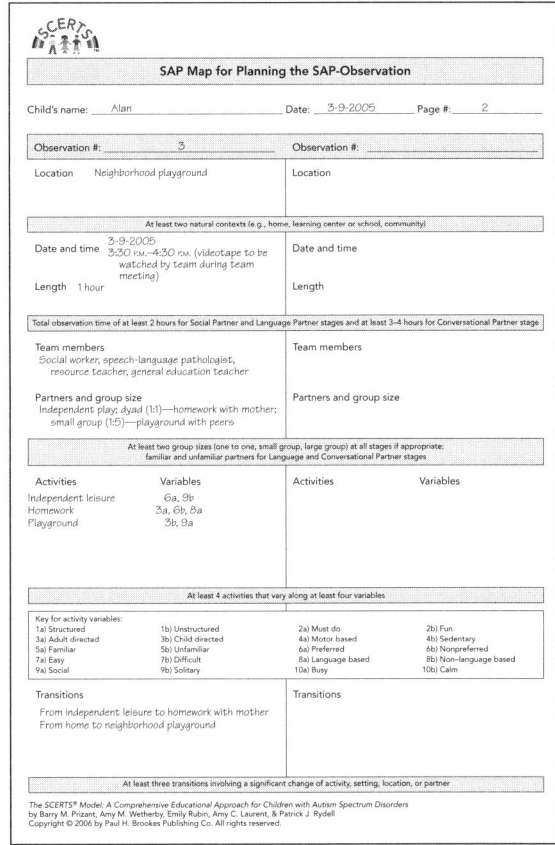

Figure 7.1A. Alan's SAP Map.

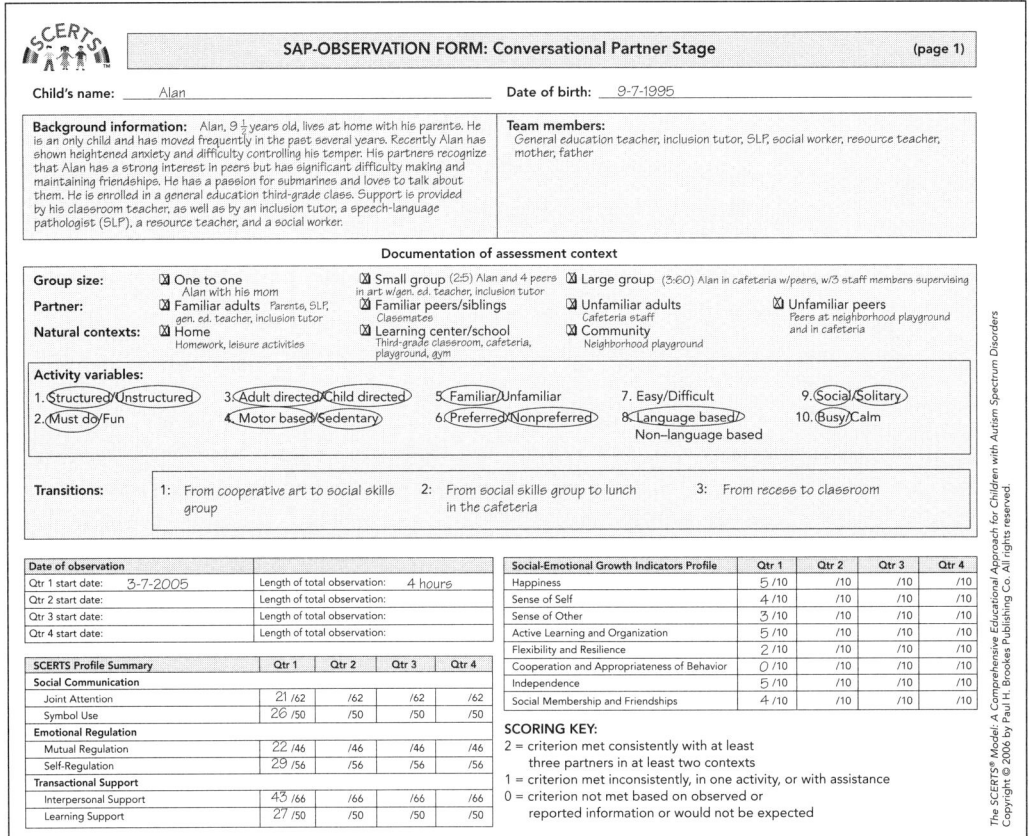

Figure 7.1B. Cover sheet (p. 1) of Alan's SAP-O Form.

ports). The team divided observational responsibilities to develop an accurate and representative developmental profile for Alan, as well as the support strategies used by his partners. The social worker and resource teacher would gather the majority of the information related to emotional regulation because they would be present at both observations and also would be viewing the videotape. Careful observation of Alan's emotional regulatory abilities would be necessary for determining appropriate steps for supporting the development of more socially appropriate coping strategies throughout his day, a critical priority. Alan's speech-language pathologist and general education teacher agreed to focus their attention on gathering information about Alan's social-communicative abilities and his partners' transactional supports and to supplement the observations made by the other team members as appropriate.

SAP Step 5: Conducting Behavior Sampling

Alan's team members briefly reviewed his SAP-O Form following the completion of the three scheduled observations, including the team's review of Alan's videotaped sessions at home and in the neighborhood. A wealth of information had been gathered from observing his interactions in natural environments and activities; however, there were a number of questions remaining regarding specific social-communicative and emotional regulatory objectives. These questions pertained to objectives that required many examples to establish that Alan had a skill solidly in his repertoire or that required observation of very specific social situations (i.e., engaging in a conversation with a peer with limited knowledge of a subject or reflecting on a strategy to support self-regulation before a dysregulating event). The team recognized that there was a need for behavior sampling, as these situations did not occur during the course of natural observations.

Thus, the team identified five areas in which behavior sampling would be required to complete the SAP-O Form. The first two areas related to Alan's capacity to understand nonverbal cues of emotional expression (JA2.6) and understand plausible causal factors for those emotions (JA2.7). In the first three observations, many instances were observed in which Alan dominated a conversation without considering a partner's obvious desire to participate and in which he tended to select the same topics of conversation regardless of his partner's apparent interest level. Although his team members speculated that these difficulties were related to Alan's limited ability to read and understand others' nonverbal cues of emotional expression, such as cues of boredom, disinterest, and annoyance, the team members felt that additional information was needed to assess this aspect of his development. Similarly, the team members were concerned that they did not yet have enough information regarding Alan's understanding of plausible causal factors for emotion. When he lashed out at a classmate who accidentally bumped into him while waiting in line for gym class, Alan did not appear to connect the negative emotional expression of his distressed classmate to his actions. He was not observed to apologize or express empathy and seemed to not even respond to his peer's shift in emotional state. Therefore, behavior sampling was considered essential to determine whether Alan was interpreting these nonverbal signals of emotional expression and was beginning to recognize plausible causal factors for emotions across adults, peers, and situations.

Next, Alan's team leader felt that she needed additional opportunities to observe Alan engaged in conversation with peers to gain a more detailed picture of his ability to *use* a variety of sentence constructions (SU5.4) to provide needed information to his peers (JA4.5). In particular, it was important to observe Alan engaging with a peer who was less familiar with Alan and his interest in submarines. Because Alan's classmates have all participated in a number of conversations related to the U-505, the Museum of Science and Industry in Chicago, and the military career of Alan's father, it had been difficult to determine Alan's ability to provide needed information based on a partner's knowledge of those topics. Therefore, the team realized that these skills needed to be sampled with a different peer or group of peers to assess whether this skill was emerging.

Alan's educational team also decided that his ability to identify and reflect on strategies to support regulation (SR4.5) was an area of skill development that needed to be explored further, as he had only occasionally been observed to reflect on a strategy for self-regulation. For example, on two occasions during a cooperative art project with his general education teacher, he commented, "I am having a hard time with this. Can I take a break? I think that would help." While completing a homework assignment with his mother, he commented, "Mrs. P said that when I write a list of things to do, I do a better job of finishing my work." This comment referred to strategies that Alan was working on with his social worker in his weekly one-to-one sessions. His generalization of this strategy was quite positive. Nevertheless, because this skill needed to be observed across at least three partners (including a peer) and two contexts, behavior sampling would be needed.

With these areas of concern in mind, Alan's educational team desired more information with respect to the following objectives:

- JA2.6—Alan's understanding of nonverbal cues related to emotional expression
- JA2.7—Alan's ability to describe plausible causal factors for emotions of himself and others
- JA4.5—Alan's ability to provide needed information based on partner's knowledge of topic
- SU5.4—Alan's understanding and use of a variety of sentence constructions
- SR4.5—Alan's identification of and reflection on strategies to support regulation

After identifying these remaining questions, Alan's educational team members considered the use of activities set up specifically to address these questions through behavior sampling. With respect to Alan's capacity to understand nonverbal cues of emotional expression (JA2.6) and plausible causal factors for those emotions (JA2.7), a behavior sampling session was scheduled that would provide the team with a chance to see Alan's nonverbal deductive skills in action. The social worker would arrange for Alan to serve as playground monitor for the third-grade students during their 30-minute recess, a job designed by the principal to ensure that all of the students were having fun. This was scheduled with a peer group that Alan does not typically interact with and during a recess time distinct from that of the third graders. In addition, because Alan's role would be to monitor as an outside observer rather than to interact with the children, the complicating variable of Alan's social anxiety might be reduced, hopefully resulting in a measure of his skills when he is better regulated. During this activity, Alan would be asked to pick students and describe to the social worker whether they were expressing a positive or negative emotion based on their gestures, facial expressions, and/or intonation (prosody). Next, he would be asked to serve as a detective and determine causal factors for the positive and negative emotions observed so that he could report his findings back to the principal, with the intent of sharing how many students were having fun and for what reasons.

Next, to gain a more detailed picture of Alan's ability to *use* a variety of sentence constructions (SU5.4) to provide needed information to his peers (JA4.5), an additional behavior sampling session was scheduled in the context of his social skills group.

An unfamiliar peer, however, would be asked to join the session for the day so that Alan and his familiar peers could share experiences with this new partner. As noted previously, this peer would likely not have the same background information related to Alan's preferred subject areas (e.g., submarines, naval history, his father's military career) as his familiar peers. Therefore, conversational sampling might elicit more instances for filling in needed information and repairing communicative breakdowns.

His resource teacher agreed to attend and observe this session and would use the Worksheet for Sentence Constructions in the Conversational Partner Stage to tally and list examples of each sentence type to assess Alan's use of a variety of sentence constructions (i.e., active declaratives, imperatives, negations, interrogatives, embedded clauses, conjoined clauses). As part of this additional session, Alan's speech-language pathologist planned for an activity designed to elicit descriptive and precise language use as well as conversations about personal interests and experiences. This Friendship Map activity would involve a worksheet that each student would complete. In the center of the page, students would draw a picture of a peer and then interview that peer to develop a list of "ideas my friend thinks about," "activities my friend enjoys," and "places my friend has been." At the end of the session, Alan's team will have a better sense of his abilities in these areas, and the students will have a quick reference to use in the future for understanding their classmates' unique perspectives.

Alan's educational team also planned behavior sampling opportunities to gain information about his ability to identify and reflect on strategies to support regulation (SR4.5). His parents were particularly intrigued with this aspect of Alan's development, as they noted far greater success in Alan's ability to remain engaged and well regulated when he could talk himself through a situation in a positive and constructive manner. Nevertheless, they felt that Alan relies heavily on adult coaching and has not yet developed the ability to identify and reflect on regulatory strategies on his own. They offered to take additional notes on his independent ability to reflect on an upcoming activity and determine potential strategies to get ready. They would then report back to the team in the next SAP team meeting, where all of this newly gathered information would be compiled and integrated along with the findings documented in the SAP-O to complete the SAP Sum.

SAP Step 6: Compiling and Integrating Information with the SAP Summary Form

Following the completion of the initial observations and the follow-up behavior sampling sessions and notes, Alan's educational team and his parents met to compile and integrate information, a step that involves two key information sources: 1) summarizing strengths and needs from the SAP-O and 2) documenting parent perception of the SAP-O results.

Key Information Source 1: Summarizing Strengths and Needs

Social Communication: Joint Attention

Alan's parents and educational team members initially focused on determining Alan's strengths and needs in joint attention. As noted, his parents had expressed that Alan often has a lot to say and can always seem to strike up a conversation, particularly if one shares his passion for the mechanical specifications of different submarines. Nevertheless, he is rarely successful at maintaining joint attention with his age peers and does not yet have a true friend. His educational team had observed these patterns during their SAP observations and felt that Alan often stands alone in his class of third graders, who not only have friends but also have networks of friends. Alan's team leader discussed how later in the Conversational Partner stage, joint attention supports the ability to select topics of conversation that a specific partner enjoys; to gauge the amount of background information to provide for a partner; and to request information about immediate, past, and future events to learn more about that partner's perspective. These abilities contribute to greater enjoyment for the child's partner and, consequently, result in an increase in the partner's motivation to maintain and seek out engagement with the child in the future, providing the foundation for friendships to emerge.

Based on information obtained through the SAP-O, it was apparent that Alan's scattered profile of abilities and needs in Joint Attention appeared to have a stigmatizing effect in his peer group. Although Alan demonstrated exceptional strengths in ability to share his intentions across a range of partners and contexts, his limited ability to understand his partners' nonverbal cues of emotional expression and limited ability to modify his language or behavior based on these reactions contributed to a very stilted and insensitive communicative style. For example, his speech-language pathologist commented that during her observation of Alan participating in a kickball activity in gym class, Alan appeared to have no difficulty sharing intentions to request desired activities (e.g., "I want to be the umpire, so I can say whether you are *safe* or *out*"). His abilities to request a break (e.g., "This is no fun. Can I take a break?"), refuse undesired activities (e.g., "I don't want to be paired with you, you are always so slow"), and regulate turns with his classmates (e.g., "You already had a turn. It's my turn now!") appear to be emerging. In fact, the speech-language pathologist noted that Alan was observed to speak his mind quite freely in this activity.

Alan's black-and-white adherence to rules appeared to contribute to his tendency to act as a disciplinarian to his classmates, talking in teacher language. For example, after the gym teacher introduced the game of kickball, Alan took over the lesson by making a comment each time a child did not adhere to instructions. Thus, he clearly demonstrated an ability to share intentions for the purposes of directing another's behavior. However, in doing so, limitations in his ability to understand nonverbal cues of emotional expression prevented him from recognizing that his friends were quite displeased with his comments and actions. His limited ability to modify his language and behavior based on his partners' emotional reaction created a pattern that eventually led to a group of his peers mimicking his actions and even teasing him behind his back.

Alan's scattered profile of abilities and needs in joint attention also appeared to affect his competence in more intimate conversational exchanges with both familiar and unfamiliar peers. Alan clearly demonstrated relative strengths in his ability to share intentions for joint attention by commenting and providing requested information about immediate, past, and imagined events. However, limitations in his ability to modify information based on a specific partner's interests and knowledge led to frequent communicative breakdowns.

During her observation of Alan's social skills group (with three familiar peers and one unfamiliar peer), his resource teacher had observed Alan's talkative and one-sided style. In this context, Alan clearly enjoyed providing information when his peers asked him a question; however, he rarely asked questions in return to learn about his peers, preferring to remain in control of the conversation. For example, when asked, "Where did you go for Thanksgiving vacation?" he responded, "I went to the Museum of Science and Industry in Chicago. The U-505 was longer than I had expected. I thought it was going to be only 212 feet long, but it was actually 251 feet long. It holds 22 torpedoes and three guns, two of which are anti-aircraft. Yesterday, I learned that when the U-505 was captured, we obtained code books to decode secret messages from the German navy."

In providing this lengthy response to the posed question, he appeared to have difficulty monitoring the emotional reactions of his peers to this information to gauge an appropriate length of turn or to determine an appropriate opportunity to ask a peer a question about his or her perspective (e.g., "Have you ever been to this museum?"). In addition, his abrupt topic shifts interfered with his ability to provide relevant and needed background information for a partner to follow his intentions. In the example just given, his resource teacher recognized that Alan had combined information about his family vacation with information he had learned through an on-line search earlier in the week, a pattern that led to a great deal of confusion on the part of his communicative partners. A complete summary of Alan's current profile of strengths and areas of need in the Joint Attention component is included in a sample SAP-O Form and a sample SAP Sum (see Figures 7.2 and 7.8).

Social Communication: Symbol Use

After establishing Alan's baseline in the SAP in Joint Attention, his educational team and family determined Alan's strengths and needs with respect to his abilities in Symbol Use. Based on information gained through both the observations and the Worksheet for Sentence Constructions in the Conversational Partner Stage, it was evident that Alan demonstrated exceptional abilities in specific aspects of symbol use, namely his ability to understand and use generative language to express meanings. In these various contexts, he communicated through a range of both simple and complex sentence constructions and was observed to use an exceptional vocabulary for a child in the third grade. Despite these strengths, Alan's educational team and parents recognized a number of vulnerabilities in Symbol Use that were clearly limiting Alan's competence as a communicator across partners and contexts.

The team discussed Alan's *use* of language as part of an expanding repertoire of learning strategies. As discussed earlier, his parents felt strongly that Alan experienced far greater success when he was able to talk himself through a social situation. Both his educational team and his parents observed that although Alan continues to rely heavily on adult coaching to identify regulatory strategies in unfamiliar situations, he has internalized an ability to use self-talk to monitor his behavior in more familiar routines. For example, his resource teacher observed that while completing a history worksheet in the classroom, Alan told himself, "Write your name at the top," "Put it in the basket," and "Clean off your desk. . . . It is time for gym class." Although he spoke somewhat loudly while using self-talk during this transition, the language clearly guided his behavior and limited his need for support by his inclusion tutor.

In contrast, the team discussed how Alan's ability to use language in collaborative learning activities with his peers was significantly limited, such as using language to successfully compromise or negotiate with a peer. For example, when playing with neighborhood children on the playground, he misinterpreted a child's initial negative response as an absolute refusal to his request to play freeze tag, as the child stated he preferred to play TV tag (i.e., a freeze tag game that requires a child to say the name of a television show to unfreeze a friend). Due to his misunderstanding and inflexibility, Alan stormed away from the kids despite their willingness to take a vote and compro-

SAP-OBSERVATION FORM: Conversational Partner Stage
Social Communication (page 2)

Child's name: Alan

		JOINT ATTENTION
1		**Shares attention**
1		JA1.1 Monitors attentional focus of a social partner (= SR1.2)
1		JA1.2 Secures attention to oneself prior to expressing intentions
0		JA1.3 Understands nonverbal cues of shifts in attentional focus
1		JA1.4 Modifies language based on what partners have seen or heard
1		JA1.5 Shares internal thoughts or mental plans with partners
2		**Shares emotion**
2		JA2.1 Understands and uses early emotion words (= MR1.1, SR3.1)
2		JA2.2 Describes others' emotional states with early emotion words
1		JA2.3 Understands and uses advanced emotion words (= MR1.2, SR3.2)
0		JA2.4 Describes others' emotional states with advanced emotion words
0		JA2.5 Understands and uses graded emotions (= MR1.3, SR3.3)
0		JA2.6 Understands nonverbal cues of emotional expression (= SU2.2)
0		JA2.7 Describes plausible causal factors for emotions of self and others
1		**Shares intentions for a variety of purposes (↔ JA5.2, SU4–SU5)**
		JA3.1 Shares intentions to regulate the behavior of others (= MR4.3)
		☒ a. requests desired objects and activities ☐ c. requests a break
		☐ b. requests help ☒ d. protests/refuses undesired objects or activities
		JA3.2 Shares intentions for social interaction (= MR4.4)
		☒ a. greets ☒ d. regulates turns ☐ g. expresses empathy
		☒ b. calls ☐ e. requests permission ☐ h. shares secrets
		☐ c. requests comfort ☐ f. praises partner
		JA3.3 Shares intentions for joint attention (= MR4.5)
		☒ a. comments on immediate, past, and imagined events
		☒ b. provides requested information about immediate and past events
		☐ c. requests information about immediate, past, and future events
		☒ d. expresses feelings and opinions
		☐ e. anticipates and plans outcomes
2		**Shares experiences in reciprocal interaction**
2		JA4.1 Shows reciprocity in speaker and listener roles to share experiences (= SR1.3)
1		JA4.2 Initiates a variety of conversational topics
0		JA4.3 Initiates and maintains conversations that relate to partners' interests
1		JA4.4 Maintains interaction by requesting or providing relevant information
0		JA4.5 Provides needed information based on partners' knowledge of topic
0		JA4.6 Gauges length and content of conversational turn based on partners
1		JA4.7 Prefers to be engaged with partners
0		JA4.8 Has friendships with partners who share interests
2		**Persists and repairs communication breakdowns**
2		JA5.1 Uses appropriate rate of communication for context
1		JA5.2 Repeats and modifies communication to repair breakdowns (↔ JA3)
0		JA5.3 Recognizes breakdowns in communication and requests clarification
1		JA5.4 Modifies language and behavior based on partners' change in agenda
0		JA5.5 Modifies language and behavior based on partners' emotional reaction
0		JA5.6 Expresses feelings of success and confidence during interactions

SCORING KEY: **2**, criterion met consistently (across three partners in two contexts); **1**, criterion met inconsistently or with assistance; **0**, criterion not met

Figure 7.2. Alan's SAP-O Form (Joint Attention component).

SAP-OBSERVATION FORM: Conversational Partner Stage
Social Communication (page 3)

Child's name: Alan

		SYMBOL USE
		1 **Learns by imitation, observation, instruction, and collaboration**
2		SU1.1 Spontaneously imitates a variety of behaviors later in a different context
1		SU1.2 Uses behaviors modeled by partners to guide social behavior (= MR3.3)
1		SU1.3 Uses internalized rules modeled by adult instruction to guide behavior (= SR4.1)
1		SU1.4 Uses self-monitoring and self-talk to guide behavior (= SR4.3)
0		SU1.5 Collaborates and negotiates with peers in problem solving (= MR3.4)
		2 **Understands nonverbal cues and nonliteral meanings in reciprocal interactions**
1		SU2.1 Understands nonverbal cues of turn taking and topic change
0		SU2.2 Understands nonverbal cues of emotional expression (= JA2.6)
1		SU2.3 Understands and uses nonliteral meanings of humor and figures of speech
0		SU2.4 Understands nonverbal cues and nonliteral meanings of teasing, sarcasm, and deception
		3 **Participates conventionally in dramatic play and recreation**
2		SU3.1 Uses logical sequences of actions in play about familiar events
2		SU3.2 Uses miniature or abstract objects as props
2		SU3.3 Uses logical sequences of actions in play about less familiar events
1		SU3.4 Takes on a role and engages in dramatic play
2		SU3.5 Plays in a common activity with other children
0		SU3.6 Takes on a role and cooperates with peers in dramatic play
1		SU3.7 Participates in rule-based group recreation
		4 **Uses appropriate gestures and nonverbal behavior for the context (↔ JA3, MR1)**
1		SU4.1 Uses appropriate facial expressions for the context and partner
0		SU4.2 Uses appropriate gestures for the context and partner
0		SU4.3 Uses appropriate body posture and proximity for the context and partner
0		SU4.4 Uses appropriate volume and intonation for the context and partner
		5 **Understands and uses generative language to express meanings (↔ JA3, MR1)**
2		SU5.1 Understands and uses a variety of advanced relational words
		☒ a. wh- words ☒ c. physical ☒ e. location ☒ g. causal
		☒ b. temporal ☒ d. numerical ☒ f. kinship
2		SU5.2 Understands and uses reference to things
		☒ a. subject pronouns ☒ b. other pronouns ☒ c. determiners ☒ d. plurals
2		SU5.3 Understands and uses a variety of verb phrases
		☒ a. main verbs ☒ c. helping verbs ☒ e. negation
		☒ b. tense markers ☒ d. modals
2		SU5.4 Understands and uses a variety of sentence constructions
		☒ a. declarative ☒ c. negative ☒ e. embedding
		☒ b. imperative ☒ d. interrogative ☒ f. conjoining
2		SU5.5 Understands and uses connected sentences in oral and written discourse
		6 **Follows rules of conversation**
0		SU6.1 Follows conventions for initiating conversation and taking turns
0		SU6.2 Follows conventions for shifting topics in conversation
0		SU6.3 Follows conventions for ending conversation
0		SU6.4 Follows conventions of politeness and register

SCORING KEY: **2**, criterion met consistently (across three partners in two contexts); **1**, criterion met inconsistently or with assistance; **0**, criterion not met

Figure 7.3. Alan's SAP-O Form (Symbol Use component).

mise. His educational team felt that Alan's limited success with using language to compromise and negotiate with his peers might be a contributing factor to problems in developing peer relationships and highlighted this objective as a critical emphasis for programming.

Next, Alan's educational team raised concerns about Alan's awareness of how nonverbal cues and behaviors can influence the meaning of a partner's message, particularly given his challenges with understanding nonverbal cues of emotional expression. His social worker commented that during his chance to serve as playground monitor, Alan could differentiate very basic facial expressions and gestures (e.g., angry, happy) but struggled with more subtle emotions (e.g., boredom, frustration, annoyance) and with using intonation to support his problem solving. These challenges appeared to underlie Alan's difficulty in understanding humor, particularly because intonation plays a critical role in this ability. On the SAP-R Form, his parents had noted, for example, that when Alan tells jokes, his tone is flat and he does not appear particularly interested in the reaction of his listeners. In fact, he often starts the next joke before even allowing them to respond to the first one. These challenges appeared to be limiting his ability to recognize or understand nonliteral meanings. During an observation of Alan in his social skills group, for example, a classmate made the comment, "I heard that the cafeteria staff cancelled lunch today because they ran out of fruit cups." Alan immediately responded with heightened anxiety, "They can't cancel lunch; it's on the schedule every day at noon." His literal understanding of the schedule coupled with his limited ability to respond to his peer's sarcastic nonverbal cues (e.g., his smile, raised eyebrows, and exaggerated intonation) clearly affected his ability to recognize that the statement was not truthful.

During their observations, Alan's educational team members also recognized Alan's difficulties in follow social conventions to guide his appropriate use of gestures, nonverbal behaviors, and conventions of conversation based on the social rules or expectations for that context. His speech-language pathologist had observed Alan using an inappropriate volume for the context of the classroom while using self-talk during the transition from completing a worksheet to going to gym class. Although she felt that it was clearly supporting his regulation during this time, his classmates had glanced over at him and then giggled to each other, clearly perceiving Alan's behavior to be odd. Thus, this aspect of his symbol use (and self-regulation) was considered an important priority, as the impressions that Alan makes in his peer network are critical to social success. Next, his resource teacher and speech-language pathologist discussed Alan's ongoing challenges with following the conventions for exchanging turns in interactions and/or ending interactions in a socially appropriate manner, as Alan had been observed to simply walk away during a conversation with a peer that was related to a topic he did not find interesting. A complete summary of Alan's current profile of strengths and areas of need in the Symbol Use component is included in a sample SAP-O Form and a sample SAP Sum (see Figures 7.3 and 7.8).

Emotional Regulation: Mutual Regulation

Alan's educational team members and parents then discussed his strengths and needs in mutual regulation. Based on information gained through the SAP-O, three primary areas of vulnerability were identified: 1) the ability to consistently understand and use emotion words, 2) the ability to understand and use graded emotions, 3) and the ability to respond to feedback provided by partners to communicate for assistance in a socially appropriate or conventional manner. The team felt that vulnerabilities in these aspects of mutual regulation have clearly contributed, at least in part, to Alan's emotional volatility and explosive nature in the classroom as well as to increased social isolation from his peer group.

First, the team discussed their impressions of Alan's ability to use early and advanced emotion words to express a range of emotions, a critical aspect of initiating requests for mutual regulation and securing assistance from partners. Although Alan clearly understands a range of emotion words and may use them in certain contexts, using these words to express his own internal state remains inconsistent according to information gained through the SAP-O. During gym class, for example, while participating in a game of kickball with his classmates, Alan was observed to become very upset and agitated when a classmate on the opposing team had caught one of his *foul* kicks. Because he had just learned how to play the game, he apparently was not aware that a *foul* kick could be caught with the same consequences as when a fair kick is caught (i.e., the kicker is "out"). Instead of using his language to express his emotion (e.g., "I didn't know that rule; that makes me mad!"), Alan began to pace feverishly back and forth in the field of play while mumbling the names of different types of submarine torpedoes that were common in the World War II era. Alan's facial expression was intense, and he was observably upset; however, he was not clearly directing these emotional signals to his classmates and/or his teacher. Thus, his educational team recognized Alan's need to solicit assistance for mutual regulation as a critical area. He continues to rely on the support of sensitive and responsive partners, typically familiar adults, to foster his regulation. In this instance, the inclusion tutor invited Alan to continue his conversation with her on the sidelines, allowing the game to continue with minimal interruptions. He was not observed, however, to recover fully and reengage in the activity.

During the SAP-O, Alan's ability to express a range of emotions appeared to be further compromised by difficulties with understanding and using graded emotions, and difficulties changing emotional expression based on the feedback of partners. Both at school and at home, Alan's range of emotional expression appeared either extremely flat or extremely volatile. His parents agreed with this description, as they have themselves described his emotional expressions as an all-or-nothing event. As noted in the SAP-R Forms, Alan's teacher had remarked that he had been explosive and unpredictable in the classroom. His teacher's observations had included instances of yelling, talking back to the teacher, and attempting to clear off the table physically when his peers made suggestions during group projects that did not coincide with his expectations.

During the SAP-O, Alan's explosive episodes appeared to occur even following rather minor instances such as a peer using his pencil during a cooperative art project and a teacher tapping on his shoulder to see if he needed assistance. Alan's reaction to these rather benign actions was surprising and extreme, as he lashed out and reprimanded his peer on realizing his pencil was missing and shoved his worksheet off his desk after his teacher asked if he needed help. The team reflected that he often appeared to perceive gestures (e.g., a peer reaching onto his desk) and nonverbal cues (e.g., a teacher tapping him on his shoulder) as threatening, particularly if they were unexpected, and he could not interpret the intent or meaning of these cues, especially if they were not paired with explicit verbal language. With limited ability to refer to social contextual cues, Alan could not tell the difference between a teacher touching his shoulder to offer assistance or to reprimand him for inappropriate behavior, leading to greater confusion and anxiety. Therefore, Alan's team reflected that without understanding his teacher's intent, he may be using an extreme emotional response as a protective mechanism. Regardless of the specific rationale, his extreme reaction punctuated his inability to express emotions in a graded manner, as even the most benign situations could produce an extreme shift in his arousal state and emotion.

In addition, Alan's limited ability to respond to his partner's feedback, which is intended to support his ability to request assistance in a socially appropriate or conventional manner, results in his difficulties in securing assistance from teachers. These difficulties also affect his ability to establish friendships among his peer group. During the SAP-O, his social worker recognized that Alan's immature and unconventional emotional expressions were clearly stigmatizing for him and were leading to increased social isolation from his peers. Nearly every partner was able to read Alan's emotional signals of anxiety, such as his tendency to pace, talk to himself, and twist his shirtsleeves and shirttails; however, his intense emotional display, his submarine talk, and his obvious internal focus served to ostracize him from his peers. For example, during the kickball game, his peers had clearly been turned off by Alan's behaviors and did not know how to successfully redirect him to play the game. When he had lashed out at his classmate in line for gym class, this peer had quickly backed away and joined another group of children. Alan's educational team discussed how these instances of high arousal and agitation were most likely to be seen in unstructured environments, transitions, and activities that required negotiation and when he experienced unanticipated events or stimulation. Therefore, the need for transactional supports to foster Alan's emotional regulation and expression in these contexts was considered a critical priority. A complete summary of Alan's current profile of strengths and areas of need in the Mutual Regulation component is included in a sample SAP-O Form and a sample SAP Sum (see Figures 7.4 and 7.8).

Emotional Regulation: Self-Regulation

Next, Alan's team members and parents discussed Alan's abilities and needs in self-regulation. Based on information gathered through the SAP, the team discussed Alan's current repertoire of self-regulatory strategies, including the behavioral, language, and metacognitive strategies that he was using to self-regulate his arousal and emotional state. The team identified two primary vulnerabilities: 1) his reliance on adult coaching or guidance to use socially conventional strategies for regulation and 2) his limited use of higher level metacognitive strategies, which would allow him to regulate his arousal not only during familiar activities but also in new and changing situations such as unstructured activities and transitions.

First, his team members listed behavioral strategies that Alan consistently used during their observations: 1) pacing, 2) twisting his shirt, and 3) walking away or fleeing from a distressing situation. More problematic and/or inappropriate attempts included 1) lashing out and 2) clearing the table or his desk. His team agreed that these strategies served as early attempts at self-regulation, as well as clear signals to partners of his dysregulation. The team also agreed that the effectiveness of these strategies was variable, as they were not always supportive of his ability to learn and interact with others. For example, although pacing supported his ability to decrease his arousal level, this strategy was not effective at supporting his reengagement with the kickball game that he had abandoned. Similarly, walking away from an interaction or fleeing clearly fostered a decrease in arousal as Alan removed himself from the stressful event; however, his actions not only prevented reengagement, but they also left a negative impression on his peers. While watching the videotape of Alan and his peers at the neighborhood playground, both his resource teacher and speech-language pathologist observed Alan simply walking away during a conversation with a peer when the topic was un-

SAP-OBSERVATION FORM: Conversational Partner Stage (page 4)
Emotional Regulation

Child's name: Alan

MUTUAL REGULATION

Qtr 1	Qtr 2	Qtr 3	Qtr 4		
				1	**Expresses range of emotions (↔ SU4–SU5)**
2				MR1.1	Understands and uses early emotion words (= JA2.1, SR3.1)
1				MR1.2	Understands and uses advanced emotion words (= JA2.3, SR3.2)
0				MR1.3	Understands and uses graded emotions (= JA2.5, SR3.3)
1				MR1.4	Changes emotional expression based on partners' feedback
1				MR1.5	Uses nonverbal cues of emotional expression
				2	**Responds to assistance offered by partners**
1				MR2.1	Soothes when comforted by partners
2				MR2.2	Engages when alerted by partners
1				MR2.3	Responds to bids for interaction
0				MR2.4	Responds to changes in partners' expression of emotion
0				MR2.5	Attunes to changes in partners' expression of emotion
0				MR2.6	Responds to information or strategies offered by partners
				3	**Responds to feedback and guidance regarding behavior**
0				MR3.1	Responds to feedback regarding the appropriateness of emotional display
1				MR3.2	Responds to feedback regarding the appropriateness of regulatory strategies
1				MR3.3	Uses behaviors modeled by partners to guide behavior (= SU1.2)
0				MR3.4	Collaborates and negotiates with peers in problem solving (= SU1.5)
0				MR3.5	Accepts ideas from partners during negotiation to reach compromise
				4	**Requests partners' assistance to regulate state**
1				MR4.1	Shares negative emotion to seek comfort
1				MR4.2	Shares positive emotion to seek interaction
1				MR4.3	Shares intentions to regulate the behavior of others (= JA3.1)
					☒ a. requests desired objects and activities
					☒ b. requests help
					☒ c. requests a break
					☒ d. protests/refuses undesired objects or activities
1				MR4.4	Shares intentions for social interaction (= JA3.2)
					☒ a. greets ☒ c. requests comfort ☐ e. requests permission ☐ g. expresses empathy
					☒ b. calls ☒ d. regulates turns ☐ f. praises partner ☐ h. shares secrets
1				MR4.5	Shares intentions for joint attention (= JA3.3)
					☒ a. comments on immediate, past, and imagined events
					☒ b. provides requested information about immediate and past events
					☐ c. requests information about immediate, past, and future events
					☒ d. expresses feelings and opinions
					☐ e. anticipates and plans outcomes
0				MR4.6	Requests assistance to resolve conflict and problem-solve situations
				5	**Recovers from extreme dysregulation with support from partners**
1				MR5.1	Responds to partners' efforts to assist with recovery by moving away from activity
1				MR5.2	Responds to partners' use of behavioral strategies
1				MR5.3	Responds to partners' use of language strategies
1				MR5.4	Responds to partners' attempts to reengage in interaction or activity
0				MR5.5	Decreases amount of time to recover from extreme dysregulation due to support from partners
0				MR5.6	Decreases intensity of dysregulated state due to support from partners

SCORING KEY: **2**, criterion met consistently (across three partners in two contexts); **1**, criterion met inconsistently or with assistance; **0**, criterion not met

Figure 7.4. Alan's SAP-O Form (Mutual Regulation component).

SAP-OBSERVATION FORM: Conversational Partner Stage (page 5)
Emotional Regulation

Child's name: Alan

SELF-REGULATION

Qtr 1	Qtr 2	Qtr 3	Qtr 4		
				1	**Demonstrates availability for learning and interacting**
2				SR1.1	Responds to sensory and social experiences with differentiated emotions
1				SR1.2	Monitors attentional focus of a social partner (= JA1.1)
1				SR1.3	Shows reciprocity in speaker and listener roles to share experiences (= JA4.1)
1				SR1.4	Demonstrates ability to inhibit actions and behaviors
1				SR1.5	Persists during tasks with reasonable demands
1				SR1.6	Demonstrates emotional expression appropriate to context
				2	**Uses behavioral strategies to regulate arousal level during familiar activities**
2				SR2.1	Uses behavioral strategies to regulate arousal level in solitary and social activities
1				SR2.2	Uses behavioral strategies modeled by partners to regulate arousal level
1				SR2.3	Uses behavioral strategies to engage productively in an extended activity
				3	**Uses language strategies to regulate arousal level during familiar activities**
2				SR3.1	Understands and uses early emotion words (= JA2.1, MR1.1)
1				SR3.2	Understands and uses advanced emotion words (= JA2.3, MR1.2)
0				SR3.3	Understands and uses graded emotions (= JA2.5, MR1.3)
1				SR3.4	Uses language strategies to regulate arousal level during solitary and social activities
1				SR3.5	Uses language strategies modeled by partners to regulate arousal level
1				SR3.6	Uses language strategies to engage productively in an extended activity
				4	**Uses metacognitive strategies to regulate arousal level during familiar activities**
1				SR4.1	Uses internalized rules modeled by adult instruction to guide behavior (SU1.3)
1				SR4.2	Uses metacognitive strategies to plan and complete activities
0				SR4.3	Uses self-monitoring and self-talk to guide behavior (SU1.4)
0				SR4.4	Uses emotional memory to assist with emotional regulation
0				SR4.5	Identifies and reflects on strategies to support regulation
				5	**Regulates emotion during new and changing situations**
2				SR5.1	Uses behavioral strategies to regulate arousal level during new and changing situations
1				SR5.2	Uses language strategies to regulate arousal level in new and changing situations
0				SR5.3	Uses metacognitive strategies to regulate arousal level in new and changing situations
2				SR5.4	Uses behavioral strategies to regulate arousal level during transitions
1				SR5.5	Uses language strategies to regulate arousal level during transitions
0				SR5.6	Uses metacognitive strategies to regulate arousal level during transitions
				6	**Recovers from extreme dysregulation by self**
1				SR6.1	Removes self from overstimulating or undesired activity
1				SR6.2	Uses behavioral strategies to recover from extreme dysregulation
1				SR6.3	Uses language strategies to recover from extreme dysregulation
1				SR6.4	Reengages in interaction or activity after recovery from extreme dysregulation
0				SR6.5	Decreases amount of time to recover from extreme dysregulation
0				SR6.6	Decreases intensity of dysregulated state

SCORING KEY: **2**, criterion met consistently (across three partners in two contexts); **1**, criterion met inconsistently or with assistance; **0**, criterion not met

Figure 7.5. Alan's SAP-O Form (Self-Regulation component).

interesting or dysregulating, which his peer viewed as quite offensive. Thus, although Alan has a broad repertoire of behavioral strategies, he is not yet using more effective and socially acceptable behavioral strategies that have been modeled by his parents and teachers, unless the strategies have been explicitly coached or encouraged in a given context.

Next, his team members read through a list of Alan's language strategies they had gathered during their observations: 1) talking himself through a specific task or routine, 2) engaging in submarine talk, and 3) writing lists about his special interests. More problematic and/or inappropriate attempts included 1) disciplining his peers, 2) reprimanding his peers, and 3) yelling at his teachers. His team agreed that these strategies served as early attempts at self-regulation, as well as signals to partners of his dysregulation; however, the effectiveness of these strategies was variable, as they were not always supportive of his ability to learn and interact with others. For example, using submarine talk by himself and with his inclusion tutor supported a well-regulated state while he was engaged in these behavioral patterns; however, it was not effective at supporting his ability to rejoin the kickball game that he had abandoned. Similarly, his social worker commented that she had observed Alan writing lists to support his ability to independently progress through a complex academic activity, such as completing his homework at home. However, Alan had been observed to go off track while writing lists in the classroom as he began listing submarine parts and specifications and became increasingly disengaged from his teacher. Thus, although Alan's ability to use language strategies to regulate his arousal is emerging, his limited use of emotion words and limited ability to understand graded emotions has prevented him from developing more consistent self-talk for self-regulation throughout most activities.

The team also discussed Alan's limited abilities and reliance on adult coaching and support to reflect on upcoming activities, to determine his own state of arousal, and to use problem-solving strategies to support his own organization and attention through metacognitive strategies. This was particularly evident when Alan was engaged in activities with his peers, as collaborative learning begins to emerge at the advanced Conversational Partner stage. Although Alan is developing the ability to use instructed learning strategies to guide himself through academic lessons (i.e., using an inner dialogue involving an instructor's cues as well as his own understanding of an event), his ability to identify and reflect on strategies to support regulation remains limited. These difficulties result from limited self-regulatory abilities and a limited awareness of socially appropriate coping strategies that he may use when experiencing dysregulated states. Among peers, Alan did not understand the use of negotiation and compromise as strategies to cope with dysregulating group dynamics, such as responding to the peer who had initially rejected his request for a specific game but who then suggested a vote. Thus, Alan reverted back to idiosyncratic behavioral and language strategies when adult coaching and support were unavailable. In this instance, he walked away and retreated into his special interest of describing submarines. A complete summary of Alan's current profile of strengths and areas of need in the Self-Regulation component is included in a sample SAP-O Form and a sample SAP Sum (see Figures 7.5 and 7.8).

Transactional Support: Interpersonal Support

Both the SAP-R and the SAP-O were reviewed to gain a sense of the strengths and needs of Alan's social network and those interpersonal supports that might be useful for facilitating his social communication and emotional regulation. Alan's team leader first focused on how Alan's challenges in the areas of social communication and emotional regulation frequently had a transactional impact on his partners, particularly his peers. For example, Alan's bias toward a high state of arousal and his difficulties using effective and socially acceptable regulatory strategies often limited his ability to maintain engagement in group recreation activities (e.g., kickball, freeze tag) with his peers. This was particularly true when the nature of the activity was unclear or when Alan was in an unstructured environment, such as the neighborhood playground. In these types of settings and activities, Alan's peer partners often perceived him as demanding and uncompromising. In turn, they appeared less inclined to seek him out or to invite him to play with them. Difficulties understanding nonverbal cues of emotional expression, such as those indicative of a partner's boredom, distress, or even humor, often led to failed interactions and socially stigmatizing behaviors.

The educational team, therefore, considered a number of transactional supports that might be effective when coaching Alan's peers. The team members determined that Alan's adult partners needed to learn strategies for providing him with guidance to foster greater success during interactions with his peers (IS5.1). For example, they discussed a number of interpersonal supports that would likely enable Alan's classmates to achieve greater success in both initiating and successfully engaging Alan in an interaction. He was more likely to initiate and participate in interactions with partners who recognized his need for activities that had a clear turn-taking structure, a predictable sequence of events, and clear guidelines or rules. Therefore, it was determined that his peers would benefit from adult coaching to be able to use supportive strategies such as suggesting several options for a group activity (IS2.1), providing an extended period to review or discuss the rules at Alan's pace before initiating the activity (IS3.2), and pairing nonverbal emotional expressions with explicit verbal language to share emotions, internal states, and mental plans with Alan (IS4.4).

By reviewing the SAP-R and SAP-O results, Alan's parents and educational team members were able to identify a number of interpersonal supports that were emerging as areas of strength in his social network and those that were considered critical areas of need. The following chart provides examples.

Interpersonal Support

Strengths	Needs
Alan's adult partners (both at school and at home) recognize signs of dysregulation and provide information or assistance to support regulation (IS1.5, IS1.6).	Alan's parents and educational team members need to learn strategies for providing guidance for success in interaction with peers (IS5.1).
Alan's educational team members are often able to recognize when Alan would benefit from a break from a complex social interaction (IS1.7).	Alan's partners (at home, at school, and in the neighborhood) need to offer choices of rule-based recreation activities (IS2.1).
Alan's parents and educational team members often interpret problem behavior as communicative and/or regulatory (IS3.3).	Alan's partners need to provide time for Alan to solve problems or complete activities at his own pace by allowing him to have time to establish rules before a group activity (IS3.2).
	Alan's partners need to consistently pair their use of nonverbal emotional expressions with explicit verbal language to share emotions, internal states, and mental plans with Alan (IS4.4).
	Alan's educational staff need to provide guidance for Alan to express emotions and understand the cause of emotions (IS5.4).
	Alan's educational staff need to learn additional strategies for supporting Alan's reengagement in activities following breaks (IS1.8).

Transactional Support: Learning Support

A complete summary of the use of various interpersonal supports by Alan's social network is provided in a sample SAP-O Form and a sample SAP Sum (see Figures 7.6 and 7.8).

Alan's team then discussed the learning supports that have already been implemented as transactional supports in his daily routines and those that should be considered to further augment his programming. During their observations, the team members noted that the learning supports that appeared to be most effective in Alan's home and school environments often had an element of predictability or provided static *written* information. At home, the use of visual support to define steps within a task (LS3.1) had been a successful accommodation for encouraging Alan to complete his homework more independently. The use of a between-task schedule with written cues helped Alan prepare for transitions and upcoming activities (LS3.3). These supports were presumed to be contributing to his emerging use of self-talk to prepare for transitions. Learning supports that had been effective in some but not all contexts included adjusting the social complexity to support organization and interaction (LS4.1), as Alan clearly had benefited from the opportunity to take breaks and problem-solve with an inclusion tutor outside of the complexity of a group activity. Alan's weekly sessions with his social worker clearly demonstrated increased use of regulatory strategies across contexts, as evidenced by his emerging ability to use self-regulatory strategies, such as writing lists. They felt that he needed more opportunities to visit this "safe" person in a safe place to discuss instances of dysregulation and appropriate strategies for regulation, as his anxiety appeared to be increasing in the classroom setting.

Alan's parents and educational team members also recognized the need to add supports to facilitate his use of emotion words for emotional expression, his understanding and use of graded emotions, and his use of language for regulate his arousal using more socially appropriate strategies. For example, they discussed implementing a written language support that would promote more accurate identification of his and others' emotions and the selection of appropriate regulatory strategies when Alan is becoming dysregulated. Next, his team members recognized a need to implement learning supports to foster Alan's ability to determine plausible causal factors for his own emotions and the emotions of others and learning supports to foster his ability to follow conversations when engaged in conversation, such as a conversation map encouraging both comments and questions. Last, they discussed the need to foster Alan's understanding of nonverbal cues of emotional expression, such as facial expressions, gestures, and intonation. Capitalizing on his interest in naval warfare, they developed a code that Alan would be able to use to search for clues in his classmates gestures, facial expressions, body language, and tone of voice. Each of these nonverbal cues would be identified by a specific color (i.e., orange for tone of voice) so that a teacher, for example, could cue Alan to think "orange" when engaged with a peer who might be telling a joke.

Thus, by reviewing the SAP-R and SAP-O results, Alan's parents and educational team members were able to identify a number of learning supports already being used that were emerging as areas of strength in his social network and those that were considered critical areas of need. The following chart provides examples of several of these areas.

SAP-OBSERVATION FORM: Conversational Partner Stage (page 6) Transactional Support				
Child's name: Alan				
Qr 1	Qr 2	Qr 3	Qr 4	INTERPERSONAL SUPPORT
				1 Partner is responsive to child
1				IS1.1 Follows child's focus of attention
1				IS1.2 Attunes to child's emotion and pace
1				IS1.3 Responds appropriately to child's signals to foster a sense of communicative competence
1				IS1.4 Recognizes and supports child's behavioral, language, and metacognitive strategies to regulate arousal level
2				IS1.5 Recognizes signs of dysregulation and offers support
2				IS1.6 Provides information or assistance to regulate state
2				IS1.7 Offers breaks from interaction or activity as needed
1				IS1.8 Facilitates reengagement in interactions and activities following breaks
				2 Partner fosters initiation
1				IS2.1 Offers choices nonverbally or verbally
2				IS2.2 Waits for and encourages initiations
2				IS2.3 Provides a balance of initiated and respondent turns
1				IS2.4 Allows child to initiate and terminate activities
				3 Partner respects child's independence
1				IS3.1 Allows child to take breaks to move about as needed
1				IS3.2 Provides time for child to solve problems or complete activities at own pace
2				IS3.3 Interprets problem behavior as communicative and/or regulatory
1				IS3.4 Honors protests, rejections, or refusals when appropriate
				4 Partner sets stage for engagement
2				IS4.1 Secures child's attention before communicating
1				IS4.2 Uses appropriate proximity and nonverbal behavior to encourage interaction
1				IS4.3 Uses appropriate words and intonation to support optimal arousal level and engagement
1				IS4.4 Shares emotions, internal states, and mental plans with child
				5 Partner provides developmental support
1				IS5.1 Provides guidance for success in interaction with peers
2				IS5.2 Attempts to repair breakdowns verbally or nonverbally
1				IS5.3 Provides guidance and feedback as needed for success in activities
1				IS5.4 Provides guidance on expressing emotions and understanding the cause of emotions
1				IS5.5 Provides guidance for interpreting others' feelings and opinions
				6 Partner adjusts language input
1				IS6.1 Uses nonverbal cues to support understanding
2				IS6.2 Adjusts complexity of language input to child's developmental level
1				IS6.3 Adjusts quality of language input to child's arousal level
				7 Partner models appropriate behaviors
1				IS7.1 Models appropriate nonverbal communication and emotional expressions
1				IS7.2 Models a range of communicative functions ☒ a. behavior regulation ☐ b. social interaction ☐ c. joint attention
2				IS7.3 Models appropriate dramatic play and recreation
1				IS7.4 Models appropriate behavior when child uses inappropriate behavior
1				IS7.5 Models "child-perspective" language and use of self-talk

SCORING KEY: **2**, criterion met consistently (across three partners in two contexts); **1**, criterion met inconsistently or with assistance; **0**, criterion not met

The SCERTS® Model: A Comprehensive Educational Approach for Children with Autism Spectrum Disorders
Copyright © 2006 by Paul H. Brookes Publishing Co. All rights reserved.

Figure 7.6. Alan's SAP-O Form (Interpersonal Support component).

SAP-OBSERVATION FORM: Conversational Partner Stage (page 7) Transactional Support				
Child's name: Alan				
Qr 1	Qr 2	Qr 3	Qr 4	LEARNING SUPPORT
				1 Partner structures activity for active participation
1				LS1.1 Defines clear beginning and ending to activity
2				LS1.2 Creates turn-taking opportunities and leaves spaces for child to fill in
1				LS1.3 Provides predictable sequence to activity
1				LS1.4 Offers repeated learning opportunities
1				LS1.5 Offers varied learning opportunities
				2 Partner uses augmentative communication support to foster development
1				LS2.1 Uses augmentative communication support to enhance child's communication and expressive language
1				LS2.2 Uses augmentative communication support to enhance child's understanding of language and behavior
1				LS2.3 Uses augmentative communication support to enhance child's expression and understanding of emotion
1				LS2.4 Uses augmentative communication support to enhance child's emotional regulation
				3 Partner uses visual and organizational support
2				LS3.1 Uses support to define steps within a task
1				LS3.2 Uses support to define steps and time for completion of activities
2				LS3.3 Uses visual support to enhance smooth transitions between activities
1				LS3.4 Uses support to organize segments of time across the day
1				LS3.5 Uses visual support to enhance attention in group activities
0				LS3.6 Uses visual support to foster active involvement in group activities
				4 Partner modifies goals, activities, and learning environment
1				LS4.1 Adjusts social complexity to support organization and interaction
1				LS4.2 Adjusts task difficulty for child success
1				LS4.3 Modifies sensory properties of learning environment
1				LS4.4 Arranges learning environment to enhance attention
1				LS4.5 Arranges learning environment to promote child initiation
1				LS4.6 Designs and modifies activities to be developmentally appropriate
1				LS4.7 Infuses motivating materials and topics in activities
1				LS4.8 Provides activities to promote initiation and extended interaction
1				LS4.9 Alternates between movement and sedentary activities as needed
1				LS4.10 "Ups the ante" or increases expectations appropriately

SCORING KEY: **2**, criterion met consistently (across three partners in two contexts); **1**, criterion met inconsistently or with assistance; **0**, criterion not met

The SCERTS® Model: A Comprehensive Educational Approach for Children with Autism Spectrum Disorders
Copyright © 2006 by Paul H. Brookes Publishing Co. All rights reserved.

Figure 7.7. Alan's SAP-O Form (Learning Support component).

Learning Support	
Strengths	**Needs**
Alan's parents often provide within-task schedules to help him define steps in his homework assignments (LS3.1). Alan's educational team members provide between-task schedules to help him anticipate transitions and upcoming activities (LS3.3).	Alan's educational team members have successfully adjusted the social complexity of some activities to support Alan's organization and interaction; however, they have identified this as a continued need (LS4.1). Alan's educational team members need to use an AAC system to foster his expression of emotion words and his emotional understanding (LS2.3) as well as his development of socially appropriate emotional regulatory strategies (LS2.4). Alan's educational team members need to use a greater range of visual support to foster active involvement in group activities and interactions with his peers (LS3.6, LS4.8).

A complete summary of the current use of various learning supports by Alan's social network is provided in a sample SAP-O Form and a sample SAP Sum (see Figures 7.7 and 7.8).

Social-Emotional Growth Indicators: Results and Impressions

Next, Alan's team calculated his baseline composite scores for his Social-Emotional Growth Indicators. These indicators would provide useful benchmarks against which to measure future gains in his general qualities of behavior. The general qualities of behavior measured by the Social-Emotional Growth Indicators include 1) Happiness, 2) Sense of Self, 3) Sense of Other, 4) Active Learning and Organization, 5) Flexibility and Resilience, 6) Cooperation and Appropriateness of Behavior, 7) Independence, and 8) Social Membership and Friendships. Alan's Social-Emotional Growth Indicators revealed a relative strength in the areas of Happiness, Active Learning and Organization, and Independence. Areas of relative weakness included Cooperation and Appropriateness of Behavior, and Flexibility and Resilience.

Key Information Source 2: Family Perception of SAP-O Results and Priorities

Before Alan's parents and his educational team the specific goals and objectives for Alan's educational program, his parents shared their perceptions of whether his behavior during SAP-O was representative of his typical behavior and whether Alan's strengths and needs were accurately captured on the SAP Sum. Alan's mother and father indicated they felt that the results of the SAP were an accurate reflection of their son's current strengths as well as his current needs. They also indicated that the SAP had accurately captured the significant challenges faced by Alan's partners when attempting to initiate and maintain engagement with him.

Following this discussion, Alan's parents were invited to reiterate their primary concerns and to discuss their hopes and expectations regarding Alan's development, to clarify goals and desired outcomes for a SCERTS Family Support Plan. Next, his parents were asked to indicate the types of information and support that would be most helpful for their family at home and in the community. Family perceptions are included on a sample SAP Sum (see Figure 7.8).

SAP Step 7: Prioritizing Goals and Objectives

Based on the information compiled and integrated throughout the SAP, Alan's parents and educational team members prioritized goals and objectives that were 1) the most *functional,* 2) directly *addressed family priorities,* and 3) matched the *developmental areas of need* revealed on the SAP Sum for both Alan and his partners. His performance on the SAP-O was not the sole factor for selecting weekly objectives, as equal consideration

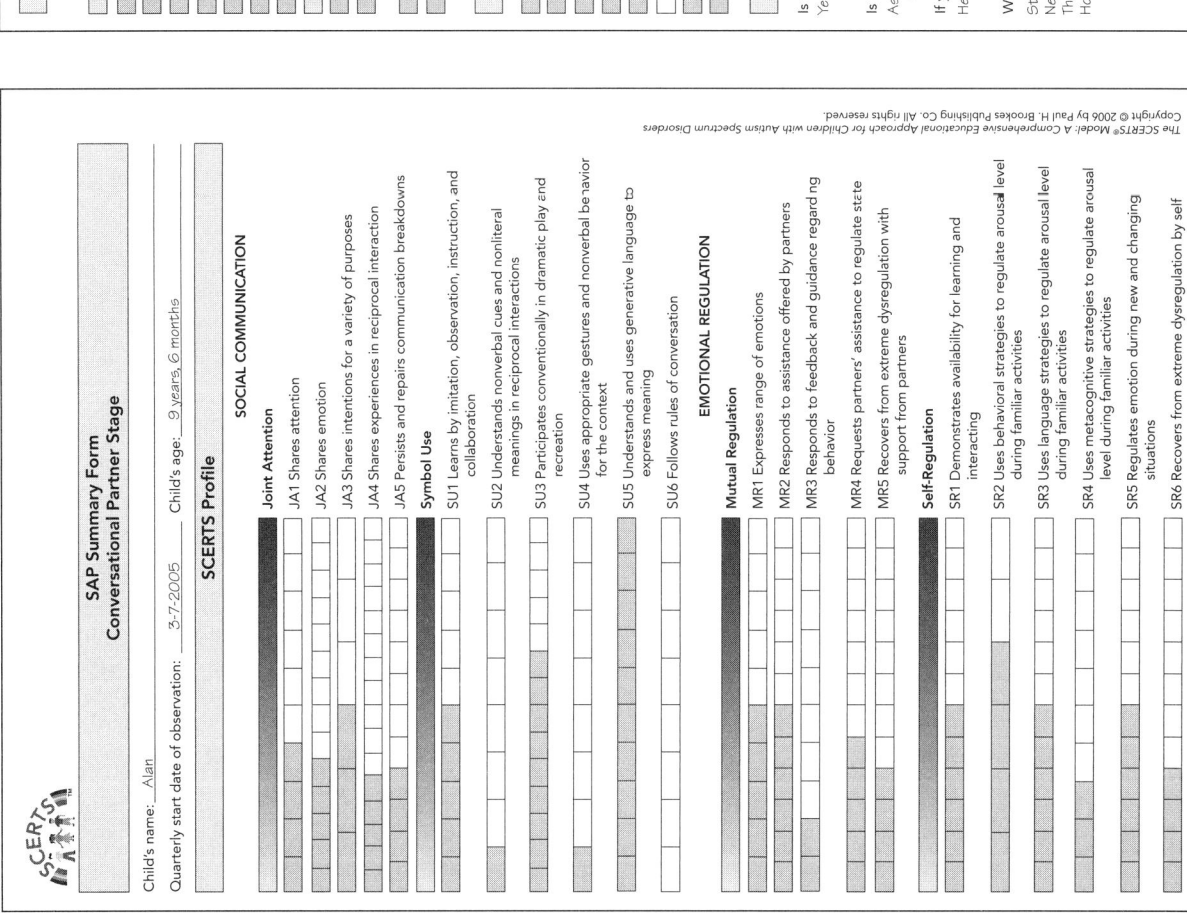

Figure 7.8. Alan's SAP Sum.

Further Assessment—Key Results or Additional Recommendations

No additional testing was completed as part of the SAP; however, the team did agree to refer Alan for an assistive technology evaluation to determine if additional transactional supports would be appropriate.

SAP Activity Planning

Identify key activities using the SAP Activity Planning Form for
☒ Morning schedule   ☒ Afternoon schedule

SCERTS Family Support Plan

Educational Support		Emotional Support	
Activity	How often	Activity	How often
Provision of educational resources Caregiver education program Caregiver development day System of daily communication	Ongoing Monthly Annual Daily	Support meetings with social worker	As needed

SCERTS Support Plan for Professionals and Service Providers

Educational Support		Emotional Support	
Activity	How often	Activity	How often
Mentoring arrangements Team meetings Crisis meetings	5 hours/week Monthly As needed	Team meetings Crisis meetings	Monthly As needed

Prioritize Weekly SCERTS Objectives

Child Social Communication and Emotional Regulation objectives	Partner Transactional Support objectives
1. Alan will initiate a variety of conversational topics (JA4.2).	1. Partner will provide time for Alan to solve problems or complete activities at own pace (IS3.2).
2. Alan will use self-monitoring and self-talk to guide behavior (SU1.4).	2. Partner will share emotions, internal states, and mental plans with Alan (IS4.4).
3. Alan will understand nonverbal cues of emotional expression (SU2.2).	3. Partner will provide guidance for success in interaction with peers (IS5.1).
4. Alan will follow conventions for initiating conversation and taking turns (SU6.1).	4. Partner will provide guidance on expressing emotions and understanding the cause of emotions (IS5.4).
5. Alan will understand and use advanced emotion words (MR1.2).	5. Partner will use augmentative communication support to enhance Alan's expression and understanding of emotion (LS2.3).
6. Alan will collaborate and negotiate with peers in problem solving (MR3.4).	6. Partner will use augmentative communication support to enhance Alan's emotional regulation (LS2.4).
7. Alan will monitor the attentional focus of a social partner (SR1.2).	7. Partner will use visual support to foster active involvement in group activities (LS3.6).
8. Alan will use behavioral strategies modeled by partners to regulate arousal level (SR2.2).	8. Partner will adjust social complexity to support organization and interaction (LS4.1).

Figure 7.8. (continued)

was given to those objectives that would be the most functional and those that most closely matched his family's priorities. Although this process occasionally results in selection of objectives that might appear out of sequence, this flexibility and individualization is actually considered critical for successful implementation of a SCERTS Model program. Please refer to Alan's sample SAP Sum (see Figure 7.8).

SAP Step 8: Recommending Further Assessment if Needed

When reviewing the SAP Sum, Alan's parents felt that a representative sample of Alan's social-communicative and emotional regulatory needs was obtained; however, they sought additional information regarding the most appropriate transactional supports through an assistive technology evaluation. In particular, they were interested whether specific hardware (i.e., a hand-held computer) and specific software (i.e., daily and weekly calendars) could assist Alan's development of language and metacognitive skills to enhance organization and attention. His educational team felt that this type of evaluation would be appropriate given Alan's learning style differences and current profile of strengths and needs. Thus, in addition to a systematic reassessment of the SAP at 3-month intervals, his team recommended that an assistive technology evaluation be provided by the school district.

SAP Step 9: Designing a SCERTS Educational Program for Alan, His Parents, and His Service Providers

Step 9 of the SAP involved identifying a number of key meaningful and purposeful activities, the complexity of social support in these activities (i.e., the roles and responsibilities of educational team members), and familiar partners who will play a critical role in service provision. Alan's team leader, the social worker, assumed the primary role of organizing the educational and support program for Alan and his family. She led a discussion about the continued need for intensive educational programming and *at least* 25 hours per week on a year-round basis of planned and developmentally appropriate learning opportunities. In addition, she indicated that continued individualized attention would be needed for Alan to remain actively engaged during his programming, especially to facilitate relationships with peers. There also was a need for the team and his family to collaboratively develop a plan for educational and emotional support, to address his parents' ongoing concerns about how best to facilitate his development in their home and in community settings such as the neighborhood playground.

This step of the SAP resulted in the development of two SAP Activity Planning Forms, each of which incorporated approximately 3 hours of meaningful and purposeful activities in Alan's natural routines. The first form outlined Alan's typical morning routines in his third-grade classroom (see Figure 7.9), and the second form outlined Alan's typical afternoon routines (see Figure 7.10). Therefore, a plan was established for approximately 6 hours per day, for a total of 30 hours per week of educational programming.

The SAP Activity Planning Forms included the specific goals that would be addressed in these activities and the complexity of social context (i.e., the degree of naturalness and the amount and frequency of one-to-one support) that would be appropriate depending on Alan's social-communication and emotional regulatory capacities. In addition, the SAP Activity Planning Forms were completed to identify the partner objectives and specific transactional supports (i.e., interpersonal supports and learning supports) that would be embedded in each activity. See Figures 7.9 and 7.10 to review these two sample SAP Activity Planning Forms for Alan and his educational team.

Next, Alan's inclusion specialist shared information provided by his family on the SAP-R as well as information obtained through the Transactional Support domain of the SAP-O to discuss with the team a SCERTS Family Support Plan. As discussed, the

Assessment to Implementation: Conversational Partner Stage

SAP Activity Planning Form

Child's name: Alan   Communication stage: Conversational Partner   Date: 3-16-2005   Page #: 1 (A.M.)

Team members and partners: General education teacher (GET), resource teacher (RT), social worker (SW), speech-language pathologist (SLP), inclusion tutor (IT), mother (M), father (F), peers (P)

Activity/time	Social complexity	Group size	Team members and partners	Alan will initiate a variety of conversational topics.	Alan will use self-monitoring and self-talk to guide behavior.	Alan will understand nonverbal cues of emotional expression.	Alan will follow conventions for initiating conversation and taking turns.	Alan will understand and use advanced emotion words.	Alan will collaborate and negotiate with peers in problem solving.	Alan will monitor the attentional focus of a social partner.	Alan will use behavioral strategies modeled by partners to regulate arousal level.	Partner will provide time for Alan to solve problems or complete activities at his own pace.	Partner will share emotions, internal states, and mental plans with Alan.	Partner will provide guidance for success in interaction with peers.	Partner will provide guidance on expressing emotions and understanding the cause of emotions.	Partner will use augmentative communication support to enhance Alan's expression and understanding of emotion.	Partner will use augmentative communication support to enhance Alan's emotional regulation.	Partner will use visual support to foster active involvement in group activities.	Partner will adjust social complexity to support organization and interaction.	Sample transactional supports
				\<-- Weekly child objectives --\>								\<-- Weekly partner objectives --\>								
History lesson (MOD) 8:30 A.M.–9:15 A.M.	1:1	25	GET, IT, P	X		X									X	X					(LS) Models of appropriate self-regulatory language (e.g., highlighting activity structure) will be provided. (LS) A pocket-size emotion wheel will be used to help guide conversation related to emotions as needed.
Music class (MOD) 9:15 A.M.–10:00 A.M.	1:1	24	IT, P	X						X		X						X			(LS) Partners will provide "break cards" and model their appropriate use (e.g., handing to teacher and going to water fountain for a drink). Partners will write the music class schedule on the chalkboard.
Cooperative art project (MOD) 10:00 A.M.–10:40 A.M.	2:5	7	GET, IT, P				X	X						X					X	X	(LS) A wipe-off board will be used to visually map out negotiations with peers and to record compromises. (LS) Group size will be limited to four students.
Social skills group (PAR) 10:30 A.M.–11:20 A.M.	1:3	4	SLP, P	X	X								X	X							(IS) Emphasis will be placed on having each peer explicitly describe his or her emotions or preferred topic rather than on nonverbal social cues. (LS) Comic Strip Conversation frames will highlight Alan's successful interaction with his peers and friends.
Lunch (NAT) 11:20 A.M.–12:00 P.M.	1:2	63	IT, P	X					X					X	X						(IS) Partners will use simple cues related to peers' interests and activities to help Alan initiate interactions with respect to peers' interests and activities. (IS) Peers will inform Alan verbally when they are bored with a conversation and would like to switch topic.

Instructions: Write the weekly Social Communication and Emotional Regulation objectives for the child and the Transactional Support objectives for the partner in the vertical boxes across the top. In the far right vertical box at the upper right-hand corner, list the team members and the child's partners and numbers or initials for each team member or partner. In each row below the column headings, write a brief description of the activity and the time, the ratio for social complexity, the group size, and the number or initials of the team members or partners participating in that activity. Then check off all of the objectives that will be targeted in each activity. Write in a brief description of sample transactional support used in each activity.

The SCERTS® Model: A Comprehensive Educational Approach for Children with Autism Spectrum Disorders
Copyright © 2006 by Paul H. Brookes Publishing Co. All rights reserved.

Figure 7.9. Alan's SAP Activity Planning Form (morning activities) (*Key:* PAR, planned activity routine; ENG, engineered activity; MOD, modified natural activity; NAT, naturally occurring event; LS, learning support; IS, interpersonal support).

provision of both educational support and emotional support to a child's immediate and extended family is a critical priority in a comprehensive program. The purpose of this aspect of the educational program was to foster his family's ability to actively and independently problem-solve and address the challenges they face, empowering and preparing them for the future.

Educational Support for Alan's Family

As noted, primary concerns expressed by Alan's parents included managing Alan's increasing anxiety; coping with his tantrums and outbursts; supporting his ability to compromise and negotiate, particularly when he perceives that his rules are being broken; and supporting his ability to develop friendships. Thus, educational support appeared to be needed in the following general areas.

Goal 1: **To provide Alan's parents with the knowledge and skills to support Alan's development in everyday activities, and to address specific issues that are identified as most stressful and challenging.** For Alan's parents, these issues included 1) supporting Alan's development of self-regulatory strategies to decrease his anxiety,

Figure 7.10. Alan's SAP Activity Planning Form (afternoon activities) (*Key:* PAR, planned activity routine; ENG, engineered activity; MOD, modified natural activity; NAT, naturally occurring event; LS, learning support; IS, interpersonal support).

2) implementing interpersonal and learning supports to prevent dysregulation and tantrums, 3) supporting Alan's ability to compromise and negotiate, and 4) supporting Alan's development of friendships.

Desired outcome: *Alan's parents will feel confident in providing the necessary supports to foster Alan's development of 1) more conventional self-regulatory strategies, 2) more sophisticated strategies for collaborating with peers, and 3) socially conventional communication to successfully establish and maintain friendships.*

Goal 2: To provide Alan's parents with information and resources to understand the nature of their child's disability (i.e., Asperger syndrome) and how it specifically affects his development

Desired outcome: *Alan's parents will become knowledgeable about Asperger syndrome and how it specifically affects their child's functional abilities in life. They will be able to use resources to find information and continue to actively learn as their child develops.*

The first step of the SCERTS Family Support Plan included the *provision of resources* by educational team members. To address the primary concerns expressed by the family, the social worker offered Alan's parents several handouts on the use of visual supports that would be appropriate for supporting his emotional expression and understanding (e.g., using written language to describe upcoming social situations and perspectives). Next, Alan's parents were provided with a variety of resources from the school's special education resource library to convey knowledge and understanding about Asperger syndrome and the unique learning style consistent with this disability.

The next step of the SCERTS Family Support Plan was to ensure that Alan's family had *access to educational resources* and that a consistent approach could be achieved across home, community, and school. Alan's parents were informed about a *caregiver education program* offered one evening per month to support families in daily routines at home and in the community. Each session would focus on a particular area from the Interpersonal Support and Learning Support components of the SCERTS Model and would be led by a professional experienced in these areas, such as a speech-language pathologist, an occupational therapist, or an inclusion specialist. Alan's parents and team members agreed that involvement in this ongoing lecture series would enhance Alan's parents' skills to address partner objectives such as *Provides guidance for success in interaction with peers* (IS5.1) and *Uses augmentative communication support to enhance a child's expression and understanding of emotion* (LS2.3). In addition to these monthly educational support activities, Alan's educational team encouraged his parents to attend an upcoming *caregiver development day,* a full day offered on an annual basis devoted to providing information and discussing resources available for parents and other family members of students with ASD. In addition, they recognized the need to arrange a monthly *team meeting* and devise an efficient *system of daily communication* between school and home to convey information related to Alan's successes and challenges in these environments.

Emotional Support for Alan's Family

Throughout the SAP, Alan's family stated they were generally satisfied with their family life; however, they did mention several challenges that they encountered due to Alan's difficulties, such as coping with his tantrums, finding a balance in their family life, and dealing with uncertainty about the implications of his social difficulties in the future. Therefore, it was apparent to the team that emotional support was also needed in the following areas.

Goal 1: **To help Alan's parents understand and gain access to the range of formal and informal emotional supports that may be available**

Desired outcome: *Alan's parents will gain access to formal and informal supports that best match their emotional needs at specific points in time.*

Goal 2: **To help Alan's parents to identify their own priorities and develop appropriate expectations and realistic, achievable goals for Alan's development and family life**

Desired outcome: *Alan's parents will be clear about the most important issues they wish to address for Alan and their family, develop realistic goals and expectations for Alan, and create a balance in family life consistent with their lifestyle and values.*

A range of options was discussed with Alan's parents regarding the available emotional supports and an appropriate plan for SCERTS Family Support. These included formal supports such as a *support group* held one evening per month at the school and community-based support groups. During the meeting, Alan's parents expressed that they were appreciative for the range of resources available; however, at this time, they felt that the supports provided by their informal social networks in their extended family and through the military community were sufficient. Based on this discussion, the staff encouraged Alan's parents to schedule *support meetings* with Alan's social worker. In this approach, a family member or both parents together would have the opportunity to meet with a staff member who knows the child and family to discuss specific acute issues or challenges that have arisen.

Support Among Professionals

As a final step in planning and designing Alan's educational program, his team leader discussed how the SCERTS Model recognizes that professionals and other service providers may face considerable challenges when implementing an intensive educational program. She also discussed the unique challenges of providing such a program in an integrated setting, such as feeling isolated from other special education service providers. For professionals and other service providers to be as effective as possible in supporting a child and family, a SCERTS Support Plan for Professionals and Service Providers would need to be developed. Because Alan's team, as described in the SAP Activity Planning Form, includes not only professionals but also a paraprofessional (i.e., an inclusion tutor), *mentoring arrangements* were scheduled on a daily basis for at least 5 hours per week of paraprofessional supervision provided by the resource teacher, the speech-language pathologist, and/or the social worker. Supervision would involve both direct educational and interactive guidance as well as one-to-one emotional support in a bimonthly supervision meeting. Additional time was included on a monthly basis for a *team meeting* to discuss Alan's progress and the need for consistency with both interpersonal and learning supports. It was agreed that the staff could call *crisis meetings* if Alan were to exhibit sudden changes in his behavior or if a staff member is having a particularly difficult time successfully implementing transactional supports.

SAP Step 10: Ongoing Tracking

Following the identification of weekly objectives for Alan and his partners, his team discussed the need to track his ongoing progress in his educational program. During their discussion, his team recognized that it would not be feasible to take data on every objective in every activity; however, it would be critical to track Alan's progress to inform decision making about the effectiveness of his program's implementation. As a result, progress with each objective would be monitored on a daily basis in one or two activities. To share responsibility for data collection, his speech-language pathologist would assume primary responsibility for collecting data related to Alan's Social Communication objectives, his inclusion tutor would assume primary responsibility for collecting data related to his Emotional Regulation objectives, and his resource teacher would be responsible for monitoring Transactional Support objectives.

Next, Alan's team formulated a plan for using the information documented on the SAP Daily Tracking Log to complete a SAP Weekly Tracking Log. They discussed having his resource teacher compile and integrate this information and take responsibility for sharing it with the team. These reviews would be essential for recognize growth and/or lack of progress in specific objectives. The SAP would then be readministered quarterly.

References

Blackburn, R. (2005, March 5). *Logically illogical: Information and insight into autism.* Paper presented at the 10th annual ASD Symposium, Providence, RI.

Bricker, D. (with Pretti-Frontczak, K., & McComas, N.). (1998). *An activity-based approach to early intervention* (2nd ed.). Baltimore: Paul H. Brookes Publishing Co.

Bricker, D., & Cripe, J.J.W. (1992). *An activity-based approach to early intervention.* Baltimore: Paul H. Brookes Publishing Co.

Brown, L., Branston, M.B., Hamre-Nietupski, S., Pumpian, L., Certo, N., & Gruenewald, L. (1979). A strategy for developing chronological age-appropriate and functional curricular content for severely handicapped adolescents and young adults. *Journal of Special Education, 13,* 81–90.

Bryson, S. (1996). Epidemiology of autism: Overview and issues outstanding. In D. Cohen & F.R. Volkmar (Eds.), *Handbook of autism and pervasive developmental disorders* (2nd ed., pp. 41–46). New York: Wiley.

Cautela, J., & Groden, J. (1981). *Relaxation procedures for persons with developmental disabilities.* Champaign, IL: Research Press.

Frost, L., & Bondy, A. (1994). *PECS: The Picture Exchange Communication System training manual.* Cherry Hill, NJ: Pyramid Educational Consultants.

Gray, C. (1994). *Comic strip conversations and Social Stories: Unique methods to improve social understanding* (Videotape and booklet). Arlington, TX: Future Horizons.

Gray, C. (1994b). *The new Social Story book.* Arlington, TX: Future Horizons.

Hodgdon, L. (1995). *Visual strategies for improving communication.* Troy, MI: Quirk Roberts Publishing.

Hodgdon, L. (1999). *Solving behavior problems in autism.* Troy, MI: Quirk Roberts Publishing.

Lord, C., & Paul, R. (1997). Language and communication in autism. In D. Cohen & F.R. Volkmar (Eds.), *Handbook of autism and pervasive developmental disorders* (2nd ed, pp. 195–225). New York: Wiley.

McDonough, S. (1998). Interaction guidance: Understanding and treating early infant-caregiver relationship disturbances. In C.H. Zeanah (Ed.), *The handbook of infant mental health* (2nd ed.). New York: Guilford Press.

National Research Council, Division of Behavioral and Social Sciences and Education, Committee on Educational Interventions for Children with Autism (NRC). (2001). *Educating children with autism.* Washington, DC: National Academies Press.

Pretti-Frontczak, K., & Bricker, D. (2004). *An activity-based approach to early intervention* (3rd ed.). Baltimore: Paul H. Brookes Publishing Co.

Prizant, B.M., Meyer, E.C., & Lobato, D. (1997). Brothers and sisters of children with communication disorders. *Seminars in Speech and Language, 18,* 263–282.

Rydell, P.J., & Prizant, B. (1995). Assessment and intervention strategies for children who use echolalia. In K. Quill (Ed.), *Teaching children with autism: Strategies to enhance communication and socialization* (pp. 105–129). Albany, NY: Delmar.

Schopler, E., Mesibov, G., & Hearsey, K. (1995). Structured teaching in the TEACCH curriculum. In E. Schopler & G. Mesibov (Eds.), *Learning and cognition in autism* (pp. 243–268). New York: Plenum Press.

Shonkoff, J., Hauser-Cram, P., Krauss, M., & Upshur, C. (1992). Development of infants with disabilities and their families: Implications for theory and service delivery. *Monographs of the Society for Research in Child Development, 57*(6, Serial No. 230).

Snyder-McLean, L., Solomonson, B., McLean, J., & Sack, S. (1984). Structuring joint action routines: A strategy for facilitating communication and language development in the classroom. *Seminars in Speech and Language, 5,* 213–228.

Sussman, F. (1999). *More than words: Helping parents promote communication and social skills in children with autism spectrum disorder.* Toronto: The Hanen Centre.

Vygotsky, L. (1986). *Thought and language* (A. Kozulin, Ed. and Trans.). Cambridge, MA: Harvard University Press.

Appendix

SCERTS Assessment Process–Quality Indicators

The following SCERTS Assessment Process–Quality Indicators (SAP-Q) scales are designed to be used by program administrators and staff to rate the quality of their program. The specific purpose of each scale is as follows.

Key Indicators of a Quality SCERTS Model Program: The first SAP-Q scale lists the essential key indicators of a quality SCERTS Model program. It can be used to determine whether the program is meeting these key indicators. Program administrators and/or staff can rate the program on each indicator using a 3-point rating scale. For any indicator with a rating of 0 or 1, an action plan and a time line should be formulated to address the shortcomings of the indicator in question.

SCERTS Program Quality Indicator Rating Scale: Support to Families: The second SAP-Q scale is designed to be used to provide specific, detailed information to program staff about whether specific quality indicators are being addressed in providing educational and emotional support to families. Program administrators and/or staff can rate the program on the *quality* of each indicator using a 3-point rating scale. For any indicator with a rating of 0 or 1, a *priority* rating of A, B, or C should be given to determine the urgency of addressing the indicator, and an action plan and a time line should be formulated to improve the ratings for A- and B-level priorities.

SCERTS Program Quality Indicator Rating Scale: Support Among Professionals: The third SAP-Q scale is designed to be used to provide specific, detailed information to program staff about whether specific quality indicators are being addressed in providing support among professionals. Program administrators and/or staff can rate the program on the *quality* of each indicator using a 3-point rating scale. For any indicator with a rating of 0 or 1, a *priority* rating of A, B, or C should be given to determine the urgency of addressing the indicator, and an action plan and a time line should be formulated to improve the ratings for A- and B-level priorities.

SAP Quality Indicator Form
Key Indicators of a Quality SCERTS Model Program (page 1)

Program name: _____ Person completing this form: _____ Date: _____

All of the following are essential key indicators of a quality SCERTS Model program. Rate your program on each indicator using the following rating scale. Formulate an action plan and a time line to improve any ratings of 0 or 1.

Quality Rating	
0	There is no or minimal evidence that this is happening.
1	There is some evidence that this is happening with at least some of the staff or some of the time.
2	This is clearly happening with most of the staff most of the time.

Quality	Program Planning, Implementation, Monitoring, and Adjustment
	1. A SCERTS Assessment Process (SAP) is completed initially and updated quarterly for each child.
	2. At least four to eight objectives addressing social communication and emotional regulation and four to eight objectives addressing transactional supports are targeted each week for each child and his or her partners.
	3. Social Communication objectives emphasize the functional use of language and communication in natural contexts, not simply teaching isolated language and speech behaviors.
	4. A child's emotional regulation and its effect on social communication and learning are always considered, and arousal states are monitored constantly.
	5. The targeted objectives are functional (i.e., the skill makes a difference in a child's life), directly address family priorities (i.e., the skill is valued by the child's family), and match the child's developmental areas of need.
	6. Objectives are targeted to support all partners, including peers, in engaging more effectively with a child with an autism spectrum disorder, with the overriding goal of supporting positive relationships.
	7. Approaches to problem behavior are fully integrated with social communication programming and are determined by understanding the range of challenges to a child's emotional regulation.
	8. A number of key meaningful activities and purposeful activities (i.e., MA & PA) have been identified for the morning and/or afternoon schedule.
	9. More than one objective is targeted for each child within each activity, and each objective is targeted within more than one activity.
	10. Activities are designed regarding the levels of support within these activities and the familiar partners who will play a critical role to address a child's objectives.
	11. Data are collected daily and tallied weekly so that all objectives are measured weekly.
	12. The team meets regularly to ensure coordination in programming.
	13. On a quarterly basis, adjustments in programming are considered and made by each child's team based on the SAP results to ensure that each child is making progress.
	14. The staff monitor the intensity of each child's program and documents that each child is actively engaged in productive learning activities at least 25 hours per week.

The SCERTS® Model: A Comprehensive Educational Approach for Children with Autism Spectrum Disorders
by Barry M. Prizant, Amy M. Wetherby, Emily Rubin, Amy C. Laurent, & Patrick J. Rydell
Copyright © 2006 by Paul H. Brookes Publishing Co. All rights reserved.

SAP Quality Indicator Form
Key Indicators of a Quality SCERTS Model Program

Quality	Transactional Support: Learning Support and Interpersonal Support
	1. Partners are responsive to children's communication and emotional expression in all learning environments.
	2. Partners foster children's initiation by offering choices, waiting, and facilitating shared control.
	3. Partners respect children's independence by allowing breaks and time for problem solving, by interpreting problem behavior as meaningful, and by honoring protests when appropriate and possible.
	4. Partners set the stage for engagement by responding to children's nonverbal and verbal communication and use of words.
	5. Partners provide development support to encourage children's participation, interaction, and success.
	6. Partners adjust language complexity and quality to match each child's developmental level.
	7. Partners model appropriate language, communication, play, and behavior.
	8. Partners structure activities throughout the day to encourage children's active participation.
	9. Partners use augmentative systems to foster expression and understanding of language and emotion.
	10. Partners use visual and organizational supports to encourage children to participate in activities and promote smooth transitions across activities.
	11. Partners modify goals, activities, and the learning environment to promote initiation of communication, emotional regulation, motivation, and independence.
Quality	**Transactional Support: Support to Families and Support Among Professionals**
	1. Family members are engaged as collaborators in efforts to support their child's development.
	2. A priority is placed on the development of mutually respectful, positive parent–professional relationships to enhance family members' and professionals' sense of competence and trust.
	3. A plan is developed and offered to families that includes educational and emotional support.
	4. A plan is developed and offered for professionals that includes educational and emotional support.

The SCERTS® Model: A Comprehensive Educational Approach for Children with Autism Spectrum Disorders
by Barry M. Prizant, Amy M. Wetherby, Emily Rubin, Amy C. Laurent, & Patrick J. Rydell
Copyright © 2006 by Paul H. Brookes Publishing Co. All rights reserved.

SAP Quality Indicator Form
SCERTS Program Quality Indicator Rating Scale: Support to Families (page 1)

Program name: _____ Person completing this form: _____ Date: _____

Rate your program on the quality of each indicator using the following rating scale. For indicators with a quality rating of 0 or 1, rate the priority of addressing each indicator. Formulate an action plan and a time line to improve any priorities with ratings of A or B.

	Quality Rating
0	There is no or minimal evidence that this is happening.
1	There is some evidence that this is happening with at least some of the staff or some of the time.
2	This is clearly happening with most of the staff most of the time.

	Priority Rating
A	Needs immediate attention, of the highest priority
B	Important issue to address, but not immediate or urgent
C	Not important or relevant now, but need to monitor for future consideration

Quality	Educational Support to Families (Child Specific)	Priority
	1. Parents are educated about their child's level of social communication, specific strategies in communicating, and specific difficulties faced in emotional regulation and related areas.	
	2. Parents are educated about the sequences and processes of language, communication, and social-emotional development relevant to their child, to develop appropriate expectations regarding their child's development.	
	3. Parents are supported in developing interactive styles that are appropriate and responsive to their child and supportive of successful communicative interactions, through hands-on guidance.	
	4. Parents are helped to identify and modify daily activities and routines and develop new activities that will support their child's social communication development and improve relationships with their child.	
	5. Parents are offered a number of opportunities to become educated and involved in their child's program (e.g., regularly scheduled progress review meetings with teachers, direct observations of the program, after-school educational seminars or discussions, systematic and regular two-way home–school communication regarding the child's participation and progress).	
	6. The program fosters coordination of educational efforts among school, home, and other agencies or service providers.	
	7. The program has a process for supporting families by addressing a child's needs outside of the school day as identified by his or her parents.	
	8. The program arranges for home-based services or home visits, depending on the needs of a family.	
	9. The program provides learning supports for home use (e.g., visual supports).	

The SCERTS® Model: A Comprehensive Educational Approach for Children with Autism Spectrum Disorders
by Barry M. Prizant, Amy M. Wetherby, Emily Rubin, Amy C. Laurent, & Patrick J. Rydell
Copyright © 2006 by Paul H. Brookes Publishing Co. All rights reserved.

	SAP Quality Indicator Form SCERTS Program Quality Indicator Rating Scale: Support to Families	(page 2)

Quality	Educational Support to Families (Child Specific) *(continued)*	Priority
	10. The staff help siblings develop the social communication skills and strategies to interact and play successfully with their brother or sister with an autism spectrum disorder (ASD) in everyday social communication and play interactions, including the ability to read the communicative and emotional regulatory signals of their brother or sister.	
	11. The staff help siblings understand that problem behaviors may be due to communicative limitations and other causes of emotional dysregulation.	
Quality	**Educational Support to Families (General)**	**Priority**
	1. The program informs parents of outside agencies or people who are able to provide support and information specific to the legal rights of their child and their family.	
	2. The program offers resources such as a lending library for books, videotapes, and DVDs.	
	3. Professionals provide information about a range of educational approaches and clearly state their biases about educational issues when relevant.	
	4. Professionals help family members deal with and develop a better understanding of the critical and often controversial information available about ASD.	
	5. The program inquires about and provides support regarding sibling issues when parents request assistance with such matters.	
	6. The program provides parents with information about ASD that is age appropriate for siblings of the child with ASD (e.g., books for children about ASD).	
	7. Parents are supported in addressing issues raised by siblings.	
	8. The program provides training and information to parents to support their efforts in fostering more successful play and social interactive experiences for siblings.	
	9. The program provides parents with material that clearly specifies the program's mission statement or philosophy, resources available, relevant policies and procedures, and the student's and parents' legal rights.	
Quality	**Emotional Support to Families**	**Priority**
	1. Staff help family members identify major sources of stress related to having a child with ASD and to develop coping strategies specific to the major sources of stress that are identified.	
	2. Staff help family members identify, develop, and/or gain access to the supports that would be helpful in addressing the family's emotional needs, including referral to outside services as needed.	
	3. There is a mechanism for program staff to respond to crises or provision of urgent, immediate support to a family.	
	4. Staff support parents in addressing difficult parent–professional relationships.	

The SCERTS® Model: A Comprehensive Educational Approach for Children with Autism Spectrum Disorders
by Barry M. Prizant, Amy M. Wetherby, Emily Rubin, Amy C. Laurent, & Patrick J. Rydell
Copyright © 2006 by Paul H. Brookes Publishing Co. All rights reserved.

SAP Quality Indicator Form
SCERTS Program Quality Indicator Rating Scale: Support to Families

	#	Indicator	
	5.	Staff support parents in dealing with stresses that arise with educational and health care systems.	
	6.	The program has clear policies and procedures for addressing parental concerns and grievances about staff or about a child's program, with timely follow-up and feedback.	
	7.	The program has clear policies and procedures for helping with stressful circumstances for families, such as transitions to summer programming and the next school year.	
	8.	Staff engage parents in discussions to identify the most crucial issues for their child and the family.	
	9.	Staff collaborate with parents to develop realistic short-term goals and expectations for their child.	
	10.	Staff encourage parents to express long-term goals for their child and family.	
	11.	Staff provide opportunities to problem-solve the challenges of bringing a balance to family life.	
	12.	Staff demonstrate respect for diversity of cultures, languages, values, and parenting styles and adjust practices accordingly for different families.	
	13.	Parents are provided opportunities to clearly state their educational priorities for their child in program planning meetings.	
	14.	Staff help parents create an atmosphere of open communication so that siblings feel comfortable in expressing feelings or raising questions about their brother or sister or about ASD.	
	15.	Staff help parents respond to siblings' questions about ASD in a manner that is appropriate to siblings' level of understanding and provide parents with resources about supporting siblings.	
	16.	The program offers sibling support activities such as sibling groups and family fun events.	

The SCERTS® Model: A Comprehensive Educational Approach for Children with Autism Spectrum Disorders
by Barry M. Prizant, Amy M. Wetherby, Emily Rubin, Amy C. Laurent, & Patrick J. Rydell
Copyright © 2006 by Paul H. Brookes Publishing Co. All rights reserved.

SAP Quality Indicator Form
SCERTS Program Quality Indicator Rating Scale: Support Among Professionals (page 1)

Program name: _____ Person completing this form: _____ Date: _____

Rate your program on the quality each indicator using the following rating scale. For indicators with a quality rating of 0 or 1, rate the priority of addressing each indicator. Formulate an action plan and a time line to improve any priorities with ratings of A or B.

Quality Rating	
0	There is no or minimal evidence that this is happening.
1	There is some evidence that this is happening with at least some of the staff or some of the time.
2	This is clearly happening with most of the staff most of the time.

Priority Rating	
A	Needs immediate attention, of the highest priority
B	Important issue to address, but not immediate or urgent
C	Not important or relevant now, but need to monitor for future consideration

Quality	Educational Support	Priority
	1. Staff participate in continuing education activities within the school or agency that are designed to further develop staff members' knowledge and skills, such as regularly scheduled staff in-service trainings or professional development days.	
	2. Staff participate in continuing education activities outside of the school setting, such as by attending regional or national conferences and workshops.	
	3. There is a mentoring system to link more experienced with less experienced professionals and/or paraprofessionals.	
	4. Professionals and paraprofessionals receive specific and direct instruction and supervision as needed regarding their responsibilities to students.	
	5. Ongoing support and technical assistance are available from individuals other than classroom staff or direct supervisors to resolve challenging issues or concerns related to specific children (e.g., outside consultants are brought into a program as needed).	
	6. Teachers and related service providers have access to students' individualized education programs (IEPs) or individualized family service plans (IFSPs) and are informed of their responsibilities for implementation.	
	7. Staff are available in a ratio sufficient to provide the support necessary to accomplish IEP or IFSP goals for children and carry out other programmatic responsibilities.	
	8. Staff plan and collaborate on students' programs using a team approach.	

The SCERTS® Model: A Comprehensive Educational Approach for Children with Autism Spectrum Disorders
by Barry M. Prizant, Amy M. Wetherby, Emily Rubin, Amy C. Laurent, & Patrick J. Rydell
Copyright © 2006 by Paul H. Brookes Publishing Co. All rights reserved.

	SAP Quality Indicator Form SCERTS Program Quality Indicator Rating Scale: Support Among Professionals	

Quality	Educational Support (continued)	Priority
	9. Sufficient time is available for collaboration.	
	10. Staff are monitored, evaluated, and given feedback regarding their effectiveness with students and participation as team members.	
	11. Staff have opportunities to be involved in research projects conducted in collaboration with university-affiliated researchers.	

Quality	Emotional Support	Priority
	1. Regularly scheduled meetings allow for discussion of emotional challenges at work.	
	2. Informal opportunities are available to address emotionally challenging issues (e.g., weekly brown bag lunches, beginning- or end-of-day sharing times).	
	3. There is a process for calling crisis meetings on an urgent, as-needed basis.	
	4. There are regularly scheduled staff retreats (annual or biannual) for program review, action planning, and similar issues.	
	5. There is a clearly defined process for staff to express concerns to supervisors, with feedback and follow-up.	
	6. There are policies to ensure that staff interact and communicate with students, families, and each other in a supportive and respectful manner, with clearly stated standards of conduct.	
	7. Staff use supportive and positive language and nonverbal behavior when interacting directly with students and parents and when discussing other staff.	
	8. Differences of opinion and conflicts among staff and between staff and families are dealt with in a respectful and constructive manner.	
	9. Staff are invited to participate in decision-making processes that directly affect them.	
	10. Recommendations are solicited from staff to improve services at a child-specific or programmatic level, including modifications in program policies and procedures.	
	11. Formal programmatic self-studies are conducted and result in action plans for program improvement.	

The SCERTS® Model: A Comprehensive Educational Approach for Children with Autism Spectrum Disorders
by Barry M. Prizant, Amy M. Wetherby, Emily Rubin, Amy C. Laurent, & Patrick J. Rydell
Copyright © 2006 by Paul H. Brookes Publishing Co. All rights reserved.

Index
Volumes I and II

This index serves both volumes of *The SCERTS™ Model: A Comprehensive Educational Approach for Children with Autism Spectrum Disorders*. I and II indicate Volumes I and II, respectively. Page numbers followed by *t* and *f* indicate tables and figures, respectively.

AAC, *see* Augmentative and alternative communication
ABA, *see* Applied behavior analysis
ABI (activity based intervention), *see* Activity-based learning approaches
Academic curricula, standard, challenges of, for children with ASD, I:82–83
Academic skills, functional, National Research Council recommendations on, I:113–114
Active learning, definition of, I:311
Active learning and organization
    definition of, I:155
    as Social-Emotional Growth Indicator, I:141, 155, 157*t*
    rationale for, I:155
Activity(ies)
    modification of, by partner, II:36–37
    see also MA & PA approach
Activity-based learning, in SCERTS Model, II:11–23, 88
    activities for, designing, II:11–12
    see also MA & PA approach
Activity-based learning approaches, I:126
    definition of, I:311
    National Research Council recommendations on, I:112
    in school setting, II:21
    see also Skill-based approaches
Affect, ability to share, I:24
Affect attunement, I:24
Affect displays, I:50
    definition of, I:313
    see also Expression of emotion
Age, and educational approaches, I:128
Analytic language, I:79
Analytic learning strategy, I:35–36, 37*t*, 38*t*, 103
Applied behavior analysis (ABA), I:111, 115, 116, 118, 129, 314
Appropriateness of behavior, *see* Cooperation and appropriateness of behavior
Arousal
    definition, I:52
    modulation of, *see* Modulation of arousal
    optimal, *see* Optimal arousal
    physiological, *see* Arousal state
Arousal bias, definition of, I:311
Arousal level, regulation of, during familiar activities
    use of behavioral strategies for
        at Conversational Partner stage, goals for, and related partner goals, II:164–165, 164*t*
        at Conversational Partner stage, SAP-O Forms and criteria for, I:230
        at Language Partner stage, goals for, and related partner goals, II:135–136, 135*t*
        at Language Partner stage, SAP-O Forms and criteria for, I:203–204
        at Social Partner stage, goals for, and related partner goals, II:108–109, 108*t*
        at Social Partner stage, SAP-O Forms and criteria for, I:177–178
    use of language strategies for
        at Conversational Partner stage, goals for, and related partner goals, II:165–166, 165*t*
        at Conversational Partner stage, SAP-O Forms and criteria for, I:230–231
        at Language Partner stage, goals for, and related partner goals, II:136–137, 136*t*
        at Language Partner stage, SAP-O Forms and criteria for, I:204–205
    use of metacognitive strategies for, at Conversational Partner stage, SAP-O Forms and criteria for, I:232
Arousal state
    definition of, I:311
    see also High state of arousal; Low state of arousal
ASD, *see* Autism spectrum disorders
Assessment
    approaches to, continuum of, from less intrusive to more intrusive, I:135, 135*f*
    definition of, I:131
    and evaluation, differentiation of, I:131
    family-centered, practices in, I:139–140
    National Research Council recommendations on, I:112
    outcome measures for, I:16–17
    procedures for, I:132
    of progress, measures for, I:16–17
    purpose of, I:131
    siblings' role in, I:138–139, II:56–59
    terms used in, definition of, I:131–132
    traditional approaches to, versus SCERTS Assessment Process, I:132–134
    see also Criterion-referenced assessment; SCERTS Assessment Process
Assistance
    offers of, response to
        at Conversational Partner stage, SAP-O Forms and criteria for, I:225–226
        at Language Partner stage
            goals for, and related partner goals, II:131–132, 131*t*
            SAP-O Forms and criteria for, I:200

Assistance—*continued*
    at Social Partner stage
        goals for, and related partner goals, II:104–105, 104*t*
        SAP-O Forms and criteria for, I:175
    in problem solving, requests for, at Conversational Partner
        stage, SAP-O Forms and criteria for, I:228
    requests for
        at Conversational Partner stage, SAP-O Forms and criteria
            for, I:227–228
        at Language Partner stage
            goals for, and related partner goals, II:132–133, 132*t*
            SAP-O Forms and criteria for, I:200–201
        at Social Partner stage
            goals for, and related partner goals, II:105–106, 105*t*
            SAP-O Forms and criteria for, I:175
    to resolve conflict, requests for, at Conversational Partner
        stage, SAP-O Forms and criteria for, I:228
Attention, ability to share, I:23
    at Conversational Partner stage, SAP-O Forms and criteria for,
        I:216–217
    at Language Partner stage
        goals for, and related partner goals, II:113–114, 113*t*
        SAP-O Forms and criteria for, I:190
    at Social Partner stage
        goals for, and related partner goals, II:90–91, 90*t*
        SAP-O Forms and criteria for, I:167
    see also Joint attention/Joint Attention (component)
Augmentative and alternative communication (AAC), I:110,
        116
    definition of, I:311
    goals and strategies for, I:129
Augmentative communication support
    at Conversational Partner stage, SAP-O Forms and criteria for,
        I:241–242
    at Language Partner stage, SAP-O Forms and criteria for,
        I:213
    at Social Partner stage, SAP-O Forms and criteria for, I:186
Autism spectrum disorders (ASD)
    as developmental disability, I:9
    diagnostic criteria for, I:9
Availability for learning
    definition of, I:311
    demonstration of
        at Conversational Partner stage
            goals for, and related partner goals, II:163–164, 163*t*
            SAP-O Forms and criteria for, I:229–230
        at Language Partner stage
            goals for, and related partner goals, II:134–135, 134*t*
            SAP-O Forms and criteria for, I:202–203
        at Social Partner stage
            goals for, and related partner goals, II:107–108, 107*t*
            SAP-O Forms and criteria for, I:176–177

Behavior
    appropriateness of, *see* Cooperation and appropriateness of
        behavior
    challenging, *see* Problem behavior
    feedback on, response to, at Conversational Partner stage,
        SAP-O Forms and criteria for, I:226–227
    guidance on, response to, at Conversational Partner stage,
        SAP-O Forms and criteria for, I:226–227

    problem, *see* Problem behavior
    socially undesirable, as communication means, I:31
    unconventional, as communication means, I:31
Behavior management, I:121–123, 122*t*
Behavior regulation
    definition of, I:311
    development, I:26
    difficulty of, for children with ASD, I:27
Behavior sampling, in SCERTS Assessment Process, I:157–161
    at Conversational Partner stage, II:317–319, 341–343
    at Language Partner stage, II:251–252, 276–277
    at Social Partner stage, II:190–191, 212–213
Behavioral strategies, I:51
    definition of, I:177, 311
    to regulate arousal level, use of
        during familiar activities
            at Conversational Partner stage, goals for, and related
                partner goals, II:164–165, 164*t*
            at Conversational Partner stage, SAP-O Forms and crite-
                ria for, I:230
        at Language Partner stage
            goals for, and related partner goals, II:135–136, 135*t*
            SAP-O Forms and criteria for, I:203–204
        during new and changing situations, at Conversational
            Partner stage, SAP-O Forms and criteria for, I:232
        at Social Partner stage, goals for, and related partner goals,
            II:108–109, 108*t*
        at Social Partner stage, SAP-O Forms and criteria for,
            I:177–178
        during transitions, at Conversational Partner stage, SAP-O
            Forms and criteria for, I:233
Benchmarks, II:6
Best practices, knowledge of, and early childhood intervention
        practices, I:110

Caregiver education programs, II:66–67
Caregiver–child coaching/guidance, II:65–66
Challenging behavior, *see* Problem behavior
Changing situations
    definition of, I:178, 311
    regulation of emotions during
        at Conversational Partner stage, goals for, and related
            partner goals, II:168–169, 168*t*
        at Conversational Partner stage, SAP-O Forms and criteria
            for, I:232–233
        at Language Partner stage, goals for, and related partner
            goals, II:137–138, 137*t*
        at Language Partner stage, SAP-O Forms and criteria for,
            I:205–206
        at Social Partner stage, goals for, and related partner goals,
            II:109–110, 109*t*
        at Social Partner stage, SAP-O Forms and criteria for, I:178
Child characteristics, educational approaches and, I:118*t*,
        127–128
Classroom structure, II:22
    definition of, I:311
Clinical experience, working with children with ASD, and
        knowledge of challenges, I:11
Cognitive appraisal, I:50
    in children with ASD, I:66
    definition of, I:311

Index, Volumes I and II

Cognitive goals
  generalization of, fostering, National Research Council recommendations on, I:113
  maintenance of, fostering, National Research Council recommendations on, I:113
Cognitive style, in children with ASD, I:78–82
Communication
  assessment of, I:132–134
    at Social Partner stage, SAP-O Forms and criteria for, I:166–174
  augmentative and alternative, *see* Augmentative and alternative communication
  challenges, of children with ASD, I:19
  development, I:21, 92–93
  functional, spontaneous; fostering, National Research Council recommendations on, I:113, 129
  intentional, *see* Intentional communication
  joint attention, *see* Joint attention/Joint Attention (component)
  multimodal, *see* Multimodal communication
  nonverbal, *see* Nonverbal communication
  problem behaviors used for, I:31
  rate of, at Conversational Partner stage, SAP-O Forms and criteria for, I:219
  receptive, development of, I:29
  reciprocal, I:31–32
  social, *see* Social communication
  spontaneous, initiated, goals and priorities for, I:129
  symbolic, acquisition of, I:32–39
  see also Functional spontaneous communication
Communication breakdown
  at Conversational Partner stage, SAP-O Forms and criteria for, I:219–220
  definition of, I:311
  at Language Partner stage, persists and repairs
    goals for, and related partner goals, II:119–120, 119t
    SAP-O Forms and criteria for, I:192–193
  at Social Partner stage
    partner's attempts to repair, SAP-O Forms and criteria for, I:183
    persists and repairs
      goals for, and related partner goals, II:96–97, 96t
      SAP-O Forms and criteria for, I:169
  see also Repair strategies
Communication partners, *see* Partners
Communication stage, of child with ASD, determination of, I:145–147, II:186, 209, 246–247, 272, 313, 336
  echolalia and, I:146–147
Communicative competence, I:19
  definition of, I:311
  development of, I:19
    factors affecting, I:19–20
Communicative exchange, *see* Exchange (social or communicative)
Communicative function, I:25
  definition of, I:312
Communicative intention, I:25–26
  definition of, I:312
Communicative means, I:4
  definition of, I:312
  presymbolic, I:4
    definition of, I:312

  symbolic, I:4
    definition of, I:312
  see also Conventional communicative means
Communicative opportunities, creating, II:20
Communicative repair, definition of, I:312
Communicative temptations, I:158–159, 159t
Consultants, working with children with ASD, knowledge of challenges, I:11
Contact gestures
  response to, at Language Partner stage, SAP-O Forms and criteria for, I:190
  understanding of
    at Language Partner stage, SAP-O Forms and criteria for, I:194
    at Social Partner stage, SAP-O Forms and criteria for, I:171
  use of, at Social Partner stage, SAP-O Forms and criteria for, I:172
Contingent response, definition of, I:312
Controlled variation, I:104
Conventional communicative means, definition of, I:312
Conversational discourse
  at Conversational Partner stage, I:44–45
    SAP-O Forms and criteria for, I:224
  definition of, I:312
  and social inflexibility, in children with ASD, I:48
  social rules of, I:23
    following, at Conversational Partner stage, SAP-O Forms and criteria for, I:224
  transition to, I:22–23
Conversational Partner stage, I:3, 20
  advanced level, assessment to implementation, II:333–362
  definition of, I:312
  domains, components, and goals, in SCERTS Assessment Process, I:144t
  emotional regulation at
    assessment of, I:144t, II:323–326, 347–351
    goals for, and related partner goals, II:156–170
    milestones in, I:97, 99t, 100
    during new and changing situations
      goals for, and related partner goals, II:168–169, 168t
      SAP-O Forms and criteria for, I:232–233
    SAP-O Forms and criteria for, I:225–234
  goals and objectives at, prioritizing, II:329, 355–358
  milestones of, I:42–48
  novice level, assessment to implementation, II:311–333
  recommending further assessment at, II:329, 358
  social communication at
    assessment of, I:144t, II:319–323, 343–347
    goals for, and related partner goals, II:141–156
    SAP-O Forms and criteria for, I:216–224
  Social-Emotional Growth Indicators at
    objectives for calculation of, I:157t
    results and impressions, II:328–329, 355
  spotlight on children at, II:311–362
  structured situations for use at, I:159, 160t
  transactional support at
    assessment of, I:144t, II:326–328, 351–355
    goals for, and related Social Communication and Emotional Regulation goals, II:140–170
    SAP-O Forms and criteria for, I:234–244
  transitions in, I:22
  see also Language Partner stage; Social Partner stage

Conversational rules, I:44
Cooperation and appropriateness of behavior
    definition of, I:156
    as Social-Emotional Growth Indicator, I:141, 156, 157t
        rationale for, I:156
Cooperative principle, in conversational discourse, I:44, 47
Cooperative turn-taking games, II:17–18, 17t
    definition of, I:312
Criterion-referenced assessment, I:132
    definition of, I:312
    see also Curriculum-based assessment
Cues
    gestural
        at Language Partner stage, SAP-O Forms and criteria for, I:194, 205
        at Social Partner stage, I:29
            SAP-O Forms and criteria for, I:170–171
    intonation
        at Language Partner stage, SAP-O Forms and criteria for, I:194–195
        at Social Partner stage, I:29
            SAP-O Forms and criteria for, I:171
    nonverbal, understanding of
        at Conversational Partner stage, SAP-O Forms and criteria for, I:218, 221–222
        at Language Partner stage
            goals for, and related partner goals, II:123–124, 123t
            SAP-O Forms and criteria for, I:194
        at Social Partner stage
            goals for, and related partner goals, II:98–99, 98t
            SAP-O Forms and criteria for, I:170–171
    situational
        at Language Partner stage, SAP-O Forms and criteria for, I:194
        at Social Partner stage, I:29
            SAP-O Forms and criteria for, I:170
    visual, understanding of
        at Language Partner stage, SAP-O Forms and criteria for, I:194, 205
        at Social Partner stage, SAP-O Forms and criteria for, I:171
Curriculum modification and adaptation, I:104–105
    definition of, I:312
Curriculum-based assessment, I:132
    definition of, I:312
    see also Criterion-referenced assessment

Data
    clinical
        and early childhood intervention practices, I:110
        and educational approach, I:16
    educational
        and early childhood intervention practices, I:110
        and educational approach, I:16
    empirical
        and early childhood intervention practices, I:110
        and educational approach, I:16
Decentration, I:38
Decontextualization, I:33–34, 38
Delayed echolalia, see Echolalia
Development
    core challenges of
        for children with ASD, I:14–15
        transactional nature of, II:83–84
    critical capacities, for children with ASD, I:19
    and educational approaches, I:128
    fostering, in children with ASD, family-centered approach to, II:70
    interrelationships/interdependencies in, I:6, 7
    Transactional Model of Development, I:6, 71–72, II:83–84
Developmental discontinuity, I:92–93
    challenge of, I:82
    definition of, I:82
Developmental framework, in SCERTS Model, rationale for, I:92–93
Developmental stages, in SCERTS Model, I:3
    see also Conversational Partner stage; Language Partner stage; Social Partner stage
Diagnosis, support to family at, II:53
Directive teaching approaches, I:119–121
    definition of, I:312
    see also Facilitative teaching approaches
Distal gestures
    understanding of
        at Language Partner stage, SAP-O Forms and criteria for, I:190, 194
        at Social Partner stage, SAP-O Forms and criteria for, I:171
    use of, at Social Partner stage, SAP-O Forms and criteria for, I:172
Dysregulation
    definition of, I:312
    extreme, see Extreme dysregulation
    factors related to, in children with ASD, I:67, 68t, 100
    recovery from, see Recovery from dysregulation
    signals of, see Signals of dysregulation

Early identification
    challenges to family in, II:51–52
    educational support and, II:51–52
    emotional support and, II:51–52
Early intervention, National Research Council recommendations on, I:111
Early word-like form, I:173
Echolalia, I:40–41, 103
    definition of, I:312
    delayed, I:31, 79–80
        definition of, I:81t, 312
        examples of, I:81t
    and determination of child's communication stage, I:146–147
    functions of, I:40
    immediate, I:79–80
        definition of, I:81t, 312
        examples of, I:81t
    mitigated, definition of, I:312
    see also Unconventional verbal behavior
Ecologically valid measures, I:17
    definition of, I:312
Educational approach(es)
    broad descriptive, I:114, 116
    categorical, I:114–116
    and child characteristics, I:118t, 127–128
    for children with ASD, similarities and differences among, I:114

consistency across settings
  challenges in ensuring, I:89–90
  National Research Council recommendations on, I:112
continuity in
  challenges in ensuring, I:89–90
  National Research Council recommendations on, I:112
continuum, I:114, 116–117
and core challenges to children with ASD, I:128–129
current landscape of, SCERTS Model and, I:114–130
developmental considerations for, I:15, 130
dimensions of, I:117–130, 118*t*
functional considerations for, I:130
individualized, I:15
learning contexts in, I:118*t*, 125–127
and long-term goals, consistency between, I:15–16
measures of progress and outcome for, I:16–17
multidimensional continua of, I:117
National Research Council recommendations on, I:113–114
and programmatic goals, I:118*t*, 128–130
sources contributing to, I:16
teaching practices in, I:117–125, 118*t*
Educational practices, dimensions of, I:117–130, 118*t*
Educational priorities
  for child with ASD, I:7
  in goal setting, I:118*t*, 128–129
Educational program, SCERTS, design of, I:163
  at Conversational Partner stage, II:329–333, 358–362
  at Language Partner stage, II:263–270, 287–290
  at Social Partner stage, II:201, 222
Educational support
  for children with ASD, goals and priorities for, I:103–105
  definition of, I:312
  for families, I:6, 105–107, II:49
    activities that provide, II:76*t*
    appropriateness to family's developmental stage, II:51
    at Conversational Partner stage, II:330–331, 359–361
    in early elementary school years, II:54–55
    and early identification, II:51–52
    goals of, II:49–50, 60*t*–61*t*
      meeting, II:59–63
    in initial planning of services, II:53
    at Language Partner stage, II:199, 221, 266–269, 287–289
    in later elementary school years, II:55–56
    providing, principles and practices for, II:63–67
    at Social Partner stage, II:201–206, 222–224
  for professionals and service providers, II:80–81, 80*t*
Elementary school
  early, transition to, support to family at, II:54–55
  later, transition to, support to family at, II:55–56
Emotion(s), I:49
  ability to share, I:24
    by children with ASD, I:27
    at Language Partner stage, SAP-O Forms and criteria for, I:190–191
    at Social Partner stage
      goals for, and related partner goals, II:91–92, 91*t*
      SAP-O Forms and criteria for, I:167–168
  causal factors for, expression of, at Conversational Partner stage, SAP-O Forms and criteria for, I:218
  dysregulation of
    extreme, *see* Extreme dysregulation
    factors affecting, I:5

graded
  at Conversational Partner stage, SAP-O Forms and criteria for, I:231
  use of, at Conversational Partner stage, SAP-O Forms and criteria for, I:217–218
intensity of, I:49
mutual regulation of, I:5
  see also Mutual regulation/Mutual Regulation (component)
negative, *see* Negative emotional display
physiological aspects of, *see* Physiological aspects of emotion
positive, *see* Positive emotion(s)
self-regulation of, I:5
  see also Self-regulation/Self-Regulation (component)
words for, at Conversational Partner stage, SAP-O Forms and criteria for, I:225, 231
see also Expression of emotion
Emotional arousal, definition of, I:312
Emotional cues, understanding, challenges faced by children with ASD, effects on partners, I:74–75
Emotional overarousal
  causes of, I:177
  definition of, I:312
Emotional regulation, 121–123, 122*t*
  and arousal, relationship between, I:52–53
  assessment of, I:132–134
    behavior sampling for, I:159–161
  capacities for, levels of development, I:51–52
  challenges faced by children with ASD, I:76–78
  at Conversational Partner stage
    assessment of, I:144*t*, II:323–326, 347–351
    goals for, and related partner goals, II:156–170
    milestones in, I:97, 99*t*, 100
    during new and changing situations
      goals for, and related partner goals, II:168–169, 168*t*
      SAP-O Forms and criteria for, I:232–233
    SAP-O Forms and criteria for, I:225–234
  as core capacity for all children, I:10
  as core challenge, I:9
  developmental milestones in, I:97, 98*t*–99*t*
  developmental perspective on, I:96–97
  difficulties with, in children with ASD, I:61–69
  dimensions of, I:49
  educational approaches and, I:128
  factors related to, in children with ASD, I:67, 68*t*
  goal-setting framework for, II:5–6
  at Language Partner stage
    assessment of, I:143*t*, II:256–259, 280–284
    goals for, and related partner goals, II:130–140
    milestones in, I:97, 98*t*, 99–100
    during new and changing situations
      goals for, and related partner goals, II:137–138, 137*t*
      SAP-O Forms and criteria for, I:205–206
    SAP-O Forms and criteria for, I:199–206, II:256–259, 258*f*
  as life-span ability, I:10
  during new and changing situations
    at Conversational Partner stage, goals for, and related partner goals, II:168–169, 168*t*
    at Conversational Partner stage, SAP-O Forms and criteria for, I:232–233
    at Language Partner stage, goals for, and related partner goals, II:137–138, 137*t*

Emotional regulation—*continued*
  at Language Partner stage, SAP-O Forms and criteria for, I:205–206
  at Social Partner stage, goals for, and related partner goals, II:109–110, 109t
  at Social Partner stage, SAP-O Forms and criteria for, I:178
  priorities for, in SCERTS Model, I:96–100
  social communication and, interdependencies in, I:96
  at Social Partner stage
    assessment of, I:142t, II:194–197
    goals for
      prioritizing, II:177–180
      and related partner goals, II:103–111
    milestones in, I:97, 98t
    during new and changing situations
      goals for, and related partner goals, II:109–110, 109t
      SAP-O Forms and criteria for, I:178
    SAP-O Forms and criteria for, I:174–179, II:194–197
  strategies for, I:97–100
  supporting, ultimate goal for, I:69–70
  see also Mutual regulation/Mutual Regulation (component); Self-regulation/Self-Regulation (component)
Emotional Regulation (domain), I:3
  definition of, I:49–51, 312
  goals of, linking to Transactional Support goals, II:86–87, 87–170
  overall goals of, I:5
  overview of, I:4–5
  see also Mutual regulation/Mutual Regulation (component); Self-regulation/Self-Regulation (component)
Emotional support
  definition of, I:312
  for families, I:6, 105–107, II:49
    activities that provide, II:76t
    appropriateness to family's developmental stage, II:51
    at Conversational Partner stage, II:332, 361–362
    in early elementary school years, II:54–55
    and early identification, II:51–52
    goals of, II:50–51, 70–75, 71t
      meeting, II:70–75
    in initial planning of services, II:53
    at Language Partner stage, II:269, 289–290
    in later elementary school years, II:55–56
    at Social Partner stage, II:201–206, 222–224
  for professionals and service providers, II:80t, 81
Emotional underarousal, causes of, I:177
Engineered activities and settings, II:13f, 14t, 15–16
  definition of, I:312
Environmental arrangement, definition of, I:312
Evaluation
  and assessment, differentiation of, I:131
  definition of, I:131
  developmental, I:131
  diagnostic, I:131
  tools and strategies for, I:131–132
Evidence-based practice, I:109–110
  definition of, I:109
  SCERTS Model and, I:110
Exchange (social or communicative)
  at Conversational Partner stage, SAP-O Forms and criteria for, I:229

  definition of, I:312
  at Language Partner stage, SAP-O Forms and criteria for, I:189, 193
Executive functioning, definition of, I:312–313
Expression of emotion
  by children with ASD, I:61–64, 65–66
  at Conversational Partner stage, SAP-O Forms and criteria for, I:217–218, 225
  definition of, I:313
  at Language Partner stage
    goals for, and related partner goals, II:114–115, 114t, 130–131, 130t
    SAP-O Forms and criteria for, I:190–191, 199, 200–201, 203
  at Social Partner stage
    goals for, and related partner goals, II:103–104, 103t
    SAP-O Forms and criteria for, I:174
Extreme dysregulation, I:67–69, 100
  definition of, I:176, 179, 313
  recovery from, I:5
    by self
      at Conversational Partner stage, goals for, and related partner goals, II:169–170, 169t
      at Conversational Partner stage, SAP-O Forms and criteria for, I:233–234
      at Language Partner stage, goals for, and related partner goals, II:139–140, 139t
      at Language Partner stage, SAP-O Forms and criteria for, I:206
      at Social Partner stage, goals for, and related partner goals, II:110–111, 110t
      at Social Partner stage, SAP-O Forms and criteria for, I:179
    with support of partners
      at Conversational Partner stage, goals for, and related partner goals, II:161–162, 161t
      at Conversational Partner stage, SAP-O Forms and criteria for, I:228–229
      at Language Partner stage, goals for, and related partner goals, II:133–134, 133t
      at Language Partner stage, SAP-O Forms and criteria for, I:201–202
      at Social Partner stage, goals for, and related partner goals, II:106–107, 106t
      at Social Partner stage, SAP-O Forms and criteria for, I:176
    see also Recovery from dysregulation

Facial expression
  understanding of
    challenges faced by children with ASD, effects on partners, I:74–75
    at Language Partner stage, SAP-O Forms and criteria for, I:194–195
    at Social Partner stage, SAP-O Forms and criteria for, I:171
  use of
    at Conversational Partner stage, SAP-O Forms and criteria for, I:222
    at Social Partner stage, SAP-O Forms and criteria for, I:172
Facilitative style, I:119–121

Facilitative teaching approaches, I:12, 119–121
  definition of, I:313
  see also Directive teaching approaches
Familiar actions and sounds
  definition of, I:170
  imitation of, at Social Partner stage, SAP-O Forms and criteria for, I:170
Family(ies)
  assessment of, I:105–107
  challenges faced by, I:83, II:46, 46t
    related to factors outside the family, I:86–87, II:46t
      SCERTS Model and, II:49
    challenges within, I:83–85, II:46t
      SCERTS Model and, II:46–47
  as communicative and social partners for children with ASD, I:76–78
  in educational programming, I:124–125
  educational support for, I:6
  emotional support for, I:6
  feeling of isolation, I:86
  and future uncertainty, I:85
  involvement of
    effect on outcomes, II:43
    National Research Council recommendations on, I:112
    in SCERTS Model, II:43
  lifestyle of, changes in, child with ASD and, I:84–85
  members' interface with social community, I:86
  members' responses to ASD, differences in, I:84
  and need to explain ASD to others, I:86–87
  ongoing support for, I:10
  priorities for, I:11
    and goal identification, II:8–9
  professional–parent interaction, challenges in, I:87–88, II:46t
  roles in, changes in, child with ASD and, I:84–85
  routines of, changes in, child with ASD and, I:84–85
  service provision to, challenges in, I:87–88, II:46t
  siblings of child with ASD in, challenges to, I:85
  understanding of ASD, I:86
  see also Support to families
Family decision making, challenges in, I:84
Family Expectations for Services and Helpful Supports (questionnaire), II:47, 48f
Family life, finding balance in, I:83–84
Family system, changes in, child with ASD and, I:84–85
Family systems theory, I:119
Family-centered intervention, I:119
Feedback, on behavior, response to, at Conversational Partner stage, SAP-O Forms and criteria for, I:226–227
Fight-or-flight reactions, definition of, I:313
First words, transition to, I:22, 32–34
Flexibility and resilience
  definition of, I:156
  as Social-Emotional Growth Indicator, I:141, 155–156, 157t
    rationale for, I:155–156
Flexibility within structure, I:104
Flow, fostering, I:69–70
Following the child's lead, I:119–120
Formal supports
  definition of, I:313
  see also Emotional support; Informal supports
Friendships, as Social-Emotional Growth Indicator, see Social membership and friendships

Functional skills, definition of, I:313
Functional spontaneous communication
  definition of, I:313
  fostering, National Research Council recommendations on, I:113, 129
Future uncertainty, I:85

Gaze
  and gestures, coordination of
    at Language Partner stage, SAP-O Forms and criteria for, I:196
    at Social Partner stage, SAP-O Forms and criteria for, I:173
  and sharing of emotion, by children with ASD, I:27
  and vocalizations, coordination of, at Social Partner stage, SAP-O Forms and criteria for, I:174
Gaze shift
  definition of, I:313
  at Language Partner stage, SAP-O Forms and criteria for, I:190
  at Social Partner stage, SAP-O Forms and criteria for, I:167
Gaze/point following, I:24
Generalization, measurement of, I:124
Gestalt language, I:79–80
  in children with ASD, I:40–41
Gestalt learning strategy, I:35–36, 37t, 38t, 103
  in children with ASD, I:40–41
Gestalt processing, in children with ASD, I:78–79
Gestures
  and gaze, coordination of
    at Language Partner stage, SAP-O Forms and criteria for, I:196
    at Social Partner stage, SAP-O Forms and criteria for, I:173
  sequence of, use of
    at Language Partner stage, SAP-O Forms and criteria for, I:196
    at Social Partner stage, SAP-O Forms and criteria for, I:173
  understanding, challenges faced by children with ASD, effects on partners, I:74–75
  use of
    at Conversational Partner stage, SAP-O Forms and criteria for, I:223
    at Language Partner stage
      goals for, and related partner goals, II:125–126, 125t
      SAP-O Forms and criteria for, I:195–196
    at Social Partner stage
      goals for, and related partner goals, II:100–101, 100t
      SAP-O Forms and criteria for, I:172–173
  see also Cues, gestural
Goal-directed activities, II:17, 17t
  definition of, I:313
Goals, for children with ASD
  addressing, setting for, II:10
  determining, II:5–11
  developmental appropriateness of, II:9–10
  and family priorities, II:8–9
  functionality of, II:6–8
  modification of, by partner, II:36–37
  multiple, targeting within activities, II:10–11, 20–21
  selection of, II:6–10

Happiness
    definition of, I:155
    as Social-Emotional Growth Indicator, I:141, 154–155, 157t
        rationale for, I:154–155
High state of arousal
    definition of, I:313
    see also Arousal state; Low state of arousal
Homeostasis, definition of, I:313
Hyperlexia, I:80

IDEA, *see* Individuals with Disabilities Education Act Amendments of 1997 (PL 105-17)
IEP, *see* Individualized education program
IFSP, *see* Individualized family service plan
Imitation
    capacity for
        at Conversational Partner stage, SAP-O Forms and criteria for, I:220–221
        at Language Partner stage
            goals for, and related partner goals, II:122–123, 122t
            SAP-O Forms and criteria for, I:193–194
        at Social Partner stage, I:29–30
            SAP-O Forms and criteria for, I:170
    deferred, I:30
    of familiar actions and sounds, at Social Partner stage
        goals for, and related partner goals, II:97–98, 97t
        SAP-O Forms and criteria for, I:170
Immediate echolalia, *see* Echolalia
Incessant questioning, I:80
    definition of, I:81t, 313
    examples of, I:81t
    see also Unconventional verbal behavior
Inclusion, successful, II:37–42
    essential programmatic elements for, II:37–39
Independence
    child's, partner's respect for, II:28–29
    definition of, I:156
    as Social-Emotional Growth Indicator, I:141, 156, 157t
        rationale for, I:156
Individual differences
    definition of, I:313
    and educational approach, I:15
Individuals with Disabilities Education Act (IDEA) Amendments of 1997 (PL 105-17, I:131
Individualized approach, National Research Council recommendations on, I:112
Individualized education program (IEP), I:7, 131, II:6
Individualized family service plan, I:131
Informal supports
    definition of, I:313
    see also Emotional support; Formal supports
Information processing, in children with ASD, I:78–79, 129
Initiated communicative behavior, definition of, I:313
Initiated mutual regulation, I:55
    definition of, I:313
    see also Mutual regulation/Mutual Regulation (component); Respondent mutual regulation
Instructional strategies, II:25
Intentional communication, I:24–25
    by children with ASD, I:27
    definition of, I:313

for joint attention
    at Conversational Partner stage, SAP-O Forms and criteria for, I:218, 227
    at Language Partner stage
        goals for, and related partner goals, II:118–119, 118t
        SAP-O Forms and criteria for, I:192
    at Social Partner stage
        goals for, and related partner goals, II:94–95, 94t
        SAP-O Forms and criteria for, I:169
nonverbal
    at Language Partner stage, SAP-O Forms and criteria for, I:195–196
    at Social Partner stage, SAP-O Forms and criteria for, I:172–173
to regulate others' behavior
    at Conversational Partner stage, SAP-O Forms and criteria for, I:218, 227
    at Language Partner stage
        goals for, and related partner goals, II:115–116, 115t
        SAP-O Forms and criteria for, I:191
    at Social Partner stage
        goals for, and related partner goals, II:92–93, 92t
        SAP-O Forms and criteria for, I:168
for social interaction
    at Conversational Partner stage, SAP-O Forms and criteria for, I:218, 227
    at Language Partner stage
        goals for, and related partner goals, II:116–117, 116t
        SAP-O Forms and criteria for, I:191–192
    at Social Partner stage
        goals for, and related partner goals, II:93–94, 93t
        SAP-O Forms and criteria for, I:168–169
Interaction
    availability for, demonstration of
        at Conversational Partner stage
            goals for, and related partner goals, II:163–164, 163t
            SAP-O Forms and criteria for, I:229–230
        at Language Partner stage
            goals for, and related partner goals, II:134–135, 134t
            SAP-O Forms and criteria for, I:202–203
        at Social Partner stage
            goals for, and related partner goals, II:107–108, 107t
            SAP-O Forms and criteria for, I:176–177
    bids for, at Language Partner stage, SAP-O Forms and criteria for, I:189, 202
    initiation of, at Language Partner stage, SAP-O Forms and criteria for, I:189, 202
    reciprocal, *see* Reciprocal interaction
Interpersonal interactions, quality and characteristics of, and children with ASD, I:72–78
Interpersonal support/Interpersonal Support (component), I:2, 3
    and challenges faced by children with ASD, I:72–73
    at Conversational Partner stage
        assessment of, I:144t, II:326–327, 351–353
        goals for
            prioritizing, II:305–308
            and related Social Communication and Emotional Regulation goals, II:140–170
        SAP-O Forms and criteria for, I:234–240, II:351–353, 354f
    core challenges requiring, I:72–78

definition of Interpersonal Support component, I:313
do's and don'ts of, II:32, 33t
goals and priorities for, II:26–32
at Language Partner stage
    assessment of, I:143t, II:259–260, 284
    goals for
        prioritizing, II:239–241
        and related Social Communication and Emotional Regulation goals, II:111–140
    SAP-O Forms and criteria for, I:207–212, II:259–260, 261f
overview of, I:5
providing, goals and priorities in, I:100–103, 101t
at Social Partner stage
    assessment of, I:142t, II:197, 219–220
    goals for
        prioritizing, II:180–182
        and related Social Communication and Emotional Regulation goals, II:89–111
    SAP-O Forms and criteria for, I:179–185, II:197, 198f
see also Learning support/Learning Support (component); Transactional support; Transactional Support (domain)
Intersubjectivity, I:26
Interventions, family's confusion about, I:87–88
Intonation, at Conversational Partner stage, SAP-O Forms and criteria for, I:223

Joint attention/Joint Attention (component), I:3–4, 20
capacity for, I:27
    assessment of, I:91
    and development at Conversational Partner stage, I:42–43
    and development at Language Partner stage, I:31–32
    and development at Social Partner stage, I:23–27
    and development of social communication, I:20
    developmental milestones in, I:93, 94t–96t
    supporting, goals and plan for, I:92
at Conversational Partner stage
    assessment of, I:144t, II:319–321, 343–345
    goals for
        prioritizing, II:294–296
        and related partner goals, II:141–147
    milestones in, I:93, 95t–96t
    SAP-O Forms and criteria for, I:216–220, II:343–345, 346f
definition of Joint Attention component, I:313
development, I:26
    challenges in
        at Conversational Partner stage, I:43
        at Language Partner stage, I:32
        at Social Partner stage, I:27–28
difficulty of, for children with ASD, I:27
goal-setting framework for, I:93–96
at Language Partner stage
    assessment of, I:143t, II:252–253, 277–279
    goals for
        prioritizing, II:229–231
        and related partner goals, II:111–121
    milestones in, I:93, 94t–95t
    SAP-O Forms and criteria for, I:189–193, II:252–253, 254f
at Social Partner stage
    assessment of, I:142t, II:191–192, 213–215

goals for
    prioritizing, II:173–174
    and related partner goals, II:89–97, 89t
milestones in, I:93, 94t
SAP-O Forms and criteria for, I:166–169, II:191–192
see also social communication; Social Communication (domain); Symbol Use (component)

Language
development, I:22
    individual differences in, I:35–36
    generative, at Conversational Partner stage, SAP-O Forms and criteria for, I:223–224
    receptive, development of, I:34
    written vs. spoken, I:80
Language abilities, positive effects of, I:4
Language acquisition
    analytic styles in, I:35–36, 37t, 38t
    by children with ASD, I:79–80
    gestalt styles in, I:35–36, 37t, 38t
    in children with ASD, I:40–41
Language learning, I:21
    activity context and, I:35–36
    cultural context and, I:35–36
Language Partner stage, I:3, 20
    advanced level, assessment to implementation, II:270–290
    definition of, I:313
    developmental transitions in, I:32–39
    domains, components, and goals, in SCERTS Assessment Process, I:143t
    emotional regulation at
        assessment of, I:143t, II:256–259, 280–284
        goals for, and related partner goals, II:130–140
        milestones in, I:97, 98t, 99–100
        during new and changing situations
            goals for, and related partner goals, II:137–138, 137t
            SAP-O Forms and criteria for, I:205–206
        SAP-O Forms and criteria for, I:199–206, II:256–259, 258f
    goals and objectives at, prioritizing, II:263, 286
    milestones of, I:31–42
    novice level, assessment to implementation, II:244–270
    recommending further assessment at, II:263, 286–287
    SAP-O criteria for, I:189
    SAP-O Forms for, I:188–189
    social communication at
        assessment of, I:143t, II:252–255, 277–280
        goals for
            prioritizing, II:229–234
            and related partner goals, II:111–130
        SAP-O Forms and criteria for, I:189–199, II:252–255, 254f
    Social-Emotional Growth Indicators at
        objectives for calculation of, I:157t
        results and impressions, II:262, 285–286
    spotlights on children at, II:244–290
    transactional support at
        assessment of, I:143t, II:259–262, 284–285
        goals for, and related Social Communication and Emotional Regulation goals, II:111–140
    transitions in, I:22
    see also Conversational Partner stage; Social Partner stage

Language processing, challenges faced by children with ASD, I:72–74
 effects on partners, I:73–74
Language strategies, I:51
 definition of, I:313
 to regulate arousal level, use of
  during familiar activities
   at Conversational Partner stage, goals for, and related partner goals, II:165–166, 165t
   at Conversational Partner stage, SAP-O Forms and criteria for, I:230–231
   at Language Partner stage, goals for, and related partner goals, II:136–137, 136t
   at Language Partner stage, SAP-O Forms and criteria for, I:204–205
  during new and changing situations, at Conversational Partner stage, SAP-O Forms and criteria for, I:233
  during transitions, at Conversational Partner stage, SAP-O Forms and criteria for, I:233
LAPP, *see* Learning and playing with peers
Learning
 active, *see* Active learning
 active engagement in, I:104
  National Research Council recommendations on, I:111
 availability for, *see* Availability for learning
 collaborative, at Conversational Partner stage, I:45–46
 core capacities need for, in all children, I:10
 definition of, II:6
 emotional regulation and, I:4–5
 experiential, I:104
 flexibility in, goals and strategies for, I:103–104
 individual differences in, educational approaches and, I:127
 instructed, at Conversational Partner stage, I:45–46
 natural environment for, I:15, 125, II:20
 observational, I:36–38
  difficulties with, at Language Partner stage, I:39
 situation-specific, *see* Situation-specific learning
 strengths and weaknesses in, in children with ASD, I:78–82, 79t
 symbol use in, at Language Partner stage, SAP-O Forms and criteria for, I:193–194
 transactional model of, I:6
Learning and playing with peers (LAPP), I:127, II:37–42
 activities for, implementing, II:39–42
 definition of, I:313
 partner's role in, II:42
Learning contexts, II:11–23
 in educational approaches, I:118t, 125–127
Learning environment, modification of, by partner, II:36–37
Learning strategies
 analytic, I:35–36, 37t, 38t
 at Conversational Partner stage, I:45–47
  SAP-O Forms and criteria for, I:220–221
 gestalt, I:35–36, 37t, 38t
  in children with ASD, I:40–41
 at Language Partner stage, I:36–39, II:122–123, 122t
 at Social Partner stage, I:29–30
Learning style
 challenges related to, I:80
 definition of, I:313
 individual differences in, I:80–82
Learning support/Learning Support (component), I:3, 71–72, II:32–37
 at Conversational Partner stage
  assessment of, I:144t, II:327–328, 353–355
  goals for
   prioritizing, II:308–311
   and related Social Communication and Emotional Regulation goals, II:140–170
  SAP-O Forms and criteria for, I:240–244, II:353–355, 354f
 core challenges requiring, I:78–83
 definition of Learning Support component, I:313
 at Language Partner stage
  assessment of, I:143t, II:260–262, 285
  goals for
   prioritizing, II:241–244
   and related Social Communication and Emotional Regulation goals, II:111–140
  SAP-O Forms and criteria for, I:212–216, II:260–262, 261f
 overview of, I:6
 providing, goals and priorities in, I:101t, 103–105
 at Social Partner stage
  assessment of, I:142t, II:197–199, 220
  goals for
   prioritizing, II:182–184
   and related Social Communication and Emotional Regulation goals, II:89–111
  SAP-O Forms and criteria for, I:185–188, II:197–199, 198f
 see also Interpersonal support/Interpersonal Support (component); Transactional support; Transactional Support (domain)
Linguistic communication system, acquisition of, I:22
Linked objectives, in SAP-O, I:152–154
 symbols for, I:165
Low state of arousal
 definition of, I:314
 see also Arousal state; High state of arousal

MA & PA (meaningful and purposeful activities) approach, II:12–16, 88
 activities in
  balancing, throughout day, II:21–22
  characteristics of, II:17
  design of, II:20
  implementing, guidelines for, II:18–22
  interrelated and interdependent skills targeted within, II:20–21
  types of, II:17–18
 and communicative opportunities, II:20
 continuum of naturalness in, levels on, II:13f, 13–16, 14t
 criteria defining, II:23
 definition of, I:314
 rationale for, II:12–13
Meaningful activities, definition of, I:314
Memory
 associative, I:78
 emotional
  in children with ASD, I:66–67
  use of, at Conversational Partner stage, SAP-O Forms and criteria for, I:232
 episodic, I:78

gestalt, I:78
rote, I:78
Mental representation, capacity for, I:33–34, 37–38
Mental-state language, I:46
Metacognitive skills/strategies, I:51
   at Conversational Partner stage
      SAP-O Forms and criteria for, I:217, 232
      used to regulate arousal level
         goals for, and related partner goals, II:167–168, 167t
         during new and changing situations, SAP-O Forms and criteria for, I:233
         SAP-O Forms and criteria for, I:232
         during transitions, SAP-O Forms and criteria for, I:233
   definition of, I:314
   for self-regulation, I:60–61, 100
Mitigated echolalia, *see* Echolalia
Modified natural activities and settings, II:13f, 14t, 16
   definition of, I:314
Modulation of arousal, I:52
   definition of, I:314
Motor actions, simple, use of, at Social Partner stage, SAP-O Forms and criteria for, I:172
Motor planning difficulties, definition of, I:314
Motoric gestures, presymbolic, I:30
Multimodal communication, I:4
   definition of, I:314
   in SCERTS Model, I:129
Multisensory teaching, definition of, I:314
Mutual regulation/Mutual Regulation (component), I:5, 53–57
   capacity for
      and development in Conversational Partner stage, I:57
      and development in Language Partner stage, I:56–57
      and development in Social Partner stage, I:54–55
   at Conversational Partner stage
      assessment of, I:144t, II:323–324, 347–349
      goals for
         prioritizing, II:299–302
         and related partner goals, II:156–162
      milestones in, I:97, 99t
      SAP-O Forms and criteria for, I:225–229, II:347–349, 350f
   and core challenges in ASD, I:61–64
   definition of Mutual Regulation component, I:314
   at Language Partner stage
      assessment of, I:143t, II:256–257, 280–282
      goals for
         prioritizing, II:234–237
         and related partner goals, II:130–134
      milestones in, I:97, 98t
      SAP-O Forms and criteria for, I:199–202, II:256–257, 258f
   milestones in, I:97, 98t–99t
   at Social Partner stage
      assessment of, I:142t, II:194–195, 216–218
      goals for
         prioritizing, II:177–178
         and related partner goals, II:103–107
      milestones in, I:97, 98t
      SAP-O Forms and criteria for, I:174–176, II:194–195, 196f
   strategies for, I:97–100
   see also Emotional regulation; Emotional Regulation (domain); Initiated mutual regulation; Respondent mutual regulation; self-regulation/Self-Regulation (component)

National Academy of Sciences expert panel, I:7
National Research Council
   instructional priorities for children with ASD, I:111, 113–114
   recommendations on educational interventions for children with ASD, I:111–112
      SCERTS Model and, I:111–112
Natural contexts, for SAP-O, I:148
Natural language paradigm, I:115, 128
Naturally occurring activities and settings, I:125, II:13f, 14t, 16
   definition of, I:314
Naturalness
   definition of, I:125
   of teaching activities or contexts, I:125
Negative emotional display, I:49
   causal factors for, expression of, at Conversational Partner stage, SAP-O Forms and criteria for, I:218
   at Conversational Partner stage, SAP-O Forms and criteria for, I:227
   definition of, I:314
   at Language Partner stage, SAP-O Forms and criteria for, I:190, 199, 200–201
   at Social Partner stage, SAP-O Forms and criteria for, I:167, 175
New situations
   definition of, I:178, 314
   regulation of emotions in
      at Conversational Partner stage, goals for, and related partner goals, II:168–169, 168t
      at Conversational Partner stage, SAP-O Forms and criteria for, I:232–233
      at Language Partner stage, goals for, and related partner goals, II:137–138, 137t
      at Language Partner stage, SAP-O Forms and criteria for, I:205–206
      at Social Partner stage, goals for, and related partner goals, II:109–110, 109t
      at Social Partner stage, SAP-O Forms and criteria for, I:178
Nonliteral meanings, understanding of, at Conversational Partner stage, SAP-O Forms and criteria for, I:221–222
Nontransient information, I:78–79, 129
Nonverbal communication, I:23
   at Conversational Partner stage, SAP-O Forms and criteria for, I:222–223
   definition of, I:314
   and development of social communication, I:20
   at Language Partner stage
      goals for, and related partner goals, II:125–126, 125t
      SAP-O Forms and criteria for, I:195–196
   at Social Partner stage, I:29
      goals for, and related partner goals, II:100–101, 100t
      SAP-O Forms and criteria for, I:172–173

Observation, capacity for, at Language Partner stage
   goals for, and related partner goals, II:122–123, 122t
   SAP-O Forms and criteria for, I:193–194
One-to-one therapy, II:22–23
On-task versus off-task behavior, I:119
Optimal arousal, I:52
   definition of, I:314
Optimal experience, fostering, I:69–70
Oral language, *See* Language

Organization, *see* Active learning and organization
Organizational supports
   at Conversational Partner stage, SAP-O Forms and criteria for, I:242
   definition, I:186
   definition of, I:314
   partner's use of, II:35–36
      at Social Partner stage, SAP-O Forms and criteria for, I:186–187
Outcome measures, I:111
Outcomes, I:7
   family involvement and, II:43
   measures for, I:16–17
Overarousal, *see* Emotional overarousal

Parents
   involvement of, in educational programming, I:124–125
   ongoing support for, I:10
   role of, in educational programming, I:124–125
   see also Professional–parent interaction
Partner(s)
   adjustment of language input, II:30–31
   assistance from, requests for, *See* Assistance
   communicative and social, for children with ASD, I:76–78
   definition of, I:314
   developmental support provided by, II:30
   initiation fostered by, II:28
   in Interpersonal Support, goals and priorities for, II:26–32
   modeling of appropriate behaviors by, II:31–32
   modification of goals, activities, and learning environment, II:36–37
   respect for child's independence, II:28–29
   responsiveness to child with ASD, II:27–28
   role of
      in learning and playing with peers (LAPP), II:42
      in transactional support, II:25–26
      in setting stage for engagement, II:29
   structuring of activity for active participation, II:34–35
   use of augmentative communication support, II:35
   use of visual and organizational support, II:35–36
PBS, *see* Positive behavior support
Peer support, I:5
   definition of, I:314
   transactional model of, I:6
Peers, typical or more developmentally advanced, in educational approaches, I:127
   see also Learning and playing with peers (LAPP)
Perseverative speech, I:80
   definition of, I:81*t*, 314
   examples of, I:81*t*
   see also Unconventional verbal behavior
Physiological arousal, I:50
   in children with ASD, I:65
   see also Arousal level; Arousal state
Physiological aspects of emotion, I:50
   in children with ASD, I:64–65
   definition of, I:314
Physiologically oriented interventions, I:115
PL 105-17, *see* Individuals with Disabilities Education Act (IDEA) Amendments of 1997

Planned activity routines, II:13*f,* 13–15, 14*t*
   definition of, I:314
Play, I:4
   among siblings, facilitating, II:68
   constructive, in children with ASD, I:42
   at Conversational Partner stage, I:45–47
   development of, in children with ASD, I:41–42
   and development of social communication, I:20
   dramatic, I:47
      at Conversational Partner stage, SAP-O Forms and criteria for, I:222
   imaginative, precursor to, I:30
   at Language Partner stage, I:36–39
      use of familiar objects in
         goals for, and related partner goals, II:124–125, 124*t*
         SAP-O Forms and criteria for, I:195
   patterns of, in children with ASD, I:41–42
   at Social Partner stage, I:28, 30
      use of familiar objects in
         goals for, and related partner goals, II:99–100, 99*t*
         SAP-O Forms and criteria for, I:171–172
   symbolic, in children with ASD, I:41–42
   symbolic nature of, I:28
Play skills, teaching of, National Research Council recommendations on, I:113
Positive behavior support (PBS), I:110, 116, 121–123, 122*t*
   definition of, I:314
Positive emotion(s), I:49
   ability to share at Conversational Partner stage, to seek interaction, SAP-O Forms and criteria for, I:227
   ability to share at Language Partner stage, SAP-O Forms and criteria for, I:190, 199, 200–201
   ability to share at Social Partner stage
      SAP-O Forms and criteria for, I:167, 175
      to seek interaction, SAP-O Forms and criteria for, I:175
   causal factors for, expression of, at Conversational Partner stage, SAP-O Forms and criteria for, I:218
Posture, use of, at Conversational Partner stage, SAP-O Forms and criteria for, I:223
Predication, I:34
Prescriptive approaches, I:119
   definition of, I:314
Problem behavior
   approaches to, I:121–123, 122*t*
      National Research Council recommendations on, I:113
   definition of, I:314–315
   educational approaches and, I:128
   prevention/lessening, with social-communicative abilities, I:4
Professional–parent interaction, I:107
   challenges in, I:87–88, II:46*t*
   SCERTS Model and, II:49–56
Professionals
   challenges faced by, I:107–108, II:79–80
   educational support for, II:80–81, 80*t*
   emotional support for, II:80*t,* 81
   relationship to child with ASD
      development of, I:88–89
      transactional model of, I:6–7
   see also Support among professionals

Programmatic goals, educational approaches and, I:118*t*, 128–130
Progress, of child with ASD
    environmental factors and, II:86
    factors affecting, II:84–86
    measurement of, I:123–124
        and carryover to natural environments, I:124
        and generalization, I:124
        qualitative versus quantitative approaches, I:123–124
    partner factors and, II:85–86
    within-child factors and, II:84–85
Protoword, I:173
Proximity, use of
    at Conversational Partner stage, SAP-O Forms and criteria for, I:223
    at Social Partner stage, SAP-O Forms and criteria for, I:172
Pull-out therapy, II:22–23

Questioning, incessant or repetitive, *see* Incessant questioning

Reciprocal interaction
    at Conversational Partner stage, SAP-O Forms and criteria for, I:218–219
    at Language Partner stage
        goals for, and related partner goals, II:111–112, 111*t*, 120–121, 120*t*
        SAP-O Forms and criteria for, I:189, 193, 202–203
    at Social Partner stage
        goals for, and related partner goals, II:89–90, 89*t*
        SAP-O Forms and criteria for, I:166
Reciprocity
    at Conversational Partner stage, SAP-O Forms and criteria for, I:218–219
    definition of, I:315
    at Language Partner stage, SAP-O Forms and criteria for, I:193
Recommended practices, educational, I:16
Recovery from autism, I:7, 111
Recovery from dysregulation, I:5, 50–51
    and core challenges of ASD, I:67–69
    definition of, I:315
Recreation, participation in, at Conversational Partner stage, SAP-O Forms and criteria for, I:222
Reenactment gesture, use of, at Social Partner stage, SAP-O Forms and criteria for, I:172
Reenactment strategies, I:30–31
Regulation of emotional and mood states, I:50
    definition of, I:315
Relationship-based approaches, I:115
Relaxation techniques, definition of, I:315
Repair strategies
    at Conversational Partner stage, SAP-O Forms and criteria for, I:220
    definition of, I:315
    at Language Partner stage, SAP-O Forms and criteria for, I:192–193
    at Social Partner stage, SAP-O Forms and criteria for, I:169
    see also Communication breakdown
Repetitive questioning, *see* Incessant questioning

Resilience, *see* Flexibility and resilience
Respondent mutual regulation, I:54
    definition of, I:315
    see also Initiated mutual regulation; Mutual regulation/Mutual Regulation (component)

SAP, *see* SCERTS Assessment Process
SAP Activity Planning Form, II:201, 204*f*, 263, 266*f*, 267*f*, 358, 359*f*, 360*f*
SAP Daily Tracking Log, I:163–164
SAP Map for Planning the SAP-Observation
    at Conversational Partner stage, II:339, 340*f*
    at Language Partner stage, II:249, 250*f*
    process for completing, I:150–151
    at Social Partner stage, II:188, 189*f*
SAP Summary Form (SAP Sum), I:161–162
SAP Weekly Tracking Log, I:164
SAP-O, *see* SCERTS Assessment Process–Observation
SAP-Q, *see* SCERTS Assessment Process–Quality Indicators
SAP-R, *see* SCERTS Assessment Process–Report
    at Conversational Partner stage, II:355, 356*f*–357*f*
    at Language Partner stage, II:263, 264*f*–265*f*
    at Social Partner stage, II:191–200, 202*f*–203*f*, 213–221
SCERTS (acronym), definition of, I:1
SCERTS Assessment Process (SAP), I:3, 17
    approaches used in, range of, I:135–137
    behavior sampling in, I:136
        at Conversational Partner stage, II:317–319, 341–343
        at Language Partner stage, II:251–252, 276–277
        at Social Partner stage, II:190–191, 212–213
    components of, I:141, 142*t*–143*t*
    core questions in, I:141
    as criterion-referenced instrument, I:132
    as curriculum-based instrument, I:132
    definition of, I:315
    design of SCERTS educational program in, I:163
    determination of child's communication stage in, I:145–147
        echolalia and, I:146–147
    domains of, I:141, 142*t*–143*t*
    elicited responses in, I:136
    forms for, I:251
    goals and objectives in, prioritizing, I:162
        at Conversational Partner stage, II:329, 355–358
        at Language Partner stage, II:263, 286
        at Social Partner stage, II:200, 221
    implementation of, I:145–164
    and individual differences, I:127
    interviews used in, I:135
    measurement of progress in, I:124
    observation of daily activities in natural environment in, I:135–136
    as ongoing process, I:140
    ongoing tracking in, I:163–164, II:207–208, 225, 270, 290, 333, 362
    overview of, I:140–144
    questionnaires used in, I:135
    and recommendation of further assessment, I:162–163
        at Conversational Partner stage, II:329, 358
        at Language Partner stage, II:263, 286–287
        at Social Partner stage, II:200–201, 221

SCERTS Assessment Process (SAP)—*continued*
  SAP Daily Tracking Log in, I:163–164
  SAP Summary Form in, I:161–162, II:6, 7*f*
    at Conversational Partner stage, II:355, 356*f*–357*f*
    at Language Partner stage, II:263, 264*f*–265*f*
    at Social Partner stage, II:191–200, 202*f*–20
  SAP Weekly Tracking Log in, I:163–164
    3*f*, 213–221
  siblings' contribution to, II:56–59
  at Social Partner stage, II:186–201
  stages in, I:141, 142*t*–143*t*
  standardized testing in, I:136
  and support to families, II:56–59
  terms used in, definition of, I:131–132
  versus traditional assessment approaches, I:132–134
SCERTS Assessment Process–Observation (SAP-O), I:136, 140, 165
  activity variables in, I:149–150
  assessment team for
    at Conversational Partner stage, II:315, 338
    identification of, I:148–151
    at Language Partner stage, II:248, 274
    at Social Partner stage, II:187–189, 211
  behavior sampling in, I:157–161
    at Conversational Partner stage, II:317–319, 341–343
    at Language Partner stage, II:251–252, 276–277
    at Social Partner stage, II:190–191, 212–213
  criteria
    at Conversational Partner stage, I:216
    for Language Partner stage, I:189
    for Social Partner stage, I:166–188
  definition of, I:315
  family response to, II:199–200, 221, 262, 286, 329, 355
  forms for, I:165, 251
    for Conversational Partner stage, I:216
    for Language Partner stage, I:188–189
    for Social Partner stage, I:166
  group size in, I:149
  implementation of, I:151–157
  length of observation for, I:148–149
  natural contexts for, I:148
  partners in, I:149
  planning for, I:148–151
    at Conversational Partner stage, II:315–316, 338–339
    at Language Partner stage, II:248–249, 274–275
    at Social Partner stage, II:187–189, 211–212
  and SAP Map for Planning the SAP-Observation
    at Conversational Partner stage, II:339, 340*f*
    at Language Partner stage, II:249, 250*f*
    process for completing, I:150–151
    at Social Partner stage, II:188, 189*f*
  SAP-O Form
    completing, I:151–157, II:190, 212, 249, 275, 316–317, 339–341
    at Conversational Partner stage, II:316–317, 339–341
    cover page, tabulation of scores on, I:154
    documenting observed behaviors in, I:152
    at Language Partner stage, II:249, 275
    linked objectives in, I:152–154
      symbols for, I:165
    ongoing tracking included in, I:163–164
  scoring system for, I:153, 153*f*
  at Social Partner stage, II:190, 212
  Social-Emotional Growth Indicators on, I:154–157, 157*t*
  transitions in, I:150
SCERTS Assessment Process–Quality Indicators (SAP-Q), II:6, 365
  definition of, I:315
  forms for
    Key Indicators of a Quality SCERTS Model Program, II:365
    SCERTS Program Quality Indicator Rating Scale: Support Among Professionals, II:365
    SCERTS Program Quality Indicator Rating Scale: Support to Families, II:365
SCERTS Assessment Process–Report (SAP-R), I:135, 140
  at Conversational Partner stage, II:314–315, 336–338
  definition of, I:315
  implementation of, I:147–148
  at Language Partner stage, II:247–248, 273–274
  siblings' contribution to, II:57
  at Social Partner stage, II:186–187, 209–211
SCERTS Model
  basic tenets of, I:14–17
  compatibility with practices and strategies from other approaches, I:13–14
  comprehensive scope of, I:2
  core domains of, I:3
    interrelationships/interdependencies in, I:7
    overview of, I:3–7
    see also Emotional regulation/Emotional Regulation; Social Communication (domain); Transactional Support (domain)
  core values of, I:17–18, II:2–3
  and current landscape of educational approaches, I:114–130
  definition of, I:1, 315
  developmental framework of, I:118
    rationale for, I:92–93
  and evidence-based practice, I:110
  Family Support Planning Form, II:77*f*–78*f*
  flexibility of, I:11–13
  guiding principles of, I:17–18, II:2–3
  as individualized approach, I:13
  innovative aspects of, I:14
  as life-span model, I:2
  as next-generation approach, I:14
  rationale for, I:7–8
  recommended practices in, I:14–17, II:3–5
  transactional principles in, I:71–72
  as values-based model, I:17–18
SCERTS Profile Summary, I:154
Self-determination, definition of, I:315
Self-regulation/Self-Regulation (component), I:5, 53–54, 57–61
  capacity for
    and development in Conversational Partner stage, I:59–61
    and development in Language Partner stage, I:58–59
    and development in Social Partner stage, I:58–59
  at Conversational Partner stage
    assessment of, I:144*t*, II:325–326, 349–351
    goals for
      prioritizing, II:302–305
      and related partner goals, II:162–170

milestones in, I:97, 99t
SAP-O Forms and criteria for, I:229–234, II:349–351, 350f
and core challenges in ASD, I:64–67
definition of Self-Regulation component, I:315
at Language Partner stage
assessment of, I:143t, II:257–259, 282–284
goals for
prioritizing, II:237–239
and related partner goals, II:130–140
milestones in, I:97, 98t
SAP-O Forms and criteria for, I:202–206, II:257–259, 258f
milestones in, I:97, 98t–99t
at Social Partner stage
assessment of, I:142t, II:195–197, 218–219
goals for
prioritizing, II:178–180
and related partner goals, II:107–111
milestones in, I:97, 98t
SAP-O Forms and criteria for, I:176–179, II:195–197, 196f
strategies for, I:97–100
see also Emotional regulation; Emotional Regulation (domain); Mutual regulation/Mutual Regulation (component)
Sense of other
definition of, I:155
as Social-Emotional Growth Indicator, I:141, 155, 157t
rationale for, I:155
Sense of self
definition of, I:155
as Social-Emotional Growth Indicator, I:141, 155, 157t
rationale for, I:155
Sensory processing disturbances
in children with ASD, effects on partners, I:76
definition of, I:315
Sensory-motor strategies, *see* Behavioral strategies
Sentence grammar
at Conversational Partner stage, I:43–44, 45t, 46t
SAP-O Forms and criteria for, I:224
definition of, I:315
transition to, I:22
Sequential organization, I:38
Service delivery systems, family's dealings with, challenges in, I:87, II:46t
SCERTS Model and, II:49–56
Service models, family's confusion about, I:87–88
Service providers
challenges faced by, II:79–80
educational support for, II:80–81, 80t
emotional support for, II:80t, 81
family's dealings with, challenges in, I:87, II:46t
SCERTS Model and, II:49–56
support among, *see* Support among professionals
Services, initial planning of, challenges to family in, II:53
Setting events, definition of, I:315
Shared control, definition of, I:315
Shared meaning, I:28–29
Shutdown
definition of, I:315
tendency toward, in children with ASD, effects on partners, I:75–76
Sibling issues, support to caregivers regarding, II:75
Siblings
in assessment, I:138–139, II:57–59
challenges to, I:85
and enhancement of social-communicative and emotional regulatory abilities in child with ASD, II:67–69
play among, facilitating, II:68
in role of teacher, support for, II:69
social communicative skills of, fostering, II:68–69
social interaction among, facilitating, II:68
Signals of dysregulation, definition of, I:315
Situations
changing, *see* Changing situations
new, *see* New situations
Situation-specific learning, I:32
definition of, I:315
Skill-based approaches, I:6, 115, 126
definition of, I:315
see also Activity-based learning approaches; Prescriptive approaches
Skills
functional, *see* Functional skills
metacognitive, *see* Metacognitive skills/strategies
Social communication, I:19–48
assessment of, I:132–134
challenges faced by children with ASD, I:20, 21, 72–73, 76–78
competence in, importance of, I:91
at Conversational Partner stage
assessment of, I:144t, II:319–323, 343–347
goals for, and related partner goals, II:141–156
SAP-O Forms and criteria for, I:216–224
as core capacity for all children, I:10
as core challenge, I:9, 20, 21
definition of, I:315
development
milestones in, I:93, 94t–96t
stages of, in SCERTS model, I:20
characteristics of, I:21–28
transitions in, I:21–28
see also Conversational Partner stage; Language Partner stage; Social Partner stage
goal-setting framework for, I:93–96, II:5–6
at Language Partner stage
assessment of, I:143t, II:252–255, 277–280
goals for
prioritizing, II:229–234
and related partner goals, II:111–130
SAP-O Forms and criteria for, I:189–199, II:252–255, 254f
as life-span ability, I:10
priorities for, in SCERTS Model, I:91–96
at Social Partner stage
assessment of, I:142t, II:191–200, 213–216
goals for
prioritizing, II:173–176
and related partner goals, II:89–103
SAP-O Forms and criteria for, I:166–174, II:191–200
see also Joint attention/Joint Attention (component); Symbol use/Symbol Use (component)

Social Communication (domain), I:3
    definition of, I:315
    developmental underpinnings, I:19
    goals of, linking to Transactional Support goals, II:86–87, 87–170
    overall goal of, I:4
    overview of, I:3–4
    see also Joint attention/Joint Attention (component); Symbol use/Symbol Use (component)
Social complexity, in educational approaches, I:126–127
Social control, definition of, I:315
Social engagement, core capacities need for, in all children, I:10
Social exchange, *see* Exchange (social or communicative)
Social instruction, National Research Council recommendations on, I:113
Social interaction
    definition of, I:315
    development, I:26
    difficulty of, for children with ASD, I:27
Social membership and friendships
    definition of, I:156
    as Social-Emotional Growth Indicator, I:141, 156–157, 157t
    rationale for, I:156
Social motivation, definition of, I:315
Social observation, learning through, difficulties with, at Language Partner stage, I:39
Social Partner stage, I:3, 20
    advanced level, assessment to implementation, II:208–225
    definition of, I:316
    domains, components, and goals, in SCERTS Assessment Process, I:142t
    emotional regulation at
        assessment of, I:142t, II:194–197
        goals for
            prioritizing, II:177–180
            and related partner goals, II:103–111
        milestones in, I:97, 98t
        during new and changing situations
            goals for, and related partner goals, II:109–110, 109t
            SAP-O Forms and criteria for, I:178
        SAP-O Forms and criteria for, I:174–179, II:194–197
    goals and objectives at, prioritizing, II:200, 221
    novice level, assessment to implementation, II:185–208
    recommending further assessment at, II:200–201, 221
    SAP-O Forms and criteria for, I:166–188
    social communication at
        assessment of, I:142t, II:191–200, 213–216
        goals for
            prioritizing, II:173–176
            and related partner goals, II:89–103
        SAP-O Forms and criteria for, I:166–174, II:191–200
    Social-Emotional Growth Indicators at
        objectives for calculation of, I:157t
        results and impressions, II:199, 221
    spotlights on children at, II:185–225
    transactional support at
        assessment of, I:142t, II:197–199, 219–220
        goals for, and related Social Communication and Emotional Regulation goals, II:89–111
        SAP-O Forms and criteria for, I:179–188, II:197–199, 198f

transitions in, I:21, 23
    see also Language Partner stage
Social referencing, I:24
Social Stories, definition of, I:316
Social understanding
    definition of, I:316
    enhancing, for children with ASD, I:104
Social values
    and early childhood intervention practices, I:110
    and educational approach, I:16
Social-Emotional Growth Indicators, I:17, 165
    at Conversational Partner stage, results and impressions, II:328–329, 355
    definition of, I:154–157, 157t, 316
    at Language Partner stage, results and impressions, II:262, 285–286
    objectives for calculation of, I:157t
    rationale for, I:154–157
    in SAP, I:141
    on SAP-O Form, I:154–157, 157t
    at Social Partner stage, results and impressions, II:199, 221
    see also specific indicators
Socialization, I:50, 56–57
    of children with ASD, I:66
    definition of, I:316
Speech, perseverative, *see* Perseverative speech
Speech production, difficulties with, in children with ASD, I:41
Standardized testing, in assessment, I:136
Strategic support, I:125
Structure, definition of, I:316
Structured situations, in SCERTS Assessment Process, I:159, 160t
Support among professionals, I:3, II:79–81
    at Conversational Partner stage, II:332–333, 362
    core challenges requiring, I:88–90
    definition of, I:316
    goals and priorities for, I:107–108
    at Language Partner stage, II:269–270, 290
    overview of, I:6
    providing, goals and priorities in, I:101t
    SCERTS Program Quality Indicator Rating Scale for, II:365
    at Social Partner stage, II:207, 224–225
Support to families, I:3, II:43–79
    activities that provide, II:76t
    assessment practices for, II:56–59
    in SCERTS Model, I:136–140
    characteristics of, II:44–46
    core challenges requiring, I:83–88
    definition of, I:316
    Family Support Planning Form for, II:77f–78f
    goals and priorities for, I:101t, 105–107, II:43–44
    overview of, I:6
    principles and practices of, implementation of, II:56–79
    SCERTS Program Quality Indicator Rating Scale for, II:365
    see also Educational support; Emotional support
Symbol use/Symbol Use (component), I:3–4
    capacity for
        assessment of, I:92
        and development at Conversational Partner stage, I:43–47
        and development at Language Partner stage, I:32–39
        and development at Social Partner stage, I:28–30